Bears Ears

Bears Ears

LANDSCAPE OF REFUGE AND RESISTANCE

ANDREW GULLIFORD

THE UNIVERSITY OF UTAH PRESS
Salt Lake City

Publication of this volume is made possible in part by the generous support of the following:
Marcey Olajos, Arizona and Colorado
Charles Redd Center for Western Studies at Brigham Young University
Fort Lewis College Foundation
Fort Lewis College Faculty Development Fund

The Defiance House Man colophon is a registered trademark of the University of Utah Press. It is based on a four-foot-tall Ancient Puebloan pictograph (late PIII) near Glen Canyon, Utah.

ISBN 978-1-64769-076-2 (hardcover)
ISBN 978-1-64769-077-9 (paper)
ISBN 978-1-64769-078-6 (ebook)

Catalog-in-Publication data for this title is available online at the Library of Congress.

Errata and further information on this and other titles available online at UofUpress.com.
Printed and bound in the United States of America.

To President Theodore Roosevelt,
who signed into law the Antiquities Act,

to Bill and Beth Sagstetter,
who first showed me Cedar Mesa,

and to BLM Grand Gulch Ranger Lynell Schalk,
who helped protect our nation's heritage.

Contents

Acknowledgments

> Here is your country. Cherish these natural wonders... Do not let selfish men or greedy interests skin your country of its beauty, its riches, or its romance.
>
> —Theodore Roosevelt

In the century since President Theodore Roosevelt signed the Antiquities Act in 1906, never had Native American tribes publicly endorsed using the federal law to establish a national monument. Then, on December 28, 2016, President Barack Obama established Bears Ears National Monument at 1.35 million acres, in part because of Native American support for the project. Yet the subsequent president, Donald Trump, shrunk the monument boundaries by 85 percent.

To understand the original impetus for the monument designation and also to understand why rural Utah citizens and politicians opposed the monument's declaration and boundaries, I set out to research and write this book. But my affinity for the canyon country of southeast Utah began decades before. To write this book, I had to build a house. To find and buy the lot, to understand the nature of the country, I spent years getting to know the Bears Ears and Cedar Mesa landscape, hiking cliff ledges, watching the full moon rise over canyon rims, and learning patterns and styles of ancient Indian rock art. Four decades ago, attracted to the slickrock country around Moab, Utah, I explored Canyonlands National Park. We dropped off Island in the Sky, got lost on our way to the Colorado River, and spent the night curled up in the sand, watching galaxies in the black sky wheel above us and wondered where we had set up our tents with warm sleeping bags cozily laid out on aired up-pads.

At dawn the next morning, we found camp with everything in place and undisturbed. I was hooked. From then on, I came to southern Utah when I could, ran desert rivers by canoe and raft, hiked remote canyons, and came to absorb the silence, solitude, and darkness found in a landscape of sandstone slickrock. But Moab got crowded with Jeepers and mountain bikers, and though I loved slickrock, what compelled me were canyon country archaeological sites south of Moab in San Juan County, Utah, on Cedar Mesa, northwest of the tiny town of Bluff.

When the chance came, we bought a lot on the western edge of Bluff at the foot of Tank Mesa. I thought I would have to convince my New Jersey–born wife who had grown up on the Jersey Shore with sandy beaches. I thought she would say no. This was all rock and sand with no ocean in sight, but I had a rationale. The San Juan River was close by so there was water. I could say this was an ocean beach sixty million years ago. Just look at all this sand.

But she didn't protest. She liked the idea of building a retirement residence in a small town at the edge of the big country of redrock canyons with the sprawling seventeen-million-acre Navajo Nation just across the river. The house took years to plan and build, but we were in no rush. Time slows down in Bluff. By building a house and becoming local taxpayers, my wife and I chose to become more engaged in the community, not just to comment as writers passing through, but as neighbors involved in San Juan County's future and the need for financial stability and opportunity for younger generations.

Some writers take a few hikes, write a few words, and are gone. My wife and I want to contribute to the dialogue of what the county can become and how it needs to diversify both culturally and economically. We also wanted to fight for landscape preservation to save the magic and mystery of Bears Ears as one of the largest intact Native American cultural landscapes in the United States. So even though some residents disdainfully label us and other couples like us "local outsiders," I'll accept that nickname and smile. Yes, we're local, and as much as we can be, yes, we're outside.

From our back patio across the fence on public Bureau of Land Management (BLM) land, we can see a small Ancestral Puebloan granary. A thirty-minute walk away is a set of rock art panels depicting 2,000 years of Native American thoughts, ideas, and beliefs carved into sandstone cliffs. I've explored archaeological sites, learned tribal histories and myths, and researched Mormon pioneers who came into the country by wagon in 1880. The landscape resonates with stories. Writer Ellen Meloy also resided in Bluff. I accept her goal of "striving to live within deep history gracefully and intuitively, to take my humble place inside the neighborhood's overlays of time."[1]

For hiker friends who went with me and also who showed me archaeological sites I never would have found, I thank Jim and Jeanette Petersen, Nik Kendziorski, Steve Jones, Rich Moser, Joe Pachak, and former BLM Ranger and Special Agent Lynell Schalk. Help and support came from Steve Allen, Roni Egan, Marcey Olajos, and other canyon hikers and explorers. I thank Jim and LuAnne Hook, owners of Recapture Lodge and hosts to visitors who want to explore "at the edge of the Big Country" in the tradition of the Recapture's founders Gene and Mary Foushee.

For funding and support, I gratefully acknowledge the Research Fellowship Program of the Charles Redd Center at Brigham Young University and the interlibrary loan librarians at Fort Lewis College who have located everything for me from rare documents to copies of recent national newspapers. Thank you, Victoria Giannola. I am also indebted to the Fort Lewis College Faculty Development Fund for travel and research assistance and to the Fort Lewis College Foundation for financial assistance with maps drawn for this book.

Thanks also go to the Utah State Historical Society and Archives to Heidi Stringham, Valerie Jacobson, and Jedediah Rogers among others. The State Records Committee works to provide state records under Utah's open records or Government Records Access & Management Act (GRAMA). They are to be commended for their public service. Brigid Carney helped me with a GRAMA request to understand historical and legal issues related to Utah's School and Institutional Trust Lands Administration (SITLA), and I am in her debt. With thousands of acres of school sections in San Juan County, understanding Ancestral Puebloan sites on those lands is important.

Retired BLM Archaeologist Michael Selle has helped me learn about evidence related to Navajo migration stories. Harvey Leake, a Wetherill descendant, assisted me with countless sources and information on Richard Wetherill and his life and times. Researcher Lee Bennett increased my knowledge of San Juan County uranium mining and explained why many local families favor a return to mining yellowcake.

Bill Boyle, editor and publisher of the *San Juan Record,* does an important job of providing a vital weekly newspaper to both local and regional readers. Being editor of the only newspaper in a county of 7,900 square miles can be a thankless task. Bill does a good job. Thanks also go to San Juan County Surveyor Kent B. (Sam) Cantrell, who shares my love of maps and has helped me with research interests. Geologist Gil Mull assisted with sources and also gave me invaluable *Desert Magazines* from the 1960s.

Peekay Briggs, Archivist & Collections Manager for the National Park Service and the Southeast Utah Group of Arches and Canyonlands National Parks, Natural Bridges, and Hovenweep National Monuments, helped me immensely. I enjoyed my time in Moab working with her and she found every file I requested. I also enjoyed seeing an ancient leather bag found at a Barrier Canyon Rock Art site, and I saw a Clovis point found in the Needles District now in the National Park Service (NPS) research collections.

Bridget Ambler and Tracy Murphy at the Canyons of the Ancients National Monument Visitor Center helped guide me through the Wetherill Papers originally archived by Fred Blackburn and many volunteers. Those papers provide an intimate look into one of the most important pioneer families in the Southwest. I am also indebted to Special Collections at the Marriott Library at the University of Utah for their research files and historical photographs. The base map for this book was drawn by cartographer Bill Nelson. Other maps and the mammoth illustration are by DJ Webb of djwebbimages.com.

Learning the archaeological landscape of Bears Ears has been one of my greatest joys. For helping me to understand prehistory and evolving archaeological theories, I want to thank archaeologists Don Simonis, Stephen Lekson, Ben Bellorado, Phil Geib, William Lipe, and the late Florence Lister, who was a joy to work with as we guided tours together at Mesa Verde National Park. Ranger Jeff Brown at Mesa Verde has also been helpful, and he has kept me up to date on Ancestral Puebloan scholarship. Scott Edwards and Laura Lantz, dedicated Kane Gulch BLM rangers, explained much to me, and I'll not forget Scott's tour of canyon sites beyond Moon House that he graciously led for the San Juan Basin Archaeological Society. Laurie Webster taught me about excavated perishable items from southeast Utah and helped me to understand catalogs and collections from the earliest digs in Bears Ears.

Al and Betty Schneider helped me to understand southeast Utah botany and the early expeditions of Alice Eastwood, who named many canyon country plants and for whom many plants are named. Steve Jones walked my socks off as we dropped into and hiked Dark Canyon,

Hammond Canyon, and Woodenshoe Canyon. Attorneys Pat Shea and Kyle Maynard assisted with my Utah GRAMA request to try to understand what happened with over $500,000 in public funds that San Juan County Commissioners spent between 2016 and 2017 trying to block President Obama's Bears Ears National Monument. The San Juan County attorney sued the State Records Committee. Finally, after reviewing over 400 emails, Zak Podmore broke the story in the *Salt Lake Tribune.*[2]

I want to thank attorney Steven Boos, attorney John Andrews, political science professor Daniel McCool, and archaeologists Kenny Wintch and Joel Boomgarden. Scholar Clyde Denis has also shared San Juan County sources on cattle grazing and Canyonlands National Park. Utah State University–Blanding librarian Heather Raisor helped me locate valuable historic photos from the San Juan Historical Commission, and Merri Shumway assisted me in better understanding her father Calvin Black and his deep commitment to southeast Utah. Lisbeth Louderback and Bruce Pavlik explained to me their work on the Four Corners potato. I'll never forget the quiet conversations I had with former Zia Pueblo governor Peter Pino about the tiny tuber's use at Zia. For three years, we co-led Mesa Verde National Park tours, and Peter taught me much about his ancestors. I wish I could have walked with him among ancestral sites in Bears Ears.

Some of the writing in this book has previously been published in my monthly newspaper column "Gulliford's Travels" in the *Durango Herald* and *Cortez Journal.* My essays have run in the *San Juan Record, High Country News, Utah Adventure Journal,* and on the editorial page of the *Salt Lake Tribune.* I am grateful to have worked with Brenden Rensink of the Charles Redd Center at Brigham Young University for a special summer seminar that resulted in his edited book *The North American West in the Twenty-first Century* published by the University of Nebraska Press. My chapter titled "The American West, Native Americans, and Controversies over the Antiquities Act: Bears Ears National Monument, a Utah Case Study," is included in this book. Thank you, University of Nebraska Press. My essay on handprints in the canyon was previously published in my edited book *Outdoors in the Southwest: An Adventure Anthology* (University of Oklahoma Press), and I am grateful for reproducing it here.

My wife of over forty-five years, Stephanie Moran, supported this project, hiked into canyons with me, camped with me, kept me slathered with sunscreen, and cooked elk and venison in those years when I was lucky enough to have successful fall hunts. She is my editor, my soulmate, and best of all she believes in the long-term projects I undertake. Of course, I also have to acknowledge the three generations of hiker dogs who have explored Bears Ears with me. First there was Charlie, a black Flat-coated Retriever. Then there was Finn, a Springer Spaniel–black Lab mix. Now I walk sometimes with Josie, a dachshund/terrier/Boxer mix, but I always hike with Fiona, a Lab/Great Pyrenees/Australian Shepherd mix who is smarter than I am.

Over the decades I've written several books about broad historical themes set in remote rural landscapes, but this is the first time I've confined my research to a single county in the American West—and what a county! The San Juan Country of southeastern Utah is five million acres with 13,000 years of human history that has captivated numerous archaeologists and historians. By using Bears Ears as a landscape of refuge and resistance for an organizing theme, I have tried to sift through a wealth of available primary and secondary sources to focus on the landscape included within the boundaries of President Barack Obama's national monument proclamation. I take comfort in the advice a Diné chanter gave Navajo scholars Klara Kelley and Harris Francis as they embarked on years of research that culminated in a unique Navajo history. Joe Dennison told them, "You know what you have to do, so just do it. People will criticize you no matter what you do."[3] I also accept that writer's reality.

I want to thank Thomas Krause at the University of Utah Press for his unwavering support of this project as well as three anonymous readers who offered their suggestions and criticism. They helped polish the manuscript and made it a tighter book. I am in their debt. I've tried to sort through primary and secondary sources to create a readable narrative. All errors with this book manuscript are my own. I welcome comments and critiques at andy@agulliford.com.

In his edited book *The Earth Will Appear as the Garden of Eden* about Mormon environmental history, Jedediah S. Rogers wrote, "We need more works that blend personal memoir and environmental history, for this combination produces a deep dive into the richness of place."[4] I am aiming for that goal. Utah history is rich with narratives and stories at the local level and in the engagement, often contentious, with federal public lands. So here is a Bears Ears history. I hope others will follow, especially books written by Native scholars who can synthesize the wealth of Native American oral tradition that surrounds this unique prehistoric and historic cultural area. For many Native peoples in the Southwest, Bears Ears is their ancestral home.

Introduction

Bears Ears and a Deep Map of Place

A lot of rocks, a lot of sand, more rocks, more sand, and wind to blow it away.

—Cowboy description of San Juan County, Utah, 1938

Rising from the center of the southeastern Utah landscape and visible from every direction are twin buttes so distinctive that in each of the Native languages of the region their name is the same: Hoon'Naqvut, Shash Jaa, Kwiyagutu Nukavachi, Ansh An Lashokdiwe or 'Bears Ears.' For hundreds of generations, Native peoples lived in the surrounding deep sandstone canyons, desert mesas, and meadow mountaintops, which constitute one of the densest and most significant cultural landscapes in the United States.

—Proclamation for Bears Ears National Monument,
President Barack Obama, 2016

Bears Ears National Monument in southeast Utah is a vast prehistoric, historic, and cultural landscape in one of the least populated areas in the United States. San Juan County, Utah, is the state's "Indian County" with five million acres, 100,000 archaeological sites, a population of only 16,000, and an original Mormon mission goal to aid and convert the Natives. San Juan County is the largest county in Utah. South of the San Juan River sprawls the Navajo Nation, the largest Indian reservation in the United States. Native Americans represent over half of San Juan County's population. South of Blanding, Utah, the White Mesa Reservation is a small community of historic Paiute and Ute Mountain Ute families. As a hiker and historian, I hope to learn the stories that go with the land. It's a harsh, dry, beautiful place to live, and humans have been here on and off for 13,000 years.

A friend and I had spent the day on the edge of Canyonlands National Park, and we were in Blanding, Utah, headed south when news came on the radio that President Barack Obama had declared Bears Ears National Monument. We looked west at the Bears Ears and thought about all that the 9,058-foot-tall landmark represented for tribes, for conservation, and for preserving archaeological sites. There was a party in Bluff that night with backslapping and congratulations all around.

After more than a decade of efforts by Utah Diné Bikéyah, the Southern Utah Wilderness Alliance, Grand Canyon Trust, Friends of Cedar Mesa, Great Old Broads for Wilderness, and other environmental and Native American groups, patience and persistence had paid off. Department of Interior Secretary Sally Jewell had come to southern Utah on July 16, 2016, to see the Bears Ears cultural landscape. She visited Moon House and was awed by the site's remoteness and its careful preservation. In Bluff, the public comment meeting on a hot July day was standing room only for speakers. They were chosen by a lottery system and allowed only three minutes to talk.

Over a century earlier, Congress had passed the Antiquities Act of 1906. This unique legislation had two important functions. This was the first cultural resources law in the world to protect unmarked Indigenous burials. Henceforth, archaeologists would be required to have permits for any excavations on federal lands. Looters or pothunters could be fined for illegal digging. The law also allowed, in brief wording, that as an executive privilege the president of the United States could set aside national monuments out of the public domain for lands that had unique historic, cultural, scientific, and scenic value. Unlike national parks, national monuments could be declared without an act of Congress.

President Barack Obama used that law to set aside 1.35 million acres in San Juan County, Utah, an expanse larger than Grand Canyon National Park. The environmental community was ecstatic. Citizens in Blanding and Monticello were not. Within a year, President Donald Trump took the unprecedented step of reducing Bears Ears National Monument. Trump eliminated important archaeological sites on Cedar Mesa. He did not include Grand Gulch, first explored in the 1890s. He deleted the historic route the Mormon Hole-in-the-Rock Expedition took down Road Canyon and through The Twist. He ignored years of careful negotiation with diverse tribes seeking a common preservation goal. Hence this book—I seek to write about prehistory, history, and current issues within the Obama-designated Bears Ears National Monument boundaries. This

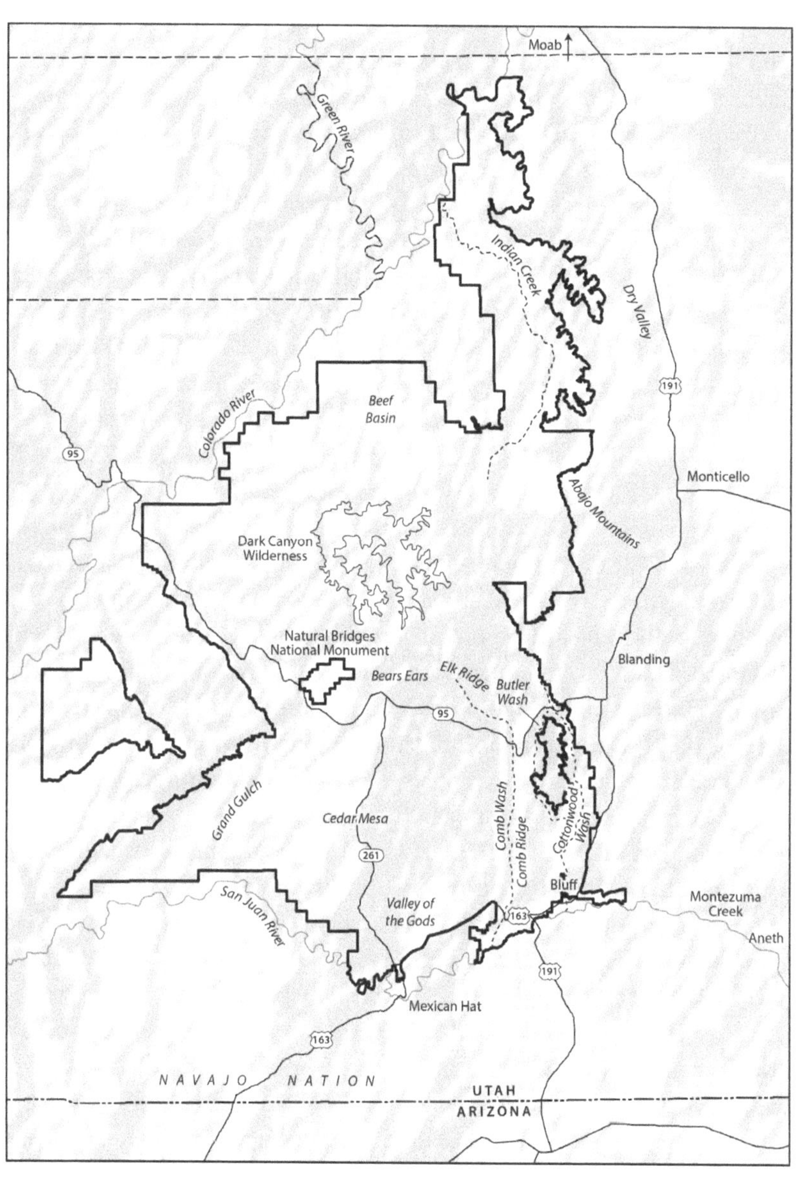

The dark line on this map shows the boundaries of the 1.35 million-acre Bears Ears National Monument in San Juan County, Utah, designated by President Barack Obama in December 2016. Five Native American tribes urged the president to use the Antiquities Act to protect their prehistoric and historic sacred and cultural sites. Map by Bill Nelson, copyright by the author.

vast area of public lands has become a twenty-first-century target for conservation goals and, alternatively, for local Utah communities saying "no" to federal proclamations. Much of nineteenth century Southwestern archaeology began within the Bears Ears boundaries. An author cannot write about Bears Ears without also writing about the adjacent, ongoing human communities both Native and non-Native.

I set out to research and write the history of Bears Ears, not just as a new national monument and a crisis over the interpretation of federal law, but also as a distinctive, remote place, a cultural landscape of unparalleled beauty. Four lawsuits have gone forward to restore Bears Ears National Monument to its original size. No president has ever before so dramatically reduced another president's executive order and national monument. Those political machinations and the desires of Utah politicians to redefine federal land management practices and uses for federal lands will be discussed. But the change in monument boundaries represents only a small segment in time in a place occupied by Native peoples for millennia.

The struggle over Bears Ears is also a fight over names upon the land and over whose stories demonstrate understanding of the landscape. Along Comb Ridge, Mormon settlers christened a distinct outcropping "Highland Lady" to commemorate their Scottish and northern European roots.[1] For the Diné or Navajo, the same dramatic rocks are labeled "Big Sheep's Balls" from a story of Indigenous hunters pursuing a large bighorn sheep ram that fled to the top of red rock cliffs. For cultural geographers, the place is "a layered, shifting reality that is constituted, lived, and contested, in part, through narrative." Cultural geographer Patricia L. Price explains, "If one digs into the history of any place, one is bound to uncover layer upon sedimented layer of historic claims to places by people who had come from other places."[2] She adds, "One has only to witness the contemporary liberation struggles of . . . Native Americans . . . to appreciate the grim reality of the blood shed and the hearts broken over such stories. These struggles are driven ultimately by stories often in direct conflict with the equally mythic, divine, or timeless claims of other groups."[3]

The importance of naming and cultural values is found in the name Bears Ears itself.[4] In *Comb Ridge and Its People: The Ethnohistory of a Rock,* Robert McPherson describes Navajo tradition and "the lengthy narrative of Changing Bear Maiden" as "a young virtuous woman who lives with her brothers. She denies many suitors but through Coyote's wily trickery, marries him and begins to change. She learns how to transform through witchcraft into an evil powerful bear then tracks down and kills all of

Naming sites is a part of claiming landscapes. Mormon pioneers, members of the Church of Jesus Christ of Latter-day Saints, called this rock outcropping on Comb Ridge "Highland Lady" to commemorate their Scottish and northern European roots. For the Diné or Navajos the same rocks are called "Big Sheep's Balls" because it is here where hunters pursued a large desert bighorn ram. Author photo.

her brothers except for the youngest one."[5] Writer Amy Irvine explains Coyote's lust and sexual appetites. Coyote will connive a way to sleep with a girl "and once he has her on all fours, howling and panting with abandon, no man will ever again satisfy her." Irvine writes that after the maiden's seduction and the murder of her brothers only the youngest brother remains. "When he realizes he cannot contain her newfound wildness, he kills and dismembers her. Her body parts are scattered across Cedar Mesa—two prominent landmarks called the Bears Ears are part of her remains."[6] They are her head and ears because she had become a bear.

This Southwest story hints of incest and rage as the virtuous maiden eliminates her brothers. It echoes the bear story from Wyoming's Devils Tower, the first national monument, in which a brother becomes a bear and pursues his sisters with sexual intent. The frightened girls climb a stump that rises into the air and transforms into a large rock outcropping clawed by the angry brother bear. The Creator saves the sisters by sending them skyward toward the heavens to become the constellation known as the Pleiades.[7]

Just as with Devils Tower, named Bears Lodge by several Great Plains tribes, so Native stories about Bears Ears and the dismemberment of a maiden who had changed into an angry bear are powerful moral tales. Stories stick to sandstone and encompass vast landscapes. For Navajos, Zunis, Hopis, Ute Mountain Utes, Utes, and Puebloans, Bears Ears is a sacred landscape of stories, homes, storage areas, and artifacts from countless Indian generations. There are cliff dwellings, refuge sites, sweat lodges, rock art of petroglyphs and pictographs, and thousands of potsherds scattered over roadless areas. It is a landscape of dry washes, steep canyons, sandstone cliffs, hidden springs, and pothole water tanks or *tinajas*.

To try to understand stories from the landscape, I'll use the same methodology I use in my classes at Fort Lewis College, where Native American students receive free tuition waivers at a school that provides unique opportunities for Indigenous students. The history of Fort Lewis College is important because it was a military fort beginning near Pagosa Springs, Colorado, and later moving southwest of Durango, Colorado. Soldiers from Fort Lewis were routinely called upon to both fight and defend American Indians in southeast Utah in a variety of skirmishes and events that lasted into the early 1900s. The fort evolved into an Indian boarding school. By an act of Congress in 1911, the federal property of the fort and over 6,000 acres became state property with our sacred trust to continue to educate Native Americans. The boarding school grew into a public high school and then a junior college. In 1956, staff and students moved to a new campus adjacent to Durango and became a four-year-degree-granting institution. We always kept the promise of free tuition for Native students from across the United States including Native Alaskan students. We now have 40 percent Native American enrollment with the highest Native American graduation rate in the nation.

Four kinds of truth are crucial in my classes and in this book. The first truth is archaeology. If an artifact was found in the ground in stratigraphic layers of undisturbed soil, or if a prehistoric site can be studied from its still standing ruins, then there is a truth. A second form of truth is Native oral traditions, which pass on stories and descriptions over centuries. A third truth is history gleaned from diaries, maps, photos, reports, and other original documents and accounts as well as secondary sources like newspapers, magazines, and books.

The fourth truth is language and how it slowly changes over time and how words and descriptions can tell us about culture, especially with legends and stories that link to specific places or settings within a landscape.

The naming of Bears Ears itself is one of those crucial and insightful stories. The goal then, through professional research as well as on-the-ground visits and reflections, is to understand Bears Ears National Monument in San Juan County, Utah, why it was declared, why it is supported by five American Indian tribes, and why local and state politicians fought so hard to reject it.

The struggle over Bears Ears is not just a fight over a million acres of federal public land. It is a contest over the very soul of a landscape. If the Native perspective is to leave land alone as the ancestors found it and to preserve this ancient landscape for quiet, respectful visitation and traditional uses, many descendants of white Mormon settlers and some Navajos want development. They want oil and gas wells, mining, and public lands grazing. They want more roads and better wages that come with industrialization and a local future for their children and grandchildren. "To Mormons, wilderness has been not Eden but a fallen landscape to be redeemed: although they live in the midst of dramatic Western scenery, Mormon advocates for wild nature have been few," writes Mark Stroll in *American Wilderness: A New History.*[8]

The local non-Native vision is often for extractive uses—holes in the ground for oil and gas wells, gouges in rock cliffs for potential uranium mines, and slender grasses clipped and eaten by cows in already overgrazed public pastures. But nothing is simple. Some Natives want development; some Anglos want preservation. There is both a conflicted vision of the past and a stark difference in perspectives on the future. For some San Juan County Commissioners, the Old West of pioneers and settlement should lead to a future of energy development and a higher county tax base.

For others, the Old West has become the New West of heritage tourism, eager hikers and vacationers, and a stable, sustainable economy based on a scenic landscape infused with the palpable remnants of a prehistoric past. "There is a complete blindness in small town Utah about us out-of-state millennials. We're living in our vans. We're here for the recreation, the outdoors, and we can revitalize local communities if we're given a chance," I was told by a guide and outfitter who added, "State government does not understand. Small towns in the West can profit from their local outdoor recreation. We can make a new economy while maintaining local community character."

The battle is over the Next West and whether "the lords of yesteryear," to use law professor Charles Wilkinson's phrase, will prevail in a landscape that epitomizes Congressional goals in the 1906 Preservation of American

Antiquities Act. The law states that presidents have the executive authority to set aside lands from the public domain in the smallest acreage possible. But who decides how small an archaeological site or landscape is? Comb Ridge, Butler Wash, Comb Wash, Indian Creek, Beef Basin, Cedar Mesa, Tank Mesa, Valley of the Gods, and all the canyons that drain Grand Gulch form vast, intact cultural landscapes. Their very value is their size. They should be left alone.

"Bears Ears, first and foremost, is Indigenous land. It is a place essential to the physical, spiritual, and cultural identity of the Hopi, Zuni, Ute, and Navajo nations. Before the advent of European settlers in the West, these people were here," wrote Angelo Baca in the *New York Times.* Baca is the cultural resources coordinator for Utah Diné Bikéyah. He explained, "We listened to the direction that tribal leaders and elders provided. After weighing many options, they decided to pursue the national monument designation, which prohibits resource exploitation of these sacred lands while explicitly allowing us to continue our many traditional uses of this living cultural landscape that needs us as much as we need it."[9]

President Barack Obama, in a magnificent, sweeping gesture, set aside acres of Bureau of Land Management (BLM), National Park Service (NPS), and US Forest Service (USFS) land as Bears Ears National Monument, permanently withdrawing lands from oil, gas, or mineral leasing. This is the first national monument enthusiastically supported by Native Americans who want protection for their cultural heritage and traditional landscapes as defined by the law. In 2017, President Donald Trump in an unprecedented action proclaimed a reduction in the monument's size of 85 percent or 1.1 million acres. Upon the recommendations of his then-Secretary of the Interior Ryan Zinke, Trump split the monument into two sections and gave each section new names. A part of Bears Ears is now called *"Shash Ja,"* or Bears Ears in Navajo, though local Navajo were never consulted. The Native coalition had agreed on the name Bears Ears in English, and to change it to a Navajo word "tramples the Native American true history of the place," explains Gavin Noyes of Utah Diné Bikéyah, which had championed the original monument and its larger boundaries. Never before has a president so drastically shrunk a national monument or so clearly ignored the conservation actions of a previous president. Nowhere in the Antiquities Act does it state that a president can undo the actions of a former administration.

Lawsuits have been filed. The environmental community is outraged; yet some San Juan County citizens express satisfaction with Trump's action. They are willing to gamble on the ups and downs of an energy and mining economy utterly vulnerable to international markets, rather than to carefully build a more substantial tourist and retiree economy. For professional archaeologists, the Trump administration's decisions are a recipe for disaster. "This is the worst possible scenario," a federal archaeologist told me. "More people. No money. No management."

The opportunity exists to create and save a stunning landscape; yet city, county, and Utah state officials opposed Bears Ears National Monument. The struggle continues over protecting the landscape but also over the political future of San Juan County with a redistricting of voter precincts to allow equitable representation of Native voters who comprise over 50 percent of San Juan County's residents. They have been underrepresented on the county school board and on the powerful board of county commissioners. A federal judge mandated redistricting. Ironically, just as the Trump administration shrunk Bears Ears boundaries against tribal wishes, a federal judge forced the expansion of Native participation as voters. For the first time in history, two Navajos elected on the Democratic ticket in 2018 assumed a Native majority on the San Juan County commission.

For the descendants of Mormon pioneers who originally came to southeast Utah on a mission to help Indians, this is a shocking turnabout. Outnumbered, they have lost their political control over the county, but not without a bitter, protracted struggle. In their first meeting, the Navajo county commissioners immediately voted to reverse the county's anti-Bears Ears position. The non-Native commissioner opposed the resolution. What the future means for land use decisions and for economic development is unknown.

Every president since Theodore Roosevelt has used the Antiquities Act. In Utah popular national parks, including Arches and Zion, began as national monuments. Local politicians have called the Obama designation a "land grab," but it is not. Every single acre set aside by President Obama was already federal public land. The critical difference is that by proclaiming a national monument, Obama used his executive authority to withdraw mineral leasing and oil exploration from within the monument. That's what some locals are incensed about, and I understand their complaint.

Only 8 percent of San Juan County, which is almost the size of Massachusetts, is private property. It has two stoplights, but one just blinks. San Juan is "the largest county in Utah, a great triangular wedge of abysmally eroded and weathered sandstone bounded on the east by the Colorado line, on the south by the Arizona line, and all along its hypotenuse by the

Colorado River," wrote Wallace Stegner in *Mormon Country*.[10] He added that its southern end is the Navajo Nation. Navajos, calling the area Diné Bikéyah or traditional tribal lands, played a major role in creation of the Bears Ears National Monument. Goals will be to protect thousand-year-old Ancestral Puebloan sites from vandalism, to maintain access to Native cultural sites for ongoing ceremonies, and to provide for hunting, plant gathering for herbs and medicines, and firewood collecting.

In 1862 when Colonel Kit Carson ordered Navajos to be rounded up and forced to walk east to Fort Sumner and Bosque Redondo in New Mexico, Navajo headman Hoskininni, or "one who passes out anger," fled west with his small band to avoid the Long Walk, one of the seminal events in Navajo history. His band learned to eke out a living in a sandstone maze. Navajo leader K'aayelli was born near Bears Ears as was Hastiin Chi'ihaajin or Manuelito.

Disputes over the new monument have been a struggle about how the land should be used, but the landscape is also contested terrain because of competing origin stories. For some Navajo and Ute bands, this is their homeland. For Puebloan peoples, this is where their ancestors lived thousands of years ago. For members of the Church of Jesus Christ of Latter-day Saints, this is where they were called to a San Juan Mission in 1879. Their relatives endured privations along the Hole-in-the-Rock Trail to establish the village of Bluff before moving north to create the towns of Blanding and Monticello.

Bluff has a Chacoan Great House and signs at the edge of town state "Bluff, established 650 AD," long before the arrival of Mormon wagons. A thousand years ago the Bluff valley may have had two to three thousand Native people farming and living in small clusters. By 1900, twenty years after Mormons settled Bluff, there were 200 residents. In 2020, there were still only 265 residents. Not much has changed, but it's about to. Too many visitors may overwhelm remote and underfunded public lands. Favorite canyons and ruins will see additional tourists. There will be more tire tracks, more crushed cacti and cryptobiotic soil.

I love Cedar Mesa for its silence, solitude, and darkness. Natural Bridges National Monument has been designated the nation's first dark sky park. Sky Rangers lead galactic tours after sunset via telescope. During the day visitors hike ancient trails in deep sandstone canyons; at night they explore the universe. "As one of the most intact and vast roadless areas in the contiguous United States, Bears Ears has that rare and arresting quality of deafening silence," reads the Obama monument proclamation.[11] Yet

The Bears Ears as seen from the Bears Ears meadow where each summer tribal peoples gather and camp to share food, stories, and cultural traditions. Author photo.

some local citizens want energy development with its concomitant roads, dust, drilling rig lights, and utilization of pure ground water to frack horizontal wells. They want good paying gas well jobs, and I sympathize with that, but energy development is not sustainable. Over time gas production diminishes. Wells falter and eventually fail. Pumpjacks squeak and groan and finally seize up.

The night sky and the ground beneath it can instead become an enduring resource for respectful, well-managed, heritage tourism. Utah favorite son Wallace Stegner wrote that mining communities often went out "like blown matches." That has happened with oil and gas, but not with tourism. Recently there has been a 1.5 hour waiting line to get into Arches National Park and on some days the park has been closed because all available parking slots are full by mid-morning.

What is it about this Bears Ears landscape that produces such intense feelings of home and sacredness? How has such a remote place with so few current inhabitants become nationally known, and how has it become a twenty-first-century case study over the future of conflicting views of the American West?

Part of the answer is understanding what nature writer Ellen Meloy described as the need for a "a deep map of place." Terry Tempest Williams also expresses the power of the red rock desert. She writes in *Red: Passion and Patience in the Desert,*

> For as far as I can see, the canyon country of southern Utah extends in all directions. No compass can orient me here, only a pledge to love and walk the terrifying distances before me. What I fear and desire most in this world is passion. I fear it because it promises to be spontaneous, out of my control, unnamed, beyond my reasonable self. I desire it because passion has color, like the landscape before me. It is not pale. It is not neutral. It reveals the backside of the heart.[12]

Some of her passion was part of the national groundswell of conservation support for Bears Ears. As a nation of over 330 million people, we need more places left alone, more landscapes protected in their entirety.

Williams explains, "As the world becomes more crowded and corroded by consumption and capitalism, this landscape of minimalism will take on greater significance, reminding us that through its blood red grandeur just how essential wild country is to our psychology, how precious the desert is to the soul of America."[13]

That old desert rat Ed Abbey, an eco-activist, writer, and former park ranger, spent time across the Colorado Plateau. He explored side canyons in Glen Canyon before 1963 when it was flooded to create Lake Powell. But he also spent days in San Juan County, perhaps more days than Sheriff Rigby Wright would have liked. As Abbey's anti-development, save-the-wilderness ideology intensified, he may have practiced some of his monkeywrenching techniques on road-building equipment used to create Highway 95, a 1976 Bicentennial Project, which constructed a two-lane asphalt highway heading west from Blanding, Utah, to Lake Powell or "Lake Foul," as Abbey christened it.

For Abbey, the magic of the canyons resulted in slickrock seduction. He admitted to a love affair with rocks. Once, he left Bluff, Utah, headed west into "the Big Country" of Valley of the Gods and Monument Valley before it became a tribal park. He drove his aging vehicle to the top of the cut in Comb Ridge and just stared at the desert stretched out before him. "We went by dusty washboard road to Bluff on the San Juan and thought we were getting pretty near the end of the known world. Following a narrow wagon road through more or less ordinary desert we climbed a notch in Comb Ridge and looked down and out from there into something else,"

Abbey wrote.[14] He was on the southern edge of Bears Ears. Exhilarated, he described,

> What you see from Comb Ridge is mostly red rock, warped and folded and corroded in various ways, all eccentric, with a number of maroon buttes, purple mesas, blue plateaus and gray dome-shaped mountains in the far-off west. Except for the thin track of the road, switchbacking down into the wash a thousand feet below our lookout point, and from there climbing up the other side and disappearing over a huge red blister on the earth's surface, we could see no sign of human life . . . Nor any sign of any kind of life, except a few acid-green cottonwoods in the canyon below. In the silence and the heat and the glare we gazed upon a seared wasteland, a sinister and savage desolation. And found it utterly fascinating.[15]

Yes, my kind of place—desolate, hot, and dangerous; no shade; only trickles of water; and circling turkey vultures. Abbey turned around. He rarely did, but on that day, he did not trust his car to continue westward. He worried about food, water, spare parts, his radiator rupturing, tires splitting, and bogging down in sand. But he would return "toward whatever lay back of that beyond."[16] On another trip he described "Bears Ears, Elk Ridge, and more fine blank areas on the maps."[17]

What Cactus Ed luxuriated in—the vast desert wasteland, the inviting sandstone curves and cliffs, the lack of water, which meant few if any people—was exactly what terrified the early Mormon settlers. They just wanted to farm. These sons and daughters of European immigrants sought deep topsoils, shade, vegetable gardens, and a pastoral landscape. Instead, they got rock and sand and convoluted canyons so complex it would take decades to map and understand them. For millennia Native Americans had adjusted and even thrived in the canyon country landscapes where Wallace Stegner once wrote about "the poetry of hidden springs" where sandstone seeps produce hanging gardens of sweet-smelling flowers and luxuriant grasses protected by shade. But acres of sustainable farmland? Not in southeast Utah.

"A country of drifting sand and bald rocks, a country of dry desolation gashed deeply with crooked gulches. Its surface had been carved by the winds into knobs and pinnacles and figures of fantastic patterns," wrote Mormon pioneer cowboy Albert Lyman. "The hellish howl of coyotes echoed back and forth in the darkness of its nights, and long green lizards raced over its hot hills in the day."[18]

Sent on a mission to create a farming community at Montezuma Creek and to begin the political creation of what would become San Juan County, Utah, the hardy Mormon pioneers, adherents of the Church of Jesus Christ of Latter-day Saints, became exhausted and never made it. Their planned six-week trip had taken six months across some of the most complicated canyons on the continent. They stopped short and established the village of Bluff, which by 1890 pretentiously called itself Bluff City. Part of the Bears Ears story is their story and the story of their descendants still tenaciously working the land and living primarily in the communities of Blanding and Monticello. The Native towns or villages are Monument Valley, Montezuma Creek, and Aneth for Navajo tribal members, and White Mesa for Paiute and Ute Indian families. Bears Ears, its past, present, and future, cannot be understood without also knowing something about the adjacent communities and the people there struggling to make a living in one of the poorest parts of Utah.

Under President Barack Obama, the new monument would have featured an unprecedented Native American commission. The Obama monument designation states, "In recognition of the importance of tribal participation to the care and management of the objects identified above, and to ensure that management decisions affecting the monument reflect tribal expertise and traditional and historical knowledge, a Bears Ears Commission is hereby established to provide guidance and recommendations."[19] That had never happened before. It did not happen under President Trump, and it has not happened yet.

"When we look at a landscape, we do not see what is there, but largely what we think is there. We attribute qualities to a landscape which it does not intrinsically possess—savageness, for example, or bleakness, and we value it accordingly," states Robert Macfarlane. "We *read* landscapes, in other words, we interpret their forms in the light of our own experience and memory and that of our shared cultural memory."[20]

So welcome to Bears Ears where an ancient landscape, rich in botany, geology, and paleontology, also represents thousands of years of human history and some of the most remote and spectacular archaeological sites and ongoing Native sacred places in the nation. This book is a chronological sampling of human history within or adjacent to the Bears Ears boundaries. It is not a guidebook, but rather an introduction to an extraordinary

Tribal elders have demonstrated the importance of Bears Ears cultural sites that go back in time for thousands of years. Former Zia Pueblo governor Peter Pino worked tirelessly with Mesa Verde National Park and Crow Canyon Archaeological Center to bring modern Pueblo peoples' perspectives to the forefront of archaeological interpretation. He strongly supported protecting Bears Ears. Author photo.

landscape now at the center of a major controversy over local and state versus federal management and control.

My preparation for researching and writing *Bears Ears: Landscape of Refuge and Resistance* grows out of years of volunteering on public land issues. For over a decade, I held a gubernatorial and presidential appointment to the Southwest Colorado Resources Advisory Council (RAC) of the BLM, where I represented history/culture and the environment. That experience helped me to learn about the agency and its dedicated staff. Much of Bears Ears is BLM and USFS land. From the USFS, I received the National Individual Volunteer Award from the Chief of the Forest Service for my work on wilderness education. For the BLM, I was asked to write "Canyons of the Ancients National Monument: Interpreting and Administering the Proclamation," appended to the CANM Management Plan. Traveling the United States, including Alaska and Hawaii, I researched and wrote *Sacred Objects and Sacred Places: Preserving Tribal Traditions*, which helped prepare me for the myriad issues related to Bears Ears. Throughout this book, I focus on refuge and resistance of both Native and white communities struggling to survive and thrive in canyon country. My own personal connections to the landscape via hikes, camping trips, and stories of people and the land are interwoven in fifteen chapters.

I begin in Chapter 1 with hunter-gatherers, deep time, and a possible woolly mammoth petroglyph at Sand Island along the San Juan River. Chapter 2 describes the critical transition from the first farmers, the Basketmakers, to the Ancestral Puebloans with their pottery and architectural traditions. Those peoples were once labeled the Anasazi by archaeologists, but now the preferred terminology advocated by their descendants is Ancestral Puebloans. Chapter 3 outlines the Pueblo III period of moving into the cliffs, or the cliff dwellings, found in canyon after canyon across Bears Ears. Next in Chapter 4 comes other Native peoples—Navajos and Utes who sometimes traded with each other and often raided each other. Canyon exploration begins in 1859 by the US military, whose expedition leader J.N. Macomb found Canyonlands valueless, though an accompanying scientist, Dr. J.S. Newberry, was captivated by the slickrock landscape and made discovery after discovery.

Chapter 5 details the Navajos' Long Walk or "The Fearing Time," where some prominent Navajo families sought refuge at Bears Ears to avoid Kit Carson's troops. I also describe the first surveyors in the Bears Ears region and their initial reactions to the hundreds of archaeological sites they encountered.

"We Thank Thee, Oh God," is a Mormon inscription at the top of San Juan Hill where missionary families faced their last serious obstacle before settling Bluff, Utah. I explain their intent to farm and their switch to cattle and sheep ranching in Chapter 6. Chapter 7 is about cowboy archaeology and the first pothunters to discover the wealth of artifacts deep in San Juan County's caves and cliffs. I write about a famous female botanist, the attempt to move Southern Utes to San Juan County from Colorado, and congressional debate and passage of the Antiquities Act in 1906.

Chapter 8 chronicles the first federal influence in San Juan County with establishment of the USFS and the Manti-La Sal National Forest, and Natural Bridges National Monument. I use a variety of sources to explain the local assault on Ute Indians as part of the pursuit of Paiute Posey by a posse during the so-called "Last Indian War" in 1923. In Chapter 9, I describe crucial events in the 1930s including adventurers getting lost, a kidnapping, a murder, and the failed attempt under the Franklin Delano Roosevelt Administration to create a huge national monument that would have embraced Bears Ears.

Chapter 10 is about uranium mining, the Atomic Age, and post-World War II tourism resulting in a Golden Circle of national parks and monuments and a full flush of tourists finding San Juan County along with establishment in 1964 of Canyonlands National Park. Chapter 11 is about Commissioner Calvin Black's pet project, highway U-95, which bisected Bears Ears and was rigorously, and possibly illegally, opposed by Edward Abbey and friends, who wanted the deep canyons of Cedar Mesa left alone. I also describe the first federal pothunting raid in Blanding in 1986 and its mixed results. The chapter chronicles tragedies related to uranium mining and the Monticello Mill where millworkers and local residents suffered, and still suffer, from radioactive poisoning.

Chapter 12 explains ongoing problems with local pothunting and the arrest of Dr. James Redd and his wife Jeanne Redd for illegally excavating an Ancestral Puebloan burial site on state trust land in 1996. Their legal battle resulted in subsequent revisions to state laws protecting all burials, not just those in fenced cemeteries. The 2009 Blanding pothunting raid is described in detail along with the suicides of two defendants and the federal government's informer and star witness. The extent of the raid and the thousands of artifacts recovered helped create Utah Diné Bikéyah, a grassroots organization committed to preserving cultural resources on traditional Navajo lands, especially Bears Ears. Multiple vectors of environmental and Native American activism resulted in tribes coming together for Bears Ears National Monument in 2016.

Chapter 13 chronicles deep local and state resistance and opposition to the Bears Ears Monument designation and challenges to the 1906 Antiquities Act, which has never been altered or amended by Congress. Chapter 14 relates new scientific discoveries in Bears Ears, including a tiny tuber or potato that the ancients cultivated and brought into Utah and new research on thousand-year-old artifacts collected by cowboy archaeologists in the 1890s now being rediscovered and analyzed in some of the nation's most prestigious museums. I also look at the value of dark skies in Bears Ears and have quotes from delighted visitors to Natural Bridges who had never seen the Milky Way or other galaxies. Chapter 15 brings us up to date with political issues involving Bears Ears and an understanding of ongoing tourist impacts as well as recent anthropological research.

Bears Ears is both a physical landmark visible for miles across the horizon and the collective name for a region in southeast Utah. In one place, prehistory, history, Native voices, and the future of federal lands in the American West all come together. Bears Ears beckons.

CHAPTER 1

Hunter-Gatherers and Deep Time

From Pleistocene Mammoths to Archaic Rock Art

> Although we will never be able to recover all the specific meanings that an artist attempted to express on the rocks in ancient times, rock art will continue to fascinate us because it offers a direct connection, however imperfect, to the individual artist who made it, and to aspects of the collective knowledge and meanings embedded in those artists' cultural worlds.
>
> —William Lipe in *Rock Art: A Vision of a Vanishing Cultural Landscape*

They moved through the canyons and down to the rivers in small groups. Always hunting, foraging, looking for food and game, sleeping in hide shelters, soaking in the morning sun after it was too late to hunt after daybreak, animals already gone. They traveled lightly across the landscape without farming, without building stone shelters. We know them by their spearpoints mostly. These Native Americans, who have been labeled Paleo-Indians, entered the Bears Ears area as early as 13,000 to 11,000 years ago in a wetter time with lush grasses, herds of big game such as deer, elk, and bighorn, and megafauna such as mammoths and huge bison.

The southeast Utah they knew had the same physical features of Comb Ridge, Cedar Mesa, and deep canyons such as Fish, Owl, Mule, Bullet, and Grand Gulch, but all those millennia ago, the landscape had groves of deciduous trees, mainly cottonwoods, and waving grasses without arroyos. A Pleistocene pack rat midden in Bears Ears at Fishmouth Cave dates from 12,770 years before present with proof of tree species including limber pine, red-osier dogwood, rose, dwarf juniper, blue spruce, and Rocky Mountain juniper. Archaeologist William Davis states, "None of these species appear at the site today," which is 5,200 feet in elevation. These species now "do not co-occur locally at elevations lower than 8,000 feet."[1]

High water tables from full aquifers made hunting easier, and springs came out of sandstone seeps bubbling, flowing water, attracting small game and the quiet movements of desert bighorns sniffing the wind, lowering their heads to drink, an older female on guard. Clovis spearpoint fragments and dozens of stone artifacts have been found on Lime Ridge at an ancient hunting stand. Davis explains that the small Clovis groups of not more than forty people were "specialized large game hunters" who moved fast, populating the American continents and "within a period of only five hundred years after crossing through the treeless arctic tundra of the Bering land bridge from Asia, the Clovis hunters had reached the end of the line at Tierra del Fuego, Argentina."[2] There may have been continental migrations even earlier than those of Clovis people, but some of these small Clovis bands came through southeast Utah.[3] They entered the vast canyon complex that other Native groups, thousands of years later, would call Bears Ears.

Davis writes that on the Colorado Plateau, "Clovis finds are surface deposits only," and in San Juan County, "eight isolated projectile points have been documented." He adds with awe, "Their sophisticated stone tool technology was equal to any in the world," with Clovis points averaging an inch wide and 2.64 inches long.[4] So, the people were here. Did they also carve rock art? In one place along the San Juan River a stretch of cliff has been an artist's canvas for thousands of years. The site offers an abundance of rock art styles and anthropomorphs carved into stone, facing south toward the flowing river and migrating geese, turkeys crossing the sandbars, bears following closely, noses down, bear paw prints covering turkey tracks. On that straight stretch of sandstone cliff, among the thousands of carved animals, human figures, spirits, snakes, and representations of corn, one petroglyph stands out, small, hard to see, but with the outline of upward pointing tusks, a Columbian mammoth or *Mammuthus columbi*, from an age and an ecosystem we can barely understand.

It takes a long time to find a mammoth, especially if it has been buried beneath tamarisk, oak brush, and Russian olive trees. I had heard rumors about a mammoth along the San Juan River in San Juan County, but a beast from the Pleistocene is hard to locate and even harder to prove. Now thanks to the Bureau of Land Management (BLM), a possibly 13,000-year-old petroglyph, one of the oldest in North America, can be visible under just the right lighting conditions. A furry elephant carved on rock in the desert of southeast Utah?

Mammoths are from not only another time, but also another climate. Proving such a find would continue to turn back the clock on human habitation in the American Southwest. The ancient hunter-gatherers moved constantly following huge megafauna then expertly dispatching them with sharp spearpoints while fearing saber-toothed tigers, huge bears, and even fifteen-foot-high ground sloths.[5]

When I had heard about a possible mammoth image along the river, I hiked in with local artist and rock art specialist Joe Pachak to see the petroglyph. I remember getting whipped in the face by bushes and branches and being unable to make out the animal's image, discernible to Joe but not to me. Then the Monticello office of Utah's BLM hydro-axed and weed-wacked tamarisk below the site. I returned for Pachak's mammoth figure, but the pachyderm was playing hide and seek. I couldn't find it. My dog, however, found all sorts of things recently revealed by the cut over landscape—bewildered skunks and porcupines that had just lost their homes and were wandering in the wood slash.

By spring 2011, Arizona rock art specialists Ekkehart Malotki of Flagstaff and Henry Wallace from Tucson photographed the mammoth.

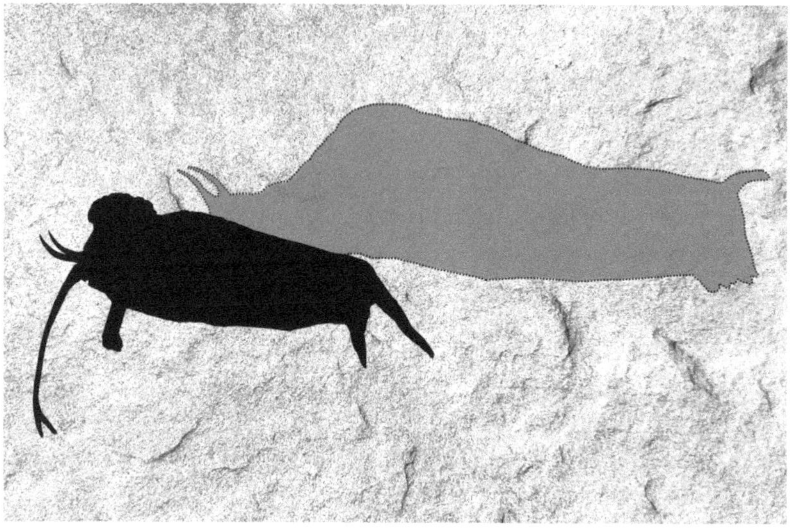

On a sandstone cliff east of Sand Island Campground a 13,000-year-old petroglyph of a Columbian mammoth, *Mammuthus columbi*, lies beneath a superimposed glyph of a Pleistocene bison or *Bison antiquus*. This may be one of the oldest examples of Native American rock art in North America. Illustration by DJ Webb based on a photo from Craig Childs, *Flying Home*. Used with permission.

The scientific community began to take notice. As Malotki and Wallace explain, "It had never been scientifically described or investigated, probably because of its difficult access more than fifteen feet above ground level. Also impeding its recognition as a mammoth is its indistinctness."[6] Local archaeologist Winston Hurst concurs. He writes, "The panel, located about fifteen feet above the modern ground surface and forty feet above the modern river level appears to depict images of Ice Age animals rendered in a style that suggests great antiquity."[7] Hurst notes that the rock art artist must have seen Columbian mammoths because of the level of detail in the petroglyph, which includes "the distinctive 'topknot' that is an identifying hallmark of mammoth skulls" and "the distinctive bifurcation at the end of the trunk that represents what mammologists refer to as 'fingers.'"[8]

Now I've seen it too. Not only does the glyph take strong side light to view the twenty-inch-long carving, but another prehistoric artist superimposed a Pleistocene bison, *Bison antiquus*, over the mammoth image. That bison species became extinct about 10,000 years ago. Equally confusing are other petroglyphs close by. Thanks to the BLM's tamarisk removal program, the mammoth's unique tusks and trunk can now be seen, but just barely. On top of it the rock art bison image also dates to the Paleo-Indian period of hunter-gatherers. The real question for geologists is how old is the sandstone cliff the artists utilized?

The petroglyphs were carved into Navajo Sandstone, a formation that is fractured and easily eroded. According to geologist Mary Gillam, angular sandstone slabs at the base of the cliff broke away from its face. The question is whether this sloughing occurred more or less than 13,000 years ago, roughly when mammoths became extinct in the region. Future geologic dating may tell us when the cliff face at the mammoth panel became stabilized. French Paleolithic rock art expert Jean Clottes believes that if the petroglyph "had been discovered in a French or Spanish cave, nobody would question its identification."[9] Meanwhile, Bluff resident Pachak appears to have been vindicated. Initially, rock art specialists disavowed his finding; yet now a *Mammuthus columbi* or Columbian mammoth seems likely in San Juan County. A story and photos of the image became a hot topic in *Pleistocene Coalition News*.

"I recognized it about 1990 when I was trying to record Archaic rock art," Pachak explains. "I took photos and discussed it with friends. It seemed apparent, but rock art specialists rejected it because they said a wall like that could not sustain an image for 13,000 years." But Pachak knew that the soft sandstone wall had an overhang above it. He had been there in driving rain and not gotten wet. "I believe there are fifteen badly eroded Paleolithic images near there." He adds that the entire site, which may be over sixty feet long, has not been adequately recorded, "which is a very difficult thing to do because you'd have to draw every rock surface."[10] How to position ladders without potentially damaging an ancient panel is complicated. Pachak urges the BLM to require special permits for such an investigation.

Who carved the mammoth? Probably a Clovis-era hunter, part of a human explosion in the use of this unique spearpoint technology that quickly spread across the continent and even down to the tip of South America before plants were domesticated.[11] The Clovis culture with its magnificent spearpoints heralded a new age of hunting technology with its basal fluting on both sides of the spearpoint. It meant the speedy demise of large beasts. The points have been found across America, but with almost no accompanying rock art.

The mammoth image along the San Juan River remains intact, undamaged, and a unique opportunity to assess Pleistocene life, when the canyons of southeast Utah had a wetter environment. Glaciers melted and carried down river cobbles on volumes of water several times current snowmelt. Cobble terraces occur nearby. Clovis-era hunters wounded large mammals like mammoths and then followed the blood trail. They moved so quickly across the continent that Clovis hunters caused not only death, but also—along with climate change—extinctions, due to environmental change, overkilling, diseases spread by humans, and fragile ecosystems.[12]

The hunters may also have inadvertently befriended another species, California condors. Grand Canyon guide Wayne Ranney believes that California Condors evolved with Paleo-Indians. He thinks that before the extinction of megafauna like woolly mammoths, when early man killed large beasts, condors cruised in for the banquet.[13] Joe Pachak has lived over four decades in Bluff. Discovering the mammoth petroglyph "was one of the most enriching things that ever happened to me. How special is it to find one of the oldest rock art sites in North America?" And if Utah can have a state bird and even a state handgun, why not a state Pleistocene pachyderm?

Who knows what else we'll find as we rid the Southwest of thirsty invasive plants like tamarisk and Russian olive? As for the mammoth, I believe Joe. I have found it again on that long, bright expanse of ancient

For years Bluff, Utah, had a unique winter solstice festival. Local artist Joe Pachak crafted large animals out of wood, willow, and brush and then they were ceremonially burned an hour or two after sunset. The burning of this mammoth, set on fire by flaming darts hurled from replica atlatls, drew hundreds of people. Author photo.

rock art especially with the slanted sunlight of fall or spring mornings close to the equinox. The image may have been there for 13,000 years or more. Now that we know about it, we need to keep it safe.

Paleo-Indian hunting parties, after the extinction of the large megafauna, concentrated on bison using smaller Folsom-style points, still fluted, but with etched ears at the bottom. Familiar herd animals in Bears Ears included elk, deer, bison, and bighorn. With the last of the Folsom fluted points, 8,000 years ago, Archaic hunters emerged near headwaters of river canyons. They specialized in atlatls or spear throwers to hunt meat, and they utilized Bears Ears in Early, Middle, and Late Archaic phases until 2,000 to 3,000 years ago.

These hunters had a different diet, demonstrated the beginnings of territoriality, and showed the first use of ground stones to utilize plant seeds such as amaranth (pigweed), Chenopodium (goosefoot), and Indian rice grass. They hunted small game like rabbits and gathered berries including hackberry, serviceberry, and the petals of wild roses. Archaic peoples used leather, wove yucca sandals (both plain weave and open twined), and had a tool kit of bone tools. Their storage areas were stone-slab-lined pits under ledges or in caves. Just like Native peoples today, Archaic peoples treasured nutritious pinyon pine nuts. Gathering them may be one of the longest continuing Native traditions in Bears Ears.

Old Man Cave, below Cedar Mesa and on the west side of Comb Wash, included the remnants of an Early Archaic sandal from approximately 7,800 years ago.[14] The Green Mask site in Grand Gulch may be early Archaic. Late Archaic peoples used hunting nets of yucca fiber and human hair. They organized communal hunts and rabbit drives and they had their own distinctive rock art. Archaic period hunter-gatherer rock art along the San Juan River is thousands of years old, but unlike the few carved mammoths, which may be unique in North America, the other hunter-gatherer style is more whimsical. As I walk the trail between cliff and river in southeast Utah, I search again for the face. It's ten inches tall. The eyes and mouth are distinctly pecked and two antennae rise above the head. I almost walk past it and then I see it again, south-facing, looking out across space and time etched on sandstone 5,000 years ago.

There's no smile, but no scowl either. Just a human face, an anthropomorph really, insect-like because of the antennae. I wonder who carved it

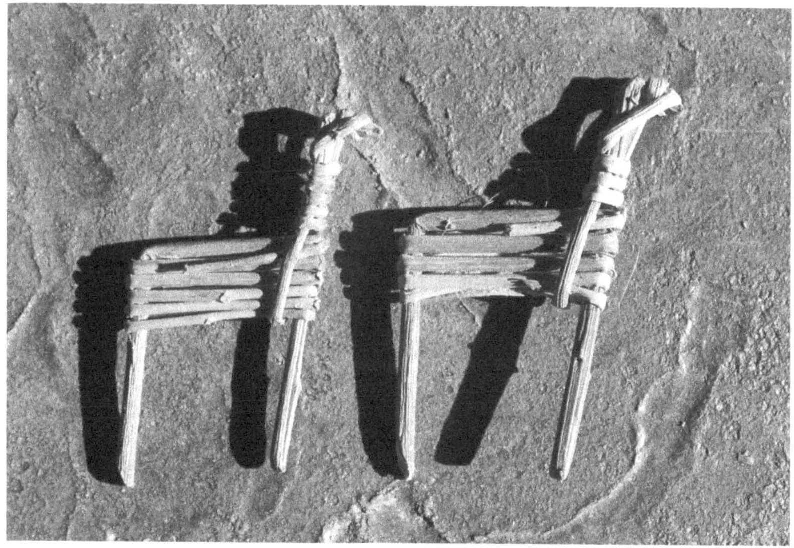

Paleo-Indians crafted split-twig figurines from bent willow twigs probably as hunting magic in the pursuit of desert bighorn sheep. These are modern replicas from Supai Village on the Havasupai Indian Reservation, Grand Canyon. Author's collection and author photo.

and why. Along this stretch of the San Juan River thousands of petroglyphs appear. Most of the images are Basketmaker II, early cousins of the Ancestral Puebloans with their large torsos, earbobs, and duck-style headdresses. The face I see is from an even older time. This Western Archaic rock art style known as Glen Canyon Linear, defined by Christy G. Turner II in 1963, was briefly investigated, described, drawn, and photographed before the captured Colorado River flooded Glen Canyon with the closure of Glen Canyon dam. Much of that rock art style is hundreds of feet under water, but traces of it can be found on cliffs along the San Juan River and on boulders at the base of Cedar Mesa. The artists preferred carving the dark desert patina of sandstone blackened by manganese oxide.

"The animals are fairly representational, but the artists added lines or crosshatching. Their sheep and deer are elegant, but there is a layer of abstraction with linear lines," explains Utah rock art photographer Diane Orr. "I'm drawn to Glen Canyon Linear because it's so beautiful and so well done. The style is defined by its exceptional quality. The groups had time to do it. They worked on it and improved it." She adds, "In hunting cultures you find more individual expression and variation than in agricultural societies."[15] Imagine a world without agriculture and with small family groups perpetually moving through a canyon landscape searching for edible roots and seeds from wild plants. Always on the alert for meat protein, from small cottontail rabbits to the delectable desert bighorn, these groups of Native Americans tilled no fields and built no architecture. Instead, they sharpened their stone knives, practiced with their atlatls, and hid near springs or stone water tanks, *tinajas*, at dawn, waiting for wildlife.

They found game trails and followed them up canyons through oak brush and pinyon-juniper forests like those on Cedar Mesa below the Bears Ears. Careful and cautious, these hunters lived from meal to meal; yet anthropologists suggest that the hunters' workday may have averaged only three hours instead of our eight or ten. "The key to understanding the style is in understanding the broad spectrum of diets of the archaic hunters and gatherers. The folks who made both the Glen Canyon Linear Rock Art and shaped the split-twig figurines were the people around when, at least in some areas, corn first made its way into the northern Southwest," explains archaeologist and ancient farming expert Ben Bellorado.[16]

Archaic shamans carved elongated figures with small faces, flowing vertical lines sometimes without hands or feet, and plenty of etched dots, circles, gridirons, diamonds, spirals, wavy zigzag lines, and the occasional

A 9,000- to 5,000-year-old rock art style, labeled Glen Canyon Linear because it was first described in Glen Canyon, can be found in the Bears Ears region and along the San Juan River corridor. Author photo.

downward pointing penis. I am captivated by this rock art style. These hunters depended upon fresh game. They left their marks on canyon cliffs, but they also twisted split-twig figurines as representations of desert bighorn sheep and mule deer. Magical offerings, still fashioned today by some tribal people, split-twig figurines have been found within Grand Canyon caves.

"These figurines were ingeniously constructed of a single long thin willow branch, split down the middle, bent and folded in such a way as to create a miniature representation of an animal," wrote Alan R. Schroedl, who added, "These figurines were probably magico-religious objects that were used in ritual activities to insure success in hunting game animals."[17] Some of the figurines have even been found ritually killed, pierced by tiny spears.

Willow twig craftsmanship continues. Archaic hunters folded figurines to bring luck. Grand Canyon river guides bend willow twigs into the same shape to garner tips. All these centuries later, it's still about making offerings. I think Archaic hunters would approve. They understood foraging. They liked rivers. Sally Cole writes in her classic rock art book *Legacy on Stone,* "The Glen Canyon Style 5 is widely dispersed across the

Colorado Plateau and appears to be most common along major rivers (Colorado, Dolores, Escalante, Green, and San Juan), indicating a relationship to Archaic populations that used these areas for such activities as gathering, hunting, fishing, ceremonies, and trade." She explains, "Panels are often loosely composed but may feature precise rows of anthropomorphs and quadrupeds," which "most frequently appear in outline with abstract interior line and dot decorations."[18]

So Archaic folks colored within the lines. Why not? They still had plenty of time for spirals, zigzags, and snakes. Their insect-like human faces have earned their rock art representations a similarity to ant people. Glen Canyon Linear style, at that transition phase from Archaic peoples to Basketmaker farmers, shows elements later used by Basketmakers. Describing the Upper Sand Island panel, Joe Pachak wrote, "The round, solidly pecked forms have wavy lines connecting strategic places on the figures. This suggests the representation of skinned human heads or masks, motifs which are common in later Basketmaker art." He adds that one long panel "may have been a ritual hunting, harvesting, and fertility narrative" with accurate depictions of elk including brow tines or antlers and dark heads.[19]

Even the writer Ed Abbey admired Archaic rock art. "Humanlike forms with helmets and goggles wave tentacles at us. What can they be? Gods? Goddesses? Cosmonauts from the Betelgeuse neighborhood? But still we ask, what does the rock art mean? Unlike the story of the cliff ruins, fairly coherent to archaeologists, we know little of the significance of this ancient work . . . Perhaps meaning is not of primary importance here. What is important is the recognition of art, wherever we may discover it, in whatever form."[20]

Abbey appreciated ancient rock art. What he could not abide was Glen Canyon Dam, which destroyed so much of it. I agree with Abbey's lament, but I still look for the Glen Canyon style rock art and I occasionally find it, far from a river's winding corridor at the base of a vast sandstone cliff. Here, a tipped-over rock rolled from hundreds of feet above and landed on its side revealing an entire tableau of Glen Canyon Linear figures. I tilt my head sideways to see them—the lines, the dots and dashes, and the small heads with their playful antennae. Archaic hunter-gatherers, poised at the edge of the transition to sedentism and dependence upon corn, beans, and squash, carved these figures. Shamans etched this great stone slab, and then it careened off a cliff to land on its sandstone shoulder. I tilt my head sideways and look again. Then I scan the horizon as they must have continually done, looking for movement, looking for meat, wondering what we gave up thousands of years ago when we traded wild foods and mobility for tiny ears of maize.

Late Archaic hunter-gatherers moved across Bears Ears from 2,000 BC to AD 200 starting to live where later peoples would also congregate. The Late Archaic period includes the first domesticated plants, bell-shaped storage pits, and beads for decoration. They built permanent villages and left evidence of spiritual ceremonies. Hunter-gatherers gave way to Basketmakers who farmed corn, beans, and squash, perfected their own unique rock art style, San Juan Anthropomorphic, and created thousands of sites in what would become the Bears Ears region of San Juan County, Utah. But theirs is a different Native story because theirs was a different age.

CHAPTER 2

From Basketmakers to Ancestral Puebloans, AD 50–1150

> Cedar Mesa . . . is a place of untrammeled natural beauty whose remoteness has secured a prehistoric microcosm from large-scale ravages of modern exploitation . . . The Cedar Mesa landscape is much like that of Mesa Verde. It . . . was a major staging area for those at the dawn of Puebloan history.
>
> —Florence Lister, *Troweling Through Time*

Hunter-gatherers with their spear-throwing atlatls and their distinctive rock art panels eventually gave way to a new cultural group labeled Basketmakers who still hunted and foraged but also settled down to plant and to farm, in a transition to sedentism that ended the Paleolithic age and began the first real settlements along the San Juan River and in adjacent drainages of Bears Ears. Maize arrived north from Mexico brought in packs by long-distance traders who developed a thriving trade in seashells. After AD 900 scarlet macaws or parrots and their feathers were traded to Basketmaker villages in the Bears Ears area along the San Juan River, Butler Wash, Comb Wash, and Cedar Mesa. Copper bells came later. Archaeologists explain that the transition occurred over decades, but the new group had distinctive cultural traits including beautiful and functional baskets, bows and arrows, pithouses dug deep into sandy soils, and a distinctive style of rock art labeled San Juan Anthropomorphic Style.[1]

Probably owing to population increase, Archaic families became more settled. By 1000/500 BC or AD 1 these people came to be known as "Basketmakers," because of their extensive use of basketry. After thousands of years of mobility and moving through the landscape pursuing game, now Indigenous people embraced the routine of farming maize. Though the small ears of corn were less than one-fourth the size of our large corn cobs, they provided steady nutrition and a chance for the people to settle down, to establish rituals and traditions, ceremonies and songs, and to plant in multiple fields always watching the way water ran off cliffs and down washes.

With digging sticks, farmers buried their precious maize seeds in sandy soils in small patches hoping and praying that if they planted six or seven areas that at least two or three would receive the proper moisture and ears of corn would burst forth from the soil. As I write this, I turn my head to see a small clay pot, and I study the brilliant red and blue colored corn cobs given to me by one of my former students, Georgie Pongyesva from Hopi, who during a cultural heritage internship learned from her elders how to plant and harvest corn. I treasure these cobs with their multiple-colored hues, every color except yellow. The genetics of this corn go back thousands of years, perhaps even to the first small maize cobs that the Archaic predecessors of the more settled Basketmakers planted in the San Juan Valley. Farming in the desert on sandy benches of soil and in the bottom of canyons could not have been easy, but these first permanent families in the Bears Ears area began to plant corn, to store the dried cobs in underground cists, and to build ovoid-shaped pithouses with storage niches, wing walls on the inside, and a roof of plastered wood. Boys and men dug the pithouses approximately two and a half feet below grade with an inside bench for sitting and for storage and a central hearth for both cooking and heating fires. Women helped roof the structures. Smoke went up through a central hole and at night starlight and moonlight shone down on the sleeping families who slept together on the earthen floor, feet to the fire.[2]

By 3,000 years ago, squash seeds came north, and then 2,500 years ago, beans arrived to make for a complete diet when supplemented with wild food gathering and hunting. Farmers planted beans whose fresh green runners climbed the corn stalks, and in the shade of the tall corn plants, squash grew underneath. The beans helped replenish nitrogen in the thin soils. The three domesticated crops—corns, beans, and squash—sustained the people for centuries and became known as the Three Sisters.

With a reliable cultivated food supply came Basketmaker pithouse villages from the beginning of the Christian era to AD 750.[3] Farmers utilized planting sticks and hoes of wood and stone and spent years watching water run off cliffs and through washes to know where to build check dams of smooth rocks or river cobbles to create farming terraces by trapping rain runoff and impeding soil erosion. In places across the Bears Ears landscape, these small check dams can still be seen though they have silted up. New crop varieties included larger cobbled maize by AD 400 and *Maize de Ocho,* which dates from the AD 600s with more calorie-dense kernels easier to grind from plants that flowered earlier and worked well with the shorter growing seasons across the Colorado Plateau. These corn plants had long, deep taproots that provided a distinct advantage in sandy soils. With successful food production and storage in underground cists and later above ground granaries mortared into canyon corners and ledges, the population expanded. Young children used throwing sticks and bows and arrows to keep rabbits and deer out of corn patches. Foraging continued, especially for a tiny potato as well as amaranth seeds.

On Cedar Mesa in the heart of the Bears Ears region and to the south of those two 9,000-foot outcroppings that from a distance look like the ears of a bear, Basketmaker people practiced low-intensity dryland farming, hunting, and foraging for pinyon nuts, grass seeds, and cactus fruit. They farmed small plots of maize in sand dunes and on canyon floors and used slash-and-burn agriculture in pinyon-juniper forests. Charred wood provided soil nutrients but for only a short time. Higher elevation plots benefited from more rainfall. Farmers understood to plant on slopes and drainages to capture moisture.

Describing Cedar Mesa, Florence Lister wrote, "It is a flat plateau averaging 6,000 to 7,000 feet in elevation, sliced by deep, sheer-walled gashes opening to the south, and having no running water except in some of the fissures." She added, in *Troweling Through Time,* "It is blanketed with the same Aeolian soils deposited by winds whirling out of Monument Valley and a dense pinyon-juniper forest that merges with taller timber in the uplands."[4] Cedar Mesa and Bears Ears area villagers kept and domesticated wild turkeys in "the only case of Native American animal domestication north of Mexico," William Lipe and other authors report.[5] Basketmaker and early Puebloan people domesticated a local Merriam subspecies of turkey for its feathers for use in rituals and turkey feather blankets, which had a warmth and loft similar to goose down and were warmer than rabbit fur. The turkeys themselves had special value and even received ritualized burials.

Grand Gulch, in the Bears Ears area, has a major archaeological site named Turkey Pen, which includes a jacal structure or enclosure made from vertical sticks, brush, and mud dried like adobe. Based on the amount of turkey droppings found, turkeys were kept there. Lipe and other scholars write that for the villagers, "maize (or corn) provided around 80 percent of their caloric needs," and "turkeys were not a regular food source" until "after about AD 1050."[6] The importance of turkeys is underscored by the number of rock art or petroglyph sites with incised, three-toed turkey tracks of varying sizes and lengths.

In ancient villages in the Bears Ears area, girls processed the carefully farmed corn and ground it up into useful flour on stone platters or metates using stone hand tools or manos. Though metates may break or crack over centuries, all across Bears Ears, bedrock metates, or grinding slicks in large sandstone boulders, can still be found. They were probably used for processing wild foods. Some bedrock metates have narrow slits parallel or perpendicular to the grinding surface, which may represent tight grooves for sharpening arrow shafts or other tools. Three adjacent metates placed together meant girls kneeled, grinding the corn into coarse, medium, and fine flour ready for cooking. As they knelt, they whispered and talked, casting side glances at any boys who may have returned successfully from the hunt perhaps with a front or back quarter of a mule deer or best meat of all—a desert bighorn sheep.[7]

Basketmaker people prized tender, succulent bighorn meat, and the wild sheep became symbols of fertility. Across the Bears Ears region, Basketmakers left thousands of examples of rock art or petroglyphs etched on stone. Though some panels contain delightful glyphs of fanciful animals, and the occasional frightening wild man with a hairy torso, big feet, and big hands, by far most of the carved animals are herds of bighorns. There can be single animals with accurate feet and horns as well as herds of half a dozen animals. Some glyphs have herds of more than twenty sheep with etched pictures of hunters nearby, arrows notched on drawn bows.

A few bighorns have large, fanciful horns swept back over their heads. Bighorns bunch together, leap apart, and also stand perfectly poised. The glyphs can be as small as your hand or the size of a dinner table, and they are everywhere. Basketmakers had begun to farm but continued to hunt. They carved panel after panel of bighorn rock art hoping to become one with the animal they pursued. Basketmaker rock art exists in dense panels along the San Juan River near Bluff, Utah, near the BLM's Sand Island Campground and on cliffs above ancient sand dunes north of the river.[8] On some sheer sandstone walls are small indented pecked cupules, about the size of a two-fingered handhold, to leave offerings of corn pollen and to say a prayer for health, fertility, and good crops.

By the Basketmaker II phase in Bears Ears, artists etched hundreds of rock art panels on canyon walls with new motifs of corn plants, segmented baskets, warriors with dramatic headdresses, feathers, earbobs, necklaces, and sometimes near their hands, skinned heads. Basketmaker II rock art

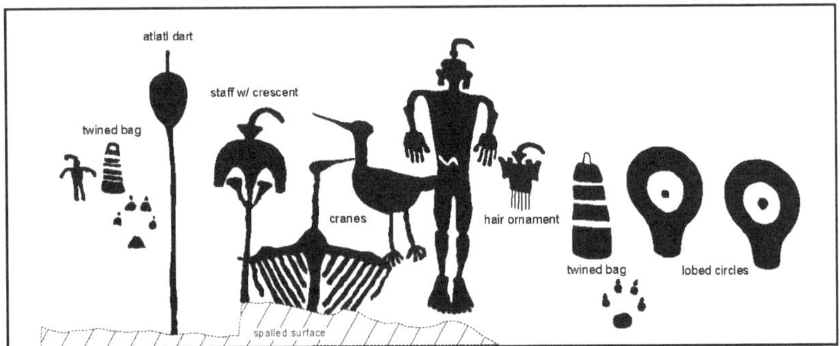

Rock art abounds in Bears Ears including this panel named Wolfman because of the wolf prints carved onto stone beneath the twined bags. This panel contains one of the most fully articulated human figures among thousands of Bears Ears rock art images. Drawing by Phil R. Geib, used with permission.

is dramatic and playful, but also serious, with large, fierce kachina-like figures and dozens of carved spirals. Along the San Juan River, dense Basketmaker rock art panels tower above the flood plain, etched deep into the dark almost black patina of weathered sandstone.

Thousands of petroglyph images depict atlatl darts, fanciful animals, human figures, deities, crookneck staffs, and unique lobed circles, looking like large lightbulbs, always found in pairs and possibly representative of religious iconography. "The lobed circles in these panels appear to be representations of actual objects, examples of which have been found with male burials . . . These objects were large pendants with a lobed-circle-shaped backing of wood onto which turquoise and shell mosaics were affixed. The lobed-circle shape has been interpreted as a representation of the womb, a powerful fertility symbol, or possibly the early Basketmaker house," note scholars in the book *Crucible of Pueblos: The Early Pueblo Period in the Northern Southwest*.[9] In some rock art panels in Bears Ears, especially along the San Juan River, warriors stand with magnificent headdresses, necklaces, earbobs, and occasionally they hold a skinned head. There are examples at the Butler Wash Kachina Panel. The meaning of those images is lost to time, but their dramatic presentation endures.[10] Basketmakers farmed but also produced intricate baskets whose "coiled basketry was a venerable and well-developed art."[11]

As soils became depleted, family groups moved on, symbolized by stone spirals that represent clan migrations over centuries, movement because of drought, soil exhaustion, and social strife.[12] I hike across Bears

Ears canyons, cliffs, and washes looking for rock art panels often dominated by Basketmaker symbols. Looking for signs from past cultures, sometimes canyon echoes reveal more about myself.

The shadows had grown long, and I knew I had to get off the slick rock and out of the canyon soon or I would never cross the wash in the proper place and find my way through the mud and the tangle of tamarisks and up the other side to my truck. The shadows lengthened. Impatient and a bit depressed, I descended the canyon. I had been trying to glean some significant sign from the ancient inhabitants.

I had spent a glorious spring afternoon high atop Comb Ridge, Utah, breathing in the wind from far across the Navajo Nation and walking slowly, deliberately, to the top of the sixty-five-million-year-old uplift with Charlie, my black flat-coated retriever mix. He eagerly led the way, tail up, nose down, and eyes bright. We had napped close to the top of the Comb in sand beneath an aging juniper tree, and I had seen a few small petroglyphs on the massive sandstone fins. I had picked up a few pottery sherds and some red chert flakes, which I put back down on the ground and covered with a thin layer of dirt. I term finding an arrowhead and

Arrowheads and spearpoints can be found across Bears Ears and they must remain on-site under penalty of federal law. Collecting artifacts is illegal. The author discovered this PI dart point of Dakota silicified sandstone dated AD 800–900, photographed it, and reburied it. Author photo.

putting it back "catch and release arrowhead hunting." Why not? It works for trophy trout and gives others the chance to catch them again.

I walked without maps wanting to discover the landscape on my own. The weather had been splendid and the temperature just right, perfect for hiking the Comb, but despite looking and searching, scanning the horizon and cliff walls with my small birder's 7.5 power binoculars, I had not seen much of consequence. I wanted to find a spectacular site that would reach out to me across time and space and jolt me out of the present, but no luck. I was tired, a little hungry, irritable, and late getting down to the truck. I hadn't gleaned anything from the landscape.

And then I saw it. High up. Higher than I could reach. My hiking sticks had been clicking down the canyon floor as I moved quickly looking for small barrel cactus, tree roots and bends in the trail. The light was gone and though the air was not yet cool, night was coming. I approached a long south-facing alcove. Suddenly, for no reason I can remember, I looked above a low Basketmaker wall from more than a thousand years ago. The Basketmakers preceded the Anasazi or Ancestral Puebloans, and this site had been severely pothunted or looted by vandals looking for bowls, baskets, or anything. The desecration meant there were no standing ruins and no need to stop, but for some reason, I looked up and what I saw rooted me to the spot. My blood pulsed through my upper body. As silence and shadow became darkness, a quick scan up the wall revealed a row of exquisite ochre red handprints. I was not alone.

In the canyons and broken terrain of Bears Ears, one frequently hikes in solitude and silence. Hours and even days go by with only the mesmerizing beauty of clouds scuttling above the tops of the Abajo Mountains vivid against the red rocks and layers of sandstone from ancient beaches. The solitude soothes and softens, but one is never alone. The Ancient Ones are present and palpable.

That day, I had found no stunning rock art panels or defensive, difficult-to-access cliff dwellings. Instead I walked, hiked, napped, shook off a few sorrows, talked to a few family ghosts, and crossed from one drainage south to another. Hurrying back against the darkness I had forgotten to look up, but now something compelled me to shift my weight and angle my shoulders, and there, like a message from the Old Ones, arched the handprints. Magnificent, they spoke as clearly as though an Ancestral Puebloan, long dark hair flowing, water dripping from cupped hands, had raised his head from the small pour-over pool I had passed moments ago.

I stopped. My dog Charlie stopped. He sniffed the air. I stared at the gallery of handprints, some adult size, many from small children. This is what I had sought all day—that moment of discovery, the thrill of finding something not on any map. A village had left its mark in this low, deep alcove centuries ago as families giggled, laughed, and stood on the rooftops of their small stone rooms. Now the ceilings were gone, rooms had toppled, and only a few low walls of rectangular, dressed stones remained. But still in place, protected from wind and rain and sun, handprints spread across the alcove, a silent gesture of kinship in the universal sign of peace and presence, an open hand pressed upon hard stone.

In the shadows as I gleaned the red hands, large and small, I looked down the alcove. A few yards away were more handprints, this time white around the edges, negative handprints made from paint held in a young man's mouth then blown against the wall perhaps by using a small reed tube. In this style of pictograph, the shape of the hand and each distinct finger was outlined in white unlike the red prints where the hands had simply been dipped in ochre paint. I stood stunned, my dog ready to spend the night.

Handprints in canyons may be positive handprints created by dipping hands in a clay paint mixture and applying hands to stone, or negative handprints like this one where paint was in the artist's mouth and then blown on to a rock face possibly with a small reed tube. Handprints signify our humanity over millennia. Children's handprints are especially endearing. Author photo.

I had not been stopped by a high cliff dwelling or an etched petroglyph, but rather by the simplicity and humanity of handprints waving to me across time, frozen forever in a moment of playfulness, asserting, "This is us. We are here. These are our hands." Down canyon the stars came out one by one. The evening star appeared and then the others shone. When I could no longer see the handprints, I finally started walking, more slowly now, at peace. I did not worry about finding my way to the truck.

The Old Ones had been there. They would always be there. The presence of the handprints in the canyon, the subtlety and intimacy struck me more deeply than if I had stumbled upon an unknown cliff dwelling. Though they had been made a thousand years ago, the red and white hands, particularly the children's prints, reached across time and space to my heart.

I came out of the canyon into a brilliant rising moon. I was flush with warmth and affection for a people who had left their telltale sign in such careful, colorful patterns. I was humbled and grateful. My dog and I stepped off the steep bank into the mud and tamarisks as moonlight glinted on my truck's windshield above us and through the trees. Then I understood the wisdom of the Old Ones. I stopped again and smiled. I had come down through the canyon too fast, in too much of a hurry, caught up in all the modern pettiness and busyness that burdens our lives. Had I not paused to study the handprints I would have hit the arroyo in the deepest dark with no moon and stars to guide me. Despite my canine companion, we probably would have gotten lost. But with the moon on my windshield, I found my truck on the arroyo's opposite bank. What had drawn me to that alcove precisely when I needed to slow down and wait for the rising moon? What had made me look up at that exact moment? I'll never know, but in Bears Ears, as across the Southwest, there are always secrets in the landscape, silent signs from those who went before. There are messages from the past to the present and stories on stones.[13]

Archaeologists have proven climate-induced strife at Ridges Basin near Durango, Colorado, and a 150-year drought that gripped the Southwest from AD 700 to 850. As farm families began to group together, ceremonies became larger and more elaborate. One rock art panel in Bears Ears National Monument several miles north of the San Juan River, almost at the top of Comb Ridge, illustrates that process.

This panel depicts a fundamental shift in the lives of prehistoric Pueblo peoples. A millennium ago individual ceremonies and rituals gave way to group events. On a massive sandstone wall, 179 carved human figures march in three lines toward a circle that probably depicts a great kiva or an underground ceremonial space. To stand before the Procession Panel is to feel the power of Basketmaker villagers coming together to dance, sing, feast, and become one. As I stood there the first time, warm from late afternoon sun and the hike up from the dry wash below, the silence of the rock contrasted with the movement etched upon it. Everywhere on this huge Navajo sandstone panel were figures moving, flowing, and walking out of a tall crack. As heat radiated off the southwest-facing rock, I took off my pack, stripped down to a t-shirt, and quietly stared, motionless. The figures seemed to move in front of me around two large etched mule deer bucks and assorted anthropomorphs or human/animal images.

As I hike across Bears Ears, I seek painted pictographs and petroglyphs carved by the ancients. I've come across dozens of desert bighorn sheep with their distinctive hooves and horns, exotic warriors and their headdresses from the Basketmaker II period, splayed Lizard Man figures with outstretched arms, legs, and genitalia, and hundreds of handprints. Many petroglyphs seem to be a random animal here, a hunter there, or perhaps a reclining flute player or two, knees bent, enjoying their own music. But the Procession Panel stands out as depicting an annual or semi-annual group event of great import and majesty. Runners have arrived carrying symbolic canes or crookneck staffs to lead families and friends. The ancients carved the five yards long, four-foot-high panel between AD 650 and 800. Like all great rock art, it tells a story, which, centuries and centuries later, we try to understand.

Among tumbled and jagged rock, interspersed with cacti, bunchgrass, small junipers, and the occasional sagebrush and ephedra or Mormon tea, the rock art panel rises above the red, sandy soils and speaks across time. The panel is close to the top of Comb Ridge near one of the dozen or so ancient crossings of the 900-foot-tall stone reef. Across the panel leaders brandish crooked-neck staffs as they lead small groups.[14] Animals, too, are carved into the smooth dark desert varnish on the rock face. The panel includes a long-horned serpent, as well as atlatl darts from prehistoric spear throwers and two lightbulb shaped images, lobed circles always in pairs, probably religious symbols shared and understood. Robert L. Powell in a seventeen-page report, wrote the first description of the Procession Panel Site for the BLM and the Utah State Archaeologist. Powell described figures on the rock and noted unique characteristics. After explaining groups of converging marchers, he stated, "The next five men are special: each one has his left arm hanging down and his right elbow

One of the most distinctive rock art panels in Bears Ears is the Procession Panel, which probably represents diverse villagers all converging on a great house for a ceremony or celebration. Composite photo by Steve Jones.

bent so that his right hand is even with his head. Each raised hand has tiny incised figures (or ceremonial wands); the lower hands do not have fingers. They all have clearly separated legs and are larger."[15]

There's a "bird man" shaman, men wearing backpacks grasping ceremonial staffs, and a desert bighorn whose front feet seem to be rotating a wheel, yet Basketmakers had no wheels, no horses, and no domesticated animals except turkeys and dogs. "An ambiguous figure is directly under the rear of the coyote and in front of the first large deer. It may be a mask with a headdress, two eyes, a large nose, and whiskers. Or it may represent two men holding hands with a square artifact above them," Powell noted. He added that one of the buck deer "in a rare and realistic manner is shown with a penis . . . but unrealistically he has five toes on his feet. Like most of the other animals he has deep indentations in his face, heart, hooves. A spear protrudes vertically from the bottom of his belly."[16]

I hope this meant that venison was served at the celebration, at the great kiva represented by the circle where all the etched figures seem to be heading.[17] Powell spent hours studying intricate details of the Procession Panel. I can only stare and wonder, trying to take it all in, caught up in the movement, realizing that where I stand near the top of the ridge is one of the few crossover places between drainages. Perhaps a group of Basketmakers came up the same incline I did, climbed over and around the same rocks, and stood beneath the panel created to honor and remember them. Scholars study relationships among great kivas and procession panels. In *Crucible of Pueblos,* the editors suggest that perhaps "procession panels do not depict actual events but are instead representations of cultural concepts and narratives." Either way, the imagery represents "public gatherings" and "the role of ritual in uniting individuals into bands or larger communities."[18]

"These gatherings would also have facilitated the long-term vitality of local residence groups by providing opportunities for the exchange of information, marriage partners, and material goods, and by providing a framework for the resolution of disputes," explains former Colorado State Archaeologist Richard H. Wilshusen and other researchers.[19] I can feel the movement of the dancers, the steps in unison. I can hear the chanting, the singing. Maybe it's only the wind coming up and over the steep escarpment, blowing out of Monument Valley, across the Navajo Nation, to where I stand in awe.

Another scholar believes that the Procession Panel represents "a community in transition . . . when the first large, above-ground multihousehold structures were built within settlements that could be characterized as 'aggregated' villages."[20] Kellam Throgmorton thinks the numerous human figures on the panel are grouped in such a way as to be actual representations of villagers coming together. He feels that the artist, or artists, may have depicted a ritual event and "the scale and composition of a seventh through ninth century community."[21] Centuries later, there would be conflict and clan violence, driving villagers into the cliffs. By 1300, the Colorado Plateau would be empty.[22] Families and clans moved to the south and southeast to become the modern Pueblo people of today at Hopi, Zuni, and in pueblos centered along the Rio Grande River. Basking in the sun, the Procession Panel high on the ridge stood there for centuries until its discovery in 1990 by biologist Chuck LaRue hiking with his two-year-old daughter. Just hiking along, they found one of the great late Basketmaker depictions of group ritual from 1,200 years ago. LaRue told a teacher from Kayenta, Arizona, and slowly the word got out.[23]

Descending the ridge, my pack felt lighter. My dog's tail wagged more often. Just why did that bighorn have its hooves on a wheel? How many figures, arms up, hands waving, are emerging from the elongated crack in the Navajo sandstone? I've been back numerous times to answer questions and to ask new ones.

If dances and processions brought people together as connected groups, body art or tattooing may have done the same. Recently a 2,000-year-old artifact from Bears Ears and the Turkey Pen site has been identified as a Basketmaker II tattooing implement made from a wooden sumac stem, spines of the prickly pear cactus, and strips of yucca leaf. Considered "the oldest Indigenous North American tattooing artifact in western North

America," this is one more scientific find among the vast canyons and cliffs of Bears Ears. Removed from the site in 1972, researchers have just now identified its purpose. "Tattooing acted as a way to negotiate and affirm group identities within an increasingly populous and complicated cultural landscape. Tattooing was an irreversible commitment to a group or status," state authors in the *Journal of Archaeological Sciences.*[24] In terms of personal adornment, Basketmaker men and women had long hair and on the sides of their heads kept it in rolled bobs with men having longer hair than women, sometimes in a single braid down their back.

Dances, tattoos, hair styles, ceremonies, and rituals created social cohesion. Basketmaker II rock art flourished, and then the next phase, harder to identify, occurred. Basketmaker III lasted a few centuries with cycles of settlement and depopulation in different areas of Bears Ears and what is considered the Northern San Juan Region. Bill Lipe explains that people lived on Cedar Mesa where there was good dry farming "in a sort of episodic fashion—occupation was more continuous in Comb Wash and probably the easternmost slopes of Cedar Mesa [with] the heaviest populations between the Comb Ridge and Mesa Verde." He argues that groups came and moved on, and then there was "the next burst of occupation" with "waves of settlement and retreat washing up onto central Cedar Mesa from the Comb Wash area." As an historian, I like the fact that Lipe uses the frontier concept. He argues, "Cedar Mesa becomes kind of a frontier area relative to the area east of the Comb Ridge/Comb Wash. People from the more populous areas east of Cedar Mesa episodically moved out onto Cedar Mesa and then withdrew, probably dependent on climate variation and also whether the core populations between the Comb and Mesa Verde were increasing."[25]

Basketmaker II farmers had diets that were 60 to 80 percent corn or maize, but they also ate squash and gourds and had dogs and turkeys. Around AD 500, Basketmaker III begins and stretches to AD 760 with permanent settlements, pottery, and the first communal architecture or an early version of great kivas. Cooking in baskets gave way to cooking in clay pots, with pottery appearing in Basketmaker III in AD 500–700. Soon ceramics would include dramatically painted pots with black and white designs and even redware. Basketmaker people transitioned into a new phase and a new culture, Ancestral Puebloans and the Pueblo I phase began from AD 750 or 760 to AD 900. Pottery-making extended across both Basketmaker and Pueblo traditions.

Specific groups fired and painted unique ceramic styles such as pots from the area near Mesa Verde, Mancos Gray from AD 875 to 975, Chapin Black-on-White from AD 575 to 900, Abajo Red-on-Orange from AD 700 to 850, Piedra Black-on-White from AD 750-900, and my favorite Bluff Black-on-Red from AD 750 to 925.[26] Pottery styles would continue to evolve with elaborate bowls, mugs, pitchers, cups, ladles, and whimsical effigy figures with their own heads, horns, and hooves. The best examples can be found at the Edge of the Cedars Museum State Park at Blanding, Utah, with numerous displays and exhibits and open storage representing various pottery types and ancient artifacts.[27] Just as ceramic styles changed and evolved, so did living arrangements and habitation sites.

"The vast majority of [Basketmaker] III sites are on mesa tops, and there are thousands of them, but we recognize that they also used the canyons," offers Ben Bellorado, who explains that, "Pueblo I starts right at AD 760 based on the construction of the first villages in the region and tree-ring dates from the first apartment complexes that they built in the upland areas in open air sites."[28] The Pueblo people moved their farm fields and their homes across valleys and mesas always in search of more

The lower story of the room block in this Bear's Ears site was built in the mid-late 1050s in a masonry style similar to rooms found at Mesa Verde and with Chaco-style great houses. The elaborate chinking stands out and was never covered with plaster. Author photo.

rainfall. Famine became a possibility, and Puebloans settled in highland villages, pooled their labor and resources, and built larger storerooms or masonry granaries to survive potential crop failures. Raiding each other's villages continued.

Though maize agriculture meant more food, constantly grinding corn by hand with manos on stone metates meant tiny pieces of stone got into daily meals, grinding down teeth and leaving Puebloans vulnerable to infections from their mouths. Though there were always revered elders and aged shamans both male and female, adult women were only about five feet tall and on average lived into their early twenties. Men grew to be five feet four to five feet six inches and lived into their mid-twenties. As in medieval Europe in the same centuries, only about half of the children born lived to maturity. Life on the mesa tops and in the canyons was short. Puebloans abandoned farming areas only to return in a few generations to farm again. People lived continuously at Mesa Verde and at other large sites across the Four Corners region where the states of Colorado, New Mexico, Utah, and Arizona meet. The Pueblo I phase ushered in Pueblo II from AD 900 to 1150 or the great era of Chaco Canyon dominance and *Pax Chaco* or the peace of Chaco.[29] The Bears Ears region represents the northern San Juan area or the northwest edge of the Ancestral Puebloan world.

Power and ceremonies emanated over one hundred miles to the southeast from a large collection of buildings constructed at Chaco Canyon in five different masonry styles. Chaco became the heart of a vast trading center, a place where turquoise and scarlet macaws were distributed or perhaps hoarded. Some food was grown nearby, but most was imported to feed the hundreds of pilgrims who came to Chaco to build and roof the large structures requiring over 150,000 ponderosa pine trees to be cut and then hauled by hand from the Chuska Mountains to the west.[30]

Over centuries, the basic shape and size of underground pithouses evolved into formal kivas lined with stone, with elaborate ventilation systems, benches, niches for sacred objects, and cribbed wooden roofs with entry via kiva ladders from the top. On the floor, near the fire pit or hearth, the ancients always dug a small sacred hole called the *sipapu* so the spirits of their ancestors could come and go from other worlds into the kivas if they wished to. The largest of all kivas could be found in the Great Houses in Chaco Canyon including Pueblo Bonito, Kin Kletso, and others. The Great Kiva at Pueblo Bonito measures sixty-five feet across, and it was roofed with hundreds of logs cut by stone axes and transported by runners

Basketmaker and early Ancestral Puebloan rock art includes images of conflict and warfare including combatants dueling with spear throwers or atlatls in Johns Canyon. Drawing by Phil R. Geib, used with permission.

whose rituals forbade setting the logs down until crews put them in place in the vast buildings.

The kings and queens at Chaco initially presided over a wetter climate and enjoyed two centuries of peace, prosperity, and stability.[31] Floodwater farming from rain runoff descending from cliffs evolved into small, efficient waffle gardens of maize planted in floodplains or along ephemeral streams. Seedlings needed to sprout before songs and ceremonies brought the blessings of summer monsoons. The Chacoan elites were well fed with elk meat, venison, corn, beans, and squash, and because of better nutrition, some of the men grew much taller than their contemporaries and reached six feet in height. Exotic grave goods in royal burials included thousands of pieces of turquoise, seashells from the Gulf of Mexico, and numerous feathers.

In Pueblo Bonito, a forty-year-old man was buried with seashells from the Pacific Coast, a conch shell trumpet, 11,000 turquoise beads, and another 3,000 shell beads, but beneath him were fourteen even more significant burials. "Scientists say they were all related to the same female ancestor, which could provide clues to the power structure of an ancient society that lived in Chaco Canyon," reported the *New York Times*.[32]

Major archaeological discoveries at Chaco Canyon include a road system pointed straight north thirty feet wide and with small berms on each

Chaco Canyon and Pueblo Bonito pictured here became the cultural center of a vast Ancestral Puebloan world, which covered 35,000 to 40,000 square miles. The Bears Ears region was the northwest edge of the Chacoan world, and it possesses Chacoan great houses and Chacoan roads. Chaco refugees fled to Bears Ears when Chaco's power structure collapsed by AD 1150. Author photo.

side; yet the Chacoans had no horses or wheels for carts or wagons. With smoke signals, the Ancestral Puebloans had real time communication among sites. Large firepits for signal fires have been found at Chimney Rock National Monument in southwest Colorado, on Huerfano Butte south of Bloomfield, New Mexico, and in Chaco itself at Pueblo Alto or high town. In the clear desert air on a windless day, they could communicate up to one hundred miles. Pueblo Alto also has a large mound, over a half-acre in size, of smashed pottery. Buried for centuries are distinctive Chacoan ceramic cylinder jars, tall without handles. One archaeologist found "evidence of eighty thousand ceramic vessels intentionally smashed at one site. He saw this as a ritual act," writes Craig Childs. "It was like casting champagne glasses into the fireplace, an exploit of stunning abundance and celebration in this crumbling, bare-bones land."[33]

Scientific analysis with electron microscopes of broken pottery sherds from straight-sided jars reveal what Chaco pilgrims drank—chocolate. Not the chocolate we would recognize sweetened with milk and sugar, but a strong, bitter caffeinated chocolate made from cocoa beans imported from Mexico. Aztecs used cacao beans for currency, and the beans became Chaco chocolate between AD 1000 and 1125. Imagine long distance traders running from Mexico, bringing up cacao beans for parties to be held among the thousands of Ancestral Puebloans who traveled to Chaco for pilgrimages, seasonal ceremonies, and observances related to solstices, equinoxes, and phases of the moon. As for Chaco chocolate, archaeologist Patricia Crown asks, "So really the questions then become how were they preparing it, what were the additives, when did it first appear, who was drinking it—just all the things about the more detailed societal information."[34] Recently researchers have also identified chocolate residue on sherds found in Utah, perhaps rituals included Bears Ears communities.

Chaco became the cultural capital of the Ancestral Puebloan world and its influence stretched northwest to Bears Ears on a network of north-directed roads. Hopi tribal members, direct descendants of Ancestral Puebloans, point out twin alcoves near Bluff, Utah, as significant shapes on a north-facing cliff that would have directed their ancestors to build the Bluff Great House between AD 1075 and 1150 on a hill on the north side of the San Juan River.[35] Across Bears Ears, Chacoan influences include rock art panels, road systems, masonry walls, and Chacoan outliers, including unexcavated Great Houses in Cottonwood Wash, Comb Wash, and further north into Ruins Canyon and Beef Basin.[36] Research also connects twined sandals as important footwear linking Chaco Canyon to Bears Ears, with a significant number of sandal petroglyphs being etched on stone after Native peoples left Chaco.[37] In the Pueblo II period, centuries of basketmaking resulted in the technological breakthrough of kiln-fired corrugated ceramic pottery that held heat longer. With more fuel-efficient cookware, families could use less firewood and gain more nutrition from the corn they cooked.

On the edge of the Chaco frontier, Bears Ears groups may have been more conservative or more liberal in their thoughts, ideas, and actions because they were farther from the cultural core's center, farther from "center place" enshrined in story cycles and oral traditions. By 1150, droughts at the end of the twelfth century caused political instability and Chaco's collapse. The reign of queens ended. The hierarchy that sustained Chaco faltered and failed. Bears Ears groups found themselves on their own as power and Chacoan refugees shifted to a new capital at Aztec, New Mexico, on the Animas River straight north along what archaeologist Stephen Lekson has called "the Chaco meridian."[38]

Chaco's collapse, the greatest historical event in thousands of years of Southwestern prehistory, sent Ancestral Puebloans into their Pueblo III phase of becoming cliff dwellers and living in dramatic, remote locations farther from their farms and fields.[39] In Bears Ears, two groups of Ancestral Puebloans diverged—a Mesa Verdean group and a second one known as the Kayenta Anasazi. For Ancestral Puebloans, survival became even more precarious.

Across Bears Ears, Basketmaker and Puebloan habitation sites with scatterings of broken potsherds and distinctive rock art can easily be found. Even more dramatic, however, are the cliff dwelling sites, proof of the need for safety and security because without the order and authority of Chacoan rulers, clan violence and raiding escalated. While Mesa Verde National Park has Cliff Palace, the largest cliff dwelling in North America, Bears Ears National Monument has much smaller Puebloan houses but in untouched locations, caught between narrow canyon ledges and blue skies the color of turquoise, Chaco's sacred stone.

CHAPTER 3

Into the Cliffs, 1150–1300

> The Pueblos are an ancient people whose history goes back into the farthest reaches of time. Archaeological exploration sufficiently confirms the fact of their occupancy of the Southwest from time immemorial. . . . Tradition was history; history was tradition.
>
> —Joe S. Sando, *Pueblo Nations*

> I had come upon the city of some extinct civilization, hidden away in this inaccessible mesa for centuries, preserved in the dry air and almost perpetual sunlight like a fly in amber.
>
> —Willa Cather, *The Professor's House*

With the fall of Chaco by AD 1150, order and stability collapsed within the Ancestral Puebloan world. Drought and time took their toll on the royal Chacoan families. Clans left, some to move toward Bears Ears and to leave telltale signs of Chacoan influence with well-built walls in Arch Canyon, rooms, and a road system at the Et Al Site on Cedar Mesa, and in the remnants of fallen great houses such as those in Cottonwood Wash, Comb Wash, Beef Basin, and on a hill in Bluff, Utah, facing two alcoves above the San Juan River. Across the Colorado Plateau, Ancestral Puebloans moved into south and east-facing cliffs and built small habitation rooms and storage granaries on narrow ledges with easy to defend access.

For 150 years Ancestral Puebloans became cliff dwellers, farming above or below where they resided in defensive structures on precarious cliffs. They looked for raiders. Women carried water up steep trails. Scarce wood for heating and for cooking came from wherever it could be found. For a century and a half, the Puebloans in Bears Ears lived in stacked stone structures engineered for defense. Then the people left.[1] After millennia of living on the Colorado Plateau and in the Bears Ears region, they walked away. Some went to the southeast: Tewa language speakers, for example, who would build the Pueblo villages at Taos and along the Rio Grande River; others such as the Kayenta Anasazi, a different Ancestral Puebloan ethnic group who would become ancestors to the Hopis, went to the southwest.

At most sites, boulders block entrances or small defensive walls represent barriers. At those choke points, Puebloans could defend against attackers. Weapons included rocks, bows, arrows, and war clubs made with dense stone found in river cobbles on terraces above the San Juan River, polished stones from the San Juan Mountains swept downstream over millions of years and then lashed to hardwood handles darkened over time with oils from men's hands. "The literature on conflict in the Greater Southwest has been growing exponentially as new theories about the roles of violence, warfare . . . conflict and raiding has become increasingly emphasized as dominant features of the ancient Pueblo world," state scholars, who describe "sustained intervillage conflict" and "fortifications, palisades, towers, communities positioned in strategic locations, walled villages and sites burned at the time of abandonment" all because of "violent interactions between groups increas[ing] over time, starting around AD 1150 and continuing through the 1300s."[2]

Within Bears Ears, these sites are intact, difficult to access, and still standing in the undisturbed cultural landscape where they were created by Ancestral Puebloans 800 years ago. Hiking to these defensive locations is to enter a cultural window in time. These small, remote sites demonstrate all aspects of humanity, from humor and fun with fanciful handprints on cliff ledges, to desperation in the last hastily constructed stacked stone barrier walls. What makes Bears Ears unique is the architectural mosaic built over centuries by clans and ethnic groups.

Across the Southwest, much larger multiroom structures have been preserved as national parks and monuments such as Chimney Rock, Mesa Verde, and Yucca House in Colorado; Pecos, Aztec, Gila Cliff Dwellings, and Chaco in New Mexico; and Betatakin, Keet Seil, White House Ruins, and Wupatki in Arizona. Southwest Colorado also has Ute Mountain Ute Tribal Park, consisting of sites and ruins south of Mesa Verde, which are much less visited with unexcavated sites and cliff dwellings almost pristine.

The Bears Ears region in Utah is unique because the best sites are small and often accessible only after driving rocky, rutted four-wheel drive roads and then hiking up and down canyons, descending from ledge to ledge and finally after a narrow traverse hundreds of feet in the air seeing rooms seldom visited. Sometimes there are no footprints. No trails. Roofs

This dramatic defensive wall halfway down into a canyon would have allowed sentries to monitor human movement in and out of the canyon as part of protecting valuable water sources on the canyon's rim. Author photo.

This refuge site in Bears Ears faces west so the author named it Sunset House. It would have been intensely hot in summer heat. Ancestral Puebloans would have fled to this site during times of conflict and warfare, but water is not readily available. Author photo.

may be intact or mostly so, with stacked stone and wood building materials lain unused for almost a thousand years, granaries still sealed with flat stone doors rimmed with a coating of adobe.[3]

Almost all the Pueblo III cliff dweller sites built between AD 1150 and 1300 in Bears Ears represent defensive architecture. Frightened families moved into the cliffs for protection. They built defensive curtain walls with numerous loopholes to shoot arrows at potential invaders just as Europeans did at the same time in their medieval castle walls. Bears Ears has distinctive refuge sites or places to retreat.[4] There is often no soot on the ceiling of these sites and no storage areas, just walls to hide behind in case of danger.[5] Archaeologist Mark Varien notes,

> I consider the following characteristics, when taken together, to make a compelling case that warfare was a serious problem in the thirteenth century: (1) the relatively inaccessible location of many sites, (2) the placement of sites and structures to provide views of people entering the area, (3) the planned intervisibility among sites, (4) the presence of site-enclosing walls and fortress-like walls with peepholes that concealed inhabitants while allowing them to see anyone approaching the area, and (5) architecture that restricts access within sites.[6]

These late Pueblo period defensive sites are concentrated in the Bears Ears area of Cottonwood Wash, Comb Ridge, Cedar Mesa, and Grand Gulch. So many questions remain. To come upon these remote sites is to sense the presence of the earlier Ancestral Puebloans. Intrepid hikers soak up the silence of centuries as dust swirls around their feet and small corn cobs without kernels lie about the rooms.

Habitation sites have level floors with dirt and sand used to smooth irregularities in rock ledges. Ceilings, now often open and exposed, show soot and signs of repeated evening fires from cold moonless nights as families huddled together for warmth beneath turkey feather blankets, dogs close by, stars pinwheeling across a black void. Ancestral Puebloans endured a cool, dry Little Ice Age with extended cold and farming seasons too short to support corn cultivation. "If growing seasons became too short to grow maize, that would explain why Pueblo people left the northern San Juan region and never returned," argues archaeologist Varien, who adds, "Emigrations from the region began relatively early and occurred over a period of many decades . . . by about 1285, everyone had left."[7]

Carefully constructed at the head of a canyon, this two-story habitation structure has a solid foundation, intact ceiling beams, and a nearby cholla cactus species that may have been introduced. Author photo.

Every time I visit Bears Ears, I want to walk more slowly to see what I might have missed before. Once halfway up a canyon we stopped to examine a small granary. Often, I take photographs. As I put down my pack to retrieve my camera, I studied the wooden lintel, still intact, above the granary doorway. By the horse collar shape of the opening, I knew it was built by Kayenta Anasazi, who did not live in large communities but instead stayed more isolated and in far off sites across western Bears Ears.

The door was no longer there, and I looked at the lintel and saw a shape, a pattern that I did not recognize. I approached with my camera dangling from my neck, took another look, and the quizzical expression on my face went from a question to a broad grin, a deep smile, and then laughter. In the adobe clay mortar used in Pueblo III room blocks and granaries, I often find preserved fingerprints and thumb prints, a telltale sign of humanity, but here was a new impression I had never seen before. I had to laugh. Just as the granary had been finished 800 years ago and wet mud was still drying, still setting up, a proud father lifted a young child and pressed the infant's feet into the moist clay. As the sun began to descend that April afternoon, I marveled at such a simple gesture.

As a father myself, I had to chuckle. No baby's sandals had been preserved; instead here were the impressions of small feet and tiny toes, still there after centuries. We walked up out of the canyon with a new respect for the Ancient Ones and their difficult lives, but just like colored handprints on canyon walls, here was a message from the past, a symbol of love and hope for the future. How could we not smile?

"It is likely that the northern San Juan region was populated by groups with distinct histories speaking distinct languages," writes archaeologist Varien.[8] Centuries of living in the Bears Ears landscape had taken its toll. Soils became depleted. Large game animals disappeared. Arrowheads got smaller as hunters pursued birds, rabbits, and even rodents. With a lack of meat protein, women suffered from anemia or low iron in their blood, making them weak and sickly with vulnerability to sprains, bruises, and broken bones and more likely to have weak babies. Scholars note in *Children in the Prehistoric Puebloan Southwest*, "If the diet was composed largely of corn . . . anemia undoubtedly increased the death rate among pregnant women and nursing mothers. . . . Sickly or very young mothers produce babies less likely to survive and thrive."[9] Then even the corn dried up.

Droughts returned. Crops withered. Environmental damage increased with scarce game, soil erosion and arroyo cutting, and a lack of wood for

This rock art panel along the San Juan River depicts warriors dueling with atlatls and other Ancestral Puebloan imagery. Drawing by Phil R. Geib, used with permission.

heat and fuel. Fewer resources on the land intensified fear of rival clans arriving at night to steal food, women, and children and to kill male adversaries, whom invaders would trap in kivas by stealing kiva ladders before dawn while men slept. Rival clan members then set the kivas on fire, trapping men inside.[10] Scholars have stated, "Increasing violence characterized many late-AD 1200s sites, often in their final use. Even though the physical landscape may have remained viable, the changed social landscape was no longer sustainable."[11]

Over a decade ago, I discovered that defensive social landscape myself, preserved in architecture. Bears Ears has always represented a landscape of refuge and resistance, and on a narrow canyon ledge, I experienced what it would have been like to live in a constant state of fear and to build rooms now inhabited by only swallows.

It has been years now since I cowered on that ledge with the canyon bottom hundreds of feet below me and the clifftop hundreds of feet above. I was terrified, unable to move from fear. Oh, I could continue to crawl alright, but the four-foot ledge angled out toward a sheer drop-off, perhaps 500 feet below. Ravens made large turns below me and then slowly ascended in updrafts. There was no way to stand up. My heart pounded against my rib cage. Sweat ran off my hands. I could not swallow, and we still had not made it around the corner to the Ancestral Puebloan ruin we sought. The morning had started off in bright sunlight, a spring

High in the middle of a sheer cliff face, this Bears Ears site demonstrates the desperation of the Pueblo III period, AD 1150–1300, when Ancient Peoples moved into sandstone cliffs for their safety and security and lived on narrow ledges. Author photo.

breeze, a walk to the edge of a cliff. With binoculars we stared down at a thin ledge on a sandstone cliff with a stacked stone mortared wall as a barrier to entry, then a habitation room block, an even narrower ledge, and a small room with a still sealed Ancestral Puebloan door. Something had been piled near the room, but even with the best of binoculars it was hard to tell what the objects were.

We stared, laughed a little nervously, and agreed that, sure, we would try to walk that ledge. My happy Lab pup had no idea what we were planning. He was just glad to be outdoors in canyon country with plenty of fresh smells and small sandstone pockets of water. As we began our descent a mile or so distant from the ruin we had spotted, I wondered how difficult the trail would be, and then I realized there was no trail. Where we were headed no one had been in years. Visualizing those sheer angles of the cliff and the narrowness of the ledge, I knew why.

My friends had spotted this remote ruin from a small airplane they had chartered to fly the canyons of Cedar Mesa in the Bears Ears region. They found the ruin on Thanksgiving Day, hence their name Thanksgiving House. It took months with a compass and maps to begin to know where it was and then even longer to actually find it on the landscape.

They had managed to climb, walk, and crawl all the way to the end of the ledge once before, but now a party of five of us would make the attempt. I had no idea how scared I would become.

Pueblo III cliff dwellings are scattered across Bears Ears and Cedar Mesa. They represent the last structures built by Ancestral Puebloans in those difficult decades between AD 1150 and 1300 when families moved into south and east-facing cliffs for protection and security against raiders. We were going to attempt to climb, without safety ropes, into one of the most difficult ruins to access.

I didn't fully understand the process until we finally made it down off the rim and around the boulders, bushes, and pinyon trees to stand at the beginning of the ledge itself. I tied up my dog, and he began to howl. This was a crucial event for both of us, and never again would he allow me to tie him to a juniper tree or anything else. Never again would he allow me to go out on such a frightening ledge. As our small group started to walk forward, my feet slid uncontrollably, and I looked down to see dozens of small pebbles on our pathway, as dangerous as ball bearings on a sidewalk. Whether they arrived there over the centuries or were placed there by the inhabitants, I'll never know. Instantly, I began to watch my step. Because I could not look up, I would have been an easy target for an archer hidden behind the wall in front of us. Another defensive technique, I thought, as I silently nodded in understanding.

Finally, after what seemed an hour of concentration but what must have been only a few minutes, we made it through the barrier wall entrance onto a safer part of the ledge and into a small room with a t-shaped doorway where we rested our backs against a smoothed surface and stared out at wide-open space in front of us. With my back against the sandstone cliff, surrounded by stone walls, soot on the roof above, and an ancient hearth in the middle of the room, I breathed easily and felt like I was back in my mother's womb after the terror of walking the cliff edge. I did not realize our adventure had only begun.

We found another way out of the room to the west, and then the sandstone cliff lowered to the top of the ledge so abruptly it was like walking the inside of a clam shell. The farther we went, the more it dropped until we had no choice but to crawl. I put my two cameras behind my back, bandolier style, and started down on my hands and knees, breathing hard and hearing the lonesome howls of my lonely dog. After just a few minutes, I knew it was not safe for me to continue. I couldn't control my body movements. I shook from fear, and my blood pressure felt like I had run uphill ten miles. The others went ahead. I found a place to lean back on the ledge without being able to sit up.

I had to calm down and fool my nervous system into thinking everything was under control. So I took out my small birder's binoculars and scanned the adjacent cliffs and canyon contours pretending that everything was much closer and easier than it was, though I knew in my heart that those ravens were still circling far below. But it worked. I slowed down my sympathetic nervous system, let the panic attack subside, and resumed crawling. In just a dozen yards, I turned on the ledge and could stand up again. My friends were examining the ruin, which had a unique two-tone exterior paint job, an intact sandstone slab door, and a roof in excellent condition. The objects we had seen far away on a facing cliff we now knew were stacked building materials, wood for beams and possibly cooking fires. Stepping into the room from another entrance, we looked out one last window. The ledge had ended.

I thought about being in the middle of a ten-floor skyscraper and poking my head and shoulders out of a window that should not have been open. I'll never forget the view, the silence, and the golden afternoon light upon the cliffs. I knew we would have to return the dangerous way we had come, but not quite yet. We had earned this silence and solitude. Few people had ever crawled in here in the last 800 years. We savored those precious moments of personal discovery. Then came the hard part—turning around.

We made it out easily enough. We had a few scratches and bruises, but no one panicked and no one fell. I cannot imagine how hard it would have been to take that route every twilight after farming small patches of corn on the canyon rim. Hauling water was women's work, and I can barely conceive of the poise and balance it would have taken girls and women to bring cool pottery jars full of water along that dangerous ledge.

When we finally made it back to the curve of the canyon with tree limbs to touch, we were laughing and joking, stunned by our own accomplishment and in awe of the persistence and determination of the elders. My Lab was overjoyed to see me and vowed never to leave me again. He didn't. We spent the next twelve years hiking canyon country, and he never left my side. I promised my wife I would never go where my dog wouldn't go, but I did not tell her that he had four-paw drive and an excellent sense of balance. I'll never forget crawling that ledge with friends and the depth of my fear as I sat immobile on a downward sloping uneven ledge. There are other places in the world where ancient peoples built defensive architecture, but in southeast Utah's Bears Ears, a few remote settings remain undisturbed, full of "the dust of centuries," as the Wetherill brothers described Puebloan ruins in the 1890s.

Brothers, uncles, friends, and children crawled that ledge with each of the stones they used to make the farthest room. Trip after trip they returned with stones, water, mortar, and wooden beams. They brought straight tree branches to that precipice eight centuries ago. Protected from rain and snow on that narrow shelf, the gathered wood lies there still. Stone rooms sit empty, entered by only starlight.

"The latest large-scale shift from mesa top occupation to the cliffs really starts at about AD 1210 according to tree ring dates taken from the cliff dwellings," confirms archaeologist Ben Bellorado, who adds, "The terminal phase of Ancestral Puebloan occupation of the Bears Ears area is more accurately portrayed as AD 1250–1275. The last structures that we have dates from are two sites on the eastern side of Cedar Mesa and they are both AD 1268."[12] So we know when wood was cut, and it was sometimes recycled, especially the insect-resistant juniper wood favored for use in ceiling beams and doorway lintels. I have often found the lintels above doorways still intact, with yucca fiber ties perfectly in place where they held juniper sticks taut as mortar dried and tightened.[13]

This site represents storage granaries, not habitation rooms, and is approached by walking a long narrow span of cliff top. Author photo.

The pottery sherds displayed on this stone represent a museum rock where visitors have made a small display. This is to be discouraged because other visitors may decide to take "just one," and thus diminish valuable artifacts found at a site. The author carefully scatters these museum piles to discourage this practice. Author photo.

Across Bears Ears, carved spirals spin on rock. The circular shapes can be found on mesa top rocks, on canyon walls, and on boulders at the base of cliffs. The spirals represent continuities in families' lives but also clan movements and migrations over centuries. Families in Bears Ears resisted change in their cliffside residences at the northern edge of the Ancestral Puebloan world, but by the late 1200s, it was time to go, to move on. Women helped to make those difficult decisions, but I am sure men, crouched in the kivas, came to nod their agreement. Leaving meant rituals of abandonment including breaking or smashing metates so no more corn could be ground. No more meals lovingly prepared. Too heavy to carry, the metates would remain. Youth helped empty granaries, carefully packing seed corn.

And so, family by family, clan by clan, the movements began to the southeast and to the southwest, out of Bears Ears and into new lives for the children and for the children to come. Not vanishing but simply moving, walking away for new opportunities of safety, security, better farming, and perhaps new religious perspectives and ideas about kachinas and their ability to bring rain following proper rituals, ceremonies, dances, and songs.[14]

After centuries living in Bears Ears, Ancestral Puebloans left. The cliff dwellings would remain vacant, the earlier Pueblo II sites covered by blowing sand and dirt. Baskets, pottery, arrow quivers, and turkey feather blankets would remain in fragments or intact. The time had come to move again, and so the clans departed but not without songs and stories that would be remembered generations later, for the landscape still calls their descendants whose languages include Piro, Hopi, Zuni, Tano—the sub-groups Tewa, Tiwa, and Towa—, and Keresan. Within the arc of history, other Native peoples would come to make Bears Ears their home, but for the Puebloans, it is a place of deep time remembrance and a connection to the land that has never been severed, never been broken.

Frequently they had buried their dead in south-facing middens or loose soil near their habitation sites, especially in winter when the ground was frozen. That custom of careful and reverent interment, often with grave goods and funerary objects, would become the focus of an intense legal debate centuries later. A key legal issue would become the rights of the dead to stay buried. Pottery fragments from pots made elsewhere prove that Puebloan relatives occasionally returned. In the Puebloan worldview, the Puebloans never really left Bears Ears. They always sought to visit again, and pottery sherds, other artifacts, and the remains of villages are the footprints of the ancestors, proof of an ancient and abiding connection to a sacred cultural landscape.

Centuries after Puebloans migrated southward, their descendants would rally to defend Bears Ears National Monument. For the first time, Native tribes would seek to preserve ancestral sites at a landscape level using the Antiquities Act of 1906, which one scholar has called "the most important piece of preservation legislation ever enacted by the United States government."[15] Ancestral Puebloans departed Bears Ears, but other native peoples moved in after AD 1400 to make their own marks upon the landscape and to shape their own stories about living in canyons and desert drainages as places of refuge, resistance, and sanctuary.

CHAPTER 4

Navajos, Utes, and Canyon Exploration, 1300–1859

Diné history is geography, so we have preserved geographical details along with the diversity and local particularity of histories that exist in pieces spread widely among the People.

—Klara Kelley and Harris Francis, *A Diné History of Navajoland*

I look upon all this region, I have yet seen [,] as being worth less than the cost of examining It . . . I cannot conceive of a more worthless and impracticable region than the one we now find ourselves in.

—Captain John N. Macomb, 1859

Archaeologists agree that by 1300 or the end of the twelfth century, the Colorado Plateau and the Bears Ears area had been abandoned by Ancestral Puebloans who had moved off the plateau to the southeast toward the Rio Grande Valley and also settled to the southwest toward the Hopi villages and the Mogollon Rim of Arizona. Cliff dwellings sat exposed to the wind. Granaries had been emptied as the migrations began. No longer heard was the rasping sound of manos against metates as girls ground corn. Dirt and dust entered empty habitation rooms and fires no longer left soot upon low ceilings. In some sites, many daily items remained untouched and in place—mugs, bowls, baskets, and burials in the backs of deep caves and in midden piles. Ancestral Puebloans had not vanished; they had simply begun a new cycle of migrations, which left Bears Ears cliff dwellings sunlit and silent on their narrow ledges.

But while Ancestral Puebloans had moved on to establish new multi-roomed villages closer to southwestern rivers, new native peoples moved onto the Colorado Plateau and into Bears Ears a century and a half later. They came from different directions. Over millennia, Athabascan-speaking peoples moved south from Alaska down the Continental Divide. In the area of Largo and Gobernador Canyons in northwest New Mexico, they developed the songs, dances, stories, and ceremonies that would bring them together as Diné people. This cultural hearth or place of coming together became known as Dinétah. Navajos would later move west from Dinétah into the Bears Ears region of southeast Utah.

At about the same time or the mid-1400s, Ute Native Americans moved east out of Nevada's Great Basin and came into the area named for them—Utah. Some groups stayed in Utah and others continued to move east to become a mountain people in the Four Corners region. They spoke an entirely different language than the Ancestral Puebloans and the incoming Navajos. Utes spoke a Shoshonean language, which is Uto-Aztecan.

For studying the past in college classrooms, I teach four truths or four types of evidence. One of those is archaeology, another is oral tradition, a third is history, and a fourth is language. Sometimes these lines of evidence conflict, and one of the significant areas for controversy is this pivotal point in Southwestern history, 1300–1450, when the prehistoric Ancestral Puebloans had left the Bears Ears region and been replaced by other Native groups on the same terrain. If some archaeologists believe that the Colorado Plateau experienced a century and a half of no human habitation, Navajo oral tradition offers a different story. Navajos argue that they have always been here, and their origin stories are explicit about being placed in the Southwest among four sacred mountains including Colorado's Mt. Blanca to the northeast, Mt. Taylor near Grants, New Mexico, to the southeast, Mt. Hesperus to the northwest near Durango, Colorado, and to the southwest the San Francisco Peaks at Flagstaff, Arizona. Those peaks represent the boundaries of the Navajo world. To achieve *hozho* or proper balance and harmony, Navajos are to always remain in the landscape bounded by those four sacred mountains or to have one or of those mountains as a distant viewpoint. For Bears Ears inhabitants, Hesperus Peak or *Dibe Nitzaa* is usually on the eastern horizon, while another sacred mountain within the storied landscape of the Navajo people is Navajo Mountain to the west.

A chronological synthesis of Navajo, Ute, and Puebloan people and where they lived on the Colorado Plateau and Bears Ears landscapes before the arrival of the Spanish in 1540 is difficult to determine. If the Navajos have a rich lore of place-based oral tradition beginning with their elaborate creation story and the two sons of Changing Woman who slayed monsters at Monument Valley, Arizona, at Shiprock, New Mexico, and at other locations to make the world safe for the People, Utes have no such recorded oral traditions.

One of the four Navajo sacred mountains is Hesperus Peak west of Durango, Colorado, also known as *Dibe Ntsaa* (or Big Sheep Mountain) in Navajo. Author photo.

Ute legends abound with animal stories and delightful tales about animals speaking to one another and establishing order out of chaos, but no origin stories link Utes to the Four Corners and Bears Ears region. "The archaeological and ethnographic records of Ute and Paiute entrance into the Four Corners region are vague," asserts Robert McPherson in his book *Viewing the Ancestors.* "Campsites and material remains are difficult to find and differentiate from those left by earlier peoples because of the small amount of pottery, nondescript dwellings, and limited technology necessitated by a hunting-and-gathering lifestyle."[1]

Navajo scholarship, however, is becoming ever more insistent that Navajo people coexisted with Ancestral Puebloans, whom they called the "Anaasazi," a name that translates as "enemy's ancestors," for indeed raiding and warfare, as well as trade and intermarriage, characterize centuries of Pueblo-Ute-Navajo interchanges. Not only is understanding these old animosities among area Native Americans an essential part of southwestern and Bears Ears history, but it also forms the backdrop for the unprecedented reconciliation in the beginning decades of the twenty-first century, when five tribes united to fight for national monument status for the landscape of refuge and resistance they had uneasily shared for at least 500 years. Because the landscape resonates with deep cultural and historical meaning, each tribe or group's time and place in Bears Ears must be chronicled.

Traditional Navajos believe they have always lived within the Four Corners area surrounded by the four sacred mountains plus Huerfano Mesa and Gobernador Knob in New Mexico. The 300,000 members of the Navajo Nation on their seventeen-million-acre reservation, which sprawls across four states, have ancestors from more than sixty clans that came from all directions into the upper San Juan River drainage of New Mexico. Over time, Navajos would move west into Arizona and Utah just as Utes moved east out of the Great Basin of Nevada into the same canyon country. "Ceremonial and clan histories establish an ancestral Diné presence on the land," explain the authors of *A Diné History of Navajoland*. They argue, "Diné ancestors have been in Navajoland since remote pre-Columbian times . . . those pre-Columbian ancestors include hunter-gatherer-farmers who lived among the village-dwelling Anaasazi."[2]

Authors Klara Kelley and Harris Francis maintain that "many Diné recognize among their pre-Columbian forebears not only the hunter-gatherer-farmers but also the Anaasazi themselves, directly or through their Puebloan descendants."[3] Puebloan families did mingle with Navajos. As the Spanish arrived in the Southwest in 1540, led by Don Francisco Vazquez de Coronado, they created havoc at Zuni Pueblo, attacking the Zunis, demanding women, corn, cloth, and other tribute before moving east, and capturing and killing other Puebloans. Coronado and his conquistador soldiers left only to have Don Juan de Onate y Salazar return to permanently colonize New Mexico. The Pueblo Indians, in their settled villages along the Rio Grande River and at Hopi and Zuni to the west, endured religious persecution and forced labor under the *encomienda* system, which required Pueblos to work and farm for the Spanish in return for their holy redemption and their saved souls. At least that was the Spanish version of the exchange—for Pueblo peoples, it was brutal work that Navajos contemptuously avoided.

Using kivas as religious and community chambers whose architectural genesis had occurred across the Bears Ears region, Puebloans watched as Spanish priests ordered kivas to be abandoned, filled with sand, covered up, and in some cases built over as happened at Pecos Pueblo. Catholic adobe churches were constructed atop older Puebloan religious sites. If the Puebloans complained or refused, the priests ordered in well-armored and sword-wielding Conquistadors to enforce their bidding.

The Puebloans found themselves forced under the Spanish yoke while Navajos generally stayed to the west of the colonized areas and kept to themselves, fully aware of this new enemy that not only had swords and guns but also tall war horses. For the descendants of Puebloans from Bears Ears, it was a time of dramatic decline. In 1638, Fray Juan de Prada calculated the number of Pueblos at about 40,000 "or a little less."[4] After decades of abuse and a dramatically shrinking Puebloan population because of disease, drought, and starvation, finally under the authority of Popé, a tall Native religious leader from San Juan Pueblo, in August 1680 the Puebloans revolted in the most successful Indian uprising in American history. The revolt forced the Spanish out of northern New Mexico and south to what is now El Paso, Texas. Twelve years later, when the Spanish returned in 1692, some Puebloans, fearing reprisals, fled north and west and joined dispersed Navajo families. By 1706, Puebloans, excluding Hopis, numbered only about 6,440.[5] Spanish domination had taken its toll. Puebloans had accepted Catholicism and priests while Navajos rarely did.

Because the Diné are matrilineal and trace their descent from their mother's side, a Puebloan woman, marrying a Navajo man, could start an entire clan. Thus, Navajo scholars are correct when they state that there are Navajo clans like the Towering House Clan descended from Ancestral Puebloan or Anaasazi blood, but whether Navajo ancestors lived near Ancestral Puebloans prior to 1300 remains disputed. I asked Puebloan elder and former Zia Governor Peter Pino, "When did the Navajos arrive?" He answered, "The evening before the Spanish," meaning long after the Puebloans from the Bears Ears area of southeast Utah had migrated to the Rio Grande Valley. Navajo and Pueblo oral histories do not agree. "The people of the Puebloan Nations of New Mexico's nineteen pueblos are the descendants of the original natives of North America's vast southwestern region. The Athabascans, ancestors of today's Apaches and Navajos, came to the Southwest between 1400 and 1525, according to social scientists," states Pueblo scholar Joe Sando.[6]

Archaeologists claim that Navajos arrived around 1500, or two centuries after Puebloans migrated southeast and southwest, while Navajo scholars state, "this notion is based on flawed assumptions and interpretations of scholarly data."[7] Kelley and Francis argue, "In 1938, 60 percent of all Navajos belonged to clans with connections to Puebloans or Anaasazi" and "[o]wing to the connection of each Navajo to three other clans besides mother's clan, most Navajos probably have a clan link to Anaasazi either directly or through more recent Puebloans . . . the southward-moving Athabaskan population was small and absorbed people from other groups along the way."[8] One place where people merged is Largo Canyon.

In northwest New Mexico in a thirty-six square mile area, small stone structures, rarely larger than four to six rooms, perch on boulders, rock outcroppings, and mesa edges. Named *pueblitos,* or little pueblos, the defensive buildings date from the early 1700s. They represent an architecture of fear and the Southwest slave trade in women and children. Standing at a site named Pork Chop Pass Pueblito, looking north up the grand sweep of Largo Canyon, I could forget the thousands of gas wells thumping away in the San Juan Basin to consider this special area known as the Dinétah or the Holy Land for the Diné, the people we now know as Navajos. By the mid-1400s, ancestors of the Navajos had settled in Largo, Gobernador, San Rafael, La Jara, Frances, Munoz, and other canyons. Here, they farmed, hunted, and began the rich ceremonial life of songs, dances, chants, and sings that characterize the Navajo today. To the south they traded with Pueblo Indians. Potsherds have been found in these canyons from Zia, Santa Ana, Acoma, and Zuni villages.

Now part of the Farmington Field Office of the BLM, centuries ago this was a cultural hearth. Ancestors to the Navajo blended their traditions with Pueblo neighbors. According to the BLM, "within Dinétah is archaeological evidence of the earliest definable aspects of modern Navajo culture."[9] Early Navajos raided Spanish settlements for trade goods, sheep, and slaves and were in turn raided by punitive Spanish expeditions. A precarious peace existed until 1680 when Pueblo Indians revolted pushing the Spanish out of New Mexico and forcing them south down the Rio Grande. As the Spanish left, Comanches, Utes, and Navajos seized coveted Spanish horses. By 1715 the largest threat to the Dinétah area were Ute and Comanche raiders carrying off Navajo women and children to sell or barter in trade fairs in Taos and Abiquiu. The captives would become household servants and weavers in Hispanic households. Thus, Ute raiders forced construction of Navajo pueblitos. Pueblito builders perched their small stone structures on hard to climb boulders or at the steep edges of rock outcroppings. If an intruder made it to the top of the boulder without being shot by arrows, then the twisted, turning, low-ceilinged entrances provided another gauntlet to run, easily defensible by Navajo grandmothers armed with rocks and sharp stones or river cobbles.

On a quiet spring morning standing at Pork Chop Pass Ruin, I pondered that dangerous, unsettled time in the Dinétah when Navajo and Pueblo families built over 200 defensive Pueblitos between 1680 and 1754 in a north-south arc 10 to 15 miles wide and 40 miles long. James Copeland, Senior Archaeologist for the Farmington Field Office of the BLM,

The cartographer Bernardo de Miera y Pacheco traveled with the Spanish friars Francisco Atanasio Dominguez and Silvestre Velez de Escalante in 1776 as they skirted the eastern edge of Bears Ears. Miera's map depicts "the provincia de Nabajo," homeland of the Navajo peoples. Bernardo de Miera y Pacheco, "Plano Geographico" (detail), Chihuahua, 1778. Courtesy of John L. Kessell.

sees pueblitos as "temporary refuge sites from raiders. There were many cultural dynamics and exchanges going on here, but you did not want hand to hand combat with adult males."[10] Natural rock outcroppings funneled human movement and pueblito builders designed walls and rooms to trap invaders in a crossfire. Larry Baker from Salmon Ruins, the San Juan County Museum in Bloomfield, New Mexico, has directed stabilization crews working on remote pueblitos. He argues the defensive structures were so well-built that "Mom and the kids could defend these places with a box of rocks because a rock coming downhill has a lot of force."[11]

Because of their remote location in the San Juan Basin, after 300 years many pueblitos remain intact with original stone walls, smaller walls as barriers to entry, parapets, pinyon or juniper wood ceilings, and escape hatches into second stories. A few prominent pueblitos are on New Mexico State Trust Land, and Trust Land Archaeologist David Eck explains, "Once the Comanches got the horse the whole world changes. Navajos,

Pueblos, and Apaches had learned to live with one another, but when you get into a period of conflict you don't know who's going to help or hurt you. Fighting's a poor option with maximum risk and minimum reward." Sheep were hard to steal so Eck says, "People and horses were the most common things taken." By sending smoke signals from rooftops, an embattled family could bring reinforcements within half an hour. Weapons of warfare included bows, arrows, and shields. A brave warrior using a toughened bison-hide shield attached to his wrist could deflect an enemy's arrows and then later reuse them. "Defenders could launch a furious amount of artillery in a short time with great effect," explains Eck.[12]

A few of the pueblitos in Gobernador and Largo Canyons retain original plaster and distinctive handprints. Broken pottery sherds represent both Navajo grayware and Navajo-made Gobernador polychromes that have a buff orange color. The sites have names like the Citadel, Three Corn, Old Fort, Truby's Tower, *Kin Naa daa* (Maize House), Tapacito, *Kin Yazhi* (Little House), Delgadito Pueblito, Shaft House, Star Rock Refuge, and Tower of the Standing God. Many pueblitos are now listed on the National Register of Historic Places. A distinctive architectural feature found at Frances Canyon Ruin is a Spanish-style hooded fireplace made of wood. I can imagine the Native woman who had seen such a fireplace and insisted her mate build one. The fireplace is a symbol of the cross-cultural currents swirling through the Dinétah—Spanish, Pueblo, Navajo, Ute, Comanche, Apache, and even Kiowa. By the 1750s, increasing pressure from raiding parties and a 40-year drought forced Navajos south and west away from their cultural homeland.

Now 15,000 to 20,000 gas wells cover the San Juan Basin, and decades of overgrazing have reduced native grasses. Weeds abound as does ubiquitous sagebrush. BLM archaeologist Copeland states, "The tribe's very interested in Dinétah as ancestral ground," yet ironically the seventeen-million-acre Navajo Nation does not include Largo and Gobernador Canyons with its historic stone pueblitos. In these canyons under threat from invaders, diverse native clans became one Diné or Navajo people.

Regardless of when Navajos arrived and how they incorporated other members in an effective, inclusive process called ethnogenesis, which allowed peoples to come together with shared stories, songs, and ceremonies, for my purpose it is the Navajo story of retreating to and residing in the Bears Ears region that is important. Just as Bears Ears was the northwest edge of the Ancestral Puebloan world, it also formed the same edge for historic Navajo peoples who used it as a retreat and a place of refuge from both Spanish and Ute incursions. A Spanish scholar wrote that the Navajo population "becomes greater as we go toward the center of their land, which extends so far in all directions that . . . it alone is vaster than all the others . . . In journeying westward through this nation, one never reaches the end of it."[13]

A key piece of evidence is tree ring dating. Dates for Ancestral Puebloan cliff dwellings can be determined by coring wood samples left in door lintels. Outward migration of Ancestral Puebloans by 1300 is partly determined by the last wood cut for ceiling beams and lintels in their stone granaries, habitation rooms, and defensive walls.[14] Athabaskan peoples who became the Diné also have distinctive architecture primarily of wood not stone—east-facing hogans, both male and female, sweat lodges, drying racks for processing wild game, and other structures.[15] As part of Navajo Land Claim Field Research for the United States Indian Claims Commission, from old hogans and other structures across the Four Corners, anthropologists and archaeologists took wood specimens and dated them through dendrochronology to determine the geographical extent of Navajo land use. In the Northern Sector along the lower San Juan River and to the north of the river, 297 specimens were collected, twelve from the Bears Ears region. The date closest to the date of use, or when the wood was cut, comes from the outermost ring. Researchers wrote, "The presence of bark on a specimen is the only definite proof that the date of the outermost ring represents the last year of growth."[16] A sweathouse with bark on it dated to 1794 and a hogan with bark to 1840. Most Bears Ears dates ranged from the early 1800s to 1868.[17] Clearly, the Navajo were deep in Utah's canyon country. Originally, they came on foot, but post-1680 everything changed.

After the Pueblo Revolt, horses got loose. Navajos and Utes may have had a few horses prior to 1680, but Popé's instructions to his followers who had routed the Spanish colonizers were not to touch anything the Spanish had brought and to abandon Spanish names, Spanish customs, Spanish food, and anything the Spanish had introduced. For the Navajos and Utes, traditional raiders of Pueblo villages, Popé's command resulted in a revolution in their lifeways. The Utes could now become mounted warriors and as they traded horses to the north, the French *couriers du bois,* or fur trappers, moved west across the Great Lakes. By the 1730s, guns had moved west and south into the northern Great Plains creating for the first time, armed Indians on horseback. Utes adopted Plains Indians' cultural traits. In addition to their brush shelter wickiups, they now had heavy bison-hide teepees because horses could pull the teepees on wooden travois. Utes developed beadwork, traded for pistols and rifles, and established their range across northern New Mexico, southern Colorado, and into the state that would be named for them—Utah. Utes hunted, gathered, and moved with the seasons while also planting small corn plots in sandy well-drained areas. They maintained goat herds for meat and milk.

Navajos took horses from the Spanish but rarely traded the equines. Instead, the Diné built up large horse herds, bred the Spanish Churro sheep, and developed a mobile lifeway that required vast grazing areas for horses, flocks of sheep, and some cattle. Navajos built hogans or octagonal one-room structures with horizontal logs for a female hogan and vertical logs for a male hogan. Each structure depended upon four upright wooden support posts to hold up the cribbed wooden roof just as the four sacred mountains supported and enclosed Navajo culture. Doorways always faced east. In Navajo oral tradition, Spider Woman taught Navajo women how to weave, though weaving probably transitioned to the Diné from male Pueblo weavers whose ancestors had first used cotton and then under Spanish domination switched to wool.

Utes traded brain-tanned deer hides while Navajo blankets became a prized trading item, with their distinctive designs and colors from organic dyes especially dark red from a small cochineal beetle that thrives on prickly pear cactus. Both groups began to raid and trade with not only the Puebloan Indians but also the Spanish when they returned in 1692. Bears Ears, in the heart of southeast Utah's canyon country, remained remote, but as Spanish populations grew in the Rio Grande Valley and Spanish colonists were forced to raid Navajo strongholds to recover lost stock and stolen women and children, Navajos moved west. They fled the Spanish who sought to capture Navajo women and children for slaves. When the Diné crossed the San Juan River, they entered traditional Ute territory and a high desert landscape occupied both by Utes as well as their Paiute cousins, also from the Great Basin.[18]

In the 1700s raiding and trading fluctuated out of Taos and Abiquiu, New Mexico. The presence of liquor could make annual trade fairs dissolve into open skirmishes among otherwise peaceful bands. Away from the Spanish settlements, Navajos and Utes established their own seasonal rounds for farming and hunting with summer camps at higher elevations and winter camps in lower river valleys and canyon bottoms, and in secret, Spanish explorers may have skirted the edges of Utah's canyons.

Small groups of Spanish traders may have ridden northwest from the settlements looking for trading opportunities. Juan Maria Antonio Rivera traveled at first illegally without consent of the New Mexican governor, but in June 1765, the governor gave permission for Rivera's *entrada* or entrance into the area for legal trading and prospecting. Actually, his goal was not so much assessing mineral riches as to attempt to determine how far any British incursions might have occurred on the Colorado Plateau. Rivera's geographic descriptions, however, remain confusing other than his crossings of the Animas River near Durango and his party's arrival on the Dolores River. Rivera may have arrived on the San Juan River, the traditional Navajo/Ute boundary with Navajos remaining south of the river and Utes to the north. Rivera's party may also have camped near Montezuma Creek close to the river's edge.

He traveled north in June, returned, and set out again on October 1, 1765 with the same men. According to historian Paul T. Nelson, "By October 10 the party was camped in a barren region somewhere between the Abajo and La Sal Mountains, perhaps at the head of Indian Creek Canyon," which would mean they had spent days traveling north and would have seen the Bears Ears from horseback.[19] They skirted the eastern edge of what would become Bears Ears National Monument and continued north toward the Colorado River crossing at Moab, Utah. Rivera's second expedition, trying to ascertain fact from fiction in a landscape full of myth and confusing Native tales, became "the first direct Spanish encounter with the Canyon Country," but it would soon be followed by two friars who brought along a mapmaker in the year of American independence.[20]

In 1776, Friars Francisco Atanasio Dominguez and Silvestre Velez de Escalante traveled north from Abiquiu, New Mexico, in search of a route to Spanish missions at Monterey in Alta California. Their travels are well-known. What is less known is information about the short, scrappy Spaniard who accompanied them, taking notes, drawing pictures, befriending Natives, and complaining about the priests' overbearing attitudes. An artist, he would become a mapmaker and give us the first map of the Four Corners and the Colorado Plateau. At only five feet tall, Bernardo de Miera y Pacheco (1713–1785) could easily be overlooked. But that would be a mistake. Indefatigable, resourceful, Miera had all the attributes of an adventurer exploring the Spanish frontier with a thirst for knowledge, a willingness to endure freezing nights, cold mornings, blistering afternoons, and a desire to learn from Native Americans.

The people who migrated south from Alaska culturally became the Diné in the area known as Dinétah, in canyon systems southeast of Farmington, New Mexico. Unique structures that combine both Pueblo and Navajo elements are called Pueblitos, which can be found in Largo and Gobernador Canyons. Author photo.

He would become an early ethnographer and provide the first assessment of where Navajos and Utes lived in the canyons, mesas, and mountains of the Southwest. A devoted family man, he was rarely home. Instead, he walked and rode on Indian trails, learning, assessing, and trying to understand the culturally complex world around him. But who really was Miera y Pacheco? Born in Spain, how and when did he get to Mexico and how did he eke out a living on Spain's northern frontier or "the ragged edge of Christendom?" I've followed Miera across the Four Corners. I've traced him from Abiquiu, New Mexico, northwest toward Moab traveling above the Abajo Mountains in Utah. He must have seen the Bears Ears. Often, Miera patiently waited with his braying burros, his lack of fresh food, dust on his clothes, his saddle bags, and his beard. The overheated friars in their dark wool cassocks complained again and again about their Ute guides. The priests occasionally running fingers over their rosary beads, muttering prayers and staring into the relentless western sun. I've followed Miera across the Colorado Plateau. I knew his route but not the man, nor did I understand his magnificent map with place names that have endured until I read historian John Kessell's *Whither the Waters: Mapping the Great Basin from Bernardo de Miera to John C. Fremont.*[21]

"My impression is that many of the names, especially the secular names, like the La Platas and the Rio de Los Pinos, were first applied by Hispanic New Mexican traders who came north to trade with the Utes," historian Kessell explains.[22] Miera put rivers and mountains on his map thus forever naming geographic features. "By 1778 Miera was the most knowledgeable person in the kingdom who understood New Mexico's human and physical environments," notes Kessell.

Despite what Kessell discovered about Miera, as an historian, he also knows what has been lost. "We do not have an original of the first map he drew in May 1777, only copies. The original we cite was his revision in 1778" held by the British Museum. Dutifully, Miera drew Indigenous peoples in their locales and habitats, yet when the Spanish Royal Engineers copied Miera's work "they left out the Indians Miera had so carefully placed on his map," Kessell comments. Miera named the Green River the Rio de San Buenaventura, though that name did not stick, and he whetted appetites for countless explorers by drawing in a westward-flowing river, the Rio de Tizon, that others later projected ran to the Pacific. No such river existed, but explorers would search for it well into the nineteenth century. Richard Francaviglia in *Mapping and Imagination in the Great Basin* writes, "The map produced by the Dominguez-Escalante Expedition was one of the landmarks in the cartographic history of the North American West. It would influence other maps for more than a generation."[23]

Despite Miera's errors, his map "represented the first attempt of any European to portray cartographically, from personal experience, the complex upper Colorado River basin," explains cartographic historian Carl Wheat.[24] But the junction of the Green River with the Colorado River, and the merging of the Colorado River with the San Juan, remained unmapped. Canyon country, with Bears Ears at its center, had not been even initially explored. There were too many confusing canyons, too many dead ends and dry, waterless routes, and too much danger, from both mixed bands of Navajos, Utes, and Paiutes, and occasional Spanish slavers who sought women and children, but who would attack and ambush anyone.

In the mid-1700s, at the time of the Dominguez-Escalante expedition, the Southwest slave trade increased with a high value placed on women who could do domestic household work and weave, and children who could be taught skills including wood cutting and sheep herding.[25] In slave raids, men were routinely killed because they would resist, fight back, and become a dangerous burden to their captors. Utes generally stayed out of the way of the Spanish or occasionally aligned with them or the Comanches, while Navajos moved further west into their stronghold at Canyon de Chelly and beyond. In *Navajo Wars,* historian Frank McNitt explains, "Always known to the Spaniards as mountain people, the Navajos withdrew to higher, more inaccessible elevations of the mesas. Here they built fortified sites of stone—large circular emplacements, houses, parapet walls, towers, and lookout points—from which they could defend themselves against surprise or heavy attack." He adds, "These sites extended southward from Gobernador and Largo canyons to the Chacra and Big Bead mesas."[26]

In the winter of 1804–05, the military campaign of Lieutenant Colonel Antonio Narbona took Navajo warfare into the heart of Navajo resistance at Canyon de Chelley filled with deep snow and dramatic pink sandstone cliffs. Hiding in a cave, considered safe from the soldiers below, a Navajo woman who had once been held captive by the Spanish, jeered the soldiers. She ridiculed them "as men who walked without eyes."[27] Hearing the taunts, the soldiers shot up into the cave from below allowing their bullets to ricochet down upon the terrified Navajos who thought they were safe high above the valley floor. That branch of the canyon is now known as Canyon del Muerto or Canyon of the Dead and within that cave the first documented evidence of Navajo weaving has been found in the fragments of clothes from those who died there.

Spanish raids gave way to Mexican raids when Mexico revolted from Spain in 1821. Navajos had by then been living north of the San Juan River and in the ponderosa pines near Bears Ears for at least two centuries. One of the great Navajo war leaders and resistance fighters, Manuelito, was born near Bears Ears. He married a daughter of the Navajo headman Narbona, not to be confused with the Spanish Colonel of the same name, and by matrilineal custom moved to her home. Manuelito became known as *Nabaah Jilt'aa* or Warrior Grabbed Enemy. His brother *K'ayelli* or One with Quiver, stayed closer to home and a spring is named after him as well as a USFS ranger station.

"Manuelito plays an important part in resisting American expansion," notes his biographer and descendant Jennifer Nez Denetdale, who argues that he "was the most vocal warrior to resist the Mexican and American invasions in the nineteenth century ... For many Navajos, Manuelito strove to keep Navajo land and believed that we should remain a sovereign people."[28] She adds, "Navajo stories and portrayals of their leader highlight his commitment to his people's survival, and his lifelong passion that Navajos retain their land for future generations."[29] Approximately two years after Manuelito's birth in 1823, Governor of New Mexico Jose Antonio Vizcarra again pursued Navajo raiders. An American in Santa Fe at the time said of the Navajos, "what they could not carry off they burned and destroyed."[30] Leaving in June 1823 with 1,500 men, Vizcarra "faced an elusive enemy. The Navajos constantly were retreating, scattering, and vanishing into hideouts."[31]

Vizcarra killed Navajo men and women, took slaves, sheep, and goats, but a smaller force under Colonel Don Francisco Salazar failed to capture much livestock. McNitt writes that the Mexican soldier "came upon a broad trail of livestock—sheep and goats, horses, and cattle—that from the signs had been traveling in the direction of the Bear's Ears, twin promontories north of the San Juan visible far in the distance."[32] He gave up the chase and turned east. Again, the rugged country of Bears Ears had proven to be a safe refuge for Navajos, a true land of resistance with deep incised canyons on both sides of the long stretch of Cedar Mesa.

Two fierce decades of Mexican raids against Navajo families and livestock gave way to American military skirmishes against the Navajo after the Mexican–American War of 1846–1848 brought all of Arizona, New Mexico, Utah, California, Nevada, and Colorado into American territorial ownership. New York newspapers had proclaimed that it was "manifest destiny" to "overspread the continent" from sea to shining sea. The Southwest would become one of the last holdouts for Native peoples to retain their original land bases.

Eastern tribes had suffered from Indian removal under President Andrew Jackson, but southwestern tribes dared to retain their homelands. American soldiers expected subservience. They thought they were better trained. They knew they had better rifles, but the Navajos understood the terrain and knew every fork in the canyons, every hidden spring and water hole, and every rock basin or *tinajas* where snowmelt collected. Concealed behind rocks and stunted pinyon trees, Navajos moved with stealth and took what they wanted from military supply lines regardless of pickets or sentries.

They also had better horses, more adaptable to local grasses, while the US cavalry mounts depended upon grain and extra forage. For the Navajo, who had fought Pueblos, Utes, Spaniards, and Mexicans, the newly arrived Americans were just one more enemy appearing on the eastern horizon.

The Hayden surveyors in Utah mapped traditional Ute and Navajo landscapes near Bears Ears. Part of the importance of the four sacred peaks to Navajos is that their medicine men or *hatali* travel to the peaks to acquire rare plants and minerals for their *jiish* or medicine bags. Photograph of Nesjaja, a Navajo medicine man, by photographer Edward Sheriff Curtis, 1904. Original Curtis photogravure print donated to the Center of Southwest Studies at Fort Lewis College by the author. Courtesy of the Center of Southwest Studies.

Skirmishes continued between Navajo raiders and American cavalrymen who used local New Mexicans and Pueblo warriors as auxiliaries with the promise they could keep whatever booty they recovered from Navajo hogans—livestock, women, children, or blankets. By the late 1850s, 12,000 Navajos owned 200,000 sheep and 60,000 horses. They lived on 45,000 square miles of mesas, canyons, and pine-covered slopes with the Bears Ears area on the northwest edge of their territory on lands also frequented by Utes. The two little peaks of the Bears Ears, which can be seen for over one hundred miles, had many historic names such *Shash Jaa* in Navajo, *Kwiyagat Nugavat* in Ute, and *Las Orejas del Oso* in Spanish.[33] For Navajos with a variety of ceremonies, dances, and traditions, the Bears Ears became a powerful sacred site with its own oral traditions and stories attached to it. Robert S. McPherson explains,

> One of the most notable sites in southeastern Utah is the Bears Ears, with stories from the Mountain Way and Upward Moving and Emergence Way associated with it. This latter ceremonial cycle contains the myth of Changing Bear Maiden, who married Coyote and learned his witchcraft. She eventually killed all but one of her brothers, lived by trickery and deceit, and used her evil knowledge to defeat others. Her youngest brother killed her and separated her body parts, tossing them in different directions. The Bears Ears are the upper portion of her head.[34]

Such a unique location provided for both good and evil with plants to pick to "cure witchcraft and incest" and as a site for a medicine man to help his patients suffering from loneliness or weight loss.[35] Such a powerful place would become a refuge and a sanctuary with many Native camps, both Navajo and Ute, in the meadows below and to the north.

Over the centuries Navajos and Utes shared what would become San Juan County, Utah, which in the mid-nineteenth century offered excellent browse for Navajo herds and for mule deer whose hides became supple skins in the hands of skilled Ute women. It was an uneasy peace, but on this northwestern edge of the Navajo world, Utes, Paiutes, and Navajos kept to their own winter and summer camps, but they also mingled. As Americans flooded into the Southwest onto lands taken during the Mexican–American War, US military expeditions sought new routes of passage. One of those military surveys entered the Bears Ears region. The military leader, worrying about his wagons and supplies, would find the area intolerable, a jumble of canyons and miles of worthless rock. In contrast, the scientist on the survey would be the first to exclaim about the beauties of a world of sandstone cliffs, junipers in canyon clefts, cottonwood trees and willows in the bottoms of washes, and as yet unnamed desert plants flowering near hidden seeps and springs.

In 1859, Captain John N. Macomb left Santa Fe to find a useful wagon route to the southern settlements in southwest Utah. Over a decade earlier in 1846, Brigham Young had departed Nauvoo, Illinois, with hundreds of his followers in the Church of Jesus Christ of Latter-day Saints to start a new life beyond the legal boundaries of the United States in the Great Salt Lake Valley. Under Young's leadership, Mormons branched out from Salt Lake City and established settlements along rivers and creeks throughout the Great Basin and land that would be called the Kingdom of Deseret. Macomb sought a route "to the southern settlements of Utah territory in the event of future conflicts with its inhabitants," meaning Mormons.[36] In 1857–1858, federal troops had clashed with Mormons near Salt Lake in what has been called the Utah War and even identified as the first Civil War. The military needed to find other routes into Utah.

Writing about Macomb's expedition and the country he traversed, historian Steven K. Madsen explains, "At its heart lies one of the largest uninhabited and undeveloped landscapes in the American West. A myriad of fanciful shapes, captured in stone, greet the eye."[37] Though Macomb was ordered to find the confluence of the Green and Colorado Rivers, which he almost did in what is now Canyonlands National Park, Bears Ears is farther south in an equally remote area—the San Juan Triangle where the Colorado River meets the San Juan. Macomb's expedition also became known as the San Juan Exploring Expedition. He took 300 soldiers, civilian employees, cattle and sheep, 6,000 pounds of provisions, and scientists who collected specimens and made daily recordings with barometers and thermometers. Albert H. Pfeiffer came because of his knowledge of Utes. John S. Newberry would become the expedition's scientific star, and he would locate the first dinosaur bones in the American West.

Macomb followed much of the Old Santa Fe Trail, which after leaving Abiquiu skirted Largo Canyon and the cultural hearth of the Navajo. Then he went west to the La Plata Mountains and on to the Blue or Abajo Mountains. Abajo means "below" in Spanish and that small range was below the Old Spanish Trail ford of the Colorado River and below the higher La Sal Mountains.[38] Off the trail and to the west, deep into the heart of slickrock canyon country "the rugged features and steep-walled gorges in the heart of the high plateau region formed an insurmountable obstacle to direct east-west travel," and a perfect place to hide stolen livestock in the region now known as Canyonlands.[39]

If Newberry loved the canyons, Macomb despised them. Macomb's expedition traveled eight and a half months and 800 miles. He named the Great Sage Plain on the Colorado-Utah border and though Macomb felt his expedition to have a tedious topographic task, scientist John Newberry delighted in the description. He wrote,

> Directly west the Sage-plain stretches out nearly horizontal, unmarked by any prominent feature, to the distance of a hundred miles. There the island-like mountains, the Sierra Abajo and Sierra LaSal, rise from its surface. South of these is the little double-peaked mountain called by the Mexicans Las Orejas del Oso—the bear's ears.[40]

Following the Old Spanish Trail, the expedition stayed east of the Bears Ears itself but later dropped into what would become the Needles District of Canyonlands on the northeast edge of Bears Ears National Monument. Soldiers and scientists began to see cliff houses. They named Labyrinth Canyon in lower Indian Creek, and as the explorers approached the Needles District, its "appearance was so strange and beautiful as to call out exclamation and delight from our party."[41] The San Juan Exploring Expedition had entered the southern edge of Canyonlands. In that world of red rock, blue skies, and white clouds, expedition member, chronicler and artist Charles H. Dimmock explained, ". . . there met our eyes such a view as is not to be seen elsewhere on earth. But few, if any other whites, were ever the beholders of so magical a variety of towering sierra-like m[e]sas, deep cut by canons, penetrating in all directions, into whose depths the sun at midday can only fall."[42] Captain Macomb, however, could see no economic or resource value in a sterile world of rock. He disliked the heat, the lack of water, and the difficult to access terrain. "I doubt not there are repetitions and *varieties* of it for hundreds of miles down the canon of the Great Colorado."[43] In that, he was correct.

The group left what would become San Juan County, Utah, without obtaining their objective—standing atop the confluence of the Green and Colorado Rivers. In those winding sandstone canyons, they could find no route opening to the west that could be utilized for military wagons. The Macomb Expedition reversed course and made its way back to Santa Fe only to have their arduous trek and their documentation of it become lost to history as the Civil War engulfed the nation by April 1860.

Two decades later another wagon train, this one full of families, men, women, children, and household goods, would also venture into the canyons but from the west. The Mormon Hole-in-the-Rock Expedition of 1879–1880 would become the largest eastbound wagon train in American history. Almost all wagon trains moved west from Missouri across the Great Plains to settle in Oregon Country or to move south toward California. This last Mormon mission reversed course. Members of the Church of Jesus Christ of Latter-day Saints, many of whom had been born in England or northern Europe, had already crossed the continent. Now at the request of church elders, they would leave farming settlements in central Utah to descend into canyons once home to Ancestral Puebloans.

Mormon scouts would navigate the deep-set canyons that seemed impassable to the US military. But first, the Civil War (1860–1865) tore the nation apart, and in the Navajo stronghold of Canyon de Chelly, the Diné would meet determined soldiers who would force them away from their native lands in a terrifying episode remembered to this day as the Long Walk. Small bands of Navajos would escape the soldiers' patrols and head into the canyon recesses below Navajo Mountain and to the safety of the pine-clad meadows of Bears Ears, to find refuge high above the desert floor.

CHAPTER 5

"The Fearing Time" and Mapping Ancient America, 1860–1875

I hope to God you will not ask me to go to any other country except my own.

—Barboncito, Navajo headman speaking at Fort Sumner, May 1868

The process of 'surveying' was more than merely measuring; it sought to define the land in terms of western concepts of nature and of capitalist concerns of value and usefulness. This meant measuring these concepts into tangible, usable, and communicable forms, such as maps, photographs, and published reports.

—Robert S. McPherson and Susan Rhodes Neel, *Mapping the Four Corners*

By September 28, 1859, Macomb's expedition dissolved. Within months, some of its members would join the Union Army and others the Confederacy. The War Between the States would be about slavery of African Americans, yet a thriving slave trade had existed in the American Southwest for centuries. The Old Spanish Trail, which Macomb had followed to the Abajo Mountains, had been a slave route for Indian captives to be taken to Los Angeles or on the return route to be taken to Santa Fe. A spur of the main trail was known as the Bears Ears Trail. The route crossed the San Juan River probably at the Rincon, or a low spot where horses could find firm footing. It's a beautiful spot. To stand there and look to the west along the river where the canyons begin to open up is one of the great views in southeast Utah. The Bears Ears Trail route went north from the Rincon along Comb Wash on the west side of 900-foot-high Comb Ridge. It is a natural pathway open to the north with almost no obstructions for horses, riders, and herds.

The Bears Ears appears northwest of Comb Ridge at the edge of Elk Ridge among stands of pinyon, juniper, and ponderosa all of it cooler, greener, and higher than the desert below. The Bears Ears Trail then angles northwest beyond White and Red Canyons toward the Green River and Spanish Bottoms.[1] It was probably this route that Navajos used when they fled across the San Juan River. Colonel Francisco Salazar saw signs on August 12, 1823 of a large herd of livestock driven north by fleeing Diné. In the decades to come, Navajos would continue to use the Bears Ears Trail, only this time to flee American soldiers, not the Spanish.

As the Civil War began to split the nation, Navajo depredations against New Mexican livestock increased in part because of continuing slave raids against the Diné, which resulted in the loss of children, women, and wives. By 1860 with the first US Census of New Mexican territory, over 5,000 household "servants" would be enumerated, many of whom had been stolen as children. In Conejos County in Colorado, 63 Navajos had been bought from Apaches, Mexicans, and Utes. In adjacent Costilla County, fifty Navajos had been purchased and placed into bondage.[2] Is it any wonder that having fought Mexicans and Spaniards for centuries, that Navajo headmen and their warriors would also turn against Americans engaged in similar raids? The Navajo nickname for whites was *Bilagaana* or "those who love to fight."[3] The excuse was that Southwestern slavery was good for the slaves because once placed in households slaves received Christian values to save their Native souls. The Superintendent of Indian Affairs at Santa Fe wrote the Indian Commissioner to explain this practice of domestic slavery. He began by stating that reports to the federal government "upon this subject have been greatly exaggerated" and that the goal in having household captives "has not been to reduce them to slavery, but rather from a Christian piety . . . to instruct and educate them in civilization" and thus such bondage has been "favorable, humane, and satisfactory."[4]

The Civil War generals in charge of New Mexico believed in Christian instruction for Native Americans as the Navajo wars ended in incarceration in a prison camp named Fort Sumner or Bosque Redondo on the southeastern New Mexican plains. Located on the east side of the Pecos River, far from the mesas and canyons of the Navajo homeland, Bosque Redondo was originally a forest of cottonwood trees in a river-shaped curve. By the 1860s, as soldiers cut down the trees to build Fort Sumner and Native prisoners needed firewood, the bosque shrank, affording no shelter or shade.[5]

At *Hweeldi*, the Navajo name for Fort Sumner, Navajos would endure ill health, dysentery, and dehydration from drinking Pecos River water

The wooden remains of Navajo hogans and sweat lodges are found across the Bears Ears region especially at the mouths of canyons where water pools. This historic forked-stick structure is along the base of Comb Ridge. Many significant Indigenous architectural features have been trampled by cattle. Author photo.

laced with sodium chloride and sodium sulphate. They suffered brutal heat, freezing winter nights, and were desperate from starvation; girls and women prostituted themselves to American soldiers for food for their families. Eleven thousand Navajos endured the Long Walk to Bosque Redondo, which is Spanish for Round Grove. Over 2,500 people died between 1863 and their final release in 1868.[6] Other Navajo families fled west and north during the Fearing Time, ahead of the soldiers' patrols. Those small bands took refuge at Bears Ears and Navajo Mountain willing to risk everything rather than be prodded by soldiers' rifles.

After years of skirmishes, reprisal raids, and failed treaties, some not ratified by the US Senate, an 1861 peace treaty with Navajos failed and fell apart even though fifty-four Navajo headmen had signed it. They said they could speak only for their extended families and could not control their younger men who stole flocks and horse herds from Hispanic settlements. With the Civil War underway back East, but effectively ended in the West after the Battle of Glorieta Pass north of Santa Fe, enlisted Union soldiers and New Mexican militia would be brought together for one final scorched earth campaign against Navajos. Lieutenant Colonel Edward Canby formulated the war policy in late 1861, but his successor Brevet Brigadier General James H. Carleton would implement it. Canby's orders to Colonel Christopher "Kit" Carson, known to the Navajos as Red Shirt, were specific. "You are directed to instruct the commanding officer not to take any male prisoners," he wrote, "and if any men fall into his hands to execute them at once. Women and children will be turned loose and ordered to go into their own country." Within two years, the orders to field commanders became even more precise. "Kill every . . . Navajo Indian who is large enough to bear arms."[7]

General James Carleton used former Indian Agent Kit Carson, commander of the Central Military District at Albuquerque who in turn asked for Captain Albert Pfeiffer, Ute Indian Agent from Abiquiu, to round up Navajos and force them east to Fort Sumner. Future plans remained vague, perhaps to send them east to Indian Territory in Oklahoma or further west beyond the Hopi villages. Contrary to orders and for which he could have been court-martialed, Colonel Carson did not have his men shoot Navajo males—unless they resisted. Carson and Pfeiffer agreed to use Hispanic and Pueblo scouts but also to use the Navajos' most feared enemy—armed Utes on horseback. Ute trackers received two horses, saddles, rifles, ammunition, blankets, food, and tobacco. The Ute auxiliaries could take anything they found including slaves. The pretext was to civilize Navajos starting with their children. A fervent Christian but also a Navajo slave owner, Carleton believed,

> Little by little, on a reservation, away from their haunts, and hills, and hiding places of their country, and then to be kind to them; there teach their children how to read and write; teach them the arts of peace . . . the truths of Christianity. Soon they would acquire new habits, new ideas, new modes of life; the old Indians (would) die off, and carry with them all the latent longings for murdering and robbing; the young (would) . . . take their places without these longings; and thus, little by little they (would) become a happy and content people and Navajo wars (would) . . . be remembered only as something that belongs entirely in the past.[8]

As the months wore on, fewer and fewer Navajos agreed to come in by the July 20, 1863 deadline to surrender at either Fort Canby or Fort Wingate.

After that date, the US Army considered Navajos "hostile." Navajos could be pursued and shot on lands where they had lived for centuries. A specific military goal was to harass them in their stronghold of Canyon de Chelly. During a winter campaign that began on January 11, 1864, Captain A.H. Pfeiffer and his troops entered Canyon Del Muerto where the Spanish governor had also brought troops over half a century earlier.

As cavalrymen rode the canyon bottom, Navajos higher on the walls above heckled the soldiers and threw rocks, sticks, and stones. If the Navajos would not surrender, then they would be starved into submission. Colonel Kit Carson returned and destroyed hogans, cornfields, acres of beans, and cut down or burned 3,200 peach trees, which had taken decades to cultivate in the sandy soils. "Those peaches which were not eaten fresh or dried for winter use were traded to other Navajos, who came from far and wide to obtain this sweet food stuff," writes Stephen Jett.[9]

The blue-coated soldiers ruined water sources and filled them with dirt, rocks, and gutted dead sheep and goats in a scorched earth policy that left no food sources for the ragged, hungry Navajos looking from cliff tops down at the devastation. Cold winter months lay ahead.

Soldiers and Utes pursued Navajos at Dennehotso, Black Mountain, Steamboat Canyon, Ganado, and Wide Ruins. By the end of 1864, 8,000 Navajos had surrendered and had begun the 300-mile Long Walk to Fort Sumner along the Pecos River. There they found bad water, alkali soil that shriveled crops, and 400 Mescalero Apache internees—a long-time enemy of the Diné who had also been forced into the flat camp devoid of shade.

Canyon de Chelly, now a national monument, is within the Navajo Nation. I have hiked down into the canyon to White House Ruin, a cliff house of the Ancient People and traditional home of Navajo deities. At twilight on the spring equinox, when day and night are equal, I have stood on the canyon rim and watched the last rays of sun climb the tall red rock spire named Spider Rock, the place in Navajo legend where Spider Woman first taught Navajo women to weave. During equinox the entire canyon grows dark. But the last light of day sets the top of Spider Rock on fire as though from a celestial searchlight.

With binoculars I've looked across the rim to Fortress Rock to see the stone barricades and ponderosa pine timbers hauled to the top of the cliff as desperate family groups staged a dramatic resistance against soldiers rounding up their kin in the canyon below. Known in Navajo as *Tselaa*, within the stronghold of Canyon de Chelly was an even more remote hideout strengthened in summer 1863 on a 243-acre summit with dwellings, stored water, latrine trenches, and minimal supplies for the Navajo, who knew the soldiers were coming and sought shelter on a red rock pinnacle. By October, 300 people lived on top quietly waiting for the Blue Coats to enter the canyon. On a winter day in 1805 Spanish troops had invaded Canyon de Chelly to punish the Navajo. A woman had shouted and jeered at them thinking her clan members were safe in a high alcove now named Massacre Cave. Spanish bullets ricocheting from the alcove's stone ceiling killed and wounded most of the trapped family members. This time there would be no taunts, no Navajo women cursing, and no jeering soldiers. Everything was quiet. Extensive preparations were complete. David Roberts writes of a dangerous approach to the summit of Fortress Rock through a narrow sandstone cleft:

> The climb to the gunsight notch, then farther upward by a series of ledges, chimneys and cliffs, was an acrobatic undertaking; from many places on the route, a simple slip meant falling to one's death… the Navajo improved the route to allow the passage of women, children and supplies. They built a kind of wooden bridge across the notch. Near the top, two blank cliffs barred the way; to tame them, the people hauled a pair of 80-foot ponderosa pines all the way from the Lukachukai Mountains, 15 or 20 miles away, somehow wrestled those timbers up the route, propped them in place, and cut alternating steps in the wood to turn them into ladders.[10]

Binoculars reveal the wooden bridge. On a cold, windy day I have speculated on all the efforts to survive on that barren rock and especially how to conserve water. Without it a stronghold could become a death trap. As Colonel Kit Carson patrolled the canyon rim, Captain Pfeiffer's troops entered the bottom, 700 feet below, with a trickle of flowing water in Tsaile Creek.[11] Everyone on top remained silent as the soldiers etched inscriptions on the rock.

Four days later Carson's men found the fortress and lay siege from the top. Riflemen shot across the canyon rim firing over the Navajo sentries to have bullets ricochet off rocks and kill those in hiding. Twenty Navajo died. Others suffered from thirst. The Diné had no choice but to make a human chain down a steep cliff edge to quietly gather water on a starlit night. Roberts writes, "A Navajo lowered one pot after another by rope, dipping and filling each in the stream. The pots were relayed to the summit through the night. Not a single stone clattered loose, not a pot was dropped, not a man fell."[12]

Setting down my binoculars, I thought of their desperation, having just seen the last of their wooden logs still atop Fortress Rock after more than a century. I thought of their deep resistance to the soldiers' encroachment on traditional Navajo lands, knowing that other families had made different choices. They had fled to the west, traveled only at night, and remained hidden during the day. The Long Walk is seared into the memory of Navajo people. Story after story tells of cruelty, with the elderly and infants being abandoned or shot if they could not keep up. Navajo scholar and oral historian Jennifer Nez Denetdale writes of the Diné, "Their remembrances tell of how their ancestors, in the face of starvation, death, and brutality were forced to abandon the elders and pregnant women who could no longer keep pace ... mothers killed their newborn infants because they did not want to see them suffer or because the children had been products of rapes by the soldiers or New Mexican raiders."[13]

A Navajo shepherd named Wolfkiller lived near Kayenta, Arizona, years after the Long Walk. He allowed his friend Louisa Wetherill to record his stories of the Fearing Time when the Navajos were being rounded up. Wolfkiller's grandfather told him, "Some of our people have brought the trouble on themselves and all the rest of us, as we who do not want to fight will have our troubles keeping out of the way of the ones who are for war, and out of the way of the soldiers."[14] Wolfkiller remembered his family going into hiding. He recalled,

> For many days, we hid in the canyons where we could find feed for our sheep and horses. The men went to the cornfields from time to time. The rains came and the corn grew very fast. The women wove blankets and gathered grass and weed seeds to store for the winter, as this year the men would not be able to hunt as they had each year before. They would not want to leave the women and children alone long enough to hunt.[15]

The soldiers and Ute scouts got nearer. "As we moved, the men sent the women, children and sheep over the rocky ridges. Then they came along behind them, walking backward and brushing out their tracks with boughs of trees at places where we crossed sand."[16]

But it was no use. Wolfkiller's family and a total of fifty Navajos peacefully surrendered and began the Long Walk. Wolfkiller remembered,

As a young boy, the Navajo sheepherder named Wolfkiller remembered his family surrendering and going on the Long Walk to Bosque Redondo. Later, he would narrate his life's story to Louisa Wetherill, who was fluent in Navajo and wrote it all down. Photo courtesy of Harvey Leake.

"Grandfather told the ones who had complained that it was their own fault. He said they had not tried to control their young men, so the whole tribe must suffer."[17] Not all Navajos surrendered. Perhaps as many as 6,000 hid on their mesa tops and canyons and some of the fiercest moved toward Bears Ears and Navajo Mountain to live lives in hiding. Of the Navajos who never submitted to Carson's Blue Coats, who eluded Ute scouts always on their trail, the venerable headman Hoskininni symbolizes resistance to American military hegemony.

For four and a half years, this leader, who may have been in his mid-thirties, kept his group hidden and safe. His small band of sixteen kinsmen including children was never apprehended; instead he fled west, moving at night, into the complicated canyon recesses of the Bears Ears region, Navajo Mountain, and Monument Valley. He fled west toward Rainbow Bridge with only twenty sheep, one old rifle, a single horse, some sharpened butcher knives, and a deep resolve to keep his band together at all costs. Other Navajos later joined them.

"One day a rider came in from the south and shouted that the soldiers were coming for us. They were so close we could see their dust. We had no time to get our horses nor prepare for a journey so each one grabbed what he could and we ran north toward the Ute country," Hoskininni's son remembered. He added, "There were some Ute scouts among the white soldiers and we were more afraid of them than the whites, as we had always been at war with them."[18] "We traveled many nights, sleeping in the daytime. We were all footsore and hungry, as we had not brought any food. We lived mostly on grass seed and sometimes a rabbit," his son said years later. "We had no meat and could find no game on the mountain. So father made everyone go out and gather grass seed and pine nuts to store for winter use. He drove everyone all day long and would never let us rest, knowing that we might starve."[19]

Hoskininni would not let his band eat any of the sheep they carefully protected. As he found hidden pockets of grass and sweet water springs, his small flock began to thrive. His tiny band of relatives could eat mutton only from sheep that had died. He never allowed them to kill a sheep or a lamb as Hoskininni counted on the natural increase. He earned the nickname "the Angry One" because he demanded complete obedience and he got it. In the depths of canyon country, he learned uses for plants and herbs and when to harvest them. He learned what was edible, inedible, and poisonous. "When we lived at Navajo Mountain my father learned much about medicine and treated the sick. He taught me many things," his son recalled.[20]

Hoskininni's group survived and thrived to the point that when the Navajos finally came west after their imprisonment at Bosque Redondo, he could magnanimously give each arriving family sheep to start their own flocks as well as skins, hides, corn, and wool. He earned a new nickname, "The Generous One." Thus, he assured prominence for his family and his son, Hoskininni-begay, in the red rock world of Monument Valley, in the canyon country of southeast Utah, a place of refuge and resistance, where Bears Ears can always be seen in the distance.

In the New Mexico prison camp, Navajos received bacon, flour, and coffee beans. They undercooked the bacon because of a lack of firewood. At first, they did not understand how to cook with flour. The coffee beans the Diné tried to eat as regular beans, throwing out the brown water the coffee beans had been boiled in. There were not enough blankets. Diseases spread, and Navajos began to die in large numbers. Food was scarce even for the soldiers because of camp mismanagement. After four long years at the prison camp of Fort Sumner, finally the US Army realized they had to decide what to do with the imprisoned Navajos. A fourth of those Diné who had been forced to make the Long Walk had died. Others remained sick and in wretched condition.

A treaty council was to be held but before it began the Navajos sought to learn the outcome. They wanted to return to their mesas and plateaus and not to be sent east to Oklahoma. Those who were healthy enough to participate joined in a secluded Enemy Way Ceremony. The Navajos incarcerated at Fort Sumner started the ceremony at a vast distance apart. Then they drew closer and closer. Within this circle they caught a coyote who stood ready to leap and run. Headman Barboncito spoke to the coyote, "put a bead in her mouth," and implored the animal to tell them the future.[21] Depending upon which way the wild creature ran, the Diné believed the coyote could predict what would happen with the Navajo people. Barboncito asked the coyote to let them all go home. Then as the chanting continued, the coyote lowered its tail and began to run to the west. The grateful Navajos knew they would be able to return home, but first there had to be a treaty, resolutions, speeches, and the concept understood of not raiding and of staying within a reservation and boundaries in a desert landscape where they had always moved with freedom.[22]

At the council, Barboncito refused a move to Oklahoma. Colonel Francis Tappan and General William T. Sherman drafted the treaty of June 1, 1868. The document was signed by twenty-nine headmen who left their marks, including Manuelito, who had been born at Bears Ears and who

Almost life-sized Navajo horse petroglyphs adorn high sandstone cliffs in Cottonwood Wash. Note the details including reins and bridles. The horses are carved over much older Basketmaker spiral glyphs. For Utes and Navajos alike, horses played a key role in allowing remote Bears Ears to become a place of refuge and resistance. Author photo.

had finally surrendered to the Blue Coats after losing his flocks and horses, but the corn he stored along his trails was never found. Navajos received 3.5 million acres for their reservation and the US Senate ratified the treaty. A few years later, in 1871, the lower house of Congress rebelled against the Senate. The House refused to authorize any payments for schools, livestock, wagons, and supplies for Native Americans. No other Indian treaties were ratified after 1871. Tribes that received reservation boundaries prior to that time generally had much more land reserved than tribal reservations established later under presidential executive orders. Within two weeks of the treaty signing Navajos began the walk home. They said, "When we saw the top of the mountain (Mt. Taylor) from Albuquerque we wondered if it was our mountain and felt like falling to the ground. We loved it so . . ."

Navajos signed their most important treaty in 1868 and began their journey home to their desert country, to their canyons and mesas, and to Bears Ears. But some Navajos had not surrendered and along with Utes and Paiutes, continued to raid from hideouts in southeast Utah. They would do so into the early twentieth century.[23] Indian Agent Pfeiffer wrote that in September 1866 a renegade band that had attacked the Hispanic settlement of Tierra Amarilla in northern New Mexico "then left that region and went to the neighborhood . . . of *Sierra Orejas* (Bears Ears) about one hundred miles from the settlements."[24] So far, small groups of whites had not traveled west into canyon country, but within a year that would change. Prospectors looking for gold and silver had begun to come into the Colorado mountains because gold had been discovered in Colorado before the Civil War. As the war ended, more prospectors flooded into the San Juan Mountains. Three of them, after searching for prospects near Silverton, Colorado, headed west into what became San Juan County, Utah, and the Bears Ears region beloved by Utes and Navajos.

Major John Wesley Powell is celebrated for his daring 1869 expedition down the Colorado River through Grand Canyon. But was he the first? Another story exists with defenders and detractors and links to Silverton and canyons in Bears Ears country. Two years before Powell and his men emerged from the Grand Canyon's depths, a sun-burnt, blistered, starved, half-clothed, and half-dead bearded man, leashed to a log raft, arrived at Callville, Nevada, on September 7, 1867. He was incoherent, barely alive, with bruises, welts, and recent scars. His skin was mahogany and his hair matted and bleached. Slowly he recovered from dehydration. His mind cleared. He called himself James White.

His story begins high in the San Juan Mountains where a party of drifters and gold-seekers under the leadership of Captain Charles Baker had returned to Baker's Park, now the site of Silverton. Baker's first venture into the high country the winter of 1860–1861 had proved disastrous with men living in brush huts working gold placer claims. The Baker Expedition had retreated south toward Santa Fe, but now the captain was back with two other men—George Strole and James White. "Baker and companions were merely examples of hordes of drifters, the flotsam and jetsam of westward migration," writes historian Virginia McConnell Simmons in *Drifting West: The Calamities of James White and Charles Baker.* Baker himself "did what he did better than anything else—promoting an enterprise for others to subsidize with provisions and labor."[25]

After a month, finding no new opportunities in Baker's Park because placer mining had yet to become the hard rock, deep shaft mining that would make Silverton boom, the small band rode south. Near what would become Durango they drifted west to follow the Mancos River where they saw small cliff dwellings or "houses built of cobblestones." Baker's party paralleled the Mancos River to the San Juan River hoping to prospect for gold in the softer sandstone. They were some of the first white men to see

An exquisite dancing Navajo Yei figure seems caught in a moment of reflection. This rare, small figure was carefully carved in a hidden cleft on a large cliff face. Author photo.

Ancestral Puebloan cliff dwellings near Mesa Verde and to venture west into Bears Ears country.

In later years, White became confused, stating that the three men went south of the river when instead they probably crossed it to the north near the Rincon or where Comb Ridge comes to the water's edge and a natural, shallow ford exists. They probably rode the Bears Ears Trail up Comb Wash and then turned west to be caught in a maze of canyons coming off Cedar Mesa toward what is now Lake Powell. White claimed to have two revolvers. He would need them both. They camped two days after leaving the San Juan River, and while the other men were exploring, White saw a Native. His partners thought he was imagining things. Riding out the next morning with Captain Baker in the lead, a rifle shot rang out. Baker fell off his horse and either died immediately or shouted to his companions, "I am killed." Another version of the story has Baker whispering, "Save yourselves." Either way, Baker died in the dust in Utah while his two companions fled down canyon for safety. They were stopped at the water's edge.[26]

Fearful of being trapped in a narrow canyon, they used their lariats to make a raft of four cottonwood logs, perhaps eight inches thick and up to ten feet long.[27] On their makeshift raft, White and Strole drifted off down Glen Canyon, named two years later by Major Powell. There are no rapids in Glen Canyon, and after a few hours or days, they could have abandoned their raft and begun to hike out. They also could have left the Colorado River near what became Lees Ferry. Instead, they stayed on their flimsy raft until at the first Grand Canyon rapid, Strole fell off never to be seen again. One writer explained, "White still clung to the logs, and it was only when the raft seemed to be floating smoothly, and the sound of the rapids was behind, that he dared to look up; then it was to find himself alone, the provisions lost, and the shadows of the black canon [*sic*] warning him of the approaching night."[28]

White drifted downriver probably making ten hours a day. Starving, he met Native Americans, possibly Yavapais, who gave him a few roasted mesquite beans near Grand Wash. He floated off, forced to chew on the leather scabbard of his knife, and finally, semiconscious, he arrived at Callville, now under the waters of Lake Mead. Two years later Powell made his epic journey. His men, aware of White's claims, thought it impossible, as did subsequent river runners. Still, the story endured.[29] I set out with a friend to find where White and Strole may have entered Glen Canyon, possibly at Moqui Canyon. We camped nearby and tried to four-wheel drive into Moqui Canyon from the top.

I thought we were in trouble when I drove over a small sand dune, wondering if we could get up it on the way out. I should have known better. Farther along we were blocked by a huge dune. Turning around, sure enough, I buried my truck to the axles. Luckily, it was still mid-morning. I've learned through the years that if you are going to make a mistake, always do it when there is plenty of daylight. I got out the shovel. My friend found flat rocks. Let air out of my tires. Slowly, a few feet at a time, we drove in low gear back up to what passes for rural roads in San Juan County. Did James White and his companion launch a log raft at Moqui Canyon, and did White survive the huge rapids of Grand Canyon?

His descendants think so and want recognition for their ancestor. Greg Adams wrote to me that James White's river tale is "a controversy that never ends and never will." He explained, "White was honest in his story," but that other writers did not want to believe that "a simple miner might have done what they couldn't . . . namely run all the rapids in Grand Canyon which they themselves found impossible to achieve."[30] Major Powell gets the credit. After all, he documented his wooden boat trip and ran the river twice—once in 1869 and again in 1871. But did James White survive solo on a tippy log raft? We'll never know, just like we'll never know what happened to the bones of Captain Charles Baker, the drifter who took one trail too many in the American Southwest and died west of Bears Ears.

The Macomb Exploring Expedition had come in 1859 into the Bears Ears region. Now another scientific and topographic group would enter southeast Utah as an extension of their mapping of Colorado. Pressure from prospectors had transformed Colorado's San Juan Mountains, the birthplace of the San Juan River, into a mining frenzy. Like their neighbors and sometimes enemies the Navajo, the Utes had also received an 1868 treaty giving them almost one-third of Colorado—the far western part generally west of the Continental Divide. But gold and silver had been discovered in the high recesses of the San Juans and prospectors had flooded in, violating the treaty. Rather than have the US Army move the prospectors, the US government found it infinitely easier to move the Native Americans. The Brunot Cession required that a significant part of the 1868 treaty be abrogated and that the San Juan Mountains be "opened up" for mining and settlement. The Utes agreed to sell the tops of the mountains, where there were little elk and deer year-round, but they insisted they never agreed to sell the valleys; yet when the Brunot Cession received Congressional approval in 1874, another large area of Indigenous land had been lost. The Southern Utes were left with a reservation at the very southern edge of Colorado—a rectangle 110 miles long and 15 miles wide.

Many Native Americans who refused to abide by reservation boundaries drifted back into southeast Utah and San Juan County where they could live unmolested and occasionally raid in any direction before retreating into the canyon systems of the Bears Ears region. Railroads had begun to stretch their iron tentacles across the West with the Denver and Rio Grande Railroad building toward mineral wealth in the San Juans. A new patented invention, barbed wire, would begin to change the western landscape forever. Over the decades, barbed wire would segment and divide thousands of acres of both public and private land; the same landscape then needed to be mapped, surveyed, and parceled out. Manifest Destiny brought more settlers and soldiers further west, and though southeast Utah and the Colorado Plateau remained a sandstone maze of cliffs and canyons, lines had to be drawn on maps and Native Americans put on reservations—out of the way of choice irrigable lands or mountain mineral deposits.

Maps are fascinating because just like words in a foreign language, they give new meaning to landscapes we think we know. Maps create worlds. They define people, places, and routes we have not yet taken. They show us where we've been and where we want to be. In the Four Corners region, one map appeals to me most of all. It's actually a series of maps—an atlas; to open this atlas on a large table or desk is to see a landscape that is both ever-present and yet has ceased to exist. It is the great-great-grandfather of all Colorado maps and stunning in beauty and prescience.

To open the 1877 Hayden Atlas is to see a masterwork of science, lithographic art, and nineteenth-century ideology. Imagine the bold and adventurous task of mapping Colorado, by hand, on foot, and on horseback. What an audacious idea, and yet the nineteenth-century West, after the Civil War, was full of men seeking to understand the landscape and themselves. On paper, they created the world in which we live. An original Hayden *Atlas* has surprisingly supple paper, yellowed at the edges. Leather bindings can be scuffed and frayed. In the middle of the Civil War the Republican Congress voted for laws that forever changed the West. The 1862 Homestead Act provided free land for farmers and settlers and the 1862 Railroad Act financed the first transcontinental railroad. As immigrants and Americans began the long journey westward in the 1870s, Congress funded four separate government surveys of the West by F.V. Hayden, John Wesley Powell, George M. Wheeler, and Clarence King. In 1880 these surveys were combined to become the US Geological Survey.

Geologist Gil Mull explains, "Of the four surveys, the Hayden Survey was the largest and of longest duration. In addition to written reports, the Hayden Survey published separate topographic, drainage, and geologic maps for many areas in Utah, Wyoming, Montana, and Idaho, but only Colorado was mapped in its entirety."[31] From our perspective in the twenty-first century, the 1877 Hayden Atlas is extraordinary. Holding it in your hands and slowly turning the pages is to travel backward in time to see what was here, and not here, over 140 years ago. The *Atlas* reveals Indian ruins, burials, and the names of historic ranches. Battle Rock in McElmo Canyon, which drains into the San Juan River, can be found as well as Hovenweep Castle and areas labeled "Ute farms" and "Indian farms." William Henry Jackson journeyed up the Mancos River, so sites are listed in what is now Ute Mountain Tribal Park including Jackson's Butte, Moss's Tower, Double Walled Tower, and Two-Story House.

The country is wide open, unfenced, and unclaimed. The maps display notations and color coding for agricultural land, pine forests, pinyon and cedar trees, and quaking aspen groves. The *Atlas* reveals sage and badlands, coal lands, and gold and silver districts. With joyous abandon the surveyors named rivers, creeks, canyons, peaks, and hot springs. In some cases, they used locally generic names, but in many instances, they simply invented names. Because they were geologists, they labeled the depositions of the earth, and the *Atlas* shows deposits from the Tertiary, Cretaceous, Jurassic, and Paleozoic eras. All of us who live in the Four Corners owe a debt of gratitude to a small man who grew up as an orphan in Ohio and possessed a penchant for frayed frock coats, battered hats, and unexpected fits of belligerence. Ferdinand Vandeveer Hayden was a quiet, dreamy, nervous student considered by his classmates at Oberlin College the least likely to succeed. Yet succeed he did, not only in helping to establish the United States Geological Survey, but also in producing reliable maps.

Historian William Goetzmann described Hayden as the quintessential "businessman's geologist" whose agenda was not just mapping the West but also uncovering its mineral wealth. Hayden saw the region as the "resource West," and in keeping with the political tenor of the times, devoted himself, in Goetzmann's words, to the "pursuit of practical prospecting in the public interest."[32]

Indian troubles were infrequent because of the patience of the Utes, but James Gardner and his small party in 1875 did run into several lodges of Native Americans in the La Sal Mountains of Utah. Chief Ouray had warned against renegade bands of Utes and Paiutes, but Gardner proceeded anyway down the Dolores River and close to the canyon country visited by the Macomb Expedition. After a lengthy skirmish near Dry Valley, with tired mules and parched throats the team sought protection from Indian bullets and finally reached Colorado territory with a loss of eight pack animals and valuable camping supplies.

Hayden's survey included William Henry Jackson, the famous pioneer photographer who first photographed southwest Colorado cliff dwellings in Mancos Canyon but missed Cliff Palace and Spruce Tree House because they had not yet been discovered. Jackson was there in 1874 in Mancos Canyon with guide John Moss. They discovered Two-Story House and other Ancestral Puebloan sites now in Ute Mountain Tribal Park. All that seminal work is clearly displayed in the Hayden Atlas of 1877. Members of the Hayden Survey kept accurate measurements. Their mapping of Colorado and southeast Utah is extraordinary. William Henry Holmes, Hayden's gifted surveyor and artist, drew vast landscapes in precise detail. In a nineteenth-century Victorian conceit, magnificent panoramic views show small figures of the surveyors themselves drawn to scale against the backdrop of southwestern Colorado mountains and the rim of Utah's canyon country. They stand at the edges of great precipices and contemplate the scenery, sketch the mountain massifs, or lean on their canes as they wear formal greatcoats and fashionable bowler hats. Mountain sheep gaze at them from the drawings' edges. Literally and figuratively Hayden's men are contemplating the West of the future, the resource-rich West they have shown on their maps. As they look down from high peaks it is almost as if they can see the farms, ranches, and towns that will emerge a century later.

Panoramic views up to thirty-eight inches long were hand-drawn, shaded pen and ink drawings completed on location by William Henry Holmes, who produced exceptional drawings. Mull explains, "In these views, Holmes not only portrayed the rugged topography, but also skillfully accentuated the rock stratification in order to show the geological structure." Mull notes that the Hayden Survey "established and published the geologic framework that all succeeding geologists in the Rockies have expanded upon and refined. Although the work was hard and dangerous, I can fantasize what it must have been like to have had the privilege to

From the top of Comb Ridge all of Cedar Mesa and Monument Valley spread out to the west with Comb Wash on the west side of the Comb and Butler Wash on the east side. Author photo.

participate in these expeditions of discovery, and the feeling of excitement when understanding a geological framework."[33]

As for place names, in the canyon country of southeast Utah, "Of significance here is that Holmes recognized the Elk Plateau for what it is but interestingly called it a name that reflected one of the most dominant features—Bear's Ears Plateau," writes historian Charles S. Peterson.[34]

People love maps because of where they can take us, and with all the public land in the Four Corners, there are plenty of places to visit. The early US geological surveyors mapped Colorado and southeast Utah and, in a sense, gave us the mountain West and a new understanding of canyon country. We live in the mapped and bounded world they helped to create, but adventure isn't found on any map. For each of us, the West and the canyon country of southeast Utah is *terra incognita* until we explore it on our own.

The best chroniclers of the Hayden Survey in the Four Corners region and in San Juan County, Utah, are Robert S. McPherson and Susan

Rhoades Neel, who in their book *Mapping the Four Corners: Narrating the Hayden Survey of 1875* describe in detail the field research that produced the magnificent Hayden Atlas. The Utes knew about surveys. They knew about survey stakes and mapping. Before John Wesley Powell rowed down the Colorado River and began to understand the West, near Meeker, Colorado, he attempted a small survey. Utes demanded he remove his stakes. He wisely did so. Utes knew who were using their trails, and they understood that prospectors and surveyors were harbingers of changes to come that would mean more restrictions for Native Americans and loss of land.

"Most of the territory that the scientists surveyed that summer was part of the traditional homeland of the Utes and Navajos," write McPherson and Neel who explain that for the Hayden survey "its overall goal, true of all federal surveys in the West, was to integrate the region into the economic and cultural system of a rapidly expanding and industrializing nation."[35] Utes and Paiutes harassed and then attacked the surveyors forcing them to abandon valuable equipment and to flee for their lives back to the La Plata Mountains and the mining camp of Parrot City where they arrived "a sad and hungry lot," according to W.H. Holmes, who was in charge of the southwestern division of the Hayden Survey.[36]

Letters written back east explain, "It will be easily seen that such a region represents nothing which is ever likely to attract any other inhabitants to it than it has now" including Utes, Navajos, and Paiutes, renegades who "congregate there for mutual protection and plunder when they dare not openly appear anywhere else."[37] An editorial in the September 9, 1875 *New York Times* explained that in southeast Utah's canyon country "[t]here yet linger some of the remnants of the wild tribes. These, for the sake of plunder, have forgotten ancient feuds, and often combine in bands which are the terror of the few white men who have occasion to penetrate that forbidding region . . . They can subsist on roots and insects, hide in the sagebrush, and scale the rocky cliffs of the region with the agility of the tiger-cat."[38]

For these "desperate rascals," Native Americans refusing to abide by an Indian Agent's stringent rules, trying to retain the last of their cultural values in a landscape they knew well, the Bears Ears region remained their refuge and retreat. Of course, they harassed any incoming whites, especially surveyors and government men. But while Native occupants in the mid-1870s frightened survey crews, the crews looked in astonishment at ancient dwellings perched high in seemingly inaccessible cliffs.

The expedition members had ridden up Comb Wash in the direction of Blue Mountain, explored Arch Canyon, now within Bears Ears National Monument, ridden over Comb Ridge and eventually into Montezuma Canyon. They would be among the first to describe Ancestral Puebloan ruins in southeast Utah and even though their job was to look for land valuable for agriculture or mining, they became enraptured by the obvious signs of a long-ago people. Utes, Paiutes, and Navajos knew about the high cliff dwellings and assorted Native villages and had left them alone out of both fear and respect. In Navajo belief a dead person's spirit may continue to reside where that person had lived and died. Their *chindi* or spirit may be lonely and seek to haunt or terrorize visitors. For surveyors on horseback, the deep canyons and tall sandstone cliffs epitomized the Southwest. Clearly, thousands of people had lived in the Bears Ears region centuries earlier.

W.H. Jackson and E.A. Barber entered Casa del Eco, now called Seventeen Room Ruin, on the San Juan River and explored down Chinle Wash south of the river to Poncho House Ruin now on the Navajo Nation and Utah's largest ruin. Barber wrote, "[A] large colony of ruined buildings was found, among which some very perfect and valuable implements, ornaments and ancient pottery were found."[39] The surveyors endured one hundred plus degree summer heat and made some of the first comparisons between prehistoric peoples in the Bears Ears region and modern Hopi Indians living on their mesas to the south.

Barber wrote in the *New York Herald* an essay headlined, "Ancient America: Races of Men Flourishing Here a Thousand Years Ago." He described ancient cliff dwelling structures "standing . . . five hundred or six hundred years."[40] America had yet to celebrate its centennial on July 4, 1876. Now in the Southwest, in southeast Utah, government surveyors had discovered ruins and remains that clearly presaged Pilgrims landing off Cape Cod. Canyon country's secrets had begun to reveal themselves. No white settlers yet lived in this rocky, waterless region inhabited by bands of renegade Indians determined to defend their sacred landscape. But if Navajos, Utes, and Paiutes evaded authority and capture and sought to live in their traditional and resilient ways, so did another group fleeing persecution. If the Bears Ears region had long been a place of refuge and resistance for Native peoples, now another group would enter, Mormons coming east from central Utah, in one of America's epic tales of migration and settlement by wagon train.

CHAPTER 6

"We Thank Thee, Oh God"

Mormons Settle Bluff and Cattle Come to the Canyons, 1876–1890

> Our first expeditions into the land of the cliff-dwellers were full of interest. We were not, however, the first explorers.
>
> —W.S. Holmes

> ... these barren valleys, these sterile mountains, this desolate waste, where only Saints can or would live.
>
> —Brigham Young

As prospectors poured into the San Juan Mountains, as railroads snaked their way toward the young, brawling gold and silver camps, leaders of the Church of Jesus Christ of Latter-day Saints in Salt Lake City took out their maps. Between 1846 and 1847, Brigham Young had brought the faithful out of Nauvoo, Illinois, where the founder of the Mormon church, Joseph Smith, had been murdered by a mob, in part because the church sanctioned polygamy or plural marriage. Devout Mormons, gathered from many northern European countries such as England, Scotland, Wales, and Denmark, had spent a freezing season at Winter Quarters near what would become Omaha, Nebraska.[1] As the snows melted, they headed west in wagons on the Mormon Trail toward open, unclaimed country because a recent report by Captain John C. Fremont described the area around Salt Lake as good country suitable for farming if irrigation canals could be dug to bring water from the Wasatch Mountains.

The Saints arrived with Brigham Young sick with mountain fever in a carriage. As they finally descended toward the valley he raised up and said, "This is the place." Mormons began to settle and farm along the Wasatch Front. Seeking isolation, wanting to be far from American legal jurisdictions, Brigham Young and the Church of Jesus Christ of Latter-day Saints sought to establish a theocracy in the heart of the American West and to claim an empire known as Deseret. They adopted the beehive as their symbol where all worked together for the common good in contrast to an era of rigorous competition back East. Mormons sought to work together, to communally develop the Great Basin with small farming towns and churches linked to bustling Salt Lake City.

The faithful, over 100,000 immigrants, established five hundred settlements north and south of the Salt Lake Basin, anywhere rivers flowed, from Salt Lake south toward Las Vegas, Nevada, southern California, and north toward Boise, Idaho, and the Upper Snake and Goose Creek Valleys. The church called settlers to create new communities and the devout sold their established farms and set out to build new Mormon villages on lands no one else wanted. These missions helped spread the Church of Jesus Christ of Latter-day Saints, fueled after 1848 with dollars brought by thousands of gentiles or non-Mormons moving through Salt Lake City on their way to the California Gold Rush and California's boisterous gold camps. The church thrived under Brigham Young's leadership and more Mormons arrived a decade later in 1856 with the Willie Handcart Company, but it proved to be the last time devotees would be encouraged to cross the Great Plains into the Salt Lake Valley only pulling handcarts.[2] The Willie group left too late, got caught in an early fall blizzard, and many suffered or froze including Jens Nielson, who would become the bishop of Bluff, Utah. He led the tiny town for years with his wise decisions and counsel despite his aching, frostbitten feet injured on the trail.

Railroads came into Utah bringing more gentiles, commerce, hard cash, and threats to the church. The idea behind a large and cohesive self-sustaining empire like Deseret became a major political issue in the late 1850s with Congress and the president determined that no separate religious theocracy should exist within American boundaries and certainly not with polygamy as a central tenet. Mormons felt frightened and defensive. To find a route for troops from New Mexico to enter Utah and cross the deeply entrenched canyon country toward settlements in southwest Utah, Captain John Macomb sought to find a wagon route. He failed.

Now in the late 1870s, after the Mountain Meadows Massacre of 1857 in which a large, well-funded wagon train from Arkansas headed to California had been attacked by Mormons disguised as Paiutes near Cedar City, Utah, tensions had eased.[3] John D. Lee, one of the organizers of the massacre, then spent years moving from place to place and wife to wife before being apprehended. Lee would be executed by a US Army firing squad after he had made his peace with God. Whether he had received orders from the church hierarchy prior to the killing of Arkansas emigrants has never been proven. Brigham Young died in August 1877. Church leadership shifted. The Quorum of the Twelve Apostles looked at what had now become the territory of Utah. They realized that the Elk Mission at Moab had failed, but it needed to be revived because Moab, situated on the Old Spanish Trail, remained one of the safest places to cross the Colorado (then named the Grand) River for hundreds of miles. But what about the rocky, formidable canyon country to the south of Moab? What about a Mormon settlement in southeast Utah, along the San Juan River to safeguard against non-Mormons moving there from Colorado, which had become a state in 1876?

How to defend against a gentile encroachment into an area where the Church sought dominance? It was decided to sponsor one more mission, one more settlement of devout church members who would be called to leave their communities to start a new one. This would be an Indian mission to extend a helping hand to the renegade Paiutes, Utes, and Navajos who lived on both sides of the San Juan River and who would be taught the Bible and to become Christians. "The proposed settlement would be started for both offensive and defensive reasons," wrote historian David S. Carpenter, "to pacify Indians in the hope of eventually converting them and to defend Zion by preempting this large section of land from outsiders."[4]

There would be many conflicts, many ideological differences, petty theft, the killing of cows, and an occasional murder, but in one realm there would be agreement. Native Americans in southeast Utah also practiced plural marriage as did members of the Church of Jesus Christ of Latter-day Saints. Native headmen had multiple wives, young and old. Native clans had similarities to extended Mormon households. On that there was agreement, and there would be resistance, both Native and Mormon, to federal oversight and restrictions, especially two years after the settlement of Bluff when polygamy prosecutions began under the Edmunds-Tucker Act of 1882. Bears Ears would become a landscape of resistance for Latter-day Saints families just as it had been for centuries for Native inhabitants fleeing first the Spanish, then the Mexicans, and finally blue-coated American soldiers.

The Church sought a new settlement in southeast Utah territory on the San Juan River at a place called Montezuma Creek. But if Brigham Young had led the Saints out of the Midwest and into the Great Salt Lake Valley based on the reconnaissance report of Captain John C. Fremont, other Mormon leaders had not read John Wesley Powell's *Report On the Lands of the Arid Region of the United States* in which Powell explained, "but little is known concerning the arable lands or volume of water in the valley of the San Juan. It flows for most of its course through a canon, and all the arable land is thought to be so much subject to overflow that cultivation is impracticable."[5] Mormon settlers would learn this the hard way, but first they had to make the trek. It needed to happen quickly because the Denver and Rio Grande Railroad's construction crews were building toward Durango and would lay track south toward Santa Fe and north to Silverton. But what route would the Mormons take who had been called to the new mission? How would recruits from Cedar City come east with their families and farming tools? Mormon scouts on horseback surveyed the area and were startled to find non-Mormons already living and farming where McElmo Creek met the San Juan River.

The logical route would be to drive wagons south toward the Hopi villages and then go east across the desert toward what is now Kayenta, Arizona, and continue east through Monument Valley until the San Juan River could be crossed. But that was Navajo territory, the northern and western edge of the Navajo Reservation, and church members feared nightly raids and the loss of livestock that they would need to establish a self-sustaining village. They believed that Paiutes and Navajos might plunder their wagon train despite night guards and sentries. A Mormon missionary had already been killed near Red Lake.[6]

Was there another route? Scouts thought the new mission could be established by bringing wagons to Escalante then down through a series of canyons toward the San Juan River. They had seen landmarks including the Abajo or Blue Mountains. They thought it could be done, but no one had ever ridden the route and certainly not attempted it with 234 people, families, small children, 83 wagons, hundreds of loose cattle, horses, and a few dairy cows. Church members were told it would take six weeks on a "shortcut" route. It took six months and resulted in near starvation, but no one died. Three babies were born. The last Mormon mission call to start a new settlement and the only large eastbound wagon train in American history would cross some of the deepest canyons on the continent through Bears Ears National Monument on a route difficult to traverse even today with modern four-wheel drive vehicles. Out of this logistical challenge would come families deeply proud of settling San Juan Country, of surviving on their home gardens and limited livestock in one of the communities farthest from a railroad in the United States.

But the mission to Montezuma Creek never made it. The exhausted settlers, having spent days and weeks navigating around tight canyons

The convoluted canyons of Cedar Mesa and the Bears Ears region are represented in this historic photograph possibly taken by Charles Goodman. #p0068n062, photo courtesy Special Collections, J. Willard Marriott Library, The University of Utah.

lined with cliff dwellings, finally skirted the southern edge of Comb Ridge to arrive at a tall sandstone escarpment of bluffs that glowed golden before sunset. The wagon train stopped seventeen miles west of their Montezuma Fort destination. They paused where Cottonwood Wash drained south from the Abajos and huge cottonwood trees spread out across the riparian zone at the river's edge. This would do. This was their place. They named it Bluff City as they began to till the soil, to plant crops, to cut cottonwood logs for cabins, and to establish the Indian Mission the Church had ordered.

"In all the annals of the West, replete with examples of courage, tenacity, and ingenuity, there is no better example of the indomitable pioneer spirit than that of the Hole-in-the-Rock expedition of the San Juan Mission," wrote David. E. Miller in his seminal book *Hole-in-the-Rock: An Epic in the Colonization of the American West.*[7] Brigham Young had conceived of this mission, but hardy pioneers did not organize the expedition until two years after Young's death. Faithful members of the Church of Jesus Christ of Latter-day Saints answered calls to missions, and "when called, most families gladly responded, often leaving well established homes, farms, and other business enterprises and taking all their possessions into rough, unknown, untried country."[8] Historian Leonard Arrington explains, "In such unlikely spots as the San Juan Country of southeastern Utah . . . Colonizing companies moved as a group, with church approval; the village form of settlement prevailed; canals were built by cooperative labor; and the small holdings of farmland and village lots were parceled out in community drawings."[9] The church goal was to establish a buffer, an outpost against other white settlers and stockmen who might move into southeast Utah as well as to become a mission to Native Americans who in church scripture were considered Lamanites or members of a lost group that if properly spoken to and taught Christian doctrine would cease to have brown skin and would become "white and delightsome" as church members. Miller explains, "To secure the San Juan region for Mormon colonization, to settle it before others could do so, was certainly a major church objective and members of the expedition recognized this."[10]

The problem was the route taken. It included building a steep dugway, a hole in a cliff or rock, named Uncle Ben's Dugway, in the sandstone canyons in what is now Glen Canyon to drop almost one thousand feet, cross the Colorado River, and then ascend upward into what is now San Juan County, Utah, headed east for Bears Ears. From a houseboat on Lake Powell boaters can stare up at the Hole-in-the-Rock the Mormon pioneers made. With binoculars I have looked incredulously at the steep canyon. I have wondered how even with oak staves pounded into the sandstone and brush, with logs and dirt used to make a narrow platform to add a few feet of width, how so many wagons, people, and livestock could have descended such a gap. But they did, always helping each other, though a Mormon friend cautioned me to think about the family with the last wagon, no one behind to help them, no one left in front of them, as the pioneer father, hands sweating but held tight to the leather reins, eased his frightened team down through the gap, kept his children behind with his wife, who stared down at the ribbon of river below.

At the bottom workmen prepared a ferry that enabled families to cross the Colorado. They breathed easily on the other side until they realized that more slickrock loomed ahead. Who had conceived of this route? Would it really work for all the families and wagons? "Some historians speculate that if Brigham Young had still been alive, he would not have allowed a wagon train to depart on an unscouted route," explains Stewart Aitchison.[11] But the faithful left the town of Escalante anyway, enjoyed themselves singing and dancing at Dance Hall Rock, came through the Hole-In-The-Rock, and now in the cold of December 1879 scouts rode ahead calculating only seventy miles further to Montezuma Fort. But that was in an impossible straight line. How to get through these canyons and to go from the Colorado River to the San Juan?

George B. Hobbs, who had been on the initial exploratory trip, Lemuel H. Redd, Sr., George W. Sevy, and George Morrell each on horseback had only two pack animals with eight days rations. As they headed across broken canyons, they encountered cliff dwellings from the first inhabitants and even segments of constructed Ancestral Puebloan roads, traces of the prehistoric past untouched in the Bears Ears region. Hobbs referred to "the old Cliff Dweller trail again," which took them over Clay Hills Pass.[12]

On December 23, with eight inches of snow on the ground, the scouts prepared a large pancake using up the last of their food supplies. Christmas found them close to Elk Ridge with no landmark and no way to find the river, lost in a maze of pinyon and juniper, dark green set amidst red rock. Looking for landmarks, Hobbs climbed a small outcropping christened Salvation or Christmas Knoll, and from that elevation he could see down the long red spine of Comb Ridge, down along the Bears Ears Trail, south toward the San Juan River with the snow-covered Abajos to the east. Now he knew where he was. He knew where they needed to go.

Salvation Knoll is marked on Highway 95 as it crosses just below the Bears Ears. An interpretive sign leads to a trail to the top of the knoll. Hiking it, one looks out at all of Cedar Mesa spread far and wide. I've marveled at the courage of the Mormon pioneers and the dedication of their scouts. After that snowy night, on horseback the scouts descended through the canyons and then rode the old Bears Ears Trail in Comb Wash on the western side of Comb Ridge and then to the south, spied another trail ascending the cliff. They had made it through Comb Wash only to be blocked by a major gulch, Butler Wash. Three days without food, the scouts sought shelter in Butler Wash, close to the river, in a small Ancestral Puebloan ruin now known as Hobbs' Ruin. I've hiked into it, alone, absorbed by the silence, the upright walls, the patterns of rock chips in the 800-year-old masonry, wooden lintels still in place, petroglyphs carved on the back wall, and a nice flat plaza area sheltered from the west wind where I imagine Hobbs had lain down his bedroll, trying to sleep, worrying about the wagons full of families days behind him, children cowering in the cold, doing his best to ignore the empty ache in his belly. Hobbs wrote, "Night overtook us. We camped in this small canyon, this being our third day without food. I cut my name in the rock with the date I was there, not knowing that I would survive the journey."[13]

Near Christmas in 1879 lost and hungry Mormon scouts tried to find a way across the sandstone canyons of the Bears Ears region to arrive at the San Juan River to start a new town and settlement. George Hobbs, one of the scouts, spent a cold night without food in this Ancestral Puebloan ruin that now bears his name. Author photo.

Finally, up and out of the wash the scouts rode toward what would become the townsite of Bluff only to find a calf that they considered butchering and eating, but they restrained themselves and a little later came across a family camp of Coloradans who had been there since August. Western hospitality prevailed. The men finally ate—fresh biscuits and roasted meat. They tried to eat slowly, tried not to show their hunger, eating every crumb of the biscuits, licking their fingers, trying to be satisfied with the food provided.

Headed to the fort at Montezuma Creek the scouts encountered two men on horseback, Ernest Mitchell and James Merrick, who first said they hoped to establish a cattle ranch but later admitted they were headed west into the red rock country, west into Monument Valley, west to find Hoskininni's lost silver mine. They invited young Hobbs to ride with them, but true to his Mormon mission, he declined. He rejoined the other scouts. As for Hoskininni, the Navajo headman discouraged all newcomers. The two would-be prospectors were found dead a year later, and the large outcroppings in the Navajo Nation's Monument Valley Tribal Park nicknamed the Mittens are also called Mitchell and Merrick

Buttes. Brigham Young had always discouraged precious metal mining. "He counseled the people to farm rather than prospect," wrote historian Thomas G. Alexander, "You cannot eat gold, he said."[14] Young sought to establish self-sustaining farm villages based on families and shared values not the helter-skelter all male world of raucous mining camps.

The scouts turned back, returned to the wagons, and led the San Juan Mission southeast across Cedar Mesa at the head of Grand Gulch. They had used fragments of Ancestral Puebloan roads and for miles the Mormon families saw the prominent Bears Ears. From Clay Hills the wagon train crossed Harmony Flat, Grand Flat, Mormon Flat, skirted Kane Gulch, and with male crews always working ahead of the wagons, created the Emigrant Trail on the edge of Owl Creek, finding springs and seeps and descending close to McLoyd Canyon and Moon House, an extraordinary late twelfth-century ruin in Bears Ears, and then down off Snow Flat to a tight cleft in the canyons called the Twist where Mormon men braced their feet hard against wagon brakes to slow their teams. Women walked behind holding their children's hands.

Driving that stretch of the Emigrant Trail in a short-wheel-based four-wheel drive, it is hard to imagine going over those rocks in a jostling, bumping, creaking wooden wagon. Yet I realize the rocky road I am driving, and the entire trail itself, a route bisecting Bears Ears from northwest to southeast, was constructed by Latter-day Saints road crews fulfilling their mission to get to the San Juan River. They wanted to return to their lives as farmers. San Juan County Road 237, known as the Emigrant or Mormon Trail, the route just north of Road Canyon, is an exciting drive. Always dropping down, finally it comes to the red dirt of Comb Wash and the Bears Ears Trail as it intersects Comb Ridge.

The scouts found a way up the ridge, but it was far too narrow for wagons. So the wagons continued south along Comb Ridge until finally reaching the river and the Rincon, the low, easy crossing of the San Juan River that Navajos, Utes, and Paiutes had used for centuries. Families rested. Children played. Down by the river in their long skirts and bonnets, women washed laundry. It was early spring and almost time to plant, but the expedition was still miles from Montezuma Creek and Fort Montezuma. They had to cross the 900-foot-tall red rock spine of Comb Ridge, but how? The last dugway had to be built, the last road segment constructed so at the base of the Comb where it comes closest to the river, work crews again built rocky ramps, filled in low spots on the sandstone, calculated the angles that the exhausted horse teams would have to pull wagons to finally top out over the Comb and head east to flat farmland ahead.

Today the site is marked. At the bottom, an interpretive sign explains the significance of San Juan Hill, their last major barrier. Historian David Miller writes, "The road up San Juan Hill is one of the most fantastic of all sections constructed by these indomitable pioneers. It angles up the face of that cliff in a manner which defies description . . . San Juan Hill proved almost too much for the worn-out teams, weakened by a long winter of hard work without sufficient feed."[15] If the horses faced fatigue, so did the wagons, leather harness, collars, reins, wagon wheels, and all the pioneers' gear—the very equipment they would need to start a new settlement. Charles Redd explained, "Aside from the Hole-in-the-Rock, itself, this was the steepest crossing on the journey. Here again seven span of horses were used, so that when some of the horses were on their knees, fighting to get up to find a foothold, the still-erect horses could plunge up against the sharp grade."[16] Mormon men had tears in their eyes as they beat their exhausted animals to give all that the horses had. Charles Redd, whose father Lemuel Redd had been on the expedition, stated, "the worst stretches could be identified by the dried blood and matted hair from the forelegs of the struggling teams."[17]

Hiking that route with a backpack, trekking poles, and a camera, I've had to stop and pace myself, catch my breath, and stare down at the river and up at summer cumulus clouds. Pieces of the constructed route can still be seen along with gouges in the redrock ramp. From the top the view looks west across the jumble of canyons jutting from Cedar Mesa and north toward the Bears Ears, which pose above a ponderosa pine forest.[18] I marvel at the dedication of the Hole-in-the-Rockers to answer the last mission call of the Latter-day Saints church to establish a new settlement whose goal was to make the desert "blossom as the rose," to bring civilization to the canyon country of southeast Utah.[19] Yet if they were on an errand to civilize a sandstone wilderness, the true treasure that they could not conquer, could not overcome, remains—the thousands of acres of wildness and designated wilderness study areas on both sides of the Emigrant Trail. To this day it is wild country that could not be farmed and could be only minimally grazed. The San Juan Mission crossed miles of sandstone domes and rock. Rock it remains.

From the top of San Juan Hill, I've looked far to the west. I've also looked down, just a little, away from the edge of the cliff, below a small outcropping to find an inscription, without a date, just words from the pioneers, a phrase from a Mormon hymn. I've climbed all the way up

San Juan Hill to see it, to photograph it, and to think of their arduous trek. The words are simple, the inscription fading, and the sentiment profound. There at the top of San Juan Hill, the second most difficult crossing the Latter-day Saints families made, are five words etched in the rock: "We thank thee, oh God." I turn away, marveling at faith, contemplating a unique American frontier religion that literally moved rock and stone and brought people across an ocean and then across a continent to stand at this point and wearily to descend, setting again the worn-out wooden wagon brakes, headed east across desert sands, too tired to take those exhausted teams of horses to Montezuma Creek, instead to found the town of Bluff, in the spring of 1880, in the same river valley where Basketmakers had built their pithouses and planted their corn in AD 650.

Over time the Hole-in-the-Rock Expedition story would shape and define descendants of those who had made the journey. "Having endured, and crossed to safety, they began at once to transform their experience into myth," Wallace Stenger wrote about the Mormon Trail, but he could easily have been describing the Hole-in-the-Rockers.[20] Unlike their predecessors on the Mormon Trail west from Nauvoo, Illinois, the Hole-in-the-Rock route was rarely used again. It was too steep, too arduous, and unnecessary. Cutting across Cedar Mesa and into the heart of the Bears Ears region, simply did not work for wagon transport or even on horseback. Easier routes were found. What was not easy, however, was trying to sustainably farm near Bluff, Utah, on sandy soil adjacent to the San Juan River that repeatedly flooded its banks or tore out irrigation canals painstakingly dug by Mormons under the guidance and authority of Bishop Jens Nielson after he had been selected. Mormon communities had a pattern and a plan. They began with wide streets, the planting of poplar trees, the building of barns, sheds, and modest houses. In Bluff a fort came first because of Indian fears, and with no close by hardwood trees, cabins constructed from cottonwood trees had walls that curved and writhed requiring extra chinking that routinely fell out exposing occupants to winter winds or summer heat. Pioneers enclosed their cabins with a juniper rip-gut fence.

In his book *The Mormon Landscape*, geographer Richard Francaviglia explains, "[T]he entire Mormon landscape involves the bold trinity of mountain, field and village."[21] Across the Latter-day Saints planned communities of Deseret, small villages set in verdant valleys backed up against mountain massifs. Cool mountain water flowed down through hand-dug ditches. Jedediah Rogers writes of "Mormons as masters of agriculture in a dry region" and notes that "The image of a Mormon village at the base of the Wasatch Mountains powerfully representing order, permanence, and godliness" became the standard Mormon geographic pattern in a land where church members felt obligated to make the desert bloom and to reflect God's kingdom on earth.[22] But the San Juan Mission settled canyon country at 4,200 feet far from winter snows and mountain streams. In Bluff City, 700-foot-tall sandstone cliffs bordered the town to the north. To the south the San Juan River formed the edge of the Navajo Reservation. Cottonwood Wash, draining the Abajos, became the town's western perimeter. To the east flowed Recapture Wash, named by Hayden Expedition artist and mapmaker W.H. Holmes, whose group had recaptured stolen horses in the lower reaches of the wash. Hot, dry, with cottonwoods only along the riverbanks, starting the isolated community would take time and patience. "Within days of the arrival of the Hole in the Rock group, bitter conflicts erupted over how to allot land to the new families," explains historian Paul Nelson.[23] Families received a town lot under an acre in size and a farming plot of eight to twenty acres dependent upon its soil and potential for irrigation.[24]

Acting Bishop Platte Lyman redistributed house and farming plots, but "this did not allay the problem that what little arable and irrigable land existed was of low quality and was certainly not what the settlers . . . had expected. The San Juan Mission was off to a very rough start."[25] Personal

A group of families from Bluff, possibly on a Sunday, pose below Locomotive Rock near Cow Canyon. Charles Goodman photo, Wanda Black Collection, courtesy of the San Juan County Historical Commission.

conflicts stemmed from the necessity for agriculture and from the Mormon belief that farming was a "divinely based endeavor."[26] In the sandy soils of San Juan County, surrounded by sandstone cliffs, a well-watered pastoral landscape seemed far removed. In terms of the US Census the unbroken line of a western frontier would be over by 1890. When the settlers came a decade earlier in 1880, "San Juan was then, and is now, the most barren frontier in the United States," Wallace Stegner proclaimed in his book *Mormon Country*.[27]

Bluff settlers had landed in one of the most remote corners of the American West. Less than a decade earlier, the Hayden Survey had termed some of the local landscape *terra incognita* or unknown land; yet here the Mormons settled at the mercy of the San Juan River. "Being dependent on the river for irrigation, it was alarming to them that they could not tame it to their use," wrote San Juan pioneer Albert R. Lyman, "It threatened the possibility of their making a living, or even part of a living, from the soil."[28] Arriving in April, disappointed by what they saw, almost one fourth of the Hole-in-the-Rock families departed before June. Those Mormons who stayed were extraordinarily young with an average age of seventeen and a half.[29] Despite repeated attempts to irrigate Bluff's bottomlands along the river, farming failed. Wing dams and ditch laterals to direct the river's flow washed out. Spring floods often brought a river load of sediment and mud roiling down from the San Juan Mountains near Pagosa Springs, Colorado. The snow-swollen river inundated plowed fields and when it subsided sand and gravel smothered young plants. To control and channel the river and to bring water to thirsty crops, "On average, each man worked ninety days building and anchoring cribs, scraping and digging the ditch itself," reports Bluff historian David S. Carpenter.[30] In all, two irrigation ditches cost thousands of dollars in man hours of labor; yet only 500 acres remained in spotty cultivation.

With fragile crops in constant jeopardy and no local source of cash, Bluff men had to do what they reviled—lend themselves out as teamsters with the nearest source of jobs being the rowdy railroad and mining town of Durango, Colorado, 130 miles to the east. Some families hoped to be released from their church mission, but two church apostles arrived, Brigham Young Jr. and Erastus Snow, who argued that the colony should stay despite the hardships. Cultural geographer D.W. Meinig describes the Bluff settlement as trying to farm "tiny, remote, restricted patches of irrigable land within the depths of the intricately sculptured terrain of the high canyonlands." He adds, "The implantation and the permanence of

"A TURN IN THE ROAD BROUGHT US TO THE TOWN ITSELF"—BLUFF CITY, NEAREST SETTLEMENT TO THE RECENTLY DISCOVERED GOLD FIELDS IN THE SAN JUAN VALLEY.

THE CHOIR, BLUFF CITY

"THE SHEEP AND GOATS WERE DRIVEN INTO A RAVINE."

Some of the first national news about the small Mormon settlement of Bluff, Utah came from Remington W. Lane in "An Artist in the San Juan Country," *Harper's Weekly*. Author's collection.

these little clusters in such difficult country is one of the remarkable achievements of Mormon colonization."[31]

Even though Bluff's remoteness made it difficult to sustain the village's livelihood, isolation also kept it safe from roving US federal marshals who might arrive after the 1882 passage of the Edmunds Anti-Polygamy Act that prohibited "unlawful cohabitation" or "bigamous" relationships. Deeply committed to plural marriage, families of the San Juan Mission knew that a federal law condemned their multiple marriage vows, but they felt safe knowing that Church practice and doctrine supported such unions. The San Juan Mission persevered and the Saints fought the river they had traveled so far to settle alongside. Still, farms failed. Drought could become rain, and in March of 1884, after three tough years of plowing and planting, the river rose seven feet. When waters ebbed, white sand smothered faltering crops.[32]

Out of desperation, and in contrast to the Mormon farming ethic, local residents residing in the newly established San Juan County of territorial Utah switched to livestock grazing of cattle and then sheep. They competed directly with Texas ranchers, Texas cowboys, and an assortment of thieves and outlaws on horseback. Sheep and cattle sales would sustain Bluff and encourage the settlement of two other towns, Blanding and Monticello. But finding grass in the bottoms of washes and on canyon rims would require all the perseverance and tenacity it had taken to get into the San Juan Country in the first place. Yet profits could be made, although difficulties with Utes, Paiutes, and Navajos only increased because more cattle meant less range for the deer and elk herds that Natives had relied on for centuries.

Settlers had passed the Bears Ears on the way to the San Juan River and what they thought would be their farming future. Now some of those same settlers returned, on horseback, with a new eye toward water holes, hidden pockets of grass, and canyon ledges to sleep under out of the wind while rounding up stray cattle. The Utah legislature had established San Juan County at 7,933 square miles, the largest in the territory. Bears Ears is near its center.

By 1884 cowboys had moved west from the Dolores River Valley in Colorado and a US Army Post, Fort Lewis, had been established south of the La Plata Mountains. Ute Indians in Colorado had been forced onto a reservation south of Durango, and the Navajos had their own reservation with the San Juan River as its northern boundary, but San Juan County remained an open frontier. Cowboys clashed with Indians and exacerbated conflicts. Generally, the Bluff Mormons adhered to Brigham Young's admonition that it was easier to feed Native Americans than to fight them, but tensions continued to escalate over slaughtered cattle left to rot by Utes and Paiutes who felt, and rightfully so, that livestock grazing impinged on their centuries-old claim to grass and game in and around Bears Ears. Conflict erupted with the incident at Soldiers' Crossing as further proof of Native American resistance to cattle incursions.

Three years earlier, Bluff residents chasing cattle stolen by Indians found the high meadows near Elk Ridge on the same elevation as Bears Ears. Now summer range for livestock could be in the higher country with winter range closer to the river and to Bluff, but Utes had begun to routinely kill cattle and steal horses to add to their large horse and goat herds. With a fast-growing market for beef in the Colorado mining camps of Ouray, Telluride, and Rico, cowboys brought cattle into southeast Utah. Utes retaliated.

The first major flare up occurred in the early summer of 1881 south of Moab in Pinhook Draw where Utes took high ground and successfully fought off Colorado cowboys who had invaded one of their camps after cowboy posses had looked for Utes along Comb Wash and Indian Creek, both in what would become Bears Ears National Monument. Better armed with Winchester repeating rifles, Utes outmaneuvered cowboys with their single-shot Sharps rifles. Utes had bought their Winchesters at trading posts and demanded the rifles from their Indian agents—for hunting purposes the agents were told. Ute and Paiute leaders who would become major obstacles to whites included Mancos Jim, Narraguinnep, Hatch, Bishop, Polk, Mariano, and Teegre. Both sides of the Pinhook fight had men killed and wounded, and Fort Lewis soldiers, charged with keeping the peace, rode 200 miles without accomplishing anything.

Two years later, the cattle conflict escalated. Huge herds covered Ute ancestral lands including cows from the Kansas and New Mexico Land and Cattle Company of Edward Carlisle and about a dozen smaller outfits. Legally, it was all open range, free public land, but local Indians considered the landscape theirs. "Me no go," proclaimed renegade Mancos or "Winchester" Jim. He said, "My father died here, my father's father die here, me die here, too."[33] In 1883 Carlisle purchased 7,000 cattle in southeast Utah and brought in thousands more scrawny Texas longhorns wild as deer and multihued.[34]

In Cottonwood Wash, I have seen the Carlisle brand etched into sandstone on a cliff wall which includes prehistoric Basketmaker rock art and a large Ute panel of a warrior on horseback wearing a long flowing headdress. This was Ute land, and at that spot in Cottonwood, a hidden pool of water collects under a sandstone spill-off close to an open grassy area that could easily have accommodated numerous Ute tipis warming in a winter sun with heat reflected off west-facing cliffs. That same year of 1883 intrepid prospectors drifted out of Colorado including Cass Hite, known for his proficiency with a pistol. Hite moved toward Dandy Crossing on the Colorado River that Platte Lyman from Bluff and others had discovered as a much easier crossing than the famed Hole-in-the-Rock route. Hite settled in after exploring and naming White Canyon in the fall of 1883 and discovering a series of three natural bridges that would become Natural Bridges National Monument directly west of Bears Ears. He found copper deposits and started an ill-fated White Canyon gold rush. He would also diligently search for Hoskininni's famed silver mine, whose pursuit had caused the death of prospectors Merrick and Mitchell. Hite would earn the Navajo nickname *Hosteen Pish-la-ki*, but despite a lasting friendship, neither Hoskininni nor his son ever revealed the location of any Navajo mine in Monument Valley.[35]

Indians could tolerate small bands of prospectors, but the livestock rush incensed them. Historian Robert McPherson explains that, by the 1880s, newspaper accounts describe,

> . . . in San Juan County alone there were 11,000 sheep and 32,000 cattle belonging to white stockmen on the range all year long and another 100,000 cattle that came in from Colorado for winter grazing. As a people dependent upon hunting and gathering, the Utes ground their teeth as they watched livestock destroy their livelihood—plants not eaten were trampled, and game not shot scared away.[36]

First had come the Pinhook Fight, now the 1884 fight at Soldiers' Crossing in the heart of Bears Ears would again prove the Utes' success at guerilla warfare and resistance against both cowboys eager to kill Indians and US cavalrymen trying to round up renegades. The incident began to the east at Mitchell's store where Montezuma Creek flows into the San Juan and where the Hole-in-the-Rockers sought to originally settle. A fight broke out. Itinerant whites killed a Navajo, wounded others, and then in the general melee the store lost thousands of dollars' worth of supplies carted off by Native Americans. Before the week was over cavalry soldiers arrived from Fort Lewis.[37] By July Bluff Mormons worried about considerable trouble approaching. Their instincts were correct.

On July 6 Captain Henry P. Perrine left Fort Lewis with forty-nine men. He also recruited volunteer cowboys numbering between 130 and 175. They rode toward a band of Ute Indians led by Mariano and Narraguinnep. The Utes had only 75 to 100 members, but they knew the country, knew the trails, and most importantly for the brutally hot days of July in canyon country, Utes knew the water holes and where to revive weary horses. "From the Round Mountain area they traveled south along Elk Ridge through the Big and Little Notches to the Bears Ears area on south Elk Ridge," explains historian McPherson. "At the springs or ponds, near the northern end of the Bears Ears the Utes rested."[38]

Before the Utes thundered off Elk Ridge for a defensive goal more than twenty miles away, they gathered water, let their livestock drink, and then ran a goat herd into their water source, which was a sandstone basin or tank where the goats not only sucked up the last of the water but also relieved themselves into the small basin, ruining any remaining water for soldiers following them. It was a masterful strategic tactic to use goats as an offensive weapon in this way, since both Navajos and Utes knew not only how to find water in a dry landscape, but also how to poison a water source for any pursuing enemies. The Utes then rode toward White Canyon. The large combined cowboy and military expedition followed leaving the cooler pines of Elk Ridge and seep springs below Bears Ears for dry exposed slopes where once again Utes sought higher ground.[39] From their defensive position the Utes could rain deadly fire down upon thirsty and dehydrated soldiers cowering behind thin shade from pinyon juniper trees and slight rock outcroppings.

"The lack of water proved crucial. It was one o'clock on a hot July afternoon, when temperatures in that country can easily rise to well over 100 degrees," explains McPherson. "The soldiers had filled their canteens that morning but were now out of water. The cowboys had even less. . . ."[40] Knowing the Bears Ears region proved providential for the Utes. They quickly ascended a hogback ridge to top out at Piute Pass, divided into three defensive bands, and took sniper positions to look down a steep talus slope near the gap. Utes waited comfortably for the cowboys to advance. When they did, the Indians fired down slope eventually killing two whites—cowboy James "Rowdy" Higgins and Joe Wormington, a military scout and packer.

Once their friends had died, neither cowboy nor cavalryman advanced. Under cover of darkness an attempt was made by five cowboys to recover the bodies, but a small band of seven armed Utes came off the rim by starlight stealing saddled horses and stripping the dead. The cowboys did not dare expose themselves at such close range, so they carefully backed down off the slope. A combined cowboy and military campaign against Ute families turned into a dusty, desperate retreat. Ute marksmanship won, but so did the lack of water. Native resistance in the Bears Ears country proved successful again. The two white men would lay unattended, unburied, bones bleaching in the sun until they were discovered by prospectors Joe Duckett and Cass Hite, who found the remains and moved them closer to the White Canyon Trail where weathered sandstone markers now signify dual graves.

If in 1884 wild landscapes of the Bears Ears region remained undisputed territory for Native groups unable to be run off or captured by either cowboys or the cavalry, back East in Washington, DC, other events were taking place that would shape the region even more profoundly. Archaeology and anthropology were in their infancy with high status archaeological sites to be found in the Holy Land, in the fallen ruins of Troy and at the buried city of Pompeii. For decades wealthy and sophisticated Europeans had toured the continent marveling at the ruins of classical Rome and Greece and speculating upon the length and duration of the continent's emerging nation states squabbling for colonies around the world. Archaeology revealed secrets from the past. Departments of Classics in America's premiere colleges taught ancient languages as professors ruminated on the birth of civilization and its democratic traditions.

The American Southwest had been home to sophisticated Native communities and at last a group of dedicated scientists sought to describe and catalog what they had seen. Published by the Government Printing Office in 1886, the *Fourth Annual Report of the Bureau of Ethnology* was issued by J.W. Powell. The one-armed major had been the first to run wooden boats through the Grand Canyon. Now as director of the Bureau of Ethnology for the prestigious Smithsonian Institution, Powell, who never carried a pistol in Indian country and instead chose to learn Native languages, published the work of one of his most outstanding contributors, William H. Holmes, who had traversed portions of southeast Utah and named the area below Elk Ridge as the Bears Ears Plateau.[41] Having traveled with Hayden's mapping expedition into Utah in 1875, a decade later Holmes published "Pottery of the Ancient Pueblos," with an early understanding of "the ancient Pueblo peoples [who] dwelt in a land of canons and high plateaus" where "there is an individuality in these Pueblo remains that separates them distinctly from all others and lends a keen pleasure to their investigation."[42]

Holmes had fond words for the San Juan River Valley and its prehistoric ruins. W.H. Jackson had named and photographed Casa del Eco, just east of Bluff on the Navajo side of the river. W.S. Holmes found much to value in what his party also discovered in the Bears Ears region. He took pleasure in their reconnaissance. He wrote, in the Bureau of Ethnology's report,

> In a number of ways the valley of the Rio San Juan possesses unusual interest to the antiquarian. Until within the latter half of the nineteenth century, it remained wholly unknown. The early Spanish expeditions are not known to have penetrated its secluded

> precincts, and its cliff-houses, its ruined pueblos and curious towers have been so long deserted that it is doubtful whether even a tradition of their occupation has been preserved, either by nomadic tribes of the district or by the modern pueblos of the south.[43]

Holmes reported on potsherds, their shapes, distribution and patterns including distinctive indentations created by Native fingernails or fingertips. If in southeast Utah cattlemen often despised and denigrated Native peoples, in the comfortable halls of America's scientific institutions a new awareness and appreciation for prehistoric Native American arts and architecture was born. Holmes relates, "The miners of the silver-bearing mountains to the north had made occasional excursions into the sinuous canons of the plateau district, and failing to bring back the coveted gold, told tales of the marvelous cities of the cliffs. . . ."[44]

W.S. Holmes explored Mancos Canyon in southwestern Colorado before traveling west into the canyon country of southeast Utah. Frontier photographer W.S. Jackson, also with the US Geological Survey, had been guided by raconteur and Ute linguist "Captain" John Moss and had photographed Two-Story House in the same canyon after spying it one night from camp just at twilight. Early the next morning Jackson made the arduous climb up the cliff to photograph the small cliff dwelling. At another site Holmes used his geologic hammer to free a corrugated coiled pot. There were two such pots, and Holmes explains, "[T]hese vessels had been placed in a small recess, where the falling walls had not reached them, and were standing just as they had been left by their ancient possessors. The more perfect one, which had lost only a small chip from the rim, I determined to bring away entire."[45] He did so and deposited it with the National Museum or the Smithsonian Institution in Washington, DC, thus beginning the start of decades of looting of ancient Ancestral Puebloan sites by professional archaeologists as well as amateurs and commercial diggers.

To be fair, both archaeology and anthropology were in their infancy. But the rush to collect pots, bowls, cups, mugs, baskets, blankets, skulls, and mummies for urban museums to be exhibited in halls funded by wealthy industrialists would consume the Southwest over the next few decades as completely as pushing cattle and sheep into ungrazed canyon bottoms. Both were extractive processes and both took from Native landscapes. Holmes recognized the impacts of looting and how some collections had "been brought east by the various expeditions without a proper record of the locality. This is to be regretted, as it makes it impossible to study the shades of distinctions between the wares of neighboring localities."[46] He also provided one of the first documentations of grave robbing when he described two high necked mugs with handles "in great favor with the San Juan potter . . . obtained by Captain Moss, of Parrott [a mining camp at the base of the La Plata Mountains] who stated that they, with other relics, had been exhumed from a grave in the San Juan Valley."[47] Robbing prehistoric Indian graves in southwest Colorado and southeast Utah was just beginning. One of the central locations for generations of such theft would be the Bears Ears region where Native peoples flourished for millennia and deeply incised canyons kept out Anglo settlement.

By 1886 Bluff residents, with the blessing of Mormon leader Francis Hammond, had moved toward communal ownership of livestock herds, pooling their resources together and creating "the Bluff Pool," where local men rode out as cowboys to watch over first cattle and then sheep. Though still overwhelmed by Texas cattle run by absentee Texas owners, Bluff men persevered. At the end of 1886 Lemuel Redd, one of the original scouts for the San Juan Mission, brought in a herd of cattle bringing the town's total to 2,000 head against the 20,000 longhorns run by the Carlisles.[48] Over time, Bluff men bought out the Texas cattle interests and established new communities north of Bluff at Blanding and at Monticello, which had been the Carlisle headquarters.

Violence both among cowboys and with Native Americans erupted occasionally, sometimes with fatal results. William Hyde built a trading post at the edge of Comb Wash at the Rincon where riders on horseback could easily ford the San Juan River most of the year. Ruins still stand of a sandstone block structure, part of a multibuilding trading post and house he constructed close to the river's edge. A large wooden water wheel, now partially buried in dirt, serviced an irrigation system. In June 1887 Bad Eye, or Old Eye, a Navajo, and another unknown Navajo, came to the fort then managed by Hyde's son in law Amasa Barton. Bad Eye sought to retrieve some pawned jewelry of his wife's, but an argument erupted over the trade. Barton wound up with a rope slipped over his head. He struggled, strangled, and in the melee the second Navajo accidentally shot his companion Bad Eye and then intentionally shot Barton twice in the head.

Miraculously, Barton hung on for seven days. Bluff residents, mainly women and children because the men were herding cows miles away, feared an Indian attack. Sixty Navajos, faces painted black, arrived to fight. Kumen Jones, the son-in-law of Bishop Jens Nielson who led the

The indomitable leader of the San Juan Mission, Bishop Jens Nielson, led Bluff's members of the Church of Jesus Christ of Latter-day Saints for decades. Guen Lyman Smith Collection, courtesy of the San Juan County Historical Commission.

Bluff community, spoke Navajo. Jones tried to negotiate and then realizing the severity of the situation stated that if a fight ensued soldiers would come. He talked about Blue Coats who had chased and captured Navajo headmen and their extended families during the Long Walk two decades earlier. Butchering and serving a steer helped mollify the angry band which left after "a general handshaking, and the war was over."[49]

In the same year of 1887, far to the east in Washington, DC, the genteel, well-dressed and well-bred members of the Friends of the Indian devised a new policy patterned after the highly popular Homestead Act of 1862, which awarded heads of household 160 acres of free land on the public domain if they built a cabin on it, fenced it, farmed it, and lived on the acreage for five years. Based on Thomas Jefferson's goal of a nation of Yeoman farmers, the Homestead Act had wide public appeal.[50] Now reformers sought a solution to the perennial "Indian Problem," and that was to replicate the Homestead Act for Native peoples by passing the Dawes Act or the General Allotment Act of 1887; only instead of parceling out the public domain, this law would fracture and splinter Indian reservations into private land holdings based on acreage for different family members. Perhaps well-intended by white Easterners, the law sought to civilize Native Americans by forcing them into farming, and incidentally paying taxes on their private land holdings. The law had devastating effects across the country and resulted in the loss of over 65 percent of tribal lands, but in southeast Utah, in the heart of the canyon country, it had almost no initial effect. But the Dawes Act was the beginning of a major policy shift as more federal laws would impact unclaimed public lands in San Juan County and penetrate even the remote recesses of the Bears Ears region.

After the Amasa Barton misfortune, Bluff citizens gratefully returned to their ranching way of life. A year later other ranchers to the east in Mancos, Colorado, made a discovery that would have profound effects on the Southwestern landscape and the preservation of ancient ruins. While Native Americans in southeast Utah continued to resist change and civilization, finding the largest cliff dwellings in North America would result in a new appreciation for cliffs and canyons and the ancient residents who had built their homes on narrow sandstone ledges.

The Wetherill family of five brothers under the patriarch B.K. Wetherill moved west of Durango into the Mancos River Valley and established the Alamo Ranch. As Quakers believing in the fundamental dignity of all peoples, they got along well with everyone. Utes allowed the brothers to run cattle on the Ute reservation and up on top of a large, long mesa christened centuries before as Mesa Verde, or green table, by the Spanish. From the top of the mesa the Four Corners region stretched for miles and far in the distance the Abajo or Blue Mountains could be seen in southeast Utah and on the edge of the long, green Elk Ridge, Bears Ears. Over time the Wetherill brothers, more than any other family, would come to know the region intimately and to spend more time in the saddle riding across the Southwest, poking into remote canyons and taking tourists to dances at Hopi villages. They would become known as cowboy archaeologists. They would lead into the field the most prominent scientific men of the day, but on that snowy December 18, 1888 the oldest son Richard Wetherill and his brother-in-law Charles Mason were just looking for lost cows.

Riding along a canyon ledge, searching through the pinyon-juniper trees, as snow drifted and swirled in front of them, they saw across the canyon a huge set of stone rooms and towers under a mammoth alcove. They named it Cliff Palace and exploring it for artifacts changed their lives. Within a year they were starting to lead tourists—writers, photographers, anyone interested, by horseback and wagon up onto Mesa Verde to see ruin after ruin, which they had named and which W.H. Jackson had originally missed as he rode and camped in Mancos Canyon without climbing higher up into the side canyons of Mesa Verde. The Wetherill brothers would climb into all those canyons, digging for artifacts, but the first collection of "Ancient Aztec Relics" would be attributed to Al Wetherill, Charles McLoyd, J.H. Graham and L. Patrick.[51] Assembled between 1888 and 1889 the collection was exhibited in Denver and so impressed its citizens that in the summer of 1889 the newly established Colorado Historical Society paid $3,000 for it, inadvertently starting a frenzy of searching for additional antiquarian relics not only in Mancos Canyon and the area of Mesa Verde but also west into Utah's Bears Ears and Grand Gulch. By 1890 the Wetherills had started a successful tourist operation headquartered at Alamo Ranch where visitors from eastern cities rested and signed the guest book before beginning the arduous trek up to Mesa Verde the next day. The Wetherill brothers would use the ranch as a base of operations before riding west toward Bluff and then leading archaeological expeditions into canyon country.

While tourists came to see the cliff dwellings and artifacts of prehistoric Native Americans, dead for centuries, Coloradans actively agitated to remove living Ute Indians and force them to San Juan County, Utah. Durango businessmen offered a plan that would place the Southern Utes "upon a reservation three times as large as the present one," but the Indian Rights Association argued in March 1890, "Removal merely shifts the burden of their presence from Colorado to Utah, and delays their final civilization."[52] The end of the decade also meant the end of ten long years at Bluff for the remnants of those families who had traveled west through the precarious Hole-in-the-Rock above the Colorado River. Latter-day

Saints stake president of San Juan County Francis A. Hammond encouraged exploration and settlement north of Bluff at a townsite that would take the name Monticello. It was close to the headquarters of the Carlisles' Kansas and New Mexico Land and Cattle Company and the LC Cattle Company. Mormons planted crops and argued with cattlemen over water rights. Mormon families determined that the Carlisles had limited legal claim to all the land they ranched on, but then neither did Bluff stockmen legally own their ranching domain. By 1888 Latter-day Saints members, having fenced 320 acres, began to uproot and burn sagebrush to construct a new town north of Bluff and south of Moab.

Bluff citizens switched to livestock, had numerous stock loans through Durango banks, and were generally prospering. "The San Juan Mission was the last gasp of mission-style settlement by the Mormon church in the West," wrote historian Paul Nelson. "By the end of the 1870s Brigham Young was dead and federal prosecution of polygamists and church leaders had become so aggressive that Young's successor John Taylor spent most of his presidency in hiding."[53] Bluff residents with their large, plural families had been relatively safe. Church leaders and community members on the bustling Wasatch Front north and south of Salt Lake City sought statehood for Utah, but it would be denied as long as polygamy was accepted throughout Utah territory. Then on September 25, 1890, Wilford Woodruff, President of the Mormon Church, described a revelation that had come to him and he issued a "Manifesto," abandoning polygamy as a practice of the Church of Jesus Christ of Latter-day Saints.

Even in remote Bluff, Mormon families now feared the arrival of federal marshals to take their beloved fathers and husbands into custody and then into jail. Having spent a decade trying to make the desert bloom and resisting other changes in America, discouraged by the shift in church policy, some families would now continue their resistance and leave southeast Utah altogether, abandoning the homes they cherished and the wide canyon country to the west with Bears Ears at its center.

CHAPTER 7

Cowboy Archaeology, a Lady Botanist, a Failed Indian Reservation, and the Antiquities Act, 1891–1906

Much Trouble, Some Expense, No Danger.

—Gustaf Nordenskiold telegraph home to Sweden

We discovered ruins that had probably never been seen by white men before, and succeeded in scaling cliffs and entering dilapidated fortresses that appeared inaccessible.

—Frederick Chapin, *The Land of the Cliff Dwellers*

The decade of the 1890s brought change to Utah's canyon country. Mormon cowboy J.A. "Al" Scorup arrived and he would push his cattle into remote reaches of an already remote landscape. Cowboy archaeologists sought collections of prehistoric artifacts, "relics," and human remains from deep within Grand Gulch, whose precipitous canyons flowed toward the San Juan River. Cowboy relic hunters were outfitted from the Mormon-owned two-story stone Bluff Co-op Building, as were itinerant prospectors. They rode through Bluff City on horseback before taking narrow wooden skiffs down into the canyons of the San Juan on a hunt for gold in a brief mining "excitement" that resulted in new trails, wagon roads, and a better understanding of the county's vast maze of sandstone canyons. More Utes would come to San Juan County, encouraged by Durango businessmen to vacate a reservation in southwest Colorado and move into Utah, with the intent of making the majority of San Juan County a Ute Indian reservation. That concept would fail because ranch families resisted, as did Utah's territorial governor. Some Bluff Mormons with polygamous families also resisted government intervention and fled to Mexico with their plural wives. Other Bluff ranchers joined in the hunt for Indian relics after being urged to procure a prehistoric Utah collection for the 1893 Chicago World's Fair.

As the twentieth century began, changes occurred with knowledge gained of prehistoric peoples and their lives in the Bears Ears region thanks to significant archaeological publications and congressional passage of the 1906 Antiquities Act. This act resulted from a public and professional outcry over prehistoric Native American artifacts collected by amateur archaeologists and relic hunters to sell for cash. A major economic depression, the Panic of 1893, collapsed cattle markets. Factory doors closed on thousands of American workers. Southwestern cowboys turned to prospecting cliff dwellings for artifact collections just as mining prospectors searched for gold and silver veins. The Wetherill brothers and one of their clients, a young Swedish nobleman, would be at the center of the collecting controversy.

Impetus for the Antiquities Act came in part from the canyons of southwest Colorado and southeast Utah. It is no coincidence that legislation creating Mesa Verde National Park and the separate law establishing fines and regulations for excavating ancient Indian sites were both signed by President Theodore Roosevelt in June 1906. The Antiquities Act not only protected unmarked Native American burials, but also allowed the US president, without Congress's consent, to declare public lands as national monuments, which Roosevelt did with vigor. How ironic that pothunting and grave robbing within Comb Ridge, Cedar Mesa, Ruins Canyon, and Grand Gulch would become a major impetus for passage of the Antiquities Act, and yet that vast prehistoric cultural landscape and those thousands of archaeological sites would not be federally protected until the twenty-first century.

For local families and out of state cattle companies, the canyon country of San Juan County, Utah, seemed to have only one purpose—grazing cattle and later sheep. As the range became divided and fully stocked, the two prominent peaks of Bears Ears played a central role in delineating range boundaries. By the 1890s the Pittsburg Land and Cattle Company ran cattle below the La Sal Mountains and across Dry Valley. The Carlisles ran cows in and around what had become the village of Monticello in 1887. The Lacy Company herded cows in Montezuma Creek. Incorporated in 1886 as the San Juan Cooperative, the Bluff Cattle Pool embraced Cottonwood Wash, Butler Wash, Comb Wash, and all of Cedar Mesa. "Aggressive action was taken by the Pool and local LDS Church leaders in rapidly expanding cattle numbers . . . maneuvering Indian land claims to the Pool's advantage, claiming springs and river crossings, expanding into remaining virgin range areas, and even buying out outside cattle and sheep interests," states author John F. Valentine.[1] By 1891 the region was fully stocked with cattle except for White Canyon and the rough country around Wooden Shoe Buttes. Into that world of sandstone cliffs and deep-set canyons rode Al Scorup from Salina, Utah, where there was no available cattle range either. Scorup faced a springtime flood.

He had hired out to a rancher named Sanford in exchange for payment in one-third of Sanford's calves. "I swam my two horses across the roaring, muddy Colorado River, climbed out on the south side of White Canyon, and began rounding up Sanford's cattle that were wild as buckskins . . . I soon ran out of grub, and I had no gun to kill the many deer I saw," he wrote in his biography. "I was desperate so I sold a big three-year-old steer of Sanford's to some placer miners for twenty dollars. It cost eleven dollars of that twenty to buy a sack of flour . . . I tell you those were dark days, but I made up my mind that this was a great country for cattle, and I was going to stay with it."[2]

After arriving in the canyon country of San Juan County at the age of nineteen, Scorup became a legend in the Southwest. He began a marathon life in the saddle, up before dawn, squatting before a small fire, drinking coffee, and then on horseback looking for cows and steers with maybe a can of beans for lunch and no dinner until dark. "He came into the country with nothing but two horses. Within seventeen years he bought the Indian Creek Cattle Company and became the largest public land grazer in the United States," notes Heidi Redd.[3] Scorup's range included parts of what is now Canyonlands National Park as well as numerous canyons and mesas within the boundaries of President Obama's Bears Ears National Monument. Al Scorup's ranch embraced one of the wildest sections of the United States called the San Juan Triangle or the then-unmapped area between the San Juan and Colorado Rivers for 1,185,000 acres of range. Scorup purchased the Dugout Ranch. The middle of all that area, which began to suffer from overgrazing, was the Bears Ears. Scorup wore out horses and cowboys, but he kept pushing cows anywhere there was grass.

At the beginning he went toe-to-toe with Texas cowboys who swore, chewed tobacco, drank whiskey, and loved to shoot their Colt .45s. Dubbed "the Mormon Cowboy" because of his religious beliefs and refined habits, Scorup had personality traits many of the Texas hands lacked—persistence, perseverance, and that do-or-die pioneer spirit, keeping him in the saddle long after tired cowpunchers stretched out in their bedrolls. Writing about Scorup, rancher and author David Lavender explained, "For 50 years Al Scorup found and loved that land. The scars of the battle are in his weather-tanned cheeks, in hands brown and gnarled as pinyon knots, in the slight limp that tells of a broken foot and shattered knee. Resilience, courage, patience—these things are obvious." Lavender continued, "But there is something more, something in his pale blue eyes, in the timbre of his deep, unhurried voice. Words cannot define it. It is that intangible quality of bigness, of understanding, of the things you sense when you stand on the desert at sunrise."[4]

Scorup's ranch hands covered a huge territory, poached deer, ate dried fruit, and slept in caves just as Ancestral Puebloans had done 1,000 years earlier. Scorup's herds evolved from rangy Texas longhorns to blooded Herefords. He made and lost money, was deep in debt, but he expanded the Dugout Ranch at Indian Creek into hayfields, ranch buildings, barns, and sheds with red rock views and the Six-Shooter Peaks just beyond. Stay with it he did, sleeping under rock shelters, riding sixteen hours a day, finding and branding calves, and working harder than half a dozen men. Scorup lived on his range for months at a time and demanded the same dedication from his brother and their hired ranch hands. Scorup outlasted the Texans. They were virile young men who knew dust and mesquite, but not the twisted canyon country with limited access to meadows and water and 900-foot drops to occasional creek beds. Al Scorup figured the Texas cowboys did not know the country. "The Texans would fail in the wild canyons of San Juan," he believed, "as they were used to the flat plains of Texas, where cattle rustled for themselves. I knew their system wouldn't work in the rock jungles of southeastern Utah."[5] The Bluff Pool also failed with 50 percent losses. Local Mormon cowboys did know the canyons, but families wanted individual not community responsibility for their own stock, so the Bluff cooperative pool fell apart. The Scorup brothers "bought it out." As local ranchers began to run their own smaller herds, the Bears Ears became a critical landmark with a north-south fence "constructed along the east side of the Bears Ears."[6]

Ranchers struggled to survive on overstocked ranges with bunch grass and Indian rice grass replaced by noxious weeds. No rules or regulations existed on who could use public lands and in what seasons. The forested areas near Bears Ears, Elk Ridge, and on the slopes of the Abajos became especially hard hit with imperiled creeks and watersheds. Back east a conservation movement had begun. In 1891 Congress passed the Forest Reserve Act establishing federal forests and removing tree-covered lands from entry for homesteads or settlement. In the canyons of southeast Utah it would be sixteen years before the regulations would begin to be enforced. Then a new type of resistance would begin—cattle and sheep ranchers intent on ignoring necessary federal regulations promulgated to protect southeast Utah's grazing landscapes to reduce erosion, save watersheds, and allow native grasses to return.

Scorup's cowboys pushed rangy steers into remote canyons. Other explorers looked for Indian ruins. One unique traveler who knew both cliff dwellings and botany wore a split skirt of her own design. Contrary to the rigid Victorian rules for females, she rode horseback.

The American West has always had extraordinary women, but few of them have stopped to pick the flowers. Alice Eastwood, a Canadian-born, 1879 Denver high school graduate, was a determined young woman who not only picked the flowers, but also named them. In turn she had plants named after her. She explored the Southwest when single women were supposed to be home, married, and raising a family. Instead she made enormous contributions to botany and plant science in her ninety-four years, and she did it all with grit and grace. In California, Alice Eastwood named 125 new plant species. The genera *Aliciella* and *Eastwoodia* were named for her. In her lifetime she wrote 310 scientific articles, named 395 plant species, and had 17 species named for her. At age sixty-eight on a botany trip in California, she walked twenty miles the first day and ten miles on day two. Eastwood officially retired at age ninety.

She became an early paleoethnobotanist. She helped identify plants unearthed in Wetherill excavations at prehistoric sites in Mesa Verde after first visiting Mancos Canyon on July 14, 1889. She helped study Ancestral Puebloans by understanding the plants they had used. She worked with Richard Wetherill at Cliff Palace in Mesa Verde, and with his brother Al she had one of the great adventures of her life in southeast Utah. Alice taught at East High School in Denver for eleven years. Because of her wise real estate purchases in Denver and Durango, she retired at age thirty-one to spend the rest of her life botanizing. Regional botanist Al Schneider told me, "The properties were bought as investments and when sold returned her sufficient money to feed her flower frenzy."[7] Eastwood became well known in Colorado and Utah and far beyond. She helped start botanical collections now at the Denver Museum of Nature and Science. She gave 1,400 plant specimens to form the nucleus of the University of Colorado herbarium including seventeen species that she named from Montezuma County, Colorado.

By 1892 Eastwood had become co-curator in San Francisco at the California Academy of Science's herbarium. She would travel the West finding

The lively and irrepressible botanist Alice Eastwood introduced Gustaf Nordenskiold to the Wetherill family and traveled horseback for days with Al Wetherill in search of plants new to science to be found in the Bears Ears region. CANM 2000.19.P.139.0. Courtesy of BLM—Canyons of the Ancients Visitor Center and Museum.

and identifying new plants. Eastwood edited *ZOE: A Biological Journal* and in 1892 she published "Notes on the Cliffdwellers" where she wrote, "Corn, squash, and beans were the chief crops; the walnuts now and then discovered were probably from further south with the cotton which has been found on the pod, spun into thread, and woven into cloth . . . seashells have been found matted in the hair of the dead . . . willow twigs fastened together something like the slats of Venetian blinds formed the outside cover, the coffin of these prehistoric people."[8] An astute observer, she noted, "Coarse grass with stiff stems, *Oryzopsis cuspidate*, was tied into bundles to make brushes, probably for their hair. The wild tobacco, *Nicotiana attenuate*, is common near their homes and in the canons where their houses stand like statues in the rocky niches the wild fruits are more abundant than elsewhere, leading to the belief that to some extent they were cultivated."[9]

Alice Eastwood's letters make clear that one of her finest collecting trips occurred across southeast Utah in 1892. She wrote about it in *ZOE* and began, "It was my good fortune the past year, toward the end of May, to travel on horseback through a part of the Great American Desert that has been but little explored."[10] Al Wetherill met her at Thompson's Spring as she stepped off the Denver and Rio Grande Railroad into a sea of sagebrush and a treeless plain. An inveterate explorer, she invented her own type of dress with a split skirt so she could ride horseback and not go side-saddle. She was prepared for anything, unlike other male adventurers who got off at the same weathered railroad station where with a four-horse wagon it was one and a half days south to Moab, two more days to Monticello, and another few days to Bluff.

Fifteen years later in 1907 an archaeological team disembarked at the same station and a squeamish young man asked the agent if he could use the urinal. "Urinal! My god, man," shrieked the agent as he swept the room with an open palm. "Right outside that door is 40,000 acres and not a tree on it," wrote Neil M. Judd in his memoirs.[11] Alice Eastwood had no such qualms, including traveling with a married man. Her epic journey with Al Wetherill meant riding to Monticello, a "Mormon settlement at the foot of the Blue Mountains," down Montezuma Canyon to the San Juan River and then McElmo Creek and the Montezuma Valley to Mancos. They would run out of food, but nothing stopped Alice from botanizing. She wrote, "It was the period when vegetation was most luxuriant, and the earth was gay with flowers."[12]

Eastwood impressed everyone. In his autobiography, Al Wetherill remembered, "She would stop to pick, or examine, some strange or rare

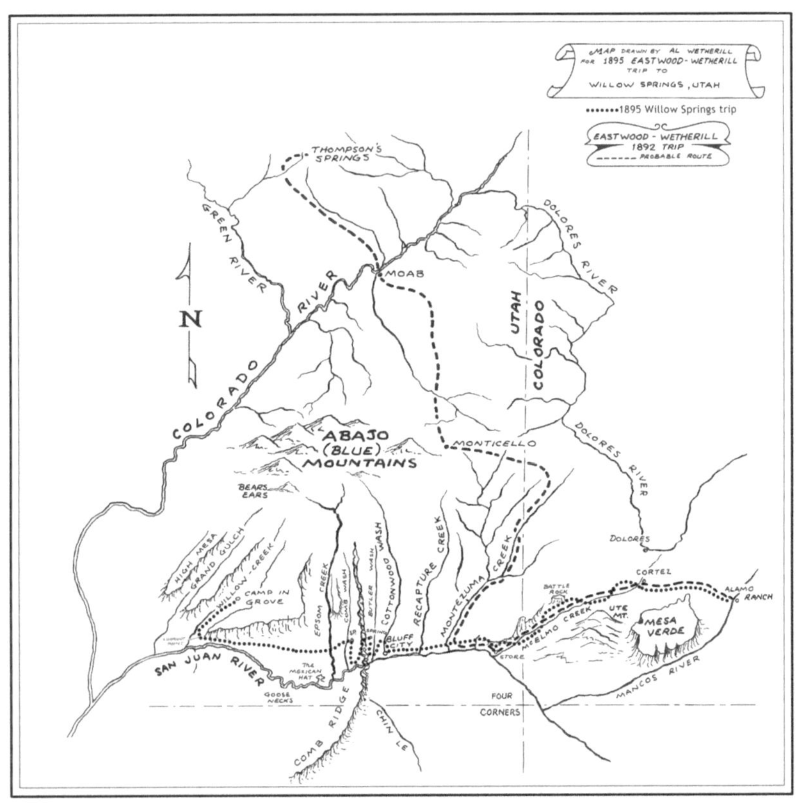

This map shows the route of Alice Eastwood and Al Wetherill as they rode horseback across southeast Utah in 1892 and 1895 in two botanical expeditions. Map combined from maps drawn by Al Wetherill and used in Maurine S. Fletcher, ed. *The Wetherills of the Mesa Verde: Autobiography of Benjamin Alfred Wetherill.*

specimen of plant that cropped up in protected places or in new territory." As for accommodations, he admitted, "We had a regular cowboy's layout—a greasy sack outfit. That meant limited camping equipment, a couple of saddle blankets, and a canvas covering for the pack. Grub was bacon, oatmeal, salt, sugar, coffee, and flour and baking powder."[13] Along the way she turned down an offer of marriage from a Mormon widower. Because she had to prepare and dry all her plant specimens, she was not prepared for a Utah wind that blew apart her samples. "She just sailed into those papers and specimens and got them all safely packed and tied in their proper places with no loss that I could see. Most of them were pretty green and had not blown far," Wetherill reminisced.[14]

She collected in Court House Wash, now in Arches National Park, and in Comb Wash and Butler Wash in Bears Ears National Monument. She named several species after Al including *Oreocarya wetherilli*. But if her gumption and perseverance were often tested in the field, the ultimate challenge came in 1906 in San Francisco during the city's epic earthquake. She thought nothing about herself or her possessions; instead, she saved plant specimens from the California Academy of Sciences. She hurried into the collapsing building to climb five stories of twisted railing on broken stairs to retrieve 1,497 specimens. Fires erupting down the block, she retrieved the Academy's historical records and irreplaceable botanical specimens by her quick thinking and by hiring a team and wagon to haul them to safety. "My own destroyed work I do not lament, but it was a joy to me while I did it, and I can still have the same joy in starting it again," she wrote. "All my pictures and books are gone and many treasures that I prized highly; but I regret nothing for I am rich in friends and things seem of small account."[15]

In her lifetime she would rebuild the Academy's collections to 300,000 specimens. I think of this amazing woman as I hike the canyons of Bears Ears looking for *Erythranthe eastwoodiae* (Eastwood's Monkeyflower) that appears in seeps and springs. The type locale, the first place where the plant was identified, is in a small alcove just east of Bluff. What a long life Eastwood lived at the intersection of archaeology, anthropology, botany, and the Old West becoming the settled West we now know. Alice Eastwood dedicated her life to science, and she enjoyed every moment of it. We should be grateful for her adventurous, pioneering spirit and also for her foresight in introducing to the Southwest a young Swedish nobleman who would become one of the first Southwestern archaeologists and who played a pivotal, if unwilling, role in establishing the Antiquities Act.

It was Alice reading in the Denver Public Library on July 31, 1891 who met Gustaf Nordenskiold, a Swedish scientist suffering from tuberculosis and who was "chasing the cure" in nineteenth century parlance. She told him of cliff dwellings recently discovered near Mesa Verde and of her friends the Wetherills from Mancos, Colorado, who could guide him. He took the train to Mancos and would become one of the first Southwestern archaeologists to study Ancestral Puebloan sites at Mesa Verde, map them, and write a book about them. But Nordenskiold also collected 610 Indian artifacts in fifteen crates and two barrels for shipment to Sweden. For that he was arrested by a US marshal in Durango, placed under house arrest in the Strater Hotel, and forced to pay $1,000 bail.

He found a lawyer and telegraphed his famous Arctic-explorer father with six brief words: "Much trouble, some expense, no danger."[16] The Nordenskiold detention and legal troubles would become an international incident involving embassies, ambassadors, the US district attorney for Colorado, and presidential cabinet members. It would become a flashpoint for the fledgling new field of archaeology and anthropology because Nordenskiold had excavated in southwestern Colorado with the Wetherills at Mesa Verde, which in the late-nineteenth century was still Ute Indian land. He dug ancient ruins without permission of the Indian Agent.

In May 1889 C.C. Graham and Charles McLoyd brought to Denver for exhibition a large collection of relics from Mesa Verde. In the first appropriation for archaeology in the state, the legislature authorized purchase of the collection for $3,000 spurring interest in additional Ancestral Puebloan artifacts. "Aware of McLoyd's success in the sale of Cliff Palace artifacts, Richard [Wetherill] and his brothers recognized the potential benefits of gathering and selling a large collection," writes Wetherill scholar Fred Blackburn. "It would not only finance their excavations, but also hold to their Quaker beliefs through the study and preservation of cliff dwellings and their contents."[17]

In Denver, Gustaf Nordenskiold saw the Mesa Verde exhibit and made plans to visit southwest Colorado. "Gustaf imagined a similar museum-quality collection of artifacts for Europe," explain Judith and David Reynolds in *Nordenskiold of Mesa Verde*. "It would be invaluable for science, [Nordenskiold] noted, 'and none such exists in Scandinavia.'" He wrote his father for funds and stated, "I could assemble a beautiful collection which ought to be most valuable. It will cost me around 400 dollars, a sum which without a doubt can be regained many times over."[18] Though prehistoric baskets, bowls, blankets, and war clubs had value, the real prizes in Indian relics were human remains—skulls and mummies.

Over a hundred miles west of Mesa Verde in southeast Utah, the Bears Ears region remained wide open to Navajos and their small sheep herds. Anglo cattlemen grazed the area with their much larger herds. In the same convoluted canyons would-be antiquarians sought to dig up artifacts and sell their assembled collections. "Mormons were pushing cattle into this rugged area, and not far behind were the archaeologists, or at least, the relic hunters. The Wetherills' Mesa Verde discoveries in the late 1880s, had stimulated public interest in Southwestern antiquities, especially in the remains of the 'cliff-dwellers,' and had created in the great cities a demand for collections and exhibits," explains William Lipe writing about collecting within the boundaries of Bears Ears National Monument. "Here were tantalizing mementos of a universally human yet terribly remote past, things preserved in the dry caves as if the stream of time had spent itself in their arid and protecting sands."[19]

As the Wetherills named, excavated, and dug Cliff Palace, Spruce Tree House, Mug House, Spring House, and other Mesa Verde ruins for a total of twenty-six sites in three months with Gustaf Nordenskiold in 1891, the brothers learned to use a trowel, not just a shovel. The cowboy archaeologists grasped camel hair brushes to carefully sweep away what Al Wetherill termed "the dust of centuries." Other collectors had less interest in science and more interest in cash. Durangoans C.C. Graham and Charles McLoyd rode horseback through Bluff prior to entering the Bears Ears area and the deep canyons of Grand Gulch. They explored in the winter of 1890 when water sources were more dependable. The pair "had heard of the splendid dry caves of Grand Gulch and . . . fielded the first of several expeditions to 'explore' them with their shovels. Their collections further aroused the late Victorian passion for withered bodies and curious relics from the Southwest's canyons," notes scholar Lipe.[20] Cowboy archaeologists, including Graham, McLoyd, and the Wetherill brothers, acquired large collections to sell to museums. Even the Reverend C.H. Green of the first Baptist Church in Durango got involved. He sponsored a Grand Gulch dig in the summer of 1891 and created a catalog for the 1893 World's Fair in Chicago. Green titled it a "Catalogue of a Unique Collection of CLIFF DWELLER RELICS . . . estimated to be The Oldest Relics in the World." Green exaggerated the age of the relics, but there was plenty of speculation about who the cliff dwellers might have been and who might have preceded them.

Unlike the Wetherills, few historic details exist about McLoyd and Graham, though a magnificent canyon on Cedar Mesa flowing east toward Comb Wash is named McLoyd Canyon. One document, however, stands out. I found it in Special Collections at the Harold B. Lee Library at Brigham Young University cataloged under Americana/Rare.

The pamphlet is old and faded. Staples have been removed, but the title and date are unmistakable: "CATALOGUE AND DESCRIPTION OF A VERY LARGE COLLECTION OF PREHISTORIC RELICS, OBTAINED IN THE CLIFF HOUSES AND CAVES OF SOUTHEASTERN UTAH." The next page proclaims, also in capital letters, "THIS COLLECTION IS FOR SALE—ADDRESS MCLOYD & GRAHAM. P.O. BOX 312, DURANGO,

COLO. EXPLORERS OF PREHISTORIC RUINS AND COLLECTORS OF RELICS. 1894."[21] The authors state that "a few ruins have been found in the Canon of the Colorado River, but they are not so large or numerous as in the side canons." The authors' first set of artifacts, Group A, in a collection that goes to Group K, consists of human remains. The catalogue explains, "Usuly (sic) the lsrger (sic) humad (sic) remains were buried in a doubled up posture, the knees drawn up against the chest, the clothing being left on the body," but without any sort of headstones or gravestones. McLoyd notes, "No land marks leading to the discovery of the general burial places of the Cliff Dwellers have yet to be found. Some of the skulls in this collection were obtained from underground rooms, that have been excavated in the clay bottoms of the caves."[22] Then the sales items were enumerated.

"No. 1 Headless mummy, of female child, that was found in Lake Canon." Followed by "No, 2. A well preserved mummy, five feet six inches in length" and "No. 3 A well preserved mummy of a child, about 3 feet high; found in a cave in Grand Gulch. It is wrapped in fur cloth, and deer skins that have been tanned with the hair on . . . the hair on the head of the child is of a red cast." The fourth sales item was also a child's remains. The catalog lists "No. 4 Mummy of a very small child that was found in a basket—23C—with another basket—12C—turned over it; was found in a cave in Colorado River Canon, just above the mouth of the San Juan."[23] The catalog continued with over fifty-four items in the human remains section detailing accompanying grave goods, described for separate sale, as well as mummified lower arms, hands, legs, feet, an assortment of skulls, human hair, scalps, and "16 lower jaws, collected from the various caves where work was done."[24] This jarring lack of respect for the dead with body parts itemized for sale coincided with a lack of respect for the living.

Victorian era Anglo and Mormon pioneers could not conceive that the ancient ancestors of Native peoples living in the Southwest could have built the astounding structures found at Chaco Canyon in New Mexico, Mesa Verde in Colorado, and in the cliffs of Utah's Bears Ears. After centuries, these structures remained intact with careful stonework, uncracked mortar, tightly woven roof beams over circular and square kivas, and original wooden doorway lintels with hand twists of yucca fiber still wrapped around small diameter juniper sticks. The builders simply had to be civilized peoples from exotic places like Mexico, hence the numerous Four Corners place names like Aztec, New Mexico, Aztec Creek and Montezuma County in Colorado, and Montezuma Creek and Montezuma Canyon in Utah.

If McLoyd and Graham looted dozens of Bears Ears sites with only vague descriptions of their site locations, Nordenskiold kept scientific notes. He was at the forefront of the key archaeological concept of stratigraphy, which is that the age and value of an artifact is dependent upon its location and depth in soil strata. His book, *The Cliff Dwellers of the Mesa Verde* published in 1893, contains detailed maps and analysis of all major sites on the mesa. It is a landmark of scientific achievement in southwestern archaeology. The appendix by a Swedish physical anthropologist describes Nordenskiold's collection of "seven perfect skulls with nearly complete skeletons, one skull with an incomplete skeleton, two partial skulls, two adult mummies so enveloped in hide and bandages as to preclude thorough study without disassembly, two child mummies, and three child skulls."[25] But before the young Swedish traveler could return to Europe, review his collection, consult his notes, and write his book, he went to court.

Beginning with the Victorian impulse to classify and categorize, gentlemen assembled curio cabinets that evolved into marble-halled museums as the Industrial Age created American millionaires intrigued by natural and human history. This was the golden age for amassing anthropological collections because everywhere Indigenous peoples were perceived to be a "vanishing race."[26] The new fields of archaeology and anthropology had fervent scholars dedicated to "salvage archaeology" and "salvage anthropology" who attempted to record and document archaeological sites before they were looted. These scholars barged into teepees, hogans, and pueblos to record and photograph Indigenous customs, culture, and ceremonies that they assumed would be lost forever. "At the turn of the century, prehistoric artifacts were the most important results of excavation. Cultural institutions and private collectors engaged in fierce competition for these spoils," writes historian Hal Rothman. "To load their halls with full museum cases, institutions cavalierly sponsored scientists who tore through southwestern archaeological sites in search of artifacts."[27] The same colonial impetus that required great nations to have empires assumed those nations would bring back to their museums immense collections of artifacts, bird specimens, reptile skins, wooden masks, totem poles, Indian dwellings, and a wide assortment of everything from human skeletal remains to war canoes. In New York City, Washington, DC, Chicago, Philadelphia, and Boston dedicated curatorial staff gathered cultural items for metropolitan and national museums.

Curators put human history into perspective and showcased both the bows and arrows of "primitive" tribesmen and the exploits and pedigrees

This collection of prehistoric ceramic vessels was probably pothunted in southeast Utah. #p1205n077, photo courtesy of Special Collections, J. Willard Marriott Library, The University of Utah.

of the ruling class. Museum staff felt confident in their role to classify and interpret the world around them and to teach visitors their place in the prevailing paradigm, which mandated white Anglo Saxon Protestants on civilization's highest rung and other peoples lower down the ladder depending upon the color of their skin and their distance from the northern latitudes.[28]

In the last decade of the nineteenth century no American law existed to protect unmarked burials or the habitation sites of Indigenous peoples. Committed to the concept of race as a defining factor in human affairs, anthropologists collected Indian skulls, and photographed and studied Native Americans convinced they would be assimilated and lose their cultural identity.[29] Museum directors hurried to assemble artifact collections for new educational institutions established in major American cities and for large crowd-pleasing events like world fairs and expositions. Hiring the Wetherills as guides and excavators to unearth artifacts at Mesa Verde was not unprecedented. Gustaf Nordenskiold's only failing was that he was a foreigner, labeled in the newspapers as a European nobleman or baron. Outraged Coloradans complained that a Swedish aristocrat had looted southwestern Colorado sites.

The lawsuit against him went forward. Then on October 5, 1891 when Judge Cyrus Newcomb convened his Durango court, attorneys stepped to the bench and charges were quickly dropped. Diplomatic overtures had succeeded including permission to ship two wooden barrels and fifteen crates of artifacts back to Sweden, though the Southern Ute Indian Agent demanded that the cargo not include "any bones or skeletons known to have belonged to any of the Southern Ute Indians, or their ancestors."[30]

Despite his father's concerns for his son's health and the impacts of rapidly worsening tuberculosis, Gustaf Nordenskiold did not immediately return home. In November 1891, he set out with Al Wetherill and a neighbor to visit the Hopi mesas on horseback. They circled back through Monument Valley, well-worn, clothing in tatters, hungry, and overjoyed to buy food on credit in Bluff at the San Juan Co-op before riding to Mancos on weary horses. In early 1892 Gustaf Nordenskiold traveled east to Stockholm. Within a year, traveling west into the Bears Ears and Grand Gulch, the Wetherills continued to dig. "When the collection the Wetherills made with Nordenskiold appeared in Sweden, American scientists howled. Wetherill offended their professional pride and they became nationalistic as they publicly castigated him," explains Rothman. "Simply put, his presence at southwestern sites threatened the fledgling profession of anthropology, and his work with foreigners gave the anthropologists an avenue to attack him."[31]

The three oldest Wetherill brothers, Richard, Al, and John, became guides and packers for tourists and scientific expeditions. They brought Frederick Chapin to Mesa Verde sites and he published *Land of the Cliff Dwellers* a year before Nordenskiold's treatise. Between 1889 and 1901 the Alamo Ranch became a well-known departure point for Mesa Verde tours with Al Wetherill estimating that almost one thousand "ordinary sight-seers, teachers, scientific men, and world travelers visited the ranch to see the cliff dwellings."[32]

Inevitably that also meant further exploration to the west, into southeast Utah, into the heart of the Bears Ears region. One scientific group that traveled from the East to study ruins and to gather a collection had a miserable time despite their high expectations. The group represented a new publication titled the *Illustrated American*, similar to *Harper's Weekly Illustrated* and what would become *National Geographic*. The Illustrated American Exploring Expedition (IAEE) of 1892 thought in a few months they could canvas the entire San Juan River area for archaeological treasures. They barely made it to Bluff City from the railhead at Durango. Some explorations into southern Utah and the Southwest became famous. Here's one expedition that did not. The explorers visited

The IAEE Exploring Expedition named numerous sites on Comb Ridge including Monarch's Cave which has recently been stabilized by the Bureau of Land Management. Author photo.

one hundred archaeological sites between Durango, Colorado, and Comb Ridge, Utah,—eighty of them never before described or recorded, but they had an awful time of it, constantly underfunded, underfed, dehydrated, and with sand in their hair, their clothing, and their food. Mainly from Ohio, the seven-man team should have had the time of their lives. Instead the group complained about the very isolation and landscapes that now draw thousands of tourists to Utah. The IAEE explored and named some of the most important Comb Ridge sites included in Bears Ears National Monument.

Fearful of local Navajos and suspicious of Mormon families, these elite Easterners bungled across the Four Corners with mules, burros, horses, wagons, and even an ill-conceived wooden boat, which almost got them drowned. Yet this was an important scientific expedition headed by Warren K. Moorehead, who had worked as an archaeologist with the Smithsonian Institution and done extensive work on the Moundbuilders of Ohio. Across America, archaeology was in its infancy. *The Illustrated American* planned an expedition into the Southwest to learn the truth about rumors of ancient people and to publicize scientific findings in a thirteen-article series written by Moorehead titled "In Search of a Lost Race." A second goal was to assemble a sizable collection of artifacts for the 1893 Chicago World's Fair or Columbian Exposition. From the beginning, nothing worked as planned. "*The Illustrated American* had been allotted space at the Columbian Exposition to display both a collection of prehistoric relics from the American Southwest and scale models of the ancient aboriginal buildings located there," writes historian James Knipmeyer in his book *In Search of a Lost Race.*[33]

The group's physician never showed up and neither did promised funding for expenses and local salaries for guides, food, and horse and burro purchases. Permits to cross the Navajo and Ute reservations never arrived. As the group made their way toward Bluff, Utah, thieves stole their burros. Of course, there were gnats, tarantulas, coyotes, and rattlesnakes. The intrepid explorers recommended when "you see a great flat-headed rattler just in the act of striking . . . put a bullet through his head." A permanent camp at Bluff and the Mormon community there provided social contact and comforts including daily baths in the muddy San Juan River. Moorehead wrote, "The country is wild, the scenery full of grand, strange beauty . . . ," but he found the canyons tiresome, and he admitted, "The main desire on the part of everyone is to get through as rapidly as possible and return to the delights of the East." This statement, written from Bluff, contrasts sharply with the expedition's original intent to archaeologically explore all the drainages of the San Juan until its confluence with the Colorado River.

They wrote in *The Illustrated American* that they had traveled "over the most forlorn looking desert that the sun ever shone upon. Or a total of one hundred and thirty miles of desert traversed by the San Juan River, and but five creeks, all of which contain water largely impregnated with alkali."[34] The explorers visited Casa del Eco or Seventeen Room Ruin on the Navajo side of the San Juan River and hiked both banks. Using ropes, they dangled on a precipice above the San Juan inspecting pottery and small stone dwellings. Eventually, they headed up Butler Wash and explored and named important sites on the east side of Comb Ridge including Monarch's Cave and Cold Spring Cave. At both locations I've found their inscriptions carved into stone with the letters and date "IAEE 1892" and the name they christened each site.

Perhaps the most audacious effort of the explorers was to enter the remote Eagle's Nest ruin high on the Comb. From across the drainage with binoculars the site looks almost perfect; it has a few small rooms in a high shallow alcove appearing like a hand-carved silhouette. Expedition members noted faint traces of carved steps and tied off on small bushes using ropes to descend into the site, which has a steep pitch. Author and canyoneer Steve Allen comments, "To think of these men, far from help in a remote land, risking it all by swinging out over the abyss to gain access to the Eagle's Nest is astounding even by today's standards in adventure sports. There were no bolts, no 'camming devices' stuck in a crack, no sheath covered perlon ropes, no mechanical ascending devices, no belays." Allen explains, "They had an old hemp or cotton rope tied to some scraggly bushes. Off the sheer cliff face they went, hanging onto the rope for dear life, looking hundreds of feet down into the void, praying the bushes would stay attached to the rock."[35] Once inside the ruin the explorers realized that this cliff dwelling had no portholes or loopholes for defense. None were needed. No enemy could easily approach because of the cliff's steepness. Today under the management plan for Bears Ears, accessing cliff dwellings by rope is not permissible without authorized research permits.

The *Illustrated American* party included Remington W. Lane, an artist and photographer who provided some of the first published drawings of the Mormon community of Bluff as well as drawings of artifacts like axes, arrowheads, spearpoints, baskets, bowls, and skeletons.[36] The IAEE

The remote Eagle's Nest site on Comb Ridge was first entered and described by the Illustrated American Exploring Expedition in 1892. It is now illegal to enter any prehistoric cliff dwellings by rope without a special research permit. Author photo.

also visited sites with local names like Long Fingers, Double-Stack, Fish Mouth Cave, Ballroom Cave, Red Knobs, and Ruin Canyon. Returning to Bluff, the explorers ran out of financial support. Funds had not arrived from the New York headquarters of *The Illustrated American*. By late May the expedition backtracked to Durango. They had acquired only forty-six artifacts for the Chicago Exposition, and trip leader Moorehead was personally out $1,900 for trip expenses.[37] He later sued the magazine.

Moorehead wrote part XII of his series on "The Great McLoyd Collection," and he explained, "The region has never been thoroughly explored, and besides, cowboys and Indians, tempted by the flattering offers made them by the traders, have despoiled the ruins of the relics easiest of access." He added, "There are a number of wealthy relic collectors in the East who have been corresponding with traders with a view to securing specimens from the caves and ruins . . . they do an immense amount of damage by encouraging the taking of pottery and other objects by persons incapable of handling finds properly." Then Moorehead opined that there were a few "collectors of judgment and discrimination," and he named Charles McLoyd.[38] In the article Moorehead published photographs of skulls collected and two mummies that McLoyd had grave robbed, probably from Grand Gulch. Moorehead interviewed McLoyd in Durango prior to returning east. In several paragraphs McLoyd discusses "the cliff-dweller problem" of trying to ascertain the age of the Ancestral Puebloans. He describes living spaces of cliff-houses, cave-dwellings, and residential rooms in which "we found sandals, arrow heads, and knives mounted in their original handles, baskets, skeletons, and a host of other things."[39]

In a subsequent issue of *The Illustrated American* Morehead wrote with grandiloquence that the McLoyd Collection was "the result of years of intelligent and difficult labor, and from it we are given food for speculation as to the habits, customs, and manners of a people who had their day before Moses led the hosts of Israel out of Egypt, or before the gardens of Babylon had been raised by their ingenious builders."[40] Such flowery phrases and exotic associations typified writers of the time with their chronological inaccuracy. The deep truths of Bears Ears' human occupation were not yet understood. Morehead arranged for the McLoyd Collection to be exhibited in Chicago at the World's Fair and to be purchased by the Smithsonian Institute though that did not happen.[41]

If the IAEE party brought back only a few artifacts, all their original notes, maps, negatives and photos burned when fire destroyed offices at *The Illustrated American*, causing Moorehead to lament, "Ill fortune seemed to pursue us even after the survey had disbanded." Author Knipmeyer does not consider the IAEE a failure. "It was the first scientific party to do any exploration and research of what came to be known as the Anasazi culture in the upper San Juan River Basin," he concludes. The explorers also chronicled and described what would become Hovenweep National Monument on the Colorado-Utah state line and their published maps and drawings are accurate representations of sites and artifacts.

Over a century later, a comprehensive archaeological study of San Juan County including the Bears Ears region is still incomplete. Blanding, Utah, archaeologist Winston Hurst explains, "After 110 years of subsequent archaeological effort, including almost 40 years of fairly intensive surveys in the oil fields, we're still not even close to achieving their goal." Hurst adds, "Now, after more than a century of relentless collecting pressure, many of the sites are so stripped of artifacts that reveal their age and cultural affiliation that we have to spend hours crawling around in weeds to find enough artifacts to establish a relatively accurate age for most sites. In many cases it's no longer possible." He continues, "That's why artifact collection is illegal on public lands."[42]

As I hike Comb Ridge in Bears Ears National Monument, I think about pothunting and site desecration. I think about the Old Ones who came before whom we now call Ancestral Puebloans and how *The Illustrated American* Exploring Expedition, for all its faults, had scientific goals that matched the ethos and ethics of their time. I contemplate the hundreds of square miles of seemingly empty canyons, mesas, and ravines in southeast Utah. Archaeology can teach us only a limited amount about the breadth and complexity of the Ancestral Puebloan world, but we learn almost nothing from pothunted sites. Cowboy archaeologists entered alcoves and ruins in Bears Ears. Their goal was to find artifacts, make large collections, and sell them. The rush to dig and find artifacts continued because of the desire to have Utah items at the World's Columbian Exposition of 1893 in Chicago. Utah had its own building at the fair where artifacts were exhibited from the Bears Ears region including Platte Lyman's mummy "the King of the Blue Mountains." The mummy earned praise from a poet who romanticized a body ripped from its rightful repose:

> Mute remnant of a long-departed race,
> Perpetual sleeper from the entombed cliff,
> That liest yucca-wrapped, immobile, stiff,
> With shriveled limbs, and meager, shrunken face.[43]

The Wetherills dug and assembled an artifact collection for the World's Fair, and then a second and third collection. In the late-nineteenth century, excavating on public lands was not illegal, but the nascent scientific community of archaeologists and anthropologists took notice. As respected Eastern scientists grappled with understanding who the Ancestral Puebloans were and when they had lived in the Southwest, cowboy archaeologists like Richard Wetherill also had insights. Wetherill and McLoyd had come to understand that beneath cliff dweller deposits in alcoves and caves, an older group of people had lived at many of the same sites and buried their dead even deeper in the backs of caves. These ancient Native Americans had no pottery, made different sandal styles, and crafted exquisite baskets. Richard Wetherill shared his knowledge with expedition sponsor Talbot Hyde who changed Richard's phrase of "Basket People" to the shorter "Basketmaker." But despite his intentions, as the head of expeditions across the Bears Ears region and into Grand Gulch, Richard Wetherill did not consistently take scientific notes, or at least not all of his notetaking and journals have been found.[44] He wrote important letters and his wife Marietta described one winter season digging in Grand Gulch caves, but some of the artifacts collected did not have the scientific provenience and the painstaking mapping of artifact locations in soil deposits that were becoming part of archaeological discipline.[45]

As more publications described the richness of Southwestern archaeology and the Bears Ears region in particular, momentum grew to condemn the cowboy collectors and to pass federal legislation to preserve a valuable part of American culture and prehistory by requiring permits to dig and also to set aside the sites themselves. The need for the 1906 Antiquities Act began with nationwide site looting and with Gustaf Nordenskiold digging artifacts at Mesa Verde, but it also included the looting of habitation sites in Cottonwood Wash, in Butler Wash, on Cedar Mesa, and down into Grand Gulch—all locations within the Bears Ears cultural landscape, homeland for Native Americans for millennia. Antiquities Act scholar Hal Rothman explains that the law

> answered an important need in a culture trying to define itself... Natural wonders and prehistoric ruins testified to a longer American past and afforded a heritage that could be compared to that of Europe with its ancient castles and temples. Amid this cultural nationalism and the contemporary pillaging of archaeological

> remains in the Southwest, it became vital to protect such features from depredation and exploitation. Hence the Antiquities Act.[46]

Scholars back East sought to protect prehistoric sites as part of America's past, to give our young nation a time frame to rival ancient European and Middle Eastern civilizations as a form of cultural nationalism. Another group of Easterners sought to permanently designate the Bears Ears region as home for a modern tribe. Most of San Juan County, Utah, almost became an Indian reservation when a decade of struggle for Bluff Mormons had just begun to pay off.

Hundreds of prospectors flowed through town buying goods and supplies as part of a brief gold boom associated with mineral deposits and placer mining along the San Juan River in the winter of 1892–1893.[47] The mining excitement did not last long because the tiny amounts of gold that existed were in flakes so small as to be compared to baking flour, not sizable nuggets but tiny "flour gold," or flakes almost invisible among the river's cobbles and sandbars. The prospecting boom quickly bust, but it began an attraction for mining and mineral extraction that would continue in San Juan County into the twenty-first century. The potential for mineral wealth helped fuel Utah territory's fierce resistance to having southeast Utah become a sizable Indian reservation just as the territory reached for statehood in 1896.

How did Bears Ears National Monument almost become an Indian reservation? Over a century ago Durango businessmen actively campaigned to remove the Southern Utes to San Juan County, Utah. Most of San Juan County would have become a new 2.9 million-acre Ute Indian reservation. The businessmen almost succeeded, but they were thwarted by a group from Philadelphia named the Indian Rights Association that interceded on the Utes' behalf. What happened, and what didn't happen, forever changed Bears Ears history, but it also established records and remarks proving Ute cultural knowledge of the landscape.

Despite their cultural biases, representatives of the Indian Rights Association also provide an interesting descriptive analysis of the Bears Ears landscape and the few small white communities that would not exist "were it not for the peculiar discipline and perseverance of the Mormon church."[48] Echoing the sentiments of Captain Macomb from 1859, unappreciative of sandstone canyons, and unaware of archaeological assets, Philadelphia-based writers complained, "Except for the purpose of stock-raising the entire country between Indian Creek and the San Juan is absolutely good for nothing."[49] They decried "the expanse of absolutely dry and useless country which forms the greater part of the proposed reservation."[50]

By 1880 the Southern Utes in Colorado were relegated to a narrow strip of land adjacent to New Mexico, 15 miles wide and 110 miles long. As Durango thrived, farmers, ranchers, and businessmen coveted the long rectangle of the Ute reservation.[51] They schemed to have the Utes move to southeast Utah onto mesas, plateaus, and deep canyons already contested between fifty Mormon families living in Bluff City, Monticello, and La Sal and large cattle companies. Both proponents and opponents of the move claimed their intentions were to benefit the Utes.

Coloradans complained that the rectangular shape of the reservation presented a barrier to whites living on each side. Proponents for Ute removal argued the Southern Utes themselves wanted more isolation in the proposed Utah reservation that lay "outside of the track of the white man, is hemmed in by rivers and canons, is adapted to grazing, and abounds in game." Utes were to receive the wild, uncharted, and unmapped San Juan Triangle or the canyon country between the San Juan River on the south and the Colorado River on the north. In 1892 Senator Edward Wolcott from Colorado introduced Senate Bill No. 362 for Ute removal to Utah. The Indian Rights Association sent a representative to scout the area. He described San Juan County as a "'no man's land' owing to the extreme scarcity of running water . . . where there is sufficient water the altitude is too great for farming, and where the altitude is not too great there is no water."[52] Along sixty-two miles of the San Juan River, only 160 acres had been farmed. For Indian advocates who sought to turn Southern Utes into farmers, that was unacceptable. The Indian Rights Association fought vigorously to prevent the move, even as Indian Agent David Day from Durango not only supported it but also told the Utes to pack their horses and teepees and head to Utah, which many families did. The Indian Rights Association argued, "No removal of Indians from their homes should be dictated purely by greed of white men for Indian land, but primarily by considerations affecting the welfare of the Indians themselves."[53]

While the Indian Rights Association protested, Day and others encouraged the Utes to move while also prodding Congress to act. In December 1894 Congress debated whether to give San Juan County, Utah, to the Southern Utes who had begun to settle in Dry Valley, which is now the flat strip of BLM land north of Monticello and south of Moab, punctuated

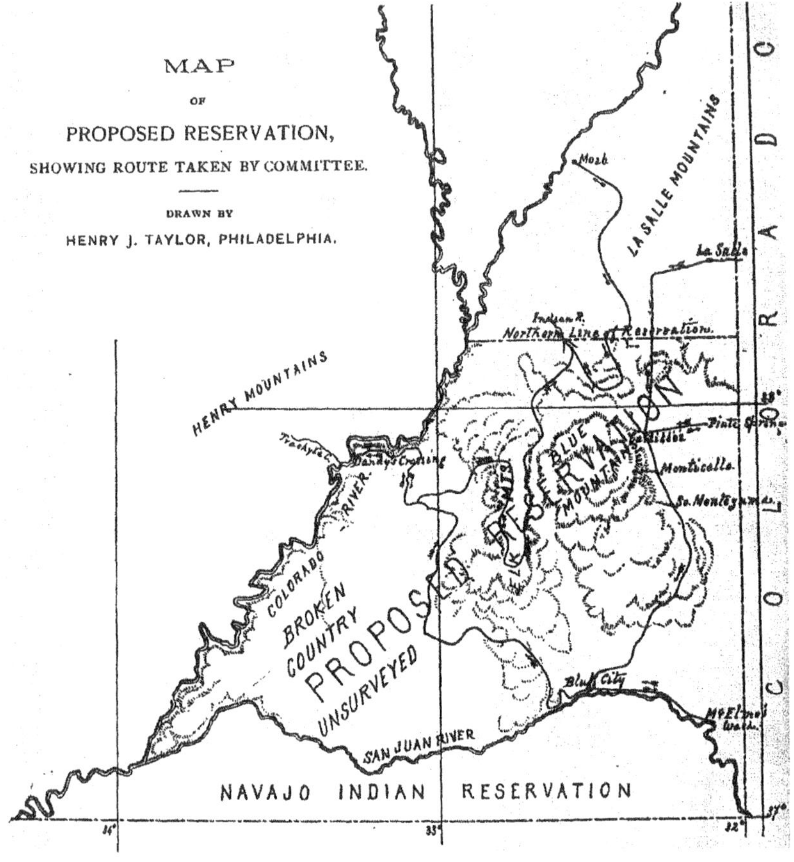

The Indian Rights Association of Philadelphia, Pennsylvania fought hard to allow the Southern Utes and Ute Mountain Utes to keep their land in Colorado rather than be moved to this proposed reservation which would have taken up all of Bears Ears and most of San Juan County, Utah. Map from the Indian Rights Association Report, 1892. Author's collection.

by Church Rock, a landmark that resembles a massive sandstone teapot. But too many cattle and sheep had already decimated the grass. Severe overgrazing had begun. Utes with their large horse herds took over water holes and springs at Hart Draw, Hatch Point, Silvey Pocket, and elsewhere. "It was a desperate situation," explained Utah pioneer Frank Silvey. "We learned that Durango people, feeling sure the Indian removable bill [would] pass the Senate and with President Cleveland's signature would become law in a few weeks, [Utes] through the Indian Agent David F. Day were told to come to San Juan County. It was theirs; 'Washington City Man' had given it to them, so the Indians were honest in this matter and were overjoyed to come here." He added, "The Southern Utes had long wished for San Juan County as their own, with at that time thousands of deer . . . thousands of acres of natural meadows at La Sal with fine clear water and many springs . . . Can you blame them?" [54]

Coloradans believed San Juan County to be "a desert country inhabited by large cattle owners and cowboys, a few Mormons, and plenty of outlaws. It was no good and the Utes should have it." Speaking at a tense public meeting in a crowded log church and meetinghouse in San Juan County, Mariano, a headman under Chief Ignacio, thundered,

> Washington City Man tell us to come here, sit down. We sit down. All over this country, it is ours. Now you say we get out and go back to our reservation. What's the matter now? We stay. Our fathers, our grandfathers, and our great-great-grandfathers have hunted here for many, many snows. We love this country, it's the 'Happy Hunting Ground' for us on earth. We feel the 'Great spirit' wants us to stay here. Washington City Man say all right, so we stay.[55]

But Utah's territorial governor Caleb West sided with Mormon settlers.[56] He said, "I feel you have been unjustly encroached upon by the Indians, although they are right in a way. They must go."[57] Meanwhile, the Indian Rights Association petitioned the halls of Congress for the Southern Utes to be returned.

On February 20, 1895 the fifty-third Congress voted on the Hunter bill, H.R. 6792 "to disapprove the treaty heretofore made with the Southern Ute Indians to be removed to the territory of Utah, and providing for settling them down in severalty where they may so elect and are qualified, and to settle all those not electing to take lands in severalty on the west forty miles of present reservation."[58] By the middle of March 1895 few Southern Utes remained in Dry Valley killing and eating Carlisle ranch cattle. Indian Police rounded up those who had stayed. By September 30, 1895, Francis E. Leupp of the Indian Rights Association published *The Latest Phase of the Southern Ute Question*. He summarized that "although the Southern Utes were disposed to be peaceful . . . the citizens of Colorado were resolved to get rid of them altogether."[59] Leupp added, "Perhaps it would be safe to say that no negotiation ever attempted with a tribe of Indians has given rise to so much public discussion as this."[60]

The Indian Rights Association demanded the Southern Utes settle down and become farmers on their Colorado reservation. This left the Bears Ears region intact as public land in San Juan County, Utah, despite Ute Indian claims to it.

Against their wishes, Southern Utes were forced to have their Colorado reservation broken up in severalty or allotments of private property in a version of the Dawes Act, which "The Friends of the Indian" had championed. Indian families took the land they wanted in minimal amounts of acreage, and then non-native families could purchase whatever land remained. Funds from the purchases were supposed to support Southern Utes who lost thousands of surface acres within their reservation but retained valuable mineral rights. Those Ute members who refused to break up Indian ownership of the reservation, including Chief Ignacio, moved to the far west end of their reservation and established the Ute Mountain Ute Reservation eventually with an agency at Towaoc. The Weminuche Band kept their property in tribal hands and later would become the administrative home for the White Mesa Band of mixed Utes and Paiutes living just south of Blanding, Utah.[61]

Lands that President Barack Obama set aside as Bears Ears National Monument in southeast Utah might have become Ute tribal lands. Certainly, the Utes felt comfortable there and wanted to own their historical landscape so they could hunt and graze their horse herds undisturbed by white men.

In the mid-1890s few settlers wanted living Native Americans in the canyon country of southeast Utah, but collectors certainly wanted dead Indians. Prehistoric mummies were sensationalized. These were human remains, reverently buried by Basketmaker people centuries ago, not cloth-wrapped like Egyptian mummies. The dry desert air in canyon country preserved these Basketmaker remains often with their own wrappings and covered in carefully woven baskets. Historical accounts refer to them as mummies. These ancient burials became highly sought after. In Bluff, Platte Lyman uncovered a mummy in Allen Canyon wrapped in a fabric and feather blanket. He stored the desiccated corpse in his cellar before it journeyed to the World's Fair. Children coming to view it nicknamed the deceased "the King of Blue Mountain."[62]

In 1894 Volume II of *The Archaeologist* published "Recent Finds in Utah" including a report of ninety-two skeletons taken from a cave with the conclusion that, "This is, by far, one of the most interesting collection[s] of human remains of a single tribe yet found in America. Each skeleton, carefully studied, reveals the manner of death. We found one interesting group, a mother with an infant on each arm, and another lying on her breast with its head under her chin."[63] The same journal reported from Salt Lake City about "Mummies in the San Juan Valley," and how "An exhibit of mummies, alleged to have been recently found in caves between the Elk and the Bule (sic) Mountains, at the head of the Comb Wash, which empties into the San Juan River, ten miles below Bluff City, Utah, was opened in a room in a hotel this week. There are six, all very well preserved."[64]

A longer and more accurate story authored by University of Utah professor Henry Montgomery went into greater detail about how "there has recently been brought to Salt Lake City a rare collection of pre-historic remains, said to have been collected by Mssers. C.B. Lang and Nielsen during the past three months in San Juan County."[65] That story also made it into a Rochester, New York newspaper that described the Bears Ears region and Allen Canyon's "cliffs and peaks of pink, vermillion, brown, white, and yellow, rising in ledges and breaking into tier above tier, story above story with intervening slopes covered with talus, the walls recessed with huge spurs and decorated with towers and pinnacles." The expedition found nearly twenty graves where "the lower caves were reached by climbing the projecting points on the bluffs; but the higher ones were reached only by ladders and ropes after incalculable labor and imminent risk of being dashed to death one hundred to two hundred feet below."[66]

The exploits of early archaeological expeditions caught the imagination of Americans fascinated by human remains, wooden artifacts, stone knives, and descriptions of Basketmaker burials with corpses tied in yucca cords, wrapped in turkey-feather blankets, and surrounded by carefully woven baskets. In southeast Utah relic hunters dug Grand Gulch the winter of 1890–1891, the summer of 1891, 1892, and the winters of 1893–1894 and 1894–1895. Charles B. Lang explored Cottonwood Canyon and Comb Wash in 1897–1898. T.M. Prudden spent various seasons from 1894 to 1902 in the San Juan Watershed. The fruits of their labors would eventually settle in a variety of prestigious eastern museums including the American Museum of Natural History in New York City, the Peabody Museum of Natural History at Harvard, the University of Pennsylvania Museum, Brigham Young University's Museum of Peoples and Cultures, the Field Museum in Chicago, the Lowie Museum of Anthropology at the University of California, Berkeley, and the National Museum of the American Indian.[67] Even as other collectors swarmed into the Bears Ears region to dig in caves and alcoves, local men acted as guides and "excavators" beginning a tradition that would last into the twenty-first century both with legal permits and without them.[68]

As Bluff men rode north to hunt for relics, a rancher from the Dugout Ranch at Indian Creek rode southwest. *The Telluride Daily Journal* on August 14, 1896 reported on the front page "Relics of a Past Age:

Richard Wetherill posed for this portrait at the 1904 St. Louis World's Fair. CANM 2001.2.P.24.0. Photo courtesy of BLM—Canyons of the Ancients Visitor Center and Museum.

An Interesting Collection of Pottery, Beads, Etc. From the Ruins of the Cliff Dwellers" discovered by rancher Ed Turner. He dug up "a large earthen vessel perfect in condition and of native workmanship," a prehistoric cotton blanket and a sixteen-foot-long string of red and black beads.[69] This blanket is the only color-dyed Ancestral Puebloan weaving known to exist. The beads, like many bodies wrenched from graves, have been lost. Across the Southwest, looting continued with the Bears Ears region a prime center for digging. Living Native peoples were forced onto reservations, the graves of their ancestors routinely desecrated.

For scholars from back East, traveling in San Juan County and through Bears Ears represented both rugged adventure and cutting-edge scientific inquiry in trying to date the age of occupation for the cliff dwellers and those who came before. Paradoxically, explorers scornfully described modern Native Americans struggling "from savagery toward civilization" and yet wrote romantically about their ancient relatives. A year after Ed Turner uncovered what became known as the Telluride blanket, physician T. Mitchell Prudden wrote in *Harper's New Monthly Magazine* about Pueblo Indians he had met. He sarcastically commented, "When such people get on cotton shirts, need coffee and sugar, want rum, and begin to name their sons after Presidents . . . they will not continue long to send messages to the gods by rattlesnakes, nor propitiate the elements with feathers and songs."[70]

Prudden hired Al Wetherill to guide him into southeast Utah where Prudden noted his bias that "access from Bluff to the plateau is mostly by dim and devious Indian trails which meander along the rough bottoms of the canyons."[71] As a New Yorker he came to respect his guides, the value of water, the coolness of a desert night after a blistering hot day, and "a nameless witchery of the air, which makes all far things strange and beautiful, and which more than all else lures back the wanderer to these hot wastes year after year."[72]

Prudden wrote about Richard Wetherill's discovery of Basketmakers living in alcove sites before the cliff dwellers, though the exact time sequence was yet unknown. "It is with Richard Wetherill's permission that I record this interesting discovery of the Basket-Makers which he and his brothers made some time ago," Prudden explained in *Harper's*. "I am eager to do this because the enthusiasm, devotion, and practical knowledge which he has brought to his life work in the cause of American archaeology should find more general appreciation."[73] But it did not. The budding field of archaeology and professionally trained archaeologists

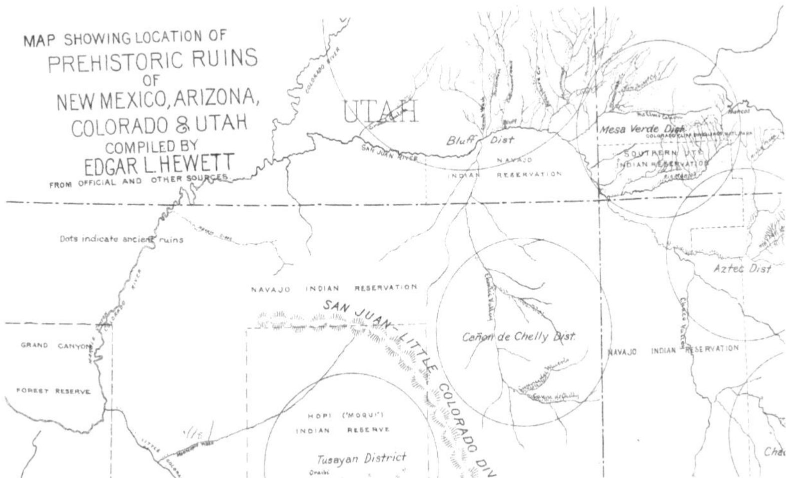

This detail of Edgar Lee Hewett's map, part of his report to Congress on the need to pass the Antiquities Act of 1906, shows the vast number of archaeological sites in the southern part of Bears Ears and in the Bluff and Mesa Verde Districts. Author's collection.

had little use for cowboy amateurs. Though the Wetherills earned the utmost respect of the scholars and tourists they guided, Richard would become a target of criticism and his collections of artifacts the impetus for a new federal law. For Richard and his brothers, "The changing times in which they lived involved pioneering efforts of exploration, discovery, and searches for meaning among ruins in an isolated, mystical landscape known as the Four Corners," notes Blackburn. "Infighting often erupted over archaeological territories, fed by political maneuvering among scholars for 'ownership' of excavations. Vehement disagreements and petty conflicts were the norm."[74] James Snead agrees. In *Ruins and Rivals* he writes about Richard, "While Wetherill's clients respected his abilities, they did not accord him the status of a scholar. The growing rift between the scholarly and public audiences for Southwest archaeology would result in resentment and resistance."[75]

As America entered the twentieth century professionals linked to academic universities or to the burgeoning field of state, regional, and national museums ironically condemned the artifact collectors whose very collections bolstered the reputation of their institutions. Writing in the *American Anthropologist* in 1903 about the prehistoric ruins of the San Juan Watershed, T. Mitchell Prudden complained that "great injury has been wrought to the interests of archaeology by the widespread, unlicensed, random digging among the ruins and burials." He concluded,

> In the early days, before the problems connected with these ruins had become clear and definite, the simple collection of pottery and other utensils was natural and not without justification. But it is now evident that to gather or exhume specimens—even though these be destined to grace a World's Fair or a noted museum—without at the same time carefully, systematically, and completely studying the ruins from which they are derived, with full records, measurements, and photographs, is to risk the permanent loss of much valuable data and to sacrifice science for the sake of plunder.[76]

One of the most aggressive critics of amateur collectors was Edgar L. Hewett. He would become the first president of New Mexico State Normal School in Las Vegas, New Mexico, help create the School of American Research in Santa Fe, and devise prehistoric exhibits for the Pan-American Exhibition in San Diego. He wrote a "Circular Relating to Historic and Prehistoric Ruins of the Southwest and Their Preservation." Published in 1904, this document became the rationale for Congressional testimony

Richard Wetherill and party working in Grand Gulch for the Whitmore Exploring Expedition, 1897. Image #338269 Courtesy of the American Museum of Natural History Library.

prior to passage of the Antiquities Act in 1906 for which Hewett laid out the provisions.

"Every cliff dwelling, every prehistoric tower, communal house, shrine and burial mound is an object which can contribute something to the advancement of knowledge, and hence is worthy of preservation," Hewett began.[77] Of the Bears Ears region he wrote, "All the ruins of the San Juan and its tributaries have suffered much from destructive collectors."[78] "Comparatively little is known of the numerous ruins in southeastern Utah. They have been explored and the district mapped by Dr. T. Mitchell Prudden, of New York City, but as yet no close investigations have been undertaken," Hewett noted. He explained that numerous ruins could be found "along Montezuma Creek, Recapture Creek, Cottonwood Creek, Butler Wash, Comb Wash, and Grand Gulch." He mentioned the Hyde Exploring Expedition led by Richard Wetherill, and he used the phrase "basket makers."[79]

W.H. Holmes, artist, surveyor, explorer, and now chief of the Bureau of Ethnology at the Smithsonian Institution, added one of many support letters to the congressional deliberations. Hewett argued that the United States had preserved its timber reserves and it should also protect its archaeological sites. With President Theodore Roosevelt in the White House, momentum increased for cultural resource protection to match natural resource protection. Roosevelt's friend Senator Henry Cabot Lodge sponsored a version of the bill in the senate. A US Senate hearing on April 20, 1904 before the Committee on Public Lands included valuable testimony.

"The general public has awakened to a realization of the importance of preserving in America these remains of the past, not simply for present interest, but for the future. They are being obliterated every day," offered Dr. Francis W. Kelsey, secretary of the Archaeological Institute of America.[80] The Reverend Dr. Henry Mason Baum referred specifically to the Wetherills when he testified, "Among the first to excavate for commercial purposes were three brothers in Colorado, who saw the commercial value of the Pueblo and Cliff ruins. They began with the Cliff Palace, in southern Colorado, which is one of the most interesting ruins in the world. They went through it thoroughly."[81] By 1904 the Wetherills had lost Alamo Ranch at Mancos. The brothers scattered to different occupations across the Southwest and established trading posts. At Chaco Canyon in northwest New Mexico Richard and brother Al began a trading post for the Navajos, whom they hired for extensive excavation for the American Museum of Natural History in New York City. The Navajos nicknamed Richard "Anasazi" because of his obsession with digging

Ancestral Puebloan remains at ancient sites like Chaco.[82] Testifying at the senate hearing about the Wetherill brothers, Baum complained, "They went through many of the ruins of the San Juan watershed, in which there are over 1,600," Baum continued. "Then they went through the Chaco Canyon, where one of them has now a large trading station."[83]

Five themes running through the human history of the Bears Ears region include adventure, archaeology, exploration, refuge, and resistance. If collecting artifacts and human remains in San Juan County helped inspire the Antiquities Act, so did its geologic wonders. In White Canyon in 1883 Cass Hite claimed to have been the first Anglo to see large stone bridges formed by water running under them. Chasing cows, rancher J.A. Scorup found the bridges in 1895. They remained more rumor than fact until Scorup guided Horace Long there in 1903. W.W. Dyar used Long's notes to write about this scientific phenomenon in *Century Magazine* and *National Geographic* in 1904.[84] Now other Utah residents, far removed from San Juan County, wanted to see the bridges too.

A canyon country trip became adventure and exploration for Salt Lake City businessmen out to promote their state. This new trend of adventure tourism would have long lasting implications for local residents who provided supplies and guides. For the first time in March 1905 visitors came to San Juan County not to exploit the landscape for grass, minerals or antiquities but who just wanted to see it. "The lone traveler—hunter, artist or recorder of places and events—was long a part of the western scene," wrote Charlie R. Steen, "With easier and faster methods of travel the trickle of tourists became an ever increasing stream, and sporadic efforts were made to open up the wilder sections of the West and to make their features known to the general public."[85] Certainly, the canyons of San Juan County, Utah, as they embraced the Bears Ears region and drained to the Colorado and San Juan Rivers, represented wild country. And it was wild country that appealed to President Roosevelt as debates over the Antiquities Act worked their way through Congress.

The businessmen of the Salt Lake Commercial Club under organizer Edwin F. Holmes expected the trip to take six weeks with local guides and cooks procured in Bluff including rancher Al Scorup as expedition field leader.[86] The group took ropes, harness, and measuring equipment to see if the bridges really were as large as had been rumored. On this first major expedition to the bridges, artist H.L.A. Culmer kept a diary and noted poor range conditions south of Moab. "Feed is scarce all along the line as the country is sheep-cursed," he wrote. "The grass that is disposed to grow freely is stamped out by the sheep."[87] Local men serving as guides and outfitters began to realize that leading tourists might be an easier occupation than cowboying, especially when groups like the Salt Lake Commercial Club willingly hired four men and twenty horses for their White Canyon trip. Sandstone scenery had new value for the descendants of families who had come through the Hole-in-the-Rock. They had spent years trying to survive in the canyons. Now tourists were coming to see a landscape the Mormon families knew well.

As the Commercial Club's springtime expedition left Bluff headed to the natural bridges, Culmer wrote, "We certainly made a startling effect as we passed thro the town of Bluff and most of the populace turned out to see us depart. I never enjoyed myself better than today." As their guides took the group over Comb Ridge, into Comb Wash and up on to Cedar Mesa and the heart of Bears Ears, Culmer exclaimed, "We were at a high altitude, and the view in every direction was superb; rocky canyons, breaks and cliffs, the Blues to the North East, the Elks to the N.W. where we were heading, and swooping swirling thunderheads everywhere. Then the rain overtook us and every rock and cliff glistened in the sunshine."[88]

As they entered an alcove and deep cave the artist Culmer commented, "Evidences of cave dwellers have almost been obliterated but are still plain, the rocks squared up and 'bonded' just as a modern mason would do." As afternoon gave way to twilight and darkness he painted a word picture in his diary, "Outside, the moon is breaking through indigo clouds, and the whole scene is weird. Tales of robbers retreats, and pictures of old time gatherings of ancient tribes in this important cave come to the mind and fill the night with strange dreams." The next day, March 13, 1905, he saw the Bears Ears themselves: "To the East was Elk Ridge, above which the flat-topped Bears Ears towered a thousand feet and [were] covered with snow."[89] He commented that their cook Franklin Adams "has had a lot of experience in digging out cave and cliff dwellings" and that he had found a large clay water jar and woven willow sticks "used for coffin making" by the Ancestral Puebloans.[90]

As the group measured and surveyed the natural bridges, they also climbed into adjacent cliff dwellings. On April 16, H.L.A. Culmer wrote, "The afternoon was spent in climbing high places in search of Moqui? Or Aztec? ruins and relics. By the aid of ropes and ladders, we got to ledges that no white man had scaled, but found little to reward our labors. Whitaker and I each drew out a stone ax or hammer, unusually well preserved with handles complete."[91] The next day he added a comment that future generations of Bears Ears tourists would agree with. Culmer claimed, "We are getting to know our feet better and fearlessly go in places that a few days ago would have taken the color from our cheeks."[92] They entered the upper level of Bare Ladder Ruin which still has well-preserved and intact roofs.[93] After leaving White Canyon, Scorup guided them through Grand Gulch, where "ruins of ancient people are around us now on every side" before the expedition returned to Bluff and home via the railroad at Dolores, Colorado.[94] As the Commercial Club returned to Salt Lake City to promote both natural bridges and its adjacent archaeology, in the halls of Congress politicians debated how to protect sites on public land that had historic and scientific value. They would do so in a single, brief federal law that provided exceptional executive powers.

Writing about the Antiquities Act, legal scholar Mark Squillace states, "There seems little doubt that the impetus for the law that would eventually become the Antiquities Act was the desire of archaeologists to protect aboriginal objects and artifacts." He adds, "Following the discovery of such noted sites as Chaco Canyon and Mesa Verde, as well as dozens of lesser sites, private collecting of artifacts on public lands by both professionals and amateurs threatened to rob the public of its cultural heritage."[95] National Park Service historian Ronald F. Lee concurs and adds that digging Chaco artifacts by the Wetherills "hastened the movement for administrative and legislative action in Washington, DC."[96] At the 1893 Chicago World's Fair the H.J. Smith Exploring Company showcased hundreds of artifacts the Wetherill brothers had dug out of ruins at Mesa Verde. The artifacts were displayed on shelves in a large replica of Battle Rock from McElmo Canyon in what is now Canyons of the Ancients National Monument in southwest Colorado.[97] For a quarter, visitors could walk through the replica rock probably made of plaster of Paris and hemp fiber over steel framing. They could see real specimens from "an extinct race, leaving no history by which modern investigators may arrive at a definite knowledge of the age in which they lived."[98]

With Nordenskiold back in Sweden, Wetherill needed a new source of funding for expeditions and excavations. He found it at the fair in two young brothers from New York, B. Talbot Hyde and Frederick E. Hyde, heirs to a fortune made from laundry soap and dedicated to collecting. The Hydes had been interested in Wetherill's work in Grand Gulch in San Juan County, Utah, but after visiting San Juan County, New Mexico, two years after the fair, Richard Wetherill proposed another field of work in Chaco Canyon. The Hydes and the Hyde Exploring Expedition created in 1896 would help fund trading posts and excavations while Frederick Putnam from Harvard University chose his student George Pepper to direct the field work. The Hydes gave many, but not all, of the artifacts to New York's American Museum of Natural History. Richard Wetherill became excavation foreman, hired numerous Navajos to dig, and began to unearth and dismantle eight centuries from the very center of the Ancestral Puebloan world. The results were staggering and earned the envy and anger of academics.

Pepper and Wetherill dug into Pueblo Bonito, a stunning five-story ruin amid the aridity of Chaco Wash on the Navajo Reservation. Despite summer heat and merciless gnats, for three summers from 1896 to 1899, Wetherill dug relentlessly 198 rooms and kivas. Special Agent J.S. Holsinger from the General Land Office reported in 1891, "Richard Wetherill and his brothers had removed entire prehistoric timbers from Pueblo Bonito, dismantled and shipped complete rooms to the American Museum of Natural History, and probably had excavated other prehistoric objects and sold them wherever they could find a market."[99]

As yet, no laws protected America's archaeological resources on public lands. What the Hydes sponsored and what Richard Wetherill directed was not illegal; however, he attempted an interesting step to consolidate this artifact-rich site. Wetherill tried to acquire it by patent under the 1862 Homestead Act which allowed anyone to go out on the public domain and claim 160 acres if their intention was to fence it, farm it, and live on it. Wetherill built a house and trading post close to Pueblo Bonito, and he continued to dig what is now a World Heritage Site and one of the great archaeological centers in North America. He also agreed to relinquish his claim and to allow the federal government to put his claims at Pueblo Bonito and other land holdings by his wife in public trust, but that story has been obscured. "We are pleased to do this as we think no Individual should have them," Wetherill wrote on January 14, 1906 to G.F. Pollock, Acting Commissioner of the General Land Office.[100] Instead of acknowledging Wetherill's role in discovering and naming the Basketmakers and his family's attempt to seek national park status for Mesa Verde, Wetherill has been vilified.

Six years before his relinquishment in Chaco Canyon, the *Santa Fe New Mexican* wrote about Richard Wetherill, "[H]e expressed a sincere hope that some early action be taken either by the national government or the New Mexican authorities looking to the preservation of the prehistoric cliff dwellings located in San Juan and Santa Fe counties." The reporter continued, "He said it was the duty of the present generation not to permit the wrecking and destruction of these communal houses by pothunters whose sole object it is to unearth their curious and varied contents and sell them to speculators."[101] Yet some historians consider Richard Wetherill to be the quintessential pothunter.

"The spectre of Richard Wetherill may well have been the most important catalyst in galvanizing support for legislation to protect southwestern antiquities," noted Rothman. "Richard Wetherill provided American preservation with a fragile consensus. The GLO [General Land Office] and its special agents advocated preservation because they saw him as a hindrance to the process of bringing law and order to the West."[102] Rothman's comments seem exaggerated, but there is no question that the Wetherills, and Richard in particular, had become scapegoats in the government's push for Progressive Era regulation and control of cultural resources on public lands. In fact, the Wetherill family had written for help from the Smithsonian Institution and urged the protection of cliff dwellings. Richard's father B.K. Wetherill stated in a letter, "I think the Mancos, and tributary canons should be reserved as a national park, in order to preserve the curious cliff houses. The country is exceedingly rough and of no earthly use, except for the curiosities."[103] In the haste to stop pothunting, the family's early advocacy for Mesa Verde National Park and its "tributary canons" would be forgotten.

At committee hearings for the Antiquities Act, archaeological experts described the destruction of remote ruins in the Southwest. They also debated provisions in the House and Senate bills that would require the Department of the Interior to issue research and excavation permits, the principle that all museums and institutions would have equal access to those permits and that no excavation could occur on public lands without a permit. Utah governor Heber M. Wells supported the legislation as did the president of the University of Utah J.T. Kingsbury who wrote, "This bill is a step in the right direction, and many regret that such a step was not taken long ago."[104] As the House and Senate hammered out compromise versions of the bill, committee members fought to preserve archaeological sites on the ground as well as to require excavation permits. The law is extraordinary in its brevity. In a single sentence, the Act for the Preservation of American Antiquities states,

> The President of the United States is authorized, in his discretion, to declare by public proclamation historic landmarks, historic and

> prehistoric structures, and other objects of historic or scientific interest that are situated upon the lands owned or controlled by the Government of the United States to be national monuments, and may reserve as a part thereof parcels of land, the limits of which in all cases shall be confined to the smallest area compatible with the proper care and management of the objects to be protected.[105]

After decades of digging on America's public lands and the looting of dozens of sites in the Bears Ears region by various groups, finally in June 1906 President Theodore Roosevelt signed into law the Antiquities Act. He protected ancient Basketmaker and Ancestral Puebloan sites and other archaeological sites around the nation. With small fines of only $500 for illegal digging and with no enforcement on public lands, the law originally had little effect. But that same month Roosevelt also signed Congressional legislation creating Mesa Verde National Park as the world's first cultural park to protect not just scenery, but the ancient ruins made famous by Gustaf Nordenskiold and the Wetherills.

At the beginning of the twentieth century, contemporary Native Americans suffered ill health, starvation, and restrictions on Indian reservations where they had few freedoms. At least now their ancestors' graves on public lands were protected by law. In San Juan County, Utah, President Roosevelt extended the Navajo reservation north of the San Juan River. In New Mexico he declared Chaco Canyon a national monument in 1907 and a year later signed into law Natural Bridges National Monument west of Blanding. In later years other presidents set aside Rainbow Bridge National Monument in San Juan County as well as Hovenweep National Monument on the Colorado-Utah border.

Pothunting continued in the Bears Ears region. Adventurers and explorers paid to travel into canyon country to see it for themselves and perhaps to find unknown sites hidden in sandstone alcoves to rival Mesa Verde's Spruce Tree House, Long House, Balcony House, or Cliff Palace. Ironically after so much looting had taken place along Comb Ridge, across Cedar Mesa, and into the depths of Grand Gulch, none of the small cliff dwellings in the Bears Ears region were declared national monuments. The digging up of baskets, pots, skeletons, and mummies, their display in urban hotel rooms and their listing in collectors' catalogs, had inspired the Antiquities Act. But the canyon country archaeological sites of San Juan County would not be declared part of a national monument until 110 years after the passage of the law. Then Bears Ears

National Monument would be supported by environmental and archaeological groups across the nation but even more importantly, and for the first time in the history of the Antiquities Act, by five Native American tribes honoring their ancestors.

In those first years of the twentieth century, Native Americans were not US citizens. They could not vote. They could not sit on juries. Their children were forcibly taken by US marshals to attend boarding schools in far-off states. Frightened children had their hair shaved, their clothes burned, replaced by starchy uniforms for boys and full-length dresses for girls. If Native American children spoke their Native tongue, they were forced to eat soap. Teachers beat them. Artifacts and archaeology of prehistoric Native Americans held scientific value, but not the actual culture of living Natives. They were to become "civilized." In the early 1900s in the Bears Ears region resistance continued against the federal government, against a law protecting antiquities, and against the new United States Forest Service.

CHAPTER 8

The US Forest Service, Natural Bridges, and the Last Indian War, 1907–1923

> There is no zest like that of exploration, no longing like that for desert places, no call like that of the unknown.
>
> —Clyde Kluckhohn, *Beyond the Rainbow*

> In the canyons of the desert country the forgotten houses of the Old People were standing—their windows black against red cliffs. Forgotten houses of a people worn out by a long struggle with drought and hail, worn out by intermarriage, moving in search of life . . .
>
> —Frances Gilmore & Louisa Wade Wetherill, *Traders to the Navajo*

In the first two decades of the twentieth century, Native and Mormon families in San Juan County continued their paths of resistance, but in starkly different ways. For many ranchers, the Bears Ears could be seen from almost anywhere as a physical landmark on public lands and as a cultural landmark for Native Americans as it always had been. Natives and Mormon ranchers adjusted to an uneasy truce except when ranchers pushed their stock into traditional grazing areas claimed by Native leaders and their kinship bands. Ranching families grazed all the range west from Bluff, established in 1880, west from Monticello, established in 1887, and west from Grayson, later Blanding, first started by Albert Lyman the same year as the US Forest Service began in 1905. These isolated, insular Mormon communities remained far from the broad sweep of American commerce.

US President from 1901 to 1909, conservationist Theodore Roosevelt understood the American West better than any president before or since. He had ranched near Medora, North Dakota, lost half his inheritance in the bitter blizzard of 1886–1887 when his cattle froze and died, and he saw firsthand the need for protection of America's forest lands because of overgrazing and soil erosion. A prominent early progressive who believed in corporate responsibility and government regulation, Roosevelt took forest reserves administered by the Department of the Interior and under the direction of his Chief Forester Gifford Pinchot, created the US Forest Service in the Department of Agriculture. In those early years of the twentieth century, Mormon sheep and cattle ranchers in San Juan County had finally outlasted the large Texas cattle herds, but grasses had suffered. Federal regulations increased with the creation of the US Forest Service and the withdrawal of public lands into the La Sal National Forest in 1906, the same year President Roosevelt signed the Antiquities Act. Roosevelt, who would declare seven new national monuments, including Natural Bridges, would also work to conserve the West's rangelands at higher elevations. Mormon ranchers resisted government regulations on Forest Service land along Elk Ridge and the base of the Blue Mountains.

Native families resisted both Mormon encroachment on their traditional pastures as well as demands that their children be educated and assimilated into white men's ways, usually by physical removal from their homelands. San Juan County had Navajos and their herds of sheep north of the San Juan River along with Utes and Paiutes with horse and goat herds from the White Mesa area south of Blanding and in camps west of Bluff and at Sand Island. Only a few Natives spoke English and almost none wanted to give up their children to distant boarding schools. Sporadic confrontations between Natives and whites occurred over horse theft, cattle theft by hungry Natives, and cattle mutilation. With the murder of a Hispanic sheepherder, federal officers arrived. Native American leaders who resisted white encroachment and Anglo-imposed cultural values included the Navajo shaman Bai-a-lil-le from Aneth along the San Juan River, and Utes Mariano, Narraguinnep, Hatch, Polk, Tse-ne-gat, and Johnny Benow. Over eighty Utes would be forced into a barbed-wire stockade in the center of Blanding in 1923 in a deplorable event known as the Last Indian War, though one historian titles the event the Last White Uprising.[1] Posey, a Paiute, resisted to the very end and died at the north edge of Comb Ridge close to the Bears Ears. Just as cowboy archaeologists had exhumed Native American burials in the nineteenth century, locals dug up Posey three times, once for grisly photographs. Later, his body disappeared.

In the first decades of the twentieth century Basketmaker and Ancestral Puebloan sites in San Juan County attracted major explorations by archaeologists and well-heeled wealthy New Yorkers. To the southwest of Bears Ears, Rainbow Bridge, the largest natural sandstone bridge in the world, became a destination for writers, hikers, and ex-presidents. San Juan County, its mesas, canyons, and remoteness, descriptively appeared in *National Geographic*. Young men on a lark came to explore canyon country in an early version of adventure tourism.

Though the canyon country landscape was large, settlements remained small and thinly populated. Mormon families who had resisted antipolygamy laws and fled to Mexico came back to San Juan County in 1914 after Pancho Villa and other leaders began the Mexican Revolution. They arrived with little more than their clothing in suitcases having to abandon carefully tended farms and irrigated fields. Some families took advantage of homestead laws to claim private land and start over again near Monticello and La Sal. They grazed livestock on federal land, opposing new rules and regulations. Beyond the Bears Ears, Wooden Shoe and Dark Canyon became summer pastures with winter forage in White Canyon and dryer areas like Beef Basin. Local ranchers doubled the number of livestock their Forest Service permits authorized. Such excessive grazing destroyed native forage.[2] "Like Utah forests elsewhere, the La Sal was critically overgrazed and seriously eroded. Range users were slow to adopt managerial practices and vigorous in their resistance to boundary changes, reduction in numbers, and escalating fees," wrote historian Charles S. Peterson in *Look to the Mountains*.

The LaSal was among the hardest forests to manage because of the "refusal of large outfits to comply with regulations. In the years before 1920 virtually every large user was charged with malpractice and deceit."[3] Into these tight-knit Mormon communities of southeastern Utah came John Riis, the son of Jacob Riis, a photographer of the infamous Lower East Side of New York City who photographed slums and recently arrived immigrants. Jacob Riis became a fast friend and frequent dining companion in the White House with President Theodore Roosevelt because they had met when Roosevelt was a New York City Police Commissioner.[4]

Roosevelt's conservation champion Gifford Pinchot promoted John Riis as a new forest ranger. Riis came into his first job at Monticello near the Blue Mountains in 1907. He wrote memorable accounts of what he experienced. "We were all in a hard place. They did not know the new forest laws and I did not know the country. They had settled it and felt it was theirs." Though Riis eventually admitted, "In later years I came to know the true worth of those rugged Mormon settlers, an industrious, law abiding and loyal people whose friendship, once won, was well worth the price."[5] Getting to know the livestock grazers, however, was not easy. They had hardened opinions and were quick to share them. Armed rancher Parley Butts, with four adult sons in tow, stormed into Riis' cabin one morning and shouted,

> We cowmen came into this country before Uncle Sam even thought it worth lookin' at. When God finished makin' the world he had a lot of rocks left over an' he threw them down here in a pile in Utah. But we took it and settled it. We've killed off the Indians and the rattlesnakes and built roads and bridges to get in here. We've put up with all hell and damnation to make our homes here and never a bit of help did we get from Uncle Sam while we were doing it. Now, when we get the country halfway fit to live in, you come in here and tell us how much grass we can have and that we have got to pay for it and that we can put our cows on this here mountain

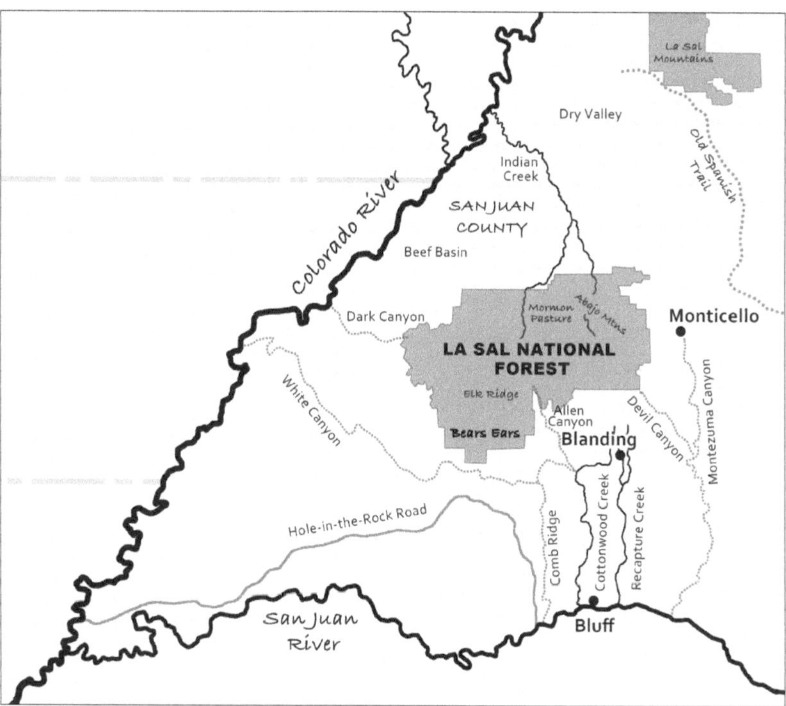

San Juan County, Utah had been wide-open public land with no rules or regulations. That began to change with establishment of the La Sal National Forest west of Blanding and Monticello in 1906. Area ranchers bitterly resisted grazing fees and stock reduction on already overgrazed lands. Map by DJ Webb © by author.

> for so long and no longer, by God! We will like hell. This is our country and we aim to keep it.[6]

Ranger Riis, caught reading in his cabin with only his long johns on, laughed. Butts wanted to know what was funny. Riis replied that he did not think Mr. Butts and his sons should start a war against Uncle Sam. They might shoot one forest ranger, but more would come.

Then Riis softened his response and reasoned, "You have to have some sort of system if the grass that is growing this year is to grow again next summer and the summer after next. The range can only stand so much and you cowmen are getting too thick on it . . . Look at it now. Do you want your cows to starve to death?"[7] Finally, moderate discussion began over allotments and grazing schedules. A focal point for the ranchers was Bears Ears. Riis described Elk Ridge as "a high mesa several miles long, its top a parkland dotted with clumps of scrub oak, aspen and pine. Its sheer walls dropping off into canyons hundreds of feet deep . . . Near its southern end two oddly shaped peaks rise for three hundred feet or more from the top of the mesa, looking for all the world like a bear's ears sticking up over the horizon."[8] Originally a city dweller, Riis loved the canyon country but shared local prejudice against the sixty or so "renegade" Ute Indians who refused to live on the reservation.

Riis wrote, "Headed by old Posey, a famous war chief in his day, and under pretext of herding their little flock of goats on the summer range, the Utes killed deer out of season, filched a mutton now and then, live a hand to mouth existence and made themselves a general nuisance" including appearing at ranchers' homes when men were away to badger women for food.[9] In his published memoir *Ranger Trails*, Riis shared a chilling story of local ranchers who returned to a mountain cabin one season "to find it had been broken into and all the provisions stolen by the Indians." In retaliation, at the end of the season in the fall before herding cows back to winter range, cowmen left in the cabin "a large batch of bread cooked up and set aside in the cupboard. They mixed in the dough two ounces of strychnine kept to poison predatory animals. Next spring the bread was gone. They never knew whether the Indians found and ate the bread but they were not troubled with housebreakers thereafter."[10] Whether a true story or just forest folklore, the idea that local ranchers would lace flour with poison would be repeated in Ute narratives.

Riis advanced from forest ranger to forest supervisor as he continued to ride the range. He met more Utes and befriended some. Others warned him not to dig for skeletal remains, which he did anyway, complaining that in a cave, "[w]e scratched around in the powder-fine dust with sticks in the hopes of stirring up a relic or two. The dust rose in a cloud, filling one's nostrils and making the throat and skin raspy and dry. Parts of four skeletons came to the surface but the skulls were missing."[11]

Like many others before and after him, Riis belittled and degraded resident Native American bands, yet was captivated by the landscape and the prehistoric past. "Here are canyons, whose walls rise for hundreds of feet, yet so narrow one can toss a stone from rim to rim with ease. Needle-like spires shoot from their depths into a turquoise sky . . . It is a land to dream over, for in some indefinable way it seems to present the story of creation; to hold locked in its rocky fastness tales that have been lost among the centuries."[12] Riis took subsequent Forest Service positions in California and Oregon. In southeast Utah he was the vanguard of government employees coming into the country with Pinchot's *Rule Book* to build cabins, fence springs, and try to enforce range regulations.

In 1907 a University of Utah expedition led by Byron Cummings visited the natural bridges in White Canyon and returned with more information, a topographic map, and photographs. Under the Antiquities Act passed by Congress the year before, the Archaeological Institute of America had transferred their research permit to all sites in Utah via the University of Utah. Edgar Lee Hewett, who had campaigned vigorously for the Act, signed the permit "for Examination, Excavation, and Gathering of Objects of Antiquity" on "the public lands of the state," effective June 1, 1907.[13]

Years later Neil M. Judd wrote a lively account of being a young archaeologist working with Professor Cummings. At one point the crew camped in Butler Wash. A Ute Indian came by on horseback to survey their camp. Through hand signals and a few words of Navajo that the Ute knew, Judd made it clear they were looking for "Anasazis, 'the ancient ones,' dead people." The Native American understood. "He knew where to find one and, for a dollar would show me. So I grabbed a shovel and plodded along behind his horse, up and over one sand dune and then another," Judd related in his memoirs. The Ute urged him on, and though fatigued, Judd kept walking until, "Finally, when I was becoming a bit weary with this endless pursuit, he stopped outside a wire fence, and pointed to the Bluff City cemetery." The budding archaeologist failed to see the humor in the Ute's escapade. Judd began the long walk back to camp.[14]

In White Canyon Cummings' crew explored ruins at short distances from each of the natural bridges. Judd described kivas, stone chambers,

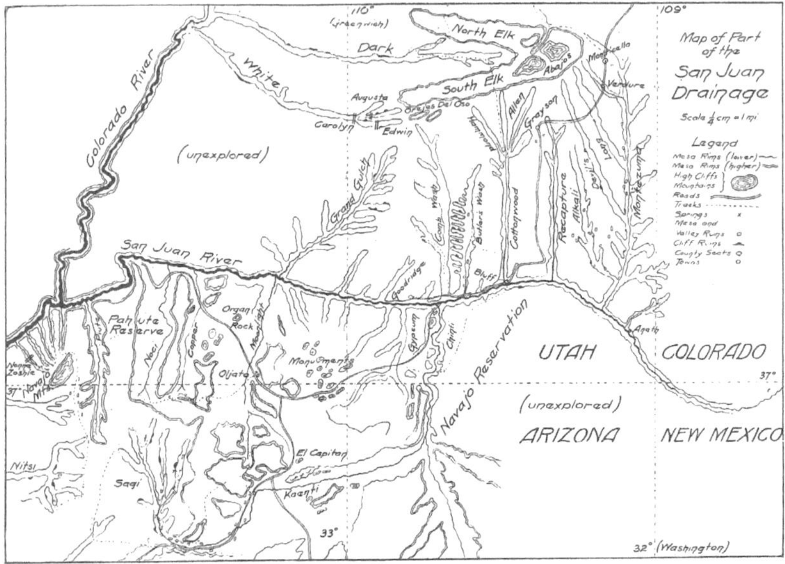

One of the first trained archaeologists to explore the Bears Ears region was Byron Cummings from the University of Utah. This map accompanied his 1910 publication *The Ancient Inhabitants of the San Juan Valley.* Note the label "unexplored" for the rocky and remote San Juan Triangle or the area between the San Juan and Colorado Rivers. Bears Ears appears in Spanish labeled *Orejas del Oso.* Author's collection.

masonry rooms, defensive walls, and "mud-plastered willows slanting up and rearward to the cliff [which] provided household granaries, each having a slanted opening framed by cedar branches and ribbed with adobe."[15] During this expedition, which was one of the first scientific explorations in the heart of the Bears Ears, the group came across ancient sites that represented different Ancestral Puebloan ethnic groups including Kayenta Anasazi who practiced a less formal masonry tradition and the use of jacal or mud and willow constructed rooms. Cummings' survey also found rooms with t-shaped doorways similar to those at Mesa Verde and ingeniously crafted doors. Judd described "a fitted sandstone door slab held in place by two cedar wedges which I found in the sand below the door and inserted into split-willow loops on either side. Elsewhere we have read of similar willow loops and of cedar wedges, but here they were found together and they belonged together." He added, "We found these ruins eroded by time but otherwise just as their builders had left them."[16]

For their natural beauty and the scientific value of the bridges to demonstrate geology as well as nearby archaeological sites, White Canyon deserved federal protection. President Theodore Roosevelt agreed. With Roosevelt's declaration of Natural Bridges National Monument on April 16, 1908, San Juan County, Utah, had one of the first national monuments. Under the twentieth century's new Antiquities Act, preservation required surveys to set aside lands. William R. Douglass came west from Washington, DC, to survey the area and he used high points of the Bears Ears themselves as part of his triangulation. He would pass through Bluff in 1908 and again two years later trying to find not just natural bridges in White Canyon, but the largest sandstone bridge in the world, a rainbow turned to stone according to Navajo legend.

In fall 1908, Douglass set boundaries for the new national monument and the three bridges originally named by Cass Hite, the President, the Senator, and the Congressman. The Salt Lake Commercial Club trip renamed them Augusta, Carolina, and Edwin.[17] Like everyone else, Douglass became fascinated by ruins of the ancients. He also had a unique assignment that honored Native Americans. Douglass was ordered to "make further investigation and inquiry concerning the Indian names of the bridges, and if possible learn the individual names by which they are known among the Indians, as it is expressly desired that these names be applied to the bridges rather than others of recent application."[18]

He inquired among Paiutes, including Posey who knew the area well, and learned that the Paiute word for the area was "Ma-vah-talk-tump," which translated as "'under a horse's belly between his fore and hind legs' in other words an arch or bridge," wrote Douglass, who acknowledged that "the original discoverers of the bridges were ancient prehistoric ancestors of the Hopi Indians, speaking their language and having their customs."[19] He recommended the names Owachomo for the 34-foot-long bridge, Kachina for the middle bridge, and Sipapu for the 68-foot-wide, 260-foot-long bridge because it represented "the gateway through which man comes to life from the underworld, and through which he must depart."[20]

Douglass predicated his work on previous surveys "noting their bearing and computing this distance, based on triangulation, from a conspicuous mountain peak known as Bear's Ears, part of Elk Ridge."[21] Because the natural bridges bisected White Canyon and could only be seen from directly above, Bears Ears conspicuously dominates the Cedar Mesa landscape so it was natural that Douglass, like explorers before him, used the Bears Ears as a vital reference point.

In his general description the surveyor explained, "The bridges are in the heart of a vast uninhabited arid region in southeast Utah." He described getting to the area via horseback from Bluff seventy miles away and two days by trail. Because of the necessity of water for travelers he added two other sites with springs to the monument's boundaries at Cigarette Cave on Road Canyon and Snow Flat Cave at the head of a branch of Fish Creek. Douglass became captivated by the adjacent ruins, describing them and enlarging Natural Bridges' boundaries to include a few archaeological sites. He explained that in a burial cave "interred in the sandy soil of the floor was found a headless mummy, with limbs doubled up, wrapped in a coarse weave of yucca cord and bound about with a rope of rabbit's fur."[22]

Douglass wrote in awe about Ancestral Puebloan ruins and yet, when he could have recommended that much of Cedar Mesa be protected as part of Natural Bridges National Monument, he did not survey expansive boundaries. He must have known the goals of the Antiquities Act, but he did not suggest a larger monument. Douglass explained that the country was "high mesa, timbered with a stunted growth of juniper and pinon, and cut by deep and impassable canyons." Yet he observed "in prehistoric times this ill-favored country supported a numerous population as is evidenced by the mounds of fallen stone, marking the sites of ancient pueblos ... About the ruin sites, the ground is covered with pottery, fragments, chiefly of whiteware, though some were of red and a few brown. The ornamentation is of geometric designs painted with black pigment as a rule, but occasionally varied with red and yellow colors."[23]

Douglass respected the cliff dwellers. He wrote, "That they were builders who builded well is vouched for by numerous time-resisting ruins. Vertical walls they built without a plumb; circular chambers without the radius; without knowledge of mechanical laws they select[ed] beams that withstand the strain; protect the openings with lintels as does the builder of today."[24] But compared to the large ruins at Mesa Verde, by then a national park, these structures perched on ledges were "small in size and few in number."

He wrote page after page in his observations, diagrammed ruins in caves, and illustrated Basketmaker petroglyphs. He drew circular kivas and Mesa Verde-style keyhole kivas, but he did not recommend a larger monument. That would come over a century later when the solitude of the immense Bears Ears region would have new meaning for twenty-first-century Americans seeking opportunities to explore a distant canyon landscape beyond the restrictions of ranger-led tours down asphalt paths. It would be the goal of five tribes to urge a Bears Ears National Monument with Bears Ears and Natural Bridges near its center. But that was in the future. In the first decade of the twentieth century Native resistance continued along the San Juan River at Aneth where the Navajo agent requested federal troops to quell a disturbance based on a headman's refusal to send Navajo children to boarding school.

Thousands of Navajos had been forced by Kit Carson on the Long Walk to Bosque Redondo, but not Navajos living along the San Juan River near Aneth, Utah. They had resisted. Under confrontational headman Bai-a-lil-le they resisted again in 1906. As Bai-a-lil-le's supernatural powers grew stronger through stargazing, local Navajos wondered if the medicine man had become a witch. He bullied and threatened villagers, made incessant demands, had thirty followers, and kept close to him belligerent young men who did his bidding. "Bai-a-lil-le did all he could to resist government intervention and consolidate his power," notes historian Robert S. McPherson.[25] Local Navajos believed the medicine man controlled thunder and lightning. Respect became fear until by October 1907 federal troops arrived at the request of former trader James M. Holley who tried to teach Navajos farming and to recruit Navajo children to attend the San Juan Boarding School at Shiprock, New Mexico, forty miles to the southeast.

As in other Native events in San Juan County, Utah, the Philadelphia-based Indian Rights Association became involved, as well as Francis E. Leupp, appointed Commissioner of Indian Affairs by President Theodore Roosevelt and a staunch advocate of "civilizing" Native Americans while also ostensibly defending their rights. Like other Indian "experts," Leupp had firm feelings about the path he wanted Native Americans to follow and he "had little patience with Indian opposition," notes historian Don Parman, who added that "the commissioner believed strongly in the 'Big Stick' brand of diplomacy," a favorite phrase of Roosevelt's.[26]

At this stage in the twentieth century, Native groups across the West often split between traditionalists who wanted to live in the old ways, though those options continued to diminish, and younger tribal members who had attended boarding schools and sought accommodations with white society. Both Roosevelt and Leupp demanded assimilation and Americanization. Mormons remained isolated in southeast Utah as did Bai-a-lil-le, who argued with progovernment Natives and quarreled with the local Indian agent over the agent's requests including dipping sheep to avoid scabies and removing school-age children to New Mexico. "Bai-a-lil-e refused to send his children and raved against what he saw as a loss of Navajo rights. He threatened to harm or kill anyone who gave their children over to the government," explains McPherson.[27] The powerful Native leader's reasons were simple. Native American children sent to boarding school often died of diseases; yet the government continued to demand more. Bai-a-lil-le fought for the old ways even as his followers fomented fear and distrust among other Natives, stealing livestock from Utes and Mormons alike.

Indian police feared the medicine man and would not arrest him. Finally, William Shelton from the Bureau of Indian Affairs asked for two troops of cavalry to intimidate Bai-a-lil-le. Captain Henry O. Williard decided to arrest the leader and his dissidents in a night raid on Bai-a-lil-le's camp on the south side of the San Juan River. The medicine man lay asleep in his hogan after conducting a curing ceremony, and he was quickly arrested along with others. Handcuffed, he growled and snarled like a bear until being pistol-whipped senseless by a soldier. As additional arrests began, fighting broke out, with cavalrymen killing two young Navajos in self-defense and wounding another. Charges against the dissident band included not only the sheep dipping refusal, but also stock theft, kidnapping, rape, polygamy, concealed weapons, and browbeating Natives cooperating with the local agent. Arresting officer Captain Williard claimed "he had never seen 'a more villainous pair'" than Bai-a-lil-le and conspirator Polly.[28] Without a trial or any formal hearing, Leupp demanded that the resisting Navajos be placed in hard labor at Fort Huachuca, Arizona, although some of the captives were released.

Local white missionary Howard R. Antes wrote letters in protest and made several false complaints.[29] Colorado Senator H.M. Teller insisted all correspondence related to the raid be sent to the Senate Indian Affairs Committee. Superintendent of the US Military Academy and investigator for the federal government Colonel Hugh L. Scott arrived six months after the event to check on Antes' allegations. They were groundless, but the trip introduced Scott to San Juan County, Utah, and he would return within a few years for another Native American incident.

The Indian Rights Association became involved over what they considered an illegal incarceration and the killing of two Navajos. Captain Williard maintained he had to arrest everyone because "all resisted." Meanwhile Bai-a-lil-le and Polly sweated during hard labor under a southern Arizona sun. A Tombstone, Arizona, lawyer became involved not because he sympathized with dissident Native Americans, but because there had been no trial or legal procedure of any sort. While visiting the prisoners, attorney O. Gibson saw a Navajo calendar marking their numerous days of imprisonment. Moved by the simple calendar, Gibson petitioned that his clients "had not been charged, tried, or sentenced in court" and should be released.[30] He argued that Native Americans had rights under the law even though, in 1909, they were not yet US citizens. Gibson stressed that the medicine man's group "numbered no more than thirty and 'at the worst were a band of ruffians, who needed to be arrested and dealt with in civil courts.'"[31]

On March 20, 1909, the Arizona Supreme Court concurred and by a unanimous decision ordered freedom for Polly and Bai-a-lil-le because the group's arrest and imprisonment had violated the hard-won Navajo Treaty of 1868 requiring that accused tribal members be turned over "to the United States, to be tried, and punished according to its laws."[32] The Navajos returned to Aneth, chastened but still resistant. Within a few years another "uprising" would occur in San Juan County, this time with Utes, national publicity, the involvement of Indian trader John Wetherill and his wife Louisa, and the return of military investigator Hugh Scott. Southeast Utah remained an ongoing Indian frontier. Living Native Americans created trouble and problems for some Mormon residents who feared them. Bureau of Indian Affairs officials tried to restrain Natives solely on reservations, even as expeditions continued to search for the remnants of prehistoric Natives in the canyons and caves of Bears Ears.

Though deep academic interest had not quite begun, the attraction for Native American relics and looting of ancient sites never diminished. In 1911 only four universities in the United States offered courses in American Anthropology.[33] Arizona and New Mexico were not yet states. Formal archaeological excavations took place in Egypt, the Middle East, the Yucatan, and other cradles of civilization. For many professors in departments of Classics trained to look only toward ancient Rome and the Middle East, the Southwest was still just home to scorpions, rattlesnakes, slickrock, and sand. Rumors circulated of more sites, of larger ancient villages in Arizona territory, and of a great stone bridge shaped like a rainbow. Louisa Wetherill had learned from Professor Cummings about his expedition to White Canyon and three natural bridges. Now stories spread of an even larger, singular sandstone bridge. In 1909 as Bai-a-li-le returned home from imprisonment, a searing summer search would begin on the Navajo Reservation for the rumored sandstone bridge.

Byron Cummings and William Douglass would compete in a race for the rainbow to find one of the natural wonders of the world and the next national monument destined to be set aside in San Juan County southwest of Bears Ears.

In August in the canyons of southern Utah, the suffocating heat at midday shrivels lizards, boots, and brains. The sun glares down. Depletion of salt from the body can lead to hallucinations; without adequate water, one's tongue becomes like soft wood. Stars speckle and pop behind sunken eyeballs. Distance and foreground merge between shimmering waves of heat, and yet over a century ago two competing groups on horseback braved insufferable August temperatures in search of a mythical Navajo rainbow that the gods had turned to stone. Before backpacks and hiking sticks, adventure in Utah required horses and mules. Intrepid explorers rode them over dangerous, steep slickrock.

Dr. Byron Cummings of the University of Utah and his team, and surveyor William B. Douglass of the General Land Office and his men with Paiute guide Jim Mike, cautiously combined efforts with trader and horse packer John Wetherill, to find a stone bridge reputedly larger than those set aside in White Canyon at Natural Bridges National Monument. Later they would be joined by Navajo guide Nasja Begay. Navajo medicine man One-Eyed Salt Clansman had spoken of the bridge to Louisa Wade Wetherill, who was fluent in Navajo, but he passed on before he could guide anyone there. He had said, "It is in the back of Navajo Mountain. It is called the Rock Rainbow that Spans the Canyon. Only a few go there. They do not know the prayers."[34] Louisa's husband John had mentioned it to Byron Cummings, one of the pioneers of Southwestern archaeology who in 1909 had a productive summer. In Tsegi Canyon he visited the magnificent ruins of Keet Seel and Inscription House, and he had paid five dollars to be led to an unnamed box canyon where they found the 150-room Betatakin.[35] Stuart M. Young, grandson of Brigham Young, was expedition photographer.[36]

They had begun to collect artifacts for the University of Utah. William Douglass complained and fired off a letter to the General Land Office demanding revocation of Cummings' permit under the recently passed Antiquities Act of 1906. Before they ever met, Douglass and Cummings opposed each other, although the quarrel was really one-sided. Cummings sought to smooth things over, but Douglass would have none of it, and now in the blistering August heat, dangerously riding and leading horses atop slick Navajo sandstone, the two men's expeditionary forces had combined under a tentative truce. Yet who would become the first white man to "discover" a rainbow turned to stone?

Fierce rivalry characterized national and international expeditions at the beginning of the twentieth century, and deep in the tight canyons of the Navajo reservation, Anglo egos continued to compete. Neill Judd, who would become famous in his own right as a southwestern archaeologist, rode with Cummings. Judd wrote, "Throughout the last day's travel, with the big bridge reported not far ahead, Mr. Douglass exhibited the uncontrolled enthusiasm of the amateur explorer and he was so disregardful of possible danger to the other members of the party as to arouse the disgust of all."[37] On narrow sandstone ledges Douglass spurred his exhausted horse. Judd commented, "Without consideration for his companions, he repeatedly crowded the other riders from the narrow trail as he forced his tired horse to the front . . . time and again he turned back from ledges he had unwisely followed, only to rush forward again at the first opportunity."[38] But if Douglass was in the lead, as they rounded a bend, Cummings, Judd, and Wetherill saw the bridge first. The trio yelled for Douglass to return and see it. Then the race was on to get there. Cummings, already on foot and leading his horse, said it would be rude to race Douglass, but mild-mannered John Wetherill had had it with the overbearing government surveyor. Wetherill spat out "[t]hen I'll be rude" and spurred his horse past Douglass to be the first known white man to stand under the bridge on August 14, 1909. Later, for one dollar a year, he would become the initial caretaker or superintendent of Rainbow Bridge National Monument, which Douglass surveyed as 160 acres with the bridge in dead center.

From the very beginning of white incursion, the sacred space of Rainbow Bridge has been contested space. Douglass and Cummings squabbled for the rest of their lives about who saw it first. Douglass returned to Cortez, Colorado, by September 11 and word leaked out in the Cortez newspaper and other papers, but Cummings scored against his competitor by writing about the bridge in *National Geographic* in February 1910 using Stuart Young's black and white photos.[39] Three months later President William Howard Taft declared it a national monument.

Formed by water, at 290 feet high with a 275-foot span that is 42 feet thick, Rainbow Bridge is tall enough to place the Statue of Liberty under it. The largest natural span in the world, Cummings described it as an "enormous flying buttress . . . chiseled out by the ages and left as a specimen of the handiwork of the Master Builder." I've been to it by boat from Lake

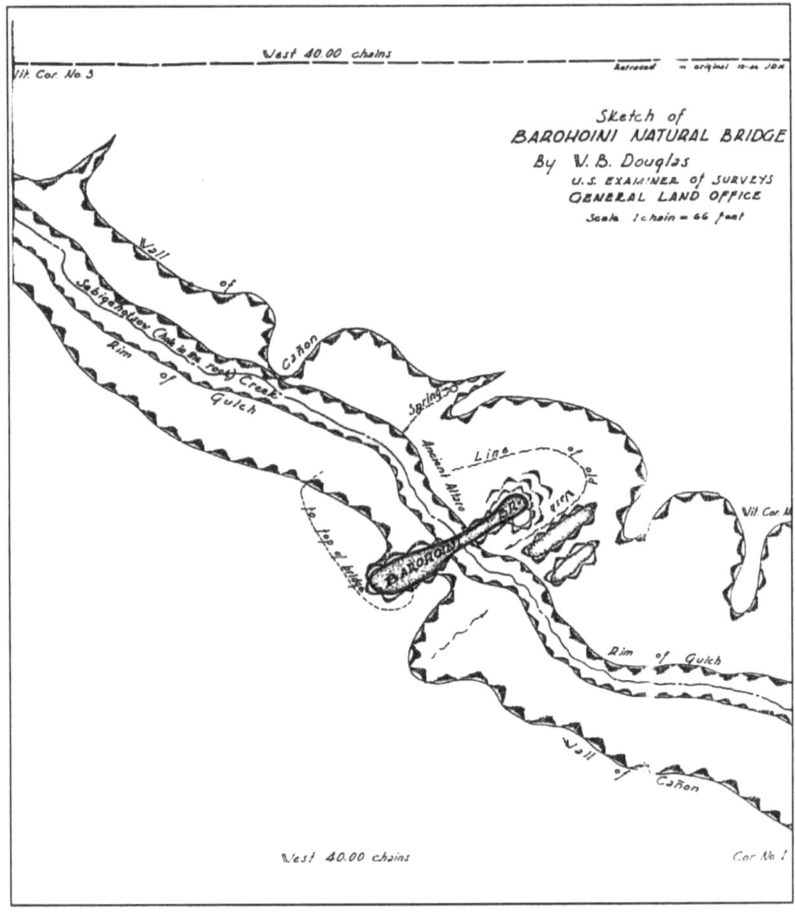

Though William B. Douglass could be rude and crass as an explorer, he was an excellent government surveyor. This is an early Douglass sketch map of Rainbow Bridge labeled Barohoini Bridge in the first decades of the twentieth century. Rainbow Bridge was the second national monument declared by presidential decree in San Juan County, Utah. Author's collection.

Powell. With a friend one September afternoon, we slowly motored up Bridge Canyon from Dangling Rope Marina and tied off to walk to the bridge. Though the massive stone arch impressed us, I'll admit that we didn't "earn" the view. Our access was too easy.

In the first decades of the twentieth century visiting the bridge became a must-see explorers' pilgrimage described by author Zane Grey and Theodore Roosevelt after he had left the presidency. Roosevelt wrote, "It is surely one of the wonders of the world. It is a triumphal arch rather than a bridge, and spans the torrent bed in a majesty never shared by any arch ever reared by the mightiest conquerors."[40] Grey explained, "This thing was glorious. It absolutely silenced me."[41]

The difficult horseback ride and hike into the bridge encouraged explorer Charles Bernheimer and his party in 1921 to work for six days and use dynamite and black powder to enlarge a slot canyon into a more respectable trail. But the ultimate indignity to the mythos of the stone rainbow came with the rising waters of Lake Powell and the failure of the Bureau of Reclamation to prohibit waters from entering the national monument via Bridge Canyon.

Lawsuits ensued first by the Sierra Club and other environmental organizations and later by Navajo singers and medicine men, but they all lost in court. Congressional legislation for the Glen Canyon Dam included wording to protect Rainbow Bridge National Monument with a smaller dam which was never funded or built. Now, instead of an arduous trek down from Navajo Mountain, over 90,000 day-trippers visit annually via tour boat. A sacred site has been compromised by too many people coming too often, but at least they respect the Navajo admonition to not walk under the natural bridge. One early morning in June we returned via a small boat and I brought one of my Navajo students, Brandon Francis, from Black Mesa. Shadows still crossed Bridge Canyon and we were alone. We made the short walk from the dock up to the famous natural bridge, and he saw for the first time the sacred stone rainbow he had always heard about. Briefly we stayed together, and then I left him alone to his thoughts and to his prayers.

"The size and grandeur of the famous arch does not hit you until it looms before you. Tradition prevents me from walking beneath it, but to gaze upon it is like listening to the Navajo creation story which takes seven nights to tell or being at an all-night Beauty Way ceremony," explained Francis. "The connection goes beyond a spiritual connection. It connects you back centuries if not thousands of years. In moments such as these, time is no longer linear but cyclical and all life stands connected, future, past, and present," he added.[42]

I want to go back to Rainbow Bridge, but this time I would like to hike in and take the tough trail down from Navajo Mountain through slickrock as the original explorers did. I would rather backpack and be one of the few instead of one of the many. I prefer to hike hard and earn the view. Then late in the afternoon we could camp in the shade about a mile up the trail and as the tour boats leave with the final trip of the day, we would have the bridge all to ourselves. We could be there as the stars come out and in silence and in shadow we could contemplate one of the great natural wonders of the world.

Rainbow Bridge became the second national monument in San Juan County, Utah. The Antiquities Act and its power to protect had become a useful tool for preservation-minded presidents. Cummings and Douglass raced to the rainbow in August 1909 with John Wetherill as guide. By October 30 of that year when Louisa Wetherill lay ill at their Oljato trading post, a significant southwestern era had almost come to an end. The great Navajo headman Hoskininni lay dying. One of his Ute slave women told Louisa that Hoskininni lay sick and needed to see her. Despite her illness, she arose from her bed and went to him.

The old man who had taken his small desperate band and fled Kit Carson during the infamous Long Walk was dying in his hogan near Monument Valley. He had allowed Louisa and John to build a trading post at Oljato, meaning Moonlight Water. Because of her fluency in Navajo, Hoskininni adopted Louisa. She had earned the Navajo nickname *Asthon Sosi* or Slim Woman. He treated her like a long-lost granddaughter. He trusted her.[43] All his relatives knew that it would be Louisa who would settle his affairs. He beckoned and she came but he was in the middle of a healing ceremony with songs and chants just beginning. She left to attend to her children and to return the next morning only to find his hogan burning as was the Navajo custom.

Hoskininni had died and the ceremonial ritual of his death and crevice burial had begun with four days of mourning. The Angry One who had successfully hidden his band of Navajos from the Blue Coats and from Red Shirt, the Navajo nickname for Kit Carson, had lived to become the Generous One because he gave sheep to Navajos moving to Navajo Mountain after the horrors of Bosque Redondo. He had represented Navajo resistance on the southwest edge of Bears Ears country. He had prospered and now he had passed on. Louisa divided up his property and then came to learn that as his administrator and his chosen granddaughter she also inherited. Settling his estate, she had asked only for his gun, but she also received his thirty-two Ute slave women who knew no other life. She awoke one day at dawn to hear their keening and crying. "She built a hogan nearby where any of them might stay. She fed them when they were hungry, gave them work to do when they asked for it." In *Traders to the Navajo,* Louisa and her co-author Frances Gilmore explained about

The aging Navajo leader Hoskininni, once known as "The Angry One," became known as "The Generous One" when he gave sheep to other Navajos returning from The Long Walk. Photo courtesy of Harvey Leake.

the slave women, "They asked her permission when they wanted to go away. When they returned, they returned as to one who had the right to decide on their coming and their going."[44] To sustain the women, Louisa divided among them some of Hoskininni's sheep.

Hoskininni's death meant the end of an era for Navajos who had endured the Long Walk and then learned to live, more or less, within reservation boundaries. Eight months later, another death also ended the initial decades of pothunting and artifact collecting for profit. Having grown less flexible and more outspoken at his Chaco Canyon trading post built adjacent to Pueblo Bonito, Richard Wetherill argued with a Navajo over unpaid debts.[45] Local Navajos claimed that one of Richard's employees, William Finn, had been stealing their livestock. Tensions rose, and Finn pistol-whipped a Navajo, knocking him unconscious in his own yard. The incident that morning resulted in Wetherill's death by the afternoon. "This man Finn was the immediate cause of Wetherill['s] being killed," wrote W.T. Shelton, Indian Service Superintendent at Shiprock.[46]

Earlier that day while Finn and Wetherill rode up Chaco Wash on June 22, 1910 gunfire erupted. Chis-Chilling-Begay shot once at Finn then turned a rifle toward Wetherill. The same shot first hit Wetherill's upraised right hand then lodged a bullet deep into his chest.[47] Richard, whom the Navajos had nicknamed "Anasazi" because of his obsession with digging up human remains, died, murdered at Chaco Canyon where the wooden cross on his lone grave, the only white burial at Chaco, fades in the sun. He had disturbed the spirits of the Ancient Ones. For the widowed Marietta, her first husband Richard Wetherill, one of the primary explorers of cliff dwellings, was dead in the southwestern landscape where he had unearthed dozens of Native American burials. Now he too lay in the same soft sandy soil.[48]

Hearing the news from a runner and having outfitted a special wagon, John Wetherill and Dr. T. Mitchell Prudden made the rough cross-country trip to Pueblo Bonito. Arriving back at Oljato, they decided to move their trading post that fall of 1910 to an open spring "Where the Water Runs like Fingers Out of a Hill" or Kayenta. At the new location in Arizona, John and Louisa continued to befriend Navajos, Utes, and Paiutes. The couple built the Wetherill Lodge at Kayenta, which would become a destination for travelers and a departure point for numerous expeditions across the Colorado Plateau and into Bears Ears. Louisa could speak Navajo, which Utes also knew. She could translate and interpret, and she had earned Native trust. Natural wonders and archaeological sites like Natural Bridges and Rainbow Bridge were being set aside in the Southwest, but Native peoples continued to resist white encroachment. The murder of a Hispanic sheepherder, apprehension of the alleged killer, and Ute demands for a fair trial all turned southeastern Utah into a state of turmoil. Isolated Bluff residents feared Ute bands camping on sand dunes just west of town. Regional newspapers raged about a Native American war that never happened. Louisa Wetherill interceded and calmed old fears.

Historian Robert McPherson explains that the Utes "unwilling to relinquish their freedom . . . continued to hunt and gather in the mountains, canyons, and desert of southeastern Utah while preying upon the livestock herds grazing on public land. Both activities proved grounds for conflict."[49] Polk and his son Tse-ne-gat, which translated as "Silver Earrings," harassed pioneer Albert Lyman, founder of Blanding, over horses. Other Utes continued to prey upon Mormon livestock, and then Tse-ne-gat in the spring of 1914 may have ambushed, killed, and robbed a Hispanic sheepherder after a gambling spree. When the herder's body was found and reported, the young Tse-ne-gat was told to come into the agency as a suspect. He and his father claimed "that they would kill Indians or white men who tried to arrest them."[50]

Louisa Wetherill hoped to intervene. With Paiutes from near Navajo Mountain, she took the two-track wagon route that hardly passed for a road from their trading post at Kayenta back to Bluff to try and convince the twenty-seven-year-old to surrender. He would not. McPherson writes, "By now the commissioner of Indian Affairs, Indian agents in both Colorado and Utah, the US Marshals Service, Governor Spry, and local citizens were well aware of the Indian resistance, more symbolic than real, mounting in San Juan County. The threat posed by Polk, Tse-ne-gat, and perhaps thirty followers needed to be stopped before infectious resistance spread."[51]

As the incident stretched from summer into fall and winter, Utes camped west of Bluff south of the sand dunes. Posey, a Paiute considered another "renegade" by locals and the son-in-law of Tse-ne-gat's father Polk, brought in his own band to stay at Sand Island. A hastily assembled posse that grew to more than seventy men, largely made up of Colorado cowboys, approached the camps and started shooting. A peaceful unarmed Ute, Chicken Jack, got shot and killed. Six Utes became jailed on the top floor of Bluff's sandstone San Juan Co-op while others fled toward Bears Ears and Butler and Comb Washes seeking a familiar place

Louisa Wetherill or "Slim Woman" as the Navajos nicknamed her, enjoys a quiet laugh with Sitsosie one of her many Navajo friends. Louisa was deeply trusted by the Navajo elder Hoskininni, became the executor of his estate, and unbeknownst to her, received thirty-two Ute slave women when Hoskininni died. Photo courtesy of Harvey Leake.

of refuge. When one hundred Utes agreed to go to Bluff for their safety and learned that instead they were being taken to the Ute reservation in southwest Colorado, "they halted in their march and refused to come in. Leaders of the band declared rather than leave their ancestral hunting grounds they would resist the white authorities," and so they headed back toward Bears Ears.[52]

As Europe fragmented over World War I, General Hugh L. Scott arrived in southeast Utah to assist with a Ute surrender. He knew the area from his previous work gathering information related to the Navajo Bai-a-li-le. Louisa Wetherill telegrammed for assurance that if Polk and his son surrendered, they would not be hanged and that justice would be served. Louisa's husband John got involved as Ute and Paiute Indian intermediaries brokered a discussion that included a fair trial for the four Utes in Salt Lake City. Tse-ne-gat would have a legal hearing in Denver. The posse had attacked without explanation. Utes shot back in self-defense. Once again, the Indian Rights Association became involved. With frequent newspaper stories siding with the Utes, legal maneuvering began including the deposition of eyewitness accounts that became discredited in court. Acquitted by a Denver jury in 1915, Tse-ne-gat returned to southeast Utah, but he would not live long because of tuberculosis. Southeast Utah locals felt that there had been too much federal intervention with unsatisfactory results. During the next Native American incident eight years later, white families handled it themselves.

If local Native bands continued to resist assimilating into American society, this lingering aspect of the Wild West attracted eastern adventurers out to see the country. San Juan County, Utah, remained at the fringe of everything, never at the center. It was that sense of isolation and expansive landscapes that brought wealthy New Yorker Charles L. Bernheimer in 1919 to Natural Bridges with a pack train led by Zeke Johnson that came up Cottonwood Wash from Blanding and followed the old trail between the Bears Ears.

Bernheimer claimed to be a cliff dweller from the canyons of Manhattan. His love for the Southwest and his interest in exploration and guiding resulted in five subsequent expeditions between 1920 and 1924 when he evolved from tourist to explorer. He funded his trips based on his corporate success in New York's garment district. He received cooperation with the American Museum of Natural History and the Carnegie Institute, which loaned archaeologist Earl Morris for scientific research. "The lure of the desert is so intense that, if my own inclinations prevail," he wrote, "each year shall find me in the saddle with my boon companions disturbing the past to inform the present."[53] Writing about the 1921 Bernheimer Expedition in an article titled "An Unexplored Area of the Southwest," Morris exclaimed, "Magnificent desolation . . . is the dominant tone of the scenery."[54]

Bernheimer's first trip with Blanding local Zeke Johnson set the pattern for all the others and "throughout their backcountry adventures Zeke was always by Bernheimer's side, assisting and protecting him."[55] Bernheimer wrote about Navajo Mountain in *National Geographic* and he wrote one of the first books on Rainbow Bridge.[56] A Southwestern aficionado, the New York shirtwaist manufacturer longed for the outdoors and slept out in the open under a blanket of stars.

"The calmness that comes over one here is something akin to celestial peace," he wrote in his Natural Bridge trip field notes. "Outside of wild cattle (no-man's property) & lizzards [sic] & swallows some humming flies & a few not very troublesome knats [sic] there seems nothing living in these unsurveyed parts of this country. Yet nature is so very beautiful."[57] Johnson and other packers came to depend on summer outings and adventure trips by wealthy easterners who brought much needed cash into San Juan County. Some expeditions were sponsored by New Yorkers who wrote the checks back East but never came west.

In Grand Gulch hundreds of Basketmaker and Ancestral Puebloan artifacts had been taken from caves and habitations sites in the 1890s by the Wetherill brothers with sponsorship from B. Talbot Hyde, heir of a soap fortune. Now in 1920 Nels C. Nelson, Curator of North American Archaeology at the American Museum of Natural History in New York City, sought to return to Grand Gulch to map it for archaeological sites and to determine from which sites and side canyons the museum's artifacts had been dug. In the introduction to his report he wrote, "The Grand Gulch region of southern Utah has been represented by extensive archaeological collections in several of our large museums for all of twenty-five years," and that the seemingly impenetrable canyons made the region "one of the most inaccessible in the United States." He complained that "pioneer relic hunters" had done quite a bit of excavation producing artifacts and that the results of "these purely mercenary efforts have been lying in several of our larger museums for nearly a quarter of a century, undescribed."[58]

L.P. Cartier of New York City, from the jewelry family, sponsored the Cartier Grand Gulch Expedition, which spent two weeks "in the great Gorge itself" exploring sixty to seventy miles within the canyon and its tributaries and mapping 110 archaeological sites. The crew included guide John Wetherill, assistant Albert Smith, Harvard medical student Oliver Rickets, and a Navajo known as Tall Singer. They used six mules and four horses, camped under the stars, and ate plenty of biscuits and beans.

As for the landscape, curator Nelson described it as "[a] great rift in the earth, tortuous and fantastic, with mushroom or toadstool rocks, monuments of standing, seated and bust figures, hats atilt ... the general course is northeast to southwest, but the hot sun makes one aware that we face in turn every point of the compass." Like all visitors, he marveled at mornings in a canyon and wrote, "Wonderful stillness of a sunny morning following a cold night—no bird or insect making a sound."[59] The Nelson report details the ruins they found on narrow ledges and the numerous rooms and different construction techniques from masonry styles to wattle and daub or jacal architecture using horizontal and vertical sticks with adobe mud on both sides. Nelson states, "Finger prints in mud numerous" meaning traces of human hands left in the wet adobe mortar as it dried. He drew samples of petroglyphs and pictographs the expedition found, and he described detailed measurements of doors, walls, rooms, ledges, and adjacent rock or talus slopes. His kiva drawings are precise with maps and measurements of benches, pillars, smoke deflectors, ventilator shafts, and layers of interior plaster.

At site #79 he wrote, "Traces of masonry, three quarters of a mile upstream or just above where the Bear's Ears become visible ... Found arrowpoint and fragments of pottery. Dug out a lot of cedar bark, corncobs, etc."[60] His final map prominently shows the Bears Ears as a distinctive landscape feature at the head of Grand Gulch, a landmark for archaeological expeditions and the ancient peoples the Easterners had come to study.

If the Cartier Grand Gulch Expedition focused on matching artifact collections in a New York museum with the habitation sites and cliff ledges from whence they had originated, other visitors had no purpose except for adventure for adventure's sake. Unlike well financed and carefully organized expeditions, then as now, some folks came to canyon country just for the adventure with little money, no expertise, and few helpful instructions. "Boys, I'd just as leave take you out and shoot you down, as let you go out there," stated Zeke Johnson, waving his arm toward the west and Natural Bridges and at two college boys, John and Robert Aird, who in the summer of 1923 arrived in Blanding and thought they would undertake their own canyon country reconnaissance. They insisted on doing the trek on their own terms and remarked, "The packers and guides had animals, but none for sale, and we refused to tie our hands with guides, packers, or even rented animals."[61]

The young men had a few vital expressions to learn in Navajo such as "Where is water?" and "Where is [the] trail?" With a small caliber .22 rifle, a recalcitrant burro, and edible supplies of flour, baking powder, beans, ham, dried fruit, macaroni, and cheese, the boys were off learning "the burro's kicking, scraping, and lying down required frequent repacking, and our first day out was both exciting and fatiguing."[62] The brothers found and followed Johnson's trail to Natural Bridges from Blanding, which was really the old Bears Ears Trail on Elk Ridge. "We passed between the Bear's Ears, two prominent buttes on the south rim of Elk Ridge. The view at that point affords one of the most extensive panoramas in southeastern Utah, from which one can see into each of the Four Corners states." Elated that they were close to Natural Bridges, they prodded their slow-moving burro. "After surveying this vast country, we continued down the broad notch between the Bear's Ears and descended into a rugged draw of high brush," Robert Aird wrote in his firsthand account. On the return trip, they descended Comb Ridge, crossed into Monument Valley, realized they would never make it to Rainbow Bridge and began a hot, dusty twenty-five-mile return trek. One of the boy's diaries records, "Long walk to Bluff. Very tired and peevish." The brothers thought their 320-mile walkabout had been valuable. They concluded,

> Although the San Juan country in 1923 was one of the wildest and most remote regions in the United States, John and I were aware of the hardships of a trip in such a country and deliberately proposed to enter it and see the worst it had to offer. Some are satisfied with the quiet beauties of nature; others seek the unusual phenomena; while in yet others it is the untamed ruggedness and the grandeur of extreme nature that touches a responsive chord, perhaps arousing and challenging some primal impulse . . . in terms of rich and unexpected experiences, which neither of us could ever forget, it far surpassed our fondest expectations.[63]

The Aird brothers represented the future for the Bears Ears region, young men out to learn the country and a little more about themselves. They admired the scenery, scouted some ruins, but did not take anything home other than personal memories.

As for Zeke, who had turned them down as a guide, he had his own routine with clients. Over time Ezekiel Johnson became custodian of Natural Bridges National Monument. As a guide he brought tourists to a cave so they could "discover" a mummy he had buried there. The story goes, "Finding an Indian mummy once, Zeke carefully reburied it in a small cave. When visitors came to see the [natural] bridges, he would suggest they climb up to this cave and scrabble for arrowheads. Invariably, with enormous excitement they would 'discover' the mummy. Zeke pulled this stunt so often he wore out the mummy," reported *National Geographic*.[64]

Finding mummies or human remains of prehistoric Native Americans may have delighted visitors to Natural Bridges, but for living Indians in San Juan County, Utah, the early 1920s remained bitterly divided between the old ways and modern pressures and economic demands. After centuries of resistance one final incident occurred that forced Utes toward assimilation and left a Paiute named Posey an historical figure in Utah history. He even got a war named after him—the last Indian War in the United States. The Aird brothers felt the conflict and chaos. "We learned that San Juan County had just passed through a bitter Indian-white conflict known as the Posey War," wrote Robert Aird, "and that things were still tense enough to render travel away from the settlements by two unarmed young men inadvisable. The Posey War seemed to be the only subject of conversation in Blanding." He explained, "Everyone had his own version of the story of forty years' pent-up frustration and tension that had erupted in the shooting deaths of two Indians, one of them Posey himself. The climate of fear and apprehension was pervasive."[65]

For decades Ute bands had pushed back against local Mormon encroachment on their range. The Utes had also resisted moving to reservations in southwest Colorado—the Southern Ute Reservation south of Durango or the Ute Mountain Ute Reservation south of Cortez. Nor would they agree to move north to the Uintah-Ouray Reservation near Vernal, Utah. Trying to live the old life, hunting, gathering, stealing a horse or cow, and breaking into remote sheep or cattle camps, there always seemed to be conflict. The last flare up which brought an armed posse to San Juan County had been the standoff over Tse-ne-gat and his refusal to surrender on a murder charge for which he was eventually acquitted. He died of tuberculosis in April 1922 in Allen Canyon, long a Ute stronghold east of Bears Ears and west of the developing Mormon town of Blanding. Ute alliances and bands shifted just as the Utes themselves moved in a rotation from summer to winter with their horse and goat herds.

By spring 1923, fifty-five-year-old William Posey had become an established renegade behind much theft, but also a leader. "His growing reputation, whether warranted or not, placed him in the spotlight, suggesting that he was behind a growing resistance," notes historian Robert McPherson.[66] Part of the struggle, as in the past, included legitimate concerns—access to good grass, grazing in the canyons and on Elk Mountain, and travel via narrow corridors that ran through historic Indian lands. Two young men began the latest confrontation by stealing and eating a calf. Dutchie's Boy and Joe Bishop's Boy admitted their theft to the older Ute named Polk, once a firebrand himself. Imprisoned in the Monticello jail, they dug themselves out and went into hiding though their parents assured authorities the boys would follow the law. They were juveniles, not quite eighteen. On his way to Natural Bridges, even the Utah Governor Charles R. Mabey became involved. In Cottonwood Wash close to Allen Canyon, he met with local Utes and said if they behaved themselves, they could stay in San Juan County and not be removed to area reservations. He posed for photographs and the expected headlines.

At trial the boys were acquitted within three hours, but then months later more thefts continued. Joe Bishop's Boy and another youth, Sanap's Boy, raided a sheep camp and took what they wanted. "The new year, 1923, began without incident," notes McPherson, "But as with previous outbreaks of violence, small acts mushroomed into larger events. While history does not repeat itself, patterns of history do."[67] The two men, now old enough to be adults, surrendered to stand trial in Blanding. Armed guards hovering around the young men disturbed the boys' fathers who came from the other Ute community in San Juan County named Westwater south of Blanding. This time the jury found the two young men guilty, but in the interval between the verdict and sentencing, their acquiescence turned to resistance. Joe Bishop's Little Boy hit Sheriff William Oliver with a stick. The sheriff tried to shoot the defendant, only to have his pistol misfire twice. Moving fast, the assailant grabbed the sheriff's gun, jumped on a horse, shot at the sheriff with his own pistol wounding the sheriff's horse, and fled town. In the melee, the other defendant, Sanap's Boy, rode hard to Westwater with Posey.

In response, and against legal precedents, locals armed themselves and started rounding up all Utes, regardless of any role in the theft, trial, or escape. The father of one of the convicted young men, Joe Bishop, made clear that he would find his son and have him return for justice. As Bishop rode away, local white resident Joe Black caught up with him and yelled,

"You old son-of-a-bitch. You turn around and go back or I'll let your guts out right here."[68]

"The news soon spread through Blanding and every man dropped what he was doing and ran for his horse and his gun and rushed to volunteer," wrote John D. Rogers.[69] Vengeful whites forced forty Utes into the schoolhouse basement until the locals constructed between the sandstone bank and the Redd Mercantile Store a military stockade of one hundred square feet with barbed-wire fences ten feet high. Eventually Utes became prisoners of war with no rights whatsoever in a confrontation that almost all local Native Americans had sought to avoid. Forced to stay there a month, young children had bitter memories of the stockade the rest of their lives.

Meanwhile Posey and others headed toward the Bears Ears and safety along Comb Ridge. Utes fled in several directions and a large posse assembled by the sheriff was told by him, "Every man here is deputized to shoot. I want you to shoot everything that looks like an Indian."[70] Posey fired back in self-defense as he fled into country he knew well. Bill Young saw Joe Bishop's Boy and Sanap's Boy riding fast toward him. He hid in

Ute Indians were forced into a stockade in Blanding, Utah during the so-called Posey War of 1923. Children who had to live behind the high barbed wire fence remembered the experience for the rest of their lives. The Indian Agent is at the far left. Verda Washburn Collection, courtesy of the San Juan County Historical Commission.

a low tree because "[t]hey were riding about fifteen or twenty feet apart, coming at full speed, standing up in their stirrups and looking for me down slope thinking I was still running." Young drew a bead on Joe Bishop's Boy, who was closest. "When he was where I could see the buttons on his shirt I took a bead on the third button and pressed the trigger . . . he was still in the saddle in a slumped position the last I saw of him."[71] Joe Bishop's Boy died of his wounds.

Within a day a Blanding posse merged with a Bluff posse and more Utes were rounded up with guards given orders to shoot to kill as unarmed Natives waited for transport after being marched down Comb Wash. The day before, the Bluff posse's leader R.L. Newman, former sheriff of Navajo County, Arizona, had given orders to his posse while searching a mesa top. "Now men, let's mark this top. Comb it out carefully and don't shoot at anything but an Indian, then shoot to kill him."[72]

While Posey hid, his relatives and friends knew his whereabouts and brought him food. "The first night we camped at the Comb and sent the Indians out with a pack mule and food and blankets to scout around and try to find Posey. Some of us were a little suspicious because they came back without any food," wrote John D. Rogers. "Several times they went out and each time they came back without food."[73] Because of the use of signal fires from cedar bark torches, the Utes knew Posey's location. Deputies interrogated captive Utes, demanding to know Posey's whereabouts. Posey's relatives never revealed where he hid, and he never surrendered even though the aging Paiute had been wounded in the hip. Fleeing up Comb Ridge and down the other side to the west, Posey died alone near Mule Canyon while eighty Ute friends and kinsmen remained behind barbed wire in Blanding. He died only a few miles from Bears Ears. He died in the canyons where his ancestors had lived for centuries. He died resisting white encroachment on traditional Ute homelands.

This time there was no intervention by General Hugh Scott or pleas from the Indian Rights Association in Philadelphia. Blanding residents took the law into their own hands. After all, Native Americans were not yet citizens, though that long overdue status would come, finally, less than a year later. "We built a barbwire stockade, a 'bullpen,' and put them in it as a bedraggled bunch of pinon busted steers," reminisced Blanding founder Albert Lyman, referring to Ute families as if they were range cattle.[74] But the disappearance and probable death of William Posey was not enough. Utes led US Marshal J. Ray Ward to Posey's grave to prove his death. Though the marshal refused to tell of the grave's location, local

Posey became a rebel and renegade as settlers' cattle and sheep continued to encroach on traditional Ute and Paiute grazing lands and hunting grounds. This photo is from 1921. He died in the Posey War of 1923 from either a gunshot wound or flour purposely poisoned with strychnine. Photo courtesy of the Utah State Historical Society.

men found out and dug it up once, then twice, and even a third time when a small group of locals posed with Posey's corpse for a grisly photograph as macabre and disgusting as other photos taken in the 1920s in the American South, where mobs grinned and glared while lynched African Americans, clothes in tatters, hung from tree limbs.[75]

Compassionate Utes, once freed from their stockade, recovered and then reburied Posey in an unknown location in the Bears Ears region. Three decades of pot hunting and grave robbing had their ultimate conclusion. Numerous mummies had been dug up in San Juan County, Utah, and now in the twentieth century another Native American, a troublemaker, had been shot and died of blood poisoning and infection, or at least that is the standard end to this sordid story. Utes felt otherwise. They believed that Posey had been killed by poisoned flour.

In the cold spring of 1923 Utes huddled around small fires and in two Navajo hogans built within their stockade. On occasion prisoners were allowed to leave to herd their livestock scattered on traditional Native lands. Posey never gave up. "The settlers could not find him and so laced a sack of flour with poison so that people released from the stockade to tend Ute animals would give it to him," wrote McPherson, describing Posey's death based on Ute oral histories.[76] Myers Cantsee, Posey's sons Anson and Jess, Marshall Ward, Jim Mike, and Jack Fly found Posey dead. His dog was dead. He had been cooking over an open campfire, and his thigh wound appeared to be healing. "Posey had made biscuits with the flour, fed some of them to his faithful dog and then ate them himself," stated Francis Posey.[77]

"They say that later, after the settlers found his body, they shot it so that they could claim that was how he died, but the white flour and bread in his hands showed what had really happened," McPherson relates.[78] Perhaps that is just folklore, a Native American tale to maintain Posey's power and resourcefulness, his reputation as a leader who would not be vanquished by whites. John Riis wrote about poisoned bread left with deadly intention in a mountain cabin a decade earlier. Somewhere between a bullet in a hip and bread in a dead man's hands lies the truth.

I've hiked the Posey Trail off US Highway 95, which bisects San Juan County and runs under Bears Ears. I've walked the slickrock uphill on an autumn afternoon and then stepped among pinyon pines as the trail rises ever higher to the height of Comb Ridge. On top there is a small saddle or flat area where a dozen people could camp with open views far to the west toward Monument Valley and Hoskininni's Navajo Mountain.

I have stood there and thought about being pursued by angry men with orders to shoot to kill.

Watching small cedar torches at night, the posse knew where Posey and his followers sought refuge. Early the next morning the posse rode up the trail only to have Posey's group dive off the steep side of Comb Ridge and other escarpments, urging their horses to jump five feet down off sandstone ledges. The Utes and their fearless ponies escaped. Posey hid. He lies somewhere in Bears Ears in a sacred Native landscape. A century later his backtrail off Comb Ridge is impossible to discern, but his memory remains, as do his bones.

CHAPTER 9

Lost in Bears Ears, Murder in Johns Canyon, and a Failed New Deal National Monument, 1924–1944

> The great caves, with their abandoned camp sites, their storage cists, or their shattered ruins, tell a mute tale of human struggles long before the written history of our continent began ... we traversed canyons perhaps never before visited by white men; we crawled through narrow doors into dwellings no booted foot had previously entered; we climbed canyon walls on trails unused for centuries.
>
> —Neil Judd, "Beyond the Clay Hills," 1924

> Ten miles of Grand Gulch is no ten cent Movie. It is grand opera. The scenery is majestic.... There are 15 cliff sites we passed within 16 miles. We visited four.
>
> —Charles Bernheimer, Field Notes, 1929

Posey was finally allowed to rest, but prehistoric Native burials were continually searched and dug. Explorers and adventurers descended on San Juan County, Utah. For such a remote, hard to get to location, from the mid-1920s through the 1930s the Bears Ears region of canyon country saw increasing visitation and scientific expeditions throughout the landscape. By the mid-1930s at least three different large-scale searches had begun for a lost artist, a lost paleontologist, and a murderer who killed a former San Juan County sheriff and his grandson in Johns Canyon, part of the expansive Bears Ears region below Elk Ridge and above the narrow, muddy San Juan River. A decade after the Last Indian War in the 1920s, San Juan County welcomed the Rainbow Bridge Expedition.

Dubbed "The Last Great Expedition," this poorly managed but well-publicized multiyear expedition began in 1934 and touched on Bears Ears where the steep canyons of Grand Gulch intersect the San Juan River. Organized by University of California graduate Ansel Hall, first naturalist for the National Park Service, the expedition was a series of summer sojourns for professors and their graduate students. It evolved into a veiled attempt to describe and rationalize a massive national park to be carved out of Monument Valley and the Navajo Reservation, just as Mesa Verde National Park had been taken unwillingly from the Ute Mountain Ute Reservation and Ute lands after 1906.[1] This time the Navajos and their vocal Indian agents successfully resisted.

San Juan County residents also helped to halt a huge Escalante National Monument proposed by Secretary of the Interior Harold Ickes in the early 1930s. Under President Franklin Roosevelt's Administration, the original Escalante National Monument would have included all of what became Canyonlands National Park, Glen Canyon National Recreation Area surrounding Lake Powell, and Bears Ears National Monument. Utah residents protested that the monument was too big and represented a federal takeover, sentiments that would be repeated in the twenty-first century. By the 1930s descendants of the original Hole-in-the-Rock settlers of Bluff had largely abandoned the town for the higher, wetter communities of Blanding and Monticello, but the stone houses they had built still stood even as sand blew down streets. Once verdant orchards died from a lack of water, yet the San Juan River continued to flood Bluff's riparian lowlands. In 1894 Utes had been told by their Indian Agent David Day to move to Dry Valley north of Monticello. In the 1930s a religious commune began at the same location, convinced that Jesus Christ would appear to them, that the climate would change, and Dry Valley would become a productive oasis. On the edge of red rock country Marie Ogden established her Home of Truth as one of the first New Age communities in the western United States. Their beliefs included reincarnation. The sect received national newspaper headlines when Ogden refused to bury a deceased follower.

Still isolated, San Juan County families suffered through the Great Depression, welcomed the occasional visitor and tourist, planted their gardens, herded their sheep, grazed their cattle, and endured increasing federal oversight of public lands including the 1934 Taylor Grazing Act, which established grazing districts. Not much changed until December 7, 1941 when Japan attacked Pearl Harbor. As America rushed to war and a secret scientific laboratory was established at Los Alamos, New Mexico, suddenly yellow rocks in different layers of the Shinarump formation had enormous value. They would be sought after and prospected in Bears Ears as World War II ended and the Cold War began. A uranium frenzy would transform San Juan County and the county seat at Monticello bringing prospectors to search the canyons for something other than lost cows and Indian relics.

Despite the Antiquities Act, site looting continued, some of it under the antiquities permit itself. Two decades after passage of the Antiquities Act, "In southern Utah ... professional archaeologists as well as avocational pot hunters burrowed into ruins, burials, and any other site that might hold objects left behind by prehistoric Indians. Today many of the efforts of even the 'trained, professional' archaeologists of the time would be classified more as looting than scientific excavation," historian Robert McPherson explains. He adds, "Collecting was everyone's intent."[2] The University of Utah was no exception. To build up campus collections, in the 1920s archaeologist Andrew Kerr, legally operating under a federal Antiquities Act permit, paid local Blanding men three dollars each for an Ancestral Puebloan basket or pot. Local men were hired for an expedition in 1925–1926 to search for Native American artifacts to add to the university's collection. The Shumway family got involved.

A.E. and Lee Shumway collected under the university's permit for the Archaeology Department at the University of Utah. Accession records at the Natural History Museum of Utah detail a wide range of items acquired including sandals, axes, bowls, awls, human hair, vessel fragments, yard cordage, and complete pots. Studying the faded blue ink of accession records at the state's natural history museum, I could trace the movement of local men as they worked south from Blanding. At Westwater Canyon on June 16, 1925 the entry reads, "surface finds near a small ruin." On February 9, 1926 twenty miles southeast of Blanding, A.E. Shumway found "small mug, black and white, neck chipped and handle gone" and a black and white seed jar "in an open grave. Very fine specimen."[3]

According to museum procedures, each item was numbered and accessioned. Notes indicate that prehistoric bowls came from public land and private homesteads. Almost all artifacts came from shallow graves. A "skull flattened in back—hence cliff dweller" was accession number 7214 found in Cottonwood Wash in what would become, decades later, Bears Ears National Monument.[4] Sanctioned by the university's permit, San Juan County locals searched for prehistoric Native American burials only two years after local Ute tribal members had been released from their forced incarceration in a World War I-style military stockade. Legally, artifact hunting was now supposed to occur only to create collections for scientific institutions, but there was no law enforcement. The USFS had rangers to check on grazing permittees and to try to limit cattle and sheep numbers to fit grazing allotments, but no one checked on pothunters. San Juan County was too remote. The local newspaper, the *San Juan Record*, would proclaim itself "Voice of America's Last Frontier."

In 1924 the year Native Americans finally received US citizenship by an act of Congress, though they still could not vote in most national elections, Neil Judd published an article in *National Geographic*. In an essay titled "Beyond the Clay Hills," he wrote about a recent National Geographic Society reconnaissance "of a previously unexplored section in Utah." San Juan County remained rural, remote, and captivating to adventurers and explorers. Judd began in the March 1924 *National Geographic*, "the fact remains that areas still exist ... about which little or nothing is definitely known. They remained in hiding when 'the last frontier' was pushed westward into the Pacific." He described, "One such area borders the Rio Colorado in Utah. East and west from this savage red river unmapped mesas stretch away mile after barren mile to green mountains, overtopping an endless distance of pink and white and brown sandstone ... Securely guarded by the Rio San Juan and the Colorado lies the least-known section, perhaps, of this gigantic rock-floored region. It remains a veritable *terra incognita*."[5]

Judd described the San Juan Triangle or that area labeled on maps as "unknown" where the San Juan River and the Colorado River met surrounded by deep canyons now partially buried under the waters of Lake Powell. He argued, "The desert possesses an impelling force—an indescribable force, infinitely magnified with greater distance and isolation from the usual haunts of men. So it was with a strange mingling of secret satisfaction and dubiousness that I accepted the National Geographic Society's recent invitation to carry its banner yet farther along untrodden trails."[6] He admitted that Mormon settlers had crossed the Clay Hills on their route to Bluff, but he sought not to replicate their route but to find more prehistoric ruins and remains. Judd explained,

> However deserted and silent this untamed country may seem to us, there was time, uncounted centuries ago, when human voices echoed through the dark recesses of the canyons: when sandaled feet stalked deer and mountain sheep along their rocky rims. The crumbling walls of crude stone dwellings, blending chameleon-like with the variegated colors of the cliffs against which they cling, mark the temporary homes of prehistoric peoples. Fragments of ancient pottery and flint chips discarded by the arrow-maker

> snap under foot as one climbs the talus to some yawning cave. And there, in the cool shadows, one observes the scattered ashes of former camp fires, the angular wall drawings of primitive artists, and daubs of mud thrown against a cavern roof by children at play.[7]

Judd was on the western edge of Bears Ears, bathed in sunlight, eating windblown sand with every meal, secure with trader John Wetherill at the head of the pack train. Judd took photographs for the world to see and documented ancient ruins in Moqui Canyon. The expedition worked to avoid quicksand. "For days we climbed canyon walls and crossed tiresome mesas, whose weathered sandstone glistened in the sunshine like whitecaps at sea," he wrote.[8] Other adventurers, some with expensive pack trains, but many on their own, would also come into the roadless Bears Ears region.

Three years after Judd's publication, another southwestern archaeological pioneer, at a conference held at Pecos Pueblo National Monument in northern New Mexico, established the time sequence for prehistoric peoples who lived in the Southwest. The first Pecos Conference, the brainchild of archaeologist A.V. Kidder, set the sequence for human habitation in a chronology beginning with Paleo-Indian hunter-gatherers, Archaic peoples, then Basketmakers I, II, and III, succeeded by Ancestral Puebloans in a PI, PII, and PIII time frame. Kidder determined that PIV meant Proto-Historic or AD 1300 to 1500 for the arrival of Navajos and Utes. The last phase PV meant the historic phase when Pueblo peoples met the Spanish with Coronado's entrance at Hawikuh at Zuni in 1540.

Now after the 1927 Pecos Conference, archaeologists had a time frame to use to interpret the artifacts they had collected and the sites they had sought out. Two years later another explorer would be back; the clothing manufacturer Charles Bernheimer would make one final expedition retracing some of Judd's route. He hired the experienced John Wetherill as a guide. It would be Bernheimer's last foray into canyon country because the Great Depression would sink his fortune just as it crushed the finances of so many Americans. Zeke Johnson also acted as a guide for the trip, though he occasionally butted heads with Wetherill and got lost in the distant canyons Judd found so compelling.

Bernheimer took the train from New York City and was met in Gallup, New Mexico, by archaeologist Earl Morris driving a Packard Six limousine that frequently broke down, got mired in sand, and became less reliable than Zeke Johnson's mules. Sponsored as the seventh Bernheimer

Charles Bernheimer posed for his photo at Keet Seel in Navajo National Monument in the 1920s. The wealthy New York shirtwaist manufacturer sponsored many trips and expeditions into the Bears Ears region. Photo courtesy of Harvey Leake.

expedition of the American Museum of Natural History, the trip included paleontologist Barnum Brown who dug dinosaur bones in the Bisti on the Navajo Reservation. They visited Pueblo Bonito and Bernheimer marveled at masonry "as delicately fitted as cabinet work" before driving on to Morris's home at Aztec, New Mexico.[9]

From Aztec they drove to Monticello then Blanding and outfitted on May 25, 1929 with forty-six animals, Wetherill, Johnson, Morris, four helpers, "and an Indian," Navajo Bill Halliday. They camped in Cottonwood Wash, where the experienced explorer wrote in his journal "very, very cold and cloudy. The sagebrush seemed to morn [sic] the absence of sun, as it had a crestfallen, dejected look. Two or three times a day I rub its young leaves in my hand and then inhale the perfume which seems very invigorating."[10] They entered the Bears Ears region as they crossed Butler Wash, Comb Wash, and rode into the bottom of Arch Canyon, always looking up and searching for ruins, though Bernheimer admitted, "Some of these ruins had previously been dug into by pot hunters."[11] By May 27 Morris and Wetherill climbed into "one of the many cliff houses to dig. The archaeologist and guide found two children['s] skeletons and one charred set of human bones which made them suspicious of cannibalism. They could explain it in no other way."[12]

After riding through Kane Gulch, the group descended into Grand Gulch. The urban dweller marveled at cottonwood trees in Grand Gulch six feet in diameter. Cloudless blue skies rose above the canyon's bottom and the weather had warmed. They kept discovering cliff dwellings every quarter mile. Their circuitous route included Clay Hills, Lake Canyon, and Slick Rock Canyon where Earl Morris brought to camp the mummified body of a young boy and hid it from the others so as not to let Native Americans see it. Bernheimer wrote, "He carried it in a sort of sneaking manner away from where we were all assembled. When asked by me he said that the superstition of the Indians is so strong as regards things found in ruins that not only will they not touch them, but there is always the risk that they may decamp."[13]

Yet the expedition continued to excavate burials of "the bodies of young beings. One of these was [the] perfectly mummified boy of about 10. He was wound with feather cloth. The head was completely wrapped. The feet protruded but were in perfect condition. Position crouching."[14] They packed out their grisly finds and continued toward their destination at the junction of the San Juan and Colorado Rivers probably inspired by Judd's *National Geographic* article from five years earlier. In Moqui Canyon they found more mummies, some with baskets over their heads, but others with no coverings such as two women and two children found on June 11. Bernheimer lamented "had they been properly covered by cedar bark they would be the most perfect specimens found."[15]

Specimens—in the late 1920s the carefully buried remains of prehistoric peoples were considered only "specimens" with no discernible thought to their relationship to living tribal peoples on the Colorado Plateau. The graves of Indian ancestors were still callously dug, the bodies rewrapped, crated, and slung on sweaty mules all in the name of science, graverobbing for prestigious Eastern museums, the "finds" cataloged and described. Bernheimer notes that the younger of the two burials, a mother "had a very young child lying across her body and another about six near her head" with an offering from her family of 250 stone beads, green, red, white, and black "partly around her neck and partly around her wrists." The older woman "was wrapped in cotton cloth, and over that was a leather blanket, and over all cedar bark held together by human hair and yucca fibre."[16] There were bone ornaments, whistles, and a perfect ear of corn. The small family lay covered in fur baskets for what their relatives thought would be eternity. They had left their loved ones in the back of a cave, cried over them and quietly keened.

Loot from the expedition included an intact atlatl arrow with affixed stone dart, a perfect wooden boomerang tool for hunting rabbits, a mountain sheep hide sewn into a bag with its hair still attached, and a pile of wooden sticks thin as pencils. The expedition left Moqui Canyon lost and found a few trails, entered Red Canyon, suffered summer gnats, and finally arrived in White Canyon at Natural Bridges where Charles Bernheimer had begun his southwestern explorations a decade earlier. His journal records no personal insights and no reflections on his travels in canyon country. He ends with a sentence about an automobile expected to meet them at noon. There is no remorse about digging sites or collecting human remains. No hint of compassion related to disturbed burials. No moral accounting. They left Bears Ears and never thought that in addition to Natural Bridges that the other canyons had value and should be protected as a national monument to honor the dead buried there and to protect cliff dwellings that they had just looted. For the Bernheimer Expedition, like so many others, it was about what the explorers could find and take, not what belonged in the landscape and certainly not what living tribal peoples might feel about their ancestral dead. A young mother had been ripped from her grave. A few small beads lay lost in sand.

Charles Bernheimer returned to the East Coast. From the West Coast came a different kind of explorer with a privately funded vision and a fleet of woody station wagons manufactured by Ford Motor Company. Ansel

Hall, Chief Naturalist for the National Park Service, was committed to exploration and education. Though the stock market had plummeted and millions of Americans were out of work, Hall enlisted elite male college students and their professors for what became known as The Last of the Great Expeditions, "large in scale, broad in scope, and romantic in inspiration."[17] Student members paid $300 to $400 each for the privilege of hard work under a hot summer sun, insect bites, sunburn, and memories.

Headed for the heart of Navajo country, Hall's scientists skirted the Bears Ears region to the south and west. The guides he employed learned valuable lessons. After the Rainbow Bridge-Monument Valley Expedition (RBMVE) ended by 1938, one of Hall's river guides, Kenny Ross, would continue to lead small expeditions into remote areas like Dark Canyon just to the north of Bears Ears. Ross's exploration down Dark Canyon from the Bears Ears Plateau to white water rapids on the Colorado River and back would set a new standard and create a new future for Bears Ears—as a challenging canyon country landscape for young men, and later women, to hone their backpacking and camping skills in wild, remote settings. But in the 1930s with the Depression raging, drought across the Navajo Reservation, and the forced slaughter of thousands of sheep as part of stock reduction, adventure education was decades into the future.

Between 1933 and 1938, Hall sought to train young men as scout naturalists, similar to the Boy Scouts' highest rank of Eagle Scouts. Over 250 people participated in this lengthy southwestern summer sojourn across the Four Corners states. Ansel Hall sought men of good physical condition who had hobbies and collected things. His goal was to create a network of young professionals once they graduated college. The adventure motif featured travel into areas "practically unexplored" like the canyons and mesas around Rainbow Bridge and briefly into Grand Gulch off the San Juan River. No comprehensive final report was ever produced. Rather than centralize research findings and collections of Native American artifacts and natural history objects, professors took their own work and that of their students to home institutions. This resulted in a massive scholarly treasure hunt decades later. For instance, a botanist from Carleton College took his plant collections back to his biology department in Minnesota. Fortunately, dozens of photographs, hand-tinted slides, and hundreds of feet of original film remain archived in good condition.[18]

Advisory board members included Harold S. Colton from the Museum of Northern Arizona, geologist Herbert E. Gregory who had studied water resources for the Navajo,[19] A.L. Kroeber, University of

California—Berkeley anthropologist, and Jesse Nusbaum, director of the anthropology laboratory in Santa Fe and former superintendent of Mesa Verde National Park. In addition to field crews of archaeologists, paleontologists, biologists, geologists, and topographical engineers, staff included mechanics for the Ford trucks, cooks, mule packers, photographers, and a pilot who took some of the first aerial photos of Monument Valley. Staff shared dishwashing chores. Each did their own laundry. An Amherst College professor dug a phytosaur skull out of sandstone. Entomologists caught insects. Herpetologists captured gopher snakes and lizards. As for artifacts, expedition scholar Andrew L. Christensen notes, "Most whole pots or perishable artifacts came from burials."[20]

Their photographic record is one of the most successful parts of the expedition, and it represents a careful chronicle of Navajo people and Four Corners sites in the mid-1930s. The Wetherill family at Kayenta was delighted that the expedition used their trading post as a base of operations. John Wetherill, who knew the country as no one else and was then in his late sixties, became associate field director. He hoped that publicity about the expedition would bring more tourists into the area. A highlight of each year was a furious tug of war with a stout hemp rope aggressively pulled between a team of local Navajos and non-native expedition members.

Lasting accomplishments of the Rainbow Bridge Monument Valley Expedition included hiring and training Navajo guides and scouts whose sons would later guide additional explorers. An important fossil discovered was a small two-footed dinosaur, *Segisaurus halli*, named after group leader Ansel Hall and found by Max Littlesalt in Navajo sandstone. Tree ring dating of wood samples for Ancestral Puebloan sites helped solidify prehistoric time sequences for the Southwest. "The RBMVE was the largest self-supporting, multidisciplinary expedition ever conducted in North America," argues Christensen. It lapped the edges on the south side of Bears Ears and "even though the National Park Service abandoned the idea for a new park in the region soon after the expedition started (apparently for political reasons) the RMBVE maintained the goal of recording the natural and cultural resources of the area."[21]

One of the reasons Monument Valley and adjacent canyons did not become a national park was due to Navajo opposition and resistance to federal interference on tribal lands. The Navajo Nation created its own tribal park a few decades later. Across the San Juan River, on public land in the center of the canyon country where Judd and Bernheimer

The Rainbow Bridge Monument Valley Expedition sought the advice and professional guidance of John and Louisa Wetherill at their Kayenta, Arizona, Trading Post. The Expedition is lampooned here in an original drawing from the post's guest register drawn by Donald Greame Kelley in July 1933. Courtesy of Harvey Leake.

had sought shaded canyons in the heat of the afternoon, another plan emerged for a huge national monument surrounding Bears Ears. Navajos opposed a national park. Utah business interests, especially mining companies, ranchers, and stockmen like Al Scorup, owner of the Dugout Ranch in Indian Creek, fought against the proposed Escalante National Monument. The attempt to create a vast New Deal national monument to embrace the cliffs and canyons of Bears Ears and much of southeast Utah failed, but not without an interesting fight.

The area to be included in a Franklin Delano Roosevelt national monument embraced the entire Colorado River drainage from the Green River south of Green River, Utah, through the canyons of the Green and Colorado rivers including the San Juan River canyons, down through Moab, Utah, and almost to Lee's Ferry, Arizona, now the official boundary for Grand Canyon National Park. The monument was to cover a whopping 350 river miles of intricate canyons. On the Green River I have canoed stretches of this canyon country landscape, and it is the largest flatwater expanse in the central Rockies with rock art panels, historic river runner inscriptions, red cliffs, blue herons, and wilderness values. The monument's size would have included the junction of the Green and Colorado Rivers, Cataract Canyon, the Fremont and Escalante riversheds, North Wash, White Canyon, Music Temple named by Major John Wesley Powell, Padre Creek, the Hole-in-the-Rock-Crossing where Mormon pioneers cut a precarious path down a sandstone cliff to cross the Colorado River, and all of Glen Canyon.

In 1935 the superintendent of the nation's first national park, Yellowstone, extolled the virtues of an as yet unnamed new national monument. "This area is the most important of the six areas of public domain now under consideration for national monuments. It is one of the greatest wilderness areas of the country," exclaimed Roger Toll in a letter to the director of the National Park Service. "The area is practically uninhabited. Civilization has not touched it. Parts of it have seldom been explored. It is rich in outstanding features of form and color. Its scenery

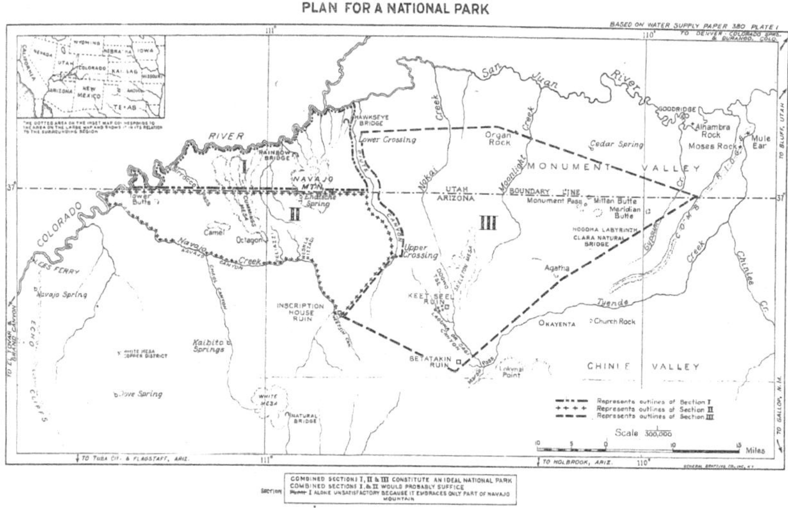

Infatuated with the canyon country of southeast Utah, explorer Charles Bernheimer proposed a Navajo National Park to the National Park Service without consulting the Navajo Nation, which rejected the idea. The park would have included canyons and drainages south of Bears Ears and the San Juan River. In early 1929 he presented the idea and this map in Washington, DC. National Archives Record Group 79 (National Park Service). Courtesy of Harvey Leake.

is varied and magnificent. It personifies silence and solitude, mystery, and enchantment."[22]

Because it was all public land, FDR could have created the West's largest national monument at 6,968 square miles or 4.8 million acres using Theodore Roosevelt's Antiquities Act.[23] "Utah state officials had been thinking more along the lines of maybe thirty-five thousand acres; grazing, mining, irrigation and commercial interests were barely able to swallow that," wryly noted T.H. Watkins, "and had no interest at all in anything bigger."[24] In the middle of the Great Depression, Congress directed Secretary of the Interior Harold Ickes to study potential recreation areas, parks, and parkways. The Utah Planning Board in 1936 proclaimed, "an extension of authority, especially of the National Park Service, would be beneficial to the people of Utah," because as historian Elmo Richardson writes, "the state's share of tourist business was far less than those of surrounding states."[25]

A National Park Service review enthusiastically supported the idea, especially at the confluence of the Green and Colorado Rivers where the colorful canyons "constitute the paramount landscape features in the entire area, and their existence alone supplies sufficient justification for the creation of a national park … Here is desolation, solitude, and peace; bringing man once more to a vivid realization of the great forces of nature."[26] Park planner Merel S. Sager in his 1937 report described flying above the area "in a northeasterly direction over the San Juan River and Grand Gulch, then [we] circled Arch Canyon south of La Sal National Forest … we found it to be as we expected, a canyon of unusual beauty, with high, many-colored pinnacles. We then passed the Bears Ears and proceeded north … we were in the air six hours, and covered approximately 600 miles of one of the most inaccessible, fantastic, and highly colored areas in America."[27] Local residents, however, wed to their extractive economies of grazing and mining, complained at public meetings and argued that in any federal reserve, prior uses should continue within the monument, and that "eastern tourists would find livestock as good an attraction as scenery."[28]

As for practicality of the monument of more than 6,000 square miles, that concept "met with strenuous opposition from the grazing interests." The NPS proposal shrank to 2,000 square miles, but still the park planner argued for protection under the Antiquities Act. "Regarding the actual need for steps taken to preserve the area, one gets the impression that because of its sheer ruggedness it will preserve itself whether in or out of

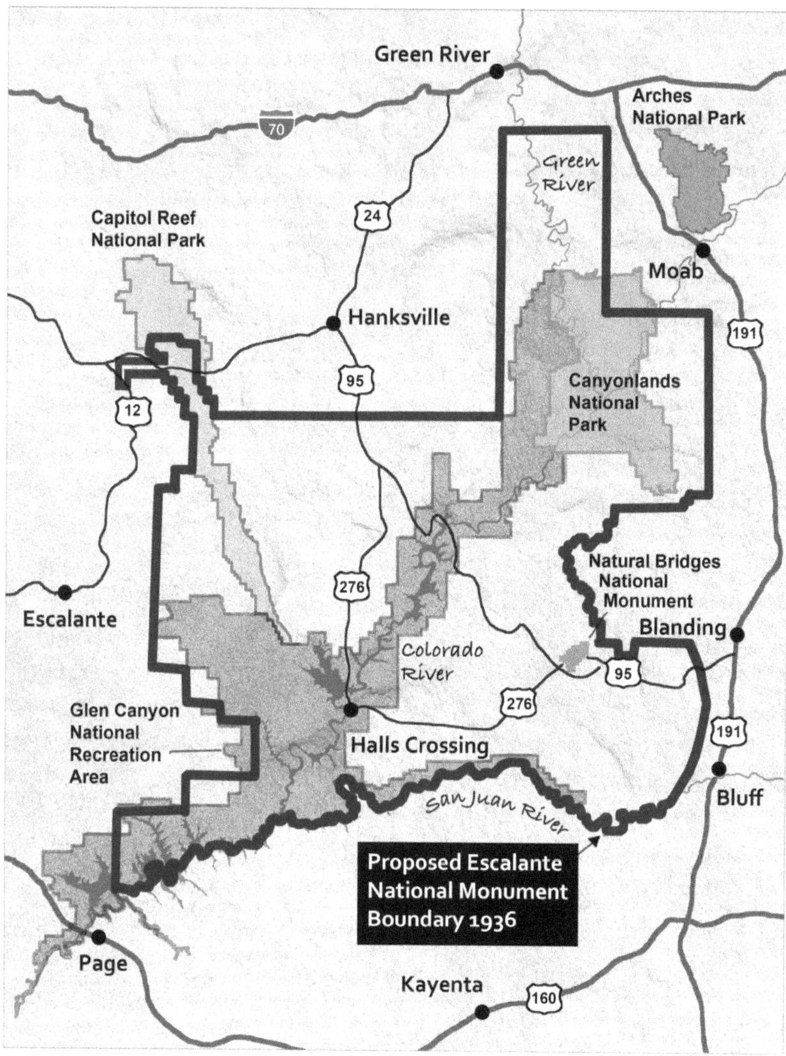

This map shows how large the Escalante National Monument of 1936 would have been compared to other national parks and national monuments in southern Utah. It would have completely enclosed the 2016 boundaries for Bears Ears National Monument. Map by DJ Webb redrawn from a modern map by NPS/Gerry Wakefield.

the Park Service. However, our past experiences," Sager argued, "should teach us that man's inherent, constitutional determination to vanquish primeval landscape is a force which has thus far never been shackled. It is well then to take steps early to set the area aside and very definitely determine the limits for its development."[29] The NPS championed natural resource protection and scenic and recreational values. Dr. Julian Steward, aware of the Bears Ears legacy of pothunting, "is outspoken in his belief that the archaeological resources are considerable and should merit attention in planning any park in the Escalante country." Supervisor of Historic Sites Ronald F. Lee stated, "It is entirely possible that more detailed examination of history and archaeology might lead to the conclusion that the area would be justified on the grounds of scientific conservation."[30]

As some groups argued to cut the proposed monument's size, others favored the complete proposal including the Southern Utah Association of Civic Clubs which met in Monticello in the summer of 1938. Two hundred of its members voted for a new national monument. Ranchers and stockmen felt otherwise. The largest ranchers in San Juan County, Al Scorup and Charlie Redd, "both were strongly against the federal government favoring tourism . . . at the expense of resource use of the area. The government was to be resisted as long as these federal domains were left alone for cattle and sheep interests."[31] President of the Utah Cattle and Horse Growers Association L.C. Montgomery agreed. He suggested legislation that would echo across the West for decades.

Unhappy with FDR's expansion of Dinosaur National Monument to include the canyons of the Green and Yampa Rivers, Montgomery sought legislation requiring local approval for presidential proclamations of national monuments in direct opposition to the Antiquities Act, which specifically spelled out executive control. By the 1930s ranchers across the West rebelled against the Antiquities Act both in Utah and in Wyoming. Economic interests worried about losing opportunities for mineral exploration and waterpower. As America entered World War II, the original proposal for Escalante National Monument, which would have enveloped Bears Ears, lost momentum. In a desperate move, Secretary Ickes tried to amend the Antiquities Act. He proposed trading executive power for declaring monuments in a swap to establish national recreation areas, specifically around New Deal dams. That failed too. "Given a choice, the westerners wanted *no* reservations, thank you very much, and probably would have abolished the Antiquities Act itself if they could," notes Watkins.[32] Despite national and some statewide enthusiasm for Utah's proposed Escalante National Monument, fears over loss of grazing rights, water rights, and mineral extraction thwarted the monument's planners.[33] The area continued to attract occasional adventurers who sought the "desolation, solitude, and peace," which park planners embraced. One of those adventurers worked briefly with the Rainbow Bridge Monument Valley Expedition and then disappeared forever.

His name was Everett Ruess, and he was an itinerant artist who walked beside burros, painted watercolors, occasionally begged food, rudely used empty Navajo hogans, and longed for desert places. Alone, he left the Utah village of Escalante, descended Davis Gulch where his two burros were later found, and vanished. He has become a southwestern legend and an icon for backpackers and wilderness wanderers. Where he may have disappeared has become its own southwestern mystery saga with one version in Davis Gulch, now under the waters of Lake Powell, and another version south of Bears Ears on the Navajo side of the San Juan River. Exploring the Southwest on foot and with burros in the early 1930s, twenty-year-old vagabond Ruess wrote, "I shall always be a lone wanderer of the wilderness. . . . I'll never stop wandering. And when the time comes to die, I'll find the wildest, loneliest, most desolate spot there is."[34] He disappeared in the fall of 1934 after telling other young boys he was headed to Fifty-Mile Mountain.

Ruess spent a few years crisscrossing the Four Corners area on the edge of Bears Ears walking from Mesa Verde to Kayenta, Arizona. He worked with the Rainbow Bridge Mesa Verde Expedition on a crew excavating archaeological sites in an alcove on remote Skeleton Mesa. Ruess has been deeply tied to wilderness issues in the American Southwest. He became a symbol for wilderness for the Southern Utah Wilderness Alliance, which continues to seek permanent protection for some of the landscapes Ruess traversed. His wanderings and abrupt disappearance have attracted searchers and researchers for decades. In his last letter written November 11, 1934 from the Escalante Rim to his brother Waldo, Ruess wrote, "As to when I shall visit civilization, it will not be soon, I think. I have not tired of the wilderness; rather I enjoy its beauty and the vagrant life I lead, more keenly all the time. I prefer the saddle to the streetcar and star-sprinkled sky to a roof, the obscure and difficult trail, leading into the unknown, to any paved highway."[35]

Volunteers searched Davis Gulch where his two burros were found in a makeshift corral. Why would he have abandoned them? Robert Lister conducted salvage archaeological work before the dam flooded Glen Canyon. Lister's wife Florence remembered, "The survey crew found a smashed tin plate and cup, a tube of mentholatum that said Owl Drug Co.—Los Angeles, and dried up tubes of paint pigment," which could have belonged to Ruess.[36] Then the trail went cold.

Riley Mitchell, Chief of Interpretation at Capitol Reef National Park, explains, "I've been out looking for Everett for years." She has used him as a metaphor to talk to visitors about why southwestern landscapes appeal to so many. To her, Ruess represents "that longing for our desire to connect with nature, to get away from cities, to touch the earth again."[37] Some of the last photos of Everett were taken in summer 1934 by members of the Rainbow Bridge Monument Valley Expedition. Ruess worked odd jobs for food. Perhaps he decided to go east instead of south for good meals and companionship. The Ruess saga has inspired books, songs, plays, and celebrations. A botched scientific analysis of his supposed DNA found in a skull, embarrassed researchers at the University of Colorado–Boulder and demonstrated errors in studying skeletal remains. In the intense publicity over finding Ruess's alleged remains, editors for *National Geographic Adventure Magazine* published an article that overlooked caution by not checking facts. Scientists ignored margins of error. A questionable oral history and a dying man's confession resulted in unearthing a historic Navajo burial on Comb Ridge near Bluff, Utah. The remains were supposed to be those of the twenty-year-old artist.

Everett Ruess has become a wilderness icon in the Southwest. He skirted the edges of Bears Ears and disappeared forever in 1936. This is one of the last photos taken of him when he briefly worked with the Rainbow Bridge Monument Valley Expedition. Photo courtesy of the Center of Southwest Studies, Fort Lewis College.

The outlines of the sensational discovery did not make sense. In 1934 Ruess's burros were found sixty miles away, yet a writer claimed Ruess's remains were discovered near Comb Ridge and Chinle Wash based on a Navajo story that Ruess had been murdered by three Utes riding horseback on the Navajo Reservation. I wrote in the *Durango Herald*,

> A 75-year-old mystery has now been solved—or has it? Did Everett Ruess visit a Navajo girlfriend? Why were his remains found 60 miles east of where he was last seen? New questions arise as old ones are laid to rest. One question is about Ruess's assailants. Would three Ute Indians have been riding horseback deep on the Navajo Reservation in 1934? Historian Robert McPherson, an expert on southeast Utah, has recorded numerous local oral histories. He told me, "I've heard nothing about the murder."[38]

Major newspapers covered the story. *National Geographic* sponsored a press conference. The DNA from the skull appeared to match the Ruess family DNA. But a BLM staffer in Monticello, Utah, intrigued by the discovery, tracked down Ruess's dental records, which verified dental work with gold fillings that the skull did not have. From the beginning of the media frenzy in 2009, Utah State Archaeologist Kevin Jones claimed that teeth in the uncovered skull showed wear patterns indicative of a Native American diet. There had been a rush to judgment, a rush to publish, and a compelling desire to have the mystery solved.

I've looked for Everett Ruess too and explored Davis Gulch off the Escalante arm of Glen Canyon National Recreation Area, much of it now buried under the receding waters of Lake Powell. I have field tested echoes and watched the moon climb slowly above the dark silhouette of canyon walls. At night, listening to summer storms rumbling down the gulch, lightning flashes pierce the blackness. I've hiked and camped in the sinuous sandstone canyons, soaked up the silence, and pondered the many nights Ruess slept alone, tired, hungry, isolated, and yet captivated by the desert Southwest.

He wrote marginal, gushing, adolescent poetry, did better with his watercolors, and excelled as an artist creating difficult block prints. A young man from Los Angeles, Ruess traveled in the depths of the Great Depression showing up uninvited at mealtimes. He routinely appropriated unused Navajo hogans. He visited remote ranches and often overstayed his welcome, yet people liked him, remembered him, and admired his perseverance because he followed his dreams. Two books help us to understand the troubled twenty-year-old, and one of the books offers the best evidence yet for why his remains were never found. *Everett Ruess: His Short Life, Mysterious Death, and Astonishing Afterlife* by Philip Fradkin can be a difficult read at times; yet we learn new details. Ruess was a pothunter, carried a pistol, and often traded his art for cash or food. In his last chapter "Resurrection, 2009," Fradkin summarizes the Ruess debacle over the unearthed remains.

Fradkin explains that just when the Ruess family thought the mystery was solved and they were preparing to cremate his remains and drop the ashes in the Pacific Ocean as is their family custom, they tried one more DNA match after contacting the Armed Forces DNA Identification Laboratory (AFDIL). Descendant Brian Ruess wrote, "The AFDIL's studies determined that [the] remains were not those of Everett Ruess." The remains had Native American DNA. Case closed. So what really happened?

The book that in my estimation finally unravels the secret of Everett's death is Flagstaff, Arizona, writer Scott Thybony's *The Disappearances: A Story of Exploration, Murder, and Mystery in the American West*. Good writers track down stories. Thybony had heard that in the 1970s human bones turned up in Davis Gulch where a Californian exploring for Indian ruins "saw bones wedged within a crack. He scaled in with a rope and saw indications of a broken hip and fractured collar bone. Leaving most of the remains in place, he took a few of the bones for identification." The tourist gave the bones to a NPS ranger, who left them with his supervisor at the Lake Powell marina at Wahweap, "and at that point they disappeared."[39]

Thybony reread the visitor's notes and set out to find the crack. He did. He also found a perfect hideaway in the sandstone—a beautiful, remote campsite in a miniature alcove where "an ancient juniper had been dragged in for firewood, and a small ring of stones had been placed against the far wall." He found a flat stone set on rocks like a small table and "by the cliffside opening, a row of stones had been laid out for leveling the sandy floor wide enough for a single bedroll. The site contained no evidence of prehistoric use, not even a potsherd or chert flake."[40]

Nearby was the unweathered inscription *NEMO 1934*. Captain Nemo piloted the submarine Jules Verne described in his fictional book *Twenty Thousand Leagues Under the Sea*. A few cryptic NEMO inscriptions have been found and photographed across the Colorado Plateau. Scholars today and previous searchers attribute the markings to Everett Ruess, who may have felt that his singularity and isolation echoed the inventive and masterful sea captain who also scorned society and social conventions.[41]

Did Scott Thybony find the last campsite of Everett Ruess? Did the young artist slip on a sandstone ledge, take a fatal fall, and die wedged in a sandstone crack? I think so. But if the mystery is solved, his legacy will endure. Everett Ruess will always be a symbol of wilderness and solo journeys across the desert Southwest. He hit the road, skirting the edges of San Juan County and the Bears Ears, establishing a wilderness hiking and personal adventure motif that still beckons today. In 1934 two other young Americans went to Bears Ears and Thybony explores their stories as well. One went as an adventure to avoid going home and the other was a young girl kidnapped by the man who murdered her father.

Like Ruess, Dan Thrapp was young, twenty-one-years-old. But unlike Ruess, Thrapp had a job and a career as a bone-hunter, a fossil finder, out to scour the West for dinosaur bones for the same New York museum that had sponsored Bernheimer's expeditions—the American Museum of Natural History. In the fall of 1934 when Ruess wrote his last letter home and disappeared never to be found again, Daniel L. Thrapp finished up work in Wyoming as part of an American Museum-Sinclair Oil Expedition and decided to verify rumors of cliff dwellings hidden in remote alcoves in southeast Utah's canyons. The summer's season had netted thirty-two tons of bones from twenty dinosaurs, packed in crates, and headed east by rail in their own boxcar.[42] Thrapp instead headed southwest by horseback into canyons south of Moab and then beyond into canyon country known only by cowboys riding ranges they patrolled. Because Thrapp did not appear when he was supposed to, search parties assembled. A ground and air search for Thrapp began in "Southern Utah Wastes" headlined the *Salt Lake Tribune*.[43]

"His reasons for being in the three-rivers country set him apart from those trying to make a living from the land. He hadn't come to punch cows, to trap or prospect," writes Scott Thybony. "His journey reflected a shift in thinking about wilderness that was beginning to take hold in the wider society. He was here for the adventure of it, to experience a pristine wilderness and uncover the clues to the past it held."[44] After cold nights alone, Thrapp arrived at the Dugout Ranch on the eastern side of Bears Ears, but his goal was the cliff dwellings hidden high in alcoves in Dark Canyon, just above and to the north of Bears Ears. Thrapp traversed the entire region. He made it to Comb Ridge, rode down the Posey Trail, still evident a decade after the Posey War, and spent a few weeks studying adjacent cliff dwellings across Cedar Mesa. Cold winter weather and gray skies in January 1935 limited his explorations, but he stayed out alone, occasionally visited by other drifters, some hiding from the law. Thrapp rode west of Clay Hills Pass, his horses exhausted, his gear falling apart, but something drove him on. "After having woven himself into the landscape so tightly, the explorer was reluctant to let it go. He had left the outer world behind to enter an elemental land and had grown accustomed to the long reaches of distances and the nearness of the past," summarizes Thybony.[45]

Expected to be gone a month, Thrapp's wilderness experience lasted three months. After staying in Comb Wash, he turned up back in Bluff. He made it easy on the search parties looking for him. He was never really lost in a physical sense, just enraptured by the desert landscape far from the cramped, confined cubicles of the American Museum of Natural History where tons of dinosaur bones remained to be unpacked and freed from their plaster casts. He simply resisted a return to civilization.

Unlike Thrapp, Lucile Garrett came into the country against her will. The man who brought her had killed her father and would kill again in a canyon south of Bears Ears. On the hot, dry prairies of Texas and Oklahoma, on the edge of the Dust Bowl in the Dirty Thirties with blowing dirt smothering corn crops and refugees driving jalopies west on US Route 66, James Clinton "Jimmy" Palmer fought fighting roosters. He encouraged Lucile Garrett and her father, a woodcutter, to work for him, but Palmer had a checkered past and a criminal record for larceny and rape. He took Lucile, better known as Lucy, west toward the Four Corners after he viciously killed her father with an ax. She did not know of the murder, only that she, a thirteen-year-old, had been forced to drive west. By July 1934 they had reached Bluff, Utah, where Palmer made a few dollars gambling. Locals whispered about the girl he was with.

Running out of money, Palmer went farther west, reaching Monument Valley and the trading post of Harry Goulding, a sheep man born in Durango who purchased Utah state land in a spectacular setting among dramatic red rocks. Navajos nicknamed Goulding "Tall Sheep" because he cast a long shadow at sunset. His flocks also set off lengthy shadows as they came in for water. Goulding had sheep to move toward grass and he could use another herder.[46] Palmer needed the money and to stay away from the law. Instead, he would shoot a sheriff.

Drought damaged the Navajo reservation, forcing Indian Commissioner John Collier to order livestock reduction and the killing of sheep, which devastated Navajo families—especially the grandmothers who owned the flocks.[47] With so little grass, Goulding pushed his flocks east from Monument Valley and into Johns Canyon or the winter range of retired Sheriff William Oliver best known for organizing posses that went after Paiute Posey. Now Oliver himself would die in canyon country in a rangeland dispute that would bring posses out to find his own body. Goulding knew that his flocks would cross close to Oliver's cattle. He told Clint Palmer to try to work things out, but he also loaned the kidnapper a pistol and a Winchester rifle for defense against coyotes hunting lambs.[48] By Thanksgiving of 1934 a pregnant Lucy moved in with the Gouldings into their two-story stone house with the trading post on the lower floor and cozy upstairs living quarters. Palmer had been moving supplies for Harry Goulding's Navajo herders while also stealing horses and putting his own JP, or Jimmy Palmer, brand on them.

Lucy gave birth. Her premature baby died a week later. She returned to Palmer, and they herded sheep on Oliver's range using a water hole desperately needed by Oliver's cattle. The old sheriff knew there would be a confrontation, and he returned to his camp armed. He was not fast enough. Jimmy Palmer shot him with a pistol, shot him with a rifle, and then, with a lariat around the dying man's neck, dragged him down the road. Lucile saw it all but was powerless to stop the psychotic Palmer, who the next day went after Oliver's grandson, Norris Shumway. Palmer fired a pistol, wounding Shumway and then in a rage again used an ax.

The killer and his kidnapped girlfriend took Oliver's car. In Monument Valley they demanded Harry Goulding turn over keys to a 1931 Chevrolet truck. They fled to Arizona and away from Johns Canyon, away from the Bears Ears. The day before he was murdered, the twenty-four-year-old Shumway carved his initials and the date on a rock at their camp called the Seeps. I have been to Johns Canyon and walked the road where "Two Gun" Jimmy Palmer dragged the dying sheriff, but I have not yet found the carved boulder. It's there undisturbed in the canyon. Bears Ears history is never erased or forgotten.

Fleeing back to Texas, Palmer was apprehended and tried for murder. At fourteen, Lucy took the witness stand. Palmer received a life sentence for the murder of her father. He was never extradited to Utah because he died in a Texas prison, but the sordid story, another in a series of Bears Ears' tales of tragedy and triumph, is still told. Goulding got his truck back but would never speak about the incident and what he had been forced to do when wild-eyed Jimmy Palmer rushed back to the trading post demanding supplies and a getaway vehicle.[49] A posse found the dead sheriff and his nearly decapitated grandson and took them home for proper burials. But in another part of San Juan County, on the eastern side of Bears Ears, a woman died and remained unburied, which resulted in a modern mummy and an additional scandal with national headlines about southeast Utah.

In 1933 in the depths of the Great Depression, forty-nine-year-old Marie Ogden, a spiritualist and millennial Christian, moved to Dry Valley in San Juan County. Ogden believed Jesus was coming to a sandstone outcropping still known as Church Rock with what looks like a door on its southern face. Ogden planned to establish a religious colony and await the end of the world. Two years later when one of the commune's members died, Ogden claimed the body was going through a transformation and left it unburied with attendants daily bathing the corpse. In the desert air of Dry Valley, the body became mummified. In Utah in 1935 there was no law about burying the dead. The story made national headlines in the *Chicago Tribune*, *Los Angeles Times*, *Milwaukee Journal*, and *Idaho Statesman*. In the 1930s there were less than forty miles of paved road in San Juan County. Settled by devout followers of the Church of Jesus Christ of Latter-day Saints, Mormon residents tolerated eccentricity and also believed in divine revelation and the kind of prophecy espoused by Marie Ogden who received revelations from her typewriter as she sat down at her desk. A former socialite and widow from Newark, New Jersey, Ogden had been married to Harry Ogden, a successful insurance executive. During World War I, she raised funds for the Red Cross and later became president of the Federated Women's Club of New Jersey. When her husband died in 1929, she and her daughter despaired. During her deep grief and soul searching, Ogden studied numerology, astrology, spiritualism, and theosophism and wrote sixty religious tracts with titles such as "Messages of the Dawn," "Wisdom," and "Truth."

"She established reading societies, study groups, spiritual soul-fights. She toured the country lecturing. The messages which came to her typewriter eventually told her to seek out the spot where the Kingdom should be built," wrote Wallace Stegner in *Mormon Country*. "Obedience, communistic living, direct revelation, personal abstemiousness and intense religious conviction, flight from the world and sanctuary in the desert, were an old story," he added.[50] Marie's followers had to give her their property, abstain from all meat, and eat only fish and vegetables. There was no alcohol, tobacco, or coffee. The one hundred or so believers lived on open

Marie Ogden founded The Home of Truth on the northeast edge of Bears Ears. This is one of the main buildings from that Depression era commune which remains along San Juan County road #211 that dips down into the Indian Creek section of Bears Ears National Monument. Author photo.

range in a world of sagebrush, sand, cactus, and low cliffs. Though it was a desert with searing summer heat and windswept winter cold, Ogden stated, "when the greater changes come we expect to have a semi-tropical climate and other changes in regard to water supply which will enable us to grow every kind of fruit and vegetable we may desire."[51]

Various articles have been written about Ogden and the Home of Truth in *Blue Mountain Shadows: The Magazine of San Juan County History*, published by the San Juan County Historical Society. Stanley J. Thayne finished his master's thesis at Brigham Young University titled, "The Home of Truth: The Metaphysical World of Marie Ogden," successfully placing her and her followers in the larger context of American millennial religious movements and calling her one of the first "New Age" religious practitioners.[52] In 1934 she wrote, "Do you know that we are approaching a New Dispensation—the Aquarian Age; the beginning of the true Christian Era when the principles of Divine law will be universally practiced as well as preached: lived as well as taught?"[53]

Ogden rejected all forms of materialism, raised followers from Boise, Idaho, and moved them to a colony fourteen miles from Monticello along

County Road 211, now the entrance to the Needles District of Canyonlands National Park and the popular rock climbing area known as Indian Creek. Her followers tried mining, farming, and gardening, but they also went hungry, worked for wages with local families, and ran San Juan County's only newspaper, the *San Juan Record*, which Ogden purchased. She published accounts of her beliefs in the newspaper and also printed religious pamphlets.

Commune carpenters built simple board and batten buildings in places called the Outer, Middle, and Inner Portal. The structures had no insulation, only tarpaper in the bedrooms. I have photographed what is left and stood in the empty doorways with door frames tilting at odd angles. Like the Ogdenites, I am also drawn to deserts for the simplicity, the clarity, and the bright stars at night. "To the deserts go prophets and hermits; through deserts go pilgrims and exiles. Here the leaders of the great religions have sought the therapeutic and spiritual values of retreat, not to escape but to find reality," wrote Paul Shepard.

Marie's followers wanted to be left alone, but publicity over the unburied corpse swirled with headlines like "Strange Cult in Desert Trying to Bring Dead Woman to Life," from the *Milwaukee Journal*. San Juan County Sheriff Lawrence Palmer visited and was turned back. Physician I.W. Allen came with nurses and determined the body of Mrs. Edith Peshak was not a health hazard. Twice daily the corpse received a salt bath and a milk enema. Eventually, the state of Utah demanded a death certificate. The woman's son, Frank Peshak, arrived. "He saw his mother's body, blue-black, mummified, shrunken, and shouted hysterically that he would take it and bury it immediately. For some reason he did not, perhaps because his father was still a cult member, still clinging to the hope that his wife would be restored, and perhaps because the nurses' report had to say in truth that the mummy was not a menace to health," wrote Stegner.[54] Secretly, in the dead of night, Marie Ogden had Mrs. Peshak cremated on a bower of cedar, pine, and juniper four feet wide, four feet high, and seven feet long. The adverse publicity of caring for a corpse diminished followers at the Home of Truth. They drifted away—some to Moab, some to Durango. "Those electing to withdraw from the sect did so completely destitute, into a largely unfamiliar region, at the harshest ebb of the worst depression in the nation's history," noted John F. Moore.[55]

The cult dispersed, but Ogden stayed, dying in a local nursing home a few weeks before turning ninety-three. She is buried with a simple gravestone in the Monticello cemetery. Her articles, diaries, and other religious tracts have been displayed at the Monticello Visitor Center. Communal living, although an interesting idea, does not often last, but I do accept Marie Ogden's belief in Utah as a magnificent landscape. Dustin Fife wrote about "Marie's references to Utah as a land of beauty and promise, [which] continued throughout her tenure as editor of the paper; more importantly, she introduced the themes of escape and renewal."[56] Sandstone salvation. The stark beauty of southeast Utah, the stunning sandstone spires of the Needles District in Canyonlands, the breadth and diversity of Bears Ears National Monument offer red rock redemption. What better place to escape to? Maybe Marie Ogden found the Home of Truth after all. In the *San Juan Record* she certainly promoted canyon country scenery and the potential for tourism.

Another newcomer from New Jersey felt the same way. Ross Musselman had learned about southeast Utah from his famous relative Roy Musselman, a government trapper who had finally killed the local wolf Bigfoot. Ross visited Roy and understood the tourist market for extended backcountry trips, having worked with youth back east from the Young Men's Christian Association (YMCA). The dedicated outdoor enthusiast moved to San Juan County in 1933 and started fourteen-day horse pack trips beginning at the Four-M Guest Ranch just east of Monticello. His exhaustive equine itinerary went into the Needles District but also stretched far to the western edge of the county via North Cottonwood, Maverick Mesa, dropping south between the Bears Ears, and exploring White Canyon's Natural Bridges and sometimes even Monument Valley.

Summers were for tours and winters for giving lectures and selling western vacations to wealthy easterners who had never seen canyon country. On Musselman's forty-person trips, sometimes five hundred miles long and a butt-bouncing twenty-five to thirty miles per day on horseback, his young visitors certainly got to experience the Bears Ears region. He was affectionately called "a one man Chamber of Commerce."[57] Ross Musselman's trips focused on geology, scenery, and Native American history and culture, but they were not archaeological expeditions like so many guided horseback trips that preceded him. Sometimes he would travel back east and then lead car caravans west to Utah. Musselman understood the need for better paved roads in the county, and so did everyone else.

"San Juan County, Utah, holds scenic phenomena and beauty unmatched by any other section of the entire world," the editor of the *San Juan Record* wrote with hyperbole on January 27, 1938 in an editorial titled "Scenery As An Asset." "Mother Nature and Father Time have dealt lavishly with this section, which is often referred to as 'the last frontier' and as 'the most primitive section of the United States.'" The editor added that roads should be improved. In contrast to decades of resistance to federal involvement the editor pleaded, "if there is a sore spot in the United States where government money is sorely needed, it is in southeastern Utah."[58]

The litany of describing spectacular scenery continued. Two months later H.E. Blake wrote in the *Record*, "The county is unique in scenic and prehistoric civilization attractions for the tourist" and "the cliff dwellings of forgotten man, or the community houses of the same races, may be sought out and studied by the seeker after such lore."[59]

But tourists needed roads, and there weren't many in San Juan County in the late 1930s. There were stretches of gravel but few miles of paved asphalt. Road building, a deep desire of county commissioners, would come only with extensive development for oil, gas, and uranium. That was in the future. Prior to World War II, two-track traces angled up and down washes and curved around canyon walls. There were few culverts and even fewer bridges. Road building became a county priority to penetrate the sandstone wilderness, which had values all its own. Despite the highway hazards, a few tourists dared to drive into the county.

In the 1930s syndicated columnist Ernie Pyle was determined to get to the Four Corners before First Lady Eleanor Roosevelt. He lampooned, "I had been holding my breath for years for fear Mrs. Roosevelt would beat me to Four Corners, but as far as I know, I made it first." Unimpressed, Pyle and a buddy kept driving through Teec Nos Pos, Arizona, and eventually arrived in Bluff, Utah, where he wrote, "Once Bluff was alive. There were cattle there, and people were rich. But that was long ago. Bluff was dead now, and well it knew it. The immense square stone houses, reminiscent of past wealth, stood like ghosts, only one or two to a block." He added, "Sand was deep in the streets. People moved slowly, for there was no competition. Nobody new ever came to Bluff."[60]

Pyle described in detail what it took to get there. He wrote, "When we started that long trip into the desert country, we prepared ourselves as though we were going from the Cape to Cairo." They outfitted their car with new tires, a shovel, a five-gallon water can for the car's radiator, and a gallon of water for the pair of them. They brought a tire pump, tire patches, extra fan belts, extra oil, gunny sacks, a snake bite kit, a first aid kit, a pistol and a rifle, and a block of wood to balance a tire jack on in soft sand. "Of all this paraphernalia, we had no need for anything except the two cans of water, the funnel, and a tin cup. We never saw a snake. We never saw anything to shoot at except some prairie dogs. We didn't eat our sardines, and the fan belt didn't break." But Pyle cautioned, "Yet if I was making the trip again, I wouldn't eliminate a thing. For it is possible to need all those things in the desert, and when you need them, you need them bad."[61]

Like the editor of the *San Juan Record*, Pyle didn't think much of local roads. He wrote,

> Just after you leave Bluff, Utah, there is a big white and black sign of the Utah State Road Commission, with this heartening message on it:
> FIFTY-ONE MILES OF NARROW, STEEP GRADES AND UNBRIDGED WASHES. DANGEROUS WHEN IN FLOOD. BE CAREFULL.
> It scares you so badly you can even excuse their poor spelling.[62]

Pyle noted that roads were bad on the Navajo Reservation, but "the worst part was the ten miles between Bluff and Comb Wash, Utah. As they term it in Bluff, the road is 'slow.' My term for it would be 'it stinks.'" Ernie didn't appreciate driving "across acres of solid sheet rock." He added, "You're through sand to the hubs. You're all the time so up-and-downish you can hardly sit in the car."

After a very slow crawl up Navajo Hill on a single lane track, he complained, "And when you finally make the summit of Comb Ridge, and swing around a hairpin turn, you are suddenly and surprisingly confronted with the steepest down-grade I've ever been on." Reporter that he was, Pyle noted that in Arizona locals said the roads were bad in Utah. In Utah they said the roads were bad in Arizona. Ernie emphasized, "[T]he truth is that nowhere on the Arizona side did we find roads as bad as Utah."[63] Off in the distance, the twin peaks of Bears Ears glittered above Elk Ridge, but Ernie, with both hands on the wheel and worried about getting stuck in sand, probably didn't see them.

Geologist Herbert E. Gregory did. He camped beneath them and agreed with his fellow scientist W.H. Holmes from the 19th century. Gregory wrote in his 1938 report, "Elk Ridge is a plateau or mesa much like Kaiparowits or Mesa Verde, and the term 'Bears Ears Plateau' as applied by Holmes is much more appropriate than the name now in use."[64] Gregory described the landscape and "the beautifully colored buttes that rise above it. Instrumental measurements show a long, flat dome—in fact, two domes separated by a shallow swale—with a top at 8,400 feet. The culminating feature is the Bears Ears, 9,040 feet," which is a condensed section of the Chinle formation from the Upper Triassic era. The ears contain red and yellow shales, thin beds of red sandstone, mud lumps, limestone conglomerates, and other colored sandstone of purple, green, red, brown, and gray.[65]

Ernie Pyle never returned to southeast Utah and the Bears Ears. He made it to Blanding, Bluff, and Mexican Hat, where he was one of the first writers to report on Norman Nevills and his Nevills Expeditions, which took Nevills's wooden boats with paying customers down the San Juan River through Glen Canyon to Lee's Ferry. Nevills would open up wild canyon country by guiding river trips just like John Wetherill and Zeke Johnson opened the Bears Ears region with their horse and mule pack trips. An eight-day trip from Mexican Hat to Lee's Ferry, including food, a cook, and sleeping bags, cost $62.50. Nevills proclaimed, "See the desert by water." When running white water he yelled, "Face Your Danger" as his passengers hung on for dear life in rapids and occasionally bashed their foreheads on Nevills's custom-made marine plywood boats. On a San Juan trip, Ernie Pyle fell forward and knocked off a boat's dashboard, which he swore had been attached with long screws. Pyle did not return to the Bears Ears country. He became one of the most celebrated World War II correspondents, and he was killed by a Japanese machine gun bullet near Okinawa. Nevills himself would die in a tragic airplane accident just as the Southwest's commercial river running industry, which he helped to launch, was beginning.[66]

If in the 1930s tourists had begun coming to Bears Ears, for Utah Navajos on the northern reservation, that decade brought drought, desperation, and resistance. Fearful that erosion in tributaries along the San Juan River would bring tons of silt and sand up against new dams being built across the Colorado Plateau, Indian Commissioner John Collier demanded stock reduction to reduce soil erosion. Navajos nicknamed him "Sheep-killer Collier." While other communities on the reservation bitterly condemned stock reduction that fell hardest on Navajo mothers and grandmothers who owned the flocks and herds, Utah Navajos in the Bears Ears region openly resisted. They especially fought reducing their beloved horses, an essential part of a male's identity. Utah Navajos remembered the Long Walk of the nineteenth century. They armed themselves to fight against grazing violations, trespass of their animals, and confiscation of their livestock.

"By summer 1941, the air sizzled with tension. A group of fifteen men attacked two range riders and released a herd of captured horses from a holding pen. Within weeks, as government officials issued trespass notices, the people around Aneth, Monument Valley, and Navajo Mountain—the descendants of Hashke Neiniih [Hoskininni] and Whiteman Killer—threatened armed resistance," wrote Marsha Weisiger. "It seemed that the northern Navajo Reservation was about to explode."[67] "Overt acts of resistance" included refusal to dip their sheep in troughs to reduce scabies and other diseases. Dipped sheep could be counted. If a family had too many, their flocks could be confiscated. As the threat of World War II increased, "an armed band of Navajos gathered near Aneth and camped on Montezuma Creek … to resist the serving of warrants for Selective Service evaders." Historian Richard White continued, "The draft was unpopular on the reservation; as one Navajo had contemptuously declared … the government, not satisfied with reducing their livestock, now intended to reduce their young men."[68] Resistance and protest at Aneth would continue decades later. In the 1940s, into that tense situation rife with cultural differences, came a man of the cloth.

Tourists arrived in Bears Ears for their own personal adventures, but one newcomer came not to visit trading posts and to buy Navajo rugs and silver jewelry, but to help the Navajos themselves. He built an Episcopal Mission and a desperately needed medical clinic. Navajos nicknamed Harry Goulding "Tall Sheep." Episcopal priest Father Harold Baxter Liebler would earn his own nickname too. Riding horseback above the San Juan River and under high sandstone cliffs, in July 1942, Father Liebler looked to establish a mission for the Navajo and to give up his ecclesiastical position in Old Greenwich, Connecticut. He sought to trade a comfortable East Coast Episcopal diocese for a financially precarious southwestern mission. As he scouted the area, similar to Marie Ogden, he had a vision. Liebler's vision, however, embraced Native Americans. He explained that he was "looking for a place where people had not come in contact with Christian teachings—a place where the best of Christianity and the Indian way of life could merge."[69]

He held mass in Mexican Hat, Utah, and then traveled back east on the road Ernie Pyle despised. After his initial visit, Father Liebler recalled years later, "I found there were no churches, no schools, and no medical care. I wrote home and told my parish that I must move here. There was a need for me. It was unbelievable that human beings were living such pitiful lives in our great country."[70] The Navajo language can be very expressive,

Ted Frank and John Billy Atcitty pose as acolytes with Episcopal Priest H. Baxter Liebler who founded St. Christopher's Mission just east of Bluff, Utah. St. Christopher's Mission Collection, courtesy of the San Juan County Historical Commission.

and nicknames often reflect a person's character or description. Father Liebler became ill after arriving in Utah so his first nickname translated as "the priest who drags his robe with a sore gut." He got better, found a cultivated area east of Bluff known as Hyrum's field, and began to build a mission that would embrace 3,000 square miles of northern Arizona and southern Utah. The Father traveled 25,000 miles a year, often using small hogans as temporary chapels. He kept his hair long, first because of a lack of a barber and then because it fit traditional Navajo ways. Thus, Liebler earned a new Navajo nickname as "drag robe with long hair" or simply "long hair." Wearing an ankle length cassock, he kept his hair Navajo style in a bun behind his head in a *tsii'eel* or "hair load."[71]

He confronted poverty, illness, and the need for education. He established a mission school and brought to southeast Utah devout Episcopal volunteers. At historic boarding schools, Native American children were forced to have their hair shorn. When Navajo parents made it clear they wanted none of that, the priest smiled, touched his own long hair, and said it would not happen in his mission school.[72] Liebler learned to talk and sing in Navajo. His newsletter reached 18,000 subscribers who donated food and clothes. Liebler ministered to the Utah Strip, or that part of the Navajo Reservation in Utah that stretches from Aneth on the east side to Navajo Mountain on the far western edge of the county. The Episcopal priest helped Navajos both north and south of the San Juan River. In 1940 despite its vast size, only 4,712 people lived in San Juan County, with 1,443 of them Navajos. South of the river, 39 of 349 homes had running water, and only 37 had electricity. Of the 18 or 20 occupied houses in Bluff in 1942, Liebler noted there were two bathtubs and only one phone for the community.[73]

The priest had entered a world still on the edge of the nineteenth century and far different from Old Greenwich, Connecticut, but he embraced it and enthusiastically set out to learn Navajo culture, customs, and traditions. He did so with occasional paternalism, but he was on a "cultural and ecclesiastical frontier" as he established St. Christopher's Mission, named after the patron saint of travelers. He became a traveler himself, preaching in Navajo, giving sacraments, blessings, and baptisms. "This New England clergyman represents the best of his kind—honest in displaying the limitations of his vision, earnest in his struggle to transcend them, and essentially peaceful in the errors he made and strove to surmount, sometimes knowingly and sometimes in spite of himself," explains Navajo scholar Paul G. Zolbrod.[74] One of Liebler's biggest challenges was dealing with the numerous cases of tuberculosis and eye disease that continued to devastate the Navajo population. He has been called "the desert priest with hard hands and a soft heart."[75]

Navajo children were born in the clinic at St. Christopher's Mission. A cemetery there holds numerous graves.[76] Father Liebler's remains repose in a small fenced area near the remnants of a stone altar, all that is left of his original chapel. When he started his mission in the early 1940s, employment options for Navajos were largely limited to sheepherding and working on railroads. World War II changed all that just as mining for carnotite, uranium, and vanadium permanently altered San Juan County and brought in new roads, new people, and community upgrades for Blanding and Monticello.

Above the San Juan River, high atop Elk Ridge, the Bears Ears continued to play a vital role in traditional Native American plant gathering, hunting, and summer camping 4,000 feet above the heat of the desert floor. Native families came to play and to pray as their ancestors had done resisting Kit Carson. In the surrounding canyons, prospectors soon arrived in Jeeps, dust on their khaki pants and boots, Geiger counters on the seat beside them.

CHAPTER 10

Yellowcake, the Atomic Age, and a Golden Circle, 1945–1970

> I suppose you had to be a little crazy and part gambler to be a miner, but it was a very fine, enjoyable occupation in many respects. I don't think miners ever worried about radiation then and they don't worry about it now.
>
> —Glen A. "Hubby" Shumway, *Blue Mountain Shadows*

> In this abundant space and isolation, the energy lords extract their bounty of natural resources, and the curators of mass destruction once mined their egregious weapons and reckless acts. It is a land of absolutes, of passion and indifference, lush textures and inscrutable tensions.
>
> —Ellen Meloy, *The Last Cheater's Waltz*

> If you live in this area long enough, the blow sand gets in your soul. That's why you stay here. No matter where you go, its charm will forever tug on you like a magnet.
>
> —Bates Wilson, first Canyonlands National Park superintendent

In San Juan County, Utah, farmers plowed more ground after World War II. A few ranchers made fortunes, but the real economic boost was oil and gas drilling near the Navajo community of Aneth and mining first for vanadium and then uranium as the newly formed Atomic Energy Commission set a base price for "yellowcake" and created a uranium boom. Mining and milling uranium paid solid wages and engaged multiple generations of local families, both Anglo and Native American. They bought new trucks, built new houses, and tried to avoid the lack of ventilation at work as daily they became covered in dangerous radioactive dust that left serious health consequences especially for miners who smoked cigarettes. The effects of radiation were not yet fully understood, and health and safety warnings were often nonexistent.

Prospecting and mining brought dirt and gravel roads to help "open up" the country. For every mile of official road, Jeeps blazed ten or more miles of two-track paths crossing washes, dodging boulders, and skirting sides of a canyon's rim. The mineral belt for uranium and vanadium included Cottonwood Wash as it drained over sixty miles from the Abajo Mountains near Blanding. Prospectors found uranium in White Canyon at the famous Happy Jack Mine and in various locations on Elk Ridge to the east and north of the Bears Ears itself.

For local families, staking, trading, and selling claims or beginning small mines of the "dog hole" variety became a satisfying way of life despite the health risks from radon gas. Blanding and Monticello families felt connected to the nation and the world because of their part in the bustling Atomic Age and what was touted as a revolutionary new energy source. Uranium processing mills opened at Monticello and near Mexican Hat. A uranium rush in Monument Valley brought work for hundreds of Navajo men who had returned home from defense plants and fighting overseas.

Of World War II inventions that changed the American West, surplus US Army Jeeps and rubber rafts had a huge impact first on uranium prospectors and then on a fledgling but expanding river running industry. The Bears Ears region would be more affected by Jeeps than rafts; yet inflatable boats going down the San Juan River from Bluff and Mexican Hat through the Goosenecks and on to Clay Hills would encourage adventure tourism. The thriving post World War II economy brought an increase in tourism and a new social movement different than anything before. In the late 1930s Theodore Roosevelt's cousin President Franklin Roosevelt signed into law some of Utah's most iconic national monuments and national parks. Now after the war with American cities sprawling into suburbs, a new land-use philosophy was evolving. Old-style conservation was about efficiency and not wasting American resources of timber, grass, water, and minerals. A new idea emerged to leave landscapes alone, to protect animals and plants in their native habitats, and to preserve remnants of the nation not for their economic potential but for the wilderness values of silence, solitude, darkness, and the adventure of crossing difficult places solo or in small groups. Not everyone in the 1950s wanted to spend their evenings eating warmed-over TV dinners in aluminum trays while sitting in front of a black-and-white television screen.

As San Juan County embraced mining, a large section of the county north of the Bears Ears became, by an act of Congress, Canyonlands

National Park. An environmental movement had begun to not only continue preserving scenery, but also limit access to back country areas by traveling only on foot, on horseback, or with a paddle or oar, no motors allowed. In 1964 President Lyndon B. Johnson signed the Wilderness Act on September 3 and authorized Canyonlands National Park on September 12. The two laws would have a huge impact on San Juan County. The new national park encompassed 580,000 acres within the county. Congress would set aside Dark Canyon as a federal wilderness and numerous wilderness study areas would be sprinkled across the Bears Ears region. Wilderness study areas (WSAs) have wilderness qualities and no roads, but they have not yet been voted on by Congress, so they are in legal limbo. Across Bears Ears, a rugged, remote landscape continued to attract a certain kind of visitor. Nicknamed "desert rats" or "canyon rats," they carried tepid water in their canteens, cooked over open fires, stared at the outstretched Milky Way as they slept under the stars, and thought the county's cliffs and canyons should be left undisturbed. This new breed of visitors wanted to preserve the wild scenery. The descendants of San Juan County's Mormon pioneers were still trying to survive it.

Because of four-wheel drive technology and new mining roads in the post-war decades, archaeological looting continued across Bears Ears, scattering precious artifacts to fireplace mantles and the grasping hands of private collectors. At least one major find, an extraordinary prehistoric feathered sash made from scarlet macaw parrot feathers, is safe in a state museum. Kent Frost discovered the unique artifact in the back of an overhang while leading a Jeep tour. The days of horseback tours with well-packed mules, loads lashed with a single rope, and diamond-hitch knots had ended. Guides and wranglers like John Wetherill and Zeke Johnson had been superseded by Frost, who started off as a boatman for Norman Nevills and decided the future for guiding in San Juan County was with Jeeps. He was right.

Another boatman, experience gained from the Rainbow Bridge Monument Valley Expedition, would also lead tours. Kenny Ross would become field manager for Ansel Hall's Explorers Club made up of adolescent boys not old enough for college but ready for the great outdoors. In the years to come, youth groups would take hundreds of trips seeking adventure in San Juan County, but one of the first descended Dark Canyon. There would be a uranium boom, a petroleum boom, and one last skirmish with Navajos over grazing in the Bears Ears region with white resistance to small Native American encampments and their flocks of sheep and horse herds. As a federal agency, the BLM was new, but BLM staff joined area stockmen in driving Navajo families south across the San Juan River away from their traditional grazing areas. It all began with a drought.

Consummate guide and archaeological explorer John Wetherill may have been the first prospector to identify a potential uranium claim in the Bears Ears region though he never filed the paperwork. Seeking summer shade in 1898, Wetherill took an archaeological group into a Red Canyon cave, where he found a petrified log that he thought contained yellow uranium. When he told Preston Redd about it in 1943, Redd found the cave and staked it as the Blue Lizard claim. Wetherill's log held no mineral value, but the area around the cave did.[1]

Writing in the local heritage publication *Blue Mountain Shadows*, researcher and consulting archaeologist Lee A. Bennett provides the best synthesis for understanding the beginning of radium, vanadium, and uranium mining in San Juan County. She describes claims along Comb Wash in the 1930s as well as detailed filings by the Shumway family—A.E., Harris, Lee, and Seth in South Cottonwood Creek. Mining claims had names like Cedar Bird, Cliff House, Last Chance, Recapture, Skunk, Chamiso, and Confusion.[2]

In a ranching economy with only a small percentage of tillable farmland, locals welcomed the new financial opportunities that came with mining. They could prospect sites, begin their own mines, and sell ore to mills owned by the Vanadium Corporation of America (VCA) or the United States Vanadium Corporation (USVC). By the late 1930s a vanadium mill had been constructed in Cottonwood Wash, and another one would be built south of Monticello. As a hardener for steel, vanadium, often found near uranium, had a definite market during World War II. Bennett notes that in Cottonwood Wash, "Mining was done by hand using star drills, hammers, shovels, and wheelbarrows. . . . Miners often worked in dust so thick their smaller carbide headlamps were almost ineffective; no ventilation fans were used at this time."[3] In Cottonwood, ore bodies were fragmentary, shallow, and not connected to each other. Mines provided a sampling of ore, but no large veins sunk deep into the earth.

The small Cottonwood mines brought in family paychecks but also new roads, including State Highway 95 west from Blanding that dropped into Westwater Canyon after Shirt Tail Junction. The gravel road meandered north and west and followed the original trail bisecting the Bears Ears before descending Elk Ridge and continuing west to White Canyon. Portions of the road are still in use but all traffic now takes US Highway 95, which cuts through Comb Ridge in a different place. The old highway signs are gone, but a few stout wooden vertical posts remain. Rains and snows have gullied out the road at the top of the Comb. Ancestral Puebloans used that route too. A prominent rock art panel depicts bighorn sheep imagery, sandals, male dancers with their legs kicked high, and what looks for all the world like an etched beer mug. I've walked along the ledge and looked down with binoculars at the old road alignment and shuddered. It was steep, narrow, and treacherous, with two hairpin turns and no guard rails. The road would have terrified truckers. A large 1960s car, rusting, glass gone, wheels taken, seems suspended in air perched on a boulder that stopped its slide to the canyon floor far below. I hope the occupants got out safely. Farther down the road a small, smashed bulldozer rusts in the sun. The fall would have been quite a ride for the Caterpillar operator. I imagine he jumped off.

Local miners made a few dollars with vanadium, but the real mining boom began with uranium. "Like the ugly duckling, uranium seemed to change overnight with the announcement on August 8, 1945 that an atomic bomb had been dropped on Hiroshima," wrote historian Gary

This photo shows old Highway 95 as it descended from Comb Ridge. In the early years of the uranium boom truckers regularly drove this road with its sharp turns and no guard rails. San Juan County Commissioner Calvin Black wanted a new paved highway; Ed Abbey liked the dangerous cliff-hanging road the way it was. Author photo.

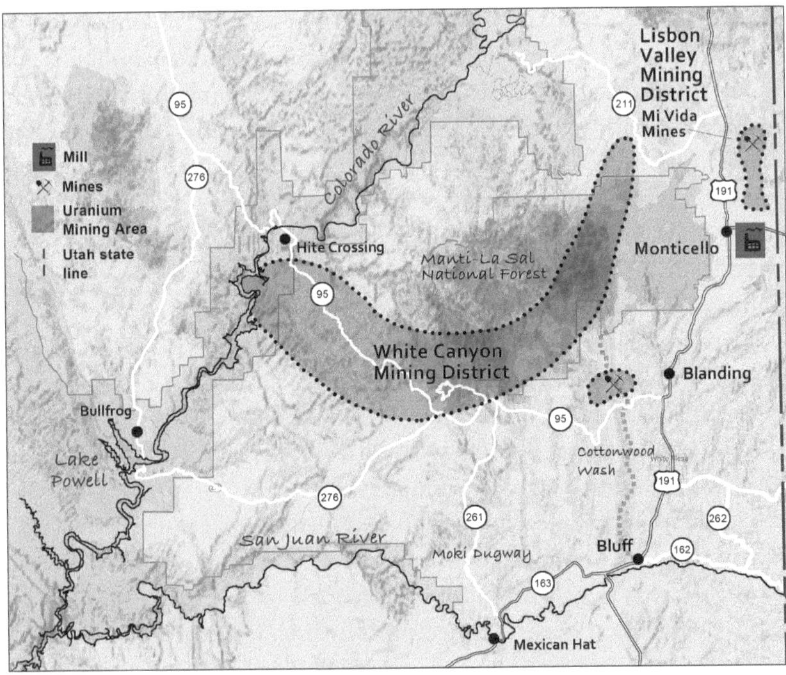

A map of potential uranium deposits within the boundaries of Bears Ears National Monument explains the mid-twentieth century mining boom that brought millions of dollars of tax revenue into San Juan County. The Atomic Energy Commission paid a fixed price for uranium ore, which now has a low market value. Map by DJ Webb © by author.

Lee Shumway. "Whereas most miners had not even considered uranium worth saving, it suddenly became the most strategically important metal in the world."[4] World War II ended, but the Cold War and an arms race immediately began with establishment of the Atomic Energy Commission (AEC) in 1946. The AEC set the price for uranium ore and purchased it to develop America's nuclear arsenal. This was a monopsony because the federal government was the only buyer for uranium ore. Beyond Natural Bridges, White Canyon had a mill by 1949. When the AEC offered a $10,000 bonus for the discovery of new uranium deposits, prospectors flooded the Colorado Plateau and San Juan County's canyon country. They came in old trucks. They drove surplus Jeeps. Their families lived in trailers along sandy washes wherever cottonwood trees provided shade.

Elk Ridge was drilled and mapped for uranium deposits with a spider web of roads bulldozed ahead of the drilling rigs. A 1950 US Geological

Survey of "uranium occurrences" in White Canyon included descriptions of the Happy Jack and Four Aces mines and claims named Scotty, Posey, Hideout No. 1, Scenic, Saddle, and Bear.[5] The geologists studied "uraniferous" deposits that were "flat-lying, roughly lenticular" across sandstones and shales, 200 to 300 feet long and five to ten feet thick.[6] A prospector could make money mining or perhaps even more dollars by consolidating and selling claims. The Shumway brothers sold eighty-four claims in Red Canyon, White Canyon, and Deer Flats for $200,000.[7]

San Juan County citizens had long resisted the federal government first over antipolygamy laws and then over grazing rights and conflicts with Native Americans. But residents embraced the government-sponsored uranium boom. The huge financial bonanza was "the first government-promoted, government-supported, and government-controlled mineral rush in American history," reported the magazine *Fortune*.[8] It would transform the county and open up new roads across the entire Colorado Plateau. "Uranium fever" took many forms including prospecting parties, celebratory wedding cakes with mushroom clouds made of white frosting, and a rapid rise in the sale of clicking Geiger counters. Every prospector wanted to peg the needle indicating a rich ore body. Few ore bodies held more than ten thousand tons of ore and prospects seemed dim for a US uranium industry—at first.

Americans love a rags-to-riches story and the tale of geologist Charlie Steen, down to his last dollar and desperately needing food and gasoline, created such a hard hat hero. To the east of Bears Ears in Lisbon Valley close to the northern edge of San Juan County, in July 1952 Steen struck a huge ore body of high-grade uranium near Big Indian Road. He made national and international news with his Mi Vida claim and the Atlas Mill he helped build along the Colorado River at Moab. Steen had suffered through hard times. For two and a half years, he begged and borrowed money, equipment, food, and stole coal to stay warm. He could not afford canned milk for his baby. With a borrowed drill from the merchant who had grubstaked him, Steen drilled down 177 feet into rock that he thought might show promise at 200 feet. The drill broke. He was broke. Dejected, he threw some sample rock into the back of his battered open Jeep and returned to Cisco, Utah, where he lived in a small shack with his family because he had been forced to sell his trailer. At the local gas station as Charlie complained about his bad luck, the attendant randomly tested the ore with a Geiger counter. Furious clicking erupted. The needle pegged. "We've struck it—it's a million-dollar lick!" Steen yelled to his wife.[9]

Geologist Charlie Steen, down to his last dollar, struck it rich with a thick seam of uranium at his Mi Vida Mine. He helped start a uranium boom that brought enormous economic benefits to San Juan County and many more roads into Bears Ears. He is pictured here at the Utah State Capitol. Photo courtesy of Utah State Historical Society.

He had found a vein containing a million tons of ore. Steen jump-started a uranium rush for concentrated uranium oxide or "yellowcake" based on the mineral carnotite found by deep drilling into the Shinarump layer, which is a member of the Chinle formation. With his sudden wealth Steen built a large contemporary-style mansion high on a hill in Moab. As the nation delighted in new television shows, Steen did too, but Moab had poor reception. If there was something he really wanted to watch, he would circle above town in his private plane to watch TV in the comfort of his aircraft. He got a clearer picture and less static that way.

Moab, Utah, claimed to be the uranium capitol of the world. In Grants, New Mexico, at the Uranium Café a miner could order a plate of yellow cakes for breakfast and for lunch or dinner the uranium burger—a hamburger slathered in Tabasco sauce. Small towns had Miss Uranium pageants and Grand Junction, Colorado, featured Miss Atomic Energy. There was a uranium rush board game where players began with a $15,000 grubstake. A popular Rockabilly song had guitarists singing "the Uranium Rock." At the dedication of Moab's new uranium mill, Steen joked,

> prospectors whose sunblistered brow, bunioned feet, seatless pants, crock haircuts, and insanely glittering eye show that they have qualified as bone-fried desert country-type prospectors and uranium hounds, thoroughly tested by blazing suns, freezing winds, reddish sandstorms, hungry scorpions, and the tall tales of crossroad and county seat barroom liars and promoters; prospectors who have blistered their rumps riding burros and jeeps, have gone without baths and women, have trekked over deserts, climbed buttes, swum rivers, run rapids, and jumped arroyos—not to mention a few claims.[10]

From mid-1952 onward, uranium strikes and uranium news covered the front page of the local *San Juan Record*. Within a year after Steen's discovery, mining claims in San Juan County jumped 400 percent. At the peak of the uranium frenzy in 1954, prospectors filed 97,661 notices at the county courthouse in Monticello.[11] Of the county's five million acres, 40 percent had been staked for uranium claims.[12] By 1955 the formerly broke geologist and mining prospector Steen began grossing $250,000 per month.[13]

Headlines included "Uranium Activities Bring Recorders Work to All Time High in San Juan" and "Utah Uranium Ore Fields Seen as Greatest in World."[14] Across the nation, but especially in Salt Lake City, Americans scrambled to buy penny stocks for potential uranium mines so they too could become overnight millionaires or at least make a few bucks. There were other San Juan success stories. Road contractor Joe Cooper from Monticello and his father-in-law paid $500 for the Happy Jack claim in White Canyon to mine copper. They couldn't. It was too contaminated with uranium and processing out the copper cost too much, so they were ready to relinquish the claim for back taxes. Then the Atomic Energy Corporation began its purchase of uranium ores. Their $500 mining claim resold for $25 million.[15]

By 1958 San Juan County produced 90 percent of Utah's uranium and 36 percent of the nation's annual production. At decade's end, 95 percent of local taxes came from uranium mines or petroleum wells resulting in better roads, schools, libraries, and water supplies.[16] "Economically speaking, San Juan County was the forgotten county of Utah—a supposedly worthless section of earth reserved for the Indians and very few whites.... Many of the citizens were living in houses without such essentials as plumbing and electrical facilities. The county school system was about the poorest (financially) in the state," wrote Robert L. Payner.[17] Everything changed with the energy boom.

"The United States' need for uranium for national defense was so urgent that the AEC created numerous incentives for prospectors and miners to search for and produce uranium," noted geologist William L. Chenoweth. "The activity created by these incentives soon grew into huge proportions."[18] As the market rose and stabilized for uranium at the mill in Monticello, prospecting in White Canyon and Red Canyon increased with finds of copper-uranium ores. The Vanadium Corporation of America built a mill at White Canyon and ore came from the Happy Jack, the Radium King, the Hideout, Markey, and Maybe mines. One corporation forever changed the Bears Ears landscape and access across Cedar Mesa.

The Texas Zinc Corporation purchased the Happy Jack Mine and decided to ship their ore to the uranium mill in Mexican Hat. There was no road from Fry Canyon, near White Canyon, down and off Cedar Mesa, so the corporation bulldozed thirty-three miles in more or less a straight line south across the heart of Cedar Mesa in 1956 and 1957. Then they came to a cliff. They went straight down it, or at least it seems that way. Driving from Bluff to Mexican Hat, on the road that Ernie Pyle felt was worthless, Cedar Mesa towers above the Valley of the Gods as a long stretch of pinyon pines and incised canyons, flat on top, but steep. Ernie's road is now US Highway 163, perfectly paved and drivable. Turning north onto State Route 261 the pavement continues until it reaches the base of Cedar Mesa where the road appears to disappear. It does not. It becomes dirt and loose gravel and goes up one of the most famous drives in the West called the Moki Dugway, which is how Texas Zinc's road crew got off the top of the mesa. They simply bulldozed and dynamited their way down in a series of curves with soft shoulders on cliffs falling away to the valley floor hundreds of feet below. There are no guard rails.

Driving off Cedar Mesa close to sunset, it is thrilling to stop at the top and walk to the edge and look toward Navajo Mountain, Monument Valley, and the San Juan River below the zigzag colored lines of Raplee's Incline. Careful scrutiny also reveals a few wrecks, just like at the old cut through Comb Ridge. Near the top of the Moki Dugway the metal frame of a truck trailer poses upside down. A little lower a yellow pickup truck lies smashed. Standing on the cliff edge, updrafts trying to steal my cap, I'm overwhelmed at the view and the audacity of the road builders. Such is the road-building legacy of uranium mining. Atop the Moki Dugway, driving north in a straight line, the Bears Ears loom ahead as an ancient landmark visible over a hundred miles in almost any direction.

At the same time as the uranium boom in spring 1956, wildcat drillers discovered a huge oil and gas field in the southeastern part of San Juan County near the Navajo community of Aneth. The first well produced 1,704 barrels of oil per day, and by the end of the year, the Aneth oil field paid out $34.5 million in bonuses and royalties.[19] Oil and gas drilling had occurred on the reservation as early as the 1920s forcing establishment of the Navajo Tribal Council to authorize oil and gas leases. The Aneth field, beginning in the mid-1950s, "perhaps the most significant field in the Rocky Mountain region," reached 500 wells with a production of 430 million barrels of oil.[20] Royalties of 62.5 percent went to the Navajo Nation and 37.5 percent to Utah Navajos to be administered by the state.[21]

Many of those dollars went for road and bridge construction while Aneth Natives remained without running water or electricity and damage done to grazing areas. Over time, "Residents near Aneth, Utah, suffered from environmental problems and cultural conflicts with oil-field workers while receiving no commensurate benefits."[22] Millions of dollars in oil had been taken from under their lands, but Aneth Navajos had nothing to show for it. In the decades ahead, they would protest against oil companies.

A Utah Indian Affairs Commission, with only one Navajo representative, was to distribute royalty funds, but commissioners quibbled over how to allocate funds and did nothing. Dollars continued to accrue. Aneth residents would join other parts of San Juan County in a landscape of resistance, especially because Native American voting had been denied for decades in Utah. As late as 1958, "all states except Utah allowed Indians, whether residing on Indian reservations or not, to vote." Finally, a lawsuit by Utes allowed Native voting for the first time in county and state elections.[23] Throughout the 1950s and 1960s, mining and oil drilling escalated in San Juan County, but so did a new industry—outdoor recreation. It did not yet have that name, and it began in fits and starts, but just as canyon country called to miners, it also called to hikers using a new technology—backpacks. Land ownership questions arose, from not only miners, but also Native land claims that tribes documented.

In 1946 the original General Land Office, whose job it was to sell the public domain, merged with the Grazing Service.[24] The new federal agency became the largest landowner in the nation—the BLM, whose holdings include 41 percent of San Juan County or 2,074,247 acres, a significant portion of which would be included in Bears Ears National Monument. After World War II, San Juan County residents continued their love-hate relationship with public lands and often focused their concerns and resentment on local BLM employees trying to enforce federal rules and regulations.

Those immediate postwar years also saw one of the last mule and horse pack archaeological expeditions into the Bears Ears region of remote western San Juan County. Expert wranglers from the Scorup-Somerville Cattle Company at the Dugout Ranch guided the scientific party that bought supplies from the Parley Redd Mercantile in Blanding. From 1945 to 1947, staff affiliated with the Carnegie Museum of Natural History in Pittsburgh, Pennsylvania surface collected artifacts from archaeological sites north of Dark Canyon in Fable Valley and north of Fry Canyon in the largely untraversed San Juan Triangle, the rocky wedge of sinuous canyons between the Colorado and San Juan Rivers. In the heat of summer, the explorers entered cliff dwellings in Cheesebox Canyon, Hideout Canyon, Deer Canyon, and in an unnamed canyon they named K & L Canyon after scientist J. LeRoy Kay and guide Henry Lyman.

The year they started, in 1945, the uranium boom helped extend Utah State Highway 95 from Natural Bridges to the Hite Ferry. At the time, the Carnegie's artifact collection was considered "the only known scientifically collected archaeological material for much of the area of southeastern Utah."[25] The expedition collected artifacts, photographed ruins, and took tree ring samples as a precursor to the massive salvage archaeological project that would precede closing the gates at Glen Canyon Dam and flooding hundreds of archaeological sites.

Archaeologist Florence Lister made the ceramic identifications. Oddly, in the far northern and western Bears Ears region of San Juan County the pottery sherds found were "overwhelmingly of the Mesa Verde tradition" by 93.2 percent with only 6.7 percent attributed to Kayenta style Ancestral Puebloans and 0.1 percent of Chaco style.[26] The exploring team found Tusayan White Ware, Tsegi Orange Ware, Mesa Verde Gray and White Ware, San Juan White and Red Ware, and a few unfired clay objects. They surface collected stone implements, ornaments, worked wood, and bighorn horn and found one burial of a middle-aged man under an overhang and sealed within a wet-laid masonry wall. A turkey skeleton rested on his rib cage identical to another turkey skeleton grave offering from a Basketmaker village on the west edge of Bluff.[27]

In the middle of the three-season archaeological project, the same year it created the BLM in 1946, Congress passed the Indian Claims Act. After years of discussion, this new law established the Indian Claims Commission to finally adjudicate over a century of broken treaties and land loss by Indigenous peoples. Many tribes sought to have their land restored. Evidence researched by Native scholars and anthropologists and brought before the Commission resulted in cash awards but few returns of original acreage. Four Corners tribes used the Claims Commission. For the Navajos it meant their first scientifically documented claims to traditional lands north of the San Juan River to the Bears Ears.[28] Researchers ingeniously used dendrochronology or tree ring dating of wood samples found in old hogans and sweat lodges to prove Native occupation decades before the arrival of Mormon pioneers.[29] This was a precursor to the cultural mapping that Utah Diné Bikéyah would use prior to Obama's 2016 Bears Ears proclamation.

Even as historic land claims were being documented, Navajo families were forced to relocate from traditional cultural areas in a concerted removal effort demanded by area ranchers. Navajo families had lived under Cedar Mesa from the Valley of the Gods east through Comb and Butler Washes in the heart of Bears Ears, though the Navajo Reservation boundary west of Bluff was the San Juan River.[30] For seventy years Navajos had peacefully shared grazing rights north of the river with tolerant Bluff stockmen, but according to anthropologist Beth King, "a series of events starting in the winter of 1950 would abruptly end that peace."[31]

Drought had decimated the range. Navajo families who lived south of the San Juan brought their livestock on to already crowded pastures north of the river and consumed valuable winter forage. With the arrival of spring, they returned. "The Navajo families who had regularly used the areas north of the San Juan remained," King explained. "They would bear the blame for the influx of Navajos into areas which the northern white stockmen considered their land."[32] The San Juan Livestock Growers Association, consisting of prominent white ranching families from Blanding and Monticello, sued individual Navajos including Joe Doe Felornia, Slim Cowboy, Hoskcon D. Begay, Adison Yanito, Old Man Blackhorse, Old Jim Joe's Girl, John Doe Yellowman, Hoskcon Deal, Little John, Tom Yellowshirt, Jean Mary's Boy, Tony Nocki, members of the Antes family, the Harvey family, Joe Ben, Ervin Navajo, Slim Todeshine, Mark Tossonie, and others.[33] The ranchers complained of a "combination, confederation, plan and conspiracy . . . to trespass, graze, take and appropriate the feed verdure and forage in said winter grazing area."[34]

The ranchers described damages from the Navajos' 3,655 sheep, goats, and horses including "great damage and injury to the plaintiffs through uncontrolled breeding resulting in lambing at other than the regular lambing period" and problems with Native rams mingling with the ranchers' ewes.[35] Ranchers threatened "a serious possibility of physical hostilities and personal conflicts and violence," which indeed came to pass.[36] The white ranchers bitterly complained about Navajos overgrazing the winter range, when the ranchers themselves overstocked the historic Navajo landscape with 27,068 sheep and 2,370 cattle.[37]

Despite the legal proceedings, or perhaps because of them, violence erupted. Hogans and corrals were burned. Navajo livestock confiscated. The legal issues dragged on and eventually rose to the Utah Supreme Court where local Navajo families lost everything. Because they could not pay fines and because the rancher plaintiffs demanded recovery of their legal fees, stolen sheep, goats, mules, burros, and horses were rarely returned. Some flocks and herds were sold to pay plaintiffs' legal expenses. Outraged, in 1953 the Navajos' lawyers argued on behalf of "aboriginal and ancestral rights of occupation" and deplored fines and penalties in excess of $20,000. The defendants' attorneys argued that bands of sheep and goats had been "unlawfully and illegally seized without warrant of law" and that the ranchers "beat up the Navajos, including some of the squaws, handcuffed them, threw them into a truck and hauled them away."[38]

I've hiked all those areas along Comb Ridge, Comb Wash, Butler Wash, and the winter grazing area of the white ranchers. I've found the remnants of sweat lodges and male forked-stick hogans at the edge of canyon folds at the intersection of canyons and washes. Where a little water trickles off the Comb, I've discovered the upturned basket-shapes of sweat lodges and river cobbles piled close by to be heated for ceremonies. At the base of Comb Ridge and across Butler Wash to Tank Mesa, these faint historic traces still exist. What remains is an archaeology of wood not stone, with evidence of cut marks by axes, circular hogan remnants, can scatters, and rare upraised wooden poles indicating a dance circle enclosure from a long ago winter chant.

I thought that these proofs of Navajo occupation meant that Navajo herders had built structures to tend flocks owned by Bluff stockmen, but these were traditional use areas held by Native families for decades. They had been driven out in one continual push. In 1952 and 1953 Native American families lost their livestock and their livelihoods and found it impossible to resist. Some abandoned the area after seeing cowboys on horseback rounding up the Indians' livestock and brandishing whips and pistols following a Utah State Supreme Court decision.

In court, white ranchers argued that they had grazing rights and grazing allotments below Bears Ears and along Comb Ridge and Butler Wash. Navajos argued that they did too, but not because of a BLM allotment process. They insisted their rights were much older and vested in the landscape. The court wrote, "The defendants are individual Navajo Indians who are joined in this action. They admit use and grazing of the lands involved, which are adjacent to the Navajo Indian Reservation, but allege that they do so under rights and continuous use handed down to them from time immemorial. They claim no fee in the lands but only exclusive grazing and possessory rights."[39]

The Navajos lost in court and were forced to abandon their traditional use areas on public lands north of the San Juan River and west of Bluff. An oral history recounts,

> There was no warning, everyone was living peacefully. We lived up Comb Ridge. People were very comfortable, very settled in that area. My mind was set to live in that area for a long time. I was the only one living in that specific area at the time. My brother made me a small home in the canyon. It was a good home for my family, our goats and sheep. Everything we needed was close by. Our

> family and friends lived in the next canyons. We used to visit each other every day. Our major transportation was by burro.[40]

Another informant told of the deep connection to Bears Ears and explained, "My grandmother's first memories of living up at the Bears Ears go back to her grand-uncle or grandfather. His name was Handsome Man. He and his family lived up around the Bears Ears. That's why they kept moving back up there, it was understood that was their area."[41]

Anger and animosity from cowboys came as a surprise because these Navajo families had moved in and out of their traditional areas staying low in winter and going higher into the pines for summer pastures. An interviewee explained, "We were there for so many years, there are many memories. Many of our loved ones are buried there. We never bothered anyone. We lived well with the people in Bluff. Some of the people we were close to, they spoke our language."[42] But soon it was over. Navajo families left the landscape of their ancestors, a storied landscape where names and tales attached to rock features, cliffs, and canyons. BLM employees and stockmen posted notices and told the Navajos to get out. But many Navajos could not yet speak English much less read it. Families fled to the new St. Christopher's Mission east of Bluff to keep their children safe and to find refuge. For the Navajos there was only confusion. Cowboys burned homes and shade shelters, impounded horses, and demanded payment to get them back. Other structures were taken apart and the wood reused to eliminate traces of Navajo occupation.

A people's history, their ties to the land and their ancestors, was severed without adequate explanation or compensation. Across the nation in the 1950s, Civil Rights issues flared up. Southeast Utah was no exception, but unlike in the American South, there were no television cameras or news reporters pursuing stories of injustice. There were only the plaintive bleats of goats and sheep being taken from families who depended on them for food and income. And after the violence, only the silence of the sandstone canyons.

Just before Native Americans were forced out of Bears Ears, hikers began to come into the country as part of a new wave of adventure exploration. Landscapes that Native peoples, Ute and Navajo, knew by heart would become summer settings for camping, hiking, team building, and personal growth. In 1946 the first documented expedition of a youth group descended Dark Canyon behind Bears Ears to the Colorado River and back. This was the first Anglo expedition on foot down Dark Canyon.

The editor of *Desert Magazine* came along for the eight-day hike. As the Rainbow Bridge Monument Valley Expedition of the 1930s faded into history, organizer Ansel Hall's vision of taking boys outdoors did not. He created an Explorer's Camp for Boys culled from well-to-do families who thought their sons should get acquainted with the Southwest as well as hiking, shooting, river running, horseback riding, and supervised digging at archaeological sites. Just as Marie Ogden's Home of Truth was one of the first examples of New Age religious beliefs, Hall's Explorer's Camp preceded the later establishment of Outward Bound camps and the National Outdoor Leadership School in Wyoming.

With a one and a half ton truck and a brand-new Jeep CJ-2A, the group arrived near Bears Ears at the head of Kigalia Canyon, a tributary to Dark Canyon, at 8,100 feet in elevation. The Jeep shuttled gear down Kigalia and Peavine Canyons then local guides helped with pack animals. The expedition covered eight miles the first day through forests of pine, aspen, and oak brush. As they descended the boys kept seeing cliff dwellings, waterfalls, and "clear water dripping from a tapestry of maidenhair fern" before they connected with the mouth of Wooden Shoe Canyon.[43] Entering a true wilderness in the dawn of the Atomic Age, *Desert Magazine* editor Randall Henderson wrote,

> Next morning I was awakened at 5:30 by the song of a canyon wren perched on the rock above my head. How I love the call of that bird! It symbolizes a world that is wild and free, and at peace with itself—where Nature's balance has not been disturbed by the follies of mankind. Coming in the stillness of early morning it is the reveille of a new day of hope and promise. . . .[44]

Soon they left their pack train and continued with only backpacks, navigating waterfalls, using hemp rope for vertical descents, and finally, after four days, reaching the roar of Cataract Canyon on the Colorado River. They drank from springs rather than the red, muddy water at their feet.

To travel fast they traveled light with less than twenty pounds in their canvas packs. The hikers, including Ansel Hall's son Roger and leader Kenny Ross, expected Ansel to airdrop more food including steaks, and he did drop supplies out of a Stinson airplane, but with parachute failure and crosswinds, the food landed on ledges out of reach. Their rations were "splattered all over the rocks and we never got anything," recalls Roger.[45] The boys would not forget swimming in plunge pools and using

Ansel Hall's dream for an Explorer's Camp for Boys brought the first backpackers into Dark Canyon in 1946, led by Kenny Ross. Here one of the hikers, Jack Pickering, poses in a cliffside ruin during their descent toward the Colorado River. Author's collection.

ropes to lower their packs down vertical canyon drops during a sixty-two-mile roundtrip.[46] "Dark canyon is a beautiful gorge in a region of indescribable grandeur," Henderson concluded. "Americans must become better acquainted with the gorgeous plateau country of southeastern Utah."[47]

Three years after hiking down Glen Canyon, editor Randall Henderson returned for one of Ross Musselman's legendary horse pack trips, which covered 353 miles in nineteen days with a circuit of red rocks, desert, cliff dwellings, rock art, tall timber, grassy meadows, water from ice cold springs, and two trips through the Bears Ears—coming and going. "The Bear's Ears are two well-known landmarks which rise several hundred feet above Elk Ridge," explained Henderson writing about the trip. "They are shaped like volcanic craters with one side of each cone broken away. Actually they are sandstone buttes formed by some strange freak of erosion. They are covered with aspen and spruce trees." Like the other riders, Henderson appreciated the view. He wrote, "From the saddle between them we could look far out across the pinyon flat which lay between us and the Natural Bridges Monument, which was our goal that day."[48]

Henderson concluded his article "19 Days on Utah Trails" with the observation that San Juan County "is comparatively poor in mineral and agricultural resources. But no region in the United States is richer in the intangible values of beauty and natural history." He prophesied, "Its limited economic resources and sparse population may become an asset as more and more Americans seek the relaxation to be found only in the great silent spaces of the desert wilderness."[49] *National Geographic* felt the same way. Six years after the Dark Canyon descent, as funding by the Atomic Energy Commission punched in new roads across the Colorado Plateau and the Bears Ears region, writer, photographer, and retired Naval officer Jack Breed wrote about "Roaming the West's Four Corners." Breed exclaimed that the landscape was "one of the largest roadless areas in the United States [and that], the region has always defied exploration by any but the hardiest and most persistent." He drove a specially outfitted woody station wagon with a full roof-rack and extra water in canvas bags. He took Kodachrome slide photographs in Monument Valley, the Needles District near Indian Creek, and he described "the forgotten Shangri-la of Chesler Park." He used local San Juan County guide Ross Musselman who knew "the Needles like a dog-eared book."[50] At the Dugout Ranch on Indian Creek, Breed refueled, filled water tanks, bought a few supplies, and then drove across a world of red sand toward the stone spires of North and South Sixshooter Peaks.

"For thousands of square miles the land was gouged into a maze of canyons and mesas, split by innumerable fingerlike reefs. In the clear, dry air, some 5,000 feet above sea level, cliffs miles away appeared to be within arrow shot," Breed noted. He also couldn't help but see all the new roads as part of uranium exploration. He cautioned, "As more are added, they will present the touring motorist with an opportunity and the Nation with a responsibility. The opportunity will be to tap a treasure-trove of spectacular, unspoiled beauty. The responsibility will be to ensure that this asset is preserved intact for the enjoyment of generations yet to come."[51] The tension began and still exists today between mining and exploiting the canyon country landscape for a brief economic boom compared to leaving it alone as a sustainable draw for tourists. In 1952 Breed and *National Geographic* advocated saving a part of the San Juan County landscape. Momentum and public sentiment grew for a new kind of wilderness park on the Colorado Plateau. A dozen years after Breed's *National Geographic*

Phil Hawkins drills a round in a uranium mine ca. 1955. Patsy Shumway photo, courtesy of the San Juan County Historical Commission.

article showed redrock country to the world, Congress voted to create Canyonlands National Park.

As with guide Ross Musselman, the push for Canyonlands also came from another local guide, Kent Frost, who knew the country and loved to drive Jeeps. Not interested in farming, he had started as a river guide for Norman Nevills. Frost decided to use his camping skills not at the river's edge but deep in a dramatic canyon landscape that he had been exploring since he was a young boy. He would take off from Blanding with a small pack and pistol and days later arrive on foot at Hite's Crossing on the Colorado River having found his way across miles of sandstone rims sleeping under rock ledges and drinking rainwater from potholes.

I met him once, and I will never forget the encounter. Close to where the Grand Canyon begins at Lees Ferry, I came out of my room at one of the lodges, and there Kent Frost stood in the parking lot, eyes crinkled, hair white, and wearing a faded blue, quilted coat with duct tape on the sleeve. As a young man, he had walked thousands of miles through canyon country, often alone. As a tour guide, he had found one of the rarest and most valuable of all prehistoric southwestern artifacts. At ninety-one, he was still alive, Kent Frost of Monticello, Utah—last of the old-time desert rats and river runners.

His friend and driver Marian Krogmann from Fruita, Colorado, introduced me, and we went into the lodge for breakfast. Over a cup of coffee,

Frost told me his story. Raised in a hardworking Mormon family on a dryland wheat farm south of Monticello, Frost wandered west early on into the slickrock following both Ancestral Puebloan and cowboy trails. Restless and bored with farming, in the late 1930s, he rowed as a boatman on the San Juan River for Norman Nevills and Mexican Hat Expeditions. Frost wanted to explore Glen Canyon, so he took off with his cousin and walked from Monticello to Hite in five days. He remembers, "We went real light—dried fruit, raisins, apricots, jerky. I didn't like carrying a rifle so I got pretty good shooting rabbits and squirrels with a .38 Special." They had no sleeping or camping gear. Frost explained, "I learned from the Navajo people to build a fire and sleep by it where there was an overhang in the rocks, which helped reflect heat down on my body."[52]

The boys met prospector Art Chaffin, and he built them a boat to float through Glen Canyon. When food ran low Frost shot a beaver, which was inedible, but it made good bait for catfish. By 1947, he was working for Nevills rowing through the Grand Canyon and impressing guests by picking rattlesnakes up by their tails.[53] Then Kent had an idea. He would do on land what Nevills did on water—he would introduce tourists to the Southwest. Kent Frost's Canyonland Tours became the first four-wheel drive tours into Canyonlands ten years before its national park status in 1964.[54]

His Jeep tours went "back of the beyond," and in 1958 for $25 a day, Frost provided all food, tents, sleeping bags, and air mattresses. The next year he guided the reconnaissance trip into the Needles with Stewart Udall, who as Secretary of the Interior would work with President John F. Kennedy and Congress to create Canyonlands National Park. Frost knew the country well. Katie Lee wrote in *All My Rivers Are Gone*, "Kent has jeeped, hiked, walked, floated, crawled, hung, climbed, swung, waded or swum about every crevasse in southeastern Utah."[55] The photographer Joseph Muench took Frost's first commercial jeep trip, and Ed Abbey used Frost as a guide for his book *Slickrock: Endangered Canyons of the Southwest.*

By Jeeping into the Needles District and Chesler Park long before paved roads existed, Frost helped create a market for Canyonlands tourism. Writers and photographers then publicized the area so it could be protected. Frost was written up in *Arizona Highways, Desert Magazine, Four Wheeler, Natural History, the Sierra Club Bulletin,* and *Sunset. Sierra Magazine* described him at sixty-five as "still a slim 150 pounds of spring steel—agile as a goat, unflappable, good-humored, always innovative. A superb outdoorsman." Marian Krogmann, his friend of thirty years who backpacked with him into the Escalante, explains, "We've done a

San Juan County native Kent Frost would hike for miles across Bears Ears and canyon country with only a pistol and a small amount of food. He became a river guide on the San Juan River for Mexican Hat Expeditions. Later, Frost launched one of the first Jeep tourist businesses into what would become Canyonlands National Park. Photo courtesy of Chris Simon, Sageland Media.

lot of exploring together. He taught me how to see. To take time and look at things instead of moving too fast."[56] It was just that technique of slow and careful observation that allowed Frost and his clients to find an extraordinary Ancestral Puebloan scarlet macaw feather sash, written up in *National Geographic* in November 1982, and now displayed at the Edge of the Cedars State Park Museum in Blanding, Utah. In perfect condition and found in 1954, the sash is 1,100 years-old, give or take thirty-five years.

Though over the years alcove sites in Bears Ears had been repeatedly pothunted and looted, this site, just a shallow overhang on BLM land at the northern edge of Bears Ears, contained a unique item and further proof of the ancient Native American presence in canyon country. Letters in the Kent Frost papers in Special Collections at the Marriott Library at the University of Utah explain the find. Mary Beckwith, who was one of Frost's clients, sent a color slide and three feathers from the sash to National Park Service archaeologist Lyndon Hargrave, collaborator in Archaeology and Ornithology. He replied, "This artifact is unique and I have never heard of anything like it from the Southwest."[57] In a subsequent letter, Beckwith responded with more detail, though she described the feathered object as a mask not a sash. She revealed, "The mask itself, when we were sitting around in the *shallow* cave in Lavender canyon getting out of the rain, was exposed, or I should say only the fur was exposed in the sand—and I at first thought it was a dead squirrel when I picked it up, well—need I say I was completely overcome! It had been folded up—and the leather ties were tied around the feathered part."[58]

Attached to the sash were bunches of maize "tied as tho for a fertility ceremony." The rare ceremonial object, probably traded north from Mexico by a runner coming on foot for hundreds of miles, had a smaller inset at the sash's center of turquoise blue macaw feathers woven into a thunderbird image. The leather ties came from a subspecies of local Abert's squirrel. The location of the find proved to be a conundrum. Beckwith notes in her May 16, 1959 letter, "The cave itself was not more than 3 feet high and perhaps 15 feet deep and about 75 feet long[.] It certainly did not in any way appear to be any kind of 'prehistoric habitation' to us who were seeking to keep dry! Sitting crosslegged in it, one's head nearly touched the ceiling."[59] She speculated that the sash bundle had not been placed in sand but that sand had blown into the sheltered area almost covering the rare object.

Decades after the find, an article in *American Antiquity* described the artifact as "unique in its integrity, construction technique, style, and materials, including multiple yucca ropes with attached scarlet macaw feathers joined to a *Scirius aberti* (tassel-eared squirrel) pelt and hide straps."[60] The authors concluded that the artifact had been crafted in the Southwest "using native materials, including the squirrel pelt and scarlet macaw feathers" and that it had not been traded whole from Mexico.

Former director of the Edge of the Cedars State Park Museum Teri Lyn Paul stated, "The sash is extremely rare—not another one has ever been found." The scarlet macaw is a warm weather parrot from equatorial Mexico. Finding this sash of yucca fiber ropes covered with feathers on the Colorado Plateau was extraordinary. Within the bright red feathers, a thunderbird shape of iridescent blue macaw feathers could be a clan symbol. "Maybe the feathers were traded from the south (northern Mexico perhaps) as loose feathers, or maybe they were traded on the yucca cords," Paul mused. "It is an object of special meaning and beauty. We are privileged to be able to care for it as part of the museum collection."[61] Kent Frost and his clients found the sash when they were resting in an overhang on BLM land. He donated the feathers to the Edge of the Cedars State Park Museum, which qualifies as a federal repository for archaeology. "I was going to sell it," Frost said over coffee with me, "but I decided it would be better to keep it in the country where I found it."[62]

The old-timers who knew the canyon country are almost gone now. They knew it not from riding ATVs or using maps and GPS units, but rather the old way, walking, on foot across the desert. By being an expert guide, Kent Frost helped Americans explore, appreciate, and protect what is now one of the most popular national parks in the Southwest. He also found and donated one of the rarest of all Ancestral Puebloan artifacts. The Glen Canyon Institute presented him with the David R. Brower Award named after the former president of the Sierra Club. That's quite a legacy for the son of a wheat farmer. Kent smiled at me as he put his coffee down, "I've had an unusual life."

In the 1950s as prospectors looked for color in outcroppings within the White Canyon Mining District, adventurers wanted to explore the canyon. One of those adventurers was a blonde-headed, long-legged, singer-songwriter named Katie Lee who would spend days floating and hiking in Glen Canyon before it was flooded by waters backed up from the Glen Canyon Dam. Much has been written about Lee, and she herself wrote books.[63] She preferred to hike naked, wearing only a straw hat and red Keds tennis shoes.[64]

Often, she went with photographer Tad Nichols and boatman Frank Wright on "We Three" trips that allowed them to explore all ninety-six side canyons off of Glen Canyon. Katie Lee, like her friend Ed Abbey, would come to represent a new kind of resistance in canyon country—a resistance to development, road building, and change. The far western edge of the Bears Ears region and San Juan County is the Colorado River, which would be forced behind Glen Canyon Dam. Ed abhorred the dam and so did Katie.

By 1957 an American baby was being born every seven seconds. Vivacious and shapely, Katie Lee was unusual for women of her generation. After World War II, American women were expected to stay home, keep the house dusted, the refrigerator full, and the floors mopped, and eagerly await husbands returning from work. Katie Lee would have none of it. She drove a 1956 "Baby Bird" Thunderbird coupe, sang songs, and played in small clubs across the nation including in Aspen, Colorado, before millionaires discovered it. The same year her car rolled off the assembly line, Congress passed the largest public works project in history to build the Interstate Highway System. Just as women's apron strings were tied to their new General Electric stoves and consumer capitalism accelerated, so did construction projects across the West. Nature was to be demolished to make way for suburbs, freeways, and dams paid for by taxpayers and built by the Bureau of Reclamation. Katie would label that sprawling federal bureaucracy "The Bureau of Wreck the Nation."

Wearing short skirts and black fishnet hosiery, she stood and sang at the center of two seismic shifts in American culture—the Women's Movement and the Environmental Movement. As change swirled around her, as she endured men's stares and solicitations, as she built her folk singing career but refused the sexual advances of Burl Ives, who could have made her famous, she sought the solitude of Utah's canyon country. A life on the road with cheap motels, smoke-filled clubs, fast food, and too many proffered cocktails left her yearning for the delicate sounds of canyon wrens. Katie explored every nook and cranny of Glen Canyon before the dam impounded millions of acre feet of Colorado River water. Katie's trips are legendary as explorations with no particular purpose other than adhering to Abbey's admonition to "[b]e as I am—a reluctant enthusiast . . . a part-time crusader, a half-hearted fanatic. Save the other half of yourselves for pleasure and adventure. It is not enough to fight for the West; it is even more important to enjoy it. While you can. While it is still here."[65]

Katie Lee, the Goddess of Glen Canyon, enjoys an intimate dip in a sandstone pothole. Katie explored many canyons in Bears Ears and was particularly taken with White Canyon. Author's collection.

That's what Katie Lee did. She lived her life, enjoyed the West, and explored Glen Canyon. The reservoir, regrettably named Lake Powell after the one-armed river runner Major John Wesley Powell, flooded 186 miles and ninety-six side canyons from the dam site near Page, Arizona, north to Hite's Crossing in Utah. Katie knew that country before the concrete. She knew it before the houseboats. She knew it before drunken Lake Powell revelers would annually leave 56,000 pounds of trash and garbage to be picked up each year by volunteers like myself as part of the National Park Service's Volunteers in the Parks (VIPs) Trash Tracker Program.

Katie walked up pristine canyons. Nearly naked, she explored a world we have lost. Abbey railed against industrial tourism at Arches National Park. Lee wrote about the canyons she loved and the respite they offered from the social confines of American suburbia and the expectations for women and wives that she refused to accept. Her interest in White Canyon, just beyond Bears Ears, is chronicled in letters she wrote to Kent Frost begging him to be her guide. Lee wrote Frost about exploring White Canyon with its frigid waters almost always in shadow. "Now darn it all

Kent you wait until next August during the hottest day of the blinkin year and we'll start from the bottom up. . . . I'll get a camera case that floats and a pair of long underwear in a plastic bag and we'll take our time going up that son-of-a-gun," Katie wrote on October 9, 1957, recalling a previous uncompleted trip. She remembered,

> There was a period in there when I could hardly tell what was going on, and yet other minutes are so vivid they are like technicolor flashing on a screen . . . the sun was blazing dead ahead on the highest ridge where the canyon turned again . . . when we finally got down I decided I couldn't swim without my clothes and put them back on again . . . but we got in and it was only up to our waist . . . I remember getting into that water was agony. . . . GAWD it was cold down there!!!!!!! I chatter every time I think about it.[66]

But despite the cold water in the canyon's bottom, Katie wanted to return. With her busy schedule of singing in small clubs and on stages across the country, she always planned for canyon trips in the fall. She begged Frost to be available "in time to be down at THAT spot on the 1st of September for the walk-wade-climb-stumble-swim-claw thru White Canyon."[67] Their letters do not reveal whether the return trip ever happened, but good guide that he was, Kent Frost kept exploring the Bears Ears region on his own. He hiked into Grand Gulch in the winter. He wrote to Lee, "There are lots of cliff dwellings and fortresses in this beautiful canyon. The last night in the canyon my water froze solid while sitting about 15 feet away from my campfire. My complete pack weighed about 20 pounds when I started and about 10 at the finish. I did not carry any bedding at all. I just slept by a camp fire and would have to put on wood every 2 hours."[68]

Frost knew that uranium mining was bringing roads into remote areas atop Cedar Mesa. When he left after four days, "I came out the upper end and caught a ride on [an] ore truck and rode back within 12 miles of the Jeep."[69] Frost played a pivotal role in canyon country preservation as he escorted tour after tour into what would become Canyonlands National Park, building a constituency of clients from around the country who would write supportive letters as well as recruiting politicians to the cause of conservation. Frost testified on behalf of the future park even though his Blanding neighbors didn't want it. Part of the attraction included secluded archaeological sites. Another guide built a motel so that his guests could visit cliff dwellings in Bears Ears.

A geologist, Gene Foushee, after hard, seasonal work in uranium exploration and managing a few mines, chose to lay down his rock hammer for a carpenter's hammer. He built a two-story motel in Bluff to accommodate a tourist boom he thought was coming. He would guide tourists to archaeological sites on Comb Ridge, in Butler Wash, and atop Cedar Mesa. Gene and Mary Foushee poured new life into the virtually abandoned community of Bluff. A travel correspondent remarked, "as late as 1953 only a pair of wheel tracks in the sand linked Bluff with the outside world."[70] The Foushees planted trees and opened a much-needed laundromat, and Gene taught area Navajos valuable construction skills. He proudly claimed the Recapture Lodge, built in 1959, as being "on the edge of the Big Country." The couple offered kitchenettes, a swimming pool, afternoon shade for patios that faced east, slide shows, and warm hospitality that brought returning guests for decades.

The Foushees took tourists to Monument Valley and the new Monument Valley Tribal Park, *Tse'Bii'Ndzisgaii*, established in 1958 at 92,000 acres as one of the first tribal parks in the nation and long advocated by trader Harry Goulding. He had worked diligently in the 1930s to convince Hollywood to use the area's stunning red rock monoliths as background for Western films. The red sandstone pillars called the Mittens would become iconic images of the American West because they dramatically demonstrate fifty million years of erosion.[71] With better highways, the tourist trickle in the 1950s would become a flood.

Flush with cash in the 1960s, San Juan County decided to fund a master plan. The planners didn't think much of historic Bluff. They wrote, "the major problem of Bluff is the need for energetic people willing to work toward improved and long-range objectives." The Salt Lake City planners argued Bluff's "general image and appearance could be improved by clean up of trash and junk cars, repairing or removing shabby fences, by keeping out drunks, and by encouraging owners of old stone houses to restore and maintain them."[72]

The Foushees tried. They spruced up their little motel, hoped for a new highway, which took years to build, and began showing tourists around. The urban planners had written, "the Indian ruins represent one of the unusual and unique aspects of the county. They should be preserved, protected, and made accessible as a visible evidence of the early culture and inhabitants of the area."[73] Gene Foushee expanded his archaeological tours, and then he wrote "What Makes Rocks Red?" in *Desert Magazine*.[74] The small billboard that advertises "Slide Shows" still stands. After six decades, the Recapture Lodge continues to welcome visitors from around the world. Bluff, once a Mormon farming and then a ranching community, is now a gateway to Bears Ears. Urban planners tried to gentrify Bluff, but a more successful effort had begun for red rock preservation in the northern part of the county.

As suggestions continued for some sort of new national park in San Juan County, archaeologists began to explore Beef Basin and the Needles District. They acknowledged Kent Frost as a "Monticello-based Jeep operator." Lloyd M. Pierson from Arches National Monument conducted an initial survey and was as impressed with the remote location as with the ruins themselves. "The archaeology of this area is neither unique to the Southwest nor to the National Park Service," he wrote, "but it is unique in its settings, its remoteness, its unspoiled freshness, the feeling of discovery present, and the particular interplay of cultures that took place here." He continued, "The various ruined villages are plentiful, some of fair size, most well preserved and with their virtues intact.... Coupled with the scenic grandeur the prehistoric works add the little touch of spice necessary to make the whole a travel gourmet[']s delight."[75]

Indeed, just as the American West had been a frontier that pushed civilization in an uneven arc across the continent, the edge of the Bears Ears area in Beef Basin and the Needles District represented an edge between the Anasazi or Ancestral Puebloan world and the Fremont culture that settled north of the Colorado River and across the Great Basin. Here in one place, now reachable by Jeep, were remnants of a great prehistoric past, the northernmost edge of the Puebloan culture that had expanded out from Chaco Canyon in the San Juan Basin, and the southern boundary for a different Indigenous people who did not wear sandals, did not build cliff dwellings, and created their own rock art imagery.

"Apparently this was a zone of contact where much of the exchange and selection of cultural traits between these two groups took place. It was a place where the ideas flowing from the more complex Anasazi group to the less complex Fremont peoples were tempered and filtered," Pierson reported.[76] Here was a prehistoric cultural edge at what would soon be another edge and boundary between BLM lands and a proposed national park. Kent Frost believed that tourism in a preserved landscape, instead of one that had been drilled, blasted, and mined, would have the most benefits for the most people and for the land itself. As the park developed, locals had high hopes for full-service lodges, motels, restaurants, and other modern tourist accommodations deep in the heart of canyon country in the Needles District. The park's first superintendent, Bates Wilson, a master at "Dutch oven diplomacy" and leading outdoor tours, had other notions in line with wilderness ideas and the burgeoning environmental movement.

Instead of paved parkways, Wilson's vision was for Canyonlands to be rugged, remote, and the first "Jeep touring" park.[77] He wanted the canyon country landscape to dominate, not the works of humans, and he sought to maintain the area's "undeveloped and primitive character."[78] The new park's boundaries, at the edge of Lavender Canyon where Frost found the macaw sash, would encompass some of the earlier 1930s vision of an Escalante National Monument, but Bears Ears, a potent Native landmark for millennia, would be excluded. Across the nation, as American Baby Boomers fled the suburbs where they had been raised, a wilderness movement began. President John F. Kennedy proclaimed, "We also need for the sixties—if we are to bequeath our full national estate to our heirs—a new long-range conservation and recreation program—expansion of our superb national parks and forests—preservation of our authentic wilderness areas."[79] But in Utah, the canyonlands controversy was whether the state should mine minerals or tourists. Different versions of a canyonlands national park bill included mining and grazing within the park in direct contradiction to National Park Service standards. Arguments continued over use of the land but not its beauty.

D. James Cannon, director of the Utah Tourist and Publicity Council, wrote in *Desert Magazine*, "Those relatively few persons who are well-acquainted with the Canyonlands region know its power to captivate completely. They who have heard its siren's song never forget, are never free . . . it is a region of bare rock, sand, and flaming color."[80] Cannon attempted to explain the governor's position on the proposed park. JFK's new Secretary of the Interior Stewart Udall had his own vision for the last sizable wilderness area south of Alaska. "Time is running out," he said, "We have only a few years left to preserve what remains of our superb original wilderness. What we save now is probably all we will ever save." Udall added, "I deplore uncontrolled, ruthless exploitation of this heritage."[81] An Arizona native with Mormon roots and a former congressman, Udall was insistent on a national park in canyon country, but he also had a larger vision that appealed to many small town shop owners and businessmen in the Southwest. Not only did he want to save the canyons, which glowed red at sunrise and sunset; he also wanted to link national parks and monuments in a "Golden Circle" of new federal paved highways to "make them accessible to those seeking recreation, relaxation, exploration, and adventure."[82] Federal dollars would help with Utah State Route 95's new bridges at White Canyon, over the Dirty Devil River, and at Hite Crossing.

On a five-day reconnaissance of Utah's red rock country by boat, helicopter, and Jeep, Udall expanded upon the Golden Circle idea after a campfire epiphany at Anderson Bottom on the Green River. He realized that a new network of highways could connect "the greatest concentration of scenic wonders to be found in the country, if not the world" to enthrall tourists with "rainbow and sunset-hued canyons, majestic spires and weird erosion formations, deep gorges, rivers, mountains, deserts, and prehistoric Indian ruins."[83] Udall believed in tourism as "one of the country's fastest growing industries. With proper development," he prophesized about Canyonlands, "such a park, together with other national parks in Utah, could assist local communities in stabilizing their economies and growth."[84] As momentum increased for a national park, San Juan County commissioners urged that park headquarters be established in Monticello as "a boost to the sagging economy," and because "it will help to replace income which may have been obtained had lands not been withdrawn."[85]

Despite letters and intercessions by Utah senators such a headquarters would not be built in Monticello. With thousands of acres changing land status from multiple use BLM lands to restricted NPS lands, county commissioners made a reasonable request. Instead, park headquarters would be constructed in Moab in Grand County, which left a bitter residue of anger against federal management and park planners. Those feelings would carry forward into the fight and resistance over Bears Ears as a national monument. While locals in Moab eagerly anticipated a new national park, the sons and daughters of Mormon pioneers in Blanding and Monticello planned a large outing of four-wheel-drive vehicles on June 4, 1963 to replicate the famous Hole-in-the-Rock trek and to honor their ancestors. Organizers expected 150 people to make the five-day strenuous outing.[86] They would drive through the heart of the Bears Ears region in a legacy landscape they claimed as their own.

Finally, after years of planning, on September 12, 1964 Canyonlands became a national park. "People are nervous in this rat race. The population is increasing. The national parks are overcrowded.... [W]e need more places of this kind, not only for our own people at present, but for the future and our children coming on. If we don't preserve it now, it won't be preserved," stated Ross Musselman, who had Jeeped Superintendent Bates Wilson into the Needles district the first time.[87]

Each year Wilson modified and diminished development plans for Canyonlands. Wilson viewed it as a philosophical choice to keep the park wild with environmental values attuned to a younger generation. He claimed, "We have a wonderful chance to provide a different park. It is more important in our estimation to let preservation of scenic values be the keynote of our policy, even if it means turning away the man with the pink Cadillac."[88] Local officials voiced their resistance. San Juan County Commissioner Calvin Black demanded more pavement and more jobs. Wilson's biographer explains, "Businessmen and local leaders didn't see dollar signs in the wilderness."[89]

Local leaders did, however, see dollars attached to the US military because beginning in 1962 and lasting for twenty years, both the Army and Air Force chose to use southeast Utah to test fire missiles and send them hurtling toward targets in White Sands Missile Base in southern New Mexico. The new Canyonlands National Park was in the way for missiles fired from Green River, Utah. Tourists might be flattened by falling missile parts, twelve-foot long first stage components of a four-stage 16,000 pound Athena missile. The military assured locals that there would be a large quarantine area of 280,000 acres as a "drop zone" and that everyone would be notified ahead of time for evacuation. The government paid ranchers whose cattle lost grazing days. They paid San Juan County residents per diem for leaving their houses.

"A friend in Moab, Utah, tells me that the area being proposed for inclusion in our National Park System as Canyonlands National Park is scheduled to be used as a missile-firing area, with booster drops into the area proposed as a park," photographer Philip Hyde wrote US Senator Clair Engle. "May I urge you to use your good offices to prevent this from being carried out?"[90] The acting director of the NPS replied to the senator that yes, there was a 5,000 acre area "within which first-stage booster rockets will fall," but he thought only 5 percent might come crashing into the ground. "Human beings" will have been evacuated and the desert would be in tiptop shape. "Considerable care has been taken to insure [sic] that there will be no undue disturbance of natural conditions. All spent rockets will be recovered by helicopter so that no vehicle tracks will scar the proposed park area," wrote the director.[91] This joint Defense Department and NPS policy would keep the cacti erect and the coyotes safe.

On September 5, 1963 a 185-vehicle convoy from Fort Sill, Oklahoma with 440 men in uniform rolled through Blanding toward a launch site at Black Mesa and a bivouac area near Bears Ears. "It was very strange—this huge, long convoy of army vehicles one after another after another, coming forever through town. I was working at my family's gas station and remember being in awe at the number of military vehicles," remembers Winston Hurst, whose father was mayor and who welcomed the military presence. Winston says, "For a little town like this, it's like all of a sudden the real world has come to Blanding in force."[92]

Beginning in 1965, a launch site from Gilson Mesa sent military hardware flying southeast across the Bears Ears region. The Air Force fired Athena missiles. The Army fired Pershing missiles to test medium-range "theatre-level nuclear capabilities" of delivering a "four-hundred kiloton warhead over four hundred miles" with "thirty times the destructive power of the bomb first dropped on Hiroshima."[93] Thankfully the hundreds of test fires did not include live nuclear war heads because occasionally missiles strayed off course.

One landed south of Durango, Colorado, near the airport. A second crashed outside of Shiprock, New Mexico, on the Navajo Reservation. A missile flew past its target and hit near Fabens, Texas. Two landed in Mexico and one of those contained radioactive cobalt-57. A Pershing missile missed Bluff, Utah, by seven miles.[94] For isolated families in Blanding, Utah, the seasonal military presence in the spring meant new faces in town in the Elk Ridge Cafe. At White Mesa the Army built bleachers so that as missiles shot up from the Black Mesa launch site, locals could sit on seats and see smoke and flames rise above the horizon before arcing across the sky. As proof of America's military might, the Army took thirty-four-foot Pershing missiles to local football games for pretend firings at half time.[95]

If the military had discovered southeast Utah, so did tourists. Canyon country was being explored thanks to a desert rat named Ed Abbey, a former Arches National Monument ranger who had lived in a trailer, hung out in Moab's bars, and written *Desert Solitare* published in 1968. His book would bring thousands of devotees to the slickrock country Cactus Ed loved. Congress preserved Canyonlands and in the same year also passed a wilderness bill. Abbey wrote, "The love of wilderness is more than a hunger for what is always beyond reach; it is also an expression of loyalty to the earth, the earth which bore us and sustains us, the only home we shall ever know, the only paradise we ever need—if only we had eyes to see . . . No, wilderness is not a luxury but a necessity of the human spirit, and as vital to our lives as water and good bread."[96]

As the wilderness movement in canyon country expanded, the Bears Ears region remained aloof and alone, except for the occasional missile, with prospectors and miners nibbling at its edges. A tumultuous post-World War II uranium mining era ended quietly at midnight on December 31, 1970. Uranium ore buying from the Atomic Energy Commission ceased. Without the government's purchase program, the market for yellowcake began its irreversible downward slide, but memories of that era would remain potent and alive among San Juan County residents.

"They clung to 1955—or to whatever year that life had last made sense—with all their might," wrote Ellen Meloy. "The uranium boom brought prosperity to their backwaters. It elevated the self-made man and his sense of control over women, children, and big-game animals. It built roads, schools, utilities, and a colossal myth." She explained,

> The myth portrayed the Colorado Plateau miners as a wholly independent lot, free to be enriched or broken by their own labors in a free market. An entrenched hatred of federal authority and 'creeping socialism'—still simmering today—denied the fact that uranium production was the tightly reined progeny of unabashed government paternalism . . . The dreaded feds, prodded by the frenetic arms race with the former Soviet Union, 'welfared' the uranium miners in every respect but their health. (Mine safety regulations were non-existent or ignored.)[97]

As the Atomic Energy Commission abandoned canyon country, the potential for tourism remained untapped. Even one of Utah's most conservative newspapers sensed a change. "It is significant that the same remoteness and primitiveness that were viewed as handicaps earlier are now cited—and properly so—as among the area's greatest assets," opined the *Deseret News*.[98]

Uranium mining faltered and declined. The age of archaeological expeditions had ended, but one of the Bears Ears region's most important archaeologists was just beginning his fascination with Cedar Mesa. With a grant from the National Geographic Society, in 1969 William Lipe began studying Basketmaker II sites on Cedar Mesa as part of an eight-week field season to try to understand the region's first farmers and their settlement patterns. By 1970 he mentored both undergraduates and graduate students from SUNY-Binghamton. Those two summers would inspire a major research project to understand Basketmaker farmers in their isolated settlements atop Cedar Mesa by applying statistical methods in a new research design.[99]

If mining uranium had ceased to be economically viable, why not turn a canyon or two into a nuclear waste dump? Commissioner Calvin Black, a successful uranium prospector and miner, opened his arms to embrace atomic waste. The health impacts of working in radiation-laced mines and mills were not yet fully understood. Local citizens in Blanding and Monticello and Navajos in Monument Valley would learn much more about the deadly daughters of radiation and the devastating spread of cancer cells.

In the next decade, the tourist trickle became a flood. Adventurers arrived to drive their Jeeps and four-wheel-drive vehicles across the dusty, rock-strewn corners of Canyonlands. "The influence of the population-leisure-travel complex since World War II has been sharply felt in our national and state parks.... In the beginning we labeled this a trend, but in the words of our park superintendents, 'it soon became a stampede,'" noted an official in the Department of the Interior.[100]

Silent and sunlit, the ruins remained. Cliff houses balanced on ledges. Small stone storage rooms sheltered in shadow with their doors still intact. Yucca ties wrapped lintel beams above narrow doorways with thumb and fingerprints pressed into adobe plaster eight hundred years earlier. Federal judges would complain that the Antiquities Act was too vague. Archaeologists and anthropologists would rally for a new law, an updated version of the Antiquities Act with stiffer penalties because an underground black market for Indian artifacts thrived in a world of cash deals and easy money made off public lands. A comprehensive federal law would make pothunting a serious crime, but graverobbing continued in Bears Ears.

CHAPTER 11

U-95, Nuclear Waste, Deadly Daughters, and Pothunting Raids, 1971–1986

> The redrock landscape of southeastern Utah has long been and will continue to be imagined and re-created. Throughout time humans have worked and reworked the land, attempting to suit their needs and expectations. This vision has butted heads with another human impulse—to keep nature as it is.
>
> —Jedediah S. Rogers, *Roads in the Wilderness*

> Uranium mining and milling have left unacknowledged and unanswered legacies in the American West, specifically impacting health and community well-being. In enhancing understanding of contested illness, it is important to recognize health impacts in rural communities such as Monticello, their contestation by the federal government, and how such contested illnesses are deeply tied to a risky industry that may be renewed.
>
> —Stephanie A. Malin and Peggy Petrzelka
> "Left in the Dust: Uranium's Legacy and Victims of Mill Tailings Exposure in Monticello, Utah"

> For three generations many of Blanding's residents dug in surrounding Indian ruins and excavated Anasazi artifacts. It was a family tradition.
>
> —Brett Shumway, "Pothunting in San Juan County"

The fifteen years between 1971 and 1986 brought ever more changes to San Juan County. New federal laws could not be ignored though local resistance to federal rules and regulations continued. The true cost of mining and milling uranium became apparent both in Monument Valley on the Navajo Nation and at the mill town of Monticello. Dozens of local citizens had worked at the mill as part of their patriotic duty during the Cold War. They began to suffer and die from cancers and leukemia. Unknowingly, children swam in a local pond laced with poisons. Laughing and yelling, they skidded and tumbled down uranium tailings filling their jeans and shirt pockets with fine toxic dust, radioactive particles in their hair, noses, mouths, and ears.

For some families, digging Native American ruins continued as part of weekend outings. As the black market for Native American antiquities skyrocketed, commercial diggers got into the act, some with loaded pistols and drug habits requiring ready cash. Utah enacted a state antiquities act to ban pothunting on state lands. Sheriff Rigby Wright began to enforce the law in San Juan County. Federally, Congress passed a new, much tougher law targeting pothunters with stiff fines, jail time, and seizure of personal possessions including pickup trucks used in the commission of a pothunting crime.

Elected Utah officials, especially Commissioner Calvin Black from San Juan County, railed against federal interference and enforcement of federal laws at the same time he sought millions of dollars in federal investment for a nuclear waste facility to be poised on the southern edge of Canyonlands and the northern edge of what would become the Indian Creek Unit of Bears Ears National Monument. As Black campaigned for a nuclear waste site, fellow San Juan County citizens began dying from exposure to radiation and deadly radon gas. San Juan County's population grew to be half Native American, largely Navajo, and yet they had little to no political representation. Of the county's small towns, writer and attorney Charles Wilkinson wrote, "From the inside, these communities are nurturing and industrious to a new and higher degree. But to many outsiders, including the Navajo, whose lands run up to the south bank of the San Juan River, the Mormon settlements more closely resemble clenched fists."[1]

For Native students, years of segregation from local schools through the 1940s and then hours spent riding school buses in subsequent decades resulted in federal lawsuits. By the 1970s Native Americans had found their voice and demanded political action including high schools closer to Native families in the southern part of San Juan County. In addition to educational inequalities, a march and sit-in near Aneth disrupted production in a major oil field as local Navajos protested and resisted environmental damage to their grazing lands.

From the 1970s forward, archaeological research on Cedar Mesa and the Bears Ears region accelerated with new studies, new theories, and new connections to Native peoples. Salvage archaeology on a well-funded highway route brought additional insights into the lives of prehistoric peoples, but the highway also produced both acclamation and antagonism. Edward Abbey squared off with Calvin Black over road building and a new, streamlined asphalt highway which bisected Bears Ears from Blanding west toward Lake Powell. Abbey and his friends resisted too. They resisted this asphalt incursion into the canyons. They abhorred the new bridges, guard rails, viewpoints, and scenic turnouts. Abbey demanded tourists get out of their cars and walk, or better yet crawl, to learn the desert's secrets.

By the mid-1980s, prices of Native American antiquities had risen dramatically. A new federal law protecting Native American sites on federal lands, the Archaeological Resources Protection Act (ARPA) of 1979, passed Congress. As the BLM employed its first rangers in the Grand Gulch Primitive Area, the full extent of looting became known. In 1986 the US attorney in Utah organized the first raid of homes and trading posts in Blanding and the Four Corners area. Local residents were livid when federal agents seized their private collections of pots, baskets, arrowheads, spearpoints, and Native American relics. The original 1906 Antiquities Act had rarely been enforced. Nothing like this had ever happened before, but it was only the beginning.

Native voices remained in the background. There were no large protests about the theft of their ancestors' bones or robbery of their graves. Indigenous people heard the stories. They learned about a site in Cottonwood Wash named Baby Mummy Cave, a fifty-foot-deep rock shelter unrecorded by archaeologists before it was ransacked by vandals. In deep sand, culture thieves found and stole almost forty infant and fetus remains as well as grave goods. Why the child burials were there in one place is lost to the centuries, but now equally lost are the remains themselves—unspeakable desecration.

Gathering roots and sacred plants on Cedar Mesa and Bears Ears, Native families saw ransacked cliff dwellings, gaping holes left by pothunters, broken walls, collapsed doorways, sunken kiva roofs. They demanded justice and equality for their own generation and that of their children while they pondered what to do about the entire Bears Ears landscape. What to do about Native peoples ripped from their burials and not allowed to continue the sacred journey of the dead? Because of taboos and traditions, Native Americans would have stayed away from cliff dwellings and cave sites. But still they saw bones and human skulls. Tossed aside. They wept and they waited.

Education for Native Americans in San Juan County had been inconsistent and unequal. Bureau of Indian Affairs boarding school superintendents recruited Native children, but San Juan County public school officials "made no effort to keep Indian children out of school, nor to recruit them."[2] Ute children forced to attend boarding school in Colorado at Ignacio or Towaoc often fled home. They walked dozens of miles to return to their reservation in Allen Canyon west of Blanding. Something had to be done. Pioneers Gladys and Albert R. Lyman established a one-room school for Native students on their own land at Westwater in 1946. They provided a daily warm meal and donated shoes and clothing. The Lymans received no county or federal aid, and their efforts met with local indifference and occasional hostility. Albert wrote about white feelings toward Natives: "As long as they were not annoying us, we felt no urge to trouble ourselves about them. We remembered, in a very passive way, that we were here to do them good."[3] Lyman recalled the original goals of the Bluff Mission to work with and to help "civilize" native tribes. Taking this on as a personal calling, he and his wife grew the school to six Paiute and twenty-one Navajo children. In 1947 the school board chose to move the classes into Blanding, but school administrators kept Native children segregated from white children.

In the same decade, Reverend Harold Liebler recalled that for Native Americans, "I found there were no churches, no schools, and no medical care," which prompted his desire to start St. Christopher's Mission east of Bluff. He said, "When we first went to Bluff the local Mormons would have almost nothing to do with a Navajo ... back in 1943 what we saw was scorn for the Navajo because of skin color. The Mormons took their money but considered the Navajo inferior."[4] School segregation occurred because white families feared that contact with Native children would spread tuberculosis and the eye disease glaucoma. School board president George Hurst worked to bring Native children into the San Juan County school system and the regular public schools in 1950 only to be met with bitter resistance. Parents believed that having Native children in school "would cause discipline, scholarship, and pupil morale to deteriorate."[5]

With the uranium and oil boom of the early 1950s, San Juan County went from being one of the poorest counties in Utah to one of the richest. San Juan County Commissioner Calvin Black wrote that assessed evaluation of the county went from $3.8 million to $132.8 million and that "it was due almost entirely to oil and uranium. A lot of the uranium was produced on the reservation ... the oil was virtually all on the reservation. So about 90 percent of our tax revenue, with which we were building libraries, recreation facilities, schools and other amenities were paid for with production of resources from the reservation."[6] Yet few of those projects benefited Native Americans. New schools were built, including elementary schools in Montezuma Creek and Bluff serving mainly Native students. Teacher salaries greatly increased. By the 1960s Native student attendance had soared; yet there were no local high schools in the southern part of the county. Navajo children had lengthy bus rides getting up before daybreak to meet the bus and arriving home after dark with little time for homework and no time for sports or other activities.

St. Christopher's Mission expanded to Hat Rock. Durango art gallery owner Jackson Clark brought wringer washing machines. Father Liebler ran the mission and his wife Joan told Clark, "The Navajo children have to have clean clothes. They ride the bus to Monticello to school every day, and they are in classes with Mormon kids who tend to look down on them anyway. Washing clothes in a muddy arroyo just won't do."[7] There were school dropouts and high absenteeism, but at least Navajo children had clean jeans.

After years of coping with white resistance to expanding equal education for Native students even after county coffers swelled with mineral and gas tax revenues, Navajo families took their own path of resistance. In the 1970s they filed a federal lawsuit *Sinajini* [Tsinnijinnie] *v. Board of Education*. The biggest issue, aside from the need for bilingual education, was to establish high schools closer to Native communities. Since World War II the Church of Jesus Christ of Latter-day Saints in an "aggressive Mormon thrust into Navajo culture" had recruited thousands of Native children into their Indian Student Placement Program where Native youth lived with Mormon families across the state of Utah during the school year and attended local schools. "However well-meaning the participating families, the program was aimed, of course, directly at the children's minds: in addition to being removed from their homes and tribes, the children faced intense pressure to convert," wrote Charles Wilkinson.[8]

Navajo families resisted. They wanted their sons and daughters closer to home, to attend ceremonies, to assist at family events, and to listen to the age-old tradition of grandfathers telling stories in winter after the last of summer's storms and before the first lightning of spring. They wanted their children home. Wilkinson became one of their attorneys. He quickly figured out that school district elections had been engineered so that an Anglo majority dominated the school board. He wrote, "the three Anglo school board members were not interested, thank you, in being told by a bunch of lawyers—and Navajo—how to run the San Juan County, Utah,

School District."[9] Some students traveled one hundred miles round trip daily to attend high school. For others it was 166 miles. "The average student spent three hours a day on a bus, traveling 15,000 miles a year. This was the equivalent of ninety student days physically riding to and from school. The students at the end of the longest bus ride traveled 30,000 miles each school year—a distance greater than the earth's circumference," explained Wilkinson.[10]

The Navajos' attorneys won with an October 1975 Agreement of Parties. Two new high schools would be built, though twice attorneys had to return to court to ask a federal judge to enforce the consent decree. Other changes occurred in San Juan County in the 1970s directly impacting Bears Ears. Commissioner Cal Black wanted more roads; Ed Abbey did not. A new type of resistance emerged with the formation of regional environmental groups committed to the wilderness qualities of San Juan County. Black saw road building as opening up and improving the county. Abbey saw it as destruction.

With the success of his book *Desert Solitaire* in 1968, Edward Abbey became a singular voice in defense of wilderness and public lands in the American Southwest. Born in Pennsylvania, he first saw the southern edge of canyon country as a hitchhiker before he enlisted in the US Army. After military service, he attended the University of New Mexico, earning a master's degree in philosophy with a thesis titled "Anarchy and the Morality of Violence."[11] For Abbey and his friends their playground and dreamscape became the Colorado Plateau with days spent poking around San Juan County in those halcyon years before paved roads. *Desert Solitare* made Abbey a new and vital voice in a growing environmental movement that challenged old assumptions and upended the status quo for mining and construction companies. Flush with his publication success, for the Sierra Club in 1971 Abbey cowrote *Slickrock: Endangered Canyons of the Southwest.* His first chapter titled "How It Was," vividly described a Bears Ears excursion.

He wrote about driving west of Bluff on the old gravel highway and ascending the top of Comb Ridge to look "down and out from there into something else. Out *over* something else. A landscape which I had not only never seen before, but which did not resemble anything I had seen before." Abbey was hooked. He would become a slickrock aficionado spending weekend after weekend in canyon country. "We were desert mystics, my few friends and I, the kind who read maps as others read their holy books."[12] But their fascination with the extremes of canyon

Ed Abbey, on the cusp of a burgeoning environmental movement in the American Southwest, railed against roads and development and particularly despised the new Highway 95, which Commissioner Cal Black supported wholeheartedly and which bisected the Bears Ears region. Drawing copyright Mike Caplanis. Used courtesy of the artist.

country did not include better roads. He deplored highway development that would become U-95 paved from Blanding west to Hall's Crossing at Lake Powell through the heart of Bears Ears and Cedar Mesa. "Most of the formerly primitive road from Blanding west has now been improved beyond recognition. All of this, the engineers and politicians and bankers will tell you, makes the region more accessible to everybody, no matter how fat, feeble, or flaccid. That is a lie."

Abbey continued his lament, "It is a lie. For those who go there now, smooth, comfortable, quick and easy, gliding through as slick as grease, will never be able to see what we saw. They will never feel what we felt. They will never learn what we knew, or understand what we cannot forget."[13] Abbey gave the 1970s West a new aesthetic and appreciation for untrammeled land. He articulated the value of wilderness and wild landscapes, and he wrote eloquently about preserving and leaving alone a region where local families sought development and full employment. Abbey wrote that Black was interested in "anything for the sake of jobs." He quoted the commissioner who said, "Our biggest export is kids and empty pop bottles."[14]

The rocks and deep set canyons that had been home to Basketmakers and Ancestral Puebloans had frustrated the original Mormon settlers in their attempts to make the desert bloom like a rose. There was just too much slickrock. Farming failed and because of overgrazing weeds replaced native grasses. The topographic ruggedness appealed to Abbey. Ever the contrarian, he valued the lack of water, the insufferable summer heat, and the serpentine canyon ledges. Describing canyon country, he wrote,

> Within this underslung lopsided rump-sprung dough-bellied highly irregular parallelogram lies the least inhabited, least inhibited, least developed, least improved, least civilized, least governed, least priest-ridden, most arid, most hostile, most lonesome, most grim bleak barren desolate and savage quarter of the state of Utah—the best part by far.[15]

And he loved the views. "From a site near the Bears Ears, for example, you can gaze out upon the four corners of four states," he exclaimed with a description of all the landmarks in every cardinal direction.[16] Abbey added, "It was not until World War II, with all the excitement and prosperity that followed, that southeast Utah became one of the West's major tourist draws." But he wasn't happy with the impacts. He opined, "As for the future, I am confident that its natural history will continue for a long time to come, give or take a few million years. The human story looks doubtful; but here, too, I believe that in the long run greed and stupidity will be overcome by intelligence, courage, and love."[17]

If Edward Abbey only visited canyon country, Calvin Black was born and lived there. Black, a uranium miner and entrepreneur, urged road construction. He fervently felt that a new highway would "not only provide for local needs," but also make scenic southeast Utah more available "for the use and enjoyment of all Americans."[18] He testified to a congressional subcommittee, "You could honestly say that when we build these roads, because of the vastness and nature of the area, it will make little more of a mark than to plow the ocean!"[19] Historian Jedediah Rogers credits Black with massive road building because he secured state and federal funds to pave roads. BLM officials believed that the county commissioner thought that "[B]lack is beautiful" meant newly laid asphalt.[20]

The same year that Navajos won their federal case against the San Juan School District, Abbey published *The Monkeywrench Gang*. He traded his park ranger memories at Arches National Monument in *Desert Solitare* for a picaresque novel about a loose band of radical revolutionaries dedicated to stopping progress by blowing up bridges, damaging construction equipment, and trying to obstruct their ultimate nemesis—Glen Canyon Dam. Black embraced the Sagebrush Rebellion, and like other Sagebrush Rebels in the American West, he tried to assert more local control over federal lands.[21] He railed against government rules and regulations on public lands in "his" county. Abbey expressed equal outrage against rapid industrial development of the West's resources. Black preached radical resistance, as did Abbey.

Not only did Cactus Ed write about "monkeywrenching" or damaging earth-moving machinery; he may also have conducted "field work" at night along the U-95 route though Sheriff Rigby Wright never gained enough evidence to pursue felony charges. Years later Abbey's friend Jack Loeffler worried about the statute of limitations on illegal activities.[22] Abbey proudly proclaimed his methods of industrial sabotage and his goal to send "those iron crocodiles" crawling back to where they came from—the Caterpillar and heavy equipment factories in the Midwest. "Wherever you go in your auto travels among the wonders of our Rocky Mountain West," he explained, always carry "a gallon or two of shellac with you, and a bucketful of fine clean sand." The shellac was intended "for the fuel tank and the sand for the crank-case" of offensive construction

Calvin Black, at left holding a camera, poses with the San Juan County Road Crew. Black would become an outspoken San Juan County Commissioner and Sagebrush Rebel always in favor of more and better county roads. Hyrum Black Collection, courtesy of the San Juan County Historical Commission.

equipment ripping up the West or specifically cutting and filling a roadway into the heart of Bears Ears.[23]

As for Abbey and Black, "Both men likely embraced their role as figureheads of ideologies at work in the West. In life they crafted their personas, and in death their adherents continue the causes for which they fought," reasons Rogers. "Each man articulated a compelling vision of the best way to act on the land."[24]

Finished in 1976, U-95 became a federal Bicentennial Highway also known as the Trail of the Ancients Scenic Byway. The route revealed extensive archaeological resources on Cedar Mesa below Bears Ears documented by archaeologists and coveted by pothunters. In the early 1970s for the first time, Cedar Mesa and the Bears Ears area had professional, systematic, careful archaeology. Archaeologists with Brigham Young University dug on Elk Ridge. Staff from the Museum of Northern Arizona surveyed Cedar Mesa. Other salvage archaeologists toiled ahead of the highway construction crews to conduct work of "an initial exploratory nature." They found a cycle of occupancy for Native peoples who had once lived at many of the small sites archaeologists uncovered.[25] Teams of archaeologists learned more about prehistoric Cedar Mesa farmers and named sites like Egg Hamlet, the Kiln Site, Center Beam Site, Surprise Village, and Rattler's Midden. Writing an overview for the highway project an editor commented, "Cedar Mesa is an extremely rich archaeological area, but to date is rather poorly known. Some work has been done on the mesa, but most is either on-going, not reported or not readily available."[26]

Both Abbey and Black were right. The new asphalt highway increased tourist traffic to Lake Powell and beyond, profiting Black who shared with Frank Wright a marina concession at Hall's Crossing. The new pavement also resulted in a different kind of profiteering—illegal pothunting for an expanding market for American Indian antiquities. Easier highway access meant more damage to and looting of canyon rim archaeological sites. Across the nation, the obsession with Native American artifacts resulted in the need for stricter legislation.

By the 1970s the Antiquities Act was seven decades old and could not keep pace with the escalating value of Native American artifacts on the black market. It was time for a new law and new responsibilities for the weakly managed BLM. Employees needed a new mission in keeping with the sweeping environmental movement and a new urgency to protect both natural and cultural resources. First came the agency's reorganization and then came a potent federal law against pothunting that would have devastating consequences in San Juan County where weekend excursions to unearth artifacts were for many a cherished family tradition. National momentum also grew to preserve roadless landscapes as part of federally designated wilderness.

Congressman Wayne Aspinall from Colorado's Fourth Congressional District forced the Wilderness Act into sixty-six rewrites before final passage in 1964. An old-style conservationist, he never met a dam he didn't like. Wayne Aspinall and Calvin Black would have immediately understood and respected each other, and they certainly would have agreed on water storage and the need for Abbey's nemesis—Glen Canyon Dam, which created Lake Powell. Required by philosophical shifts in the Democratic Party to embrace a wilderness act, Aspinall, powerful chair of the House Interior and Insular Affairs Committee, responded by demanding a complete congressional review of two centuries of public land laws. During this comprehensive review, Congress omitted dozens of antiquated laws, but one law they did not touch was the 1906 Antiquities Act, which gave the president executive authority to set aside national monuments from federal public lands. Decades later when President Obama's Bears Ears National Monument would be thrown into federal courts, this 1970s congressional review would be an important consideration of legal precedent.

The Federal Land Policy Management Act (FLPMA) of 1976 consolidated public land laws and became the organic act for the BLM. For the first time in American history, Congress established a new policy of managing all federal lands rather than trying to disperse them into private hands, which had been the historic role of the General Land Office (GLO). BLM staffers now had roles in natural and cultural resources protection including using the National Environmental Policy Act (NEPA) from 1970 to study and heal range lands damaged by overgrazing. BLM rangers began to patrol Grand Gulch, designated a primitive area. The agency still did not have armed law enforcement rangers who could write tickets and make arrests, but that was on the horizon. The immediate goal was to deter pothunters especially after passage in 1979 of the ARPA, which established stiff fines and penalties for the theft of Native American antiquities from public lands. ARPA made it a federal crime to remove, damage, alter, and/or deface archaeological resources defined as an item of past human existence or archaeological interest more than a hundred years old. Judges could now give fines and jail time for damage to archaeological sites by looters who not only tossed aside human skulls but who knocked down ancient walls, broke into kiva roofs, and destroyed archaeological contexts as they dug deep into cliff dwellings.

The archaeological awareness that prompted federal passage of the ARPA also had impacts on Utah's state trust lands. San Juan County became the center of an important archaeological controversy that eventually lead to an extension of federal-level protection of cultural resources on state trust lands in Utah. State lands in Utah had traditionally been managed for sale and lease to provide funds for public schools and other eligible public institutions. There had been no consideration of archaeology or cultural resources as being valuable to the state's educational mission. That would all change when on Cedar Mesa a rancher chained state land.

Chaining is a controversial practice of running a stout anchor chain called an Ely-chain between two bulldozers to smash and dislodge pinyon-juniper trees and other undergrowth supposedly to grow more grass for cattle. Each link in the massive chain can weigh forty-five to ninety pounds. Damage to archaeological sites can be enormous and that's exactly what happened adjacent to a spectacular late Pueblo III site named Cave Towers. Ancestral Puebloans had built seven masonry structures including towers near a spring on the edge of Cedar Mesa. Earlier sites existed close by. The public outcry from Utah citizens, archaeologists, and anthropology professors at the state's preeminent public universities demanded that "historic and archaeological resources be given consideration and protection whenever possible." Archaeologist Kenny Wintch explains that this "was the tipping point in the public's battle to win CRM (cultural resources management) on state trust land."[27]

With over 100,000 archaeological sites and a significant share of state school trust sections, San Juan County played a pivotal role in this new mission for what would later become SITLA. "Utah has had its fair share of tension and controversy over what constitutes the appropriate use of trust lands. One source of tension has been the nature and extent of cultural resource protection on trust lands," Wintch wrote. "The tension between trust lands managers and archaeologists began in the autumn of 1979, when a San Juan County rancher secured federal assistance to chain a square-mile section of school trust land" in what would become Bears Ears National Monument.[28] Wintch argues that Cave Towers "was one of the most well-loved sites in the state" and that even if the towers were not harmed "dozens of other Anasazi sites on this school trust section were badly damaged, if not completely destroyed, by the chaining."[29] The resultant outcry began a series of changes to state law to replicate cultural resource protections outlined in the National Historic Preservation Act (1966) and to extend full protection of cultural resources to lands managed by SITLA. At the federal level, by 1983 the US Geological Survey (USGS) took archaeological sites off their maps in a belated attempt to curb pothunting.

Archaeology transformed the BLM. ARPA required active enforcement. The law initiated slow, tentative steps for archaeologists to consult with living Native Americans about the value and importance of artifacts stolen from their ancestors' graves. Rarely had that happened. In the late 1970s and early 1980s, interest in Native American antiquities fueled a burgeoning black market. Pothunters scoured maps, used helicopters, airplanes, and backhoes, and made thousands of dollars stealing and then selling American heritage. In the Southwest, two hot spots for pothunting were the Mimbres area of southwest New Mexico near Silver City and the Bears Ears region of southeast Utah west of Blanding.[30]

In San Juan County, some local white residents ignored and resisted the new federal legislation, while Native Americans near Aneth decided to do some resisting on their own. After years of environmental degradation in the rich Aneth oil field and having endured slights and insults from out of state oil and gas workers, Navajos living in Aneth rose up in protest for a variety of reasons. One story has oil field roughnecks shooting at Ella Sakizzie's son-in-law when he was on horseback herding sheep. The loud sounds caused his horse to buck. Another version possibly "embellished with retelling" has roughnecks torturing a boy's goats and then shooting at him.[31] In this version, riding up on horseback, eighteen-year-old Peter Benally searched for his flock when he heard the plaintive bleating of one of his goats. As he topped a mesa he found three oil workers tossing and teasing one of his goats. Benally yelled for them to stop. They swore back shouting at him to "get [his] god'damn goats out of here." He argued that he was on tribal grazing lands. One of the roustabouts then ran to his truck, drew a pistol, and fired four rounds at Benally and his horse.[32]

That was March 13, 1978. The incident stiffened Native resistance. Within seventeen days, a hundred Navajos took over a Texaco pumping station near Aneth demanding changes, better environmental conditions, and a share in the profits. "Residents still lacked running water and electricity despite the millions in oil taken from beneath their land," writes historian Kathleen P. Chamberlain, who adds, "As the American public filled its chrome-laden gas guzzlers for a couple of dollars per tank and warmed suburban homes with cheap energy, Utah Navajos in particular lived in extreme poverty."[33] A fund had been established resulting from the 1933 extension of the Paiute Strip, which granted 37.5 percent of royalties to Utah Natives from Navajo Mountain on the west to Aneth on the eastern side of San Juan County. The dollars remained largely unspent by the state's Indian Affairs Commission, chaired by Salt Lake City attorney John S. Boyden. It would be years before Boyden's surreptitious contracts and cross-dealings with tribes would be uncovered. He was the legal mastermind behind Peabody Coal Company's Black Mesa Mine, which used Navajo and Hopi coal and Hopi water.[34]

Navajos in Aneth did not understand why the Indian Affairs Commission had only one Navajo on the board and why commissioners sought to use funds to pay the state back for public health and welfare programs.[35] The 1978 Aneth Takeover and sit-in culminated from years of frustration and resentment. Protestors stopped oil field production and listed thirteen demands to be met by Continental, Phillips, Superior, and Texaco, all of which operated the area's 200 wells.[36] Complaints included harassment or stealing of livestock, personal threats against Native residents, chemicals found in the stomachs of dead livestock, Navajo women molested by oil field workers, "and families offered liquor and drugs in exchange for their daughters."[37]

Environmental complaints included damage to air, water, and special gathering areas where grandmothers collected herbs and medicinal plants. By November 1978 Navajos west of Aneth in nearby Montezuma Creek, Utah, began a protest walk to Navajo tribal headquarters in Window Rock, Arizona, to honor Mother Earth, demand fiscal accountability, and correct mismanagement of funds "for our elders, young ones, and the Navajo people's future generation[s]."[38] Navajo resistance brought water, electricity, and new housing to Aneth. Area residents complained bitterly about energy development and a lack of local representation on oil and gas field management plans. A year after the takeover, sit-in, and protest walk, an even more potentially hazardous event occurred in San Juan County with the 1979 licensing of the White Mesa Uranium Mill adjacent to the White Mesa community of Ute families south of Blanding. Uranium production continued to spiral downward. The mill had a fifteen-year life span. Its future remained uncertain. But just as uranium mining declined because of massive stockpiles of yellowcake, Commissioner Cal Black campaigned for a high-level nuclear waste dump on the northern edge of Bears Ears. The proposed site was less than a mile from Canyonlands National Park.

In the early 1980s, I remember driving through San Juan County and stopping to get gas in either Blanding or Monticello. In those days you had to go into the gas station to pay. As I handed the clerk my credit card, I looked down on the counter to see a petition urging the governor of Utah to approve a nuclear waste facility for the county. "This is a joke, right?" I asked the clerk. "Oh, no," he said. "We really want our own waste dump. It'll bring plenty of jobs which we need. Please sign the petition." I laughed and told the clerk he was crazy. How could you have tourism and nuclear waste in the same place? But decades later, as I began researching in the Canyonlands National Park Archives, I learned just how bizarre the plan actually was in the Ronald Reagan Era of "voodoo economics," when massive projects proposed across the West "for energy independence" included an oil shale industry, dozens of coal mines, new railroads, oil and gas fields, and, yes, disposal sites for high level nuclear waste.

The clerk was right about one thing. In 1983 unemployment in San Juan County ran 12 percent compared to the state's average of 7.7 percent.

After digging up the Southwest for uranium ore, a national problem had become what to do with high-level nuclear waste generated by nuclear reactors. The newly created Department of Energy (DOE), which included the former Atomic Energy Commission, identified potential disposal sites across the nation as part of the Nuclear Waste Policy Act (NWPA) of 1982. The goal was to store waste deep in the earth in salt domes that geologists believed to be stable and impermeable in a region they labeled Gibson Dome. Two Gibson Dome sites in Utah included Lavender Canyon, where Kent Frost had found the unique Ancestral Puebloan scarlet macaw sash, and Davis Canyon adjacent to the Needles District of Canyonlands National Park and not far from South Sixshooter Peak. The Gibson Dome area became "the preferred spot for a national nuclear waste repository."[39]

The DOE planned a large underground mine, tunnels, and disturbance of 400 acres of surface ground adjacent to Canyonlands and close to a tributary of Indian Creek. Miners would stockpile twenty-one million tons of salt working twenty-four hours a day with night lighting and plenty of fugitive dust.[40] The draft environmental assessment estimated 4,510 people moving to Moab, which then had a population of 5,333 and $3.2 billion in operating costs "that would be recirculated locally."[41] During a seven-year period, 1,850 workers would be on site followed by a 900 worker maintenance staff.[42] Construction crews would need to build thirty-seven miles of railroad and a new bridge over the Colorado River so waste could arrive at the site. The authors admitted there would be "radiological risks, which would result from the direct external radiation emitted by the radioactive waste as a shipment passes by."

On the bright side, they speculated, "It is likely that radioactivity will not escape the host rock for over 100,000 years even assuming package failure."[43] What the authors didn't admit is that the waste would be dangerously radioactive for 250,000 years. In a statement, the NPS reminded officials that unique rock art and archaeological sites had been the reason to establish a "Salt Creek Archaeological District" on the National Register of Historic Places and that all the construction activity was close to wilderness study areas including Bridger Jack Mesa. The DOE's environmental assessment admitted, "The Canyonlands National Park and other recreational areas in the vicinity of the site could lose some tourists who would [otherwise] come to the area to seek a wilderness experience."[44] Suddenly a slice of Bears Ears that nobody wanted, everybody wanted. Congress had just a few years before voted to create Canyonlands National

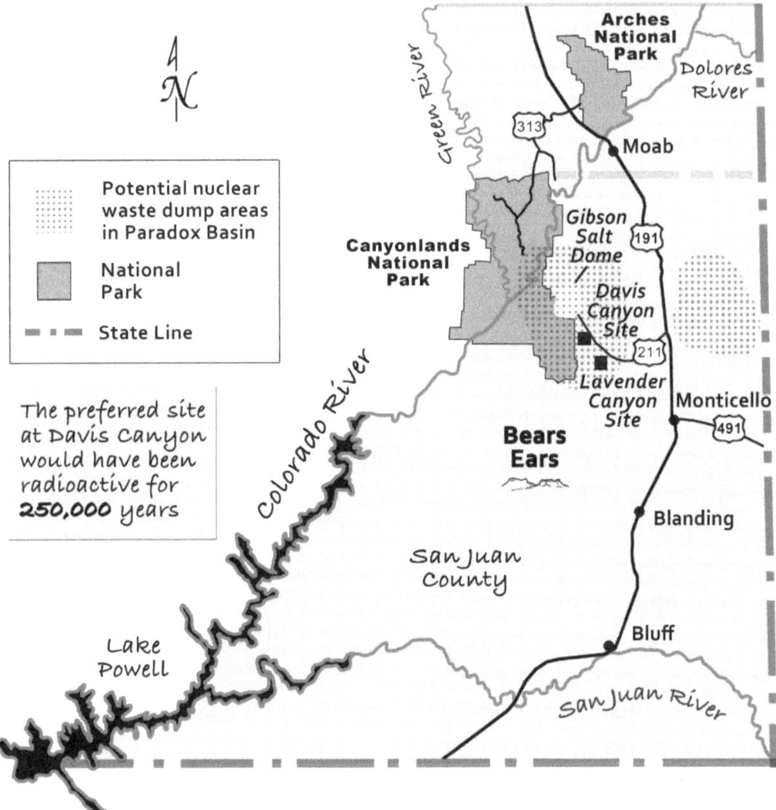

Commissioner Calvin Black supported uranium mining. When mining revenues drastically fell in San Juan County, Black then promoted a nuclear waste dump adjacent to Canyonlands National Park and what would become the Indian Creek District of Bears Ears National Monument. Map by DJ Webb, © by author.

Park, and here was a major environmental threat. Other plans included exploring for potential salt domes on Elk Ridge in the heart of Bears Ears by digging two 5,000-foot-deep holes to assess the potential for "national waste terminal storage."[45]

Politicians fielded letters. Public relations firms funded by the nuclear industry geared up. Would it be canyonlands or waste lands? A "Don't Waste Utah" campaign began with press releases that explained, "A nuclear waste dump means a huge, mile square, 24-hour industrial operation on the doorstep of an incredibly beautiful and wild national park. It means newly constructed railroad and trucking operations along the Park's eastern border."[46] The three white San Juan County Commissioners were all for it.

They wanted to revitalize a sagging uranium mining industry. For them it was a simple equation—jobs versus the environment. All three commissioners signed a letter favoring a national nuclear waste facility to be sited in San Juan County. The commissioners urged, "[T]he people of this county must show active support of the project if they do not want to miss an economic opportunity."[47] Interviewed in the *Salt Lake Tribune*, Cal Black stated he was "knee deep" in the battle to bring nuclear waste to his home county. "You have to make a living and we like to share our beauty with others," the former uranium miner offered. "I keep hoping to convert environmentalists. I once told a gal, 'We really try to forgive you people for being wrong,' he said."[48] But other Utah politicians felt differently. US Senator Orrin Hatch and Congressman Dan Marriott opposed the DOE's plans. Marriott even argued that if an eastern state benefited from nuclear power then they "should be held responsible for their own nuclear waste problem. And the prerequisite for building a plant should be a state's willingness to dispose of its own wastes."[49]

Canyonland hikers had their own ideas. A visitor register from the Needles District contains remarks from the public including "No Nukes (Store it at the White House)" and "No National Sacrifice Area." Other visitors pleaded "Don't Give Canyonlands the Shaft," "Nuclear Waste in Canyonlands is SACRILEGE," "Fantastic scenery," and "It's Disneyland for backpackers."[50] Former Secretary of the Interior Stewart Udall, who had actively promoted Canyonlands as a park, returned to Moab and in a public meeting said residents had every right to be "skeptical" and that the effects of uranium mining and nuclear tests were only beginning to be understood.[51]

Utah governor Scott Matheson made the difference. The governor's office stood firmly against the Department of Energy's plan and repeatedly challenged scientific assertions about salt dome stability and safety.[52] In the end, there was no railroad, no huge shafts sunk deep into the ground near Indian Creek, and no influx of construction workers or fleets of eighteen-wheel haul trucks constantly traveling a dangerous two-lane road. The eastern edge of Canyonlands abuts BLM land at Bears Ears. The area is now protected as the Indian Creek Unit of Bears Ears National Monument, part of the original landscape set aside by President Barack

Obama. Jobs for workers at a national nuclear waste repository never happened.

What did happen, however, was a gut-wrenching, painful reappraisal of the health impacts of the Monticello uranium mill from the Cold War Era. The mill had spewed radioactive dust through the small town causing a variety of cancers and illnesses. Black wanted a nuclear waste depository to bring federal funds to San Juan County. They came, not because of the nuclear depository, but because the Environmental Protection Agency listed the Monticello Mill as a Superfund National Priority cleanup site along with Monticello Radioactively Contaminated Properties. Millions were spent on the cleanup.

When the *Salt Lake Tribune* asked Black about potential danger from uranium waste, he stated that uranium miners had not suffered from exposure to radon gas and that he had been a miner with no ill effects. He wore a bolo tie adorned with uranium. He died of cancer. His granite headstone in the Blanding cemetery contains etched images of things that he loved—an airplane, a Jeep, a houseboat on Lake Powell, an eighteen-wheeled semi-truck, a miner's pick and shovel, an elephant with the letters GOP, a prehistoric pot, the slogan "Sagebrush Rebel," and these words from the Greek statesman and orator Demosthenes: "A leader is to discern events in their beginnings, to foresee what is coming, and to forewarn others."

The Cold War ended. Uranium mining ceased; yet local families still pine for those glory days of large paychecks and a meaningful occupation promoted as essential to national defense. What is hard to reconcile are the impacts of the Monticello Mill and the early deaths of fathers, sons, mothers, and daughters. Why would communities that had lost loved ones to radiation poisoning favor a return to uranium mining? What is it about an attraction to yellowcake? Residents in the town of Monticello still grieve.

Tourists flock to Monument Valley, Utah, where red sandstone spires of the Mitten Buttes rise above desert sands. Publicity promotions of that iconic geology omit reference to the two nearby uranium mines, Monument #1 and Monument #2, which employed hundreds of Navajo miners who would die at an early age of various cancers.[53] The Four Corners towns of Durango, Gateway, Mexican Hat, Moab, Monticello, Shiprock, and Tuba City all had uranium mills spewing poisons into the clean air of the Colorado Plateau. At Monticello, Utah, housewives gathering in their laundry off the line found it coated with yellow dust. Many became ill. Some died of leukemia.

The Four Corners economy once heavily depended on uranium exploration and mining. It was a different era and locals embraced the Atomic Age because World War II blended seamlessly with the Cold War. We needed nuclear weapons to deter Russian aggression. The 1950s spawned the Baby Boom, fast cars with long fins, rock and roll music, and a radical, revealing, two-piece swimsuit named the bikini that was "hot," just like the island atoll in the Pacific Ocean of the same name that the United States had blasted with an atomic bomb. Attractive women were considered "bombshells," and thousands of prospectors swarmed the Colorado Plateau because "[u]ranium was suddenly the most critical material the United States had ever known. It fueled atomic weapons. It promised environmentally-clean electrical power, gas-free operation of cars, planes and locomotives . . . Uncle Sam was desperate for the mineral and willing to pay for it. By law, the federal government was the only buyer," writes Raye Ringholz in *Uranium Frenzy: Boom and Bust on the Colorado Plateau.*[54]

Texas geologist Charlie Steen struck it rich near Moab with his Mi Vida Mine and made national headlines. Prospectors filed claims and opened small "dog-hole" mines to get the ore out. The Atomic Energy Commission built new bridges and roads, especially across the Navajo reservation, but few researchers worried about the effects of radiation and the impacts of radon gas. No set health standards existed for uranium miners or millworkers. Scientists thought they knew about radiation's role in creating cancers, but federal agencies said that health monitoring and mine safety was a state responsibility and state public health inspectors in the Four Corners had limited budgets and unclear directives. To inspect mines, the public health agencies needed permission from the mine corporations, which felt obligated to maximize production, not to spend extra money per ton of ore on better ventilation systems, and showers and changing facilities for miners' work clothes. Uranium mines allowed few inspectors.[55]

So miners worked all day around deadly radon gas. They ate lunch in the mines sitting on radioactive rocks. Navajo miners went home covered in dust, hugged their wives, embraced their children, and fed their livestock without taking off their work clothes. "As for the miners, they were traditionally inured to dangers underground. Hazardous conditions were just part of the mining game. Radiation was just a new name for it," writes Ringholz.[56] "Most of the miners thought they were all right. The radon gas was something you couldn't see, taste or smell. They thought as long as it was sand and not silica, they were safe. It was hard to teach these people that something was wrong," explained a former Colorado State mine inspector in *Uranium Frenzy*.[57] Radiation takes time to show its deadly effects. Radon gas decays into solid microscopic particles called daughters. Some have half-lives of a few seconds or minutes, but others become Polonium-218, Bismuth-214, or Polonium-214. As radon breaks down, a new daughter is formed, and without proper mine ventilation, the tiny nuclear particles collected on suspended dust worked their way into men's lungs—first into soft tissue and then into bone.

"The Navajo uranium miners averaged cumulative exposures that were about forty-four times higher than the levels at Hiroshima and Nagasaki," reveals environmental writer Judy Pasternak in her book *Yellow Dirt: A Poisoned Land and the Betrayal of the Navajos*.[58] Frantic prospecting for uranium mines was followed by the mines' development. Drivers trucked valuable ore off to the many mills in uncovered loads rattling yellow dust every mile.

A Navajo miner works in Monument Mine #2. Corporations never told Native miners about the dangers of radioactivity which caused illnesses, birth defects, and early deaths across the Navajo Nation. Courtesy of the Center of Southwest Studies, Fort Lewis College.

"When I used to go to Bluff Elementary, there was a whole slough of semi-trucks going through Bluff right in front of the elementary school. There used to be these materials that would fall off," recalls Kenneth Maryboy. "Now I know it was yellowcake—nobody told us not to play with it. We'd mark on the road and play with it all day long. The kids I played with back then, a lot of them are gone from some kind of cancer or illness, and nobody wants to talk about that."[59]

No environmental protection agency existed. No careful monitoring occurred. Later when the Atomic Energy Commission had stockpiled enough yellowcake the mining and milling stopped. The uranium boom ended, but not the work of the deadly radon daughters. That had just begun.

Most of the mine and mill sites have been reclaimed at the taxpayers' cost of millions of dollars—$250 million for Grand Junction, Colorado, and the same amount for Monticello, Utah. Because of worldwide nuclear fears, the bottom has dropped out of the uranium market. Mining has ended. Moab, which once boasted it was the uranium capital of the world, is now flooded with tourists and Jeeps and has a thriving recreational economy. Durango's uranium mill became a superfund site below Smelter Mountain and is now a dog park with the hazardous material buried elsewhere. Only Monticello is interpreting its poisoned past.

I found the road signs and drove to where the seventy-eight-acre Monticello mill had been in a creek bottom just below the highway. The mill site is now a reclaimed natural area with newly planted pine trees, fruit trees, elms, willows, cottonwoods, and pampas grass. Some of the trees have signs hung on them, like headstones, in memory of millworkers or residents who died of cancer-related deaths. Like names on the Wall of the Vietnam Memorial or the stark white marble at Pearl Harbor that describes sailors who died on the USS Arizona, the kiosk at the Monticello Mill site erected by the Monticello Victims of Mill Tailings Committee tells a powerful story. The interpretation begins,

> The Monticello Mill . . . heralded at one time as an economic boom for Monticello, providing needed jobs and promising a future of energy and defense for a nation . . . left quite another impact . . . The government-owned mill provided a patriotic heartbeat for the community of family oriented pioneers, offering them a united cause for their nation.
>
> During the Cold War, we fought against communist ideology with a strategy of nuclear deterrence, but it was ourselves we were

> killing. By 1957, at the Monticello mill 214 workers daily processed 600 tons of ore. Each day the mill spewed out 2,600 pounds of heavy metals, sulfates, carbonates, lead, arsenic, asbestos, selenium, manganese, molybdenum, and gases like hydrogen chloride and vanadium pentoxide. Chrome came off car bumpers. Screen doors changed color. Fumes from the plant were "inhaled in the lungs of young and old alike; mill workers, miners, ore haulers, city residents, families and children."

One side of the kiosk has facts about the plant, which closed in 1962, but the tailings were left exposed. Gophers aerating the tailings were shot and killed after being tracked by Geiger counters. The other side of the kiosk bears witness in vivid descriptions from the families of victims who died of brain tumors, leukemia, and lung diseases. A physician explains, "I moved to Monticello thinking I would have a typical rural small town practice; instead I walked into a cancer factory." A high school principal bemoans ever coming to Monticello. He describes the heartbreak of having his son, captain of the basketball team, die of leukemia two months before turning seventeen. Stunned, I left the kiosk to walk the trail. Thunderstorms came from the west. A few raindrops landed in the dust, and I thought of all the sad stories yet untold of uranium mining across the Colorado Plateau. For Monticello, scholarly studies tell a tragic tale.

In their article "Left in the Dust: Uranium's Legacy and Victims of Mill Tailings Exposure in Monticello, Utah," authors Stephanie A. Malin and Peggy Petrzelka begin,

> "You do what you have to do to provide for your family and put a roof over your head. They [my parents' generation] were so happy to have employment they didn't think there might be danger." These are the words of Fritz—lifelong resident of Monticello, sufferer from chronic lymphocytic leukemia, and activist for Victims of Mill Tailings Exposure (VMTE). Fritz lives each day with a reminder of his exposure to uranium, an element creating renewed interest on the Colorado Plateau.[60]

The authors explain about environmental health movements, community-wide uranium exposure and local resistance to being ignored, left out, and denied adequate healthcare for families who just did what they were told. They went to work—in a mill that processed uranium and vanadium owned by the government. They were never told about health risks. The authors write, "The voices of those who have been impacted most by uranium mining and milling have been too long ignored—by scholars and policymakers."[61]

The mill shut its doors when more than 86 percent of San Juan County's workers were employed in the mineral industry. The mill closed. The radiation remained. Former workers began to fight for their lives and for federal recognition because "environmentally induced diseases are often contested illnesses, or illnesses whose causes or very existence do not have a scientific consensus . . . They are either not recognized by science without prolonged struggle . . . or are formally recognized diseases . . . but with unsubstantiated links to environmental exposure."[62] Mill workers from Monticello believed they were front line fighters in the Cold War. They believed they were soldiers in civilian clothes milling minerals for the Atomic Energy Commission that would save America from the Soviets.

Utah has had twenty-two sites on the National Priorities List of the Environmental Protection Agency (EPA). These are the most toxic and hazardous environmental sites in the nation, but Utah "is the only state in which so few people have expressed concern about a site's danger or the quality of its cleanup." The authors focused on Monticello as a case study because of the local activist group VMTE, which is another example of San Juan County resistance and anger at the federal government.[63] By 1990 the VMTE became a subcommittee of the City of Monticello with activist members, regularly scheduled meetings, issues raised before the City Council, and a campaign for federal dollars to compensate bereaved families. The interpretive plaque at the former mill site reads,

> In the 1940s and 1950s, as World War II came to an end, and the Cold War gained strength, patriotism was high, and uranium was framed as a miracle element, an element helping to strengthen economies, fight the communists and even cure cancer. . . . Little did [families] realize the price they would pay, young and old alike, as the "Mill" would extract a deadly cost on the unsuspecting public in its quest for high grade uranium for the developing Atomic Weapons Age . . . The unenlisted patriots' service for their country was never recognized, many lives were cut short and families were left to struggle, an unreasonable price for all to pay. The trials continue.[64]

Daily, Monticello's mill spewed 2,600 pounds of particulates. The mill closed in 1962, but the heartache had only begun.

Editor of the *San Juan Record* Bill Boyle explained to me that the mill "was the front line of the Cold War. My father died of cancer and my brother died of cancer. He swam in the tailings pond." The mill closed but its corporate operators left over 100,000 cubic yards of contaminated soil and two million tons of toxic waste including building materials used throughout town for homes and road base.[65] Toxic dust blew in every direction and through open windows in the heat of summer. To pay for cancer treatments, Monticello residents have put second mortgages on their homes or declared bankruptcy. They've asked for federal support but received little assistance. "For a few years after my brother died someone from either the state or federal government would come to our house and draw blood samples from all of us. The Government did the big clean up and claims all contaminated materials are gone, but I still wonder," Robert Maughan told me.[66]

Monticello is on the northeastern edge of Bears Ears. Monument Valley is on the southwestern edge where dozens of Navajos who worked in uranium mines and mills have suffered or died. Their families continue to grieve, some of them living in cinder block houses built on radioactive foundations. Angered over so much illness, loss, and death, and with numerous uncovered mine sites still blowing poisonous dust across the Navajo Reservation, the Navajo Nation tribal government has permanently banned any future uranium mining on its seventeen million acres. The loss is too great. The cleanup still undone.

Under President Obama's Bears Ears National Monument, potential uranium mine sites would have been permanently closed. The Trump Administration cut the monument's boundaries by 85 percent to keep open the potential for uranium mining. The White Mesa Mill is still licensed. Some San Juan County residents wanted the county to have the nation's largest nuclear waste dump. Other residents resisted the federal government over the Monticello Mill and its poisonous past. "Government studies and memos clearly show that the government was aware of risks posed by uranium exposure yet failed to inform the community." Malin and Petrzelka argue, "Government's failure to act, failure to protect Monticello citizens, was the single biggest contributor to feelings of deception by residents."[67] In San Juan County in the late-twentieth century, some landscapes were poisoned. Others were protected.

In 1984 Congress created the Dark Canyon Wilderness, the only federally designated wilderness in southeast Utah. Now the task would be reseeding and revegetating Dark Canyon and its tributary canyons damaged for decades by Al Scorup's cows. Some of the deep arroyo cutting in what were once lush meadows may never be repaired. Bluff, where Scorup had once built a fine stone house, slumbered on. In an article titled "Bluff: Dead or Alive, the Best Old Town in Utah," author Katherine Metcalf Nelson explained, "Bluff is its people—missionary, merchant, sheriff, teacher, bartender, farmer, innkeeper, children. It's those familiar faces as well as a familiar bend in the river that give the town its flavor and bring outsiders back." She described Gene and Mary Foushee, the Recapture Lodge, and how "[t]his town has become a dependable, dearly loved place in our desert travels. Our wanderings have led us all over the Four Corners in search of Anasazi cliff dwellings and remote vistas, but almost always our journey begins and ends here." In *Utah Holiday* magazine, Nelson rhapsodized about Bluff,

> It is a worn, old Mormon quilt of wood and stone, pieced together amid small squares of pasture and field, a pioneer design that rests quietly on the bedrock of a native culture much older than its own. Like the formations that surround it, Bluff is many layered, rich in shades of color and crossbedding.... In morning small birds sing up the sun over the bluffs to the east, and the air smells of earth and river. In the evening the whole town is blond, then pink before sunset. At night when the moon rises, the red sand in the washes turns silver, and the stars tell you exactly where you stand beneath them.[68]

But if Bluff and its residents minded their business and kept to a slow pace, in other parts of San Juan County, anger at the federal government and local resistance in the 1980s continued with ongoing pothunting and illegal digging of Native American graves at prehistoric sites. Across the Bears Ears region, multigenerational families continued their traditions of digging sites on weekends. With the passage of the 1979 ARPA and BLM law enforcement rangers on patrol, the stage was set for Blanding's first big pothunting raid in 1986. Change comes hard in canyon country.

I understand the attraction of finding artifacts. I know what it is like to be walking down an arroyo and suddenly trip in the dirt, fall forward, and expose a thousand-year-old spearpoint. In Bears Ears, I've found arrowheads, potsherds, and several spearpoints from white to gray to brilliant red in color. I once found an Ancestral Puebloan knife. I let out such a yell that my hiking companions thought I'd been bitten by a rattlesnake.

They came running. We looked at the artifact, turned it over and over, photographed it, exclaimed about it, and reburied it on the spot. I call that "catch-and-release arrowhead hunting."[69] The thrill is still there as well as the story, but any found item is not mine to keep. But I do understand the excitement of holding in my hands an item crafted millennia ago shaped from stone with prayers and incantations and then used and reused, possibly lost and recovered by a different people from a different culture and then lost again. Ancient stories stay with spearpoints. When I find them, it heightens my senses. I ask how did this get here. How long has it been here? What does it mean that this object from centuries ago has revealed itself to me right now, right here, in this place with the sun going down and a brilliant red hue splashed against the cliffs behind me?

I can only imagine what it is like to find a whole pot, nested baskets, ancient effigies, or tools shaped from wood and polished by the oils from a farmer's hardened hands. In southwest New Mexico I was part of a team looking to recover an ancient jar found in a slender cave in the Gila National Forest. The cave turned out to be a mountain lion's den, and the jar was the largest intact Mogollon olla or corrugated water jar ever found in the state. Long ago packrats had devoured the contents, and a small piece of the rim was missing, but overall it was an astonishing find—a true museum piece and a one-of-a-kind storage jar that could have contained enough dried corn to feed an entire village for months or provided seed corn for several villages.

I remember sitting in the cave staring at the jar and realizing that my knowledge of our nation's history—the entire span of wars and events, of movements west, of victories and defeats, of forests leveled and fields cleared and farmed, the rise of cities and the birth of highways—had been encompassed in the life of this one jar. It had sat undisturbed in a quiet cave for centuries.[70] So I know the feeling when ancient artifacts are unearthed.

In Tony Hillerman's book *A Thief of Time* he writes about high-end collectors who covet artifacts, wealthy connoisseurs of cultures who feed the black market by buying the past. In Hillerman's novel, the aged collector Richard DuMont says, "One doesn't buy merely the object. One wants what goes with it. The history." He comments to Navajo detective Joe Leaphorn,

> "And this Anasazi pot of yours. Why is it worth five thousand dollars?" He laughed, a small tinkling sound. "It's not much of

> a pot, really. But the Anasazi! Such mysterious people. You hold this pot, and think of the day it was made. A civilization that had grown a thousand years was dying." He stared into Leaphorn's eyes. "As ours is surely dying. Its great houses were standing empty. No more great ceremonials in the kivas. This is about when my pot was made—so my appraisers tell me. Right at the end. The twilight. In the dying days."[71]

For DuMont as for so many collectors, it's not just the object but also the story of its creation and its use, its link to the past as a mnemonic or memory device to recall an ancient time and a vanished cultural era.

In *Finders Keepers*, Craig Childs writes about finding the past in backcountry known only to hikers willing to cover miles and go deep into canyons far from roads and water. "Part of it was the rush of discovery, the surprise of a sugar-white spearhead or a thatched cradleboard half submerged in dust. It was about being human, moving like a human, finding what humans left behind." He added, "You would come to a place to sit and rest, and then realize someone else had done the same a thousand years earlier, knapping an arrowhead and leaving a ring of flaked stone at your feet."[72]

I realize the bragging rights finding a rare artifact would bring in a small southeast Utah community surrounded by archaeological sites. The very essence of the find would prove your knowledge of an ancient landscape, your ability to traverse its remoteness, and your sensitive skill in decoding hidden cache sites and in uncovering a piece of the past. But I also understand the law. What I find I leave alone. It's not mine to take, not mine to keep. Citizens from Blanding, however, got caught.

Local citizens had been encouraged by an archaeologist at the University of Utah to dig prehistoric ceramics for the university's collections. Later a different university archaeologist Julian Steward would find that practice unethical. He tried to establish scientific excavation teams, but he failed. Brett Shumway wrote,

> For three generations many of Blanding's residents dug in surrounding Indian ruins and excavated Anasazi artifacts. It was a family tradition. The art of pot digging was taught to the children by their fathers. Camp outs, picnics, wood-gathering expeditions, and mining activities also included arrowhead hunting and pot digging.[73]

In the decades following World War II, the local lure of discovering antiquities continued, especially among members of the Shumway family. But times and laws had changed.

After passage of ARPA, on November 15, 1984, Earl Shumway was federally indicted on two counts involving theft and destroying government property and two counts of pothunting. In Allen Canyon on the Manti-La Sal National Forest in the Bears Ears region, Shumway found an extraordinary basket cache. He stole thirty-four rare Basketmaker baskets and jewelry with a black market value of $110,000.[74] Some of the baskets nested inside each other. A few had a unique indented shape like the curve of a fiddle. One journalist wrote, "With the Shumway arrest, US Attorney Ward is clearly giving the ARPA law some teeth. A message is undoubtedly being sent to pot hunters. . . ."[75] DNA evidence on a cigarette butt left in a dirt spoils pile at the ravaged site helped convict Shumway. Mountain Dew cans lay scattered about.

Earl Shumway styled himself as a Sagebrush Rebel and canyon country expert who had robbed "thousands and thousands" of ancient sites. He pled guilty to one charge and received probation on the other charges because he was already in prison for a different theft. Shumway would go on to inform against pothunters. At trial Shumway, who loved the limelight and attention, boasted of using a bulldozer to scalp centuries of dirt off a site.[76] Shumway, a notorious pothunter himself, was used to finger additional local looters prior to a May 8, 1986 pothunting raid in Blanding at dawn. Family traditions brought felony charges. This was the first major raid against pothunters and collectors under ARPA and it took place in San Juan County, Utah. Many of the sites from which items had been stolen were taken from cliff dwellings and caves in Bears Ears. Similar sites had been looted a century earlier.

Writing about Ancestral Puebloans in the *Los Angeles Times*, Tamara Jones explained, "Still hidden in buried pueblos, dry caves and cliff dwellings are the treasures of their lost civilization ... For generations, local families, archaeologists and occasional outsiders have combed the ruins for the beautiful pottery, jewelry and other souvenirs of the Anasazi. 'Like a big Easter egg-hunt,' said Winston Hurst, curator of the Edge of the Cedars State Park Museum in Blanding." Jones added, "The fun ended ... when law and tradition collided in the Four Corners."[77]

Federal agents raided seventeen homes and trading posts in Utah and Colorado. Two of those homes belonged to San Juan County commissioners. Agents also targeted the mayor's brother in Blanding. Law enforcement officers seized 325 Native American artifacts presumed stolen off southeast Utah's public lands.[78] "Word of the raids traveled like wildfire through the dry brush country of the southwest. It ignited the tempers of dealers and collectors, some of whom claimed they had dug up the pieces on private property," stated the *New York Times*.[79] "Blanding's general store used to swap a candy bar or pack of gum for an arrowhead. And, like many local children, Devar Shumway learned early to spot ruins and excavate them," the *Los Angeles Times* reported.[80] ARPA regulations stipulate pothunting on federal lands as a crime with up to a $10,000 fine and a year in jail plus costs for stabilizing and restoring a site to mitigate damage done. Devar Shumway's son Casey was the first person prosecuted for pothunting in San Juan County. He received a minimal $700 fine and probation.[81]

Seven months after the federal raid, sixty artifacts had been returned by federal law enforcement officers because it could not be proven the objects came from public lands. No indictments had been issued. The US attorney in Utah, Brent Ward, believed the raid had reduced pothunting, but as much as 80 percent of the area's sites had already been looted. The raids "rubbed a stick in the open sore of the cultural values of southern Utah," said Winston Hurst. "This is Sagebrush Rebellion country out here; people don't like it when the Government marches into their homes like cavalry."[82]

Devar Shumway, Earl Shumway's uncle, complained, "The government and archaeologists are using scare tactics against amateur archaeologists—they're stirring up hate."[83] Devar's father had begun the family tradition collecting pots for the University of Utah. "For three summers during the Depression, pothunting was my father's only job," Shumway remembered.[84] Earl Shumway testified in court against Buddy Black, San Juan County Commissioner Calvin Black's son. Buddy Black was acquitted of the charges and his father suggested that "amateur" archaeologists be given excavation permits just like trained professionals.[85] Calvin Black labeled the raids an act "of terrorism" and filed suit to have the objects returned that were taken from his house.[86]

Digging antiquities had become big business. The BLM finally employed two law enforcement rangers for the San Juan Resource Area, which includes the Bears Ears region. Winston Hurt discussed small groups of pothunters with specific territories and claimed "one pothunting party prefaced their looting by laying a line of cocaine on their front shovel blade. Everyone took a hit of coke before they got into a frenzy of excavation."[87] A Utah magazine published "Raiders of the Lost Art: Outlaw Diggers of Anasazi Ruins," and stated, "Ruin diggers are described as Robin Hoods, free spirits, desert rats and frontiersmen as well as deadbeats, outlaws and looters. Many vandals, native to the Four Corners region, are seen as passionately bonded to the land and to the prehistoric ruins they exploit."[88] Curator Hurst described "hundreds of examples of totaled out or mostly destroyed cultural deposits," often where human remains had been dug up and then carelessly laid aside or damaged by picks and shovels. "I used to get physically ill when I had to deal with human remains, especially when I saw burials torn up."[89]

I've hiked down to Baby Mummy Cave but never gone into it. I've walked beside it and dropped lower to admire centuries of rock art on the bottom of cliff faces. In that part of Cottonwood Wash, there are sites everywhere with pieces of stone walls, sentry posts, and small slivers of red chert, the makings of arrowheads and spearpoints. It's a quiet area with plenty of room for corn fields. Centuries after Ancestral Puebloans departed came the tall teepees of Utes who left their own petroglyphs as did the cowboys who followed them. There's a small pool of water and thick grass surrounding a natural pour off falling from a sandstone cliff. It's a special place lived in by different cultures over millennia, but now sites have been looted, dug, and torn apart. I think of the baby burial chamber as I walk down canyon with a backward view of two small alcoves that look like a rattlesnake's eye sockets. A huge sandstone snake's head stares at me as I return in late afternoon. Shadows have shifted. I think of why almost forty infant burials would have been in one place. What tears would have been shed. What sobs would have come from families. Then I think of the brutal vandalism and lack of respect for those who came before. Disgusted, I climb out of the wash.

Using Utah's own antiquities act, San Juan County Sheriff Rigby Wright charged a local looter in the first case in the state, though a Monticello judge gave the vandal only a one hundred dollar fine. Though sympathetic with collectors, Wright enforced the state law. He realized that with the decline in the uranium industry "some of the young people have turned to pot hunting." The sheriff understood, "We've got some deadbeats around here who do it. Put them in jail and we're moving in the right direction. Get some of the arrested pot hunters to talk about who else is doing it and who they sell to, and we'll put a stop to it."[90]

If some Shumways had been pothunters, other family members donated a large collection to help form the Edge of the Cedars State Park

Museum and to keep ancient artifacts in secure storage and on display close to home rather than in museums across the country. An argument that pothunters have used is that unlike professional archaeologists who dig artifacts and take them away to their institutions, collections dug by locals stay in the area. Convicted pothunter Casey Shumway argued, "I hate to see artifacts leave San Juan County, and what I do keeps them from getting squashed under books in some university basement."[91] Brett Shumway concurred. He wrote, "The war between the pothunters and the law enforcement agencies is not the only war brewing. Local residents of San Juan County also resent professional archaeologists. Many residents contend that archaeologists themselves are taking advantage of their positions to gain possession of Indian relics." Shumway added, "probably 95 percent of the relics that have been excavated have not been returned to San Juan County."[92] The Edge of the Cedars State Park Museum changed all that. The museum has been a huge success in keeping Ancestral Puebloan items within their original cultural landscape.

The 1986 Blanding raid left bitter feelings about government overreach and enforcement of federal law. Local pothunting declined, for a short period anyway, but national momentum to protect and honor Native American artifacts and cultural beliefs accelerated. American Indians had become fed up with the warehousing of their ancestors' bones. In 1990 there would be a new federal law protecting Native human remains and funerary items and requiring consultation with culturally affiliated tribes.

In the twenty-first century, there would be another Blanding raid against pothunters and their collections, but this time it would be more comprehensive and more deadly. Three men would commit suicide. Anger about the incident, another raid at dawn with federal agents coming into homes, would imperil plans to create a national monument. Local hostility against the federal government would reach a fever pitch of resistance. Simultaneously, newly energized Native groups vowed to protect their sacred and historic landscape in their own form of resistance. The battle over Bears Ears would begin.

CHAPTER 12

Tribes Come Together for Bears Ears National Monument, 1987–2016

> This is Native American heritage, but it's also American heritage and when it's locked away in private possession, the people lose.
>
> —Emily Palus, BLM National Curator

> We can still hear the songs and prayers of our ancestors on every mesa and in every canyon.
>
> —Malcolm Lehi, Ute Mountain Ute

Blanding, Utah, locals were targeted in two federal pothunting raids. Two years before the first raid, Commissioner Calvin Black had suggested that San Juan County grant local citizens permits for "excavation of Indian ruins." When Mark Maryboy became the first Native American elected to the county commission in 1986, he argued to preserve all Native American ruins in the county.[1] That deep divide between whites and Natives continued for decades as did rancor over the pothunting raids that resulted in probation and no jail sentences. The raids created enormous anger and antagonism against federal officials, the FBI, and the BLM.[2] That antagonism would ultimately result in fierce local resistance by whites and some Navajos to Bears Ears National Monument. Native support of the monument was suppressed and ignored.

In 1990 Congress passed the Native American Graves Protection and Repatriation Act (NAGPRA) requiring museums, historical societies, universities, and any institution receiving federal funds to account for Native American human remains and associated grave items in their collections. For the first time, archaeologists and National Park Service planners were required to consult with tribes over Native American artifacts and how they should be interpreted. Native voices grew stronger and Native groups evolved to focus on cultural preservation and finally received federal support to match state historic preservation programs.[3]

As the BLM established more rules, especially about driving ATVs, San Juan County commissioners used an 1872 mining law to claim public roads. Part of the nineteenth century mining law, the RS 2477 rule, stipulates public access to mining claims. Some Utah officials have argued for faint two-track traces and creek bottoms as historic roads and as a rationale to drive into canyons closed by the BLM. The canyon country had been discovered. As visitation rose at Arches National Monument and Canyonlands National Park visitors also crossed into the Bears Ears region to camp, hike, and explore.

Archaeological adventure tourism developed its own cachet in slickrock country as conservation and environmental groups like the Southern Utah Wilderness Alliance, Grand Canyon Trust, Great Old Broads for Wilderness, and Friends of Cedar Mesa flourished to preserve wilderness and roadless areas in canyons, plateaus, and red rock forests. The Nature Conservancy bought the Dugout Ranch in Indian Creek and became the county's largest private property owner. Indian Creek became a mecca for crack-climbers as one of the best climbing sites on BLM lands anywhere in the American West. Climbers came outfitted in their own vans and may not have spent much money in San Juan County, but they came nonetheless as a new type of recreation-user on public lands.

With four-wheel drive vehicles, better roads, wealthier tourists, and international visitors cruising the Golden Circle of national parks, remote San Juan County didn't seem remote anymore. Locals created a group named SPEAR (San Juan Public Entry and Access Rights) to protect and expand ATV routes and to promote off-highway motorized recreation to increase tourism, but the economy sagged with few opportunities for young people. The older generation pined for the fun, frolic, and paychecks that came with the uranium boom, but those days had sputtered to a close. The future seemed uncertain, but the prehistoric past still held its allure.

Earl Shumway would again be convicted of illegally digging an archaeological site. This time he would face a jail term and the stiffest sentence yet handed out under ARPA. With a helicopter, he had returned to the same site he had looted a decade earlier. In the 1990s a well-known and respected local physician and his wife from Blanding would be caught digging on state land. The lawsuit brought against them and years of legal maneuvering would result in precedent-setting amendments to Utah state laws to clarify that the remains of ancient Native Americans interred centuries ago in caves and rock shelters had the same legal protections as whites buried in historic cemeteries.

The uranium industry had ceased. Oil and gas revenues declined because the dozens of wells near Aneth had earlier reached their maximum production capacity. Agriculture struggled with up and down markets, but tourism and visits to cafes, restaurants, motels, national monuments, state parks, and national parks continued to increase. As a retired secretary of the interior, Stewart Udall worked compassionately for federal legislation to cover health costs for uranium miners, millers, and haul-truck drivers. Finally, Congress agreed in 1990 and passed the Radiation Exposure Compensation Act (RECA) cosponsored by Utah Senator Orrin Hatch. The law would help victims' families in Monticello, Monument Valley, and other San Juan County communities. Later, the Navajo Nation would ban uranium mining and processing on its seventeen million acres after forty years of largely unregulated mining and hundreds of unsafe radioactive mine sites. Delegate to the Navajo Nation Council Mark Maryboy said, "Our people are still dying from this. This legislation was important to [the] Navajo Nation, a very big step for Navajo people. It's very simple—uranium kills."[4]

Deep in Grand Gulch, archaeologists, historians, photographers, and other researchers spent time in the 1990s trying to understand which caves and cliff dwellings had been dug a century before. The process earned the name "reverse archaeology" in a successful attempt to link artifacts in Eastern museums with Bears Ears canyons like Lake Canyon, Allen Canyon, and other locales. Excellent detective work and hours spent in archives and in the field paid off. Winston Hurst, Ann Phillips, Fred Blackburn, and a team of volunteers helped identify historic inscriptions written on cave and kiva walls. Part of San Juan County's past was finally becoming understood with additional insights into the lives of Basketmakers and Ancestral Puebloans who had lived and farmed in canyons.

In the 1990s the NPS finally fulfilled a promise to San Juan County to develop a visitor center and other facilities in the Needles District of Canyonlands northwest of Monticello. For years local citizens had hoped for a massive resort with a lodge, restaurants, shops, plenty of paved parking, and opportunities for sales tax revenue. It didn't happen. The primitive, wilderness nature of the dramatic rock formations in the Needles prevailed. But the roads got better, and with a formal visitor center, staff housing, and accessible park rangers, perhaps tourists would tarry and stay longer.

Certainly, tourism success came to Monument Valley on the southwest edge of Bears Ears. John Wayne may have said, "Monument Valley is where God put the West," but that's also where Harry Goulding put his two-story stone trading post that grew into a lodge, gift shop, motel, gas station, trailer spaces, cabins, and even a small airport runway. The "Duke" filmed five feature films in Monument Valley. Movie companies paid Navajos as extras, built over 260 miles of roads, and set the stage for the successful Navajo Nation Monument Valley Tribal Park, which by the 1990s welcomed visitors from around the world.[5]

Bears Ears as a landmark atop Cedar Mesa continued to have a powerful pull for whites as well as Natives. A cowboy turned heavy-equipment operator had to leave the area to find work. While running equipment on the Kaiparowits Plateau in another county on the other side of the Colorado River, he looked east toward home. "I looked over across the country there one day and saw the Bear's [*sic*] Ears, and I got so homesick I couldn't stand it," he related.[6]

In the 1990s some pothunters went to jail. Others went to court for months and even years. The black market for illegally obtained Native American antiquities only increased. Private collections grew. Then in 2009 dozens of armed federal agents descended on Blanding for a huge pothunting raid to recover artifacts largely taken from the Bears Ears region and to make arrests. The unexpected raid and its bungled aftermath further drove a wedge between local whites who claimed a birthright to canyon country and its resources, including Native American artifacts, and other Americans who sought landscape preservation. Native peoples had had enough. They organized. Momentum increased to protect the Bears Ears area including Cedar Mesa, Grand Gulch, Comb Ridge, Beef Basin, Valley of the Gods, and the diverse public land landscape that had been home to Native Americans for millennia. After the Blanding pothunting raid, efforts to protect the entire sacred landscape accelerated. Two options seemed open.

Because the BLM supervised the land, a national conservation area (NCA) requiring an act of Congress was one path. A second path was asking President Obama to use the century-old Antiquities Act of 1906 to declare a Bears Ears National Monument. Environmental groups had spent years promoting a Red Rock Wilderness Act embracing much of San Juan County, but it never received legislative traction. Commissioner Calvin Black had warned of "a plan by environmentalists to turn most of southeastern Utah into a 'giant wilderness park.'"[7] Now Native Americans, disgusted with decades of looting of their ancestors' sites, formed Utah Diné Bikéyah to honor traditional Navajo lands. They began with cultural mapping and interviewing elders about specific Native connections to the landscape. Later an Inter-Tribal Coalition of Navajo, Zunis, Utes, and Hopis evolved to pursue protection of the Bears Ears landscape in their own way, in their own words. In a landscape of resistance, diverse Native voices spoke as one.

When census records verified Natives exceeded half of the county's population, Natives challenged white-dominated elections in San Juan County. Voting districts did not reflect Native voters who could be outnumbered by whites who voted in a bloc against Native candidates. In 1984 the Department of Justice became involved because the county had violated portions of the Voting Rights Act. In a subsequent case, expert witness Daniel McCool described the aftermath of federal involvement resulting in "animosity, racial hostility, and polarization."[8] He cited a chain of letters from Gail Johnson, county clerk in 1990, who wrote the Utah lieutenant governor and stated, "I am asking for your visible and concrete support in assisting San Juan County in these negotiations with the Justice Dept.... I do not want to appear to have any desire to deny any one's right to the political process. But the heavy and oppressive methods of the federal government in marching through counties individually makes me uncomfortable and defensive."[9]

Once redistricting had begun as mandated by the federal Voting Rights Act, in 1986 Mark Maryboy became the first elected Native American commissioner in the history of San Juan County. Other Navajos supported Maryboy and so did his Ute and Anglo constituents in the southern half of San Juan County. Because residents in Blanding and Monticello had voted Republican for decades, Maryboy ran on the Democratic ticket and for the first time in 1990 a full slate of other Natives also ran on the Democratic ticket. They called their campaign "It's Our Turn," which translated into Navajo as *"Niha whol zhiizh."* The campaign earned state and national attention, but because Native candidates ran for at-large county offices, they lost.[10] Maryboy won reelection. He began to voice Native needs including better roads, libraries, and healthcare.

Whites in San Juan County, fearful of Native influence, suggested splitting the county in half to create a northern county that would include Blanding and Monticello and a southern county largely Native American. A blue ribbon commission met to analyze the issue and held extensive public meetings eventually concluding that such a split would be "infeasible for financial reasons." A county split into a northern and southern section would leave the oil and gas resources from the Aneth oil field with

Navajos. Even if well production had declined, this would eliminate revenue for county coffers. Then federal contracts were studied. Because dollars supported tribal members, those funds would no longer flow through the county administration. A county split in half left only more rancor and division. "The local white Mormon population has fought every right Natives ever wanted, every step of the way, from serving on juries to better schools and healthcare to holding elected office," states retired University of Utah professor McCool.[11]

Navajos successfully claimed systematic discrimination in the selection of jurors in San Juan County. Navajo Loren Crank Jr. filed a class-action lawsuit in 1993 against three judges and the state judicial council for more Native tribal members to be admitted to the San Juan County jury pool. At that time 52 percent of the county's residents were Native American. The American Civil Liberties Union (ACLU) took the case and argued for more Native jurors. Director of the ACLU's Utah Chapter, Carol Gnade, said, "We thought they were making a good-faith effort to really change, not to have San Juan County be like the South in the 1950s."[12] Navajo and Ute tribal members argued "discrimination of American Indians in the selection of jurors in San Juan County was one of the worst ethnic inequalities in the US justice system." In 1996 state court officials agreed to develop a more representative and equitable San Juan County jury pool.[13]

As Native resistance to long-established white-dominated jury selection and voting practices continued, so did grave robbing of Native American burial sites by non-Natives. But the laws had evolved. One law in particular was a human rights victory for Native Americans. Congress passed it the same year that Utah Navajos sought election to San Juan County offices. Racism in America had included the disregard of Native American human remains. In the nineteenth century Native skulls were routinely collected and studied to prove racial hierarchies in the pseudoscience of "phrenology," and the false belief that white Anglo-Saxon Protestants had superior intellect because of larger brain cavities. In 1868 a US Army surgeon sent a memo to all military physicians stating, "The Surgeon General is anxious that our collection of Indian crania, already quite large, should be made as complete as possible." Native scholar Gerald Vizenor would conclude, "White bones are reburied, tribal bones are studied in racist institutions. . . . The tribal dead become the academic chattel, the aboriginal bone slaves to advance archaeological technicism and the political power of institutional science."[14]

The American Association of Museums reported that 163 museums held 43,306 sets of Native American skeletal remains. The Smithsonian Institution alone held 18,600 remains and thousands of burial artifacts. Native peoples had not been consulted about any of this. Their thoughts and philosophies had been ignored. Thomas King explained Native perspectives and "the rights of the dead themselves, toward whom the living bear responsibility." He argued, "The living are responsible for the dead, and the dead—often seen not as being really 'dead' but as transformed and still powerful—must be treated with respect."[15]

Testifying before the US Senate, anthropologist Deward Walker stated, "Everywhere in Native North America one encounters a great religious importance attached to the dead who are believed to have a continuing influence on the lives of their descendants and other survivors." He continued, "Given proper rituals and proper respect, [the dead] are believed to provide assistance in curing illnesses, in determining the future, in guaranteeing the outcome of risky events, and in other general ways helping make the lives of the living more secure."[16] Congress finally came to see the Native perspective. To correct a century of wrongs, Congress passed NAGPRA in 1990. The law began attempts to inventory Native human remains in dozens of museum basements and storage areas and to require consultation with federally recognized tribes on any action that might result in damage to Native American burial sites either prehistoric or historic. States like Utah passed their own burial bills, but pothunters kept digging at night under full moons and in caves and alcoves with sentries posted.

The pothunting poster child for southeast Utah, and the entire Southwest, was Earl Shumway who liked to swagger and boast of all the sites he had looted, earning himself a reputation as a PhD—pothunter deluxe—and the ire of law enforcement who tried to catch him in the act. Federal agents feared him because he threatened to shoot any rangers with a .44 magnum pistol. Shumway grew up in a family that had pothunted Native American sites in San Juan County for three generations. Some family members thought it was their right to dig sites in search of pottery, baskets, arrowheads, blanket fragments, or sandals. While some local families in the county collected arrowheads and artifacts for recreation, Shumway had moved into the world of pothunting as a commercial collector looking for unique, one-of-a-kind objects to sell on a growing black market. He boasted he could make $5,000 a day.[17]

Locals knew there were state and federal anti-pothunting laws, but they resisted and dug anyway. In the 1990s across the Bears Ears landscape and into Canyonlands National Park, pothunters persisted. Two case studies of arrest and prosecution involve Shumway, known to be a thief who had stolen other items, and the respectable physician James or "Jim" Redd and his wife Jeanne. The Redds were caught digging on Utah state land managed by SITLA. Shumway went to prison and the Redds went to court. In both cases, they impacted existing laws and further focused state and national attention on Utah's Native American heritage and the sanctity of ancient Native American burials.

As late as 1994, angry sentiments still simmered over the May 1986 pothunting raids in San Juan County. Commissioner Calvin Black had filed a $3.7 million slander suit against US Attorney Brent Ward. The criminal trial against alleged pothunters had been postponed and in a congressional hearing, residents complained about the raid and what they considered federal overreach. More than 300 artifacts had been taken from sixteen residences in Colorado and Utah and those items had been forfeited to the federal government or returned. Ownership of the 105 items taken from San Juan County homes remained unresolved so the US attorney's office, in a gesture of conciliation, agreed that a citizen's committee, rather than a judge, could weigh evidence as to whether the antiquities in question came from public or private land.

If off private land, then the items would be returned. If off public land, then the artifacts would be curated at the Edge of the Cedars State Park Museum in Blanding. Committee members included former sheriff Rigby Wright, local US Magistrate Bennion Redd, and businessman Howard Randall. It seemed like a good solution. "That raid was so badly conceived that we are, still today, trying to get over the negative reactions in the community," explained archaeologist Winston Hurst to the *Deseret News*. He added, "Some families have gone out on the weekends with their kids and hunted artifacts. They have a hard time admitting that what they have done as a family for so long is now wrong."[18]

Against that backdrop and peace offering by the US attorney's office, site digging continued. In March 1994 the artifact committee began its work. Seven months later Earl Shumway, described as "a snitch, a burglar and a pothunter" was indicted by a federal grand jury for excavating in Bears Ears in an Ancestral Puebloan alcove in the North Whiskers area of Cedar Mesa. He had been arrested a decade earlier and had become an informant, leading agents to local houses for the 1986 raid. Now he and Peter Verchick had been indicted. "Earl's a fairly well-known character in southeastern Utah," State Archaeologist David Madsen explained.

"He used to claim he could outsmart anybody and that he'd never get caught doing it."[19] Shumway said about pothunting, "Around here, it's not a crime. It's a way of life."

Shumway was also under indictment for digging Dop-Ki Cave in Canyonlands and Horse Rock Ruin on the Manti-La Sal National Forest in Bears Ears. In both cases he had arrived by helicopter. Because Shumway never paid the $5,000 helicopter use fee, the pilot turned state's evidence as did another co-conspirator. A decade earlier Shumway had looted thirty-four baskets and jewelry from another site on the national forest and received only probation. These additional repeat offenses would result in fines, jail time, and new public awareness of ARPA. By August 1995 a federal jury convicted Shumway on four charges of looting and destroying two Ancestral Puebloan sites. "Within the national archaeological community, Mr. Shumway is widely known as a looter who has done unestimable damage to archaeological resources of the Anasazi culture and earlier prehistoric peoples and cultures," stated Assistant US Attorney Wayne Dance.[20] "He's the No. 1 looter in the United States," claimed David Tarler, who tracked archaeological crimes for the NPS. At the Canyonlands site Shumway found the grave of an infant, tore away the blanket it was buried in, robbed the grave, and scattered the human bones. Native Americans would not forget that desecration.

"What he did in Dop-Ki Cave is just sacrilege," stated Joe Dishta in the *New York Times*. As heritage and historic preservation director for Zuni Pueblo, Dishta explained, "They are our ancestors. They were put in the grave in such a way to effect their journey to the spirit world."[21] BLM Agents Rudy Mauldin and Bart Fitzgerald felt evidence might be missing. Julie Cart wrote in the *Los Angeles Times* from Blanding,

> As he raced his white Ford pickup south from Moab toward the red sandstone canyons here, Rudy Mauldin kicked himself for not thinking of it before. That morning, he and his partner, fellow Bureau of Land Management special agent Bart Fitzgerald, had turned the case over and over with another investigator. What were they missing? They knew that priceless artifacts had been looted from a remote Indian grave site. They knew that a burial blanket had been stripped off the remains of an infant and the skull tossed on a trash heap. They had a suspect but no link to the crime. Then they remembered the backfill, the pile of dirt left by the digger.[22]

The successful conclusion to this case depended on DNA evidence from a cigarette filter tip found in the dirt pile. This unique use of DNA evidence became an important breakthrough because "More ARPA crimes are prosecuted in Utah than anywhere else in the nation."[23] Agents also took casts of holes made by shovels in case notches or nicks on the shovel might provide evidence of a pothunter's tools. For Earl Shumway, evidence included his cigarette butt and the soda pop brand he preferred. "Earl was known for drinking Mountain Dew at his sites. We found the cans all over the place and could tie him to scenes because of that," Mauldin explained.[24]

The conviction became a watershed moment in the prosecution of ARPA cases that occur in remote locales often with no witnesses. This was the first successful use of DNA evidence in an ARPA case and the longest criminal sentence ever imposed under ARPA. Convicted of seven felony counts, Shumway received six and a half years in prison and a $3,500 fine. On appeal the sentence was reduced to five years and three months, but justice takes many forms.[25]

For years Native Americans have told me that pothunters often die early, painful deaths. Not only have they robbed sites, but pothunters have also disturbed souls in their journey through the afterlife. Earl Shumway died of cancer at only 46, but not before a different kind of justice was meted out—and not by a judge in black robes. While in custody of the US Bureau of Prisons at the Federal Transfer Center in Oklahoma, Native American prisoners severely beat him. Shumway suffered broken ribs, a broken jaw, and additional injuries.[26] Dr. James Redd would also die an untimely death but by his own hand.

In January 1996 while Earl Shumway sat in prison for graverobbing on federal lands, Blanding physician James Redd, his wife, and their children dug a site on Utah state land in Bears Ears in Cottonwood Wash just north of Bluff. I have hiked down an old stockman's trail from the top on eight- to ten-inch wide steps carved into sandstone so cattle could be driven up out of the canyon. Once down the steps into Canyon #2, it is a quiet walk west and then south to what is now known as the Redd Site in one of the widest parts of Cottonwood Wash with steep cliffs in every direction. I have stood there and admired the Ancestral Puebloan site, which had a commanding view.

Two residents spotted the Redd family digging and contacted authorities. A deputy sheriff arrived and found a turquoise green Dodge Ram pickup with the Utah license plate ANASAZI parked off the road.[27] Dr. Redd intercepted the deputy. Redd claimed that he and his family had permission to dig the archaeological site, which he insisted was on private land. But according to the sheriff's office report, property owner Erv Guymon, "stated that he had given permission to the Redds to be on the property [but] he said that he never told them that they could dig there."[28] The deputy did not issue a citation, but he did file an incident report. Further analysis and surveying revealed the site to be on state trust land, 200 feet from private land, thus beginning one of the major cases in Utah history involving desecration and removal of human remains, which is a third-degree felony offense. The Redd case went from district court to the court of appeal, to the Utah State Supreme Court in legal maneuvering that lasted years. The lawsuit and subsequent judicial decisions finally resulted in modifications by the state legislature to rewrite a Utah law protecting human remains and "dead bodies shown to have been intentionally deposited in a place of repose," with a revised definition of a dead human body to include "thousand-year-old human remains discovered in an ancient ruin" and not just white pioneers buried in historic cemeteries.[29]

The persistence of lawyers working for SITLA is to be commended. They helped change Utah history on a vital legal issue involving human remains and basic human rights, but it was a difficult legal process. The story deserves to be told. The site, approximately three miles north of Bluff, had been eligible for the National Register of Historic Places and was a "scientifically-important Anasazi period occupation site appearing to contain the remains of habitation structures, a courtyard, a ceremonial kiva, and an associated midden."[30] Use of the midden by Ancestral Puebloan peoples would be key to the legal importance of the site because Puebloans often buried their dead in south-facing middens.

An investigation by staff of the BLM proved the site had been recently dug with an excavated area twenty feet long and three to six feet wide. BLM staff reported, "Material had been put through a three or four stage screening process, removing large rocks, pottery shards and bone fragments first and progressing down to very fine screening."[31] There were screen-mesh impressions in the back-dirt piles and traces of human bone. An accurate BLM survey concluded the site was on a section of school trust land, so BLM staff forwarded the case report to employees at SITLA.

The San Juan County sheriff's office submitted their report to the county attorney, who recused himself because Dr. Redd had delivered his children. Grand County attorney Bill Benge from Moab agreed to take the case. SITLA pledged support for prosecution to send a strong message that cultural resources and human remains would be protected on state lands. Benge filed two state-code criminal charges: (1) abuse or desecration of a dead human body, a felony charge, and (2) trespassing on state trust lands, a misdemeanor.[32] The trespassing charge could be filed only related to state lands, but the state law prohibiting abuse or desecration of a body applied equally across public and private property. Delays occurred and the Hopi Tribe wrote Benge on July 11, 1996, explaining,

> The vandalism and destruction of archaeological sites is a serious and revolting matter to the Hopi people. These archaeological sites represent verification of the traditional histories of the many Hopi clans that migrated throughout the southwest prior to residing at their final destiny, the Hopi mesas. Moreover, our ancestors were laid to rest at these archaeological sites and continue to act as spiritual stewards over these sites . . . the act of vandalizing our ancestral homes and disrupting the final resting place of our ancestors is exceedingly offensive to our culture and religion.[33]

The Hopis, under tribal chairman Ferrell Secakuku, had taken a formal step to defend and protect their ancestors' graves in the area that would be designated two decades later as Bears Ears National Monument. Newspaper accounts covered the evolving story including "Pothunters in Cottonwood Wash," in *Canyon Echo*, and "S. Utah Couple Want Grave-Robbing Charges Dismissed" in the *Salt Lake Tribune*.[34]

At a preliminary hearing in Monticello on March 20, 1997, Judge Lyle Anderson ruled that the felony charge did not apply because he believed that Indigenous human remains interred in a cave or alcove should not receive the same protections as bodies buried in cemeteries. The court transcript offers insights into the judge's thinking. He stated, "From the evidence that's been presented here, I find that there is probable cause to believe that the defendant's [sic] did trespass on state lands, I also find probable cause to believe that they—that they did disturb these—or even disinterred these remains"; yet he was not sure a felony crime had occurred. Judge Anderson explained, "I guess there's one school of thought that it doesn't matter how old the remains are, they're still human remains, and they need to be protected from being disturbed . . . these people probably have descendants living today who care that they be treated with respect.

The descendant's (sic) of these people probably are the Pueblo Indians, if—if any descendants exist."[35]

Judge Anderson worried about the effect a trial would have upon the defendants. He stated, "But, I have to decide as a magistrate, whether I will bind over and hold the—the Redd's (sic) for trial on these charges... they'll endure the expense and trauma of a—of a trial on a felony charge."[36] The judge did not bind over the Redds on a felony charge. Three weeks after the preliminary hearing, Judge Anderson disclosed that Dr. Redd had provided medical care to the judge's wife and delivered the judge's son. The judge then recused himself from the case.[37]

Thus, began a seven-year legal struggle over the rights of Native American dead in Utah to remain undisturbed. Archaeologists explained that the Native dead had been interred according to prehistoric customs and cultural norms. These were not untended human remains. These were careful burials. Assistant Attorney General Joanne Slotnik argued that the Utah grave-robbing statute was "so unworkable and so racist" that Anderson's interpretation of the law "offends public policy." She wrote in a legal brief filed with the Utah Court of Appeals, "Those buried 'recently' in Utah—for example, pioneers buried in established Anglo cemeteries—would be protected, and the law would punish violators as a felony," yet "In contrast, those buried 'long ago,' for example, the ancient peoples who lived here centuries ago and were buried in ways customary to their culture but foreign to modern peoples would not be so protected." Slotnik concluded, "The obvious racism inherent in such an interpretation renders it contrary to both common sense and public policy."[38]

The Utah Court of Appeals, however, agreed with Judge Anderson's decision that a person could not be convicted of disturbing a human grave without evidence that it was a grave. The court decided that state attorneys had failed to prove the disturbed site was a graveyard noting that "the bones were unearthed from a midden area at an ancient dwelling site."[39] Later in a subsequent court hearing, archaeologists described the use of middens by Ancestral Puebloan people. Leigh Kuwanawisiwma, director of the Hopi Tribe's Cultural Preservation Office, also testified about ancient burials. He explained Hopi clan and tribal traditions and that Hopis have ten clans with ties and links to Cedar Mesa and Bears Ears.

Kuwanawisiwma testified how petroglyphs "are connected to Hopi because we still use those symbols in our ceremonies and some of our social activities out on Hopi. The burial customs that we currently employ, the traditional burial customs are again manifested in the way those burials

All across Bears Ears and Cedar Mesa dozens of Ancestral Puebloan ruins like this small granary are to be found on cliff ledges. Author photo.

are currently being shown to us from archaeology a thousand years old." He explained the use of middens for burials because they were easier to dig in winter and close to the villages. "We find that the area most popular for the burying of deceased a long time ago was in midden areas," and he concluded, "With our clan connection into this particular region and the beliefs associated with death and dying and certainly the passing on of our ancestral people, the burials that we now encounter are hallowed ground. The ground itself contains the remains of our ancestral people. They were left to rest. So, in many ways we do have the living spiritual connection to these areas."[40]

As the legal issues spiraled up to the Utah Supreme Court, SITLA also filed a civil complaint seeking restitution for the damaged archaeological site. A state law allowed SITLA to seek treble damages. The amount rose to $250,000.[41] The Redds' attorneys appealed three times to dismiss felony charges related to disturbing the Indigenous dead. In many states if physicians are convicted of a felony, they can lose their medical license. In December 1999 the Utah State Supreme Court ruled in favor of the state and remanded the case back for trial including both felony and misdemeanor charges.[42] Earlier in the year the Utah legislature passed HB192 with new language about desecration of a human body adding protection for "any part of a human body in any state of decomposition including ancient human remains."[43] By 2001, for the second time in three years, the Utah Supreme Court ordered the Blanding couple bound over for trial.[44] But there was no trial. There was no conviction on a felony charge. Before the trial could occur, the Redds offered a settlement to SITLA that included $10,000 in restitution.[45] The settlement was accepted, but that was not the culmination of this unfortunate incident. The Utah State Legislature upgraded two laws to eliminate future legal loopholes.

The legislature amended the abuse or desecration of human remains law to explicitly include Native American burials. Legislators also changed the Cultural Sites Protection Act, which is the state's version of the federal ARPA law.[46] Previously, a violation of the law was only a misdemeanor. The new revision criminalized digging antiquities on any state or private land without the express written permission of the landowner. It became a felony charge if damage to the site exceeded $500 or if it was a second offense. The state legislature modified both laws in 2003. A major pothunting raid would occur again in Blanding six years later resulting in vehement complaints, outrage, and stiff resistance to federal enforcement. But federal law enforcement officers, just like deputy sheriffs, the BLM staff, and SITLA attorneys were only doing their job—protecting cultural resources in a state that deeply prizes its history and its heritage. Native peoples took notice. It was time for something else, something more, some level of protection to honor their ancestors and the sacred landscape where they had lived for thousands of years.

In 1996, the same year the Redds illegally dug an Ancestral Puebloan site, Navajos still struggled to vote. "Racial hostility and political polarization [had] become a way of life in San Juan County," wrote Daniel McCool in his expert witness report in a long simmering lawsuit.[47] In that election year, US Attorney General Janet Reno ordered seventeen observers sent to watch San Juan County voting polling places. She explained, "Our democracy rests on the right to vote. The observers will help ensure that every American has a fair opportunity to cast their ballot."[48]

In the 1990s environmental damage to the Bears Ears landscape was finally recognized. The BLM knew it had to make changes to grazing practices, recreational uses, and confront ongoing pothunting and vandalism. After a lawsuit and an administrative judge's decision, the BLM issued a new management plan and retired grazing in the archaeologically sensitive Road, Fish, Owl, Mule, and Arch Canyons. Two new presidential executive orders under President William Clinton required the agency to consider "Native American traditional needs and rights" and "traditional uses such as harvest, grazing, access to areas of religious importance, [and] collection and use of plants and woodland materials."[49]

In a unique acknowledgment of the ancient Native American presence on Comb Ridge and Comb Wash, the BLM offered,

> It will be the Bureau's intent to ensure the strictest compliance with these policies given the national significance of the cultural treasures found in this watershed. Monitoring of cultural properties will continue with the overall aim of determining impacts and subsequent mitigation of these impacts. The Bureau will take any necessary action to protect these resources including but not limited to fencing, recordation, excavation, or additional closures if necessary.[50]

Finally, the Bears Ears landscape was being understood for its cultural significance. Over 400 archaeological sites had been recorded. That was just the beginning. The BLM explained,

> The Comb Wash watershed is a vast outdoor museum of North American archaeology and history. This can be attributed to the area's topographic diversity and long use by humans," wrote the BLM. "The mesas and canyons of the watershed provided a wide variety of environments for people to exploit. . . . Researchers have just begun to examine the vast collection of rock art in the canyons of the watershed. The scientific importance of the cultural resources of the Comb Wash Watershed is unquestioned.[51]

This is why—two decades later—President Obama would declare it part of Bears Ears National Monument. When the BLM reassessed its management plan it noted, "Almost the entire sequence of North American prehistory is represented in the sites recorded in the immediate vicinity of the Comb Wash watershed. The physical remains of all time periods are fragile; the Archaic and Basketmaker remains can be very fragile indeed."[52] If the BLM was recognizing the cultural values of the southern Bears Ears region, in the northern part of Bears Ears the Nature Conservancy bought the historic Dugout Ranch on the threshold of Canyonlands' Needles District, adjacent to Indian Creek, a rock climber's mecca.

Al Scorup had used the red rock canyons for cattle. Now those huge slabs of perpendicular Wingate sandstone beckoned climbers from around the world eager to slip their fingers and toes into ancient stone cracks and spider their way up named and designated routes labeled Supercrack and Battle of the Bulge Buttress. Remote Indian Creek found new friends among environmental groups like the Access Fund and the American Alpine Club. Remoteness no longer mattered. San Juan County, Utah, had been discovered and a tourist economy began to supersede the old style extraction industries of grazing, mining, oil and gas, and a small amount of lumbering. A new environmental question arose: Do climbers do as much environmental damage as cows? "Climber sprawl" is real, as climbers, committed to a free and unfettered lifestyle, pay few fees to camp on public land and believe they have a right to climb without restrictions.

Cattle ranching has damaged soils and watersheds and spread non-native plants including the fire-resistant cheat grass (*Bromis tectorim*), but like cattle, climbers also leave their spoor. Amy Irvine wrote of Indian Creek in the spring and fall,

> Hordes of climbers stand like rush-hour crowds on subway platforms, jostling each other for a burn on some of the world's finest crack climbs. Across the road, toward Beef Basin, new campsites are scattered like buckshot across the desert floor. Late-risers cloister there, plunging French press pots and taping their hands for the day's projects. Beyond them, a labyrinth of trails leads into bushes and telltale piles of used toilet paper.[53]

Climbers began to police themselves. They joined forces with other environmental groups and realized the need for management at Indian Creek. Climbers wanted to preserve their opportunities to climb long, vertical, red rock cracks. Off road vehicle users wanted to drive canyon bottoms adjacent to archaeological sites.

A flash point between BLM land managers and ATV-users became sinuous Arch Canyon in the heart of Cedar Mesa just east of Bears Ears. From the top of Arch, I've hiked into an ancient cave shielded by towering ponderosa pines. Inside in the shaded coolness are ancient petroglyphs, modern graffiti, and a rare black pictograph of a bear, an important symbol for Ute peoples who are the only Native tribe to have an annual spring bear dance. Not far from the cave is a dramatic view of Pueblo III cliff dwellings precariously perched on narrow ledges. With binoculars, hikers can see room after room of ancient masonry walls, collapsed kivas, and stacked stone alignments intended to be barriers to entry to prevent intruders. Some prehistoric building materials remain untouched. It's one of my favorite views in all of Bears Ears.

At the bottom of Arch Canyon where ATVs enter Arch, in addition to several ruins and archaeological sites is a Chacoan-style perfectly fitted stone wall, proof that Chacoan refugees from over one hundred miles to the southeast migrated to the Bears Ears region sometime between AD 1100 and 1200. I've stood there admiring and photographing the Chacoan wall as ATVs rumbled past headed up canyon. Arch Canyon is "a major Ancestral Puebloan site," writes Jedediah Rogers who adds, "Indeed, around every turn is a new and delightful site, some near the base, others situated higher up on the canyon walls."[54] The canyon contains magnificent arches named Cathedral, Angel, and Keystone. Pothunters have done considerable damage and the BLM's management has been inconsistent.

The canyon bottom became a flash point over ATV use and was once a location for a Jeep Jamboree. Unrestricted ATV access resulted in complaints by the Sierra Club and lawsuits by the Southern Utah Wilderness Alliance (SUWA), which for decades had a Red Rock Wilderness plan inching its way through Congress. SUWA filed a 400-page "Petition to Preserve Arch Canyon's Natural and Cultural Heritage." The BLM seesawed between opening and closing the canyon to ATV access and San Juan County Commissioner Lynn Stevens led a motorized jamboree up the canyon disregarding BLM rules.[55] Another San Juan County commissioner, Phil Lyman, would repeat his act of resistance in a much smaller canyon named Recapture. Only this time there would be federal prosecution, a hefty fine, and ten days in jail.

Under President Bill Clinton and his Secretary of the Interior Bruce Babbitt, more national monuments were proclaimed across the Southwest, including Canyons of the Ancients in Colorado, Grand Canyon-Parashant and Vermilion Cliffs in Arizona, and the controversial Grand Staircase-Escalante in Utah. Local and state officials in the Beehive State decried the lack of local involvement and consultation. Democrats vowed to do better. Then another surge in pothunting and an escalating black market for antiquities brought a second federal raid to Blanding. Like the first pothunting bust in 1986, there would be no jail time for those arrested, but unlike the first bust, this sting would result in three suicides.

Spirits of the native dead had been disturbed, their spirit journey interrupted. The Navajo word is "*Chindi*," which speaks of evil spirits that may stay in a place and remain with human bones and burial goods. That's why even though Navajos had come into San Juan County centuries before Mormon settlers, the Ancestral Puebloan ruins across Bears Ears had remained untouched and unvisited. "It's wrong," said Navajo Melinda Cottman. "We were taught not to touch artifacts, not to dig, to leave the dead alone. To do otherwise is to bring sickness and bad luck. To bring the Chindi."[56]

In the predawn hours of June 10, 2009, 150 federal agents swept across the Four Corners region culminating a two-and-a-half-year pothunting sting named "Cerberus Action" after the Greek three-headed dog that guarded the entrance for the dead crossing the river Styx. Agents wearing bulletproof vests and tactical defensive gear arrested twenty-six people, charging them with illegal digging and trafficking of Native American artifacts stolen from public and tribal lands. Seventeen of those arrested, many handcuffed and shackled, which is standard practice, came from Blanding. Those arrested included Harold Lyman, a seventy-eight-year-old member of the Utah Tourism Hall of Fame whose grandfather had founded the town, and David Lacy, the fifty-five-year-old brother of the county sheriff and math teacher at the local high school. Also arrested were sixty-year-old physician Jim Redd, his wife, and his adult daughter. Just as in 1986, twenty-three years earlier, locals deplored the arrests. The day after the raid, Austin Lyman wrote a poem titled "Paradise Has Been Raided Again." The lines start:

> Like Jackals from hell they came,
> With bullet proof vests and guns,
> They came to arrest old men.[57]

Three of Lyman's brothers were arrested in the early morning raid. Over time the facts came out.

The sting operation included Ted Gardiner, a so-called "amateur archaeologist," collector, and dealer who received $224,000 in payment for meeting with pothunters and other collectors. He wore a wire so conversations could be recorded. He took photographs and bought rare antiquities for cash. The FBI provided the dollars and monitored his moves, and Gardiner ingratiated himself with other collectors as he lavishly spent $335,685 purchasing 256 items from the defendants including pottery, jewelry, sandals, a rare buffalo headdress, ceremonial masks, and burial objects.[58] For $11,000 he bought a menstrual loincloth, a turkey feather blanket, a wooden digging stick, and other items from David Lacy. In case files Gardiner is known as "the Source."

The swiftness of the raid opened emotional wounds across Blanding. Sheriff Mike Lacy said, "Blanding will never get over it. And it's not going to stop people collecting."[59] Archaeologist Winston Hurst complained, "They still came in this time and arrested these guys who have no criminal records and have never entertained a violent thought toward another human being. They go in with half a dozen guys, with automatic weapons, flak jackets, and black FBI suits and not only arrest them, but put them in leg chains and handcuffs." Hurst felt, "It's nothing but theater." He added, "I grew up in this town. Collecting artifacts is in the water here. You grow up, you collect artifacts. Hell, when I was a teenage kid, I was digging ruins. I didn't know any better. I didn't know it was illegal until I was in college taking classes in archaeology."[60]

For law enforcement officers, the arrest tactics were justified. US Senators Orrin Hatch and Bob Bennett complained of "heavy-handed" conduct, yet intelligence gathered before the raid indicated that many of the defendants owned guns. Twelve different teams of eight to ten agents transported suspects to Moab to appear before a US magistrate. Standing behind a federal podium, wearing a cowboy hat and bolo tie, on national television, US Interior Secretary Ken Salazar proclaimed, "Let this case serve notice to anyone who is considering breaking these laws and trampling our nation's cultural heritage that the [BLM], the Department of Justice, and the federal government will track you down and bring you to justice."[61]

Brett Tolman, US attorney in Utah, explained, "This case involves significant collections of Indian artifacts taken from public and tribal lands by excavators, sellers and collectors, including priceless artifacts sacred to Native Americans." He defended the use of force and well-armed agents as "standard operating procedures . . . to protect the safety of the agents and any occupants . . . and the need to prevent the destruction or concealment of evidence."[62] From the Redds' home agents took computers and artifacts listed on their search warrant. Half a dozen vehicles were parked in the driveway of the Redd's Pueblo-style residence with its Ponderosa pine ceilings and six fireplaces.

Smithsonian Magazine stated, "The haul from the raid was spectacular. In one suspect's home, a team of 50 agents and archaeologists spent two days cataloging more than 5,000 artifacts, packing them into museum-quality storage boxes and loading those boxes into five U-Haul trucks."[63] A former governor of the New Mexico Pueblo of Tesuque commented, "How would you feel if a Native American dug up your grandmother and took her jewelry and clothes and sold them to the highest bidder?"[64] Winston Hurst and Jim Redd, both Blanding locals, had grown up together, "but their friendship faltered over artifacts. While Redd continued digging and collecting, Hurst became a champion of preservation, passionate about the need to leave pieces of the past in place."[65] Despite agents seizing 40,000 objects that required storage in a 2,300 square foot warehouse, local resistance to the raid continued along with a sense of entitlement to acquire antiquities. "There are artifacts all over this county. There are artifacts in every farmer's field. There are artifacts on every trail," argued County Commissioner Bruce Adams. "If anybody finds half a pot out of the ground, most of them would dig it up and take it home because it's a treasure, and they found it."[66]

On Boy Scout hikes, scouts were encouraged to look for artifacts. They were taught to dig artifacts for an archaeology merit badge. "There's going to be a scar for a long time," lamented retired teacher Lynette Adams. "There are some pretty strong feelings—not about what people are accused of, but how they were arrested. These aren't terrorists. They're not rapists and murderers."[67]

A white bird pendant carved from shell made the difference. Dr. Redd was accused of owning it. BLM archaeologists estimated the artifact's worth at $1,000. Because it came off Navajo Nation lands, "that was enough to charge Redd with theft from a tribe, a felony charge that carries five times as much prison time as theft from an archaeological site."[68] Redd was charged with one felony count of tribal property theft. Felony charges require a stolen item to have a specific dollar amount. Someone had made a mistake, a fatal mistake. Later, the *Los Angeles Times* determined that the value of the white bird pendant was far less—somewhere between $40 and $200.[69]

The night of the raid, Dr. Redd checked on his nursing home patients and gave orders for prescriptions for his other patients. The next day the beloved local physician drove out on his property east of Blanding near his massive Southwest-style house that sits on a hill looking west toward Bears Ears. He parked close to a pond where he had prayed the night before. He connected a garden hose to the exhaust pipe of his silver Jeep and pulled the hose in the window on the driver's side. He died from suicide, from carbon monoxide poisoning.[70] Describing the arrest and the impact of dozens of federal agents, Austin Lyman told National Public Radio, "I blame them for Dr. Redd's death. He wouldn't have done it without the shame and the guilt, and the stuff they put him through there at his house."[71] Another friend of the physician's family explained about Dr. Redd in the *Los Angeles Times*, "You know he was the lifeblood of this community for years, the only doctor we had, gave his life to this community. And the damn feds come and killed him."[72]

Dr. Redd spoke a little Navajo and Ute. He had devoted Native American clients, but "[e]ven Navajo patients who revered Redd spoke sorrowfully over how the chindi had ruined his life," one reporter wrote.[73] In a town of 3,300, over 900 people attended Dr. Redd's funeral, many blaming the federal government for his death. The Blanding mayor denounced the FBI and BLM agents as "storm troopers." In a proud gesture to commemorate their success, the federal task force "minted oversized coins with the words 'Cerberus Action' and an image of the three-headed hellhound."[74]

National coverage of the Blanding raid included Craig Childs writing in the *Los Angeles Times*, "Pulling artifacts from the land without documentation and adding them to private collections is a form of archaeological genocide, erasing the record of a people from a place." He added, "Yet for many in the Four Corners area, it is like collecting seashells. Sunday picnics used to include shovels."[75] For the Archaeological Conservancy Mark Michael wrote, "It was the biggest such raid in the nation's history and long overdue. For too many years federal law enforcement has turned a blind eye to the rape of the nation's cultural heritage, taking action only when a lonely looter was caught in the act."[76] *Smithsonian Magazine* called the raid "the nation's largest investigation of archaeological and cultural artifact thefts." The magazine's lavishly photographed article was titled "An Exclusive Look at the Greatest Haul of Native American Artifacts, Ever."[77]

Operation "Cerberus Action" began to unravel. The well-planned raid had surprised and excluded the local sheriff, police chief, and BLM employees. Defendant Jim Redd was dead before he could go to trial. A week later defendant Steven Shrader from Santa Fe, New Mexico, shot himself twice in the chest. Informant Ted Gardiner killed himself, eliminating the prosecution's star witness and deflating the federal case. Gardiner's carefully gathered evidence lost its value in court because in death he could not be subject to cross examination.[78] Guilt and grief killed Gardiner. He'd had trouble with alcohol and with relationships. He had spiraled downward from being a grocery chain chief executive officer. As the full weight of the investigation and criminal proceedings became apparent, he lamented, "These people thought I was their friend. I'm such a liar. I pretended to be their friend. . . . I caused two deaths. I killed two people."[79] *The Los Angeles Times* reported that when Gardiner shot himself in the head during a standoff with police, he died with a Cerberus Action coin in his pocket.[80]

Many of the stolen items came from the Bears Ears region. Half of the people arrested were in their sixties and seventies. Jeanne Redd received thirty-six months of probation that included no access to public or tribal lands during that time and a $2,000 fine after pleading guilty to seven felony counts of theft and trafficking.[81] She faced a prison term of eighteen to twenty-four months, but to the dismay of prosecutors US District Judge Clark Waddoups bypassed federal sentencing guidelines. He stated in court that Blanding "is a community where this conduct is culturally accepted, if not tolerated. That doesn't justify it, but it helps explain what went on."[82] The judge added, "I know this has been a terrible experience for all of you."[83]

He did not consider Native American perspectives. For many tribal members graverobbing and artifact theft is evil and criminal behavior. The judge did not consider that the first pothunting conviction in San Juan County occurred almost thirty years before. The judge did not consider that a San Juan County man, Earl Shumway, had received the longest prison term ever given under ARPA. The judge did not consider those historical facts. Native peoples did.

"The sentence is disappointing," said Mark Michel of the Archaeological Conservancy. "And I'm afraid it sends a message that this is not serious criminal activity."[84] All the defendants received probation. No one went to jail. "The judges let everyone off the hook," complained Ute tribal member Forrest Cuch, director of the Utah Division of Indian Affairs. "I'm very disappointed. Everyone should have gone to jail and got heavy fines. We have a good-old-boys network in our state."[85]

Did the laws, arrests, and penalties make a difference? Will they do so in the future? "As archaeologists, we've become a little numb to it because we see it everywhere we go," Utah State Archaeologist Kevin Jones commented on looted and pothunted sites. He added that, without federal laws, "we would have nothing left."[86] Former County Commissioner Mark Maryboy, who had campaigned to protect Native ruins in San Juan County, expressed his own sympathy for the death of Dr. Redd. "I'm very sad. Dr. Redd was a good friend of mine," Maryboy commented. "Dr. Redd was one of a kind; he was good to everyone. The federal government has a responsibility to protect antiquities, but they have a responsibility to protect people, too. Anytime somebody loses his or her life like Dr. Redd, it's gone too far."[87] Blanding teacher Ron Atkinson was less sympathetic. Dr. Redd was his physician, but he stated of the doctor, "You had your hand slapped once. You should have learned something."[88]

Jeanne Redd later filed a wrongful death lawsuit against the federal government for her husband's death, but it was dismissed.[89] Her daughter Jerrica received twenty-four months of probation and a $300 fine for digging artifacts on the Navajo Nation.[90] Navajo artist Curtis Yanito, from his Bluff, Utah, gallery, said, "The cliff dwellings are ALL grave sites and everyone knows that." He added, "The dead should be left alone."[91] Pothunters, nicknamed "Moki Poachers," may continue their illicit trade. Some may not get caught, but there are always consequences.

Richard Wetherill, nicknamed "Anasazi" by the Navajo because of his obsession with digging rooms at Chaco Canyon, lies in a single grave below Chaco's cliffs. The Redd family owned a vehicle with the Utah license plate ANASAZI, and now Dr. Redd rests in the Blanding Cemetery. Beliefs in spirits and in *Chindi* coming back to haunt the living may be just that—beliefs and superstitions—but in the cliffs and canyons of Bears Ears, the Native presence is always manifest. It is never far and it never leaves.

Native voices, silent for generations, began to coalesce and to consider new options to protect their sacred Bears Ears landscape. "For Native American groups, the raid was a much-needed crackdown on looting in a unique archaeologically-rich region. Concern about the illegal artifact trade," reported the *Washington Post*, "was instrumental in the Obama administration's decision in December 2016 to designate the area targeted by the operation as the Bears Ears National Monument, named for a pair of buttes that resemble the ears of bears."[92]

Stored in a warehouse near Salt Lake City, the horde of artifacts included one 6,000-year-old item. They sat on shelves, disconnected from the graves and sites where they had been placed. Lost in time, it was unclear what would happen to them.[93] Ripped out of context, they sat safely on padded shelves, but the sites themselves—the caves and alcoves, the kiva floors and specially constructed niches in kiva walls, and the earlier Basketmaker sites—remained vulnerable, a sensitive landscape under siege. The time for waiting had ended. Tribal voices spoke.

Tribes initiated extensive planning and establishment of Utah Diné Bikéyah in 2009, the same year as the Blanding raid. Diné Bikéyah means Navajo native lands and the organization originally began as a Navajo initiative. Part of the reason for starting Utah Diné Bikéyah was that despite decades of state and federal laws, pothunting in San Juan County had never ceased. Native American sites and graves continued to be robbed a century after passage of the Antiquities Act. The federal raid in the Four Corners resulted in the confiscation of 40,000 objects, twenty-six arrests, and three suicides. For Natives, these were all further proof of the need for site protection in Bears Ears. For BLM employees, it was a time of fear. They were told not to be seen alone and to travel only in pairs. In Blanding someone dressed up a dummy in brown BLM clothes, put a noose around its neck, and dragged it behind a vehicle. BLM employees endured personal threats and nighttime trespass at their private residences. Some staff relocated or retired.

Beginning in June 2010, to provide a background for Native land claims, tribes used oral histories and traditional stories to document cultural mapping in San Juan County. Final maps depicted areas important for Native American hunting, fishing, and gathering; showed ceremonial land use; delineated sacred areas; and showed areas important for Native American history and crucial wildlife habitat. After centuries of disagreements and hostility, as well as traditional kinship ties, five tribes came together in an extraordinary coalition for the single purpose of protecting the Bears Ears landscape. The Zuni, Hopi, Navajo, Ute Mountain Ute, and Northern Ute nations agreed to form an unprecedented Inter-Tribal Coalition "to step forward to elevate our voice. We came together for a common cause . . . for tomorrow for our children and our own grandchildren," explained Regina Lopez Whiteskunk, a former Ute Mountain Ute Tribal Council member. The goal was "to leverage the sovereign voice of each other" as "a calling from our ancestors and a need for the future. We were speaking for our people and all people. This was an awakening from tribal peoples and it radiated out. It was about healing—to move past broken promises and broken treaties."[94]

Some local white families felt it was important to keep artifact collections in San Juan County. As proof of ongoing community support for the Edge of the Cedars State Park Museum, a family donated a valuable ceramic collection found on their ranch. I interviewed Richard Perkins from Montezuma Creek, who explained that the Richard and Evelynn Perkins Collection "came from the ranch itself or around the ranch on deeded property." Heir to a pioneering Mormon family, Perkins said, "in early times a lot was found," and some of the eighty pieces "washed out of irrigation ditches."[95] He explained that family members weren't looking for artifacts, but over the years ceramic pieces worked out of the ground. "My favorite one is a figure of a man with a bow and arrow and a long bird," the rancher told me at his home in Blanding. He also admired a rare "flute with a bird on the end, but I never tried to blow a tune."

"The collection is significant to Edge of the Cedars State Park Museum in that it enhances the museum's relatively small collections of late Puebloan pottery," Curator Deborah Westfall explained, "and it contains good examples of ceramics from northwest New Mexico and northeast Arizona." Those items may have been traded into Montezuma Creek during the Pueblo III phase, AD 1150–1300. A few items date to Pueblo IV, AD 1300–1600. "The family carefully collected the pieces from their property over several generations," explained museum director Teri Paul, who added, "This is a wonderful addition to the museum. They recognized the value of the collection to the public and wished to make it available so that it could be enjoyed by everyone."[96] Richard Perkins confirmed his family's intentions. He told me, "I'm getting older and I just decided the museum could have it because they've got better facilities to take care of it. I wanted the collection kept in the county."[97] Indian artifacts were being preserved. Native Americans also wanted preservation of their traditional Bears Ears landscape.

In the same year the Perkins family donated the artifacts, Navajo President Ben Shirley asked Secretary of the Interior Ken Salazar in 2011 to protect Bears Ears as a national monument. Shirley proclaimed it one of the country's "crown jewels." The Navajo Nation Division of Natural Resources began formal land planning for the Bears Ears region. In the next few years planning continued, but as a Utah congressional bill titled the Public Lands Initiative (PLI) sought public input, once again Native participants were not included. Native American tribes asked to be involved. They wanted to help create a national conservation area for Bears Ears, which would have required congressional approval, but the bill for a Utah PLI never emerged from committee.[98]

Resistance of Natives to whites, whites to Natives, and locals to the federal government only intensified. Because an illegal ATV trail had been constructed in Recapture Canyon on BLM lands near Blanding, archaeological sites had been impacted by the trail's construction. With a professional photographer, I walked the canyon, and we documented the damage to ancient cedar trees, a kiva, and other archaeological sites in a place I called "a mini-Mesa Verde."[99] With an intact riparian zone along the creek bottom, a few beaver lodges, and ancient stone granaries lining the canyon, it seemed like an idyllic residence for the Ancestral

Puebloans and a fine place for a day hike. After an extensive investigation, two Blanding men received $35,000 in fines for building the trail that included culverts and a small wooden bridge.

I wrote, "Whatever possessed these men to think it was alright to build seven miles of illegal trail straight down Recapture Wash by cutting 300-year-old juniper trees and damaging Ancestral Puebloan sites? To the shame of other law-abiding Utah citizens, these men broke federal laws, including provisions of the Archaeological Resources Protection and National Historic Preservation acts."[100]

There was no permit and no environmental assessment—just a newly constructed ATV route with a metal stile for access possibly even built in the San Juan County shop. I walked the path again with a former BLM ranger and special agent. We recorded more damage. The Great Old Broads for Wilderness, a national organization headquartered in Durango, Colorado, got involved and protested the route to BLM officials while county commissioners belatedly sought approval for something that had been illegally constructed. BLM closed the canyon, posting signs at each end of the route. Someone threatened the environmental group the Great Old Broads by placing posters on the closure signs with a black-and-white skull and crossbones and the words "Great Old Broads for Wilderness wanted dead or alive in San Juan County, Utah." Though he was notified, the sheriff did little about the threats. Archaeologists assessed the considerable damage to archaeological sites in the canyon at over $100,000.

As Native peoples pursued opportunities to preserve Cedar Mesa and Bears Ears, Blanding residents complained about the closure of Recapture Canyon. San Juan County Commissioner Phil Lyman threatened to ignore the formal closure and lead an ATV ride through the canyon anyway. The state BLM director called Lyman trying to talk him out of it and warning him of criminal and civil penalties. Lyman ignored the advice. In 2014 Lyman led an illegal Recapture ride, which included members of the Nevada-based Bundy family toting guns and vowing to "open" all public lands. This was more attention than what local ATV riders wanted. The outsiders, bearded, in camouflage clothing, with pistols on their hips, and with automatic rifles in scabbards atop ATV handlebars, scared everyone. BLM officers stayed out of the way and recorded the ride, a well-publicized act of resistance. Later, a federal jury convicted Lyman of criminal trespass and conspiracy, both misdemeanors. Lyman received a $96,000 fine and served ten days in jail.[101]

Because the Great Old Broads for Wilderness, a national environmental group, pushed the BLM to investigate locals who had illegally built an ATV trail in Recapture Canyon, this threatening poster appeared in San Juan County. Always ready to defend public lands, the Broads used it as a design on t-shirts to raise more funds. Courtesy Great Old Broads for Wilderness.

Political fissures in the county, as deep as its canyons, continued. The Navajo Nation demanded newly drawn voting districts to accurately reflect modern census data. County commissioners feared they would lose white majority control of the county. They fought back against new voting districts spending over $1.5 million dollars on legal fees. They also fought against further protections of the Bears Ears landscape and asked for help from the state legislature. In March 2015 the Utah State legislature passed HB3931 designating Bears Ears as an "energy zone" and stating that grazing, energy, and mineral development were to be "the highest and best use" of those public lands.[102] Native peoples felt shunned.

In April the BLM issued an environmental assessment for a trekking permit for the Hole-in-the-Rock Foundation.[103] In Bluff, the nonprofit Hole-in-the Rock Foundation had replicated historic cabins around the original Bluff fort and even rebuilt the stone co-op building that had once served both Mormon families and dozens of cowboys, outfitters, and Bears Ears explorers. Having resumed a presence in the small town and after becoming a tourist stop, the Hole-in-the-Rock Foundation now sought BLM permits to stage heritage-style treks of groups from the Church of Jesus Christ of Latter-day Saints.

In the same landscape that the state legislature proclaimed as valuable only as an "energy zone," the Hole-in-the-Rock Foundation sought special recreation permits to walk with handcarts across Cedar Mesa on the Salvation Knoll Route, Long Flat Route, and San Juan Hill Route. These trips were to stimulate interest in local Mormon history and heritage tourism, but handcarts were never used in southeast Utah. The original Hole-in-the-Rock mission arrived from the west by wagons. Serious questions arose about how to handle human waste, what might happen to trekkers in the scorching heat of summer during high use from June 1 to August 31, and the potential influx of noxious weeds.

On Cedar Mesa private and commercial group size is limited to twelve for hiking across BLM lands; yet these handcart groups asked for much larger group sizes of up to 250 people. Because of the sensitive prehistoric and historic sites, consultation over cultural resources had been initiated with the Utah State Historic Preservation Officer and eleven Native American tribes. By July 2015 the Bears Ears Inter-Tribal Coalition had abandoned a legislative solution for Bears Ears and met with federal officials to explore national monument status.

In September the National Congress of American Indians passed a resolution explaining,

> [S]ince time immemorial, the Bears Ears and surrounding land in Southeastern Utah have been a homeland and place of spiritual and cultural significance to tribal people. This living landscape continues to nurture, strengthen, and sustain tribal people, and tribal people remain dependent on these public lands to maintain

our traditional livelihoods and cultural practices, such as hunting, gathering, and ceremonial uses.

The NCAI urged President Obama "to use his powers under the Antiquities Act to declare the Bears Ears National Monument and, by doing so, provide permanent protection for these lands."[104]

In an unprecedented show of support in October 2015, twenty-five tribal governments endorsed Bears Ears as either a national conservation area or a national monument at 1.9 million acres. "We're backed by prayers? We're backed by ceremonies? How could we not do this?" argued Whiteskunk.[105] The Inter-Tribal Coalition submitted a proposal to the White House and explained that Bears Ears "is one large cultural landscape with extraordinary scientific and historical objects that should be managed as one."[106] Former Canyonlands National Park superintendent Walt Dabney wrote in the *Denver Post* about the Inter-Tribal Coalition. He stated,

> We enthusiastically support both the proposal and the designation of Native American tribes as collaborative managers of a national monument where they have been present for time immemorial. The Bears Ears National Monument proposal is unprecedented in its recognition of the importance of tribal involvement. It presents a new model, where tribal representatives and federal land managers will work side by side to manage land for the benefit of all Americans. In pursuing a monument designation of this magnitude and significance, the coalition is aligning itself with the expansive vision of Theodore Roosevelt when he signed the Antiquities Act into law in 1906.[107]

Though the tribes had hoped for a legislative compromise, an executive declaration seemed to be the only solution. *The Salt Lake Tribune* reported on December 31, 2015, "The tribal group is incensed by the Utah delegation's apparent refusal to incorporate a conservation vision for the scenic and sacred landscape . . . blowing one deadline after another." The *Tribune* reported that tribes felt, "Our strenuous efforts to participate in the PLI and related proceedings . . . over the course of the past six years have been stonewalled. We have never been taken seriously. Our five sovereign tribal nations, and our carefully crafted proposal, deserve far more than that."[108] Finally, after more than a century, the Antiquities Act would be invoked to protect prehistoric and historic Native American sites as championed by the first Americans themselves.

As envisioned, this would be the first national monument with Native American co-management. The Bears Ears Inter-Tribal Coalition explains, "The Bears Ears region is not a series of isolated objects, but the object itself, a connected, living landscape, where the place, not a collection of items, must be protected. You cannot reduce the size without harming the whole."[109] The struggle over Bears Ears is a contest over the soul of a landscape. Archaeologists claim that the Bears Ears area, as an ancient homeland for the Basketmaker and Ancestral Puebloan peoples, has cultural resources found nowhere else. Natural resources abound as well as scientific prospects. For Native peoples the goal is to make Bears Ears a living laboratory for the study and understanding of plants, animals, landscape, and traditional ecological knowledge (TEK), which would be unique among all national monuments. Traditional knowledge would guide monument management and land planning.[110]

Paleontologists assert that sites within Bears Ears are crucial to understanding deep time. Fossils found in the Valley of the Gods and at Indian Creek help scientists define how dinosaurs crowded out earlier life forms of crocodile-sized amphibians. "Paleontological resources in the Bears Ears area are among the richest and most significant in the United States," explained scientists.[111] The struggle continued with Native Americans, scientists, and local non-native residents at cross purposes. The year 2016 began with the Monticello BLM field manager issuing a "Finding of No Significant Impact" for the Hole-in-the-Rock Foundation's trekking special recreation permit, though much of Cedar Mesa and Bears Ears remained an area of critical environmental concern (ACEC).[112]

Six months later in July 2016, Secretary of the Interior Sally Jewell traveled to Bluff, Utah, and Bears Ears to listen at a public hearing and to learn about the landscape. She visited the archaeological site named Moon House on Cedar Mesa and she heard eloquent testimony both for and against a national monument. A friend who was there told me, "The crowd was reminded many times to refrain from showing emotion and to let the speakers speak. It seemed that only the Native Americans were being interrupted."[113] Predictions from a century before had come true. "There is no richer locality in this country for the ruins of cliff-dwellings than Butler's Wash, Comb Wash, and the unexplored regions to the south and west," wrote Lewis W. Gunckel in 1892. "A rich reward

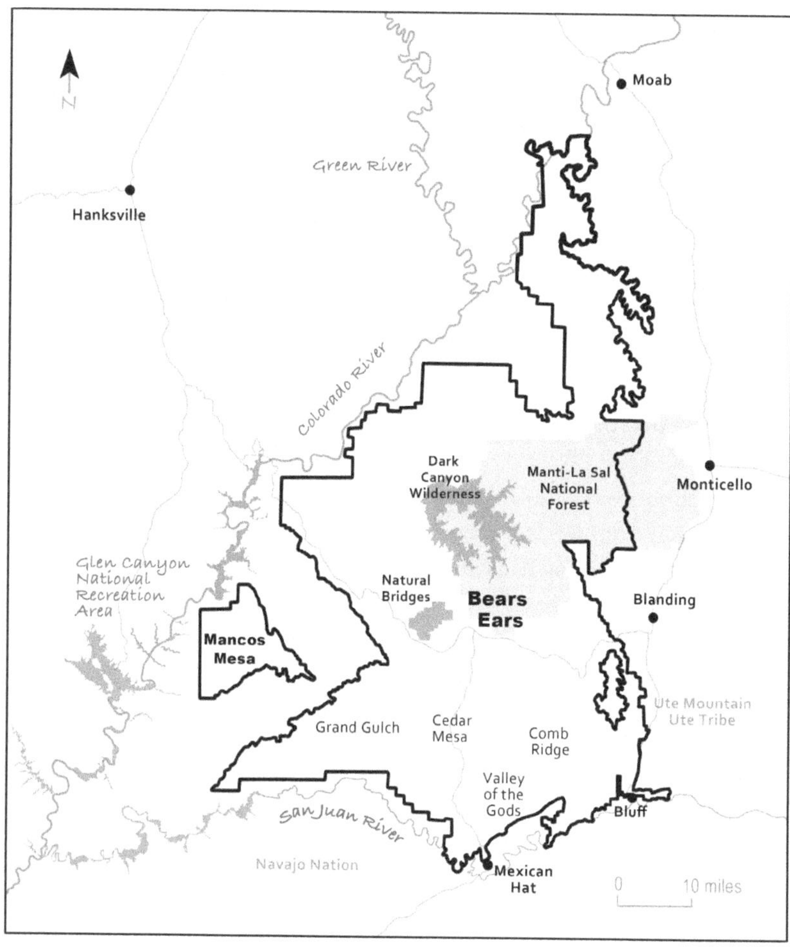

The original 2017 map for Bears Ears National Monument shows the boundaries designated by President Barack Obama in December 2016. Map courtesy of the BLM. Color map revised in black and white by DJ Webb.

awaits the archaeologist who thoroughly explores the more remote canons and gorges in this desolate and unknown region."[114]

Three months after Sally Jewell's visit, the Bears Ears Inter-Tribal Coalition issued another report titled "Protecting the Whole Bears Ears Landscape: A Call to Honor the Full Cultural and Ecological Boundaries."[115] In fall 2016 Scott Groene wrote for SUWA that after years of championing red rock wilderness, "There have been few moments in our 30-year-history where things changed so dramatically, quickly and for the better. The Bears

Ears campaign is not ours; it was created and is driven by the Tribes, but we'll do whatever we can to assist." He added, "The Tribes' proposal would protect the same lands that we've worked to conserve for three decades."[116] Longtime SUWA organizer Terri Martin concurs. She explains,

> The Bears Ears idea and effort was Tribal driven. We were constantly reminded to not get out ahead of the Tribes, and that our job was to support not decide. That was the prevalent practice in the conservation community. It arose out of a respect for sovereignty and also a political pragmatism. The proposal had its best chance if it continued to be seen as what it was—a Tribal initiated and created proposal.[117]

Writing about Bears Ears for the Grand Canyon Trust, Executive Director Bill Hedden noted, "The tribes hope to blend traditional and modern ways of understanding the world in the management of this place where their ancestors lived and where they still go to visit sacred sites and gather medicines and fuel. The idea has electrified public opinion and caught the attention of indigenous peoples around the world."[118]

The National Trust for Historic Preservation put Bears Ears and Ancestral Places of Southeast Utah on their 2016 "11 Most Endangered Places" list. Robert Redford wrote an editorial in *Time Magazine* arguing, "Despite the cultural significance of this area for Native people—and in a sense, because of it—Bears Ears is facing serious threats. Looting, vandalism, and grave robbing continue to this day, with half a dozen cases reported so far in 2016 alone." He added, "As Americans, we would never tolerate desecration of the cemeteries of our pioneers or founding fathers."[119]

Jonathan Thompson, for *High Country News*, covering the Bears Ears issue with all its local conflicts, concluded that landscape preservation would not be the only outcome. National monument notoriety would bring more visitors who would unknowingly damage archaeological sites. Indeed, with all the Bears Ears publicity, in spring 2016 BLM volunteers and rangers at the Kane Gulch Ranger Station on Cedar Mesa had three times the number of visitors in March and April then they'd had in the previous fourteen years. Thompson wrote,

> Maybe this particular monument isn't about preservation so much as it is about justice and freedom, about giving the most deeply rooted Americans some say over the landscapes that shaped them.

> More importantly, it gives them the freedom to tell their own stories of that landscape in their own ways, given just as much weight as conventional science and archaeology.[120]

Most San Juan County Native Americans supported the national monument, but some who were members of the Church of Jesus Christ of Latter-day Saints did not. Opposition and resistance intensified. The town of Monticello, Utah, passed a resolution against a Bears Ears National Monument and claimed "unanimous opposition of city, county, and state officials."[121] The British newspaper *The Guardian* reported forged letters and flyers appearing at gas stations and post offices in southeast Utah claiming that a monument would force four million acres of the Navajo Reservation to "revert" to the federal government. Letters claimed there would be a celebration party for monument status, but that Navajos would not be welcome.[122] Signs appeared at trail heads stating "open season" on Colorado backpackers.[123]

At an outdoor rendezvous in October 2016, members of the Great Old Broads for Wilderness met for a "broadwalk" in the meadow below Bears Ears. They wrote individual letters to President Barack Obama supporting the Inter-Tribal Coalition in their goal to proclaim a Bears Ears National Monument. Author photo.

A group named "Save the Bears Ears" fought monument designation and listed websites and articles published in *The Washington Times, The National Review,* and *Free Range Report.* The organization Stewards of San Juan County was formed. The organization's treasurer Wendy Black wrote letters to the editor to the *San Juan Record* claiming a Bears Ears monument would disregard existing rights. She wrote that, in Garfield County, Utah, because of Grand Staircase Escalante National Monument, the county "has seen increased alcohol and drug use, domestic violence, increased juvenile delinquency, and a 66 percent drop in high school enrollment." She added, "The rangers for the Grand Staircase National Monument have also reported 1,234 square feet of vandalism to the park in the last year, along with rapes, murders, and domestic violence and other violent crimes." Black concluded, "Federal decisions should not degrade, put at risk or have negative consequences on the locals."[124]

Local and state politicians determined to resist the Antiquities Act just as they had done in the 1930s with Escalante National Monument. Despite millions of dollars in revenue from Utah's national parks, Utah politicians took a dim view of federal land ownership and repeatedly sought a legal basis for state ownership of BLM and USFS acreage. The State of Utah even passed a Transfer of Public Lands Act, though it has no jurisdiction over federal lands.[125] San Juan County commissioners, in the poorest county in the state with 57 percent Native residents, spent over $500,000 with the New Orleans law firm the Davillier Group trying to block Bears Ears.[126] The county commissioned a report from the Kansas firm Stillwater Technical Solutions to evaluate the Antiquities Act and goals of the Inter-Tribal Coalition. The report included the premise that a San Juan County Land Use Master Plan would override a national monument designation on public lands.[127]

Commissioner Bruce Adams defended the county's decision to hire the Davillier Law Group to work on fighting Bears Ears. In the *Salt Lake Tribune* Adams stated, "The three county commissioners made a decision to go with the guy with the biggest and best gun. When you find the best, sometimes it's expensive."[128] Yet the *Tribune* could locate no record of a bid process for hiring the attorneys. "Legal battles were initiated and carried out largely behind closed doors," stated the *Salt Lake Tribune,* though "County policy typically requires public notice of any procurement of more than $5,000 and most contracts over $1,000 require competitive bidding." Commissioner Phil Lyman added, "I was very committed to having them [the out-of-state attorneys] do their job and spending whatever it took."[129]

Much of the resistance to a Bears Ears National Monument centered on San Juan County residents who sought to revive a failed uranium industry with known uranium ore deposits in Cottonwood Canyon, in a mineral belt south of Bears Ears, and to the west near Mancos Mesa and Red Canyon. In hopes of appeasing Utah politicians, administrative officials in the Department of Interior excluded those areas in the western region reducing the original tribal proposal of 1.9 million acres to 1.35 million acres. After months of consultation, in the last days of his eight-year presidency, Barack Obama chose to use executive powers first wielded by President Theodore Roosevelt. Obama declared Bears Ears National Monument.

When national news of the proclamation came on the radio, I was in Blanding with a friend, ready to drive south to Bluff. We looked to the west to see the Bears Ears itself, those two distinctive buttes on the horizon beneath a cloudless blue sky. We wondered what would happen to one of the most remote landscapes in the United States, an historical landscape of refuge and resistance. In San Juan County, Utah, many of the descendants of Mormon pioneers felt betrayed. For most descendants of Native American tribes, there was elation and the satisfaction of finally being heard. But a new president had been elected. Both sides braced for a monumental fight.

CHAPTER 13

Resistance and Challenge to Bears Ears and the Antiquities Act

> We're not going anywhere. We're not going to back out. We're not going to hedge. We're not going to roll over. We're going to stick by this, and we'll do what's necessary to make sure it's realized and that we actually do have a place at the table. It's part of our cultural identity. If we don't fight for it, then who will?
>
> —Carleton Bowekaty, Zuni councilman, in *Voices From Bears Ears*

> Bears Ears, as a national monument, is also about respect. The designation is a long-overdue acknowledgment [of] the need for tribal input on policies affecting this land, and of the fact that previous treaties should have ensured the right of indigenous communities to govern and maintain that which is theirs. It is not right to go back on those promises now.
>
> —Angelo Baca, "Bears Ears Is Here to Stay," *New York Times*

For millennia Bears Ears had been on the edge, a distinctive geological outcropping seen for over a hundred miles across the Colorado Plateau, a unique place where the redrock ecosystem of deserts and canyons meet the tall, cool ponderosa pines and profuse grasses of Elk Ridge. Ancient trails had come to Bears Ears from all directions. Basketmakers and Ancestral Puebloans had lived for 3,000 years on both sides of Comb Ridge, across Cedar Mesa, and in the sinuous canyons of Grand Gulch. In the historic period Bears Ears had been a place of refuge and resistance where Navajos and Utes had fled from Spanish, Mexican, and later American military expeditions. The Navajo leader Hoskininni took his small, starving band of followers and a few bedraggled sheep west toward Navajo Mountain but he also knew the Bears Ears country as he fled the blue-coated soldiers of Kit Carson. Navajo warrior Manuelito had been born near the Bears Ears as was Kigalia and others.

Always on the edge, never at the center of either prehistoric or historic Native cultures, Bears Ears became intimately known by numerous tribes. Each Native nation has its own story about how the Bears Ears came to be and named the formation in their own language. Anthropologist Keith Basso explains,

> What do people make of places? The question is as old as people and places themselves, as old as human attachments to portions of the earth. As old, perhaps, as the idea of home, of 'our territory' as opposed to 'their territory,' of entire regions and local landscapes where groups of men and women have invested themselves (their thoughts, their values, their collective sensibilities) and to which they belong.[1]

Bears Ears is a place, a physical landmark on the Colorado Plateau, but it also collects rain, snow, and stories, a place where the past and present are braided together, where trails met and diverged. Bears Ears is a place of "deep maps . . . that register history, and that acknowledge the way memory and landscape layer and interleave."[2] Through timeless ages a foot path went between the Bears Ears becoming a trail, later a route for horses, flocks of sheep, and cattle. The trail became a road, never paved, but always an ancient access between two separate and distinct ecosystems—the pinyon-covered mesa below stretching south to the San Juan River and then to the north into a wide, verdant forest where other trails descended into canyon after canyon, beige and pink sandstone walls arching toward the sky.

At night, the stars swirl above in one of the darkest places in the continental United States. Stories swirl, too, but they are also grounded there, fixed in time and yet flowing between languages and cultures. The power of place cannot be belittled or diminished. It resonates and echoes sometimes with the loud crash of a boulder falling and sometimes with the stark notes of a Canyon Wren singing up the sun and bringing on the dawn. Basso explains the profound linkage between Native Americans and place. He writes, "The people's sense of place, their sense of their tribal past, and their vibrant sense of themselves are inseparably intertwined. Their identity has persisted. Their ancestors saw to this, and in the country of the past, where the ancestors come alive in resonating place-worlds, they do so still today." He concludes, "Their voices are strong and firm."[3]

Stories come from Bears Ears. Stories reach across the hundreds of panels of rock art, petroglyphs, and pictographs etched into numerous canyon walls with the soft songs of girls and women grinding corn, moving forward and back to the rhythm of stone manos rasping across bedrock metates. In Bears Ears long distance runners gathered strength as darkness descended. At Bears Ears past and present fuse together.

Nearby, after decades of quarreling and livestock loss, in 1923 the descendants of Mormon settlers used the escape of two Ute boys fleeing from a trial to start what became known as the Posey War, the last Native American uprising in the United States. Paiute Posey was shot and wounded, one of two Native casualties. He rode deep into the Bears Ears for refuge. According to whites, he died in a cave from a bullet wound; he died from poisoned white flour according to Ute oral histories. Ute friends had secretly brought him food not knowing that it contained strychnine. Respected historian Robert McPherson wrote that the Posey War was not the last Indian uprising. He labeled it "the last white uprising" by the descendants of Mormon settlers angry at Native Americans into whose land they had come.[4] I think the recent Bears Ears fight about landscape preservation is another white uprising. Though Bears Ears is without doubt an ancient Indian landscape, it is now a political landscape. After centuries of being on the edge, with President Obama's declaration of Bears Ears National Monument, the small buttes moved to the center in a fight over the future of federal lands. Two powerful vectors of Bears Ears resistance collided from opposite directions.

Native Americans in San Juan County, Utah, at 57 percent of the county's population, moved to redraw voting districts as part of a federal lawsuit begun in 2012 by the Navajo Nation. White resistance in the county fought redistricting just as white politicians fought the federal government's actions. President Barack Obama, the nation's first Black president, declared 1.35 million acres as Bears Ears National Monument. Local and state officials fought the monument's designation just as Natives fought for the right to elect their own candidates in equalized voting districts. With the November 2016 election of President Donald Trump, environmental groups and tribes feared a challenge to Obama's Bears Ears National Monument. In the first weeks and months of 2017, positions hardened. Utah politicians reached out to the White House. *The Washington Post* reported that Senator Orrin Hatch stated that President Trump was "eager to work with" other Republicans on Bears Ears and that "Secretary of the Interior [Ryan] Zinke will play a key role in this fight, but in the end, changes to a national monument have to come from the president himself," Hatch explained. He added, "That's why I raised it with the president directly. And not only is he willing to listen; he's eager to work with me to address this."[5]

The Southern Utah Wilderness Alliance wrote elatedly that Bears Ear National Monument was "the first truly Native American National Monument in history!" It was "the biggest conservation gain for Utah in 20 years, and a huge victory for Native American tribes."[6] Obama's proclamation stated, "As one of the most intact and least roaded areas in the contiguous United States, Bears Ears has that rare and arresting quality of deafening silence."[7] But by spring 2017 there was no silence about Bears Ears. Instead, the two lone buttes caused a media furor. On January 7, 2017 over 400 people turned out at the Monument Valley Welcome Center. Navajo Nation President Russell Begaye exclaimed, "It's a great day to celebrate. This is what we all did. This is what working together is all about. We are a powerful voice."[8] City councils in Blanding and Monticello spent hours debating how to respond, and in a local protest, residents held signs stating, "Rural Lives Should Matter" and "Trump This Monument."[9] Outdoor retail businesses also responded in a dramatic stand against Utah's divisive public land politics.

Because the Utah state legislature had criticized federal public lands and openly supported shrinking Bears Ears National Monument, a coalition of outdoor recreation businesses, which for years had held its highly lucrative Outdoor Retailer tradeshow in Salt Lake City, threatened to withdraw from the state. The show, which featured new outdoor products such as camping equipment, tents, stoves, clothing, and climbing gear, met twice a year. Now, as Utah politicians threatened federal public lands in Utah, and Bears Ears in particular, the outdoor retailers debated leaving the state. Their highly successful trade show generated $45 million a year in annual spending.

Peter Metcalf of Black Diamond, a company that makes climbing gear, led the charge. Twenty years earlier he had brought the trade show to Salt Lake City. Before that he had relocated his business to Utah. In an opinion essay for the *Salt Lake Tribune,* Metcalf explained that the outdoor industry created 12,000 jobs in the state and annually brought in $12 billion dollars. He argued, "Our trade show, Utah's outdoor recreation industry and the relocating of many high-tech businesses to the state are predicated in great part on the thoughtful public policy that includes unparalleled access to well-protected, stewarded and wild public lands."

He added, "Tragically, Utah's governor, congressional delegation and state Legislature leadership fail to understand this critical relationship between our healthy public lands and the vitality of Utah's growing economy." He claimed that the Utah delegation had enacted "their destructive agenda" and that outdoor retailers "must respond boldly."[10] They did. The trade show left for Denver.

By February 2017 a state law asking President Trump to rescind Bears Ears "flew through the Utah legislature" after a delegation of San Juan County residents made the 600-mile-round trip to Salt Lake City to lobby for it.[11] The Congressional Research Service, however, in a special report titled "Antiquities Act: Scope of Authority for Modification of National Monuments" noted, "No President has ever abolished or revoked a national monument proclamation . . . the Antiquities Act, by its terms, does not authorize the President to repeal proclamations and that the President also lacks implied authority to do so . . . only Congress can undo that protection."[12] A battle of legal experts started a scrum over the Antiquities Act.

While in hearings to be confirmed as Secretary of the Interior, Montana Congressman Ryan Zinke proclaimed, "I am absolutely committed to restoring trust. If confirmed, I have committed to coming to Utah first and talking to the Governor and talking to the people on the ground."[13] The roll call had begun to rescind Bears Ears National Monument.[14] On March 15, 2017 one of Utah Senator Orrin Hatch's aides sent an email to a senior Interior Department staff member to ask about shrinking Bears Ears. He sent a map that would "resolve all known mineral conflicts" and delete oil and gas deposits within the monument's boundaries.[15]

Pacific Legal Foundation authors John Yoo and Todd Gaziano released through the American Enterprise Institute a study that claimed presidents can revoke or reduce national monuments but admitted, "An attorney general opinion in 1938 concluded that the statutory power granted to the president to create national monuments does not include the power to revoke prior designations."[16] An earlier article had asked the rhetorical question, "Why is it that presidential use of the Antiquities Act triggers over and over the same concern about procedural fairness and yet the act has still not been repealed or amended?" James R. Rasband, in his article "The Future of the Antiquities Act," stated that "the act is likely to remain unamended and aggressively employed, and local participation will remain minimal and largely illusory."[17]

Newspaper and magazine coverage of Bears Ears brought southeast Utah into focus for people around the world. In addition to extensive coverage of Bears Ears in the *San Juan Record* and *Salt Lake Tribune*, the *Washington Post*, *Denver Post*, *New York Times*, and diverse magazines covered the topic. Periodicals like *Time Magazine*, *The Economist*, and *The Week* wrote about Utah. Whites in San Juan County, and some tribal members, may have wanted Bears Ears limited or reduced as a national monument, but because of Native American involvement, nationally the concept met with great success.

Preservation published an article titled "Ancient Echoes: A New National Monument Is Designated—And Immediately Threatened."[18] "Thirty sovereign Tribal Nations and the National Congress of American Indians passed resolutions in support of monument protection for Bears Ears," argued *Time Magazine*. "President Trump and Secretary of Interior Ryan Zinke should honor the tribes, respect the unique importance of Bears Ears, and reject short-sighted, politically motivated demands for its reversal."[19] That advice went unheeded. Other journalists compared two San Juan County towns. Tiny Bluff at 260 residents, generally supported the monument. Blanding with 3,300 residents generally did not.[20]

In May 2017 President Donald Trump signed an executive order requiring the Secretary of the Interior to review recent national monuments. Secretary Ryan Zinke claimed that the process "finally gives a voice to local communities and states." During the rushed, four-month review period, of twenty-seven monuments to be considered, Zinke visited eight. Bears Ears was singled out. It was the only monument with a fifteen-day comment period, one-quarter of the sixty-day comment period allowed for the other monuments. On May 25, 2017 the Commission for the Stewardship of Public Lands from the state of Utah sent a lengthy report to Secretary Zinke complaining that President Obama's proclamation was "an illegal use of the Antiquities Act." On page one the first footnote acknowledged that comments were prepared by staff of the Davillier Law Group from Louisiana.[21]

Utah politicians called Obama's national monument designation a "midnight land grab" and complained that there had been no consultation or discussion with state officials. The Utah governor and elected officials protested that the White House had shown "little regard" for state perspectives; yet the *Salt Lake Tribune* reported that based on "thousands of pages of documents" that "the Interior Department had worked and

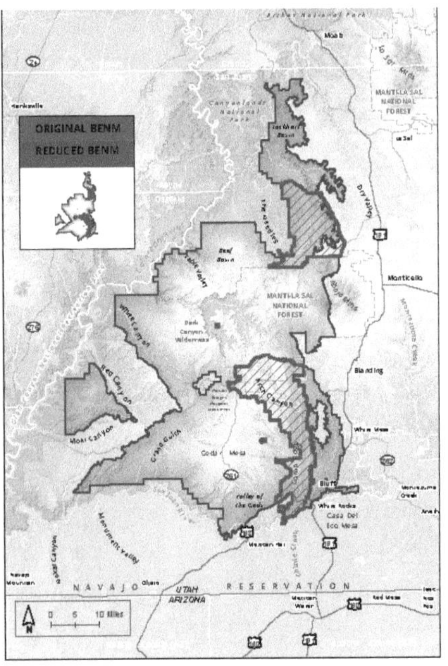

This 2018 map used by the Bears Ears Inter-Tribal Coalition and the Friends of Cedar Mesa clearly shows the impact of President Donald Trump shrinking Bears Ears National Monument by 85%. Courtesy of the Friends of Cedar Mesa.

communicated with Utah elected leaders," including eleven emails sent to the governor's office and congressmen.[22]

"If anyone wants to paint Bears Ears National Monument as a surprise or the product of a rushed or incomplete planning, they'll have to explain hundreds of emails and dozens of pages of shared work product," countered Rep. Raúl Grijalva of Arizona, who sat on the Natural Resources Committee.[23] He added, "These documents are an exemplary record of public servants going above and beyond to find a workable solution to a complicated issue, and they show Democrats and Republicans working together more often than not."[24] Grijalva referred to the failed legislative solution. No Bears Ears National Conservation Area (NCA) made it through Congress, which is why in the last days of his presidency, Obama used his executive authority under the Antiquities Act.

To the delight of many San Juan County residents, Interior Secretary Zinke flew to Utah and held a press conference on May 8 at the Butler Wash Trailhead on Highway 95, Utah's "Trail of the Ancients" and that old, paved nemesis of Edward Abbey. Highway promoter Cal Black would have been proud. Monument supporters greeted Zinke, but monument detractors seemed to have his ear. According to accounts on the ground, including film footage by the University of Utah's television station KUED, Zinke spent "much of his tour with people adamantly against the monument."[25]

On June 9, 2017 the *Virginia Law Review* posted an online essay titled "Presidents Lack the Authority to Abolish or Diminish National Monuments."[26] The public also weighed in. As the monument review continued, 2.8 million Americans responded, but the majority of their opinions were ignored. Over 59,000 comments were specific to Bears Ears and 95 percent opposed making any changes to the new monument. Only one comment was publicized and that comment San Juan County commissioners paid for. "If the [President of the United States] has authority to designate a monument of any size, shape, or area—for any reason—then what is to stop POTUS from withdrawing large swaths, regions, or even entire States under the cover of the Antiquities Act?" Jim Carlson concluded in a cultural resources report written by his Kansas firm.[27]

By September 17, 2017 Zinke summarized his review of designations under the Antiquities Act. The Interior Department released only a two-page summary despite thousands of submitted comments. Bears Ears came up first and Zinke recommended boundary revisions. On the same day, federal lands consultant and attorney Pamela Baldwin released her report titled "Presidential Authority to Modify or Revoke National Monuments," which explained Congress never altered the Antiquities Act. Even after passage in 1976 of the Federal Land Policy Management Act (FLPMA) that reviewed all federal land laws and repealed dozens of others, Congress did not touch the Antiquities Act, which is silent on a president's ability to modify or reverse another president's actions.[28] As one scholar noted, "Under the Act, lame duck presidents have withdrawn and will continue to withdraw public lands at their discretion, remaining completely unaccountable to the public."[29] Trump decided to act. The White House began plans for Air Force One to travel to Utah, one of the first trips out of the Washington, DC, beltway for the new president.

As Trump flew to Salt Lake City, protestors swarmed the state capitol where he would speak and sign his own executive order on Bears Ears. A remote outcropping on the edge of Cedar Mesa had become a national symbol pitting Native American values and landscape preservation against potential economic uses like mining, grazing, and drilling for oil and gas.

On the steps of the Utah State Capitol, Native drummers pounded a large powwow style drum. There was singing, chanting, and shouting. Peaceful protestors waved homemade signs and wore face paint and

Pat Bagley for the *Salt Lake Tribune* drew newspaper editorial cartoons depicting the struggle over Bears Ears. This image shows Secretary of the Interior Ryan Zinke listening to corporate interests and ignoring the public and Native peoples. Courtesy of the *Salt Lake Tribune.*

traditional Native dress. Inside the building folding chairs quickly filled. Invited guests wore suits, ties, dresses, and high heels. Some sported red baseball caps with the slogan MAGA, or "Make America Great Again."

San Juan County Commissioner Bruce Adams wore a white cowboy hat with that slogan. As Adams beamed before the cameras, President Trump autographed Adams' hat. San Juan County Commissioner Rebecca Benally, a Navajo from Aneth, spoke about her opposition to Bears Ears. Indeed, the Aneth Chapter House, a part of local Navajo self-governance, voted against the Bears Ears designation, the only Navajo chapter house to do so. The event ended. Crowds dispersed.[30] Tribes filed federal lawsuits the same day.

Media awareness heightened. The world would come to know this distinctive outcropping on the Colorado Plateau. From the edge to the center of the public land wars, Bears Ears had become a rallying cry in defense of a century-old law, the Antiquities Act, which had enabled presidents to set aside national monuments, many of which evolved into cherished national parks. But in Utah the established white power structure scorned federal land ownership while reveling in the $1 billion tourists brought to the state each year as they visited "The Mighty Five"—Bryce, Canyonlands, Arches, Capitol Reef, and Zion National Parks. Ironically, four of those national parks began as presidentially decreed national monuments. The state spends $12 million a year on tourist promotion and reports "that its investment returns six times that much in income to local businesses."[31]

Bears Ears National Monument, its past and its future, has become one of the most important issues about public lands management in the twenty-first-century American West. San Juan County, Utah, has become a bullseye for conflict among states' rights advocates, environmental groups, and activist Native Americans. Since passage of the Antiquities Act in 1906, this is the first monument supported by five Native American tribes; yet President Donald Trump at the Utah state capitol on December 4, 2017 shrunk the monument by 85 percent.[32] Trump drastically reduced the monument's size because of intense local opposition from non-natives in San Juan County and the Utah political delegation.

The Trump Administration split Bears Ears National Monument into two sections. The southern section is the *Shash Jaa* unit of Butler Wash, Comb Ridge, Comb Wash, Arch Canyon, and Bears Ears at 129,980 acres, explored by the Illustrated American Exploring Expedition in 1892, and lauded by the National Park Service in the mid-1930s for inclusion in the failed Escalante National Monument. The northern unit of Bears Ears is the Indian Creek Unit of 71,896 acres adjacent to Canyonlands National Park and Beef Basin where in 1896 rancher Ed Turner discovered the only hand-colored Ancestral Puebloan blanket ever found. The blanket may have been left in its buried location as a ritual of abandonment when at the end of the thirteenth century Ancestral Puebloan clans began their migrations south toward Acoma, Hopi, Zuni, and the Rio Grande Valley. Turner managed the Dugout Ranch. A subsequent owner, Heidi Redd, pleaded with Zinke to leave the area surrounding Indian Creek within Bears Ears boundaries. He did.

Litigants suing President Trump included the Hopi Tribe, Utah Diné Bikéyah, Natural Resources Defense Council and associated parties.[33] "Trump's actions were an unprecedented setback for the conservation of public lands, and they have unleashed a torrent of litigation. The plaintiffs include five tribes, archaeologists, paleontologists, photographers, climbers, and businesses—and all of them have done their homework," wrote Elizabeth Shogren for *High Country News*. "They have extensive reports documenting the rich cultural, scenic, and recreational resources that Trump has

Resistance to Bears Ears was widespread in the northern half of San Juan County and in parts of the Four Corners. The mining and oil industries got involved. This large eighteen-wheel oil truck displays a "No Monument" logo also seen on vehicles and in store windows. Author photo.

removed from Bears Ears and Grand Staircase [Escalante National Monument], and they are determined to use the courts to restore the original boundaries and uphold the principle that only Congress can eliminate a national monument and the high level of protection it affords."[34]

Legal scholars squabbling over the Antiquities Act and its language to set aside sites in "the smallest area possible" consider Bears Ears a landscape-level monument. "In the case of landscape-level monuments, the proclamations are careful to describe in sweeping terms the 'objects of historic or scientific interest' to be protected," notes James R. Rasband. "The beautifully written Bears Ears National Monument proclamation, for example, refers to the 'land,' the 'landscape,' the 'area's stunning geology,' the 'paleontological resources,' the 'diversity of the soils,' and the wonders of the region from 'earth to sky.'" Rasband argues, "In the case of landscape-level monuments, like Bears Ears . . . the 'object' to be protected includes the very acreage proclaimed as a monument."[35]

Many groups use the area for hiking, camping, and hunting, but not all are conservationists or environmentalists. Cedar Mesa and the Bears Ears area is large enough to accommodate extended Mormon or Church of Jesus Christ of Latter-day Saints families with trailers and all-terrain vehicles (ATVs) camping out for long weekends, as well as backpackers dropping into the Grand Gulch Primitive Area after securing permits at the Kane Gulch Ranger Station. A mixed group of citizens and international travelers uses this plateau landscape for recreation. From the very beginning of white settlement and the establishment of Bluff City as an outpost, San Juan County offered unique opportunities for adventure.

Hikers value the isolation and dark skies. The Obama monument boundaries include seven wilderness study areas, a variety of ecological habitats, and dozens of remote sandstone canyons. Archaeologists claim that the Bears Ears area, as an ancient homeland for the Basketmaker and Ancestral Puebloan peoples, has cultural resources found nowhere else. These include cliff dwellings tucked away on narrow stone ledges with dramatic drops to canyon floors. "An important aspect of cultural preservation, from the Hopi perspective, requires that one be able to journey back to those places and see first-hand how their ancestors lived," explains Hopi archaeologist Lyle Balenquah. "These experiences are afforded us because many of the landscapes of the Bears Ears remain in relatively pristine condition . . . Protection of this landscape allows us to share with the outside world that we are more than historical footnotes, to show that our connections to ancestral lands traverse distance and time."[36]

Connecting to ancestral lands had been a priority for Utah Diné Bikéyah, but making that ancestral connection work required modern political strength. The Navajo Nation sued in federal court over voter discrimination. In 2016 US District Judge Robert Shelby declared San Juan County's voting districts unconstitutional. He appointed an independent special master to redraw them. The judge personally attended meetings in local communities to get public input on the redistricting plan and one of my students attended the meeting in Bluff to help with documents, map displays, and the sound system. That night at the Bluff Community Center someone threw a rock through the windshield of her rental car.[37]

The same month that President Trump shrank Bears Ears, Judge Shelby handed down new boundaries. Native American resistance had paid off. "These boundaries are fair and ensure Navajo votes will matter," said Navajo Nation Attorney General Ethel Branch. "We really look forward to what the elections will bring in terms of truly representative leadership."[38] Previously, District 1 and District 2 held 60 percent non-Native voters with District 3 having 93 percent Native voters. Now under the new map District 1 was 11 percent Native, District 2 was 65 percent Native, and District 3 became 79 percent Native opening the possibility for two Native county commissioners by shifting the balance of power in San Juan County.[39] Democrat Kenneth Maryboy won the primary for the traditional Native American seat in District 3, but a huge fight began over District 1 and whether Democratic candidate Willie Grayeyes legally resided in San Juan County. White resistance to a second Native American county commissioner intensified. Grayeyes submitted documents proving his residency. He also stated, "I was born about one mile southeast of my current residence, on land within San Juan County, Utah, and my umbilical cord is buried near my place of birth." He added, "According to Navajo tradition, which I believe, the area where I was born and where my umbilical cord is buried is my permanent place of residence."[40]

The county clerk disagreed, started an investigation, and disqualified Grayeyes. The *Salt Lake Tribune* decried that it was just "another chapter in the abysmal treatment of Navajos in San Juan County."[41] A judge decided in favor of Grayeyes' Utah residency. After a forty-year fight for reapportionment, the November 2018 election made history as the long simmering lawsuit brought by the Navajo Nation, which had resulted in redistricting, tipped the balance on the county commission. The political power in San Juan County segued to two Navajo Democrats holding county commission seats.[42]

The Bears Ears fight continued like an unexpected wind blasting up a canyon. After Trump's proclamation shrinking the monument, the political landscape in Utah began to seismically shift. Twenty-one mayors and council members from across Utah signed briefs in support of lawsuits filed against the Trump administration.[43] The Rural Utah Project, a partner of the Southern Utah Wilderness Alliance (SUWA), registered more Navajo voters. In remote San Juan County, one of the first agenda items for the two Navajo commissioners was to reverse the county's position on Bears Ears, to drop ongoing litigation to block Bears Ears, and to support the monument not only at 1.35 million acres but at the tribes' original request of 1.9 million acres.[44] Referring to Bears Ears, the Navajo Nation Attorney General stated, "We want to ensure that those lands and the knowledge tied to those lands are preserved and protected."[45]

An article in the *Harvard Environmental Law Review* focused on Bears Ears and President Trump's actions. "No credible claim can be made that the reduction advanced the Antiquities Act's goal of protecting lands and objects that are valuable to culture, history, and science . . . President Trump simply decided that energy development was more important than resource protection," John C. Ruple explained.[46] Indeed, within the original Bears Ears boundaries land that President Trump removed included prior uranium claims and abandoned oil and gas exploration sites. The *Washington Post* reported that lobbyists successfully argued for retaining potential uranium deposits.[47] Yet county residents still suffered from cancers and other illnesses after years of exposure to radioactivity.

As for upset local and state citizens who denounced Obama's proclamation, Ruple offered, "Those seeking redress for perceived injury are not without remedy, but that remedy resides in the halls of Congress, which unquestionably has the power to create, modify, or even revoke national monument designations."[48] For the first time in our nation's history tribes asked that a century-old law be used for co-management of their ancestral lands. Now and in the future, Native Americans may choose to use the Antiquities Act for protection of traditional cultural values and to preserve ancient landscapes. "If history is any guide, it seems likely that twenty or even ten years from now most will look out upon the dramatic western landscapes that have been set aside and be grateful," one scholar muses about the presidential declaration of national monuments. "The dubious means of their designation will be unknown and forgotten to all but a few. . . ."[49]

In San Juan County, the year 2019 started with deep resentment over the two new Navajo county commissioners. Writing for the *Salt Lake*

Tribune, Robert Gehrke began, "Maybe we shouldn't be surprised at what we are witnessing playing out in San Juan County. After all, when the deck has been so heavily stacked in your favor for generations, it would be hard to give that up without a fight."[50] Yet the new Navajo commissioner asked for reconciliation. At the first county commissioners meeting Willie Grayeyes offered, "I'm sure it's a culture shock for most of you that we have two Native Americans sitting on the county seat, but nevertheless, we will do what we can to make better lives for those of you that reside in San Juan County."[51]

Despite a sheriff deputy's investigation, questions continued to be raised about Willie Grayeyes' residency. According to the deputy's deposition, Grayeyes "resides all over the place," but the deputy concluded, "his home is Piute Mesa, Navajo Mountain," a remote part of San Juan County.[52] Former county commissioner Phil Lyman floated the idea of splitting the county in half to create two counties, though that concept had failed twenty years earlier.[53] Other citizens wanted to change local government altogether. After more than a century of having three county commissioners, white residents of Blanding suddenly felt they needed a five-member commission. Phil Lyman's relative Joe B. Lyman circulated a petition to change county government requiring an expensive November 2019 special election—for a single question. His goal was to create a formal study committee to analyze whether "a Five Member County Commission makes sense." His primary reason was that "it provides a greater voice to the people."[54]

Democrats urged voters to vote no and argued, "This ballot question is not really about a change in government, but rather about a change in 'who' is governing. We need unity, not more division—so why not give the Navajo-majority commission a chance to govern?"[55] A rigorous get out the vote campaign ensued among Navajo voters living in far flung parts of the county, and just as before, the county clerk made serious errors which the American Civil Liberties Union (ACLU) identified as irregularities in early voting and possibly electioneering. At poll locations ACLU monitors found a letter from Joe B. Lyman giving reasons to support Proposition 10. Joe Lyman's letter to the editor in the *San Juan Record* "was outlined in highlighter and available next to official election materials provided by the county," Zak Podmore reported.[56]

The ACLU defines electioneering as "a deliberate attempt inside or nearby a polling location to influence voters for a particular candidate or issue," which is a Class A misdemeanor that in Utah carries a $2,500 fine and a year's jail time. The county clerk admitted that he had distributed the letter at six early voting locations adjacent to or on the Navajo Reservation "in an attempt to educate residents."[57] No charges were filed against him. In the end, it didn't matter. By a 52 percent to 48 percent margin the proposition died. The proposition's defeat made regional and national news with a major story in *The Wall Street Journal* quoting the lone Republican county commissioner Bruce Adams who said that judges "packed two districts with a majority of Navajos, and we are seeing the results of that." Joe Lyman added, "A three-member commission is dangerous because it can become a dictatorship." The story ended with Navajo Nation President Jonathan Nez prophesizing, "The Navajo people and non-Native people aren't going anywhere. We have to work together."[58] In the landscape of resistance, working together may require generational change.

The county's general fund reserves plummeted under the former county commissioners. The county spent $1.5 million on lawyers fighting redistricting. Under provisions of the Voting Rights Act, the county also owed the Navajo Nation its legal fees and expenses of $3 million dollars. With the two new Navajo commissioners in place, a final negotiated settlement came to $2.6 million owed to the Navajo Nation by the poorest county in the state with the highest tax rates. Remote San Juan County, Utah, stayed in the headlines with a retrospective Bears Ears story in the *Washington Post* that began, "The stories of these earlier peoples are still here, told by the places and things they left behind. And for a century the region has been at the heart of an unresolved American argument over public lands and what should be done with them." The authors explained,

> Over hundreds of generations the region has seen multiple periods of huge population and rapid depopulation. Today, what's left behind is a dense assemblage of artifacts and dwellings from different eras and groups. A twenty-first century visitor can span thousands of years in a single stride. The concentration of humanity over a few thousand years left behind artifacts that give us insight into the past, including tools, buildings and even food.[59]

Bears Ears, a place of refuge and resistance, had become center stage in a public lands debate. By May 2019 additional arguments flared over who did and who did not get selected for the inaugural Bears Ears National Monument Advisory Committee. Utah Diné Bikéyah complained about the selection process administered by the Utah governor's office and the BLM. Utah Diné Bikéyah argued that not a single person recommended by the tribes was appointed and that the racial composition of the committee "did not reflect the Native American majority in San Juan County."[60]

Legislative battles over the Antiquities Act linger in Congress. Legislation may die in committee or have a longer legislative life. Utah politicians would gut the Antiquities Act; other congressmen and senators seek to strengthen it.[61] Judges have yet to rule on the pending federal lawsuits, but a major victory for plaintiffs was to have their cases heard where they were filed in Washington, DC, rather than in the federal court in Salt Lake City. The Navajo Nation leads the legal charge to restore Bears Ears' boundaries, though if its attorneys seek to use the argument of sacred sites as essential to Native American religious freedom, a previous law, the American Indian Religious Freedom Act (1978) did not fare well with the US Supreme Court.[62]

State, national, and international interest in Bears Ears continues. *The New York Times* ran a headline stating, "Bears Ears and Notre-Dame Named to 2020 World Monuments Watch."[63] Reporter Lauren Messman wrote, "The Notre-Dame de Paris, which suffered a devastating fire earlier this year, and Bears Ears National Monument in Utah, which is the subject of a legal battle with implications for the future of protected public lands across the United States, have been named to the 2020 World Monuments Watch, a biennial list of cultural sites that are in urgent need of conservation."[64] Bears Ears was only one of three places named in the United States. "Inclusion in the Watch helps people know that it's on the level of importance of places like Easter Island, like Notre-Dame de Paris, like the Sacred Valley of the Incas in Peru," stated Josh Ewing of Friends of Cedar Mesa. "That this is not some backwater area in southeastern Utah that nobody has heard about. It's really significant on a global scale."[65]

Public interest in Bears Ears National Monument, both for and against the monument's declaration, remains critical to the future of America's western landscapes. What happens with Bears Ears may define the scope and application of the Antiquities Act in the twenty-first century, just as over a century ago pothunting in the cliffs and canyons of Bears Ears helped justify Congressional passage of the law. But tourists have limited opportunities to find information about Bears Ears. There is no visitor center staffed by a federal agency.[66] Instead, tourism is picking up in southern San Juan County along the San Juan River where it borders the Navajo Reservation. A dozen new tourist cabins have been built in Bluff, Utah,

A rare wattle and daub or jacal structure still survives in the Bears Ears back country after 800 years. Author photo.

along with a fifty-four-unit destination resort complete with conference rooms. The word is out. Tourists are coming to Bears Ears to embrace a new concept—visiting remote sites for archaeological adventure tourism. Unfortunately, so may pothunters, looters, and vandals. Without additional law enforcement rangers, archaeological sites will be picked over, potsherds and arrowheads stolen, and intact 800-year-old ruins damaged.

What are other conflicts with a tourist-based economy? Critics state, "Tourism is another form of exploitation … in which avaricious mainstream society consumes the virtues of distinctive cultures in its midst."[67] Historian Hal Rothman argues, "In areas too weak to replace faltering economic activities, tourism has often come to play an important role in the regional economy … People often find that the changes tourism brings outweigh the material advantages that accrue from its presence." Because in Rothman's words, "Tourism is a devil's bargain, a choice between change and the remaking of sociocultural lines or stasis and … ongoing poverty … In this sense, tourism is a trap, a sink to which places fall, an end-of-the-road option chosen above few others."[68]

Tourism creates complex tensions not easy to resolve. Writer Jim Stiles has argued about "industrial tourism," his friend Ed Abbey's phrase, and demanded that "Utah environmentalists sever their ties to the relentless recreation economy." Stiles continued, "Tourism can be as devastating to natural values as energy development, and both must be scrutinized."[69] The Salt Lake City Chamber of Commerce disagrees. Their publication "Life in Utah: Utah's Premiere Lifestyle and Relocation Guide" featuring "Quality Living the Utah Way—Work, Learn, Live, Play" highlighted a Bears Ears road trip of three days and 320 miles.[70]

In contrast to tourism and an influx of outsiders, some of the descendants of the original Hole-in-the-Rock Mormon settlers support an energy economy. They seem to have forgotten the hundreds of county residents who became sick or died from radiation exposure at the Monticello uranium mill. The Trump administration adjusted boundaries to favor uranium mining. The White Mesa mill, just a few miles from Blanding, is the only uranium mill with an active permit in the United States. The *Washington Post* reported that Energy Fuels Resources, a subsidiary of a Canadian firm, asked to shrink the monument in a May 25, 2017 letter to the Interior Department.[71] Historically, there were small uranium mines up Cottonwood Wash, which left potential hazardous waste in Cottonwood Creek adjacent to Ancestral Puebloan kivas, ruins, and rock art.[72] The *Washington Post* reported that a law firm was paid $30,000 to lobby for the monument's reduction in size to prepare for a new uranium boom linked to the aging 1978 White Mesa mill, with an annual capacity to process eight million pounds of uranium ore.[73] "A toxic history of failed uranium projects litter the Southwest, especially on tribal lands," stated Greg Zimmerman from the Center for Western Priorities. "That President Trump and Secretary Zinke have the audacity to sell out Bears Ears, and its thousands of unique archaeological sites to a uranium extraction company is beyond the pale."[74]

The Obama monument designation stated, "In recognition of the importance of tribal participation to the care and management of the objects identified above, and to ensure that management decisions affecting the monument reflect tribal expertise and traditional and historical knowledge, a Bears Ears Commission is hereby established to provide guidance and recommendations. . . ."[75] Such a commission had never happened before. It did not happen under the Trump Administration. What happened were lawsuits and pending legislation. On the litigation front, the State of Utah, three Utah counties, and the American Farm Bureau joined the Trump Administration to dismiss the pending federal lawsuits.

Meanwhile, the land sits patiently waiting. An unequaled landscape of vivid night skies and sun-soaked canyons awaits the turn of hikers' boots on steep sandstone trails. "Landscape is a work of the mind. Its scenery is built up as much from strata of memory as from layers of rock," notes geographer Simon Schama. Basketmaker images of males and females, anthropomorphs, and bighorn sheep reflect values, beliefs, and dreams from centuries ago. Opportunities exist for self-discovery, quiet campsites, and the thrill of finding ancient cliff dwellings in hidden alcoves. In one place, prehistory, history, Native voices, and future use of the Antiquities Act on public lands may all come together. But defining that future may take judges' rulings and court decisions. More than a century ago President Theodore Roosevelt declared national monuments with ease, but the frontier West has filled up, and in the modern West, even in remote, rural areas, everyone has a stake in public lands.

CHAPTER 14

Tiny Tubers, Dark Skies, and the Future of a Sacred Native Landscape

> It is the belief of indigenous peoples here in the Southwest that the land within the Bears Ears National Monument was made by the Creator and consecrated to spiritual sojourners since the Ancient Ones roamed the area. The land itself should be honored today, just like it was in the beginning of time. The area is considered sacred, like a church sanctuary.
>
> —Jonah Yellowman and Richard Silversmith

> This landscape has been called home by so many Native American cultures over several millennia, so it is the right approach to protect the Bears Ears landscape as a coalition of tribal nations.
>
> —Hopi Vice Chairman Alfred Lomahquahu

Across Bears Ears opportunities for discovery await an open mind. Few places in America possess the Native past with such profound presence—from panel after panel of rock art to habitation sites tucked away on canyon ledges, to tiny corncobs scattered near midden or refuse piles. In a single site may rest half a dozen styles of broken pottery, sherds from centuries past, embedded in soft clay. But in addition to remnants from ancient Indian cultures, there is the evocative Bears Ears landscape itself including Cedar Mesa. David Petersen wrote,

> Cedar Mesa, in southeast Utah, is a uniquely magical place. Elevation varies wildly but averages 6,000 feet. It is sandy mesas and slickrock escarpments. It is deep-blue skies and dark-green mountains far away . . . Here lurks an ethereal *power*, an otherworldly feeling that defies description yet is palpable as you descend into the slickrock canyons and hike the gritty mesas—beneath the vaulting sky, through the profound silence, breathing deep the sweet clean air that grants and unites all life. This is a place frozen

in time; a time frozen in place; a rolling sea of rock-hard waves: desert-hot in summer, cold as snow in winter.[1]

In his book *Cedar Mesa: A Place Where Spirits Dwell*, Petersen eloquently describes the landscape, the awe of hiking Natural Bridges National Monument, and an uncanny encounter with a mountain lion. As Petersen slept naked in his sleeping bag, the lion approached, watched, sniffed, swished its great tail in the sandy soil, and then sauntered off in supreme darkness. Bears Ears is like that. Nature still abides. The presence of the Ancient Ones is palpable.

Once in January with that glorious, slanted, saturated winter light, I climbed Comb Ridge with my trusty canine companion Finn. A Springador, half Labrador and half Springer Spaniel, Finn enjoyed Bears Ears like the perpetual puppy that he was, racing around on slickrock, nose down, tail up, ahead of me on countless trails. That day we had hiked almost to the top of the Comb, and I turned around to catch the last of the afternoon light across Butler Wash. Twilight splashed against Tank Mesa. Scanning slowly with my birder's binoculars, I thought I saw a dark window on a cliff face. That made no sense. Why would a cliff have a shadow from an open window?

I put down the binoculars, scratched my head, raised the lenses up again and realized that what I thought was a window was a door. I had located a stone ruin that perfectly matched the surrounding cliff. It was a eureka moment of discovery and later I spent several months hiking and climbing trying to find on the ground what I had seen across the valley floor. When I found it, I named the site Sunset House because although most Pueblo III ruins face south or east, this one faced due west and would have been unbearably hot after the summer solstice. Though I have hiked to the ledge of Sunset House, I've never climbed in it. It stands on its own pinnacle of rock thirty yards high and a dozen feet from the cliff ledge behind it. A large boulder blocks entrance along a narrow ledge with a defensive wall behind the boulder, a barrier to entry, that could easily have been a sentry's hiding place. This was a refuge site. A place to quickly flee to from the valley floor if invaders arrived. Across the enormity of Bears Ears hundreds of such sites hug sandstone cliffs. I've even found a few with building materials still there and ceiling beams from a thousand years ago, waiting to be set atop stone walls. How do we protect such a place? How do we preserve a sacred Native landscape that clearly knew strife, but also served as a landscape of small farming plots, untrammeled, with only the wind now blowing through dark doorways? Cultural complexities confuse.

"With these holy places in the Bears Ears Monument region, we cannot be fighting over land or we are going to hurt the plants and animals there, thus hurting ourselves and future generations. We might even hurt each other. If we do that, there will be bleeding; there will be a scar there," wrote Jonah Yellowman, spiritual advisor for Utah Diné Bikéyah, and Richard Silversmith with the Christian Indian Center in Denver. They added, "What we are trying to heal now is the wound that is there from past mining activities and ongoing looting. . . . If we lose the songs of our culture and the songs of creation, we will have nothing; we won't have a shield. Our shield is Bears Ears where most of our prayers are sent and issued to protect ourselves and the rest of the world."[2]

Terry Tempest Williams agrees. She wrote an editorial using a Navajo word: "*Nahodishgish*: A place to be left alone." She praised the language in President Obama's Bears Ears National Monument proclamation. Williams supported the tribal perspective that "asked for the protection of their ancestral lands to both honor the graves of the Ancient Ones and ensure the collection of medicinal plants, that they might continue the sacred nature of their ceremonies for future generations. Traditional knowledge in partnership with scientific knowledge inspires us to see the world interconnected and interrelated."[3] The Navajos call Bears Ears *Nahhonidzo* or "the escaping place" where many fled to avoid the troops of Kit Carson and where Navajo clans originated like the *Bi'ahnii* Clan of Manuelito, the *Hashthlishnii* (Mud) Clan, and the Many Hogans Clan or *Hooghan lani*.[4]

But San Juan County is both a Native American landscape and a Mormon landscape. Descendants of the pioneers who entered the county through the Hole-in-the-Rock have a different perspective. They believe not in leaving the landscape alone, but in changing it, improving it, using it as good stewards of a canyon country ordained to them by God and earned by constant trials. "In southeastern Utah, the notion of supreme local control and sovereignty over the land derives from religiously learned and culturally inherited ideas. They do not easily evaporate," offered Jedediah Rogers.[5] He explained, "Any land-use plan must acknowledge—and perhaps reflect—the values and traditions of the residents who make it home."[6]

So, for local members of the Church of Jesus Christ of Latter-day Saints, for an American president to declare a 1.35 million acre national monument made no sense and certainly did nothing for a sagging county tax base. But why sacrifice for short-term fiscal gains a diverse cultural landscape like Bears Ears that even now we do not fully understand? Traditions and tensions continue. Scholars explain that mining is only one percent of Utah's economy. Ranching accounts for less than one percent yet "in some rural communities these traditional extractive activities are essential to their continued viability."[7] Doug Goodman and Daniel McCool write, "In the rural West, the nature of the land determines population patterns, economic activity, and social and recreational activity. Thus, it makes sense that any effort to preserve the land must be tied to an effort to preserve the rural West."[8] Yes, but how to do that? How can remote San Juan County transition from old-style twentieth-century extractive industries into something else? And what if some residents want change and others do not?

Ranchers are a case in point. They are often wedded to the land and in San Juan County that may mean generations of families either using the same public lands for grazing or acquiring other ranchers' permits. The huge Scorup Ranch had to be whittled down. A friend and I went looking for part of the old ranch in the heart of Bears Ears deep in the bottom of Dark Canyon. Scorup's Dugout Ranch at Indian Creek now fosters science and conservation.

It was early morning when we dropped into the Dark Canyon Wilderness looking for Al Scorup's cabin, but we couldn't find the trail. Those little black dots on a USFS map that indicate a trail look simple to find, but when you're descending from ledge to ledge and the old growth ponderosa pines grow higher and thicker, doubts arise. But here's the thing about canyons: They always have a bottom and that's usually where the trail is. We found it and kept walking west as Dark Canyon opened up with side canyons branching off and arroyos in the center cut twenty to thirty feet deep—often a sign of overgrazing. We found arches, lovely sandstone outcroppings, and at least one hidden ruin, Kayenta style from the end of the Ancestral Puebloan period. Five miles in we spied the cabin complete with vintage Majestic cookstove, washtubs on an outside wall, mounted deer antlers, empty bed springs, and plenty of mouse and packrat droppings scattered around the two rooms.

Al brought his brother John to work with him. The siblings found country wild and remote. They saw two buttes shaped like one of their grandmother's wooden shoes so they named the outcropping the Wooden Shoe. There's a separate Wooden Shoe Trail into Dark Canyon and I've hiked that too. Old-time cowboy camps can still be found in the Bears Ears at Collins Canyon in Grand Gulch and in the Needles District of Canyonlands. These camps include wooden shelving, wire for hanging pots, and an assortment of cans scattered under a canyon overhang, just deep enough to get out of the rain and wind, a place to put your saddle and to leave grub, bacon, beans, and biscuit fixings, a cast iron frying pan and a Dutch oven.

Scorup's wife died during the Spanish Flu. The Scorup-Sommerville Ranch grew larger with summer range in the Abajo or Blue Mountains and winter range at the Dugout Ranch. When Al remarried, he scandalized the country by wedding his ranch cook. When he passed on, his five combined ranches came up for sale. Charlie Redd bought them to purchase a coveted 15,000 acres of private ground in the La Sals. Heidi and Robert Redd bought the home place of the Scorup empire, the Dugout Ranch, and when it came time to sell, she sought a conservation buyer. She found one in the Nature Conservancy, which purchased the historic 5,200 acre ranch along Indian Creek.

Where Herefords once grazed, the Conservancy, with Heidi's son as ranch manager, now runs smaller, nimble Raramuri Criollo cattle out of Mexico, compact cousins of original longhorns. They are tough little hombres that move "like a deer without antlers" and can travel further from water and survive on less forage. The unique Raramuri Criollo is one of thirty-three heritage biotypes of cattle from the Native Tarahumara communities of Copper Canyon in Chihuahua, Mexico. Bred for endurance and canyon country adaptability in a canyon system longer and deeper than the Grand Canyon, Criollo cattle have high fertility, longevity, and a mild temperament. "They are lighter on the land," says Heidi who reminisces that splitting up with her husband helped to save the ranch. "If Robert hadn't wanted his money out and if I hadn't wanted to stay, there would not have been the Nature Conservancy purchase which has been the best thing for the Dugout Ranch."[9] Conservancy-sponsored scientific projects now study how to live and ranch in a changing, drying climate and what can be done to preserve fragile biocrusts on delicate sandy soil. The US Department of Agriculture claims the Raramuri Criollo represents old genetics for new landscapes.[10]

I've been to the Dugout and talked to Heidi. I drove in marveling at the brilliant red rocks, blue sky, and well-watered fields. At Scorup's cabin a friend and I came in on foot. It's federal wilderness after all, deep in the heart of Bears Ears, and after lunch it was time to leave and head up

Rancher Heidi Redd, who sold the Dugout Ranch to the Nature Conservancy, has long advocated for wilderness. She helped convince Secretary of the Interior Ryan Zinke to leave untouched the Indian Creek District of Bears Ears National Monument. Author photo.

canyon. The cabin isn't logs. It's board and batten in an L-shape, hauled in from a mining site in Rig Canyon, but it's historic nonetheless. Hiking sticks in hand, I led off, striking the wrong trail and having to backtrack. As we left, I thought about history's cycles and a different kind of backtracking. I pondered how public land in canyon country had become a private cattle empire and then reverted to less-grazed public land. After a century, a classic western ranch had evolved into a conservation-minded, future-focused agricultural enterprise. Heidi Redd believes in wilderness. She says, "We need more wilderness designations." As my friend and I hiked out of Dark Canyon, I thought of Al, but also in my mind I thanked Heidi for her wilderness dedication. Sandstone cliffs receded in every direction. We saw no one.

"It is a diverse, iconic, some say spiritual landscape," explained Matt Redd, Heidi's son, about Indian Creek, his photograph on the cover of *National Geographic* for an article titled "Battle for the American West." Author Hannah Nordhaus encapsulated the Bears Ears controversy. "For years native leaders negotiated with local, state, and federal officials, seeking a legislative compromise on how the land should be managed," she wrote. "As the effort floundered in Congress, tribal and conservation groups pushed Obama to designate a monument before he left office."[11] He did, to the delight of many and the scorn of others.

Visitors are awed and attracted by the Bears Ears landscape, but local families need to survive economically. A love of the land connects and binds folks who live in southeast Utah, and the redrock inspires an increasing number of tourists, but how to live and work in that sparse sandstone ecosystem remains as complicated as threading a pathway through the canyons themselves. Perhaps potatoes can help. Science has always been essential to creating national monuments, and scientific research connected to Bears Ears is only just beginning.

For years, we've learned that Ancestral Puebloans depended on corn, beans, and squash, nicknamed the Three Sisters, for sustenance. Well, move over sisters. Little brother spud is about to take the stage. With a $225,000 National Science Foundation grant, researchers at the University of Utah hope to prove that a tiny tuber, *Solanum jamesii*, was an important part of ancient Native diets. This potato fits in a soup spoon. It balances on a fork. Not a big, heavy Idaho Russet baking potato, *Solanum tubersuom*, but a unique Four Corners potato. Starch granules from *Solanum jamesii* have been found preserved on a 10,900-year-old stone metate at Escalante, Utah, making it the earliest known evidence of wild potato use in North America. Ancient peoples transported, grew, and possibly domesticated this tiny tuber.

I've been on the trail of this potato that may have disease-resistant and drought-resistant genes. I am fascinated by its history, use, and future. Lisbeth Louderback, assistant professor of anthropology and curator of archaeology at the Natural History Museum of Utah, explains, "This potato could be just as important as those we eat today not only in terms of a food plant from the past, but as a potential food source for the future."[12] With an earthy, nutty taste and a skin that gets crinkly, the potato's insides remain fluffy. The size of a penny, these potatoes "fit nicely on your spoon," explains Louderback with a smile. In a refrigerator, the tubers keep for a year. Because the tubers occasionally taste bitter, Navajos and Hopis boiled the potatoes with white clay to reduce the toxic glycoalkaloids. Tribal knowledge of this food includes Apache, Hopi, Navajo, Pueblo, Southern Paiute, Zuni, and Zia elders.

Found in the Four Corners region and along the Mogollon Rim in northern Arizona and in the highlands of New Mexico, Native Americans possibly brought the potato north into central Utah. Mormon pioneers found it in abundance. During the Great Depression, remote rural families ate the potato. "It comes up in response to monsoons," notes Bruce Pavlik, director of conservation at Red Butte Gardens on the University of Utah campus. When I visited him in his office, he explained that the potato has the perfect "strategy of a wild plant, it disperses buds ('eyes') up to a meter away."

"I've worked a lot on conservation of landscapes and this potato captures public interest like no other project," he says with a grin, which is why Pavlik has a US Department of Agriculture (USDA) grant. "We are interested in more Native American farmers who want to grow this commercially."[13] At Red Butte Gardens I visited the potato experiment station with *Solanum jamesii* successfully growing in galvanized metal horse troughs whose interiors were covered with burlap out of Native respect for the plant not to touch metal. The two-foot-deep horse troughs made perfect test plots and could easily be watered with a drip system. There may be five useful genotypes of this small spud; scientists are not sure, but Pavlik explains, "how lush the potatoes get if you give them water." By the end of August and the cessation of summer monsoons, in a natural setting the plant puts its energy underground.

There's even a publication *The Four Corners Potato Gazette* "updating our partners on recent advances" including information on the archaeology, culture, and biology of this unique spud. According to the *Gazette*, at a workshop, Native farmers "enthusiastically spoke of returning this potato to the people of the region, with cultural, spiritual, health, and economic benefits." Hold the butter, sour cream, and chives for this protein powerhouse. Nutritional data on this tiny tuber indicates it has "three times the protein, twice the vitamin B1, calcium, phosphorus, magnesium, [and] manganese" of the standard grocery store potato. Bigger is not necessarily better, which is why locavores will love this spud that has already been served in Utah at the Hells Backbone Grill in Boulder, the Twin Rocks Café in Bluff, and soon North Creek Grill and Fourth West Pub in Escalante will be serving it.

"The plants themselves stay low to the ground. They are dark brown in color with grayish blue leaves. We don't plant them. They come out of the ground and we collect them," explained former Zia Pueblo Governor and elder Peter Pino. "We eat them raw. Some tribal members wash and cook them. We used the potato when food was scarce and in a springtime ceremony related to cleaning our irrigation ditches."[14] At a social dance, "one of the staples they took for the dance into the kivas was this potato.

My mother used them in the 1920s and 1930s," says Pino, who adds, "It was the best snack for social dances in the kiva for ceremonies between ditch cleaning and before planting. We still eat them." The thumbnail tubers, well-balanced in carbohydrates and proteins, may have been stashed along travel routes by Hopis because the potato represents "perfect fuel for runners," notes Pino who says, "And it was a food source we did not tell the Spanish about."

Vital research on *Solanum jamesii* continues. Both the Grand Staircase-Escalante and Bears Ears National Monuments may hold the key to understanding how this potato was dispersed. The latest research technique is for archaeobotanists and Native plant specialists to visit archaeological habitation sites to look for the plant. One plant was found in Bears Ears at a two-story cliff dwelling "where a slickrock waterfall came down into a bowl of sand" that provided habitat. This potato is "disease-resistant, which is why the USDA is so interested, and frost tolerant unlike other potatoes," Pavlik tells me in the University of Utah's greenhouse, where we observe the plants thriving. He states with satisfaction, "Archaeology, plant ecology, landscape conservation. I feel my whole career has been working up to this."[15]

Yes, there's a lot of spud success to share. "I really feel that traditional knowledge is as important as Western knowledge. And then there's the value of bringing back this agricultural heritage," Louderback tells me. "It's a plant species, an ancient food source that is part of the livelihood for native tribes. The Bureau of Land Management (BLM) protects archaeological sites, but what about the plants that are just as sacred to the Indigenous groups as the sacred sites? I do not want to speak for the tribes, but this is important to them, because the potato is of conservation concern in southeast Utah." Louderback explains, "There are populations [of the potato] within President Obama's Bears Ears boundaries, but when Trump shrunk it those populations are no longer protected." Because the original 1906 Antiquities Act had science at the heart of presidential land withdrawals for national monuments, the presence of this tiny tuber may be useful in the four federal lawsuits going forward to reverse the Bears Ears' reduction.

Questions remain as to which spud populations have higher or lower nutritional value and which of these potatoes may have a low glycemic index to aid modern Native peoples battling diabetes. For Utah Diné Bikéyah, Cynthia Wilson directs the Traditional Foods Program, which focuses on holistic health and reclaiming ancestral knowledge of Native foods. These special potatoes play a part in that social movement. From a snack in ancient kivas to cutting edge science defending a national monument's size, the importance of *Solanum jamesii,* is only now being understood. These are not just small potatoes. They are an ancient agricultural legacy, an Indigenous farming heritage, and new research shows that the tiny tubers are only one example of ethnographically significant plant species.

Matching Bears Ears archaeological sites with important Native plant species like the Four Corners potato (*Solanum jamesii*), sumac (*Rhus trilobata*), wolfberry (*Lycium pallidum*), and goosefoot (*Chenopodium*) Native American plant specialists and archaeoethnobotanists have found a direct connection, centuries old. Ancient peoples transported and cultivated certain plants, whether intentionally or not, to create archaeo-ecosystems with "high-priority" plant species. In a major new study, researchers used paired archaeological and ecological survey data for 265 sites spread across a million acres within Bears Ears National Monument to confirm ethnographic species richness (ESR) that matches TEK. They confirmed thirty-one plant species important to Navajo, Apache, Hopi, Zuni, and Ute Mountain Ute tribes. Some of these plants are "held sacred as lifeway medicines" and are found on Cedar Mesa and Mancos Mesa in the heart of Bears Ears.[16]

The research may have major implications for managing Bears Ears both for existing grazing allotments and for tourist visitation. The authors state, "These plant populations should be documented in detail, monitored and targeted for special actions (e.g., visitation restrictions, improved footpaths, limited grazing, interpretive signage, and designated tour guides)." Science has long been a goal of national monument designations, and the authors conclude, "Formally embedding traditional ecological knowledge into land management decisions would improve federal stewardship and promote the longstanding linkages between Indigenous people and their ancestral lands."[17]

Cynthia Wilson explains, "The medicines on the landscape all have a story. In terms of management, traditional ecological knowledge is crucial to protect the entire ecosystem as a cultural living landscape. Our ancestors tended to these ancient gardens." The plants are still there centuries or millennia later. "People brought propagules [seeds or buds] of the species in with them," offers lead author Bruce Pavlik. He states, "This is one of the rare times in the archaeological literature where people invested in native species and brought them to their habitations. It indicates this higher level of landscape manipulation, what we call an 'ecological legacy' of past human occupation."[18]

Another Bears Ears legacy dates back to the first caves explored and looted in Grand Gulch, Allen Canyon, and in canyons stretching to the Colorado River. Grand Gulch is a world unto itself. I've just embraced the edges with a winter hike to Perfect Kiva and a spring trek down Collins Canyon passing an old cowboy camp, walking toward a solid wall of painted handprints. I've paddled through the lower San Juan River canyons, but I want to immerse myself in Grand Gulch, though finding water can be tricky, and it's no place for a solo jaunt. Seasoned journalist Rob Schultheis wrote, "This is the wildest part of the San Juan River system, and one of the wildest places in the world. There are canyons down there that are like passages of time. . . . Hiking down an arroyo, following it down as it becomes a chasm, one recapitulates the whole of America's past." He added, "You break through the Iron Age, thin and brilliant as an oil slick, descend down through the Navajo, the Piute, the Anasazi and the Basketmaker down into, finally, the prehuman bedrock of the continent."[19]

Schultheis and a girlfriend found Native American ruins everywhere, drank water that tasted like stone, laughed, cried, fought, and kept hiking knowing that there may not have been another person around for miles. "It was a precious feeling to be so alone," he reminisced and explained, "If there were any saints, any shamans or medicine men left, that was their kind of territory."[20] After descending deeper and deeper the couple finally climbed out, the girlfriend cursing him, no food or water left, a long flat slog back to the truck, but with a revelation that "[e]verything seems lost in the desert. There always seems to be another twist in the canyon wall, another crook in the cliff. Gods sing to you and then drop down a trap door into the past."[21] Schultheis and his companion were hikers lost in a maze of canyons. But what about the first white explorers into Grand Gulch? What were they looking for?

In the 1890s cowboy archaeologists dug caves in remote sections of Utah's Bears Ears National Monument.[22] They created Basketmaker and Ancestral Puebloan artifact collections that have been hidden away for over a century in prestigious museums. Now a group of scholars and researchers is focusing on those thousand-year-old perishable artifacts to see what might be learned about not only the past, but also cultural continuity and revitalization. In the 1990s team members on the Grand Gulch-Wetherill Project determined which sites had been excavated on public lands in Utah and where the collections resided.[23] In a careful and systematic process of reverse archaeology, scholars like Fred Blackburn, Ann Phillips, and Winston Hurst located where those collections had gone. They matched the artifacts to their original sites despite years of catalog confusion and curatorial indifference. Now Laurie Webster and her team, including Native American scholars, are visiting those collections and learning even more.

Since 2011 the Cedar Mesa Perishables Project (CMPP) has brought scholars to study these artifact collections rarely seen by the public. Most importantly, this latest project involves Native American scholars who are viewing for the first-time artifacts their ancestors crafted and used. These scholars are bringing valuable insights and understandings into temperature and humidity-controlled museum storage areas.

"Of the roughly 5,000 artifacts taken out of alcoves in southeast Utah, 4,000 are perishable items of wood, hides, feathers, and textiles including sandals, baskets, and blankets," explains project director Laurie Webster. "We have used the original collectors' catalogs and notes to try and understand where they worked and what was excavated. We're working with five different historic collectors and each had a different collection strategy."[24] Team members include Webster, a textile expert who has studied ethnographic and prehistoric artifacts, archaeologist Erin Gearty who works for the National Park Service, and biologist Chuck LaRue who identifies feathers and species of wood the Ancients used and who replicates prehistoric wooden tools. Louie Garcia is a Tiwa/Piro fiber artist and teacher also on the team. Chris Lewis from Zuni is a fiber artist and basket weaver, and Mary Weahkee, Santa Clara and Comanche, creates modern turkey feather blankets and has revitalized other ancient crafts.

"It's been wonderful. We work as a team. We share information," states Webster who says, "We look at the same objects but in different ways. Everyone is interested in the same thing—cultural preservation and revitalization." The CMPP has received diverse funding and it is a sponsored project of the nonprofit Friends of Cedar Mesa. Just as the public has rarely seen these perishable items, neither have the descendants of Ancestral Puebloans who made them. The project brings Native researchers and scholars into collection rooms where their ancestors' everyday objects can be seen, admired, and studied. "These items are still living, breathing, feeling, even if they were made 1,000 years ago," explains Louie Garcia. He comments, "The textiles are the way they are for a reason and we shouldn't change that. I've tried to revive what was woven a thousand years ago." Garcia tells me, "This research has informed my work as a

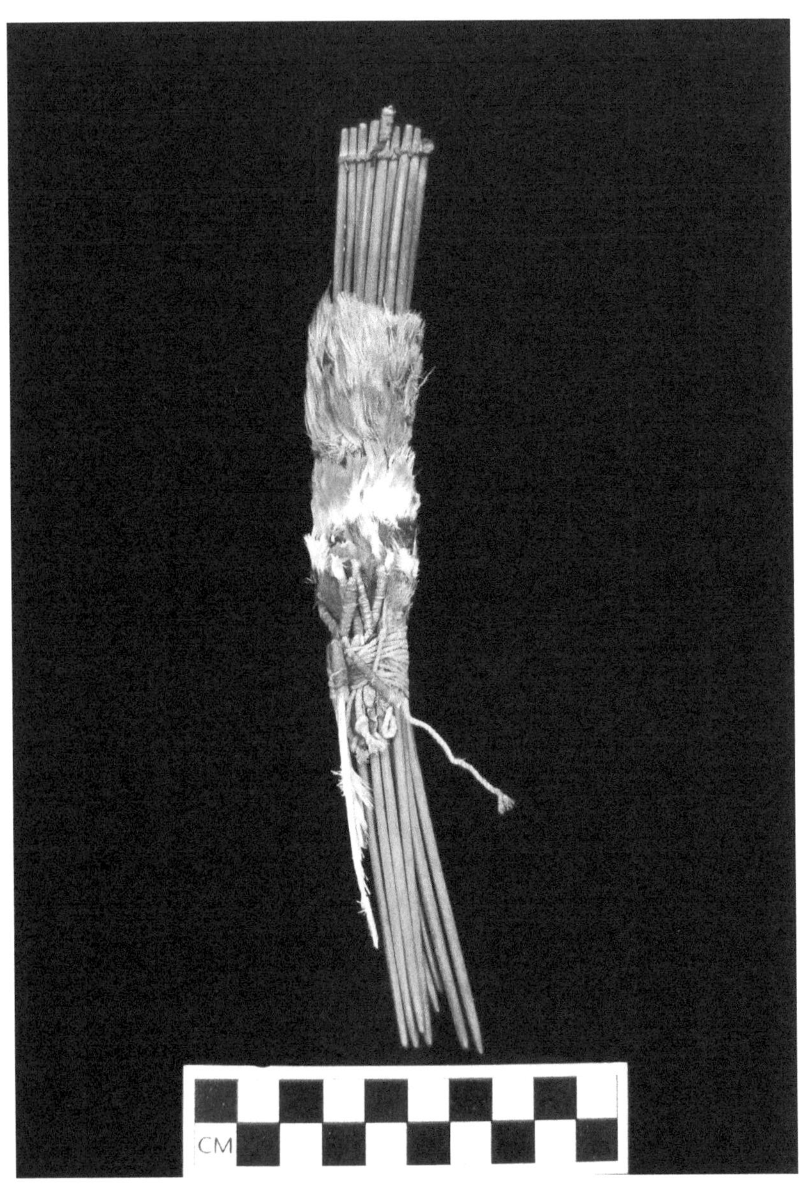

Basketmaker men from 1,200 years ago wore hair ornaments adorned with a variety of bird feathers. This is a rare intact adornment with bluebird, sapsucker and junco feathers analyzed by scholars with the Cedar Mesa Perishables Project. MPC 1995.2.378.1. Photo courtesy Brigham Young University's Museum of Peoples and Cultures.

Pueblo fiber artist as well as gaining a better understanding and appreciation of my Pueblo heritage."[25]

What is significant about the CMPP is relocating collections from those early sites and putting that knowledge, especially about the Basketmakers, to use. Approximately 40 percent of the collections may date to the Basketmaker II phase or the years AD 1–200. Webster helps us see that carved petroglyphs and pictographs often represent cultural items. One panel in the Comb Ridge or *Shash Jaa* unit of Bears Ears National Monument has etched on rock both a large coiled basket and a segmented twined bag. Many of the Basketmaker II human figures have headdresses. Webster relays that those male headdresses in Basketmaker rock art represent hair ornaments of parallel sticks decorated with feathers from turkeys, bluebirds, sapsuckers, juncos, or other birds. A topknot on the hair ornament featured a special dangling feather often facing right. A few of these stick bundles still have their original feathers.

The CMPP team has studied wooden implements, woven baskets, bags, and cotton blanket fragments, pairs of crutches, bundles of prepared yucca fiber, and crookneck staffs made from Gambel oak. Across Cedar Mesa are etched dozens of petroglyphs with crookneck staffs. The team has documented many original examples. Chuck LaRue uses his replica staffs to knock down pinyon nuts and as lightweight hiking poles. He claims that in the ancient Pueblo world crookneck staffs were "as handy as a pocket on a shirt." I agree, and like La Rue and other scholars, I think the staffs also had ceremonial uses as a symbol of authority or social standing. At one rock art site high on Comb Ridge dozens of etched figures are being led to a social event. For each group of villagers there's one individual brandishing a crookneck staff.

To open these long-closed cabinet drawers, Dr. Webster and her team have traveled to the American Museum of Natural History in New York City, the Field Museum of Natural History in Chicago, the Museum of Peoples and Cultures at Brigham Young University, the National Museum of the American Indian of the Smithsonian Institution in Washington, DC, the Phoebe Hearst Museum at the University of California—Berkeley, and the University of Pennsylvania Museum in Philadelphia. Wearing white cotton gloves, deep in museum storage, Zuni scholar and weaver Chris Lewis makes a profound connection with prehistoric tools created from living plants. "Inanimate objects still have a life, still have a soul. When I go through the collections I talk to them. I say I'm sorry you have to be locked in the dark, but we can come and visit you," he explains.[26]

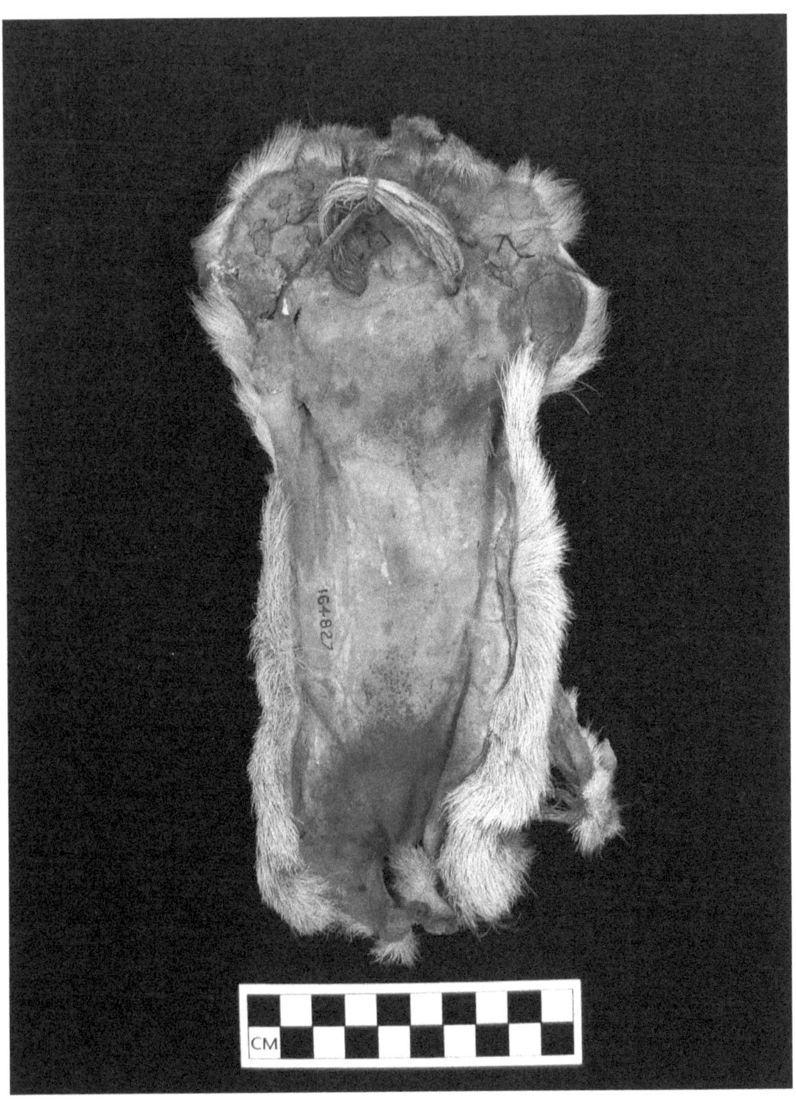

As part of the Cedar Mesa Perishables Project scholars are studying a variety of Native American artifacts from Bears Ears including this hide sandal made from a mountain lion paw. This is the upper face. FMNH 164827. Photo courtesy Field Museum of Natural History.

To understand this remarkable project, Durango filmmaker Larry Ruiz has produced a documentary film, the third in his series titled "The Languages of the Landscape." He says of Laurie Webster, "The results of her research will be known and used for years to come. People, including the Native community, have already gained valuable knowledge from the Project's investigations." I think of Ancestral Puebloan rock art spirals and cycles of nature and human nature. What was taken has now been found. The Ancients and their artifacts have more stories to tell. But as always, there's the question of how much visitation these fragile sites can endure. What are the downsides to increased visitation in Bears Ears National Monument? What are the impacts of archaeological adventure tourism?

Writing in *National Geographic*, Hannah Nordhaus explained, "The area's arid climate and profound isolation had long helped protect its archaeological treasures—the rock art, potsherds, and tools, the human remains, the thumb-sized corncobs. But our era of geotagged photos has made it easy to locate obscure sites. In the decade before the monument was created, visits to the area surged."[27] Part of that surge came from enthusiasm for David Roberts' book *In Search of the Old Ones*. Roberts chronicled hiking and backpacking with friends into remote ruins in the Bears Ears region. He wrote, "There before me ... sat an intact Anasazi pot. Slowly I approached. A branch of dead juniper had fallen to the ledge, close to the pot; now it guarded it like a fence. I got on my knees to peer close."[28] He deduced that the pot was too big to carry away centuries ago, so it had been purposely hidden. "For at least seven hundred years the pot had rested in its niche, saved from the weather by the overhang alone, preserved by the dry desert air. During those centuries of gnawing time, how many human eyes had gazed on the pot between the last Anasazi's and mine?" Roberts asked.[29]

I know the feeling having helped to recover the largest prehistoric olla or storage jar ever found in New Mexico. The archaeologist in charge of that section of the Gila National Forest, close to Gila National Monument, thought we should remove the olla. I disagreed. I thought we should leave it in place, which was also David Roberts' decision about the pot he found. He prized not just the artifact, but also its location. "You cannot, of course, set out to find such a pot. It must burst upon you by accident, when you expect nothing but another corner in the sandstone." He concluded, "the most impressive thing about the Anasazi is ... their thorough permeation of a country so difficult to travel in today that most of it remains uninhabited."[30] Yet the telltale signs of the Ancients are everywhere, potsherds, arrowheads, occasional spearpoints, stone tools, and dramatic cliff dwellings straddling ledges hundreds of feet above canyon floors.

Roberts wrote more in "Canyon Confidential" for *National Geographic Adventure*. The article began with this teaser: "The obscure redrock sanctums of southeastern Utah hide stellar ruins and rock art. But as word of these wonders leaks out, so come the crowds, careless tramplers, and souvenir hunters. Does that mean there's no longer any way to find solitude in the canyons? No. (Here's the secret)."[31] Ah, secrets—the canyons of Bears Ears are large enough to hold innumerable secrets as well as ancient cultural wisdom and the origins of tribal clans and stories. Not everything can be known, nor should it be. Artifacts like Roberts' grayware corrugated pot should be left alone, in place, in an outdoor museum.

Bears Ears should have no trail markers, no interpretive signs, no paved parking lots. Leave the large landscape of twisted canyons and dry mesa tops alone, intact, and let it tell its own tales for those hardy adventurers willing to get lost as they wend their way. The sense of discovery is paramount in Bears Ears requiring a unique form of management and tribal consultation. Hopi Vice Chair Clark Tenakhongva explained at a Friends of Cedar Mesa conference held in Bluff, "There's a reason that people left evidence behind. You have large, very large rock art panels. But be cautious of how you approach the places here. The traffic, the amount of people has quadrupled. How much more exploitation do we need?"[32] Fred Blackburn and Ray Williamson concluded in *Cowboys & Cave Dwellers*, "As more and more visitors flock to enjoy the Southwest's scenic canyons and to marvel at the signs of Ancestral Pueblo survival skills, archaeological sites are beginning to show all the hallmarks of an endangered species."[33]

I remember sitting in an ancient room, cross-legged in front of a dressed stone masonry wall that showed thumb and fingerprints in the mortar from centuries ago. Two feet up from the floor was painted a white band six inches high and at intervals along the wall the moon appeared in its phases as unpainted or negative space against the reddish plaster. Above the white band an artist had spaced white thumbprints. To enter the room, which was permissible two decades ago, I had stepped into an enclosed courtyard. Between doorways an extended white mural also had thumbprints above it. I had entered one of the great residential chambers in Bears Ears built at the end of centuries of Ancestral Puebloan occupation. I sat silently in one of the rooms, soot on the ceiling, stones polished over generations by other hands, legs, and thighs. A zigzag snake motif stretched across one end of the open courtyard. Standing at a defensive wall protecting the courtyard, I looked out across the canyon we had descended. To reach the hushed rooms we had crossed a trickle of water and stepped under a burst of colored cottonwoods, leaves ablaze in yellows and orange at the end of fall.

Snug in the small room, my eyes adjusting to the darkness, I heard voices, not ancient voices. These sounds were visitors ready to drop into the canyon. They couldn't see me, but I could hear them. I've wondered why we've done so little to understand acoustics as an integral part of Ancestral Puebloan defensive architecture. Standing on a wide stone shelf, looking cross canyon as mid-morning sun lit the opposite side, I had stood in silence viewing Moon House for the first time. I stared at the complex of 800-year-old rooms with multiple doorways. Here was an entire stone village with both McElmo style and Mesa Verde masonry. Moon House has Kayenta Anasazi-style granaries with rounded horse-collar shaped doorways, and jacal construction of upright woven willows and adobe. In the canyon's quiet, with a breeze moving the cottonwood leaves below, I felt suspended in time. It's that sense of self-discovery that the BLM in their Monticello, Utah, field office seeks to preserve in this unit of Bears Ears National Monument.

The magic of Moon House is not only the approach, the steep descent, and the route-finding up the other side, but also the inner chamber with its protective curtain wall containing thirty-one intentional loopholes strategically placed to aim arrows at intruders. Erected in AD 1262, as determined by tree-ring dating of wood samples, the wall shields a hidden courtyard similar to features in Medieval European castles built in the same time period. Behind the stone wall a suite of rooms contains original 800-year-old plaster. Soot from ancient fires covers the ceiling. Ancestral Puebloan finger impressions remain pressed into the adobe wattle-and-daub walls. Architectural aspects of Moon House were designed for defense. The BLM obtained a "Save America's Treasures" grant, and with the assistance of the National Park Service, mapped the entire forty-nine-room Moon House complex that stretches one-quarter mile in McLoyd Canyon. Volunteers carried in 750 pounds of sand to place on the rooms' floors to absorb moisture from human breath, which can damage the delicate moon-phase paintings. For further protection, entering the rooms is now prohibited.

Southwestern archaeologist William Lipe knew such rules were coming. To the west of Cedar Mesa is the Grand Gulch Wilderness Study Area and Lipe wrote, "In Grand Gulch we are moving into an era of managed

One of the rare Ancestral Puebloans sites on Cedar Mesa in Bears Ears National Monument has rooms off an inner courtyard and original wall paintings or murals. Author photo.

remoteness, of planned romance. I think that is probably how it has to be if we are to preserve the qualities of the area at all in an increasingly mobile and exploitative society." He added, "The challenge is to have effective management that does not itself overwhelm the values it is designed to protect."[34]

Because over 3,000 visitors annually hike into Grand Gulch, backpackers must get overnight permits at the Kane Gulch Ranger Station. Hikers need day use permits for a 1,600-acre two-mile stretch of McLoyd Canyon with Moon House in the middle between two large sandstone pour-offs within the Fish Creek Canyon Wilderness Study Area. Dogs, overnight camping, and campfires along the rim are not permitted. To maintain that sense of self-discovery, daily visitation is limited to twenty people. Group size may not exceed twelve. Former Monticello BLM field manager Tom Heinlein, with 1.8 million acres to oversee, explained to me that Moon House is "part of one huge Anasazi cultural landscape" and at forty-nine rooms one of the largest sites on Cedar Mesa. Heinlein said, "People come from around the world to visit southeast Utah, and we must maintain that backcountry discovery experience where eco-tourism success depends upon respectful visitors."[35]

Heinlein's staff recommended that Moon House receive additional protections because like other Cedar Mesa sites now well-known because of the internet, "the land is being hammered." He continued, "We're trying to be as flexible as we can to balance the protection of these fragile resources, while accommodating an appropriate level of heritage tourism." Occupied for only forty years and built in three distinct phases, archaeologist Lipe explains, "Moon House is important to the public because its wonderful preservation makes it easy for visitors to imagine what it would have been like to have lived there."[36] Across Bears Ears hundreds of Basketmaker, Pueblo I, and Pueblo II sites can be found at the entrance to canyons or on valley floors, but the truly breathtaking sites are Pueblo III sites like Moon House isolated on ledges, caught between mesa tops and canyon bottoms, rigorous to hike to and profoundly moving to explore.

Management of Bears Ears must be carefully considered with tribal values paramount. Not only must sites be protected from vandals, pothunters, wandering cows, and careless tourists, but the night sky above Bears Ears deserves equal protection. It offers one of the darkest skies in the United States. A visitor can look up and see what the ancients saw. Because of light pollution a third of the global population cannot see the Milky Way. "Two-thirds of the world's population—including 99 percent of people living in the continental United States and western Europe—no longer experience a truly dark night, a night untouched by artificial electric light," writes Paul Bogard in *The End of Night*.[37] In Bears Ears, stars are scattered from horizon to horizon and planets appear in their stately processions. The International Dark-Sky Association certifies national and state parks as an International Dark Sky Park. The first one designated was just below Bears Ears in White Canyon at Natural Bridges National Monument.

We live with too much artificial light and not enough darkness. In the twenty-first century Americans have lost silence, solitude, and darkness, but now the NPS has new initiatives to preserve and appreciate our dark skies, especially on the Colorado Plateau. At Natural Bridges National Monument west of Blanding, Utah, visitors are encouraged not only to see the massive Sipapu, Kachina, and Owachomo Bridges, but also to look up at night into the heavens to find our place in the universe as the Ancestral Puebloans did a millennia ago.

Across the entire United States only 1 percent of NPS sites are as dark at night as Natural Bridges. Gordon Gower is the park's astronomer and

"Sky Ranger." Bring a fleece jacket and a camp chair to his 16.5-inch telescope, and he'll show you galaxies. Gower explains, "I want people to make a connection to the sky and to learn how the National Park Service has come to recognize that the sky is also part of our resources. We're training rangers in dark sky interpretation. It's just as much our job to protect the night sky as wildlife and all the rest."[38]

At Natural Bridges, 6,500 feet in elevation, in the heart of Bears Ears, the universe awaits those who turn to the skies. Sky Ranger Gower takes complicated astronomical ideas and makes them simple. Stacks of visitor comment cards prove his success. Gower states, "Most folks only see the moon and two or three bright stars. We have people come here who've never seen the Milky Way." A family from Germany wrote him about his evening program and exclaimed, "That was a night we'll never forget." San Juan County, Utah, has actively promoted dark sky tourism to Europeans and Japanese, who in their busy industrial cities cannot see what we take for granted in the southwestern United States—brilliant stars and planets stream across a black infinity. Chief Ranger Jim Dougan at Natural Bridges says, "When I walk out at night there's absolute quiet and I see the Milky Way as a tangible presence. We get more positive letters to the park's superintendent on the Dark Sky Initiative than any other program in the park."[39] A typical astronomy program starts at twilight and takes thirty to forty-five minutes, but Gordon Gower's programs last two to three hours. He has a clear ending to his presentations, but no one wants to leave. Visitors quietly ask questions and keep looking up.

Across the Colorado Plateau, national parks are engaged with this new evolving mission. Bears Ears will be no exception. The NPS's Dark Skies program connects us with deep time. When we look up at the night sky, we're doing what humans have always done—studying stars, asking profound questions, and wondering about our place in the universe. President Obama's Bears Ears proclamation made clear, "From earth to sky, the region is unsurpassed in wonders. The star-filled nights and natural quiet of the Bears Ears area transport visitors to an earlier eon. Against an absolutely black night sky, our galaxy and others more distant leap into view." On a good night, in a dark place, you should be able to see 2,500 stars. In Bears Ears, that's possible.

Hiking down from the canyon rim to sit beneath the large stone bridges, Paul Bogard wrote about stargazing at Natural Bridges. He wrote, "The longer you stay, the darker it gets, and the darker it gets the more sounds arise—crows and frogs in the canyons, crickets all around . . . You lie on your back with your hands across your eyes like blinders, making the world that much darker, then open them to reveal the sky. . . . each time the sky is a little brighter, each time more peppered with stars."[40] He refers to a geography of night, and though he traveled to dark places across the world, his favorite locale was the American Southwest. At Natural Bridges, if he would have walked to the head of White Canyon and kept walking, he would have come close to the Bears Ears themselves, another perfect place to watch the stars.

Native Americans understand Bears Ears as a sacred landscape. Astronomers value its dark skies. Some San Juan County citizens seek energy development, and no type of development creates more controversy than mining and milling uranium, which from the 1940s through the 1980s transformed the county and provided a tax base like no other. Local families, Native and white alike, had good paying jobs and at last felt linked to the American dream. But that dream turned into a nightmare as family members developed cancers, had difficulty breathing, experienced ongoing medical problems, and died prematurely.

Across the sprawling Navajo Nation, a public art project of painted murals sends the message that "Radioactive Pollution Kills. It's time to clean up the mines."[41] Just south of Blanding, and north of the historic Paiute and Ute community of White Mesa, a uranium mill sits mostly idle. The White Mesa Mill, licensed in 1979, was supposed to operate with a fifteen-year life span. The mill is licensed by the Utah Division of Waste Management and Radiation Control and is the only conventional uranium mill operating in the United States that can annually process eight million pounds of uranium. Its owner Energy Fuels recently applied to accept radioactive waste from overseas.[42]

The mill would process the foreign uranium waste, extract the small amount of uranium present, less than half of one percent, and dump remaining waste into pits. White Mesa Utes worry about groundwater contamination and cumulative impacts over decades as well as dangers inherent in transporting the waste.[43] A Navajo-run anti-uranium activist group has the title "Haul No!" President Trump's deletion of thousands of acres from Bears Ears National Monument included a belt of potential uranium mines along Elk Ridge, in Cottonwood Canyon, and close to the White Mesa Mill. State Representative Phil Lyman writes a column in the *San Juan Record*. He titles it "Report from the Yellowcake Caucus," which is a group he organized for communication and strategy with other politicians.[44]

Lawsuits against the White Mesa Mill include those supported by the Grand Canyon Trust, which also helped produce a film titled "Half Life: The Story of America's Last Uranium Mill." In his book *Confluence*, Bluff resident and writer Zak Podmore explained, "Now the Ute community members speak out against the dust and the tailings creeping into aquifers. The white workers see a brewing battle for their homeland. They fear a future where real, honest work is an abstraction, where everyone is a hotel manager or a guide for tourists."[45]

White Mesa residents worry about toxic spills and dangers to their drinking water. "Indigenous homelands are often considered sacrifice zones, and we, the Indigenous peoples, are not seen or heard. Our tribal communities continue to live with the permanent radioactive wastes left behind by uranium companies without our consent," Talia Boyd wrote in *The Salt Lake Tribune*. She added, "The consequences of mining, milling and waste are burdens we will all carry for generations. As our communities work to heal, we continue to face nuclear colonialism, but we will never stop fighting."[46] I think about the location of the uranium and vanadium mill on the south side of Monticello, how the site is now a park after a Superfund cleanup, and how kiosks and interpretive signs help visitors to honor and remember the dead and those patriotic families who lost loved ones who worked in the mill. Uranium mining and protecting a sacred landscape seem incongruous, but those are just a few examples of ongoing social tensions in San Juan County.

Summer gatherings at Bears Ears sponsored by the Bears Ears Inter-Tribal Coalition have brought dozens of families, respected elders, and young children to the meadow north of the Bears Ears for days of talks, discussions, and sharing traditional foods. On horseback, Willie Grayeyes has visited remnants of historic Navajo hogans. At one event, the Lummi Nation gave to the Coalition a nine-foot tall, one-ton, earth-tone painted Bear Totem Pole in honor of tribal work defending Bears Ears. That same summer participants were harassed by monument opponents who stole signs making it difficult for newcomers to find the camp. "Twice I had to go do a sign check. Someone threw (one of the event signs) in the bush. The signs were taken. There was a big one and I had to (replace) it," explained Davina Smith, director of operations for Utah Diné Bikéyah.[47] Resistance continues. The question remains: Whose monument is it? Whose landscape? Whose homeland?

One of Bluff, Utah's hardest working couples has now passed on. After sixty years of marriage, Gene and Mary Foushee died just nine days apart.

The couple was eighty-eight years old and had lived a rich, full life. They will be remembered for many things, but their most important achievement was saving the small town of Bluff and building Recapture Lodge. A spectacled geologist with an empty wallet, Gene's mind brimmed with ideas. He always pointed a stubby pencil at two-by-fours, friends, and neighbors—anyone who would listen. He led some of the first tours into Monument Valley. An April 1963 ad in *Desert Magazine* proclaimed, "RECAPTURE! The fun of adventure in the Red Rock Country ... beauty and serenity in Indian Country ... DISCOVER the excitement of geology in textbook country, Recapture Court Motel, Historic Bluff, Utah, ... P.S. Everything for the traveler." Except good roads—they had yet to come. In the early 1960s, asphalt ended at Cottonwood Wash. The road west was dirt and gravel. Bluff was the end of the road, but Gene Foushee had a vision.

When the Foushees arrived in Bluff, the Mormon village had been almost abandoned by families who had moved north to Blanding and Monticello because all too often, the San Juan River raged, flooded, and ruined their farms. Navajo Reservoir would tame the muddy river, but modern civilization took a long time getting to Bluff. Electricity arrived in 1957. The Foushees built a motel, a few rooms at a time, with doors facing east, which is Navajo tradition, and they had the only automatic washing machine. When they were finished cleaning and folding motel sheets, Navajo women who had been standing in line got to use the washer.

When US Highway 160 went south of the San Juan River and largely bypassed Utah, that asphalt alignment set Bluff back two decades, but Gene Foushee was patient. He had to be. In the 1960s San Juan County, Utah, had "a little bit of ranching, oil and gas was starting, but it was pretty bleak," states Bluff resident Jim Hook. Uranium mining boomed and busted. "You could have bought Moab if you had a good credit rating. The only place to get a piece of pie was the Atomic Café."[48] Born in North Carolina in the Great Depression, Foushee knew how to straighten nails, reuse lumber, work hard, and encourage others. He lived by the Depression adage, "Use it up, wear it out, make it do or do without." He had been on Union Carbide's payroll in Uravan, Colorado, but when he moved to Bluff, "there were some skinny years there in the beginning."

"It was exhausting to work with him. He had so many ideas about what to do. Everyone who ever met him had a list given to him by Gene. I still haven't done everything on the first list he gave me and that was over 25 years ago," smiles Hook who with his wife Luanne bought the

Gene and Mary Foushee opened the Recapture Lodge in Bluff and also helped to save many of the town's original nineteenth and early-twentieth century sandstone houses. Author Tony Hillerman wrote, "The Recapture Lodge has been Bluff's center of hospitality." Author photo.

Recapture Lodge from the Foushees after they'd run it for thirty years. The Hooks, originally from the Fort Collins, Colorado, area, had "ten years of wrangling llamas and we were ready to do something else" so they took over as managers of Recapture Lodge. "I learned how to fold towels and do whatever. In a year they started talking about selling it to us, but we had no money," Jim Hook remembers. The Foushees gave them a raise so they could make the down payment and begin a mortgage. No bank, just credit and carry back the loan based on their character. "They were like our parents. He was always the visionary. We really miss them," states Luanne Hook with a tear in her eye and a catch in her throat. "They were a unit together. He was the face of the community, but she was behind the scenes, the bookkeeper. She was actually the nuts and bolts, the welcoming face at the front desk. They were the saviors of Bluff."

Gene would get a project started, move it along, then pass it on for someone else to finish. He would begin a different project. He lobbied for better roads. He planted shrubs, river privets, currants, lilacs, and dozens of trees including Carolina poplars, pecans, mulberries and fruit trees whose shade today's residents enjoy. He found funds for a small airplane strip at Bluff and he built a hanger for visiting aircraft. He created the town's first water system from shallow wells and an artesian well. And one by one he restored the town's historic stone houses built in the 1890s and early 1900s by successful Mormon ranchers and merchants.

"Gene saw the beauty and craftsmanship that went into the Mormon pioneer homes constructed by the brave souls who came through the Hole in the Rock in 1880, and then were abandoned and left to fall down or in some cases burn," wrote Alvin Reiner in the *San Juan Record*. "One by one, and brick by brick, Gene salvaged as many as he could."[49] The preserved houses in Bluff's historic district, most of native sandstone, include the Jens House, the Adams House (which is on the National Register of Historic Places), the Decker House, and the Olin Oliver House. Rancher Al Scorup's house is also on the National Register. The Lyman House and the stone mansion of Lemuel Hardison Redd have been preserved. Over the years, Gene Foushee repaired, repainted, and reroofed all of them. He would buy the houses, fix them up, get somebody living in them, and tackle another one. The Adams House had pallid bats in the upper story and "you could have thrown a cat through the roof anywhere."

Pioneer rancher Al Scorup ran cattle across the northern Bears Ears region and he built this fine sandstone home in Bluff though he was rarely there. Several stone pioneer homes still stand in Bluff's historic district. Author photo.

"Everybody has stories about him. Almost all local Navajo families have someone who worked for him at one time or another," states Hook. "He mentored a lot of Navajo kids," offers guide and outfitter Vaughn Hadenfeldt:

> Foushee was a recycler. It was too far to go to get supplies so everything got re-used. In fact, Gene probably never knew this, but the Navajo language is flexible and adaptive. They came up with the phrase 'to Foushee it,' which meant to make do with what you had. I've seen him re-use old plumbing pipes which appalled me, but it was just his generation. They made do. Gene was always drawing pictures in the dirt to explain things. He had a tape measure on his belt. He was always in construction mode.[50]

Slowly, carefully, the Foushees brought Bluff back to life, preserving the history and heritage as much as possible. The Southwest Heritage Foundation maintains Bluff's Chacoan-era Great House. The Jones Farm has a conservation easement on its one hundred plus acres to prevent Moab-style development. There's a river trail south of the Recapture Lodge and plans for a trail to go from Bluff to the BLM's Sand Island Boat Launch and Campground.

There's a Bluff Historic Preservation Association, which Foushee started, the original Bluff Fort, an annual balloon rally in January, and Bluff proudly proclaims itself as the gateway to Bears Ears National Monument. Tourists come from across the United States and England, France, Italy, Germany, Argentina, Brazil, Switzerland, Australia, and China. In November 2018 Bluff residents voted on incorporating not only the town but also the entire Bluff Valley to control development and their deep well water sources in the sandstone benches north of town. The Foushees would have been proud. Their vision is coming true. Jim Hook's eyes well up. He's remembering Gene Foushee. "Who gets to go and build a town? Nothing gets done unless you do it. There's no way he could have been in a nursing home. He'd have brought his tool belt and remodeled the windows."

The small desert town of Bluff is experiencing a canyon country renaissance as a gateway community to Bears Ears. A former trading post is a thriving restaurant, and the old Silver Dollar Bar built in 1955 has found new life as the Bears Ears Education Center because the federal government has not provided a separate facility for Bears Ears interpretation despite the popularity of the new national monument.

Bluff is on the southern end of the controversial Bears Ears National Monument and local citizens, Bluffoons as we call ourselves, are proud of it. The Silver Dollar Bar, once home to beer and burgers, now serves up tourist information and cautionary comments about desert hiking and visiting archaeological sites with respect. Purchased by the Friends of Cedar Mesa, the Silver Dollar Bar once catered to sheepherders, truckers, uranium miners, and "just whoever came down the road," states eighty-four-year-old Duke Simpson. "There was all kinds who came to Bluff over the years." As for dancing at the bar, Duke says, "It was Saturday night live" with patrons waltzing into the wee hours of Sunday morning.[51] Writing about a bar fight in Alaska, Ed Abbey waxed nostalgic. He described it as "[j]ust like down home: The Club 66 in Flag, the Eagle in Gallup, or the Silver Dollar in Bluff, on the edge of the Navajo Reservation—the only bar in Utah where you can hear squaw dance music on the jukebox."[52]

"I went in and ordered a hamburger," Simpson told me, "and the old man who was cooking tipped his head back and spit on the grill to make sure it was hot enough. Then he plopped down a beef patty and proceeded to cook the burger. But after watching his grilling style, I declined the sandwich."[53] The Silver Dollar catered to locals and the occasional tourist willing to risk dusty roads to get to Bluff. "Everyone going through Bluff, just kept going," remembers BLM River Ranger Larry Beck. "A few river runners stopped in, but it was lonely at the counter, often only me and the bartender. I used to walk to the bar and then walk home. I liked to joke that when I left Bluff that the poor bar might go out of business with my departure." That was in the 1980s.

Over the years, Bluff's three bars disappeared, as restaurants developed to serve beer and wine. The tourists passing through are now staying. Bluff is emerging as a vital destination between the Grand Canyon, with its six million annual visitors, and Arches and Canyonlands National Parks, with over two million tourists. National monument status for Bears Ears has brought a new generation of canyon country hikers trying to avoid crowds and to find wilderness values. But there's no USFS or BLM information center and no local source of maps, directions, or suggestions, though the *San Juan Record* reports that visitation to southeast Utah BLM lands is up 35 percent.

To the north in Monticello on its new campus, the Canyon Country Discovery Center orients travelers to the entire Colorado Plateau. For years the Four Corners Outdoors School introduced visitors to the San Juan River and the plateau before finally finding a permanent home as the

Discovery Center.[54] The BLM has an office in Monticello but no place to host displays or to engage visitors. In Blanding, the Edge of the Cedars Museum State Park does a superb job of interpreting Ancestral Puebloan artifacts with engaging exhibits on historic and prehistoric themes, but it functions as a museum not as a public lands visitor center. Up on Cedar Mesa, volunteers at the Kane Gulch Ranger Station do their best to answer questions, but in their small space, they are frequently swamped. So the Friends of Cedar Mesa raised funds and volunteer labor to do what the federal government currently does not have the budget or the staffing to accomplish.

"Right now, it feels like the Bears Ears Education Center is one of the only positive things happening for the monument. The incredible national support we've seen for the Center indicates people's hunger for positive, proactive actions to take on behalf of public lands," states Amanda Podmore, former assistant director of Friends of Cedar Mesa. "It's exciting to turn this historic bar and community space into a venue where visitors, locals, and friends from everywhere can 'belly up' for information about how to visit Bears Ears with respect."[55]

Indeed, in true western fashion, the outside of the building facing the highway has glass block walls so patrons inside could not be seen. Most laborers in the working West heading to a bar after work had already spent plenty of time outside. The last thing they wanted was a window with a view. They preferred to see cold beer and an array of whiskey bottles. At the old Silver Dollar, the bar is still there, as is the back bar with its wooden drawers and refrigerated cases. Over the years, the Silver Dollar became a private residence with the nickname of the Nada Bar, or not-a-bar. Children and adults playfully placed painted handprints all over the ceiling and front of the bar.

Why not? Handprints are found in canyon alcoves and above room blocks and habitation sites across Bears Ears, so why not in a saloon? Former owner Kyle Bauman is pleased with the sale and says his vintage bar building "was handed off to an organization which will continue the tradition of a community-based location for keeping the community united in art, information, and adventure." The 3,800 square foot building on 0.43 acres has been transformed. Extra rooms have become office space, meeting space, and staff living quarters. There are outdoor patios, courtyards, and parking in the back. "We are extremely grateful and excited to have received such broad support for our efforts to create the Bears Ears Education Center," adds board president Vaughn Hadenfeldt. Friends and neighbors have fond memories of the Nada Bar, and now it will take on a new life.

In Bluff, support and respect for Bears Ears is woven through the community. For the Basketmakers and Ancestral Puebloans, Bears Ears was home and a place of refuge. For historic Navajos and Utes, Bears Ears offered a sanctuary from cowboy and cavalry patrols. Some Mormon families fled San Juan County over polygamy and fear of US marshals, but as the Mexican Revolution unsettled northern Mexico, they came back. They also sought refuge, particularly in the towns of Blanding and Monticello. They began again with their families, friends, and deep faith. These Latter-day Saints descendants see the landscape as a godly gift to be used to provide wages, income, and economic viability in remote southeast Utah.

Others see Bears Ears as valuable because it never has been developed. The canyons are too big, the mesas too wide, with few roads and little water. It's a world of tapering ledges and sandstone cliffs that hold heat and sunlight and tiny traces of snow. "If any place on the continent can stay off the cluttered map of human activity, this is it, this place that even determined Mormon settlers had a hard time entering, the grooves of their wagon wheels still visible where they chopped their way into sandstone canyons looking for a promised land," writes Craig Childs. "This is what you feel out here, the music of darkness. . . . We look to the land as possibility, a place with its own agency, and it teaches us, heals us, gives us space from the press of humanity." Childs explains, "To take this away would rob us of a resource that may be the rarest of them all. This is why I fight for Bears Ears."[56]

How to define a homeland while also defining a place that should be visited like wilderness "where man is a visitor who does not remain?" Obama's monument boundaries included seven wilderness study areas. I've visited a few of them, but I want to hike in all of them. What will become of this landscape of refuge and resistance?

"Many who live in the towns around Bears Ears believe you're not a local unless you can claim six or seven generations there. But imagine familial and cultural ties that stretch back 600 generations or more," writes Tim Petersen in the *Colorado Plateau Advocate*. "Consider that tens of thousands of indigenous people alive today have ancestors who have known this place for hundreds of generations, but they each know it a bit differently based on their own cosmologies, languages, prayers formed and honed and polished here."[57] I agree with Angelo Baca, cultural resources coordinator for Utah Diné Bikéyah. He wrote, "The land is still here. The people will still be here. Bears Ears will always be indigenous land, and nothing will change that."[58]

Rain comes to red rock country and canyons become slickrock. We had hiked up a drainage and then skirted around a cliff face angling ever higher. Light rain, the first of summer, scented the sage. I pulled a few sage leaves, turned them slowly between my fingers then placed them in my nostrils for stamina and good luck. Higher we went. Just as we saw a rainbow off to the south, we spied an intricately built rock wall hundreds of feet beneath us. It was a carefully constructed refuge site or sentry point protecting an ancient trail headed toward the top of a rocky ridge—all of Cedar Mesa and Bears Ears beyond.

We stared at the wall with binoculars, admiring the craftsmanship and careful, patient placement of dressed stones set on a narrow ledge. I pivoted 180 degrees and found more ruins, wall segments, and a few small rooms rounding the base of a solid sandstone pinnacle jutting into the sky. Rain cleared and slickrock shone in sparkling light, pools of water in every direction. We stood silent surveying a wide sweep of canyon below us and two unexplored sites to either side. We would have to come back. As the sun dipped we turned and began our long walk away from the cliff edge. A turkey vulture circled left, a red tail hawk called from below.

CHAPTER 15

Bears Ears Restored?

Coming Full Circle in Canyon Country

Early mornings in the canyon have a distinct quality; they are a time I cherish. Out here there is time to watch the day begin, hear the small secret sounds that no one else is awake to hear, time to watch the light change, to anticipate the coming day, all the good hours stacked ahead. Cool dawn, in these dry canyons, is a time of rare perfection, fresh beginnings, infinite peace, total awareness. . . .

—Ann Zwinger, *Wind in the Rock*

And there are the desert wilds, where anything can happen. Where the only thing that marks the way is redrock and ruins. Where the only certainties are beauty and destruction.

—Amy Irvine, *Trespass*

Becoming "native to a place" doesn't have to be about secured boundaries of blood and territory but can allude to a deep, growing knowledge of that place. The way one feasts on it and becomes nourished and gives thanks. And hands it over to be shared.

—Gretel Ehrlich, *Unsolaced*

President Donald Trump's Administration, to the applause of many rural Utahans, reduced Bears Ears National Monument by 85 percent and left those lands vulnerable to oil, gas, and uranium exploration at a time when international markets for those resources have dramatically shrunk if not completely collapsed. "How much longer are we going to persist with the idea that the path to prosperity in some of the most beautiful places on earth is to drill oil wells and drag chains across the desert?" asked the editorial board of the *Salt Lake Tribune* referring to both Bears Ears and Grand Staircase-Escalante National Monuments. "The reason they became national monuments is because they are unique. Shouldn't we trade on that rather than trying to use them to produce commodities that are already cheaper from elsewhere?"[1]

By December 2020, several Navajo Nation chapter houses and the Utah Navajo Commission passed resolutions supporting the reinstatement of the full-sized Bears Ears National Monument, as did the San Juan County Commissioners on a two-to-one vote. "We did the right thing," Commissioner Grayeyes explained. He added, "I'm hoping the changes will come in our favor. We stand together."[2] Meanwhile back at the ranch, or at least at the headquarters of the Department of the Interior in Washington, DC, a portrait painting of former Secretary of the Interior Ryan Zinke was unveiled. The painting shows Zinke on a handsome multihued paint horse that he rode when he visited Bears Ears as part of his "listening session" in southeast Utah. The painting's background echoes Bears Ears.

According to tribes, Zinke did not listen to them. He recommended that the monument be severely reduced. Zinke resigned under a mushroom cloud of ethics scandals after facing almost twenty federal investigations. "He testified to Congress that tribal 'sovereignty meant something' while he ignored the clear statements of five sovereign tribal governments that the Bears Ears landscape needs and deserves protection," argued Ute tribal member Shaun Chapoose. "His official portrait is another desperate attempt to rewrite history. What you don't see, what he doesn't tell you, is that we are still here defending and protecting our lands."[3] In the portrait, Zinke's cowboy hat appears to be on backward as it often was when he posed for photographs amidst iconic western scenes.

Deb Haaland, President Joe Biden's Secretary of the Interior, has her law degree from the University of New Mexico. She is a former Congressional representative, a member of the Laguna Pueblo, and a thirty-fifth generation New Mexican. She brought a very different environmental and cultural awareness to the president's cabinet, and she is the first Native American to hold the office of Secretary of the Interior. Native Americans across the nation applauded her Senate confirmation.

With the change in presidential administrations after the 2020 election and a return to valuing cultural resources and Indigenous perspectives, President Obama's boundaries for Bears Ears National Monument were reinstated October 8, 2021, just in time for Indigenous Peoples' Day—the former Columbus Day. President Biden's campaign website had proclaimed, "[H]is administration will work with tribal governments and Congress to protect sacred sites and public lands and waters with high conservation and cultural values."[4] He kept his promise especially after a three-day on the ground review of Bears Ears by Secretary Haaland and her formal "Report on Restoring National Monuments" from June 2021.[5] Biden had ordered the review on his first day in the Oval Office. He also retained within Bears Ears boundaries an intriguing 11,200-acre addition that President Trump had added in the Indian Creek unit near Hatch Point and Canyonlands. The addition includes Shay Canyon, which has rare dinosaur prints and significant rock art panels.

Biden's Proclamation 10285 echoed Bears Ears themes that I have researched and written about in this book. The White House concurred, "[P]reserving the sacred landscape and unique cultural resources in the Bears Ears region was an impetus for passage of the Antiquities Act in 1906," and "few national monuments more clearly meet the Antiquities Act's criteria for protection than the Bears Ears buttes and surrounding areas." President Biden explained, "[F]or more than one hundred years, indigenous people, historians, conservationists, scientists, archaeologists, and other groups advocated unsuccessfully for protection of the Bears Ears landscape." Biden referred often to President Barack Obama's Proclamation 9558 and reiterated "the compelling need to protect one of the most extraordinary cultural landscapes in the United States."[6]

Navajo Nation President Jonathan Nez attended the White House signing ceremony and stated, "The protection of Bears Ears has been fought for by many tribal nations for many years." He told the *Navajo Times,* "It's a win for our people, our ancestors, and generations to come."[7] But Utah's largely Mormon political delegation did not think so. They responded in an opinion piece in the *Deseret News* titled "A Monumental Insult." The politicians argued that Biden's proclamation "perpetuates a cycle of abuse under the Antiquities Act," and that it happened "once again without local input," which is false because elected county commissions in San Juan County and Grand County, and the city council in Bluff, all voted to restore the original Bears Ears boundaries. The Utah politicians' real whopper, however, was the statement that Biden's proclamation "fails to include the crucial input and involvement of local tribes in protecting and highlighting their own cultural heritage."[8] Not so—governing bodies of the Navajo, Hopi, Zuni, Ute Mountain Ute, and Northern Ute Nations have all gone on record in favor of Bears Ears and their support has been unwavering.

On behalf of the Northern Utes and the Bears Ears Inter-Tribal Coalition, Shaun Chapoose explained, "The Monument represents a historic opportunity for the federal government to learn and incorporate our tribal land management practices that we developed over centuries and are needed more now than ever. We battled for this Monument because it matters."[9] A poll reveals that 74 percent of Utah residents support monument restoration, but Utah politicians continued to ignore the public and sovereign Native nations. By the end of October 2021, the state's attorney general had requested bids for a legal team and senior attorneys with "experience arguing appeals to the United States Supreme Court and United States Circuit Courts of Appeals."[10] The State of Utah will sue the federal government over Biden's Bears Ears restoration to avenge a perceived "monumental insult."

In their editorial in the *Deseret News,* Utah's political delegation referred to San Juan County as "the poorest county of Utah," yet the authors failed to acknowledge that in the state's history other national monuments evolved into national parks that have brought millions of dollars annually into rural areas. Mukuntuweap National Monument became Zion National Park. Both Arches and Capitol Reef began as national monuments. Why not let Bears Ears National Monument, with effective Indigenous management, take its own course?

When will the opposition and legal controversies end? Will it take congressional action or more years in the courts? Over a century ago, Congress passed and Theodore Roosevelt signed the Antiquities Act to protect "objects of historic and scientific interest" using the "smallest area compatible with the proper care and management of the objects to be protected." That language has already been to the nation's highest court. When Roosevelt designated Grand Canyon as a national monument with over 800,000 acres, the Supreme Court said, yes, the President has that right and authority. A careful reading of Biden's fourteen-page Proclamation 10285 reveals paragraph after paragraph that confirms the entire region is one landscape, one "object to be protected." Biden's proclamation stated,

> The Bears Ears landscape . . . is not just a series of isolated objects, but is, itself, an object of historic and scientific interest requiring protection under the Antiquities Act. Bears Ears is a sacred land of spiritual significance, a historic homeland, and a place of belonging for indigenous people from the Southwest. Bears Ears is a living, breathing landscape that—owing to the area's arid environment and overall remoteness, as well as the building techniques which its inhabitants employed—retains remarkably and spiritually significant evidence of Indigenous use and habitation since time immemorial.[11]

There is not yet resolution of the vexing political question of the appropriate size for Bears Ears and whether the land should be open for drilling and mining. Once at the edge of the Ancestral Puebloan world a thousand years ago, Bears Ears is now at the center of a public lands debate swirling in the American West, but research continues and momentum for preservation only builds.

Bears Ears will remain a poster child for presidential use of the Antiquities Act and successful collaboration with Native peoples. Withdrawing special landscapes for scientific and historical purposes is at the heart of the Antiquities Act. Anthropologists, archaeologists, and historians continue to learn new truths about Bears Ears and the peoples who have lived in canyon country. Winston Hurst, Cathy Cameron, and an exemplary cast of committed archaeologists have completed the massive Comb Ridge Heritage Initiative Project. New scientific understandings of the area's rock art images include doctoral dissertations such as Phil R. Geib's on Basketmaker II warfare and fending sticks (2016) and Ben Bellorado's "Leaving Footprints in the Ancient Southwest" (2020) on sandal imagery and unique patterns of twined sandals used across Bears Ears with ties to

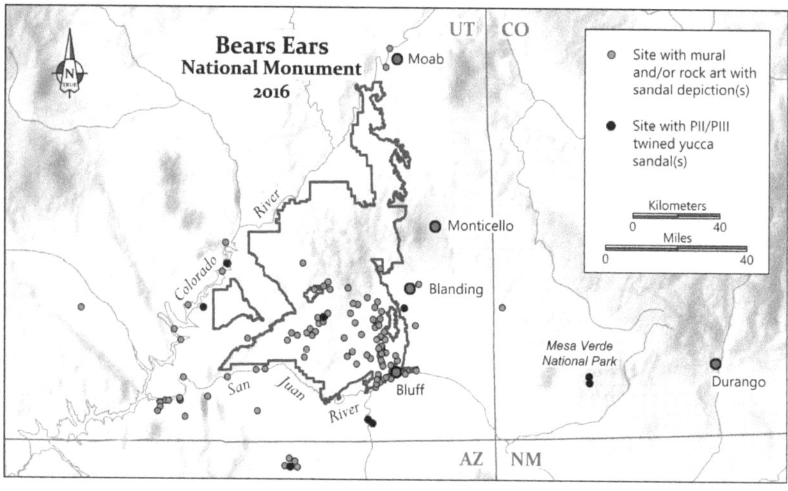

From the beginnings of the Antiquities Act in 1906, national monuments have been designated by presidents for their scientific value. Research in Bears Ears National Monument continues in the fields of archaeology, botany, geology, paleontology, and history. In his doctoral dissertation, Benjamin Bellorado explains the importance of ancient twined sandals and the number of sandal images depicted as petroglyphs on rock art. Map detail courtesy of *Archaeology Southwest* Magazine.

Chaco Canyon residents in the Chaco and post-Chaco eras (AD 850–1300).[12] Many rock art sites have petroglyphs of turkey tracks. Now there is recent research on turkey feather blankets. The past is coming full circle. An ancient craft is being revived.

I love seeing turkeys in ponderosa woods moving slowly uphill like priests absorbed in morning prayers. At twilight they are dark shapes seeking acorns and insects, always leaving their distinctive three-toed tracks. Ancestral Puebloans had a special relationship with turkeys too because it was turkey feather blankets, with loft like our modern insulated jackets, that kept the Ancient Ones warm on winter nights. Research shows that not only did Ancestral Puebloans domesticate wild turkeys, but Native women also painstakingly crafted turkey feather blankets for the same reason we sleep under puffy quilts in winter and wear lightweight puff jackets. New Mexican cultural anthropologist Mary Weahkee of the Santa Clara Pueblo and Comanche tribes recently replicated one of the first turkey feather blankets crafted in the last 800 years. She spent hours making cord from narrow leaf yucca fibers and then skillfully wove soft, short, wet feathers into the tight cordage. Her three-by-four-foot cloak or mini-blanket took 300 feet of cordage and 17,000 turkey feathers.

What a labor of love and what a way to honor the ancestors! As we study the past in the present, our respect for Ancestral Puebloans who lived in Bears Ears grows. Research is revealing that turkeys had special purposes in Ancestral Puebloan villages and that every family would have made their own blankets. Blanket-making was not a specialized trade. There is so much to learn about turkeys and how they were embedded in Puebloan life for centuries. Weahkee says that for her ancestors, turkeys were the "main herd animals," and indeed Ancestral Puebloans had only had two domesticated animals—dogs and turkeys. In the upland areas of the Southwest, turkeys were bred over several thousand square miles and for 1,600 years.

Turkeys were kept for ritual uses and turkey carcasses and bones have been found formally interred themselves and also lain to rest atop deceased Ancient Ones. Turkey burials have been found in Canyon de Chelly, at Mesa Verde, and at different sites across Bears Ears. The earliest evidence of turkey keeping, of turkey husbandry, seems to have come from Cedar Mesa within the original boundaries of Bears Ears National Monument. Ancestral Puebloans grew and harvested corn and fed part of their crops to turkeys.

During the Basketmaker II period, or 1200 BC to AD 50, as more turkeys became domesticated, the shift began from blankets made of furry

Bears Ears National Monument is a touchstone for Native peoples of the Southwest whose ancient practices can still be replicated and understood. Archaeologist and anthropologist Mary Weahkee from the New Mexico State Cultural Affairs Office poses with the turkey feather blanket she made using 17,000 feathers. Weahkee made all the yucca fiber cordage and then inserted each single feather. Photo by Martin Perea, New Mexico, Division of Game & Fish.

strips of rabbit hide to turkey feather blankets using the downy portion of the small feathers, not the larger wing feathers. Though I love the traditional turkey dinner at Thanksgiving, for centuries Ancestral Puebloans did not eat turkeys. Instead, they sustainably harvested turkey feathers with a single bird able to yield 600 feathers annually. Mary Weahkee explains that turkeys are the only bird from which feathers can be taken without causing the bird to bleed. It molts twice a year and a flock of turkeys can produce a sizable number of feathers. The birds live up to ten years and can produce numerous soft, downy feathers each year. She marvels at her ancestors' ingenious blankets.

"Inventing a blanket that thermally insulates the body by creating pockets of non-moving air thus traps in heat and prevents heat loss. This is not a new technology because the ancestors used the technology during harsh winters, in the terrain they lived in," offers Weahkee. She says, "If you wrap the feathers around cordage making the down stand up you create a structure that maintains air pockets that captures heat. Modern down and other synthetic insulated jackets do the same thing."[13] Other researchers are also focusing on the use of turkeys and their feathers.

"As ancestral Pueblo farming populations flourished, many thousands of feather blankets would likely have been in circulation at any one time," explains Shannon Tushingham of Washington State University. "It is likely that every member of an ancestral Pueblo community, from infants to adults, possessed one." Recently she worked with the dean of Bears Ears archaeology, William Lipe from Washington State University, to study cordage left from a turkey feather blanket now housed at the Edge of the Cedars State Park Museum. Lipe says, "When the blanket we analyzed for our study was made, we think in the early 1200s CE [Common Era], the birds that supplied the feathers were likely treated as individuals important to the household and would have been buried complete." Lipe explains, "This reverence for turkeys and their feathers is still evident today in Pueblo dances and rituals. They are right up there with eagle feathers as being symbolically and culturally important."[14]

Their research, published in the December 2020 issue of *Journal of Archaeological Science: Reports,* reveals that the blanket they studied at the Edge of the Cedars State Park Museum used 11,500 feathers from four to ten turkeys. They hypothesize that all the feathers came from live birds. As a former museum director, I can attest to the fact that ancient, feathered artifacts are some of the hardest cultural items to find and preserve because insects love to munch on feathers. All too often what remains is just the cordage they were attached to, and it is that cordage, looking like a complicated fish net, which has been on display at the Edge of the Cedars. Now, thanks to new research, we know much more.

The authors state, "Once a blanket was made, it likely would have lasted for a number of years. A household of five or six persons would probably not have had to produce a new adult-size blanket very frequently." As wild game populations diminished, by about AD 1050 turkeys became a food source for Ancestral Puebloans. "Previous research by Lipe and his colleagues has shown that turkeys were domesticated in southeast Utah by about AD 100, yet it took almost a thousand years before people began eating them as a regular source of food," explains textile expert Laurie Webster. "From the beginning, these birds appear to have been revered for their feathers."[15] The ritual value of their feathers continues today for use attached to prayer or *paho* sticks, as fans for dancers, and for other purposes. Maybe that astute observer of human nature Benjamin Franklin was right when he recommended that the wild turkey become our national bird.

As we gain more understanding of ancient peoples, modern Native Americans living in the Bears Ears region are speaking up. The Navajo Nation seeks to obtain free hunting permits in San Juan County and across Utah arguing that such provisions can be interpreted as part of Article IX of the Navajo Treaty of 1868.[16] A major defender of Navajo sovereignty was Chief Manuelito, who faced incarceration at Fort Sumner but lived to return to his homelands. He was born near Bears Ears. In a cycle of culture coming full circle to honor Manuelito and to help the Navajo Nation, the Office of Navajo Nation Scholarship and Financial Assistance offers the prestigious Chief Manuelito Scholars program. This assistance is for exemplary students who are college bound. Bears Ears is a national monument, but it also represents a birthplace, a homeland. Its preservation will serve as a touchstone for future tribal generations.

For San Juan County residents, one of the legacies of County Commissioner Calvin Black is the Calvin Black Memorial Scholarship program for students who live in the county and seek to attend Utah State University—Blanding. Just like the Manuelito Scholarship, the goal is to educate local students who will stay in the area and have their careers in canyon country. The four scholarships, including an achievement scholarship for a graduate of each of the county's six high schools, extend Black's vision into opportunity for local families. The General Scholarship category is open to all ages so San Juan County residents can use it for graduate school or to improve their employment skills. Cal Black always believed in compound interest and long-term planning. The scholarship program that bears his name began with $17,000 and now approaches $5 million in restricted funds.

Across Bears Ears, Hopis claim numerous petroglyphs of spirals as proof of their clan migrations. The Bears Ears region has always been about circles, about coming and going over generations and centuries, and one of those circles at the genesis of the Antiquities Act has now been completed. Congress passed the Antiquities Act in 1906 in response to widespread looting of Native American artifacts at different locations in the United States, but specifically across the Southwest and the Four Corners region. Before Mesa Verde National Park had been created the Wetherill brothers guided Swedish scientist Gustaf Nordenskiold into the canyons draining into the Mancos River. In 1891 he dug up and shipped to Europe ancient skeletons and grave offerings that were finally returned from Finland in the fall of 2020.

Twenty Ancestral Puebloans and twenty-eight funerary objects were reburied in a quiet, private ceremony at the national park. The affiliated tribes observed four days of official mourning after the reburial. The cycle of life, death, and interment has now been allowed to continue. "Our hearts are happy that our ancestors have made their journey home and are at rest where they belong," stated Fredrick Medina, Governor of the Pueblo of Zia.[17] "As their descendants, the A:shiwi continue to practice the shared Puebloan values and ways of life to this day. Even as modern-day boundaries and jurisdictions disrupt our dedication, through our age-old prayers, we have realized this event. In doing so, we honor their vision and intent to share resources, blood, and resiliency. *Elahkwa*." explained Val R. Panteah Sr., Governor of the Pueblo of Zuni.[18] The Mesa Verde reburial of human remains dug up by the Wetherills and Gustaf Nordenskiold is a memorable start. A significant beginning. But dozens if not hundreds of human remains were dug up and taken from Bears Ears sites and have yet to be returned to affiliated tribes.

Another circle is closing. Hundreds of artifacts recovered in the 2009 raid in Blanding are being returned to the Edge of the Cedars State Park Museum over a decade after they were seized by federal agents. The objects have been cataloged, inventoried, and photographed at the Natural History Museum of Utah. Lost in time, ripped from their caves and contexts, at least now the Basketmaker and Ancestral Puebloan artifacts will come home. Named the Cerberus Collection, most artifacts will remain in storage but perhaps a few items will be carefully displayed and interpreted.

The transfer of thousands of acres of Utah State Trust lands within the monument's boundaries has not yet occurred, but the land exchange process has begun. In another circle and cycle of the Bears Ears landscape, federal land that had been given to the State of Utah will now once again become federal land. Most of us go shopping with cash or credit cards. Imagine looking for land with a grocery cart full of blue squares. That's the analogy attorney Michael Johnson gave me on behalf of Utah's State Institutional Trust Lands Administration (SITLA). He may soon work with other staff to explore an exchange of 120,000 acres of state trust lands surrounded by federal land. On a color-coded map of Obama's original Bears Ears National Monument, plenty of blue squares stand out—sections of state trust land in 640-acre parcels.

In a letter to the Utah governor, former Secretary of the Interior Sally Jewell described "significant progress toward developing a conceptual framework and map for a land exchange that would benefit the State's schoolchildren and enhance protection of cultural and biological treasures." Jewell wrote, "I have great confidence, however, that these efforts will be carried forward in the next Administration and that a commonsense land exchange . . . will come to fruition."[19] It did not. Lobbyists from the energy and uranium industries got to the Trump Administration first. The goals of Native peoples were ignored.

But now an exchange may occur. We're back to square one or at least back to little blue squares. SITLA staff are dusting off the work they did a few years back, but exactly how do you swap 120,000 acres of Utah State Trust land for income-producing federal land? And how did the map get blue squares in the first place?

As Utah evolved from a territory to a state in 1896, the state's enabling act stipulated that for every township of about 23,000 acres, four sections of 640 acres each would be set aside as state land. All the rest remained federal land open to federal laws including homesteading, mining, and grazing. Utah received sections numbered 2, 16, 32, and 36. These are the little blue squares on a land ownership map different from green squares for USFS, beige for the BLM, and white for private property. Attorney Johnson explains that Utah received more state land than some other Western states because "it is an arid state, so the acreage grant got bumped up."[20]

Part of the future of Bears Ears National Monument will be respectful archaeological adventure tourism. In this photo, a group visits a dramatic Bears Ears site, which includes a room with an intact roof that is the earliest tree-ring dated cliff dwelling in the greater Cedar Mesa area. It dates from the AD 860s. Author photo.

Johnson's office will work on the land swap. Most state inholdings within Bears Ears will become federal land. But who wants to trade and for what? Before the dominoes can fall, an elaborate chess game must take place including approval by the Utah State Legislature and then the US Congress. SITLA's mission is clear—create funding for statewide educational institutions, grade schools to universities, from "lands held in trust for beneficiaries." Johnson will "look for anything that can be used to generate revenue and the more the better" to add to the $2.3 billion now administered by the State Treasurer's Office.[21] What is at stake is protecting the vast Bears Ears landscape, which includes Ancestral Puebloan roads, shrines, pueblos, cliff dwellings, and, according to Friends of Cedar Mesa, "what may be Utah's highest concentration of Navajo and Ute archaeology, including rare petroglyph panels."

"The scattered sections within the monument will likely be traded out," Johnson agrees, especially those "rich in cultural resources and topographically challenging." This land exchange is a giant game of Monopoly, only instead of buying Park Place and Baltic Avenue, it's about the state "trading into" federal acreage. Johnson says with a sigh, "There are a lot of moving parts particularly when you intend to seek an act of Congress." SITLA is not obligated to exchange for federal lands within San Juan County though there might be political pressure to do so. Attorney Johnson states, "There will always be people who question the lands we select, but we have to move forward."[22] Hopefully, full and complete protection of Bears Ears is on its way. Hopefully, we will soon preserve an intact Native landscape to honor the Ancient Ones whose spirits remain in the cliffs and canyons.

On the bright side, new Bears Ears National Monument staff have been hired. They continue twenty years of extensive monitoring of raptors in the Indian Creek area of the monument. BLM biologists intercede between rock climbers and eagles, falcons, and other migratory birds using the same cliffs but for different purposes. Climbers climb while raptors nest. Potential conflict exists at well-known climbing routes like the Wall, Far Side, the Meat Walls, Disappointment Cliffs, Fin Wall, Broken Tooth, Cat Wall, Slug Wall, and Reservoir Wall. Each spring the BLM announces updated climbing avoidance areas. Climbers make room for peregrine falcons that can rocket by at seventy miles per hour and free fall dive at 240 miles per hour—neither of which are speeds climbers want to achieve, especially in descent.

Bears Ears has hundreds of remote archaeological sites, some of which have been stabilized. Prehistoric structures may be found on narrow sandstone ledges, which are difficult and dangerous to access. Author photo.

I have not come nose to nose with a peregrine on a cliff, but I have been intrigued by bat monitoring equipment set up in upper Butler Wash where the monument biologist is trying to determine via bioacoustics monitoring which bat species live in Bears Ears. That's just one more piece of science we do not yet understand about the vast Bears Ears landscape. Perhaps with monument management and Native involvement biologists can even return desert bighorns featured on most Basketmaker and Ancestral Puebloan rock art panels. The State of Utah reintroduced desert bighorns close to Johns Canyon, White Canyon, and Mossback Butte, but Bears Ears is big enough to take many more of these iconic animals.

Tourism will inevitably increase, and that's the trade-off for monument designation—more people, more visitors, but also the opportunity for education and better archaeological and cultural site protection. The tourism push into the area began with local chambers of commerce in the 1960s and numerous articles in *Desert Magazine.* One such article from 1966 described a shift in the style of family vacations. "There are some who think Southeastern Utah's scenery is inspiration to adults and boredom to children. They roar along freeways towards beaches or Disneylands, they fill trailers with fishing rods and water-skis, and vow that the only way to family vacation is 'go where there's plenty of action,'" wrote Raye Price, who added, "We tried it the other way. A few experiences in back country had taught us the satisfactions of bumping along trackless roads in dusty deserts to ogle wind-carved formations, study prehistoric ruins, and swallow red dirt with tuna fish sandwiches on a tail-gate picnic."[23]

What began as a vacation trickle has become a deluge as younger generations value hiking in remote places, steering their four-wheel-drive vehicles up rocky, rutted roads, and camping far from developed campgrounds. Visits to public lands are increasing. Americans are spending more on trail sports gear than on home entertainment. The national outdoor recreation economy annually generates billions in consumer spending.[24]

Bears Ears has now become a destination with an estimated 425,000 visitors in 2020.[25] Thankfully, preservation groups like Friends of Cedar Mesa have been awarded $300,000 as part of a $1 million campaign to protect at-risk sites in the new national monument.[26] There are preservation success stories. In previous decades ranchers used bulldozers and logging chains on Cedar Mesa to level pinyon and juniper trees to supposedly make more room for grass to feed cattle. But such indiscriminate chaining leveled ancient archaeological sites. A case study of decimation and now preservation includes the acreage around Cave Towers on State

High school teacher Ashley Carruth, a veteran bikepacker and explorer, has pedaled 500 miles across Bears Ears National Monument. Remote outdoor recreation and visitation will be a hallmark of the monument. Carruth likes to quote Terry Tempest Williams, who wrote, "We, too, can humbly raise our hands with those who have gone before and those who will follow." Photo by Sarah Tescher.

Institutional Trust Administration Lands. New parking, interpretive signs, and wooden fencing, with much work done by volunteers from Friends of Cedar Mesa, now beckon visitors to where Ancestral Puebloans built towers and structures in the last years of their Bears Ears occupation. The landscape slowly recovers.

But if tourists are coming, in some of southeast Utah's small towns they are not welcome. "San Juan County has never been a bubbling bastion of enthusiasm for tourism, the recreation industry or any business attached to the legal designation of wilderness," writes canyon country curmudgeon Jim Stiles. "Its hostility toward non-motorized activities like backpacking is almost legendary. It has exhibited an almost pathological loathing of environmentalists and wilderness groups like SUWA [Southern Utah Wilderness Alliance]."[27] Stiles worries about the impact of "industrial tourism," Ed Abbey's phrase. Indeed, in recent years the paved entrance to Arches National Park near Moab, Utah, has looked like a parking lot with eager visitors stuck in idling vehicles, trapped in long, static waiting lines.

According to Stiles, what is at stake is not just resource damage to archaeological sites but also "the same kind of demographic change that happened in Moab. This is about changing the social fabric of a small town [Blanding or Monticello] from one that is essentially rural and conservative to a more 'progressive/mainstream green' New West population center."[28] A former resident of San Juan County, Amy Irvine adds, "And so I finally see to truly inhabit a place is to learn to dwell with the differences that threaten to divide it."[29] Local Bluff writer Zak Podmore also ponders community and the role of newcomers. He understands it to be a process of compassion and commitment over decades. He writes, "As our bones go into the ground, as our dust blows across the land—that, maybe, is how we begin to belong."[30]

The themes of this book echo over centuries—Bears Ears as a place of refuge and as a place of resistance. It has been and will continue to be both. Bluff, Utah, a truly small town, welcomes visitors but resists development. To avoid exponential growth from tourism and to shun Moab's madness, Bluff residents continue to vote against a town sewer system—no sewers, no chain restaurants, and no chain motels. Outside of conservative Blanding, Utah, a highway sign boasts "BLANDING: BASE CAMP FOR ADVENTURE." Note that's not Blanding: Base Camp for Ranching or Base Camp for Gas Drilling. Perhaps Blanding may join the New West after all. South of town westward on Highway 95, which was Cal Black's pride and Ed Abbey's nemesis, is another sign. This one is for a real estate subdivision that proclaims, "Rural Lots—Best Views of Bears Ears." A billboard greets tourists as they enter Monument Valley. It shouts, "SAN JUAN COUNTY: THE WORLD'S GREATEST OUTDOOR MUSEUM," and that's fairly accurate. Certainly, it is true for Bears Ears National Monument.

Ironically, after San Juan County politicians fought so hard against Obama's Bears Ears and congratulated themselves on Trump shrinking the national monument, the county tourism committee came up with a new slogan to boost San Juan County—"Make it Monumental!"

Oldtimers may grumble over changes, but tourists are on their way. Each spring, summer, and fall tourists drive their rental cars, campers, and trailers between Mesa Verde, Grand Canyon, Arches, and Canyonlands with Bears Ears National Monument now cozily in the middle.

In response to increased visitation, I've become a cairn kicker. As I hike the Bears Ears back country and see excessive stone cairns leading to remote sites, I give them a little nod with my hiking boots and stacked stones tumble off sandstone ledges. Ed Abbey pulled up wooden highway stakes in Arches where surveyors had planned a new road. Cactus Ed did so to slow the very outcome that occurred—a two-lane asphalt roadbed leading toward Delicate Arch with numerous tourist turnouts. One way to preserve sites in Bears Ears is to make tourists find their own routes into the canyons. Topple a few cairns. Why not? That's what adventure is for.

A little route finding for a slick rock descent never hurt anyone. After all, one of the slogans for hiking in wilderness and natural areas is to "Leave No Trace." I have disassembled a homemade ladder at the mouth of a cave. It was positioned to ascend to a habitation site built on centuries of deposition. Forty feet above me I saw soot from ancient fires covering a ceiling. Beside me the ladder crafted from cottonwood branches balanced precariously in soft soil. Placement of the ladder exposed stacked stone from a kiva wall a few feet away. I untied the wooden branches used to make the rustic ladder. I tossed them into oak brush and gathered the climbers' cord to recycle it again.

The BLM now considers approximately fourteen archaeological sites in Bears Ears "hardened" and available for regular tourist visitation. Thankfully, thousands of sites exist for which there are no directions. The hope is Bears Ears will be a landscape laboratory for Indigenous archaeology where visitors will travel with respect. "The proof of our ancestral presence is found in the archaeological record in the form of ancestral villages ("ruins"), rock art, ceramics, textiles, lithics, burials, shrines, and many other 'artifacts,'" explains Hopi archaeologist Lyle Balenquah. "In the Hopi perspective, all of these are viewed as 'footprints of the ancestors,' left in place to one day prove our previous occupations in these areas. In doing so, these landscapes become holy ground where ancestors dwell."[31]

Over the last two decades, I have found manos, metates, arrowheads, spearpoints, stone knife blades, and small and large pottery sherds. I have left each one in place or perhaps covered it with soft sand to avoid detection. Sadly, some sites have now been picked clean of their once numerous pottery sherds, reducing the Hopi concept of ancestral footprints and an Indigenous archaeological opportunity for research. Ancestral villages still stand tucked under sandstone ledges—some with geometric patterns of diamonds and triangles in the chipped stones inserted into mortar centuries ago. There are patterns from indented footprints, fingerprints, and whimsical impressions from corncobs pressed into wet adobe mud, all of which speaks across time to the humanity and artistry

Hiking in Bears Ears can reveal outstanding surprises across the landscape of cliff dwellings and approaches to Ancestral Puebloan sites carefully constructed eight centuries ago. Author photo.

of the ancients, the Old Ones, who migrated in and out of the canyons but whose spirits remain.

In Bears Ears the value of silence, solitude, and darkness is unparalleled. All three are getting a little harder to find, but for the intrepid back country hiker, there are still archaeological sites with intact roofs, original stone doors, and no trails to them. In remote washes I swear I've heard the laughing chatter of children only to hike up canyon to find ravens carrying on private conversations, muttering to themselves beneath arching alcoves.

In 1872 in Wyoming and Montana, Yellowstone became the first national park. In June 1906 when Theodore Roosevelt signed into law the Antiquities Act, he also signed legislation creating Mesa Verde National Park as the world's first cultural park. He set it aside for its cliff dwellings and cultural values unlike Yellowstone, which Congress saved for its geysers, its wildlife, and its scenery. Seven decades after Roosevelt signed the Antiquities Act, President Jimmy Carter used the law to proclaim national monuments in Alaska as a sweeping gesture of conservation and preservation in the twentieth century. Angry Alaskans burned Carter in effigy and threatened incoming park rangers.

In December 2016 President Barack Obama designated Bears Ears National Monument combining BLM, USFS, and NPS land. It was a marvelous twenty-first century use of an historic law, and this time, for the first time, Native tribes asked for preservation of their own cultural heritage. The Bears Ears Inter-Tribal Coalition succeeded. "The partnership demonstrated an unprecedented reliance on tribal consultation for the federal government. For many Indigenous leaders, it became a blueprint for how to involve tribes in the stewardship of lands that were originally stolen from them but are also important to the country as a whole," reports *High Country News*.[32] Other publications also support Bears Ears as a vital new national monument.[33]

Ute Mountain Ute tribal member Ernest House Jr. concurs: "It's been said that collaboration happens at the speed of trust. If done correctly and with tribal voices at the table, Bears Ears has the potential to re-shape the federal, tribal, state, and local collaborative process based on respect, understanding, and trust."[34] Bears Ears—a Mesa Verde for the twenty-first century—will hopefully remain back country with few if any trail signs, no pavement, no turnouts, and with Native consultation on interpretation and site preservation.

A few decades after Carter's designation of Alaskan national monuments, as Alaskans came to see the economic value of tourism, small towns officially rescinded their resolutions opposing President Carter using the Antiquities Act. No such change in political posturing has yet happened in San Juan County. In early 2021 Blanding and Monticello city councils passed a joint resolution opposing the reinstatement of Bears Ears monument. Grand County commissioners and the town of Moab voted to support the original monument boundaries. The town council of Bluff voted to support the boundaries and expand them to the tribes' initial request of 1.9 million acres.[35] Whatever happens, the canyons have their own sweep of time.

Star-strewn night skies soar above Bears Ears. Under a full moon it can be so bright as to banish sleep but not the magic and mystery of such a storied landscape. There are so many things to discover and so many riddles to ponder if one moves slowly. Once hiking on a ledge directly below a smooth sandstone cliff, I sat on a large ponderosa log both coming and going. It was big enough to block the faint route. As I leaned against it a second time, I suddenly realized there was no wood like this anywhere near. All around me were pinyon-juniper trees. Then I questioned if the log had been a ladder, now fallen, brought there by Ancestral Puebloans and placed against a cleft in the cliff as an ingenious way to descend from the mesa top above. I marveled at the prodigious effort moving this log might have meant because the nearest tall trees were seven miles away. Slowly walking back along the ledge, I wondered what else I had missed in the quiet of the canyon.

Notes

ACKNOWLEDGMENTS

1. Ellen Meloy, *The Last Cheater's Waltz* (New York: Henry Holt, 1999), 202.
2. Zak Podmore, "'We Will Circle All the Wagons,': Newly Obtained Emails Show San Juan County's Push to Reduce Bears Ears," *Salt Lake Tribune*, April 8, 2021.
3. Klara Kelley and Harris Francis, *A Diné History of Navajoland* (Tucson: University of Arizona Press, 2019), 83.
4. Jedediah S. Rogers and Mathew C. Godfrey, eds., *The Earth Will Appear as the Garden of Eden* (Salt Lake City: University of Utah Press, 2019), 24.

INTRODUCTION

1. Robert S. McPherson, *Comb Ridge and Its People: The Ethnohistory of a Rock* (Logan: Utah State University Press, 2009), 24–5.
2. Patricia L. Price, *Dry Place: Landscapes of Belonging and Exclusion* (Minneapolis: University of Minnesota Press, 2004), xiii, xvi.
3. Price, 34.
4. Naming sites on local landscapes is well-documented in memory studies and historical geography which both describe the politics of place-naming. In Ireland, the Irish have brought back Gaelic names after centuries of English place names. See Robert Macfarlane, *The Wild Places* (New York: Penguin Books, 2007). A standard reference for Native American place names is Keith Basso, *Wisdom Sits in Places* (University of New Mexico Press, 1996). For place names in the Grand Canyon, see Stephen Hirst, *I Am the Grand Canyon: The Story of the Havasupai People* (Grand Canyon, AZ: Grand Canyon Association, 2006), and Barbara J. Morehouse, *A Place Called Grand Canyon: Contested Geographies* (Tucson: University of Arizona Press, 1996).
5. McPherson, *Comb Ridge*, 76.
6. Amy Irvine, *Trespass: Living at the Edge of the Promised Land* (New York: North Point Press, 2008), 110.

7. For Devils Tower, see Hal Rothman, *America's National Monuments: The Politics of Preservation* (Lawrence: University Press of Kansas, 1989). For the Kiowa story of Bear's Lodge, see N. Scott Momaday, *The Way to Rainy Mountain* (Albuquerque: University of New Mexico Press, 1969).
8. Mark Stoll, "Religion Irradiates the Wilderness," in Michael Lewis, ed. *American Wilderness: A New History* (New York: Oxford University Press, 2004), 43.
9. Angelo Baca, "Bears Ears Is Here to Stay," *New York Times*, December 8, 2017.
10. Wallace Stegner, *Mormon Country* (Lincoln: University of Nebraska Press, 2003), 331.
11. Barack Obama, Proclamation 9558, "Proclamation—Establishment of the Bears Ears National Monument," The White House, December 28, 2016.
12. Terry Tempest Williams, *Red: Passion and Patience in the Desert* (New York: Random House, 2001), 195.
13. Williams, 6.
14. Edward Abbey, *Beyond the Wall* (New York: Henry Holt, 1984), 54.
15. Abbey, 55.
16. Abbey, 55.
17. Abbey, 58. Note the reference to blank spots on the map is from Aldo Leopold, *A Sand County Almanac* (New York: Ballantine Books). The full quote is, "Of what avail are forty freedoms without a blank spot on the map?"
18. Gary Topping, *Glen Canyon and the San Juan Country* (Moscow: University of Idaho Press, 1997), 151.
19. Barack Obama, Proclamation 9558.
20. Robert Macfarlane, *Mountains of the Mind: Adventures in Reaching the Summit* (New York: Vintage Books, 2004), 18.

CHAPTER 1

1. William E. Davis, "The First Americans in San Juan County," *Blue Mountain Shadows* 13 (Summer 1994): 6.
2. Davis, 6.
3. The idea of "Clovis first" people migrating across the Western United States may now be discredited with a cave site in central Mexico that dates 33,000 years before present. But if that date is correct, additional collaborative dates of sites used by migrating peoples traveling south from the Arctic need to be confirmed.
4. Davis, "The First Americans," 4. For the migration of early Paleo-Indians see Craig Childs, *Atlas of a Lost World: Travels in Ice Age America* (New York: Pantheon Books, 2018).
5. For an interesting perspective on those Archaic hunters, see Doug Peacock, *In the Shadow of the Sabertooth: Global Warming, the Origins of the*

First Americans, and the Terrible Beasts of the Pleistocene (Oakland, CA: Counter Punch and AK Press, 2013).

6. Ekkehart Malotki and Henry D. Wallace, "Columbian Mammoth Petroglyphs from the San Juan River near Bluff, Utah, United States," *Rock Art Research* 28, no. 2: 143–52.
7. Winston Hurst, "Ice Age Rock Art on the San Juan River?", *Blue Mountain Shadows* 44 (Fall 2011), San Juan County Historical Commission, Monticello, Utah.
8. Hurst, 6.
9. Hurst, 6.
10. Andrew Gulliford, "How to Find a 13,000-Year-Old Mammoth," *High Country News*, January 19, 2012.
11. To understand the importance of the Clovis find in New Mexico and the Black cowboy who made the discovery, see Tony Hillerman, "The Hunt for the Lost American," in *The Great Taos Bank Robbery and other Indian Country Affairs* (Albuquerque: University of New Mexico Press, 1973).
12. For one scholar's perspective on the speed and effectiveness of Clovis hunting groups, see Shepard Krech III, "Pleistocene Extinctions," in *The Ecological Indian: Myth and History* (New York: Pantheon, 1999).
13. Andrew Gulliford, "Condors in the Canyons," *Archaeology Southwest* 33, nos. 1 & 2 (Winter & Spring 2019): 15.
14. Dale Davidson, Phil Geib, and Nancy Coulam, "San Juan County Almost 8,000 Years Ago: Ongoing Excavations at Old Man Cave," *Blue Mountain Shadows* 13 (Summer 1994): 7–12.
15. Andrew Gulliford, "Hunters and Artists: Glen Canyon Rock Art Created by an Ancient Culture on the Move," *Durango Herald*, May 11, 2019.
16. Gulliford.
17. Alan R. Schroedl, "The Grand Canyon Figurine Complex," *American Antiquity* 42, no. 2 (April 1977): 254–65.
18. Sally J. Cole, *Legacy on Stone: Rock Art of the Colorado Plateau and Four Corners Region* (Boulder, CO: Johnson Books, 1990), 63–8.
19. Joe Pachak, "Early Rock Art on the San Juan River," *Blue Mountain Shadows* 13 (Summer 1994): 16–22.
20. Edward Abbey, *Beyond the Wall* (New York: Henry Holt, 1984), 91–3. For another perspective on rock art as art see Kevin T. Jones, *Standing on the Walls of Time: Ancient Art of Utah's Cliffs and Canyons* (Salt Lake City: University of Utah Press, 2019). Former state archaeologist Jones campaigned for rock art to become a state symbol, which it did under Utah Code 63G-1-601.

CHAPTER 2

1. An important resource to begin to understand Basketmaker culture and sites is Victoria M. Atkins, ed., *Anasazi Basketmaker: Papers from the 1990 Wetherill—Grand Gulch Symposium*, Cultural Resource Series no. 24,

United States Department of the Interior, Bureau of Land Management, Salt Lake City, Utah, November 1993. An excellent popular version of this research with stunning color photographs is Fred M. Blackburn and Ray A. Williamson, *Cowboys & Cave Dwellers: Basketmaker Archaeology in Utah's Grand Gulch* (Santa Fe, NM: School of American Research, 1997). For San Juan Anthropomorphic rock art style, see Sally Cole, *Legacy on Stone: Rock Art of the Colorado Plateau and Four Corners Region* (Boulder, CO: Johnson Books, 1990).

2. This reference to Basketmaker people sleeping with their feet to the fire was told to me by Zia elder Peter Pino during our Mesa Verde National Park tour as a benefit for the Mesa Verde Foundation in October 2019.
3. An excellent recent overview of Basketmaker research with specific references to Comb Ridge and Cedar Mesa in Bears Ears National Monument is Sally J. Cole, ed. *Regional Perspectives on Basketmaker II, Southwestern Lore* 77, nos. 2 & 3 (Summer/Fall 2011).
4. Florence Lister, *Troweling Through Time* (Albuquerque: University of New Mexico Press, 2004).
5. William D. Lipe et al., "Cultural and Genetic Contexts for Early Turkey Domestication in the Northern Southwest," *American Antiquity* 81, no. 1 (2016): 97.
6. Lipe et al., 99–100.
7. To understand desert bighorns as a species, see Ellen Meloy, *Eating Stone: Imagination and the Loss of the Wild* (New York: Vintage Books, 2005).
8. For drawings and photographs of Basketmaker rock art, see Polly Schaafsma, "The Rock Art of Utah from the Donald Scott Collections," *Papers of the Peabody Museum of Archaeology and Ethnology Vol. 65* (Cambridge, MA: Harvard University, 1971), and the updated version, Schaafsma, *The Rock Art of Utah* (Salt Lake City: University of Utah Press, 1994). Also see Dave Manley, *Ancient Galleries of Cedar Mesa* (Moab, UT: Canyonlands Natural History Association, 2016).
9. Richard H. Wilshusen, Gregson Schachner, and James R. Allison, *Crucible of Pueblos: The Early Pueblo Period in the Northern Southwest*, Monograph 71 (Los Angeles: Cotsen Institute of Archaeology Press, University of California, 2012), 209. Also see Steven James Manning, "The Lobed-Circle Image in the Basketmaker Petroglyphs of Southeastern Utah," *Utah Archaeology* 5, no. 1 (1992): 1–38.
10. To understand Basketmaker rock art and skinned heads, also described as scalps, see Alfred Vincent Kidder and Samuel J. Guernsey, *Archaeological Explorations in Northeastern Arizona*, Smithsonian Institution, Bureau of American Ethnology, Bulletin 65 (Washington, DC: Government Printing Office, 1919), 190–2. In a personal communication with me, Bill Lipe explained, "Sally Cole was early to recognize the depictions of full-face scalps in some of the Cedar Mesa rock art, and to link it to the occurrence

of actual full-face scalps from rock shelters in Northeast Arizona." Sally J. Cole, "Additional information on Basketmaker mask or face representations in rock art of Southeastern Utah," *Southwest Lore* 51, no. 1 (1985): 14–8; Cole, "Iconography and Symbolism in Basketmaker Rock Art," in Jane S. Day, Paul O. Friedman, and Marcia J. Tate, eds. *Rock Art of the Western Canyons,* Cultural Resource Series 28 (Denver: Colorado Bureau of Land Management, 1990), 59–85; Cole, "Basketmaker rock art at the Green Mask site, southeastern Utah," in Victoria M. Atkins, ed. *Anasazi Basketmaker: Papers from the 1990 Wetherill—Grand Gulch Symposium,* Cultural Resource Series 4 (Salt Lake City: Bureau of Land Management, 1990), 193–222. Also see Polly Schaafsma, "Head Trophies and Scalping," in R.J. Chacon and D.H. Dye, eds., *The Taking and Displaying of Human Body Parts as Trophies of Amerindians—Interdisciplinary Contributions to Archaeology* (Boston: Springer Publications, 2007); Phil R. Geib, "Basketmaker II Warfare and Fending Sticks in the North American Southwest," (PhD diss., University of New Mexico, 2016), 111–24.

11. Earl H. Morris and Robert F. Burgh, *Anasazi Basketry Basketmaker II through Pueblo III: A Study Based on Specimens from the San Juan River Country,* Publication 533 (Washington, DC: Carnegie Institute of Washington, 1941), 57.
12. Spirals on rock, rock art imagery, may also mean wind, water, snakes, and symbols of past events.
13. An earlier version of this essay appeared in Andrew Gulliford, ed., *Outdoors in the Southwest: An Adventure Anthology* (Norman: University of Oklahoma Press, 2015). For an excellent fiction and nonfiction anthology related to the Anasazi, see Ruben Ellis, *Stories on Stone: Tales from the Anasazi Heartland* (Boulder, CO: Pruett Publishing, 1997), and to learn more about Comb Ridge, see Robert S. McPherson, *Comb Ridge and Its People: The Ethnohistory of a Rock* (Logan: Utah State University Press, 2009).
14. An original ancient, crooked neck staff can be seen on display at the Edge of the Cedars Museum and State Park in Blanding, Utah.
15. Robert L. Powell, "Procession Panel Site Comb Ridge, San Juan County, Utah, 42SA21153," 1991.
16. Powell.
17. A former BLM archaeologist thinks that the circle, which represents a great kiva, may actually be the great kiva site six to seven miles north in Comb Wash.
18. Wilshusen et al., 122, 209.
19. Wilshusen et al.
20. Kellam Throgmorton, "Rock Art, Architecture, and Social Groups at the Basketmaker III–Pueblo I Transition: Evidence from the Procession Panel, Southeast Utah," *Kiva: Journal of Southwestern Anthropology and History* 83, no. 2: 137–61.

21. Throgmorton.
22. For a generalized look at violence see Steven A. LeBlanc, *Constant Battles: The Myth of the Peaceful, Noble Savage* (New York: St. Martin's Press, 2003).
23. Chuck LaRue, personal communication by telephone, December 3, 2020.
24. Andrew Gillreath-Brown et al., "Redefining the Age of Tattooing in Western North America: A 2,000-Year-Old Artifact from Utah," *Journal of Archaeological Science: Reports* (February 10, 2019). According to a retired BLM agent, a similar tattoo implement is in government-recovered collections at the Edge of the Cedars State Park Museum in Blanding, Utah.
25. Bill Lipe, personal communication, November 25, 2020.
26. For a quick overview of pottery styles, see Louis A. Green, *Layman's Field Guide to Ancestral Puebloan Pottery Northern San Juan/Mesa Verde Region* (Montgomery, AL: Minuteman Press, 2010). For an even faster reference for hikers, drawings of pottery sherds have been reproduced on a cotton bandana easy to pull out of a pack. The fifteen-dollar bandana, sold locally in San Juan County, Utah, has drawings of sherds and the admonition "Leave it where you find it." To understand trade networks and ceramics of Ancestral Puebloans, see Norman T. Oppelt, "Pottery and Other Intrusive Materials in Mesa Verde National Park," *Southwestern Lore* 68, no. 4 (Winter 2002): 1–10.
27. See Teri L. Paul, ed., *Edge of the Cedars State Park Museum, COLLECTIONS* (Virginia Beach, VA: Donning Company Publishers, 2009).
28. Ben Bellorado, personal communication, December 6, 2020.
29. There are numerous books on the Chaco Canyon phenomenon, but start with Stephen Lekson, *A History of the Ancient Southwest* (Santa Fe, NM: School of American Research, 2008); Brian Fagan, *Chaco Canyon* (New York: Oxford University Press, 2005); and David E. Stuart, *Anasazi America* (Albuquerque: University of New Mexico Press, 2000).
30. For a brief, well-illustrated book on Chaco, see Michal Strutin, *Chaco: A Cultural Legacy* (Tucson, AZ: Southwest Parks & Monuments Association, 1994).
31. Instead of egalitarian Native peoples, elites ruled Chaco. See Stephen Lekson, *A History of the Ancient Southwest* (Santa Fe, NM: School of American Research, 2008).
32. Joanna Klein, "In an Ancient Burial Place, 3 Centuries of One Woman's Descendants," *New York Times*, February 24, 2017. To understand Chaco's vast turquoise trade, see Sharon Hull et al., "Turquoise Trade of the Ancestral Puebloan: Chaco and Beyond," *Journal of Archaeological Science* 45 (2014): 187–95.
33. Craig Childs, *House of Rain* (New York: Little, Brown, 2006), 20.
34. Susan Montoya Brown, "Chocolate's Ancient Path Leads to Chaco Canyon," *Durango Herald*, September 28, 2019. For cacao use near Bears Ears, see Dorothy K. Washburn, William N. Washburn, and Petia A. Shipkova,

"Cacao Consumption During the 8th Century at Alkali Ridge, Southeastern Utah," *Journal of Archaeological Science* 40, no. 4 (2013): 2007–13. Refer also to the Utah Chocolate Story at the Natural History Museum of Utah.

35. To understand the Bluff Great House site and area trade networks, see Catherine M. Cameron, *Chaco and After in the Northern San Juan* (Tucson: University of Arizona Press, 2009).
36. For understanding a Chacoan outlier on the northeast edge of the Chacoan world see Florence C. Lister, *In the Shadow of the Rocks: Archaeology of the Chimney Rock District in Southwest Colorado*, 2nd ed. (Durango, CO: Durango Herald Small Press, 2011). President Obama declared Chimney Rock a national monument now administered by the USFS.
37. Benjamin A. Bellorado, "Leaving Footprints in the Ancient Southwest: Visible Indicators of Group Affiliation and Social Position in the Chaco and Post-Chaco Eras (AD 850–1300)," (PhD diss., University of Arizona, 2020). For a synopsis, see Bellorado, "Sandals and Sandal Symbolism in Greater Bears Ears and Beyond," *Archaeology Southwest* (2018): 39–41.
38. Stephen Lekson, *The Chaco Meridian: One Thousand Years of Political and Religious Power in the Ancient Southwest*, 2nd ed. (New York: Rowman & Littlefield, 2015).
39. Chaco's collapse brought about more prehistoric warfare. See Douglas Preston, "A Reporter at Large: Cannibals of the Canyon," *The New Yorker*, November 30, 1998; Christy G. Turner, "A Reign of Terror: Butchered Human Bones Point to Cannibals in Chaco Canyon," *Discovering Archaeology*, May/June 1999; and Stephen Lekson, "War in the Southwest, War in the World," *American Antiquity* 67, no. 4 (2002): 607–24. To put Chaco's collapse in context, see Lekson, *A Study of Southwestern Archaeology* (Salt Lake City: University of Utah Press, 2018).

CHAPTER 3

1. For photographs and historic anthropological drawings that explain the defensive nature of cliff dwellings, see Beth and Bill Sagstetter, *The Cliff Dwellings Speak: Exploring the Ancient Ruins of the Greater American Southwest* (Denver, CO: Benchmark Publishing, 2010). For defensive architecture at Mesa Verde, see Larry V. Nordby, "Control Point/Defensive Architecture at Mesa Verde During the 13th Century," Paper presented at the 67th Annual Meeting, Society for American Archaeology, Denver, Colorado, March 2002.
2. Debra L. Martin, "Ripped Flesh and Torn Souls," in *Invisible Citizens: Captives and Their Consequences*, Catherine M. Cameron, ed. (Salt Lake City: University of Utah Press, Foundations of Archaeological Inquiry, 2008), 165.
3. For excellent photographic documentation of Bears Ears area cliff dwellings, see Don Kirby and Joan Gentry, *The Anasazi Project* (Portland, OR:

Nazraeli Press, 2012); Donald J. Rommes and William D. Lipe, *Cliff Dwellers of Cedar Mesa: The Culture, Sites, and Exodus of the Ancestral Puebloans* (Moab, UT: Canyonlands Natural History Association, 2013); William D. Lipe, ed., "Tortuous and Fantastic: Culture and Natural Wonders of Greater Cedar Mesa," *Archaeology Southwest* 28, nos. 3 & 4, (Summer/Fall 2014); and Jonathan Bailey, *Rock Art: A Vision of a Vanishing Cultural Landscape* (Denver, CO: Johnson Books, 2019).

4. One of my Hopi students at Fort Lewis College explained to me that the word for these refuge sites has not changed in thousands of years. The word was learned by children so they would know where to flee to. When in modern times Hopis tried to prevent their children from attending boarding schools, elders used the same word so children would flee to a refuge or safe location known by only a few.
5. A few authors believe that Ancestral Puebloan violence included cannibalism. See Christy G. Turner II and Jacqueline A. Turner, *Man Corn: Cannibalism and Violence in the Prehistoric American Southwest* (Salt Lake City: University of Utah Press, 1999). Also see Joseph B. Verrengia, "Ancient Southwestern Tribe Ate Humans, Researchers Say," *Portland Oregonian*, September 7, 2000, A2.
6. Timothy A. Kohler, Mark D. Varien, and Aaron M. Wright, eds., *Leaving Mesa Verde: Peril and Change in the Thirteenth Century Southwest* (Tucson: University of Arizona Press, Amerind Studies in Archaeology, 2010), 10. For a general photographic overview of Ancestral Puebloan sites, see William M. Ferguson and Arthur H. Rohn, *Anasazi Ruins of the Southwest in Color* (Albuquerque: University of New Mexico Press, 1994), and William M. Ferguson, *The Anasazi of Mesa Verde and the Four Corners* (Niwot: University Press of Colorado, 1996).
7. Kohler et al., *Leaving Mesa Verde*, 15.
8. Kohler et al., 7.
9. Kathryn A. Kamp, *Children in the Prehistoric Puebloan Southwest* (Salt Lake City: University of Utah Press, 2002), 160.
10. To understand Puebloan violence in the historic period and its ramifications for warfare in prehistory, see James F. Brooks, *Mesa of Sorrows: A History of the Awat'Ovi Massacre* (New York: Norton, 2016). For a milder version of Utah prehistory, see Jesse D. Jennings, "Early Man in Utah," *Utah Historical Quarterly* (January 1960): 3–28.
11. Kohler et al., *Leaving Mesa Verde*, 179.
12. Ben Bellorado, personal communication, December 6, 2020.
13. To understand the many uses of juniper, see Kristen Rogers-Iversen, *Interwoven: Junipers and the Web of Being* (Salt Lake City: University of Utah Press, 2018).
14. For an excellent, easy to read understanding of archaeological sites and clan migrations at the end of the thirteenth century, see Craig Childs, *House of*

Rain: Tracking a Vanished Civilization Across the American Southwest (New York: Little Brown, 2006).

15. Hal Rothman, "The Antiquities Act and National Monuments: A Progressive Conservation Legacy," *CRM*, no. 4: 199.

CHAPTER 4

1. Robert S. McPherson, *Viewing the Ancestors* (Norman: University of Oklahoma Press, 2014), 30–1.
2. Klara Kelley and Harris Francis, *A Diné History of Navajoland* (Tucson: University of Arizona Press, 2019), 14, 31.
3. Kelley and Francis, 31. Whether Navajo ancestors of Athabaskan descent lived in the Southwest at the same time as Ancestral Puebloans is disputed, but an intriguing story about Chaco Canyon does create a link two both groups. Ancestral Puebloans and Navajos have oral traditions about a powerful male gambler at Chaco who took people's possessions and then took their souls. See "The Great Gambler: Icon of Destruction, Example for the Future," ch. 4 in Robert S. McPherson, *Viewing the Ancestors* (Norman: University of Oklahoma Press, 2014). Also see Florence Lister, *Chaco's Vanished Past: Hogans, Tents, and Ruins* (Durango, CO: Durango Herald Small Press, 2008), and Alexandra Witze, "When the Gambler Came to Chaco," *American Archaeology* 22, no. 2 (Summer 2018).
4. Andrew Knaut, *The Pueblo Revolt of 1680* (Norman: University of Oklahoma Press, 1995), 155.
5. Knaut, 155.
6. Joe Sando, *Pueblo Nations: Eight Centuries of Pueblo Indian History* (Santa Fe, NM: Clear Light Publishers, 1992), 1.
7. Kelley and Francis, *A Diné History*, 103.
8. Kelley and Francis. Recent scholarship on Diné migrations include Deni J. Seymour, ed., *From the Land of Ever Winter to the American Southwest: Athabaskan Migration, Mobility, and Ethnogenesis* (Salt Lake City: University of Utah Press, 2012), and Karen Coates, "Walking into New Worlds: Native Traditions and Novel Discoveries Tell the Migration Story of the Ancestors of the Navajo and Apache," *Archaeology Magazine* (August/September 2020). For an explanation as to why Diné migrations may have started south from Alaska, see Briana N. Doering et al., "A Multiscalar Consideration of the Athabaskan Migration," *American Antiquity* 85, no. 3 (2020): 470–91.
9. Andrew Gulliford, "Pueblitos Give Glimpse into Time of Danger," *Durango Herald*, June 19, 2010.
10. Gulliford.
11. Gulliford.
12. Gulliford.

13. Frank McNitt, *Navajo Wars: Military Campaigns, Slave Raids, and Reprisals* (Albuquerque: University of New Mexico Press, 1972), 6.
14. M.A. Stokes and T.L. Smiley, "Tree-Ring Dates from the Navajo Land Claim I. The Northern Sector," *Tree-Ring Bulletin* 25, nos. 3 & 4 (1963): 8–18. For instance, the last piece of wood estimated to have been cut for a Mesa Verde cliff dwelling was AD 1276.
15. For Navajo architectural types and geographic distribution, see Stephen C. Jett and Virginia E. Spencer, "Areal and Temporal Distribution of Dwelling Types," in *Navajo Architecture: Forms, History, Distributions* (Tucson: University of Arizona Press, 1981).
16. Stokes and Smiley, "Tree-Ring Dates," 12–3.
17. Stokes and Smiley.
18. Navajos crossed the San Juan River west of Bluff at the Rincon and then further west at the mouths of Paiute Creek and Oljato Creek, among other crossings.
19. Paul T. Nelson, *Wrecks of Human Ambition: A History of Utah's Canyon Country to 1936* (Salt Lake City: University of Utah Press, 2014), 48.
20. Nelson, 50.
21. John Kessell, *Whither the Waters: Mapping the Great Basin from Bernardo de Miera to John C. Fremont* (Albuquerque: University of New Mexico Press, 2017).
22. Andrew Gulliford, "Miera y Pacheco was First European to create maps of the Four Corners Region," *Durango Herald*, April 14, 2018.
23. Richard Francaviglia, *Mapping and Imagination in the Great Basin* (Reno: University of Nevada Press, 2005), 36.
24. Francaviglia, 39.
25. James F. Brooks, *Captives and Cousins: Slavery and Kinship in the Southwest Borderlands* (Chapel Hill: Omohundro Institute of Early American History & Culture and the University of North Carolina Press, 2002).
26. McNitt, *Navajo Wars*, 23.
27. McNitt, 43.
28. Jennifer Nez Denetdale, *Reclaiming Diné History: The Legacies of Navajo Chief Manuelito and Juanita* (Tucson: University of Arizona Press, 2007), 5.
29. Denetdale, 15.
30. McNitt, *Navajo Wars*, 53.
31. David M. Brugge, "Vizcarra's Campaign of 1823," *Arizona and the West* 6, no. 3 (Autumn 1964): 225.
32. McNitt, *Navajo Wars*, 63.
33. Steve Allen, *Utah's Canyon Country Place Names Vol. I* (Durango, CO: Canyon Country Press, 2012), 43.
34. Robert S. McPherson, *Dinéjí Na 'Nitin: Navajo Traditional Teachings and History* (Boulder: University Press of Colorado, 2012), 82. McPherson

notes that on one of the prominent ears may be a hole in the rocks where bones of the dead were hidden.

35. McPherson, 83.
36. Steven K. Madsen, *Exploring Desert Stone: John N. Macomb's 1859 Expedition to the Canyonlands of the Colorado* (Logan: Utah State University Press, 2010), xvi.
37. Madsen, xvii.
38. Allen, *Utah's Canyon Country Place Names*, 15.
39. Madsen, *Exploring Desert* Stone, 11.
40. J.N. Macomb and J.S. Newberry, *Report of the Exploring Expedition from Santa Fe, New Mexico to the Junction of the Grand and Green Rivers of the Great Colorado of the West, in 1859; With Geological Report* (Washington, DC: Government Printing Office, 1876), 85.
41. Macomb and Newberry, 94.
42. Madsen, *Exploring Desert Stone*, 75.
43. Macomb and Newberry, *Report of the Exploring Expedition*, 6.

CHAPTER 5

1. Robert S. McPherson, *As if the Land Owned Us: An Ethnohistory of the White Mesa Utes* (Salt Lake City: University of Utah Press, 2011), 80.
2. Frank McNitt, *Navajo Wars* (Albuquerque: University of New Mexico Press, 1972), 444–6.
3. *Bilagaana* may be a version of a Spanish word, but it also resembles the Navajo verb "to massacre."
4. McNitt, *Navajo Wars*, 441.
5. Realizing the ecological disaster he had created, General Carleton ordered more cottonwoods to be planted and by April 1865, 12,000 trees had been planted where the original grove had been. See Harry R. Parsons and Joanna Pace, "Bosque Redondo: A History Lesson," *American Forests* 100, nos. 9/10 (1994).
6. On Bosque Redondo, see Laurance D. Linford, *Navajo Places: History, Legend, Landscape* (Salt Lake City: University of Utah Press, 2000), 207. For Navajos forced on the Long Walk and the numbers who died, see Jennifer Nez Denetdale, *Reclaiming Diné History: The Legacies of Navajo Chief Manuelito and Juanita* (Tucson: University of Arizona Press, 2007), 75.
7. McNitt, *Navajo Wars*, 429.
8. The Long Walk, 148. For Carleton's Navajo slave ownership, see Denetdale, *Reclaiming Diné History*, 72.
9. Stephen C. Jett and John Thompson, "The Destruction of Navajo Orchards in 1864: Captain John Thompson's Report," *Arizona and the West* 16, no. 4 (Winter 1974): 369.
10. David Roberts, *A Newer World: Kit Carson, John C. Fremont and the Claiming of the American West* (New York: Simon & Schuster, 2000), 266.

11. Pfeiffer was an interesting historical character, probably an alcoholic who styled himself as an "Indian fighter." He certainly traveled the Southwest. A bronze plaque just west of Pagosa Springs, Colorado, describes a knife fight where, naked, he faced off a Navajo adversary for control of the local hot springs on behalf of Utes. I think the story is set in the wrong time and place though the nakedness may not be. See Andrew Gulliford, "The Truth Behind a Frontier Myth in Pagosa Springs," *Durango Herald*, June 10, 2017.
12. Gulliford, 268.
13. Denetdale, *Reclaiming Diné History*, 73–4.
14. Louisa Wade Wetherill and Harvey Leake, *Wolfkiller: Wisdom from a Nineteenth Century Navajo Shepherd* (Salt Lake City, UT: Gibbs Smith Publisher, 2007), 70.
15. Wetherill and Leake, *Wolfkiller*, 75.
16. Wetherill and Leake, 80. To understand Navajos in hiding and then being forced to go on the Long Walk, the young adult book *Sing Down the Moon* encapsulates the story for teenage readers.
17. Wetherill and Leake, *Wolfkiller*, 86.
18. Charles Kelley, "Chief Hoskaninni," *Utah Historical Quarterly*, 220.
19. Kelley, 221.
20. Kelley, 225.
21. Klara Kelley and Harris Francis, *A Diné History of Navajoland* (Tucson: University of Arizona Press, 2019), 17.
22. Navajo oral tradition states that Barboncito tied a billy goat to a post at Bosque Redondo where it continued to thrash and butt until it broke its neck. Barboncito did so as a warning to young men who might want to raid and steal and thus break the new treaty. For the treaty deliberations, see *Treaty Between the United States of America and the Navajo Tribe of Indians, with a Record of the Discussions that Led to its Signing*, published in cooperation with the Navajo Tribe as the eighth in a continuing series commemorating the Navajo Centennial (Las Vegas: KC Publications, 1968).
23. Linford, 294, explains that raiders moved from the La Sal Mountains toward Bears Ears in 1866.
24. Robert S. McPherson, *Fighting in Indian Country: Native American Conflict, 500 AD to the 1920s* (Indianapolis, IN: Dog Ear Publishing, 2016), 97.
25. Virginia McConnell Simmons, *Drifting West: The Calamities of James White and Charles Baker* (Boulder: University Press of Colorado, 2007), 12.
26. An earlier version of this essay appeared in Andrew Gulliford, "Did James White run the Grand Canyon before John Wesley Powell?" *Durango Herald*, September 14, 2019.
27. Robert Brewster Stanton, *Colorado River Controversies*, 1932, reprint (Evergreen, CO: Westwater Books, 1982).
28. Gulliford, "Did James White run the Grand Canyon before John Wesley Powell?" *Durango Herald*, September 14, 2019.

29. Eilean Adams, *Hell or High Water: James White's Disputed Passage through Grand Canyon, 1867* (Logan: Utah State University Press, 2001).
30. Greg Adams, personal communication with author, June 12, 2017.
31. This excerpt is from Andrew Gulliford, "Mapping Colorado: The Hayden Atlas turns 130 years old," *Inside/Outside Southwest* (April/May 2007).
32. William H. Goetzmann, *Exploration & Empire* (New York: Vintage Books, 1966), 498.
33. Gulliford, "Mapping Colorado: The Hayden Atlas turns 130 years old," *Inside/Outside Southwest* (April/May 2007).
34. Charles S. Peterson, *Look to the Mountains: Southeastern Utah and the La Sal National Forest* (Provo, UT: Brigham Young University Press, 1975), 24.
35. Robert S. McPherson and Susan Rhoades Neel, *Mapping the Four Corners: Narrating the Hayden Survey of 1875* (Norman: University of Oklahoma Press, 2016), 6–7.
36. McPherson, *As if the Land Owned Us*, 115.
37. McPherson and Neel, *Mapping the Four Corners*, 125.
38. McPherson and Neel, 225.
39. McPherson and Neel, 130.
40. McPherson and Neel, 129.

CHAPTER 6

1. To understand the early history of the Church of Jesus Christ of Latter-day Saints and the route taken to Salt Lake City see Wallace Stegner, *The Gathering of Zion: The Story of the Mormon Trail* (Lincoln, NE: Bison Books, 1992).
2. See Stegner, "Ordeal by Handcart," in *The Gathering of Zion*, 221–48.
3. Juanita Brooks, *The Mountain Meadows Massacre* (Norman: University of Oklahoma Press, 1991).
4. David S. Carpenter, *Jens Nielson, Bishop of Bluff* (Provo, UT: BYU Studies, 2011), 29.
5. John Wesley Powell, *Report on the Lands of the Arid Regions of the United States*, 2nd ed. (Washington, DC: Government Printing Office, 1879), 163.
6. Stewart Aitchison, *A Guide to Southern Utah's Hole-In-The-Rock-Trail* (Salt Lake City: University of Utah Press, 2005), 9.
7. David E. Miller, *Hole-In-The-Rock: An Epic in the Colonization of the American West* (Salt Lake City: University of Utah Press, 1966), ix.
8. Miller, 4.
9. Leonard J. Arrington, *Great Basin Kingdom* (Cambridge, MA: Harvard University Press, 1958), 354.
10. Miller, *Hole-In-The-Rock*, 5.
11. Aitchison, *A Guide to Southern Utah's*, 13.
12. Aitchison, 38.

13. Andrew Gulliford, "Lost and Hungry Scouts: A Mormon Christmas Story," *Durango Herald*, December 12, 2020.
14. Thomas G. Alexander, "Brigham Young and the Transformation of Utah Wilderness," *Journal of Mormon History* (Winter 2015), 111.
15. Miller, *Hole-In-The-Rock*, 138.
16. Miller.
17. Miller.
18. I have thought about the dedication of those pioneers and wondered about my own ancestor, Martin Harris, who was there at the beginning of the church when Joseph Smith received his revelation and the Angel Moroni pointed to where to dig on a New York hill to reveal the golden tablets that would become the basis for The Book of Mormon, published because Harris mortgaged his farm to do so and sacrificed his first marriage. I agree with Wallace Stegner's words from *The Gathering of Zion* (13) where he wrote about Mormons in his introduction: "That I do not accept the faith that possessed them does not mean I doubt their frequent devotion and heroism in its service."
19. The phrase "blossom as the rose" comes from the Bible and Isaiah 35:1. In 1854 Brigham Young urged his followers to farm, to be good stewards of the land, and to "make the Earth like the Garden of Eden." See Alexander, "Brigham Young and the Transformation of Utah Wilderness," 104.
20. Stegner, 3.
21. Richard Francaviglia, *The Mormon Landscape* (New York: AMS Press, 1978), 10. Also see P.A.M. Taylor and L.J. Arrington, "Religion and Planning the Far West: The First Generation of Mormons in Utah," *The Economic History Review* 11, no. 1 (1958).
22. Jedediah S. Rogers and Matthew C. Godfrey, eds., *The Earth Will Appear as the Garden of Eden: Essays on Mormon Environmental History* (Salt Lake City: University of Utah, 2019), 9.
23. Paul T. Nelson, *Wrecks of Human Ambition: A History of Utah's Canyon Country to 1936* (Salt Lake City: University of Utah Press, 2014), 165.
24. Carpenter, *Jens Nielson*, 41.
25. Carpenter.
26. Rogers and Godfrey, *The Earth Will Appear as the Garden of Eden*, 5.
27. Wallace Stegner, *Mormon Country* (Lincoln: University of Nebraska Press, 2003), 229.
28. Albert R. Lyman, *Indians and Outlaws: Settling of the San Juan frontier* (Salt Lake City, UT: Publishers Press, 1962), 37. Other standard histories for San Juan County include Cornelia Adams Perkins, Marian Gardner Nielson, and Lenora Butt Jones, *Saga of San Juan* (San Juan County Chapter Daughters of Utah Pioneers, 1968); Allan Kent Powell, ed. *San Juan County, Utah: People, Resources and History* (Salt Lake City: Utah State Historical Society, 1983); Robert S. McPherson, *A History of San Juan*

County: In the Palm of Time (Salt Lake City: Utah State Historical Society and San Juan County Commission, 1995), and for a slightly broader perspective, see Gary Topping, *Glen Canyon and the San Juan Country* (Moscow: University of Idaho Press, 1997).

29. The most detailed analysis of the early Bluff community is by Carpenter, who accessed numerous records and Latter-day Saints dairies. Carpenter, *Jens Nielson,* 44.
30. Carpenter, 87.
31. D.W. Meinig, "The Mormon Culture Region: Strategies and Patterns in the Geography of the American West, 1847–1964," *Annals of the Association of American Geographers* 55, no. 2 (June 1965): 203.
32. To best understand the history of the San Juan River, see James M. Aton and Robert S. McPherson, *River Flowing from the Sunrise: An Environmental History of the Lower San Juan* (Logan: Utah State University Press, 2000).
33. Robert S. McPherson, *As if the Land Owned Us: An Ethnohistory of the White Mesa Utes* (Salt Lake City: University of Utah Press, 2011), 152.
34. Don D. Walker, "The Carlisles: Cattle Barons of the Upper Basin," *Utah Historical Quarterly* 32 (1964).
35. For the best treatment of Cass Hite's peripatetic life see James H. Knipmeyer, *Cass Hite: The Life of an Old Prospector* (Salt Lake City: University of Utah Press, 2016).
36. McPherson, *As if the Land Owned Us*, 155.
37. Henry Mitchell liked to argue, complain, and have soldiers spend money at his store. See Robert S. McPherson, "Navajos, Mormons, and Henry L. Mitchell: Cauldron of Conflict on the San Juan," *Utah Historical Quarterly* 55 (1987).
38. McPherson, *As if the Land Owned Us,* 158.
39. For analysis of Native fighting techniques see Robert S. McPherson, *Fighting in Canyon Country: Native American Conflict, 500 AD to the 1920s,* (Indianapolis, IN: Dog Ear Publishing, 2016).
40. McPherson, *As if the Land Owned Us,* 159.
41. Powell, not only interested in Native Americans, also pioneered studies of water, and the lack of it, on the Colorado Plateau and in Utah's canyon country. For his seminal report see Powell, *Report on the Lands of the Arid Regions of the United States.*
42. William H. Holmes, "Pottery of the Ancient Pueblos," in *Fourth Annual Report of the Bureau of Ethnology to the Secretary of the Smithsonian Institution*, 1882–3, 48th Congress, mis. doc., no. 42 (Washington, DC: Government Printing Office, 1886), 284. For a modern version of a horseback ride and camping trip into Mancos Canyon see Andrew Gulliford, "Flash Floods and Cliff Dwellings in Ute Mountain Tribal Park," in Gulliford, ed. *Outdoors in the Southwest: An Adventure Anthology* (Norman: University of Oklahoma Press, 2015), 194–200.

43. Holmes, "Pottery of the Ancient Pueblos," 315.
44. Holmes, 284.
45. Holmes, 285. For context for Holmes' writing also see his "Report on the Ancient Ruins of Southwestern Colorado, examined during the summers of 1875 and 1876," extracted from the Tenth Annual Report of the Survey for the Year 1876 (Washington, DC: Government Printing Office, 1879).
46. Holmes, 316.
47. Holmes, 319.
48. Carpenter, *Jens Nielson*, 124.
49. McPherson, *Fighting in Indian Country*, 164.
50. For a more detailed understanding of the Homestead Act see Andrew Gulliford, *The Woolly West: Colorado's Hidden History of Sheepscapes* (College Station: Texas A&M University Press, 2018), 87–9.
51. Victoria M. Atkins, "Anasazi Basketmaker: Papers from the 1990 Wetherill—Grand Gulch Symposium," Cultural Resource Series no. 24, (Salt Lake City, UT: US Department of the Interior, Bureau of Land Management, November 1993) Appendix H. Also see Jean Pinkley, MVNP archaeologist, Mesa Verde National Park, Administrative History, Appendix B "Early Museum Collections from Mesa Verde," ca. 1960s.
52. T.J. Morgan, Commissioner, "Protest of the Indian Rights Association Against the Proposed Removal of the Southern Ute Indians," Philadelphia, Indian Rights Association, March 1890, 7.
53. Nelson, *Jens Nielson*, 169.

CHAPTER 7

1. John F. Valentine, *Lonesome Trails of San Juan: The Ranching Legacy of J.A. (Al) Scorup* (Provo, UT: Privately printed, 2002), 19.
2. Valentine, 22.
3. Heidi Redd, interview with author at the Dugout Ranch, September 2019.
4. David Lavender. "Mormon Cowboy," *Desert Magazine*, October 1940, and Lavender, *One Man's West* (Lincoln: University of Nebraska Press, 1977).
5. Lavender, *One Man's West,* 87. Other information on Al Scorup can be found in Lavender, "Mormon Cowboy," and Lavender, *One Man's West.*
6. Lavender, *One Man's West,* 28. Also see Neal Lambert, "Al Scorup: Cattleman of the Canyons," *Utah Historical Quarterly* 32, issue 3 (Summer 1964), and Karl Young, "Wild Cows of the San Juan," *Utah Historical Quarterly* 32, issue 3 (Summer 1964).
7. Andrew Gulliford, "Go Ask Alice: A Famous Botanist who Picked Flowers in Southeast Utah," *San Juan Record*, April 22, 2020.
8. Alice Eastwood, "Notes on the Cliffdwellers," *Zoe: A Biological Journal* Vol. III (1892): 375–6.
9. Eastwood.
10. Alice Eastwood, "General Notes on a Trip Through Southeastern Utah," *Zoe: A Biological Journal* Vol. III (January 1893), 354–61.

11. Neil M. Judd, *Men Met Along the Trail: Adventures in Archaeology* (Salt Lake City: University of Utah Press, 2009), 5.
12. Alice Eastwood, "General Notes on a Trip Through Southeastern Utah," 354–61.
13. Maurine S. Fletcher, ed. *The Wetherills of the Mesa Verde: Autobiography of Benjamin Alfred Wetherill* (Lincoln: University of Nebraska Press, 1977), 197.
14. Fletcher, 202.
15. Alice Eastwood, "Letter: May 7, 1906," in Marcia Myers Bonta, ed. *American Women Afield: Writings by Pioneering Women Naturalists* (College Station: Texas A&M University Press, 1995), 89.
16. A copy of the original telegram sent by Nordenskiold to his father can be seen in the archives at the Center of Southwest Studies, Fort Lewis College, courtesy of Judith Reynolds.
17. Fred Blackburn, *The Wetherills: Friends of Mesa Verde* (Durango, CO: Durango Herald Small Press, 2006), 42.
18. Judith Reynolds and David Reynolds, *Nordenskiold of Mesa Verde* (Privately printed, Xlibris, 2006), 57.
19. William D. Lipe, "Grand Gulch: Three Days on the Road from Bluff," in Marnie Gaede, ed. *Camera, Spade and Pen: An Inside View of Southwestern Archaeology* (Tucson: University of Arizona Press, 1980), 52.
20. Lipe.
21. C.C. Graham and Charles McLoyd, "Catalogue and Description of a Very Large Collection of Prehistoric Relics, Obtained in the Cliff Houses and Caves of Southeastern Utah," 1894, pamphlet located in Special Collections at the Library, Brigham Young University, Provo, Utah.
22. Graham and McLoyd.
23. Graham and McLoyd. For additional information on McLoyd see Fred M. Blackburn and Ray A. Williamson, *Cowboys & Cave Dwellers* (Santa Fe, NM: School of American Research, 1997).
24. McLoyd and Graham, "Catalogue." Also see the C.H. Green "Catalogue of a Unique Collection of Cliff Dweller Ruins taken from the Lately Descovered [sic] ruins of Southwestern Colorado and adjacent parts of Utah, New Mexico and Arizona, scientifically estimated to be The Oldest Relics in the World," ca. 1891. Digital copy courtesy of Harvey Leake.
25. Reynolds, 122.
26. See Robert E. Bieder, *Science Encounters the Indian, 1820–1880: The Early Years of American Ethnology* (Norman: University of Oklahoma Press, 1986).
27. Hal Rothman, *America's National Monuments: The Politics of Preservation* (Lawrence: University Press of Kansas), 19–20.
28. Excerpted from Andrew Gulliford, "Headnotes: Exhibitions, Museums, and Interpreting Culture," in Gulliford, ed. *Preserving Western History* (Albuquerque: University of New Mexico Press, 2005), 45.

29. Because Native Americans were supposed to be vanishing, and indeed in 1890 their numbers had shrunk from approximately seventeen million in 1492 to less than 200,000 people, scholars sought to record Native cultures and to photograph Native racial types. See Brian W. Dippie, *The Vanishing American: White Attitudes & U.S. Indian Policy* (Lawrence: University Press of Kansas, 1982), and Timothy Egan, *Short Nights of the Shadow Catcher: The Epic Life and Immortal Photographs of Edward Curtis* (Boston: Houghton Mifflin, 2012).
30. Reynolds, 79. In the spring of 2020 representatives from the US government and Finland agreed to repatriate the Mesa Verde human remains now in Finland. That process had now been completed.
31. Rothman, 19. Wetherill scholar Harvey Leake points out that Rothman does not identify his sources for these comments and that initially anthropologists were not much interested in the American Southwest.
32. Fletcher, ed. *The Wetherills of the Mesa Verde,* 179–81.
33. James H. Knipmeyer, *In Search of a Lost Race* (privately printed, Xlibris, 2006). The book reprints all the original essays from *The Illustrated American* with modern photographs taken from settings that match historic photos from the magazine.
34. *The Illustrated American*, July 16, 1892, 411. Series began April 2, 1892 and ended August 27, 1892.
35. From Andrew Gulliford, "Four Corners Odyssey: The Ill-fated 1892 *Illustrated American* Exploring Expedition," *Inside/Outside Southwest* (April 2009).
36. See Remington W. Lane, "An Artist in the San Juan Country," *Harper's Weekly*, December 9, 1893, 1174.
37. After the World's Fair, the forty-six artifacts collected by the IAAA were donated to the Field Museum in Chicago.
38. *The Illustrated American*, August 20, 1892, 23. Historian Knipmeyer also found at the Ohio Historical Society a printed document by Warren K. Moorehead titled "The Field Diary of an Archaeological Collector" from 1902, but it is unclear where it was printed and published. The diary contains most of the material from *The Illustrated American* but with additional background and clarification.
39. *The Illustrated American*, 25
40. XIII "Relics of the Cliff-Dwellers: Mr. Moorehead's Purchase of the McLoyd Collection for the World's Fair," *The Illustrated American*, August 27, 1892, 71.
41. Knipmeyer explains that the Smithsonian did not purchase McLoyd's collection after the World's Columbian Exhibition in 1893 where it was displayed as part of the H. Jay Smith Exploring Company items. McLoyd sold it to D.C. Hazzard. Phoebe Apperson Hearst purchased it for the University of Pennsylvania Museum of Archaeology and Anthropology where it is part of the Hazzard Collection. Knipmeyer, 145.

42. Gulliford, "Four Corners Odyssey: The Ill-Fated 1892 *Illustrated American* Exploring Expedition," *Inside/Outside Southwest* (April 2009).
43. Floyd W. Sharrock, "The Hazzard Collection," Archives of Archaeology, no. 23 (Washington, DC, and Madison, WI: Society for American Archaeology and the University of Wisconsin Press), 1963.
44. No notes have been found for Richard Wetherill's 1893–1894 expedition, but notes from his 1896–1897 expedition are in the collections at the American Museum of Natural History in New York City.
45. For a descriptive letter by Richard Wetherill on prehistoric sandals, see Letter to the Editor, *The Antiquarian* I (1897): 248. For his wife's observations and descriptions of excavating a site see Blackburn and Williamson, 60–1.
46. Rothman, "The Antiquities Act and National Monuments: A Progressive Conservation Legacy," *CRM*, no. 4 (1999).
47. David S. Carpenter, *Jens Nielson: Bishop of Bluff* (Provo, UT: Brigham Young University Press, 2011), 211–6. For the best description of the brief gold boom see James M. Aton and Robert S. McPherson, "Mining: Black and Yellow Gold in Redrock Country," in *River Flowing from the Sunrise: An Environmental History of the Lower San Juan* (Logan: Utah State University Press, 2000).
48. Francis Fisher Kane and Frank M. Riter, "A Further Report to the Indian Rights Association on the Proposed Removal of the Southern Utes," Philadelphia, Indian Rights Association, January 20, 1892, 8.
49. Kane and Riter, 18.
50. Kane and Riter, 25.
51. T.J. Morgan, Commissioner, "Protest of the Indian Rights Association Against the Proposed Removal of the Southern Ute Indians, Reasons Urged for this Removal," Philadelphia, Indian Rights Association, March 1890.
52. Kane and Riter, 9.
53. Kane and Riter.
54. Frank Silvey, "When San Juan County was Given to the Southern Ute Indians. A Historical Experience of the Early Nineties," typescript, Utah State Historical Society, A-S-I3 (13).
55. Silvey.
56. Bill Boyle, editor and publisher of *The San Juan Record,* believes, "Mormon settlement and cattle operations in 1895 are well known, but it was possibly the mining interests that swung the opinion of the Territorial Governor." Personal communication via email to author, February 10, 2020.
57. Silver typescript.
58. 53rd Congress, Sess. III, Chap. 113, February 20, 1895.
59. Francis E. Leupp, Washington Agent of the Indian Rights Association, The Latest Phase of the Southern Ute Question: A Report, Philadelphia, Office of the Indian Rights Association, September 30, 1895, 4. President Theodore Roosevelt would appoint Leupp as Indian Commissioner. Leupp

would visit the Southwest, marry into a Navajo family, and have a town named for him in Arizona.

60. Leupp.
61. See Robert S. McPherson, *As if the Land Owned Us: An Ethnohistory of the White Mesa Utes* (Logan: Utah State University Press, 2011).
62. Carpenter, 203, and Winston Hurst "Colonizing the Dead: Early Archaeology in Western San Juan County," *Blue Mountain Shadows* 17, 1996.
63. *The Archaeologist*, Waterloo, Iowa, 1894, Vol. II, 154–5.
64. *The Archaeologist*, 190–1.
65. *The Archaeologist*, Waterloo, Iowa, 1894, Vol. II, no. 8, 227.
66. *Democrat & Chronicle*, Rochester, New York, July 15, 1894, 5.
67. See Victoria M. Atkins, ed., *Anasazi Basketmaker: Papers from the 1990 Wetherill-Grand Gulch Symposium*, Cultural Resource Series no. 24 (Salt Lake City, UT: US Department of the Interior, Bureau of Land Management) November 1992. For an excellent narrative analysis, with photographs, of these expeditions, see Fred M. Blackburn and Ray A. Williamson, *Cowboys & Cave Dwellers* (Santa Fe, NM: School of American Research Press, 1997).
68. Carpenter (202–3) describes Jens Peter Nielson and Charles Lang helping to guide the McLoyd expedition in 1890 and 1891 and interest in artifacts being shown by Platte Lyman, Samuel Wood, Hans Bayles, and the Perkins brothers. "None of them knew much about the relics or how to excavate them, usually labeling them all Aztec ruins. But they uncovered a lot of interesting items."
69. "Relics of a Past Age," *The [Telluride] Daily Journal* III, no. 7 (August 14, 1896): 1–2.
70. T. Mitchell Prudden, "An Elder Brother to the Cliff-Dwellers," *Harpers New Monthly Magazine* 95 (1897): 57.
71. Prudden, 59.
72. Prudden, 60. Also see Prudden's book *On the Great American Plateau* (New York: G.P. Putnam, 1906).
73. Prudden, 62.
74. Blackburn, XXIV.
75. James E. Snead, *Ruins and Rivals: The Making of Southwest Archaeology* (Tucson: University of Arizona Press, 2001), 21.
76. T. Mitchell Prudden, "The Prehistoric Ruins of the San Juan Watershed in Utah, Arizona, Colorado, and New Mexico," *American Anthropologist* 5, no. 2 (1903): 288.
77. Edgar L. Hewett, "Circular relating to Historic and Prehistoric Ruins of the Southwest," Department of the Interior, General Land Office (Washington, DC: Government Printing Office, 1904), 3.
78. Hewett, 7. To understand more about Hewett, his admirers, and his enemies, see James E. Snead, *Ruins and Rivals: The Making of Southwest Archaeology* (Tucson: University of Arizona Press, 2001).

79. Hewett, 8. In reference to the San Juan River region, archaeologist Hewett cites Chapin's book *In the Land of the Cliffdwellers* (1892), Prudden's work, and George H. Pepper's "The Ancient Basket Makers of Southeastern Utah," Supplement to *American Museum Journal*, American Museum of Natural History ii, no. 4 (April 1902): Guide Leaflet No. 6. Pepper describes both Wetherill and McLoyd and Graham collections of baskets.
80. "Preservation of Historic and Prehistoric Ruins, Etc.," Hearing before the Subcommittee of the Committee on Public Lands of the US Senate on Bill S.1427 and S.5603 (Washington, DC: Government Printing Office, 1904), 5.
81. "Preservation of Historic and Prehistoric Ruins, Etc.," 8.
82. For the classic biography on the eldest Wetherill brother, see Frank McNitt, *Richard Wetherill Anasazi: Pioneer Explorer of Southwestern Ruins* (Albuquerque: University of New Mexico Press, 1957).
83. McNitt.
84. W.W. Dyar, "The Colossal Bridges of Utah: A Recent Discovery of Natural Wonders," *Century Magazine* 68 (August 1904), and a summary in "Colossal Natural Bridges of Utah," *National Geographic Magazine* 15 (September 1904).
85. Charlie R. Steen, "The Natural Bridges of White Canyon: A Diary of H.L.A. Culmer, 1905," *Utah Historical Quarterly.*
86. In later years Blanding became the outfitting point for expeditions to Natural Bridges under Zeke Johnson who became its first caretaker or superintendent.
87. Steen, "The Natural Bridges of White Canyon," 65. For an appraisal of the impacts of sheep in the rural west, see Andrew Gulliford, *The Woolly West: Colorado's Hidden History of Sheepscapes* (College Station: Texas A&M University Press, 2018).
88. Gulliford, 71.
89. Gulliford, 72.
90. Gulliford, 75. In White Canyon the expedition found inscriptions by W.C. McLoyd and C.C. Graham from 1892 to 1893. The diarist noted that their collection had been exhibited in Durango and later sold "to Eastern parties for over $5,000" (p. 76).
91. Gulliford, 77.
92. Gulliford, 78.
93. Bare Ladder Ruin may be misspelled or an error in nomenclature. In the vernacular of the Four Corners a bear ladder is a tree that has had the limbs clipped off so one can climb the ladder on the stubs of the tree like a bear would. It is possible that the original name was spelled Bear Ladder Ruin because of that kind of pioneer access. In contrast, another version of the name in local folklore is that the name Bare Ladder referred to the bare "stripped of branches" tree, which could be climbed to get into the site.

94. Steen, "The Natural Bridges of White Canyon," 82.
95. Mark Squillace, "The Monumental Legacy of the Antiquities Act of 1906," *Georgia Law Review* 37 (2003), 477.
96. Squillace, 478.
97. "Dead Past: The Cliffdwellers' Exhibit for the World's Fair," *Star Tribune* (Minneapolis, MN) Sunday, April 16, 1893, 6.
98. "The Cliff Dwellers," pamphlet, The H. Jay Smith Exploring Company, World's Columbian Exposition, 1893.
99. Lee, 26.
100. Richard Wetherill to G.F. Pollock, Acting Commissioner, Land Office, Washington, DC, from Putnam, NM, January 14, 1906. Copy courtesy of Harvey Leake.
101. "Wonderful Ruins, Scientific Exploration of the Cliff Dwellings in Chaco Canyon, San Juan County, At Work for Four Years, Wealthy New Yorkers Are Interested in the Investigation—the Relics are Sent to the American Museum of Natural History," front page, *Santa Fe New Mexican*, May 16, 1900.
102. Rothman, 34.
103. B.K. Wetherill to Superintendent, Smithsonian Institute, Washington, DC, [1889?]. Copy courtesy of Harvey Leake. Also see Fred Blackburn, *The Wetherills: Friends of Mesa Verde* (Durango, CO: Durango Herald Small Press, 2006), 21–3.
104. "Preservation of Historic and Prehistoric Ruins, Etc.," 15.
105. Act for the Preservation of American Antiquities, Antiquities Act (16 U.S.C. §§ 431) of 1906.

CHAPTER 8

1. Robert S. McPherson, *As if the Land Owned Us: An Ethnohistory of the White Mesa Utes* (Salt Lake City: University of Utah Press, 2011). See Chapter 12 "Posey and the Last White Uprising."
2. Charles S. Peterson, *Look to the Mountains: Southeastern Utah and the La Sal National Forest* (Provo, UT: Brigham Young University Press, 1975), 153.
3. Peterson, 176.
4. Jacob Riis and Theodore Roosevelt became good friends when Roosevelt was New York City Police Commissioner. They raided and photographed immigrants in slums at night and roused sleeping policemen. See Riis, *How the Other Half Lives.*
5. John Riis, *Ranger Trails* (Richmond, VA: The Dietz Press, 1937), reprinted by Wilderness Associates, Bend, Oregon, 2008, 32–3.
6. Riis, 51.
7. Riis, 52.
8. Riis, 35–6.

9. Riis, 53. In Oklahoma, Osage Indians were poisoned by strychnine. For one victim "his final hours would have been a hideous torment; his muscles convulsing, as if he were being jolted with electricity; his neck craning and his jaw tightening; his lungs constricting as he tried to breathe, until at last he suffocated." See David Graham, *Killers of the Flower Moon: The Osage Murders and the Birth of the FBI* (New York: Vintage Books, 2018), 73.
10. Riis, *Ranger Trails*, 75.
11. Riis, 59.
12. Riis, 62.
13. To the Secretary of the Interior, Archaeological Institute of America Application for Permit for Examination, Excavation, and Gathering of Objects of Antiquity in the state of Utah, signed as Director of Work, Edgar L. Hewett, June 1, 1907. Reproduced from the National Archives, copy from the Utah Museum of Natural History.
14. Neil M. Judd, *Men Met Along the Trail: Adventures in Archaeology* (Salt Lake City: University of Utah Press, 2009), 16.
15. Judd, 12.
16. Judd, 13. For an early archaeological summary of what they found, see "The Ancient Inhabitants of the San Juan Valley," *Bulletin of the University of Utah* III, no. 3, part 2 (November 1910).
17. J. Wiley Redd, "History of the Natural Bridges," one-page typescript, n.d., NABR 65/06-156, Natural Bridges National Monument Records, Southeast Utah Group Archives, National Park Service.
18. William B. Douglass, Special Instructions, Field Notes of the Survey of the Reservations embracing Natural Bridges National Monument, the Cigarette Cave and the Snow Flat Cave (or Prehistoric Cave Springs nos. 1 and 2), Survey Commenced September 12, 1908, completed October 3, 1908. P. 50. NABR 65/06-162. Natural Bridges National Monument Records, Southeast Utah Group Archives, National Park Service.
19. Douglass, 51–2.
20. Douglass, 52.
21. Douglass, 53. The best short book on Natural Bridges is David Petersen, *Natural Bridges: The Story of Wind, Water & Sand* (Moab, UT: Canyonlands Natural History Association, 2014).
22. Douglass, 57.
23. Douglass, 59. Natural Bridges has had three different proclamations by three different presidents: Theodore Roosevelt, William Taft, and Woodrow Wilson all with slightly different boundary adjustments. On October 25, 1949 archaeologist Jesse Nusbaum recommended eliminating the original caves protected for their valuable springs. Taft proclamation, NABR 65/06-156; Wilson proclamation, NABR 65/06-156; and Nusbaum memo, NABR 65/05-123 in Natural Bridges National Monument Records, Southeast Utah Group Archives, National Park Service.

24. Douglass, 63.
25. Robert S. McPherson, "Bai-a-lil-e and the 1907 Aneth Brawl: Power, Progress and Principle," in *Fighting in Indian Country* (Indianapolis, IN: Dog Ear Publishing, 2016), 203.
26. Donald L. Parman, "The 'Big Stick' in Indian Affairs: The Bai-A-Lil-Le Incident in 1909," *Arizona and the West* 20, no. 4 (Winter 1978): 345.
27. McPherson, "Bai-a-lil-e and the 1907 Aneth Brawl," 205.
28. Parman, "The 'Big Stick' in Indian Affairs," 347.
29. Robert S. McPherson has written an excellent essay on the quirky Antes who nevertheless successfully argued for an extension of the Navajo Reservation north of the San Juan River which Theodore Roosevelt agreed to. Roosevelt signed Executive Order 324A on May 15, 1905. See McPherson, "Howard R. Antes and the Navajo Faith Mission: Evangelist of Southeastern Utah," *Utah Historical Quarterly* 65, no. 1 (Winter 1997).
30. Parman, "The 'Big Stick' in Indian Affairs," 354.
31. Parman, 357. Commissioner of Indian Affairs Francis E. Leupp paternalistically wrote about Native wrongdoers, "If they are still in a state of barbarism, I try to deal out justice as well as I know how . . . by humane though firm measures which will prevent their continuing in their evil courses, teach them a better way of life and impress them with a sense of the magnitude and the power of the Government they are defying . . . Indeed, I have been breaking up reservations as fast as I could, so that there might soon be none to which the Indians could be confined." Francis E. Leupp, "'Law or no Law' in Indian Administration," *Outlook*, January 30, 1909.
32. Leupp, 359.
33. Mary Apolline Comfort, *Rainbow to Yesterday* (New York: Vantage Press, 1980), 188.
34. Andrew Gulliford, "Under the Rainbow," *Durango Herald*, April 9, 2009.
35. John Wetherill, Custodian, "Betatakin," Supplement of the June Report of the Southwestern Monuments, June 1934.
36. Cummings returned to the area in the summer of 1912 with photographer Stewart Young. See "To Explore Old Cliff Dwelling," *Grand Valley Times*, Moab, Utah, July 26, 1912.
37. Judd quote cited in David Kent Sproul, "A Bridge Between Cultures: An Administrative History of Rainbow Bridge National Monument," Cultural Resources Selections, no. 18, Intermountain Region, National Park Service, 2001, 63. Also see Hank Haskell, "From Shadow into Light: The Discovery of Rainbow Bridge," *Rainbow Bridge: An Illustrated History* (Logan: Utah State University Press, 1999), 49–50; and James E. Babbitt, ed. *Rainbow Trails: Early-Day Adventures in Rainbow Bridge Country* (Page, AZ: Glen Canyon Natural History Association, 1990).
38. Gulliford, "Under the Rainbow," *Durango Herald*, April 9, 2009.
39. Byron Cummings, "Great Natural Bridges of Utah," *National Geographic* 21 (February 1910): 157–67.

40. Theodore Roosevelt quote in Haskell, *Rainbow Bridge: An Illustrated History*, 69.
41. Haskell, 67.
42. Gulliford, "Under the Rainbow."
43. Part of that trust included passing on years of Hoskininni's knowledge of area plants and their medicinal uses. Louisa's work on that topic was published posthumously. "When I first knew her in 1923 this [plant] collection was largely complete, and she was very proud of it. She had worked hard at the project over a period of years, making many difficult trips and sparing no pains to secure the best possible Navaho informants," wrote Harvard anthropologist Clyde Kluckhohn. "Her heart went into this work." See Leland C. Wyman and Stuart K. Harris, *The Ethnobotany of the Kayenta Navajo: An Analysis of the John and Louisa Wetherill Ethnobotanical Collection*, University of New Mexico Publications in Biology no. 5 (Albuquerque: University of New Mexico Press, 1951).
44. Frances Gilmore and Louisa Wade Wetherill, *Traders to the Navajo* (Albuquerque: University of New Mexico Press, 1953), 180. For more on Louisa also see Comfort, *Rainbow to Yesterday* and the well-illustrated booklet by Harvey Leake, *Slim Woman: Louisa Wade Wetherill of Kayenta* (Blanding, UT: Edge of the Cedars State Park Museum, 2018, 2nd printing).
45. At his death, Navajos owed Richard Wetherill $8,000 for trade items. He had only $74 in the bank. Frank McNitt, *Richard Wetherill: Anasazi* (Albuquerque: University of New Mexico Press, 1999, first published 1957), 314.
46. Letter of W.T. Shelton, San Juan School, Shiprock, New Mexico, to the Commissioner of Indian Affairs, July 19, 1910. Copy courtesy of Harvey Leake, Prescott, Arizona.
47. See the last chapters in McNitt, *Richard Wetherill: Anasazi*. The Navajo served "just short of three years" in state prison and died in 1950.
48. Richard Wetherill's widow, Marietta, remarried. Her second marriage a few years after Richard's death was to William Finn whose actions may have started the chain of events which caused Richard's murder. The couple was living near Cuba, New Mexico, until Finn "died mysteriously in the late teens [the end of WWI]. There are rumors that a family member contributed to his demise," explains Harvey Leake, personal communication to author, August 23, 2020.
49. McPherson, *As if the Land Owned Us*, 208.
50. McPherson, 213. For recent scholarship on Tse-Ne-Gat see Reilly Ben Hatch, "'Because of His Wild Blood': Race, the Frontier, and the American Imagination in the Bluff War and the Trial of Tse-Ne-Gat," *New Mexico Historical Review*, forthcoming.
51. McPherson, 214. For Louisa's account of the 1915 affair, see the chapter "Asthon Sosi's Paiutes," in Gilmore and Wetherill, *Traders to the Navajo.*
52. McPherson, 217–8.

53. Charles L. Bernheimer, *Rainbow Bridge* (Albuquerque, NM: Center for Anthropological Studies, 1999, first published 1924), 6.
54. Earl H. Morris, "An Unexplored Area of the Southwest," *Natural History* 22 (November-December 1922): 499.
55. Bernheimer, *Rainbow Bridge*, 29.
56. Bernheimer, *Rainbow Bridge*, and Charles L. Bernheimer, "Encircling Navajo Mountain with a Pack-Train," *National Geographic* (February 1923).
57. Charles L. Bernheimer Field Notes—1919, typescript copy courtesy of Harvey Leake, Prescott, Arizona.
58. Nels Nelson, "Grand Gulch Region, Utah, 1920," report for the American Museum of Natural History, New York City.
59. Nelson.
60. Nelson.
61. Robert B. Aird and Gary Topping, ed., "An Adventure for Adventure's Sake Recounted by Robert B. Aird," *Utah Historical Quarterly* 62 (Summer 1994): 276.
62. Aird and Topping, 278.
63. Aird and Topping, 287–8. Locals also visited Natural Bridges in the 1920s. See Josephine Bayles, "A Trip to the Natural Bridges," *Blue Mountain Shadows* 7 (Winter 1990): 72–4.
64. Jack Breed, "Roaming the West's Fantastic Four Corners," *National Geographic* 101, no. 6: 305–42.
65. Aird and Topping, 276.
66. McPherson, *As if the Land Owned Us*, 229.
67. McPherson, 236.
68. McPherson, 237. For some reproduced documents and additional historical photographs, see Steve Lacey and Pearl Baker, *Posey: The Last Indian War* (Salt Lake City, UT: Gibbs Smith, 2007).
69. John D. Rogers, "Piute Posey and the Last Indian Uprising," typescript. Filed in Lloyd. L. Young Folder, Utah State Historical Society, Salt Lake City, Utah.
70. McPherson, 239. For an earlier version, see McPherson, "Paiute Posey and the Last White Uprising," *Utah Historical Quarterly* 53 (1985): 248–67. Also see the short synopsis by Charles Kelly, "The Poke and Posey Wars," *Desert Magazine* (May 1965): 18–9.
71. William R. Young, "The 1923 Indian Uprising in San Juan County, Utah," typescript. Filed in Lloyd. L. Young Folder, Utah State Historical Society, Salt Lake City, Utah.
72. Ellen Lefler, "Sheriff Newman and the Posey War," *Blue Mountain Shadows* IV (Spring 1989): 26.
73. Rogers, "Piute Posey and the Last Indian Uprising," typescript, 9.
74. Quoted in McPherson, *As if the Land Owned Us*, 243. For an updated interpretation of the Posey War, see Reilly Ben Hatch, "The Posey Wars: Race, Religion, and Settler Colonialism in Progressive-Era America," (PhD diss., University of New Mexico, 2020).

75. This grisly photo is at the History Research Center of the Utah State Historical Society photo number 87278/s67h1v68. The image is described as having "sensitive content."
76. McPherson, *As if the Land Owned Us*, 242.
77. Buckley Jensen, "Fascinating Life of Chief Posey," *San Juan Record*, September 23, 2009. Another variant of the flour story is that Posey used it to pack flour into his wounded hip. See Lefler, "Sheriff Newman and the Posey War," 27.
78. McPherson, *As if the Land Owned Us*, 242.

CHAPTER 9

1. David Harmon, Francis P. McMannon, and Dwight T. Pitcaithley, eds., *The Antiquities Act: A Century of American Archaeology, Historic Preservation, and Nature Conservation* (Tucson: University of Arizona Press, 2006), 44.
2. Robert S. McPherson, *Dinéjí Na 'Nitin: Navajo Traditional Teachings and History* (Boulder: University Press of Colorado, 2012), 188–9.
3. Accession Record of the University of Utah 1925–1926 Collections in southeast Utah, Natural History Museum of Utah.
4. Accession Record of the University of Utah, #7214.
5. Neil M. Judd, "Beyond the Clay Hills," *National Geographic* (March 1924): 275.
6. Judd, 277.
7. Judd, 279.
8. Judd, 291.
9. C.L. Bernheimer, Field Notes, Expedition 1929; typescript courtesy of Harvey Leake, 2.
10. Bernheimer, 6.
11. Bernheimer, 7.
12. Bernheimer.
13. Bernheimer, 17.
14. Bernheimer.
15. Bernheimer, 24.
16. Bernheimer.
17. Andrew L. Christenson, "The Last of the Great Expeditions: The Rainbow Bridge/Monument Valley Expedition, 1933–1938," *Plateau,* Museum of Northern Arizona 58, no. 4 (1987): 3.
18. Thanks to descendants of Ansel Hall from Mancos and Cortez, Colorado, a large collection of photographs, films, and documents from the Rainbow Bridge Exploring Expedition are cataloged and processed in the archives at the Center of Southwest Studies, Fort Lewis College, Durango.
19. For a geological assessment on Navajo water sources, see Herbert E. Gregory, *The Navajo Country*, Water-Supply Paper 380, (US Geological Survey, Washington, DC: Government Printing Office, 1916).

20. Christenson, "The Last of the Great Expeditions," 15.
21. Christenson, 30.
22. Roger W. Toll, letter to the director of the National Park Service, September 21, 1935, CANY 339/007-654, The Canyonlands NP Administrative Collection, Records, Southeast Utah Group Archives, National Park Service.
23. Charles Kelly, "Proposed Escalante National Monument," *Desert Magazine*, February 1941.
24. T.H. Watkins, *Righteous Pilgrim: The Life and Times of Harold L. Ickes, 1874–1952* (New York: Henry Holt, 1990), 382–3.
25. Elmo Richardson, "Federal Park Policy in Utah: The Escalante National Monument Controversy of 1935–1940," *Utah Historical Quarterly* 33, no. 2 (Spring 1965): 112
26. Merel S. Sager's comments are edited in Jesse L. Nusbaum, "Certain Aspects of the Proposed Escalante National Monument in Southeastern Utah," in *Region III Quarterly* 1, no. 2 (October 1939): 30.
27. Merel S. Sager, report submitted February 17, 1937, 13. Folder 654A, CANY 36607, The Canyonlands NP Administrative Collection, Records, Southeast Utah Group Archives, National Park Service.
28. Richardson, "Federal Park Policy in Utah," 116.
29. Sager, 25.
30. Ronald F. Lee, Supervisor of Historic Sites, Memorandum for the Director of the National Park Service, Re: Proposed Escalante National Park, February 25, 1940. The Canyonlands NP Administrative Collection, Records, Southeast Utah Group Archives, National Park Service.
31. Denis Clyde, "Opening the Road to Chesler Park: How Al Scorup Inadvertently Helped Create Canyonlands National Park," *Utah Historical Quarterly* 88, no. 3: 213.
32. Watkins, *Righteous Pilgrim*, 383.
33. See telegram from Harry H. Blood, Governor of Utah, October 14, 1938 to the Assistant Secretary of the Interior, CANY 339/007-654 and Gus P. Backman, Secretary, Chamber of Commerce of Salt Lake City, letter to the Director of the National Park Service, December 12, 1938, CANY 339/007-654 in the Canyonlands NP Administrative Collection, Records, Southeast Utah Group Archives, National Park Service.
34. Andrew Gulliford, "End of the Trail?" *Durango Herald*, May 10, 2009, and "Putting Ruess to rest: An end to a desert mystery?" *Durango Herald*, May 17, 2017.
35. See Philip Fradkin, *Everett Ruess: His Short Life, Mysterious Death, and Astonishing After Life* (Berkeley: University of California Press, 2011), and the film on Ruess, "Lost Forever," produced and directed by Diane Orr.
36. Interview with author for my *Durango Herald* story. Also William Lipe and Lynell Schalk, personal communication verifying Lister's discovery, December 3, 2016.

37. Gulliford, "End of the Trail?" *Durango Herald*, May 10, 2009.
38. Gulliford.
39. Scott Thybony, *The Disappearances: A Story of Exploration, Murder, and Mystery in the American West* (Salt Lake City: University of Utah Press, 2016), 240–1.
40. Thybony.
41. *NEMO* is Latin for "no one." In *Twenty Thousand Leagues Under the Sea*, Captain Nemo reveals, "I'm not what you would call a civilized man. I've broken with society." In many ways, so had Everett Ruess.
42. Thybony, *The Disappearances*, 18.
43. Thybony, 3.
44. Thybony, 38.
45. Thybony, 79.
46. Samuel Moon, *Tall Sheep: Harry Goulding Monument Valley Trader* (Norman: University of Oklahoma Press, 1992), xiv.
47. To understand the lasting impacts of stock reduction on Navajo families, see Marsha Weisiger, *Dreaming of Sheep in Navajo Country* (Seattle: University of Washington Press, 2009).
48. Thybony, *The Disappearances*, 125. A fictional version of Lucy's story but written by a trial attorney is C. Joseph Greaves's novel *Hard Twisted* (New York: Bloomsbury, 2012).
49. Moon, *Tall Sheep*, 87.
50. Wallace Stegner, *Mormon Country* (Lincoln, NE: Bison Books, 2003, first published 1942), 337.
51. Andrew Gulliford, "Marie Ogden's Search for Truth in the Utah Desert," *Durango Herald*, March 9, 2017.
52. Stanley J. Thayne, "The Home of Truth: The Metaphysical World of Marie Ogden," (MA thesis, Brigham Young University, November 2009).
53. Andrew Gulliford, "Marie Ogden and the Home of Truth," *Utah Adventure Journal*, May 16, 2017.
54. Stegner, *Mormon Country*, 340. To understand Marie Ogden's thinking see Marjorie C. Jones, "The Millennium as Envisioned by Marie Ogden," *Blue Mountain Shadows* 22 (Summer 2000): 72–7.
55. John F. Moore III, "The Enigma of Marie Ogden," *Blue Mountain Shadows* 36 (Spring 2007): 78. Also see Lee Bennett, "Marie Ogden's Monticello Garden," *Blue Mountain Shadows* 28 (Spring 2003): 65–71. For a child's memory of Marie Ogden, see Steve Jensen, personal communication to author, June 23, 2017.
56. Fife quote in Gulliford, "Marie Ogden's Search for Truth."
57. Clyde, "Opening the Road to Chesler Park," 206–7.
58. "Scenery as an Asset," *San Juan Record*, January 27, 1938.
59. H.E. Blake, "San Juan County Has Unique Scenic, Industrial Endowments," *San Juan Record*, March 3, 1938.

60. Ernie Pyle, *Home Country* (New York: William Sloane Associates, 1947), 395.
61. Pyle, 396.
62. Ernie Pyle, *Ernie Pyle's Southwest* (Desert-Southwest Publishers, 2003), 39. H. Jackson Clark remembered taking the same drive west of Bluff with his family in a new 1937 Buick. He wrote, "The road, a dimly marked path over the rock mesas, wound through a series of arroyos piled with rocks and debris. After we got down into the arroyo Dad had second thoughts about the trip. 'I heard that this might be a miserable road, but I didn't think it would be this bad. Maybe we'd better find a place to turn around and go back to Bluff.'" Instead they continued. H. Jackson Clark, *The Owl in Monument Canyon and other stories from Indian Country* (Salt Lake City: University of Utah Press, 1993), 15.
63. Pyle, *Ernie Pyle's Southwest*, 46.
64. Herbert E. Gregory, *The San Juan Country: A Geographic and Geologic Reconnaissance of Southeastern Utah*, Professional Paper 188, US Geological Survey (Washington, DC: US Government Printing Office, 1938), 10.
65. Gregory, 73.
66. "He conquered the river and died in an airplane," *Desert Magazine*, 1947, and a remembrance of Nevills by Randall Henderson, "Just Between You and Me" in the same issue. Also see Nancy Nelson, *Any Time, Any Place, Any River: The Nevills of Mexican Hat* (Flagstaff, AZ: Red Lake Books, 1991).
67. Marsha Weisiger, *Dreaming of Sheep in Navajo Country* (Seattle: University of Washington Press, 2009), 218. Also see Peter Iverson, *Diné: A History of the Navajos* (Albuquerque: University of New Mexico Press, 2002), 164.
68. Richard White, *The Roots of Dependency* (Lincoln: University of Nebraska Press, 1983), 306. For the best, most detailed analysis of this confrontation at Aneth, see "History Repeats Itself: Navajo Livestock Reduction in Southeastern Utah, 1933–1946," in Robert S. McPherson, *Navajo Land, Navajo Culture: The Utah Experience in the Twentieth Century* (Norman: University of Oklahoma Press, 2001).
69. Frank Jensen, "He Founded: '. . . A Place Where the Best of Christianity and the Indian Way of Life Could Merge," *Desert Magazine* (May 1962): 12.
70. Clark, *The Owl in Monument Canyon,* 69.
71. Clark, 67.
72. Clark, 72.
73. H. Baxter Liebler, *Boil My Heart for Me* (Salt Lake City: University of Utah Press, 1994), 24.
74. Liebler, xvi.
75. Liebler, 97.
76. McPherson, *Dinéjí Na 'Nitin: Navajo Traditional Teachings and History*, 180.

CHAPTER 10

1. Three special issues of *Blue Mountain Shadows* focus on Cottonwood Creek mining. See Lee Bennett, "Uranium Mining in San Juan County, Utah: South Cottonwood Creek and Elk Ridge," *Blue Mountain Shadows* 26 (Winter 2001–2002): 14. The reference to John Wetherill's discovery is also in Gary L. Shumway, "A History of the Uranium Industry on the Colorado Plateau," (PhD diss., University of Southern California, Los Angeles, 1970), 278. In those early years, Wetherill would have been looking for vanadium not uranium as that market did not yet exist.
2. Bennett, "Uranium Mining in San Juan County," 18.
3. Bennett, 25.
4. Gary Lee Shumway, "The Development of the Uranium Industry in San Juan County, Utah," (Master's thesis, Brigham Young University, 1964), 52.
5. H.C. Granger and E.P. Beroni, "Uranium occurrences in the White Canyon Area, San Juan County, Utah," Trace Elements Memorandum Report 7, US Geological Survey, December 1950.
6. Granger and Beroni, 13.
7. Shumway, "The Development of the Uranium Industry," 69.
8. Perrin Stryker, "The Great Uranium Rush," *Fortune* 1, issue 8 (August 1954): 90.
9. Stryker, 148.
10. Raye C. Ringholz, *Uranium Frenzy: Boom and Bust on the Colorado Plateau* (New York: Norton, 1989), 160.
11. Bennett, "Uranium Mining in San Juan County," 32.
12. Shumway, "The Development of the Uranium Industry," 80. Also see Dan Sorenson, "Wonder Mineral: Utah's Uranium," *Utah Historical Quarterly* XXXI (Summer 1963).
13. Shumway, 90.
14. For *San Juan Record* Headlines in early 1954, see January 14 "Standard Uranium Corporation Formed for the Development of the Big Buck Mines in San Juan County, Utah"; January 21, "Uranium Activities Bring Recorders Work to All Time High in San Juan"; February 25, "Utah Uranium Ore Fields Seen as Greatest in World" and "Uranium Miners Paid Over $3,000,000 in bonuses"; and March 4, "Rich Uranium-Vanadium Strike Hit in San Juan CO; Twenty Miles Southeast of Scenic Monticello, Utah."
15. Ringholz, 77. To understand the impacts of uranium on small towns, see Michael A. Amundson, *Yellowcake Towns: Uranium Mining Communities in the American West* (Boulder: University Press of Colorado, 2002).
16. Shumway, "The Development of the Uranium Industry," 92, 98.
17. Robert L. Payner, "The Effect of the Uranium and Petroleum Industries Upon the Economy of San Juan County, Utah," (Master's thesis, Brigham Young University, 1964), 5.
18. William L. Chenoweth, *The Geology and Production History of the Uranium Deposits in the White Canyon Mining District, San Juan County,*

Utah, Miscellaneous Publication 93-3, Utah Geological Survey, March 1993, 11.

19. Kathleen P. Chamberlin, *Under Sacred Ground: A History of Navajo Oil, 1922–1982* (Albuquerque: University of New Mexico Press, 2000), 89, 100.
20. Chamberlin, 89.
21. Chamberlin, 71.
22. Marjane Ambler, *Breaking the Iron Bonds: Indian Control of Energy Development* (Lawrence: University of Kansas Press, 1990), 74.
23. "Ute Indians Get Voting Rights for First Time in Coming County, State Elections," *Uintah Basin Standard,* September 4, 1958.
24. As chairman of the House Committee on the Public Lands, Utah Republican Congressman Don B. Colton drafted most of the Taylor Grazing Act, but he lost his congressional seat in the Franklin Roosevelt landslide after the advent of the Great Depression and the act was passed under Colorado congressman Edward T. Taylor. See Benjamin Kiser, "Bucking the White Elephant: Utah's Fight for Federal Management of the Public Domain, 1923–1934," *Utah Historical Quarterly* 88, no. 2 (Spring 2020).
25. Floyd W. Sharrock and Edward G. Keane, *Carnegie Museum Collection from Southeast Utah,* University of Utah Department of Anthropology, Anthropological Papers, no. 57, Glen Canyon Series, no. 16 (January 1962): 5.
26. Sharrock and Keane, 10. For an excellent analysis and summation of their work see the chapter "Moki Canyon" in David Roberts *In Search of the Old Ones* (New York: Simon & Schuster, 1996).
27. Sharrock and Keane, 63, and see Ellen Meloy, *The Last Cheater's Waltz* (New York: Henry Holt, 1999), 129–33.
28. Navajo Nation lands do spread north of the river thanks to the Aneth Extension sought by a quirky Methodist-related minister who successfully appealed to President Theodore Roosevelt in 1905 to grant Navajos grazing land north of the river at the community named Aneth, which is a Hebrew word.
29. M.A. Stokes and T.L. Smiley, "Tree-Ring Dates from the Navajo Land Claim I, The Northern Sector," *Tree-Ring Bulletin* 25, nos. 3–4: 8–18.
30. East of Bluff and west of the Colorado state line, Navajos continue to live and raise livestock on the Aneth Extension including lower Montezuma Creek and McCracken Mesa.
31. Beth King, "The Utah Navajos Relocation in the 1950s: Life Along the San Juan River," originally published by the *Canyon Echo* and the San Juan County Historical Commission in July 1996. Posted online August 16, 2019 on the new online *Canyon Echo.*
32. King.
33. District Court of San Juan County, Complaint No. 727, January 25, 1951, 105.

34. District Court of San Juan County, 106.
35. District Court of San Juan County, 109.
36. District Court of San Juan County, 110.
37. District Court of San Juan County, 113.
38. District Court of San Juan County, Utah, brief filed March 5, 1953, 2–4. Civil Case 784. Also see Case Files 727 and 728.
39. Young et al. v. Felornia et al. (two cases) No. 7772, Supreme Court of Utah, May 21, 1952, 646.
40. King, "The Utah Navajos Relocation in the 1950s." To better understand traditional Navajo land use rights see Jennifer Nez Denetdale, *Reclaiming Diné History* (Tucson: University of Arizona Press, 2007), and Klara Kelley and Harris Francis, *A Diné History of Navajoland* (Tucson: University of Arizona Press, 2019).
41. King, "The Utah Navajos Relocation in the 1950s."
42. King. Though the valuable land around Comb Ridge and the Bears Ears was not returned to the Navajos, farther to the east Navajos gained land north of the San Juan River in 1958 around the Hatch Trading Post and lower Montezuma Creek and McCracken Mesa. This was in exchange for land that became the town of Page, Arizona, staging site for the Glen Canyon Dam. Congress authorized the exchange on September 2, 1968.
43. Randall Henderson, "We Explored Dark Canyon," *Desert Magazine* (December 1946): 6.
44. Henderson.
45. Andrew Gulliford, "Outside Chances," *Durango Herald*, May 9, 2010.
46. Gene M. Stevenson, *Canyon Country Explorations & River Lore: The Remarkable Resilient Life of Kenny Frost* (Bluff, UT: Living Earth Studios, 2019), 108–14.
47. Henderson, "We Explored Dark Canyon," 9.
48. Randall Henderson, "19 Days on Utah Trails," *Desert Magazine* (October 1949 and November 1949). Quote from November issue.
49. Henderson.
50. Jack Breed, "Roaming the West's Fantastic Four Corners," *National Geographic* CI, no. 6 (June 1952): 704–6.
51. Breed, 704.
52. Andrew Gulliford, "Kent Frost: Last of the Desert Rats," *Durango Herald*, June 2008. Also see Buckley Jensen, "Kent Frost Honored," *San Juan Record*, February 11, 2009.
53. To learn Kent Frost's river running history, see the interview with him in *Boatman's Quarterly Review* 8, issue 4 (Fall 1995). On river historian Doc Marston's list of the first 100 people through the Grand Canyon by water, Frost came in at #88.
54. For other Jeep tours into the area, see W.G. Carroll, "Jeep Trail into Utah's Rugged Needles Country," *Desert Magazine*, November 1956. For photos

of Kent and Fern Frost see Charles E. Shelton, "Mechanical 'Mules,'" *Desert Magazine*, February 1960, 16–9.

55. Katie Lee, *All My Rivers Are Gone* (Boulder, CO: Johnson Books, 1998), 176.
56. Marian Krogmann, interview with author, Ouray, Colorado, July 16, 2019.
57. Lyndon L. Hargrave letter to Mary Beckwith, April 28, 1959. Kent Frost Papers, Accession 1687; Macaw Sash, Box 23; Folder 6; Special Collections, Marriott Library, University of Utah.
58. Mary Beckwith letter to Lyndon L. Hargrave, May 16, 1959. Kent Frost Papers, Accession 1687; Macaw Sash, Box 23; Folder 6; Special Collections, Marriott Library, University of Utah.
59. Beckwith.
60. Nancy Borson, Frances Berdan, Edward Stark, Jack States, and Peter J. Wettstein, "Origins of an Anasazi Scarlet Macaw Feather Artifact," *American Antiquity* 63, no. 1 (1998): 131–42. Also see "Macaw sash finds permanent home," *San Juan Record*, July 5, 2006, 6.
61. Teri Lynn Paul, personal communication, February 3, 2011.
62. Gulliford, "Kent Frost: Last of the Desert Rats," *Durango Herald*, June 2008.
63. Katie Lee, *All My Rivers Are Gone*; *Sandstone Seduction: Rivers and Lovers, Canyons and Friends* (Boulder, CO: Johnson Books, 2004), and *The Ghosts of Dandy Crossing* (Salt Lake City, UT: Dream Garden Press, 2014).
64. Andrew Gulliford, "Remembering the Goddess of Glen Canyon: Katie Lee," *Utah Adventure Journal*, January 16, 2018.
65. In the late 1970s, Abbey made these remarks in a speech to a meeting of environmental activists, but exactly where is unclear—some sources state it was a Vail, Colorado, conference in 1976, and others that it was at a meeting in Missoula, Montana in 1978. Cited in Gulliford, ed., *Outdoors in the Southwest: An Adventure Anthology* (Norman: University of Oklahoma Press, 2014), 12, and Steve Van Matre and Bill Weiler, eds., *The Earth Speaks* (Greenville, WV: Institute for Earth Education, 1983), 57.
66. Katie Lee letter to Kent and Fern Frost, October 9, 1957, Kent Frost Papers, Accession 1687; Katie Lee, Box 25; Folder 12; Special Collections, Marriott Library, University of Utah.
67. Katie Lee letter to Kent Frost, July 30, 1958, Kent Frost Papers, Accession 1687; Katie Lee, Box 25; Folder 12; Special Collections, Marriott Library, University of Utah.
68. Kent Frost letter to Katie Lee, January 20, 1958, Kent Frost Papers, Accession 1687; Katie Lee, Box 25; Folder 12; Special Collections, Marriott Library, University of Utah.
69. Kent Frost letter to Katie Lee. For more on Frost, see Kent Frost, *My Canyonlands* (New York: Abelard-Schuman, 1971), and the film by Chris Simon, "My Canyonlands: The Adventurous Life of Kent Frost," Sageland

Media, Salt Lake City, 2008. For a cover photo of Frost and an article on Utah's Canyonlands, see *Desert Magazine*, May 1967.

70. Frank Jensen, "A Long Weekend in Southeastern Utah," *Desert Magazine*, August 1960, 35.
71. To understand the history of moviemaking in Monument Valley see Samuel Moon, *Tall Sheep: Harry Goulding Monument Valley Trader* (Norman: University of Oklahoma Press, 1992), and Thomas J. Harvey, *Rainbow Bridge to Monument Valley: Making the Modern Old West* (Norman: University of Oklahoma Press, 2011).
72. Planning and Research Associates, Salt Lake City, "Master Plan Goals and Policies, San Juan County, Utah," Bureau of Community Development, University of Utah, September 1967, 44–5. Document in the Kent Frost Papers at the Marriott Library.
73. Planning and Research Associates, 3.
74. Gene Foushee, "What Makes Rocks Red?" *Desert Magazine*, June 1968. For another timely tourist essay see Walter Ford, "Down Utah's San Juan River," *Desert Magazine*, June 1969.
75. Lloyd Pierson, "Archaeological Resources of the Beef Basin, Needles, Salt Creek Mesa Area," Field Investigation Report, Proposed Needles Recreation Area, September 1959, August 1960 revised, US Department of the Interior, Region III, National Park Service, CANY 36607, Folder 659—Needles Area Report, 17. Records, Southeast Utah Group Archives, National Park Service.
76. Pierson.
77. Jen Jackson Quintano, *Blow Sand in His Soul: Bates Wilson, the Heart of Canyonland* (Moab, UT: Friends of Arches and Canyonlands National Parks, Bates Wilson Legacy Fund, 2014), 122. To understand early planning for Canyonlands, also see Lloyd M. Pierson, "The New Park Studies at Canyonlands National Park, 1959 and 1960, and Events Leading Up to Them," 1985, Records, Southeast Utah Group Archives, National Park Service.
78. Samuel J. Schmieding, "From Controversy to Compromise to Cooperation: The Administrative History of Canyonlands National Park," National Park Service, 2008, 176.
79. John F. Kennedy, Presidential State of the Union Address, January 11, 1962.
80. D. James Cannon, "Canyonlands Controversy: Should Utah Mine Minerals or Tourists?" *Desert Magazine* (April 1963): 31.
81. Weldon F. Heald, "Bold Plan to Save the Canyonlands," *Desert Magazine* (April 1962): 20.
82. Heald, 21.
83. Secretary of the Interior Udall Envisions a "Golden Circle" of National Parks and Monuments, National Park Service, Region Three Office, Santa Fe, New Mexico, news release for release August 2, 1961, CANY 339, Folder 124. Records, Southeast Utah Group Archives, National Park Service.

84. Secretary of the Interior Udall. To understand the impacts of Udall's golden circle concept see Arthur R. Gomez, *Quest for the Golden Circle: The Four Corners and the Metropolitan West, 1945–1970* (Albuquerque: University of New Mexico Press, 1994).
85. Letter to Honorable Wallace F. Bennett, US Senator from the San Juan County Commission, October 2, 1963 and associated letters from Senator Bennett and US Senator Frank E. Moss, CANY 339, Folder 671, Records, Southeast Utah Group Archives, National Park Service.
86. "Hole-in-the-Rock," *Desert Magazine* 26, no. 6 (June 1963): 3.
87. Quintano, 117.
88. Quintano, 138. For an evocative hiker's perspective on Canyonlands see Craig Childs, *Stone Desert: A Naturalist's Exploration of Canyonlands National Park* (Englewood, CO: Westcliffe Publishers, 1995).
89. Quintano, 142.
90. Philip Hyde letter to Senator Clair Engle, August 30, 1963. L58-RNPP CANY Archives.
91. Clarence P. Montgomery, Acting Director, NPS to Senator Clair Engle, October 16, 1963. L58-RNPP CANY Archives. Apparently, the BLM, the agency that would lose lands being converted into Canyonlands National Park, had granted a special use permit to the military and had not bothered to alert the NPS about the Department of Defense's proposed missile program. See memo from the Acting Regional Director to the Director, June 7, 1963, L58 CANY.
92. A. Chase Chamberlain and Robert S. McPherson, "Desert Cold Warriors," *Utah Historical Quarterly* 83, no. 2: 123.
93. Chamberlain and McPherson, 121.
94. Chamberlain and McPherson, 126–7. Also see CANY Folder 744, Series 1, Subseries 5, Athena Missile Program
95. Chamberlain and McPherson, 123.
96. Ed Abbey, *Desert Solitare* (New York: Ballantine Books, 1968, 1988), 189–90, 192.
97. Meloy, *The Last Cheater's Waltz*, 115–6. Also see Richard Q. Lewis and Russell H. Campbell, "Geology and Uranium Deposits of Elk Ridge and Vicinity, San Juan County, Utah," Geological Survey Professional Paper 474-B, prepared on behalf of the US Atomic Energy Commission (Washington, DC: Government Printing Office, 1965). Chenoweth in his earlier cited work on the White Canyon Mining District confirms that the boom years were 1955–1961.
98. Quintano, 133. Canyonlands have become so popular that there is a separate National Geographic guidebook for the area. See Scott Thybony, *Canyon Country Parklands: Treasures of the Great Plateau* (Washington, DC: National Geographic Society, 1993).
99. Bill Lipe, "Recollections of Cedar Mesa Archaeology," *Blue Mountain Shadows* 50 (Fall 2014): 9–11.

100. Quintano, 65. As Canyonlands National Park took shape, so did local tourism. See Royce Rollins, "It's Never Drab in Moab," *Desert Magazine*, December 1964.

CHAPTER 11

1. Charles Wilkinson, *Fire on the Plateau* (Washington, DC: Island Press, 1999), 55.
2. Ryan Roberts and Jenny Hurst, "Indian Education," *Blue Mountain Shadows* 9 (Winter 1991): 70.
3. Roberts and Hurst, 70.
4. H. Jackson Clark, *The Owl in Monument Canyon* (Salt Lake City: University of Utah Press, 1993), 69, 78.
5. Roberts and Hurst, "Indian Education," 72.
6. Calvin Black, "San Juan County Roads and Resources," in Allan Kent Powell, ed., *San Juan County, Utah: People, Resources, and History* (Salt Lake City: Utah State Historical Society, 1983), 252.
7. Clark, *The Owl in Monument Canyon*, 77.
8. Wilkinson, *Fire on the Plateau*, 59.
9. Wilkinson, 62.
10. Wilkinson, 65.
11. Edward Abbey, "Anarchy and the Morality of Violence," (Master's thesis, Department of Philosophy, University of New Mexico, 1959).
12. Edward Abbey and Philip Hyde, "How It Was," in *Slickrock: Endangered Canyons of the Southwest* (New York: Sierra Club/Charles Scribner's Sons), 20.
13. For a slightly different version and for this direct quote see Edward Abbey, "How it Was" in *Beyond the Wall* (New York: Henry Holt, 1971), 67.
14. Abbey and Hyde, "How It Was," 77.
15. Abbey and Hyde, 33.
16. Abbey and Hyde, 37. To understand Ed Abbey in context, see David Gessner, *All the Wild That Remains* (New York: W.W. Norton, 2015).
17. Abbey and Hyde, 44.
18. Jedediah S. Rogers, *Roads in the Wilderness: Conflict in Canyon Country* (Salt Lake City: University of Utah Press, 2013), 46.
19. Rogers, 56. Also see Black, "Roads and Resources of San Juan County."
20. Rogers, 57.
21. See Wayne E. Hage, *Storm Over Range Lands: Private Rights in Federal Lands* (Bellevue: Free Enterprise Press, 1989).
22. See the film "A Voice in the Wilderness" about Edward Abbey and his monkeywrenching as "field work" for research on his novel *The Monkeywrench Gang* (1975). Also see Rogers, *Roads in the Wilderness*, 51.
23. Abbey quotes from Vail Symposium VI, 1976, cited in Andrew Gulliford, *Boomtown Blues: Colorado Oil Shale* (Boulder: University Press of Colorado, 2003), 10–11.
24. Rogers, *Roads in the Wilderness*, 62.

25. Gardiner F. Dalley, ed., "Highway U-95 Archaeology: Comb Wash to Grand Flat" (Salt Lake City: University of Utah, May 1973), 11–2.
26. Dalley, 11.
27. Kenny Wintch, personal communication with author, August 5, 2020.
28. Kenneth L. Wintch, "The Miracle of CRM on Trust Lands," *Utah Archaeology* 21, no. 1 (2008): 122–3.
29. Wintch, 123.
30. See Andrew Gulliford, "The Pothunting Problem: Thieves of Time in the American Southwest," *Utah Adventure Journal*, May 16, 2012 and Gulliford, "Stories on Stone: Protecting Prehistoric Rock Art," in Jonathan Bailey, ed., *Rock Art: A Vision of a Vanishing Cultural Landscape* (Denver, CO: Johnson Books, 2019).
31. The most detailed description of events leading up to the Aneth oil field protest is in the chapter "Poverty, Politics, and Petroleum," in Robert S. McPherson, *Navajo Land, Navajo Culture: The Utah Experience in the Twentieth Century* (Norman: University of Oklahoma Press, 2001). See page 189 for versions of the shooting incident.
32. Kathleen P. Chamberlain, *Under Sacred Ground: A History of Navajo Oil, 1922–1982* (Albuquerque: University of New Mexico Press, 2000), 99.
33. Chamberlain, 99–100. Also see Al Henderson, "The Aneth Community: Oil Crisis in Navajoland," *The Indian Historian* 12, no. 1 (Winter 1979): 33–6.
34. See the chapter titled "Black Mesa" in Wilkinson *Fire on the Plateau.* Also see Andrew Gulliford, "Smokestacks Come Down: An Era of Deception, Exploitation Ends in Page, Arizona," *Durango Herald*, January 9–10, 2021.
35. In 1971 the Utah Navajo Development Council, with only Navajos on the board, would be created. It too would face audits and charges of fraud and fiscal mismanagement.
36. Robert S. McPherson, *A History of San Juan County: In the Palm of Time* (Salt Lake City: Utah State Historical Society & San Juan County Commission, 1995), 210–2.
37. Chamberlain, *Under Sacred Ground*, 112.
38. Chamberlain. Also see "Poverty, Politics, and Petroleum," in Robert S. McPherson, *Navajo Land, Navajo Culture: The Utah Experience in the Twentieth Century.*
39. Charles Seldin, "DOE Says It Favors Gibson Dome Site," *Salt Lake Tribune*, August 13, 1982.
40. "Dear Park Visitor," information letter, National Park Service, Arches and Canyonlands National Parks & Natural Bridges National Monument, L24, September 1982, CANY 299/01-02. At the CANY archives see "The Proposed Nuclear Waste Repository Collection (1980–1988).
41. Draft Environmental Assessment, Davis Canyon Site, Utah, US Department of Energy, Office of Civilian Radioactive Waste Management, Nuclear Waste Policy Act, Section 112, December 1984, 16.

42. National Park Service Position Statement, Proposed Nuclear Waste Repository—Gibson Dome, July 1982, CANY 200/03-69.
43. National Park Service, 16, 6-216
44. Draft Environmental Assessment, Davis Canyon Site, 13.
45. Nuclear Repository Elk Ridge site with map, Information on Waste Terminal Storage Program Activities in Utah, n.d., CANY 299, 03-69.
46. Don't Waste Utah Campaign, "Don't Waste Utah," press release, December 11, 1984. CANY 299, 03-58.
47. Clark Eisemann, "Commission Favors Nuclear Repository," *San Juan Record,* March 11, 1982.
48. Layne Miller, "Black Loves Southern Utah, Says N-Waste Dump Won't Hurt Tourism There," *Salt Lake Tribune*, September 7, 1982.
49. "Hatch, Marriott Oppose Plans for S.E. Utah Waste Facility," *Moab Times Independent*, April 29, 1982.
50. Needles District, Canyonlands National Park Visitor Register, n.d., CANY 299/02-51.
51. "Anti-Nuclear Waste Seminar Brought Large Group to Moab," *Times Independent*, August 26, 1982. Also see Sandy Graham, "N-Dump Unsettles Utah: Study by DOE Sparks Debate," *Rocky Mountain News*, July 4, 1982.
52. Scott M. Matheson, governor of Utah, to Mr. Charles R. Head, Acting Director, Operations Division, Office of Civilian Radioactive Waste Management, US Department of Energy, July 9, 1984. CANY 299/03-77. Also see Clark Eisemann, "As the Governor Views Repository," *San Juan Record*, May 13, 1982.
53. Andrew Gulliford, "Deadly Daughters, a Poisonous Past, and the Monticello Uranium Mill," *San Juan Record*, December 13, 2017.
54. Raye C. Ringholz, *Uranium Frenzy: Boom and Bust on the Colorado Plateau* (New York: Norton, 1989), 24.
55. Robert C. Dawes, personal communication, December 17, 2017. Dawes is a retired attorney who represented injured miners in claims for workers compensation benefits.
56. Gulliford, "Deadly Daughters."
57. Ringholz, *Uranium Frenzy*, 87.
58. Standard references on Four Corners area uranium mining and its economic and social impacts include Raye C. Ringholz, *Uranium Frenzy: Boom and Bust on the Colorado Plateau* (New York: Norton, 1989); Judy Pasternak, *Yellow Dirt* (New York: Free Press, 2011); and Doug Brugge, Timothy Benally, and Esther Yazzie-Lewis, *The Navajo People and Uranium Mining* (Albuquerque: University of New Mexico Press, 2006). Also see Don Unger, "A Brief History of Mining Reclamation in Navajo Country," report for the Navajo Abandoned Mining Lands Program © 2019, Navajo Tribal Authority. Report submitted January 2019.
59. David Boyle, "Energy Fuels Plans to Process Monazite Sands," *San Juan Record*, December 23, 2020.

60. Stephanie A. Malin and Peggy Petrzelka, "Left in the Dust: Uranium's Legacy and Victims of Mill Tailings Exposure in Monticello, Utah," *Society and Natural Resources* 23, no. 12 (2010): 1187.
61. Malin and Petrzelka, 1188.
62. Malin and Petrzelka, 1189. Also see Stephanie Malin, *The Price of Nuclear Power: Uranium Communities and Environmental Justice* (New Brunswick, NJ: Rutgers University Press, 2015).
63. Malin and Petrzelka, 1191. Also see Ken Silver, "The Yellowed Archives of Yellowcake," *Public Health Reports* 111, no. 2 (March-April, 1996).
64. Monticello Mill Interpretive Plaque, 2017.
65. Malin and Petrzelka, 1193. Also see Amy Joi O'Donoghue, "Monticello Mill Victims Seek Help on Utah's Capitol Hill," *Deseret News*, February 24, 2013.
66. Robert Maughan, personal communication to author, March 20, 2019.
67. Malin and Petrzelka, 1196.
68. Katherine Metcalf Nelson, "Bluff: Dead or Alive, the Best Old Town in Utah," *Utah Holiday* (June 1985): 69–74.
69. Andrew Gulliford, ed., *Outdoors in the Southwest: An Adventure Anthology* (Norman: University of Oklahoma Press, 2014), 67.
70. Gulliford, "Into the Mountain Lion's Den," 72–6.
71. Tony Hillerman, *A Thief of Time* (New York: Harper Row, 1988), 127–8.
72. Craig Childs, *Finders Keepers* (New York: Little, Brown & Co. 2010), 53.
73. Brett Shumway, "Pot Hunting in San Juan County," *Beehive History* 012 (1986): 30.
74. Brent Israelsen, "Pothunter Is in Grave Trouble Again," *Deseret News*, November 23, 1994.
75. Christian Lund, "Raiders of the Lost Art: Outlaw Diggers of Anasazi Ruins," *Utah Holiday* (February 1985): 46.
76. Lund. As director of the Western New Mexico University Museum in Silver City, New Mexico, I also saw pothunters using a bulldozer to loot Mimbres culture sites. My photo of a bulldozer quickly removing centuries of soil from an ancient village has been used in exhibits on cultural resource protection.
77. Tamara Jones, "Residents 'Pillaging and Sacking San Juan County for 100 Years': Pothunters Resent Enforcement of Federal Law," *Los Angeles Times*, December 28, 1986.
78. Sid Kane, "The Big—And Illegal—Business of Indian Artifacts," *New York Times*, September 7, 1986.
79. Kane.
80. Jones, "Residents 'Pillaging and Sacking.'" Also see Jim Robbins, "The Great Artifact [sic] Grab," *Chicago Tribune*, August 10, 1986.
81. Israelsen and Jones.
82. Kane, "The Big—And Illegal—Business of Indian Artifacts."
83. Lund, "Raiders of the Lost Art," 40.

84. Tamara Jones, "'Time Bandits' Ransacking History," *The Herald Magazine*, Provo, Utah, January 14, 1987.
85. Lund, 46; Israelsen, "Pothunter Is in Grave Trouble Again."
86. Scott Armstrong, "'Culture Thieves' Filch US History," *Christian Science Monitor*, June 16, 1986.
87. Lund, "Raiders of the Lost Art," 40.
88. Lund. To try and explain the value of scientific archaeology, the Utah State Historical Society in *Beehive History 003* published an article by Kay Sargent, "On a Dig in Southeastern Utah" (1978). Unfortunately, the description of digging a site close to Blanding, Westwater Ruin, may have only resulted in more vandalism.
89. Lund, "Raiders of the Lost Art," 42.
90. Lund, 44.
91. Jones, "'Time Bandits' Ransacking History."
92. Shumway, 31.

CHAPTER 12

1. Daniel McCool, Expert Witness Report in the case of Navajo Nation v. San Juan County, UT, Case. No. 2:12-cv-00039-RS, August 18, 2015, 117.
2. With the 1986 San Juan County pothunting raid the USFS got the search warrants. With the 2009 raid, it was the BLM and FBI.
3. See Patricia L. Parker, "Keepers of the Treasures: Protecting Historic Properties and Cultural Traditions on Indian Lands: A Report on Tribal Preservation Funding Needs Submitted to Congress" (Washington, DC: US Department of the Interior, National Park Service, Interagency Resources Division, 1990) and Advisory Council on Historic Preservation, Report to the President and Congress of the United States, 1993.
4. "Navajo Council Bans Uranium Mining," *Deseret News*, April 23, 2005.
5. Janet Wilcox, "Movies that Memorialized Monument Valley," *San Juan Record*, March 7, 2018; Robert McPherson, "Navajos and the Film Industry in Monument Valley, 1930–1964," *Blue Mountain Shadows*, no. 39, and Thomas J. Harvey, "John Ford and Monument Valley: The Production of a Mythical National Space" and "Salting the Scenery: Modern Tourists in the Modern Landscape," in *Rainbow Bridge to Monument Valley* (Norman: University of Oklahoma Press, 2011).
6. Gary Topping, *Glen Canyon and the San Juan Country* (Moscow: University of Idaho Press, 1997), 158.
7. Jim Woolf, "Canyonlands Park Expansion Proposed to Foil N-Dump Plan," *Salt Lake Tribune*, April 27, 1982.
8. McCool, Expert Witness Report, 172.
9. McCool, 173.
10. Cited in McCool, see Hector Tobar, "Navajos Try to Seize Power in Sweeping Bid for Office: Politics: An All-Indian Slate Runs in County

Election in Southern Utah, with the Goal of Redistributing Funds," *Los Angeles Times*, August 27, 1990; Carol Sisco, "Navajos Build Pathway to Added Clout," *Salt Lake Tribune*, June 24, 1990; and Sisco, "Navajos Flock to Polls in Historic San Juan Vote," *Salt Lake Tribune*, November 7, 1990.

11. Daniel McCool, personal communication and interview, July 22, 2020. The blue ribbon commission met and did its work in 1995 using the Center for Public Policy and Administration from the University of Utah. A copy of their final report is in Special Collections at the Marriott Library.
12. Christopher Smith, "Indians Say Put Judge in Jail," *Salt Lake Tribune*, September 17, 1997.
13. Christopher Smith, "Anasazi Graves No Different, State to Argue," *Salt Lake Tribune*, August 31, 1997.
14. Andrew Gulliford, *Sacred Objects and Sacred Places: Preserving Tribal Traditions* (Boulder: University Press of Colorado, 2000), 13.
15. Gulliford, 14. To understand tribal perspectives, also see Patricia L. Parker, ed., "Traditional Cultural Properties: What You Do and How We Think," *CRM* 16 (1993).
16. Gulliford, 15.
17. Timothy Egan, "In the Southwest, Heritage Takes a Hit," *New York Times*, November 2, 1995.
18. Marianne Funk, "Who Gets to Keep 105 Seized Artifacts? Judge to Let 3 Blanding Residents Decide," *Deseret News*, March 5, 1994.
19. Brent Israelsen, "Pothunter Is in Grave Trouble Again," *Deseret News*, Nov. 23, 1994; and Israelsen, "Will Repeat Pothunter Get More Than 'Slap'?" *Deseret News,* September 22, 1995.
20. Brent Israelsen, "Notorious Utah Pothunter Found Guilty on 4 Counts," *Deseret News*, August 3, 1995
21. Egan, "In the Southwest, Heritage Takes a Hit."
22. Julie Cart, "Looting Indian Graves Is Big Business in Utah/BLM Agents Fight Continuing Battle Against Robbers," *Los Angeles Times*, April 8, 2001. The agents remembered to return to the back dirt pile, but they should have looked at it in the first place. Going through back dirt at an archaeological crime site is taught in standard ARPA investigative training.
23. Cart.
24. Cart.
25. US Court of Appeals, Tenth Circuit, United States of America, Plaintiff-Appellee, V. Earl K. Shumway, Defendant-Appellant, Nos. 95-4201, 96-4000, decided May 6, 1997.
26. Joe Costanzo, "Pot-Hunter Sentence Reduced," *Deseret News*, June 7, 1997.
27. References to the unique Utah license plate ANASAZI appear in numerous newspaper accounts and investigation reports about the Redds. The *Salt Lake Tribune* reported, "The vehicle used by the couple bore vanity license plates with the single word ANASAZI." Assistant Attorney General

Joanne Slotnik commented that was a "fair implication" the Redds "had a significant interest in and knowledge of the Anasazi culture." See Christopher Smith, "Anasazi Grave No Different, State to Argue," *Salt Lake Tribune*, August 31, 1997.

28. Report, San Juan County Sheriff's Office, Case #9601-26, Ben Naranjo, Deputy, n.d. Redd Files, State Institutional Trust Land Administration. Also see Witness Interview—Rigby Wright, retired San Juan County Sheriff, interview by Dawn J. Soper, SITLA attorney, February 23, 1998. Redd Files, State Institutional Trust Land Administration.
29. Utah Code Annotated, Volume 1B, 2019 Replacement, Titles 1-9, Lexis Nexis (1953), 644–5.
30. Utah School and Institutional Trust Lands Administration v. Dr. James R. Redd and Jeanne Redd, Complaint Civil No. 9707-15, filed in the Seventh District Court for San Juan County, State of Utah, February 24, 1997. Redd Files, State Institutional Trust Land Administration.
31. US Department of the Interior, Bureau of Land Management, Incident Record, February 9, 1996, Redd Files, State Institutional Trust Land Administration.
32. Abuse or desecration of a dead human body (Utah Code Ann. [UCA] 76-9-704) and trespassing on state trust lands (UCA Title 53C). This sequence of events comes from personal communication with attorney John Andrews, chief legal counsel for SITLA from 1996–2018. Author interview, August 4, 2020.
33. Letter from Ferrell Secakuku to William Benge, Grand County Attorney, May 16, 1996, SITLA files.
34. "Pothunters in Cottonwood Wash," *Canyon Echo*, February 1996, and Christopher Smith, "S. Utah Couple Want Grave-Robbing Charges Dismissed," *Salt Lake Tribune*, January 10, 1997.
35. Preliminary Hearing, State of Utah v. Jeanne and James Redd, March 20, 1997, in the Seventh Judicial District Court, Monticello Court, San Juan County State of Utah, 46–8.
36. Preliminary Hearing, State of Utah v. Jeanne and James Redd. Also see Christopher Smith, "Charges Dismissed Against Couple Who Dug Up Ancient Burial Site," *Salt Lake Tribune*, March 21, 1997.
37. Christopher Smith, "Judge Admits Conflict in Pothunting Case," *Salt Lake Tribune*, April 13, 1997.
38. Christopher Smith, "Anasazi Graves No Different, State to Argue," *Salt Lake Tribune,* August 31, 1997.
39. Joe Costanzo, "Doctor Didn't Desecrate Indian Site, Court Rules," *Deseret News*, February 20, 1998.
40. State of Utah v. Jeanne Redd, Preliminary Hearing Case No. 9827-63, in the Seventh Judicial District Court in and for San Juan County, Utah, October 8, 1998.

41. Because UCA Title 53C allows for treble damages the amount rose to $250,000.
42. Joe Bauman, "New Life for Utah Anasazi Case: Utah Supreme Court Rules Ancient Remains Are Protected by Law," *Deseret News*, December 29, 1999.
43. Bauman.
44. Christopher Smith, "Was Pit a Grave or Scrap Pile?" *Salt Lake Tribune*, January 8, 2001, and Christopher Smith, "High Court: Grave-Robbing Charge Sticks," *Salt Lake Tribune*, December 29, 2001.
45. Utah School and Institutional Trust Lands Administration vs. Dr. James R. Redd and Jeanne Redd, Stipulation of Settlement, Case No. 9707-15CV, January 14, 2003.
46. They changed the Cultural Sites Protection Act (CSPA) or UCA 76-6-901, which is the state's version of the federal ARPA law.
47. McCool, Expert Witness Report, 128.
48. McCool, 172.
49. Utah Bureau of Land Management Proposed Comb Wash Integrated Watershed Plan and San Juan Resource Management Plan Amendment, 1997–1998, December 1997, 4. The presidential executive orders include Executive Order #12898, February 16, 1994 to address environmental justice in minority populations and low-income populations and Executive Order #13007 Indian Sacred Sites, May 24, 1996.
50. McCool.
51. Utah BLM Proposed Comb Wash Integrated Watershed Plan, 35.
52. Bureau of Land Management Proposed Comb Wash Integrated Watershed Plan and San Juan Resource Area Management Plan Amendment and Revised Environmental Assessment, February 1999, 43. Note these BLM reports are in Box 77, Folder 9 of the Kent Frost Papers, Marriott Library, University of Utah.
53. Amy Irvine, "Open Wide: Can Indian Creek Swallow the Agendas of Climbers, Cowgirls and Conservationists?" *Climbing*, no. 216 (November 1, 2002): 65.
54. Jedediah S. Rogers, *Roads in the Wilderness: Conflict in Canyon Country* (Salt Lake City: University of Utah Press, 2013), 154. Rogers has an entire chapter in his book about access issues in Arch Canyon.
55. Rogers, 160.
56. Helen O'Neill, "Blanding: A Town's Love for Indian Artifacts Backfires," *Salt Lake Tribune*, October 3, 2009
57. O'Neill. Also see Brendan Borrell, "FBI Sting Catches Alleged Archaeological Thieves in Southwest," *Scientific American*, June 16, 2009.
58. Howard Berkes, "Artifact Sting Stuns Utah Town," Morning Edition, National Public Radio, July 1, 2009.
59. O'Neill, "Blanding: A Town's Love for Indian Artifacts Backfires."

60. "Conversation: The Looters Next Door," *Archaeology* 62, no. 5 (September/October 2009).
61. Brandon Loomis, "18 Months After Utah Raid, Do Artifact Laws Stop Theft?" *Salt Lake Tribune*, January 3, 2011.
62. Berkes, "Artifact Sting Stuns Utah Town."
63. Kathleen Sharp, "The Rescue Mission: An Exclusive Look at the Greatest Haul of Native American Artifacts, Ever," *Smithsonian Magazine*, November 2015. Also see Brandon Loomis, "Officials Say the Collection Was Partly Stored and Partly on Display at the Home," *Salt Lake Tribune*, July 8, 2009.
64. Sharp.
65. O'Neill, "Blanding: A Town's Love for Indian Artifacts Backfires."
66. Berkes, "Artifact Sting Stuns Utah Town."
67. Berkes.
68. Joe Mozingo, "A Sting in the Desert," *Los Angeles Times*, September 21, 2014.
69. Mozingo. In Utah, an item stolen worth more than $1,500 but less than $5,000 is a third-degree felony. In Arizona, a Class 6 felony is a stolen item of $1,000 or more but less than $2,000. Tribal laws may differ.
70. Mozingo.
71. Berkes, "Artifact Sting Stuns Utah Town."
72. Mozingo story requoted in Kyle Swenson, "2009 Sting Contributes to Bears Ears Controversy" *The Washington Post*, reprinted in the *Durango Herald*, December 6, 2017.
73. O'Neill, "Blanding: A Town's Love for Indian Artifacts Backfires."
74. O'Neill. Also see Mark Rose, "Beyond Stone & Bone: Hearts and Minds in Utah," *Archaeology Magazine*, Archaeological Institute of America, October 9, 2009.
75. Craig Childs, "The Good Ol' Artifact Boys," *Los Angeles Times*, June 15, 2009. Also see Beth Kampschror, "In Pothunter Country, a Small Effort at Healing," writers on the Range of *High Country News* in *The Park Record*, July 29–31, 2009.
76. "In the News: Project Cerberus," *American Archaeology* 13, no. 3 (2009): 2.
77. Sharp, "The Rescue Mission."
78. Emiley Morgan, "Two Plead Guilty in 'Isolated' Indian Artifacts Deal," *Deseret News*, March 30, 2010.
79. Joe Mozingo, "A Sting in the Desert," *Los Angeles Times*, September 21, 2014.
80. Mozingo.
81. Mozingo.
82. Howard Berkes, "Mother, Daughter Get Probation in Artifacts Theft," National Public Radio, September 16, 2009.
83. Mozingo.
84. Berkes, "Mother, Daughter Get Probation in Artifacts Theft."

85. Loomis, "18 Months After Utah Raid."
86. Loomis.
87. Maryboy quote cited in Jim Stiles, "The Blanding Raids: Shame and Hypocrisy All Around," *The Canyon Country Zephyr*, July 30, 2019.
88. Brandon Loomis, "Officials Say the Collection Was Partly Stored and Partly on Display at the Home," *Salt Lake Tribune*, July 8, 2009.
89. Paul Foy, "Feds Seek to Dismiss Artifact-Raid Lawsuit," *Cortez Journal*, June 16, 2012, and Sandi Gurman and Brady McCombs, "Utah Family Wants Day in Court after Suicide," *Durango Herald*, September 21, 2016.
90. Mark Rose, "Hearts and Minds in Utah," Beyond Stone & Bone, *Archaeology: Archaeological Institute of America*, October 9, 2009, and Joe Mozingo, *Los Angeles Times.*
91. O'Neill, "Blanding: A Town's Love for Indian Artifacts Backfires."
92. Kyle Swenson, "Pilfered Artifacts, Three Suicides and the Struggle Over Federal Land in Utah," *The Washington Post*, December 5, 2017.
93. FederalGrantsWire, "Project Title: BLM-Utah, Cerberus Collection Interpretive Plan Partnership," n.d.
94. Regina Lopez Whiteskunk, "Bears Ears our Sacred Space," talk at Durango, Colorado, Public Library, May 7, 2019. To understand Native American sacred places, see Andrew Gulliford, *Sacred Objects and Sacred Places: Preserving Tribal Traditions* (Boulder: University Press of Colorado, 2000), and Todd Allin Morman, *Many Nations Under Many Gods: Public Land Management and American Indian Sacred Sites* (Norman: University Press of Oklahoma, 2018).
95. Andrew Gulliford, "Proud of its Past—Edge of the Cedars: What's Found in Utah, Stays in Utah," *Durango Herald*, February 12, 2011.
96. Gulliford.
97. Gulliford.
98. To understand this process, see Rebecca M. Robinson, *Voices from Bears Ears: Seeking Common Ground on Sacred Land* (Tucson: University of Arizona Press, 2018).
99. Andrew Gulliford, "Only the Beginning in Recapture Wash," *Salt Lake Tribune*, February 5, 2011.
100. Gulliford.
101. Zak Podmore, "Utah Lawmaker Phil Lyman Sues Feds Over Recapture Canyon Dispute, Seeks $10M in Damages," *Salt Lake Tribune*, November 10, 2019. San Juan County spent $440,000 with the California-firm of JW Howard Attorneys attempting to sue the federal government over the Recapture Canyon ATV route. The county's claim is now part of a larger statewide RS 2477 claim on 35,000 miles of roads statewide. See Zak Podmore, "Recapture Canyon Case Costs San Juan County $440,000," *Salt Lake Tribune*, February 10, 2020.
102. Brian Maffly, "Legislative Resolution: Drilling Is 'Best Use' for Cedar Mesa and San Rafael Swell," *Salt Lake Tribune*, March 9, 2015.

103. US Department of the Interior, Bureau of Land Management, Environmental Assessment, DOI-BLM-UT-Y020-2012-0001, Hole-in-the-Rock Foundation Trekking SRP, April 2015.
104. National Congress of American Indians, Resolution #EC-15-002, "Supporting the Presidential Proclamation of the Bears Ears National Monument, Including Collaborative Management Between Tribal Nations and the Federal Agencies," September 20, 2015.
105. Whiteskunk speech. Also see Andrew Gulliford, "Canyon Country Controversy," *Durango Herald*, March 8, 2015.
106. Bears Ears Inter-Tribal Coalition, "Proposal to President Barack Obama for the Creation of Bears Ears National Monument," October 15, 2015, 30.
107. Walt Dabney, opinion, "Guest Commentary: Make Bears Ears a National Monument," *Denver Post*, November 24, 2015.
108. Brian Maffly, "Unhappy with 'Lip Service' from Utah Delegation, Tribes to Take Request for Bears Ears Monument Straight to Obama," *Salt Lake Tribune*, December 31, 2015.
109. "Bears Ears Inter-Tribal Coalition Condemns Zinke Recommendation to Eviscerate Bears Ears National Monument," press release, Monument Valley, Utah, June 12, 2017.
110. Charles Wilkinson, "The Greatness of the Bears Ears National Monument," Fort Lewis College Campus, Durango, Colorado, sponsored lecture by the Center of Southwest Studies, March 22, 2018.
111. Barack Obama, Proclamation 9558, "Proclamation—Establishment of the Bears Ears National Monument," The White House, December 28, 2016. Also see April Reese, "Scientists sue to protect Utah monument—and fossils that could rewrite Earth's history," *Science Magazine*, January 17, 2019. Also see Jessica Uglesich et al., "Paleontology of Bears Ears National Monument (Utah, USA): History of Exploration, Study, and Designation," *Geology of the Intermountain West* 7 (2020).
112. US Department of the Interior, Bureau of Land Management, Environmental Assessment, DOI-BLM-UT-Y020-2012-0001, Hole-in-the-Rock Foundation Trekking SRP, Finding of No Significant Impact, December 2015, signed January 12, 2016.
113. The public had only two minutes to speak, but non-native locals booed and interrupted Native speakers. Richard Robinson, personal communication, email to author, February 6, 2017. On that day, 2,000 people came to Bluff and 200 were allowed to speak for two minutes each. Source from Charles Wilkinson, "The Greatness of the Bears Ears National Monument."
114. Knipmeyer, 123.
115. Bears Ears Inter-Tribal Coalition, "Protecting the Whole Bears Ears Landscape: A Call to Honor the Full Cultural and Ecological Boundaries," October 18, 2016, 3.
116. Scott Groene, Executive Director, Southern Utah Wilderness Alliance membership letter, Fall 2016.

117. Terri Martin, personal communication to author, July 22, 2020.
118. Bill Hedden, Executive Director, Grand Canyon Trust membership letter, October 2016.
119. Robert Redford, "Obama Must Protect Sacred Utah Land," *Time*, August 16, 2016.
120. Jonathan Thompson, "A Monumental Divide: Whose Homeland?" *High Country News*, October 31, 2016. This well-researched article is probably the best synthesis of local Utah opposition and support for a Bears Ears National Monument in fall 2016.
121. Monticello City Council, Bears Ears National Monument Opposition, Resolution No. 2016-10, August 9, 2016.
122. Griselda Nevarez, "Forged Letters Mislead Utah Residents About Native American Land Proposal," *The Guardian*, June 5, 2016.
123. Thompson, 20.
124. Wendy Black, "Bears Ears Proposal Disregards Existing Rights," letter to the editor, *San Juan Record*, November 23, 2016.
125. John C. Ruple, "The Transfer of Public Lands Movement: The Battle to Take 'Back' Lands That Were Never Theirs," *Colorado Natural Resources, Energy & Environmental Review* 29, no. 1. Also see John D. Leshy, "Are U.S. Public Lands Unconstitutional?" *Hastings Law Journal* 69, (February 2018), and *Debunking Creation Myths About America's Public Lands*, 2018 Wallace Stegner Lecture (Salt Lake City: University of Utah Press, 2018).
126. This author filed a Utah open records act request in 2019 or a GRAMA filing to gain public records including emails, letters, drafts, reports, invoices, and attachments paid for by $500,000 of public funds to the Davillier Group. *The Salt Lake Tribune* has reported that a lot of those funds were used for lobbying. Zak Podmore, "San Juan County Paid Nearly $500K to Louisiana Law Firm to Lobby for Bears Ears Reductions," *Salt Lake Tribune*, July 28, 2019. A review of the invoices prove that over $130,000 dollars were paid to third parties that were security firms specializing in the Middle East. What those firms may have had to do with lobbying Secretary of the Interior Ryan Zinke, a former Navy Seal, was somewhat clarified by the *Salt Lake Tribune*. See Zak Podmore, "'We Will Circle All The Wagons,': Newly Obtained Emails Show San Juan County's Push to Reduce Bears Ears," *Salt Lake Tribune*, April 8, 2021.
127. J.R. Carlson, Stillwater Technical Solutions, "The Advisability of Designating the Bears Ears as a Monument Under the Antiquities Act," October 2016.
128. Zak Podmore, "San Juan County Frustrations Spill Out in the Open with Ballot Drive and Allegations of Racism," *Salt Lake Tribune*, August 25, 2019.
129. Zak Podmore, "Phil Lyman on the Costs of His County's Legal Battles," *Four Corners Free Press*, May 2, 2018.

CHAPTER 13

1. Keith H. Basso, *Wisdom Sits in Places: Landscape and Language among the Western Apache* (Albuquerque: University of New Mexico Press, 1996), xiii.
2. Robert Macfarlane, *The Wild Places* (New York: Penguin Books, 2007), 145.
3. Basso, *Wisdom Sits in Places*, 35.
4. Robert S. McPherson, *As if the Land Owned Us: An Ethnohistory of the White Mesa Utes* (Salt Lake City: University of Utah Press, 2011). See Chapter 12, "Posey and the Last White Uprising."
5. Juliet Eilperin, "Trump Is Eager to Undo Sacred Tribal Monument, Says Orrin Hatch," *Washington Post*, January 27, 2017. Also see Tom Kenworthy, "Republicans Spoiling to Undo Bears Ears, Gut Antiquities Act," *Navajo Times*, January 5, 2017; Jonathan Thompson, "Bears Ears National Monument Is a Go: Despite Compromises, Opposition Is Riled Up," *High Country News*, January 23, 2017.
6. Southern Utah Wilderness Alliance, "Bears Ears National Monument: The First Truly Native American National Monument in History!" flyer, 2017.
7. Barack Obama, Proclamation 9558, "Proclamation—Establishment of the Bears Ears National Monument," The White House, December 28, 2016.
8. "Hundreds turn out to celebrate Bears Ears Ntl Monument," *San Juan Record*, January 11, 2017.
9. "Joy, Rage Greet Bears Ears," *Four Corners Free Press*, January 2017. Eric Niven, "Monticello City Council Addresses Bears Ears Issues," and Kara Laws, "Blanding City Council Addresses Bears Ears Issues," *San Juan Record*, January 18, 2017. Brady McCombs, "Bears Ears Supporters Worried Trump Might Undermine Efforts," *Navajo Times*, January 5, 2017. Kara Laws, "Blanding States Position on Bears Ears Nat'l Mon," and Bill Boyle, "Fate of State Trust Land In Bears Ears NM Unresolved," *San Juan Record*, February 1, 2017.
10. Peter Metcalf, "Op-ed: Time for Outdoor Retailers to Leave Utah and its Anti-Recreation Politics," *Salt Lake Tribune*, January 11, 2017. Also see Barry McCombs, "Black Diamond Founder: Outdoor Retail Show Should Leave Utah," *Denver Post*, January 10, 2017; Luke Perkins, "Utah's Stance Costs it $45M," *Durango Herald*, February 18, 2017; "Patagonia Is Gearing Up for War with Utah Republicans Over National Monument," *Huffington Post*, January 13, 2017; and Tom Diegel, "Bears Ears Is Good Business," *Utah Adventure Journal* (Mid-Winter 2017).
11. "Utah Passes Bill to Rescind Bears Ears Ntl Monument," *San Juan Record*, February 8, 2017.
12. Alexandra M. Wyatt, "Antiquities Act: Scope of Authority for Modification of National Monuments," Congressional Research Service, CRS Report No. R44687, Nov. 14, 2016.
13. "San Juan County Will Be First Stop if New Interior Secretary Is Appointed," *San Juan Record*, January 25, 2017.

14. David Sharp, "Republicans in Utah Seek Reversal on Bears Ears," *Durango Herald*, March 6, 2017; also see the same article titled "GOP in Maine, Utah Wants Trump to Undo Monuments," *Wyoming Tribune Eagle*, March 6, 2017.
15. Eric Lipton and Lisa Friedman, "Oil was Central in Decision to Shrink Bears Ears Monument, Emails Show," *New York Times*, March 2, 2018.
16. John Yoo and Todd Gaziano, "Presidential Authority to Revoke or Reduce National Monument Designations," American Enterprise Institute, March 2017. See March 29, 2017 AEI key points, 2.
17. James R. Rasband, "The Future of the Antiquities Act," *Journal of Land, Resources, and Environmental Law* 21 (2001): 620, 624.
18. Meghan Drueding, "Ancient Echoes: A New National Monument is Designated—And Immediately Threatened," *Preservation* (Spring 2017): 61. Also see Justin McBrayer and Sarah Roberts-Cady, "The Case for Preserving Bears Ears," *Ethics Policy & Environment* 21, no. 1 (2018): 48–51.
19. Heidi McIntosh, "Gutting America's National Treasures is Unlawful and Unwise," *Time Magazine*, March 31, 2017.
20. John Dougherty, "The Fight Over Bears Ears: A Tale of Two Towns," *The Revelator*, an initiative of the Center for Biological Diversity, June 28, 2017.
21. Commission for the Stewardship of Public Lands, Utah State Capitol Complex, report to Ryan Zinke, Secretary of the Department of the Interior, May 25, 2017.
22. Thomas Burr, "House Dems: Documents Show Feds Consulted with Utah Leaders on Bears Ears Before Designation," *Salt Lake Tribune*, April 14, 2017.
23. Burr.
24. Burr.
25. Rebecca Worby, "Zinke Listened at Bears Ears, but Supporters Felt Unheard," *High Country News*, May 29, 2017, 5. Also see KUED, Public Television, Salt Lake City, Utah, "Battle Over Bears Ears," aired November 16, 2018, a Public Broadcasting System affiliate.
26. Mark Squillace et al., "Presidents Lack the Authority to Abolish or Diminish National Monuments," *Virginia Law Review Online* 103, no. 55 (2017).
27. To understand how comments were used or not see Chris D'Angelo, "Emails Show Interior Expected to Learn Nothing from Public Input on Bears Ears Review," *Politics: Huffington Post*, May 17, 2018. Also see J.R. Carlson, Stillwater Technical Solutions, "The Advisability of Designating the Bears Ears as a Monument Under the Antiquities Act," October 2016.
28. Pamela Baldwin, "Presidential Authority to Modify or Revoke National Monuments," September 17, 2017, manuscript in possession of the author. Two other land management laws—the Forest Service Organic Act of 1897 and the Pickett Act of 1910 both authorized the president to withdraw

certain types of public land and specifically stated that the Chief Executive could modify or change those actions—but not the Antiquities Act. For a different perspective arguing repeal of the Antiquities Act see John F. Shepherd, "Up the Grand Staircase: Executive Withdrawals and the Future of the Antiquities Act," Proceedings of the Forty-Third Annual Rocky Mountain Mineral Law Institute, 1997.

29. Johannsen, 458.
30. See KUED, "Battle Over Bears Ears."
31. Heidi McIntosh, "Gutting America's National Treasures Is Unlawful and Unwise," *Time Magazine*, March 31, 2017.
32. Donald Trump, Proclamation 9861, "Presidential Proclamation Modifying the Bears Ears National Monument," The White House, December 4, 2017.
33. Partners in the lawsuits include the Navajo Nation, the National Parks Conservation Association, the Sierra Club, Grand Canyon Trust, Defenders of Wildlife, Great Old Broads for Wilderness, Western Watersheds Project, Wild Earth Guardians, Center for Biological Diversity, Friends of Cedar Mesa, Southern Utah Wilderness Alliance and amicus briefs including one from the American Anthropological Association and one from US Senator Tom Udall from New Mexico and US Representative Raúl M. Grijalva from Arizona representing 118 members of Congress.
34. Elizabeth Shogren, "Lawsuits Challenge Trump's Trim of Utah monuments," *High Country News*, December 19, 2017.
35. James B. Rasband, "Stroke of the Pen, Law of the Land?" J. Reuben Clark Law School, Brigham Young University, Research Paper No. 17-31, Proceedings of the 63rd Annual Rocky Mountain Mineral Law Institute, 21-1, Rocky Mountain Mineral Law Foundation, 2017, 21-18.
36. Lyle Balenquah, "Spirit of Place: Preserving the Cultural Landscape of the Bears Ears," in Jacqueline Keeler, ed., *Edge of Morning: Native Voices Speak for the Bears Ears* (Salt Lake City, UT: Torrey House Press, 2017), 77–8.
37. Steve Boos, personal communication to author, August 2, 2020.
38. Lindsay Whitehurst and Brady McCombs, "New Voting Districts Drawn in Navajo Discrimination Suit," *Durango Herald*, December 23–24, 2017, 5A.
39. To see the original and revised San Juan County district maps with voter percentages see Sofia Bosch and Terry Nguyen, "San Juan County prepares for 2018 special election," Discovering & Covering San Juan County, special supplement to the *San Juan Record*, May 30, 2018.
40. "Residency Claim May Rest on Umbilical Cord," *San Juan Record*, May 2, 2018.
41. Robert Gehrke, "A County Clerk's Deceptive Attempt to Keep Grayeyes Out of the San Juan Commission Race Should Lead to Criminal Charges," *Salt Lake Tribune*, August 8, 2018.
42. Sonja Horoshko, "And Then There Were Two," *Four Corners Free Press*, December 2018, 8–10.

43. Taylor Stevens, "More Than 20 Utah Local Leaders File Court Briefs Opposing Shrinkage of Bears Ears, Grand Staircase Monuments," *Salt Lake Tribune*, November 19, 2018.
44. Jim Carlton, "After 150 years, Navajos Win Back Political Power in Utah," *Wall Street Journal*, November 4, 2019.
45. Shogren, "Lawsuits Challenge Trump's Trim of Utah monuments."
46. John C. Ruple, "The Trump Administration and Lessons Not Learned from Prior National Monument Modifications," *Harvard Environmental Law Review* 43: 76.
47. Juliet Eilperin, "Uranium Firm Sought Access to Bears Ears, Documents Say," *Washington Post*, December 8, 2017; Missy Votel, "Radioactive Dealings," *Durango Telegraph*, December 14, 2017; Hiroko Tabuchi, "Uranium Miners Pushed Hard for a Comeback. They Got Their Wish," *New York Times*, January 13, 2018; Brian Maffly, "Oil and Gas Drove Trump's Call to Shrink Bears Ears and Grand Staircase, According to Insider Emails Released by Court Order," *Salt Lake Tribune*, March 2, 2018.
48. Maffly. Also see Ruple, "Can Trump Redevelop America's Monumental Legacy?" *Public Land and Resources Committee Newsletter*, Section of Environment, Energy, and Resources, American Bar Association 15, no. 1 (December 2017).
49. Rasband, "The Future of the Antiquities Act," 620.
50. Robert Gehrke, "The Old Boys Network in San Juan County Isn't Going to Give Up Power Without a Fight," *Salt Lake Tribune*, January 7, 2019.
51. Taylor Stevens, "'I'm Sure It's a Culture Shock for Most of You': Navajos Take the Majority on the San Juan County Commission," *Salt Lake Tribune*, January 8, 2019.
52. Stevens.
53. Bethany Rodgers, "A State Lawmaker Says a San Juan County Split Should Be on the Table, After a Court-Ordered Redistricting that 'Disenfranchises' His Voters," *Salt Lake Tribune*, February 7, 2019.
54. Joe B. Lyman, "Six Reasons to Support a Look at a Change in County Government," *San Juan Record*, October 9, 2019.
55. San Juan County Democratic Party, "Wolf in Sheep's Clothing—Vote No on Proposition #10 on November 5," *San Juan Record*, October 9, 2019.
56. Zak Podmore, "Potential Electioneering by San Juan County Clerk Adds Controversy to Already Heated Special Election," *Salt Lake Tribune*, October 24, 2019.
57. Podmore.
58. Jim Carlton, "After 150 Years, Navajo Win Back Political Power in Utah," *Wall Street Journal*, November 4, 2019.
59. Joe Fox et al., "What Remains of Bears Ears," *The Washington Post*, April 2, 2019.
60. Utah Diné Bikéyah, "Disappointed," letter to the editor, *San Juan Record*, May 8, 2019.

61. Proposed legislation with interesting titles includes HR3990 (Representative Rob Bishop) "National Monument Creation and Protection Act"; HR4532 (Representative John Curtis) "To create the first tribally managed national monument and for other purposes. 'Shash Jaa National Monument and Indian Creek National Monument Act, January 30, 2018; HR871 (Representative Ruben Gallego) "Bears Ears Expansion and Respect for Sovereignty (BEARS) Act, February 2019; S.2354 (Senator Tom Udall) "America's Natural Treasures of Immeasurable Quality, Unite, Inspire, and Together Improve the Economies of States Act (ANTIQUITIES) Act—The Antiquities Act of 2019," February 2019; S.3193 (Senator Mike Lee) Protecting Utah's Rural Economy (PURE) Act, July 11,2018. Bishop's bill would seriously diminish presidential powers to enact national monuments. The Curtis bill gives legislative cover or consent to what may have been an illegal monument shrinkage by President Trump. Passage of the bill might nullify or alter any later judicial decisions. Udall's bill reconfirms presidential authority to declare national monuments. Senator Lee's bill legislates the smaller size of Bears Ears National Monument and prohibits further presidential monument declarations in Utah replicating previous Congressional action restricting monuments in Wyoming and Alaska.
62. For the failure of the American Indian Religious Freedom Act (AIRFA), see Thomas F. King, *Cultural Resource Laws & Practice* (Walnut Creek, CA: AltaMira, 1998). Also see AIRFA in Andrew Gulliford, *Sacred Objects and Sacred Places: Preserving Tribal Traditions*, (Boulder: University Press of Colorado, 2000).
63. Lauren Messman, "Bears Ears and Notre-Dame Named to 2020 World Monuments Watch List," *New York Times*, October 29, 2019; Fox et al., "What Remains of Bears Ears"; and Carlton, "After 150 years, Navajos Win Back Political Power in Utah," *Wall Street Journal*.
64. Messman, "Bears Ears and Notre-Dame Named to 2020 World Monuments Watch List."
65. Messman.
66. Andrew Gulliford, "From the Silver Dollar Bar to the Bears Ears Education Center," *Durango Herald*, August 3, 2018, and Nick Davidson, "Bears Ears' Only Visitor Center Isn't Run by the Feds," *High Country News*, May 13, 2019.
67. Hal Rothman, "Pokey's Paradox: Tourism and Transformation on the Western Navajo Reservation," in Rothman, ed., *Reopening the American West* (Tucson: University of Arizona Press, 1998), 91.
68. Rothman, 91. Also see Hal K. Rothman, *Devil's Bargains: Tourism in the Twentieth-Century American West* (Lawrence: University Press of Kansas, 1998); and Jim Stiles, *Brave New West: Morphing Moab at the Speed of Greed* (Tucson: University of Arizona Press, 2007).
69. Jim Stiles, "Monument Status May Damage Bears Ears," *Durango Herald*, April 8–9, 2017.
70. SLChamber, *Life in Utah 2019*, 82–3.

71. Zinke quote from Juliet Eilperin, "Uranium Firm Sought Access to Bears Ears, Documents Say," *Washington Post*, December 8, 2017. Also see Eric Lipton and Lisa Friedman, "Oil Was Central in Decision to Shrink Bears Ears Monument, Emails Show," *New York Times*, March 2, 2018.
72. For an historical overview of uranium mining in San Juan County, see Gary Shumway, ed., "Cottonwood Mining," *Blue Mountain Shadows* 25 (Winter 2001).
73. Juliet Eilperin, "Uranium Firm Sought Access to Bears Ears, Documents Say," *Washington Post*, December 8, 2017, and Hiroko Tabuchi, "Uranium Miners Pushed Hard for a Comeback. They Got Their Wish," *New York Times*, January 13, 2018.
74. Missy Votel, "Radioactive Dealings: Energy Fuels Hired Big Guns to Lobby for Downsizing Bears Ears," *Durango Telegraph*, December 14, 2017.
75. Barack Obama, Proclamation 9558, "Proclamation—Establishment of the Bears Ears National Monument," The White House, December 28, 2016.

CHAPTER 14

1. David Petersen, *Cedar Mesa: A Place Where Spirits Dwell* (Tucson: University of Arizona Press, 2002), 4.
2. Jonah Yellowman and Richard Silversmith, "Bears Ears: Don't Dismantle the Sacred Spirit of the Land," *Durango Herald*, July 21–22, 2018.
3. Terry Tempest Williams, "*Nahodishgish*: A Place to Be Left Alone," *Durango Herald*, January 3, 2017.
4. Alistair Lee Bitsoi, "The LAND Is What I'm Here For," Grand Canyon Trust, *Colorado Plateau Advocate* (Fall/Winter 2015): 7.
5. Jedediah S. Rogers, *Roads in the Wilderness* (Salt Lake City: University of Utah Press, 2013), 186.
6. Rogers, 185. To understand Mormons and their attitudes toward the environment, also see Lori M. Hunter and Michael B. Toney, "Religion and Attitudes Toward the Environment: A Comparison of Mormons and the General U.S. Population," *The Social Science Journal* 42 (2005): 25–38.
7. Doug Goodman and Daniel McCool, eds., *Contested Landscape: The Politics of Wilderness in Utah and the West* (Salt Lake City: University of Utah Press, 1999), 251.
8. Goodman and McCool, 236.
9. Redd, interview with author.
10. USDA fact sheet, January 2020, on Criollo cattle.
11. Hannah Nordhaus, "Battle for the American West," *National Geographic* (November 2018): 58.
12. Andrew Gulliford, "On the Trail of Tiny Tubers: Tracking the Four Corners Potato," *San Juan Record*, January 22, 2020. Also see Lisbeth A. Louderback, "Ancient Four Corners Potato," *Archaeology Southwest* 33, nos. 1 and 2 (Winter and Spring 2019): 53–4.

13. Gulliford, "On the Trail of Tiny Tubers."
14. Gulliford.
15. Gulliford.
16. Bruce M. Pavlik et al., "Plant Species Richness at Archaeological Sites Suggest Ecological Legacy of Indigenous Subsistence on the Colorado Plateau," *Proceedings of the National Academy of Sciences* 118, no. 21 (2021). Also see Alastair Lee Bitsoi, "Tiny Tuber 'Rematriated' to Indigenous Farmers," *Navajo Times*, May 27, 2021.
17. Bitsoi.
18. Brian Maffly, "Ancient Native Americans May Have Cultivated Medicinal Plants in Bears Ears, Study Finds," *Salt Lake Tribune*, May 17, 2021.
19. Rob Schultheis, *The Hidden West* (New York: Lyons & Burford, 1996), 29.
20. Schultheis, 38, 42.
21. Schultheis, 47.
22. The best book on this subject is Fred M. Blackburn and Ray A. Williamson, *Cowboys & Cave Dwellers: Basketmaker Archaeology in Utah's Grand Gulch* (Santa Fe, NM: School of American Research 1997). For diary entries for one of the explorers, see the Charles Cary Graham diary in Helen Sloan Daniels, *Adventures with the Anasazi of Falls Creek* (Durango, CO: Fort Lewis College), Occasional Papers of the Center of Southwest Studies of Fort Lewis College, Paper No. 3, September 1976).
23. The project began in the 1980s and museum visits happened in the late 1980s. Results were published in the 1990s. Ann Phillips did much of the archival research and also traced locations of collections.
24. Andrew Gulliford, "Revitalizing an Ancient Past," *Durango Herald*, July 11–12, 2020. Also see Wayne Curtis, "Reexcavating the Collections," *American Archaeology* 21, no. 1 (Spring 2017): 12–9.
25. Quote from Larry Ruiz film "The Languages of the Landscape: The Cedar Mesa Perishables Project," Cloudy Ridge Productions, © 2021.
26. Ruiz, "The Languages of the Landscape."
27. Nordhaus, 58–9.
28. David Roberts, *In Search of the Old Ones* (New York: Simon & Schuster, 1996), 19.
29. Roberts, 20.
30. Roberts, 21. Others Bears Ears adventurers are bikepacking across the area's diverse ecosystems and then slipping on a pack and descending canyons. See Ashley Carruth, "Breaking Trail: Bikepacking through the heart of Bears Ears National Monument," *The Gulch*, issue 4 (August/September 2018).
31. David Roberts, "Canyon Confidential," *National Geographic Adventure* (March/April 2001): 92.
32. Hopi Vice Chair Clark Tenakhongva speaking at the Friends of Cedar Mesa Annual Conference, Bluff, Utah, March 7, 2020.
33. Blackburn and Williamson, *Cowboys & Cave Dwellers*, 147.

34. Andrew Gulliford, "Man and the Moon: For Those Visiting a Popular Ancestral Puebloan Dwelling, New Rules Apply," *Durango Herald*, December 13, 2009. For the full text of William D. Lipe's quote, see William Lipe, "Three Days on the Road from Bluff," in Mark Gaede, photographer and Marnie Gaede, ed., *Camera, Spade and Pen: An Inside View of Southwestern Archaeology* (Tucson: University of Arizona Press, 1980), 52–9.
35. Gulliford, "Man and the Moon."
36. William Lipe, personal communication with author, November 16, 2009, and interview with Scott Edwards, Kane Gulch Ranger, October 1, 2009. Also see William W. Bloomer, "Moon House Group," presented during the 53rd Annual Meeting of the Society for American Archaeology, Phoenix, Arizona, April 1988.
37. Paul Bogard, *The End of Night* (New York: Little, Brown & Co., 2013), 25.
38. Andrew Gulliford, "Rare Eclipse a Real Treat: National Park Service Trying to Protect its Dark Skies," *Durango Herald*, May 12, 2012.
39. Gulliford.
40. Bogard, *The End of Night*, 265.
41. Morgan Sjogren, "Drive Thru-Protest," *The Gulch*, issue 9 (2019).
42. Missy Votel, "Waste Not, Want Not," *Durango Telegraph*, June 25, 2020.
43. Talia Boyd, "The World's Radioactive Waste Is Not Welcome Here," *Salt Lake Tribune*, June 24, 2020.
44. Phil Lyman, "Report from the Yellowcake Caucus," *San Juan Record*, February 12, 2020.
45. Zak Podmore, *Confluence* (Salt Lake City, UT: Torrey House Press, 2019), 27.
46. Boyd, "World's Radioactive Waste Not Welcome." Also see Jim Miamaga, "Utah Residents Fear Contamination from Uranium Mill," *Durango Herald*, October 8, 2016.
47. Krista Allen, "Native American Groups Gather at Bears Ears," *Lake Powell Chronicle*, June 25, 2018. Also see "Large Group Attends Gathering at Bears Ears," *San Juan Record*, August 1, 2018.
48. Andrew Gulliford, "The Soul of Bluff: Visionary Gene Foushee Built, Restored Desert Town," *Durango Herald*, October 13, 2017.
49. Gulliford.
50. Gulliford.
51. Andrew Gulliford, "In Bluff, the Silver Dollar Bar Becomes the Bears Ears Education Center," *Durango Herald*, May 13, 2018. Also see Nick Davidson, "Bears Ears' Guerrilla Visitor Center," *High Country News*, May 13, 2019, 5.
52. Edward Abbey, "How It Was," in *Beyond the Wall* (New York: Henry Holt, 1971), 191.
53. Gulliford, "In Bluff, the Silver Dollar Bar Becomes the Bears Ears Education Center."

54. Andrew Gulliford, "School with Dreams as Big as Old West: Educating People about Colorado Plateau Is the Goal," *Durango Herald*, March 10, 2012.
55. Gulliford.
56. Craig Childs, *Flying Home* (Flagstaff, AZ: Peaks, Plateaus, and Canyons Association, 2017), 76–7.
57. Tim Petersen, "People Often Ask Me about Bears Ears," *Colorado Plateau Advocate*, Grand Canyon Trust (Spring-Summer 2020).
58. Angelo Baca, "Bears Ears Is Here to Stay," *New York Times*, December 8, 2017.

CHAPTER 15

1. "Tribune Editorial: Yesterday's Solutions Drive National Monument Plans," *Salt Lake Tribune*, February 10, 2020.
2. Zak Podmore, "San Juan County Asks President-Elect Joe Biden to Immediately Restore Bears Ears National Monument," *Salt Lake Tribune*, December 3, 2020.
3. Chris D'Angelo, "Ryan Zinke's Official Portrait a Final Slap in the Face of Native American Tribes," *Huffington Post*, December 10, 2020.
4. Brian Maffly, "With a Biden Win, Bears Ears and Grand Staircase Monuments May Soon Be Restored," *Salt Lake Tribune*, December 10, 2020.
5. US Department of the Interior, "Report on Restoring National Monuments: Prepared in Response to Executive Order 13990," June 2021.
6. Joe Biden, Proclamation 10285, "A Proclamation on Bears Ears National Monument," October 8, 2021, 86 FR 57321, Federal Register, Document Number 2021-22672.
7. Krista Allen, "'The Fight Will Continue': Biden Restores Shasha Jaa, Reversing Trump Cut," *Navajo Times*, October 14, 2021. Also see Coral Davenport, "Biden to Restore Three National Monuments in Utah and New England," *New York Times*, October 7, 2021, and Stephen Trimble, "Op-Ed: Biden Brings Back Bears Ears and Grand Staircase-Escalante, in All Their Glory," *Los Angeles Times*, October 19, 2021.
8. Mike Lee et al., "A Monumental Insult," *Deseret News*, October 8, 2021.
9. Bears Ears Inter-Tribal Coalition, "Bears Ears Inter-Tribal Coalition Says Restoring Bears Ears Is a Step Forward," *San Juan Record*, October 13, 2021.
10. Brian Maffly, "Utah AG Mounting Legal Challenge to Biden's Order Restoring Bears Ears and Grand Staircase Monuments," *Salt Lake Tribune*, October 21, 2021.
11. Biden, Proclamation 10285.
12. Phil R. Geib, "Basketmaker II Warfare and Fending Sticks in the North American Southwest," (PhD diss., University of New Mexico, 2016), and Benjamin A. Bellorado, "Leaving Footprints in the Ancient Southwest: Visible Indicators of Group Affiliation and Social Position in the Chaco and Post-Chaco Eras (AD 850–1300)," (PhD diss., University of Arizona, 2020).

13. Andrew Gulliford, "Keeping the Ancients Warm," *Durango Herald,* February 13–14, 2021.
14. Will Ferguson, "Ancient blanket made with 11,500 turkey feathers," press release, Washington State University News, November 25, 2020; also see the article by William Lipe and Shannon Tushingham in *Journal of Archaeological Science: Reports* (November 2020).
15. Gulliford, "Keeping the Ancients Warm."
16. David Boyle, "Commission Addresses Native Hunting Access," *San Juan Record,* August 12, 2020.
17. Press Release, Mesa Verde Foundation, October 8, 2020.
18. "Tribes Celebrate Mesa Verde repatriation," *Indian Country Today*, September 17, 2020, and Press Release, Mesa Verde Foundation, October 8, 2020.
19. Sally Jewell, Secretary of the Interior, letter to Gary Herbert, Governor of Utah, January 18, 2017, SITLA files accessed through a GRAMA request by author.
20. Mike Johnson, Assistant Director & Chief Legal Counsel, Utah SITLA, interviews with author, November 30, 2020 and December 29, 2020.
21. Johnson interview.
22. Johnson interview.
23. Raye Price, "Family Adventure," *Desert Magazine*, May 1966, 28–30.
24. Kate Schimel and Brooke Warren, "Recreation Is Redefining the Value of the West's Public Lands," *High Country News*, May 14, 2018, 9. Also see Jason Blevins, "Nature an Economic Force," *Durango Herald*, November 28–29, 2020. Blevins states that for 2019 outdoor recreation accounts for $788 billion in economic impact. For a more nuanced look at recreation in the West, see Liza Nicholas, Elaine M. Bapis, and Thomas J. Harvey, eds. *Imagining the Big Open: Nature, Identity, and Play in the New West* (Salt Lake City: University of Utah Press, 2003).
25. Brady McCombs and Patrick Whittle, "Biden to review changes to Bears Ears," *Durango Herald*, January 23–24, 2021.
26. Jim Mimiaga, "Friends of Cedar Mesa Is Awarded $300,000," *Durango Herald*, August 1–2, 2020.
27. Jim Stiles, "The Industrial Borg Comes to San Juan County: Is Resistance Futile?," *Blue Mountain Shadows* (Spring 2018): 73. Also see M. John Fayhee, "'Clinging Hopelessly to the Past': The Cantankerous Gospel of Jim Stiles and *The Canyon Country Zephyr*," *High Country News*, May 29, 2006.
28. Stiles, "The Industrial Borg," 74.
29. Amy Irvine, *Trespass* (New York: North Point Press, 2008), 260.
30. Zak Podmore, *Confluence* (Salt Lake City, UT: Torrey House Press, 2019), 34.
31. Lyle Balenquah, Afterword in R.E. Burillo, *Beyond Bears Ears*, (Salt Lake City, UT: Torrey House Press, 2020), 396. Also see Balenquah, "Spirit

of Place: Preserving the Cultural Landscape of the Bears Ears," in Jacqueline Keeler ed., *Edge of Morning: Native Voices Speak for the Bears Ears* (Salt Lake City, UT: Torrey House Press, 2017), 77–8. New published scholarship on Bears Ears includes David Gessner's *Leave It as It Is* (New York: Simon & Schuster, 2020), a study of Theodore Roosevelt and the Antiquities Act; and David Roberts' adventure writing in *The Bears Ears: A Human History of America's Most Endangered Wilderness* (New York: Norton, 2021). Hopefully a book incorporating Native voices and generations of Bears Ears stories is also in preparation.

32. Jessica Douglas and Graham Lee Brewer, "Bears Ears Is Just the Beginning," *High Country News*, February 2021, 10.
33. See Joshua Partlow, "Crowds Flood Bears Ears as Biden Mulls Protection," *Washington Post*, April 8, 2021; Krista Allen, "'I'm Here to Listen,': Haaland Visit to Bears Ears Balances Diverging Interests," *Navajo Times*, April 22, 2021; Elouise Wilson et al., "Women of Bears Ears Are Asking You to Help Save It," *New York Times*, April 25, 2021; and Lyle Balenquah, "The Indigenous Future of Bears Ears," *Colorado Plateau Advocate* (Spring/Summer 2021).
34. Ernest House Jr., personal communication to the author, February 26, 2021. House is a Senior Policy Director and Director of the American Indian/Alaska Native Program of the Keystone Policy Center in Denver. For additional opinions, see Stephen Trimble, "Restore Utah's National Monuments: Congress Should Act to Permanently Protect Bears Ears and Grand Staircase," *Los Angeles Times*, February 15, 2021, and David Roberts, "A Sacred Place Undone by Trump Must Be Saved by Biden," *New York Times*, February 26, 2021.
35. Zak Podmore, "Utah's Grand County Asks President-Elect Joe Biden to Restore Bears Ears Monument Borders," *Salt Lake Tribune*, January 12, 2021, and Resolution 12-8-2020-1, "A Joint Resolution Opposing the San Juan County Commission's Resolution Regarding Bears Ears," *San Juan Record*, January 18, 2021.

Bibliography

Abbey, Edward. "Anarchy and the Morality of Violence." Master's thesis, University of New Mexico, 1959.

Abbey, Edward. *Beyond the Wall.* New York: Henry Holt, 1984.

Abbey, Edward. *Desert Solitaire.* New York: Ballantine Books, 1968.

Abbey, Edward. *The Monkey Wrench Gang.* Philadelphia: Lippincott, 1975.

Abbey, Edward, and Philip Hyde. *Slickrock: Endangered Canyons of the Southwest.* New York: Sierra Club/Charles Scribner's Sons, 1971.

Access Fun. "Trump's Quest for Energy Dominance Weakens Public Lands Process." *The Vertical Times,* Winter 2017.

Adams, Eilean. *Hell or High Water: James White's Disputed Passage through Grand Canyon, 1867.* Logan: Utah State University Press, 2001.

Advisory Council on Historic Preservation. "Report to the President and Congress of the United States" (1993).

Aird, Robert B. "An Adventure for Adventure's Sake." Edited by Gary Topping, *Utah Historical Quarterly* 62 (Summer 1994): 77–90.

Aitchison, Stewart. *A Guide to Southern Utah's Hole-In-The-Rock Trail.* Salt Lake City: University of Utah Press, 2005.

Aitchison, Stewart. "Wilderness Areas of the Colorado Plateau," *Plateau* 60, no. 4 (January 1989).

Alexander, Thomas G. "Brigham Young and the Transformation of Utah Wilderness, 1847–58" *Journal of Mormon History* 41, no. 1 (January 1, 2015): 103–24.

Alexander, Thomas G. "Lost Memory and Environmentalism: Mormons on the Wasatch Front, 1847-1930." In Jedediah S. Rogers and Mathew C. Godfrey, eds. *The Earth Will Appear as the Garden of Eden: Essays on Mormon Environmental History.* Salt Lake City, UT: University of Utah Press, 2019.

Allen, Krista. "'The Fight Will Continue': Biden Restores Shasha Jaa, Reversing Trump Cut." *Navajo Times,* October 14, 2021.

Allen, Steve. *Utah's Canyon Country Place Names.* Durango, CO: Canyon Country Press, 2012.

Ambler, Marjane. *Breaking the Iron Bonds: Indian Control of Energy Development*. Lawrence: University Press of Kansas, 1990.

Amundson, Michael A. *Yellowcake Towns: Uranium Mining Communities in the American West*. Boulder: University Press of Colorado, 2002.

"An Act to Disapprove the Treaty Heretofore Made with the Southern Ute Indians to Be Removed to the Territory of Utah." 53rd Cong. Session III. Chs. 112, 113, 1895. Chap. 113. February 20, 1895.

Antiquities Act of 1906, 16 U.S.C. §§ 431.

Archaeological Resources Protection Act of 1979, 16 U.S.C ch. 1b §§ 470aa–470mm (1988).

Archaeology Southwest. "Comments on the Bears Ears National Monument Unit Draft Monument Management Plan & Draft Environmental Impact Statement." November 15, 2018.

Arnold, Carrie. "Once Upon a Mine: The Legacy of Uranium on the Navajo Nation." *Environmental Health Perspectives* 122, no. 2 (February 2014). https://doi.org/10.1289/ehp.122-A44.

Arrhenius, Olof. *Stones Speak and Waters Sing: The Life and Works of Gustaf Nordenskiold.* Mesa Verde National Park, CO: Mesa Verde Museum Association, n.d.

Arrington, Leonard J. *Charlie Redd: Utah's Audacious Stockman*. Provo: Utah State University Press and The Charles Redd Center for Western Studies, 1995.

Arrington, Leonard J. *Great Basin Kingdom.* Cambridge, MA: Harvard University Press, 1958.

Ashley, Amanda. "Breaking Up Is Hard to Do: The Outdoor Retailer Show Prepares to Leave Utah." *Utah Adventure Journal* (Early Spring 2017): 18–21.

Ashley, Amanda. "Hans Cole on Bears Ears and Conservation." *Utah Adventure Journal* (Mid-Winter 2019): 16–8.

Atkins, Victoria M., ed. *Anasazi Basketmaker: Papers from the 1990 Wetherill-Grand Gulch Symposium*. Cultural Resource Series no. 24. Salt Lake City, UT: Bureau of Land Management, 1993.

Aton, James M., and Robert S. McPherson. *River Flowing from the Sunrise: An Environmental History of the Lower San Juan*. Logan: Utah State University, 2000.

Babbitt, James E., ed. *Rainbow Trails: Early-Day Adventures in Rainbow Bridge Country*. Page, AZ: Glen Canyon Natural History Association, 1990.

Backman, Gus P. Secretary, Chamber of Commerce of Salt Lake City letter to the Director of the National Park Service. December 12, 1938. CANY 339/007-654, Canyonlands NP Administrative Collection. Records. Southeast Utah Group Archives, National Park Service.

Bailey, Alfred M. "Desert River Through Navajo Land." *National Geographic* XCII, no. 2 (August 1947): 149–72.

Bailey, Jonathan. *Rock Art: A Vision of a Vanishing Cultural Landscape*. Denver: Bower House Books, 2019.

Baldwin, Pamela. "Presidential Authority to Modify or Revoke National Monuments." Legal Brief, September 17, 2017.

Balenquah, Lyle. Afterword to *Beyond Bears Ears* by R.E. Burillo. Salt Lake City, UT: Torrey House Press, 2020.

Balenquah, Lyle. "Spirit of Place: Preserving the Cultural Landscape of the Bears Ears." In *Edge of Morning: Native Voices Speak for the Bears Ears,* edited by Jacqueline Keeler. Salt Lake City, UT: Torrey House Press, 2017.

Balenquah, Lyle. "The Indigenous Future of Bears Ears." *Colorado Plateau Advocate* (Spring/Summer 2021): 4–9.

Bassett, Carol Ann. "The Culture Thieves." *Science* 249 (July/August 1986): 22–9.

Basso, Keith. *Wisdom Sits in Places.* Albuquerque: University of New Mexico Press, 1996.

Bayles, Josephine. "A Trip to the Natural Bridges." *Blue Mountain Shadows* 7 (Winter 1990): 72–9.

Bears Ears Coalition. Native American Use Atlas. San Juan County, Utah, January 18, 2017.

"Bears Ears Hangs in the Balance." *Redrock Wilderness* 34, no. 2 (Summer 2017).

Bears Ears Inter-Tribal Coalition. "Bears Ears Inter-Tribal Coalition Says Restoring Bears Ears Is a Step Forward." *San Juan Record,* October 13, 2021.

Bears Ears Inter-Tribal Coalition. "Condemns Zinke Recommendation to Eviscerate Bears Ears National Monument." Press release. Monument Valley, Utah. June 12, 2017.

Bears Ears Inter-Tribal Coalition. "Proposal to President Barack Obama for the Creation of Bears Ears National Monument." October 15, 2015.

Bears Ears Inter-Tribal Coalition. "Protecting the Whole Bears Ears Landscape: A Call to Honor the Full Cultural and Ecological Boundaries." October 18, 2016.

Bears Ears National Monument. Comparison map of land status between the Obama and Trump Administrations. April 9, 2018.

Bears Ears National Monument. Department of Interior. ca. January 2017.

"Bears Ears National Monument." Grand Canyon Trust Report to Donors, 2017.

"Bears Ears National Monument, Utah." *The Week,* September 8, 2017.

Beckwith, Mary. Letter to Lyndon L. Hargrave. May 16, 1959. Kent Frost Papers. Accession 1687; Macaw Sash, Box 23; Folder 6; Special Collections. Marriott Library, University of Utah.

Bellorado, Benjamin A. "Leaving Footprints in the Ancient Southwest: Visible Indicators of Group Affiliation and Social Position in the Chaco and Post-Chaco Eras (AD 850–1300)." PhD diss., University of Arizona, 2020.

Bellorado, Benjamin. "Sandals and Sandal Symbolism in Greater Bears Ears and Beyond." *Archaeology Southwest* 32, no. 1 (2018): 39–41.

Benally, Rebecca. Testimony before the House Committee on Natural Resources. January 30, 2018.

Bennett, Lee. "Marie Ogden's Monticello Garden," *Blue Mountain Shadows* 28 (Spring 2003): 65–71.

Bennett, Lee. "Uranium Mining in San Juan County, Utah: South Cottonwood Creek and Elk Ridge." *Blue Mountain Shadows* 26, (Winter 2001–2002): 14–46.

Benson, Larry, and Michael S. Berry. "Climate Change and Cultural Response in the Prehistoric American Southwest." *Kiva: Journal of Southwestern Anthropology and History* 75, no. 1 (Fall 2009): 89–119.

Berkes, Howard. "Artifact Sting Stuns Utah Town." National Public Radio, July 1, 2009.

Berkes, Howard. "Mother, Daughter Get Probation in Artifacts Theft." National Public Radio, September 16, 2009.

Bernheimer, Charles. "Encircling Navajo Mountain with a Pack-Train," *National Geographic* 43 (February 1923): 197–224.

Bernheimer, Charles L. Field notes. Expedition 1919. Typescript copy courtesy of Harvey Leake. Prescott, AZ.

Bernheimer, Charles L. Field notes. Expedition 1929. Typescript courtesy of Harvey Leake. Prescott, AZ.

Bernheimer, Charles L. *Rainbow Bridge: Circling Navajo Mountain and Explorations in the "Badlands" of Southern Utah and Northern Arizona.* Albuquerque, NM: Center for Anthropological Studies, 1999. First published 1924.

Biden, Joe. Proclamation 10285. "A Proclamation on Bears Ears National Monument." October 8, 2021. 86 FR 57321. Federal Register. Document Number 2021-22762.

Bieder, Robert E. *Science Encounters the Indian, 1820–1880: The Early Years of American Ethnology*. Norman: University of Oklahoma Press, 1986.

Bitsoi, Alastair Lee. "The LAND Is What I'm Here For: Tribes Unite to Protect the Bears Ears." *Colorado Plateau Advocate* (Fall/Winter 2015): 4–9.

Blackburn, Fred M., and Ray A. Williamson. *Cowboys & Cave Dwellers: Basketmaker Archaeology in Utah's Grand Gulch*. Santa Fe, NM: School of American Research Press, 1997.

Blackburn, Fred, and Winston Hurst. "Charley Lang: Pioneer Photographer, Musician, and Archaeologist." *Blue Mountain Shadows* 14 (1994): 5–13.

Blackburn, Fred. *The Wetherills: Friends of Mesa Verde*. Durango, CO: Durango Herald Small Press, 2006.

Black, Calvin. "San Juan County Roads and Resources." In *San Juan County, Utah: People, Resources, and History,* edited by Allan Kent Powell. Salt Lake City: Utah State Historical Society, 1983.

Blood, Harry H. Governor of Utah letter to the Assistant Secretary of the Interior, October 14, 1938. CANY 339/007-654, Canyonlands NP Administrative Collection. Records. Southeast Utah Group Archives. National Park Service.

Bloom, David. *Indian Creek: A Climbing Guide.* 3rd ed. Boulder, CO: Sharp End Publishing, 2009.

Bloomer, William W. "Moon House Group." Presented during the 53rd Annual Meeting of the Society for American Archaeology. Phoenix, AZ, April 1988.

Bogard, Paul. *The End of Night*. New York: Little, Brown & Co., 2013.

Borrell, Brendan. "FBI Sting Catches Alleged Archaeological Thieves in Southwest." *Scientific American* (June 16, 2009).

Borson, Nancy, et al. "Origins of an Anasazi Scarlet Macaw Feather Artifact." *American Antiquity* 63, no. 1 (1998): 131–42.

Bouse, Derek. "Culture as Nature: How Native American Antiquities Became Part of the Natural World." *The Public Historian* 18, no. 4 (Fall 1996): 75–98.

Breed, Jack, and Charles W. Herbert. "Better Days for the Navajos." *National Geographic* 101, no. 6 (December 1958): 809–47.

Breed, Jack, and Charles W. Herbert. "Roaming the West's Fantastic Four Corners," *National Geographic* 101, no. 6: 305–42.

"Briefing: The Fight Over U.S. National Monuments." *The Week,* January 26, 2018.

Brooks, James F. *Captives and Cousins: Slavery and Kinship in the Southwest Borderlands.* Chapel Hill: Omohundro Institute of Early American History & Culture and the University of North Carolina Press, 2002.

Brooks, James F. *Mesa of Sorrows: A History of the Awat'ovi Massacre*. New York: W.W. Norton, 2016.

Brooks, Juanita. *The Mountain Meadows Massacre*. Norman: University of Oklahoma Press, 1991.

Broussard, Brian. "Uncharted Waters: The Scope and Revocation of Presidential Withdrawals Under the Outer Continental Shelf Lands Act Section 12(A)." *Public Land and Resources Committee Newsletter* by American Bar Association: Section of Environment, Energy, and Resources 15, no. 1 (December 2017).

Brown, Kenneth A. *Four Corners: History, Land, and People of the Desert Southwest*. New York: Harper, 1995.

Brugge, David M. "Vizcarra's Campaign of 1823." *Arizona and the West* 6, no. 3 (Autumn 1964): 223–44.

Brugge, Doug, and Rob Goble. "The History of Uranium Mining and the Navajo People," *Public Health Then and Now, American Journal of Public Health* 92, no. 9 (September 2002): 223–44.

Brugge, Doug, Timothy Benally, and Esther Yazzie-Lewis. *The Navajo People and Uranium Mining*. Albuquerque: University of New Mexico Press, 2006.

Bryner, Nicholas, et al. "President Trump's National Monument Rollback Is Illegal and Likely to Be Reversed in Court." *The Conversation* UCLA Law Review, December 4, 2017.

Bureau of Land Management. *Blanding: Surface Management Status.* Washington, DC: US Department of the Interior, 2007.

Bureau of Land Management. *Bluff: Surface Management Status.* Washington, DC: US Department of the Interior, 1998.

Bureau of Land Management. *Utah: Monticello Field Office Travel and Recreation Opportunities.* Washington, DC: US Department of the Interior, August 2016.

Cain, Tyler. Letter to the author from the Office of Governor Gary R. Herbert. January 6, 2017.

Calef, Wesley. *Private Grazing and Public Lands: Studies of the Local Management of the Taylor Grazing Act*. Chicago: University of Chicago Press, 1960.

Cameron, Catherine. *Chaco and After in the Northern San Juan: Excavations at the Bluff Great House*. Tucson: University of Arizona Press, 2009.

"Campaigning for a Bears Ears National Monument." Grand Canyon Trust Report to Donors, 2015.

Canby, Thomas Y. "The Anasazi: Riddles in the Ruins." *National Geographic* (November 1982): 562–92.

Cannon, D. James. "Canyonlands Controversy: Should Utah Mine Minerals or Tourists?" *Desert Magazine* (April 1963): 31–4.

CANY Folder 744. Series 1. Subseries 5. Athena Missile Program. Canyonlands NP Administrative Collection. Records. Southeast Utah Group Archives. National Park Service.

Cardenas, Mark, Rebecca Chavez-Houck, and Mo Denis. "Opinion—We All Must Speak Up to Protect National Monuments." *The Hill,* December 1, 2018.

Carlson, J.R., Stillwater Technical Solutions. "The Advisability of Designating the Bears Ears as a Monument Under the Antiquities Act." Prepared for the San Juan County Commission. October 2016.

Carpenter, David S. *Jens Nielson: Bishop of Bluff.* Provo, UT: Brigham Young University, 2011.

Carroll, W.G. "Jeep Trail into Utah's Rugged Needles Country." *Desert Magazine* (November 1956): 5–9.

Carruth, Ashley. "Breaking Trail: Bikepacking Through the Heart of Bears Ears National Monument." *The Gulch,* issue 4 (August/September 2018): 8–16.

Center for Western Priorities. "Newly-Released Documents Reveal Extensive Communication Between Interior and Utah Officials Before Bears Ears Designation." April 13, 2017.

Chamberlain, A. Chase, and Robert S. McPherson. "Desert Cold Warriors." *Utah Historical Quarterly* 83, no. 2 (Spring 2015): 116–31.

Chamberlin, Kathleen P. *Under Sacred Ground: A History of Navajo Oil, 1922–1982*. Albuquerque: University of New Mexico Press, 2000.

Chapin, Frederick Hastings. *In the Land of the Cliffdwellers*. Boston: Appalachian Mountain Club, 1892.

Chenoweth, William L. "The Geology and Production History of the Uranium-Vanadium Deposits in Monument Valley, San Juan County, Utah." Contract Report 91-4. Utah Geological and Mineral Survey. Utah Department of Natural Resources. February 1991.

Chenoweth, William L. "The Geology and Production History of the Uranium Deposits in the White Canyon Mining District, San Juan County, Utah." Miscellaneous Publication 93-3. Utah Geological Survey. March 1993.

Childs, Craig. *Atlas of a Lost World: Travels in Ice Age America*. New York: Pantheon Books, 2018.
Childs, Craig. *Finders Keepers*. New York: Little, Brown, 2010.
Childs, Craig. *Flying Home*. Flagstaff, AZ: Peaks, Plateaus, and Canyons Association, 2017.
Childs, Craig. *House of Rain: Tracking a Vanished Civilization Across the American Southwest* New York: Little Brown, 2006.
Childs, Craig. *The Secret Knowledge of Water*. Boston: Back Bay Books, 2000.
Childs, Craig. *Soul of Nowhere*. New York: Little, Brown, 2002.
Childs, Craig. *Stone Desert: A Naturalist's Exploration of Canyonlands National Park*. Englewood, CO: Westcliffe Publishers, 1995.
Childs, Craig. *The Way Out*. New York: Little, Brown, 2004.
Christenson, Andrew L. "The Last of the Great Expeditions: The Rainbow Bridge/Monument Valley Expedition, 1933–1938." *Plateau* 58, no. 4 (1987): 4–32.
Clark, H. Jackson. *The Owl in Monument Canyon and Other Stories from Indian Country*. Salt Lake City: University of Utah Press, 1993.
Clyde, Denis. "Opening the Road to Chesler Park: How Al Scorup Inadvertently Helped Create Canyonlands National Park." *Utah Historical Quarterly* 88 (Summer 2020): 202–18.
Coates, Karen. "Walking into New Worlds: Native Traditions and Novel Discoveries Tell the Migration Story of the Ancestors of the Navajo and Apache." *Archaeology Magazine* (September/October 2020).
Cole, Sally. "Additional Information on Basketmaker Mask or Face Representations in Rock Art of Southeastern Utah." *Southwestern Lore* 51, no. 1 (1985): 14–8.
Cole, Sally. "Basketmaker Rock Art at the Green Mask Site, Southeastern Utah." In *Anasazi Basketmaker: Papers from the 1990 Wetherill-Grand Gulch Symposium,* Cultural Resource Series 4, edited by Victoria M. Atkins. Salt Lake City, UT: Bureau of Land Management.
Cole, Sally. "Iconography and Symbolism in Basketmaker Rock Art." *In Rock Art of the Western Canyons,* Cultural Resource Series 28, edited by Jane S. Day, Paul D. Friedman, and Marcia J. Tate. Denver: Colorado Bureau of Land Management, 1990.
Cole, Sally. *Legacy on Stone: Rock Art of the Colorado Plateau and Four Corners Region*. Boulder: Johnson Books, 1990.
Cole, Sally, ed. "Regional Perspectives on Basketmaker II." *Southwestern Lore* 77, nos. 2 and 3 (Summer/Fall 2011): 3–128.
Comfort, Mary Apolline. *Rainbow to Yesterday*. New York: Vantage Press, 1980.
"Conversation: The Looters Next Door." *Archaeology* 62, no. 5 (September/October 2009).
Correll, J. Lee. "Navajo Frontiers in Utah and Troublous Times in Monument Valley." *Utah Historical Quarterly* 39 (Spring 1971): 145–61.
Crampton, C. Gregory. *Standing Up Country: The Canyon Lands of Utah and Arizona*. Tucson: Rio Nuevo Publishers, 2000.

Cummings, Byron. "Great Natural Bridges of Utah." *National Geographic* 21 (February 1910): 157–67.
Cummings, Bryon. "The Ancient Inhabitants of the San Juan Valley." *Bulletin of the University of Utah* Second Archaeological Number III, no. 3, part 2 (November 1910): 1–45.
Curtis, Wayne. "Reexcavating the Collections." *American Archaeology* 21, no. 1 (Spring 2017): 12–9.
Dabney, Walt. "Guest Commentary: Make Bears Ears a National Monument." *Denver Post*, November 24, 2015.
Dalley, Gardiner F., ed. "Highway U-95 Archaeology: Comb Wash to Grand Flat." Salt Lake City: University of Utah, May 1973.
D'Angelo, Chris. "Ryan Zinke's Official Portrait a Final Slap in the Face of Native American Tribes." *Huffington Post*, December 10, 2020.
Day, Franklin D. "Cattle Industry of San Juan County, 1875–1900." Master's thesis, Brigham Young University, 1958.
Davidson, Dale, Phil Geib, and Nancy Coulam. "San Juan County Almost 8,000 Years Ago: Ongoing Excavations at Old Man Cave." *Blue Mountain Shadows* 13 (Summer 1994): 7–12.
Davidson, Nick. "Bears Ears' Only Visitor Center Isn't Run by the Feds." *High Country News* (May 13, 2019): 5.
Davis, William E. "The First Americans in San Juan County." *Blue Mountain Shadows* 13 (Summer 1994): 4–6.
"Dear Park Visitor." Information letter. National Park Service. Arches and Canyonlands National Parks and Natural Bridges National Monument. L24. September 1982. "The Proposed Nuclear Waste Repository Collection." 1980–1988. CANY 299/01-02, Canyonlands NP Administrative Collection. Records. Southeast Utah Group Archives. National Park Service.
DeBuys, William. *A Great Aridness*. New York: Oxford University Press, 2011.
Decker, Peter R. *"The Utes Must Go!" American Expansion and the Removal of a People*. Golden, CO: Fulcrum Publishing, 2004.
Denetdale, Jennifer Nez. *Reclaiming Diné History: The Legacies of Navajo Chief Manuelito and Juanita*. Tucson: University of Arizona Press, 2007.
Department of City and Metropolitan Planning. "Listening to Bluff." Urban Ecology Capstone, University of Utah. December 2016.
Diegel, Tom. "Bears Ears Is Good Business." *Utah Adventure Journal* (Mid-Winter 2017): 7.
Dippie, Brian W. *The Vanishing American: White Attitudes & U.S. Indian Policy*. Lawrence: University Press of Kansas, 1982.
District Court of San Juan County. Complaint No. 727. January 25, 1951, 105.
District Court of San Juan County, Utah. Brief filed March 5, 1953, 2–4. Civil Case 784.
Doering, Briana N., et al. "A Multiscalar Consideration of the Athabaskan Migration." *American Antiquity* 85, no. 3 (July 2020): 470–91.

Donahue, Debra L. *The Western Range Revisited: Removing Livestock from Public Lands to Conserve Native Biodiversity*. Norman: University of Oklahoma Press, 1999.

Don't Waste Utah Campaign. "Don't Waste Utah," press release, December 11, 1984. CANY 299, 03-58, Canyonlands NP Administrative Collection. Records. Southeast Utah Group Archives. National Park Service.

Dott, Cynthia, "Disturbance and Plant Communities in a Dynamic Landscape: Canyons of the Colorado Plateau, Southeast Utah." PhD diss., University of Wisconsin—Madison, 1996.

Dougherty, John. "The Fight Over Bears Ears: A Tale of Two Towns." *The Revelator*. Center for Biological Diversity. June 30, 2017.

Douglas, Jessica, and Graham Lee Brewer. "Bears Ears Is Just the Beginning." *High Country News* (February 2021): 10–1.

Douglass, William B. Special Instructions. Field Notes of the Survey of the Reservations embracing Natural Bridges National Monument, the Cigarette Cave, and the Snow Flat Cave (or Prehistoric Cave Springs nos. 1 and 2). Survey Commenced September 12, 1908, completed October 3, 1908. NABR 65/06-162, Natural Bridges National Monument Records. Southeast Utah Group Archives. National Park Service.

Draft Environmental Assessment. Davis Canyon Site, Utah. US Department of Energy. Office of Civilian Radioactive Waste Management. Nuclear Waste Policy Act. Section 112. December 1984. Canyonlands NP Administrative Collection. Records. Southeast Utah Group Archives. National Park Service.

Drueding, Meghan. "Ancient Echoes: A New National Monument Is Designated—And Immediately Threatened." *Preservation* (Spring 2017): 61.

Duff, U. Francis. "Some Exploded Theories Concerning Southwestern Archaeology." *American Anthropologist* 6 (1904): 303–6.

Duncan, David, and Ken Burns. *The National Parks*. New York: Knopf, 2009.

Dyar, W.W. "Colossal Natural Bridges of Utah" *National Geographic* 15 (September 1904): 367–9.

Dyk, Walter. *Son of Old Man Hat: A Navajo Autobiography*, 1938. Lincoln: University of Nebraska Press, 1967.

Eastwood, Alice. "General Notes on a Trip Through Southeastern Utah." *Zoe: A Biological Journal* III (January 1893): 354–61.

Eastwood, Alice. "Letter: May 7, 1906." In *American Women Afield: Writings by Pioneering Women Naturalists* edited by Marcia Myers Bota. College Station: Texas A&M University Press, 1995.

Eastwood, Alice, ed. "Notes on the Cliff Dwellers." *Zoe* III (1892).

Eastwood, Alice. "Report on a Collection of Plants from San Juan County, Southeastern Utah." *California Academy of Sciences Proceedings* [2nd series] 6 (August 1896): 271–329.

Edge of the Cedars State Park Museum. "Prehistoric Rock Art of Southeast Utah: Exhibit Guide for the Earthwatch—Bureau of Land Management Rock Art Exhibit." Utah State Parks, n.d.

Egan, Timothy. *Short Nights of the Shadow Catcher: The Epic Life and Immortal Photographs of Edward Curtis*. Boston: Houghton Mifflin, 2012.

Ehrlich, Gretel. *Unsolaced*. New York: Pantheon, 2021.

Ellis, Ruben, ed. *Stories on Stone: Tales from the Anasazi Heartland*. Boulder, CO: Pruett Publishing, 1997.

Emmitt, Robert. *The Last War Trail: The Utes & the Settlement of Colorado*. Boulder: University Press of Colorado, 2000.

Ewing, Josh. "The Bears Ears National Monument: No Place More Deserving." Friends of Cedar Mesa, 2016.

Fagan, Brian. *Chaco Canyon*. New York: Oxford University Press, 2005.

Farnsworth, Reed W. "Herbert Ernest Gregory: Pioneer Geologist of Southern Utah." *Utah Historical Quarterly* 30 (Winter 1962): 76–84.

Faunce, Hilda. *Desert Wife*. Lincoln: University of Nebraska Press, 1981. First published 1928.

Federal Land Policy and Management Act of 1976, 43 U.S.C ch. 35 §§ 1701–87 (1976).

FederalGrantsWire. "Project Title: BLM-Utah, Cerberus Collection Interpretive Plan Partnership." n.d.

Ferguson, William M., and Arthur H. Rohn. *Anasazi Ruins of the Southwest in Color*. Albuquerque: University of New Mexico Press, 1994.

Ferguson, William M., and Arthur H. Rohn. *The Anasazi of Mesa Verde and the Four Corners*. Niwot, CO: University Press of Colorado, 1996.

Ferguson, Will. "Ancient blanket made with 11,500 turkey feathers," press release, Washington State University News. November 25, 2020.

Fletcher, Maurine S., ed. *The Wetherills of the Mesa Verde: Autobiography of Benjamin Alfred Wetherill*. Lincoln: University of Nebraska Press, 1977.

Ford, Walter. "Down Utah's San Juan River." *Desert Magazine* (June 1969): 26–30.

Ford, Walter. "San Juan Outpost in Utah's Red Rock Canyon." *Desert Magazine* (July 1969): 20–23.

Foushee, Gene. "The Moki Myth." *Desert Magazine* (May 1965): 14–5.

Foushee, Gene. "What Makes Rocks Red?" *Desert Magazine* (June 1968): 22–4.

Fradkin, Phillip. *Everett Ruess: His Short Life, Mysterious Death, and Astonishing Afterlife*. Berkeley: University of California Press, 2011.

Francaviglia, Richard V. *Mapping and Imagination in the Great Basin*. Reno: University of Nevada Press, 2005.

Francaviglia, Richard V. *The Mormon Landscape*. New York: AMS Press, 1978.

Frost, Kent. Letter to Katie Lee. January 20, 1958. Kent Frost Papers. Accession 1687; Katie Lee. Box 25; Folder 12; Special Collections. Marriott Library. University of Utah.

Frost, Kent. *My Canyonlands*. New York: Abelard-Schuman, 1971.

Frost, Melvin J. "Factors that Influenced Homesteading and Land Abandonment in San Juan County, Utah." Master's thesis, Brigham Young University, 1960.

Gangloff, Deborah. "Bosque Redondo: A History Lesson." *American Forests.* September 1, 1994.

Gaziano, Todd, and John Yoo. "Presidential Authority to Revoke or Reduce National Monument Designation." American Enterprise Institute. March 28, 2017.

Geib, Phil R., "Basketmaker II Warfare and Fending Sticks in the North American Southwest." PhD diss., University of New Mexico, 2016.

Gessner, David. *All the Wild That Remains.* New York: W.W. Norton, 2015.

Gessner, David. *Leave It as It Is.* New York: Simon & Schuster, 2020.

Gillmor, Frances, and Louisa Wade Wetherill. *Traders to the Navajos.* Albuquerque: University of New Mexico Press, 1953.

Gillreath-Brown, Andrew, et al. "Redefining the Age of Tattooing in Western North America: A 2000-Year-Old Artifact from Utah." *Journal of Archaeological Science: Reports* (February 15, 2019): 1–12.

Goetzmann, William H. *Exploration & Empire.* New York: Vintage Books, 1966.

Gomez, Arthur R. *Quest for the Golden Circle: The Four Corners and the Metropolitan West, 1945–1970.* Albuquerque: University of New Mexico Press, 1994.

Goodman, Doug, and Daniel McCool, eds. *Contested Landscape: The Politics of Wilderness in Utah and the West.* Salt Lake City: University of Utah Press, 1999.

Goulding, Harry. "The Navajos Hunt Big Game . . . Uranium." *Popular Mechanics* (June 1950): 89–92, 236–40.

Graham, C.C., and Charles McLoyd. "Catalogue and Description of a Very Large Collection of Prehistoric Relics, Obtained in the Cliff Houses and Caves of Southeastern Utah." 1894. Pamphlet located in Special Collections. Harold B. Lee Library. Brigham Young University, Provo, Utah.

Graham, Charles Cary. Diary in Helen Sloan Daniels. *Adventures with the Anasazi of Falls Creek.* Durango: Fort Lewis College. Occasional Papers of the Center of Southwest Studies of Fort Lewis College. Paper no. 3. September 1976.

Graham, David. *Killers of the Flower Moon: The Osage Murders and the Birth of the FBI.* New York: Vintage Books, 2018.

Grayeyes, Willie. "Bears Ears: Mapping a Cultural Landscape." *Redrock Wilderness* 33, no. 2 (Summer 2016).

Greaves, C. Joseph. *Hard Twisted.* New York: Bloomsbury, 2012.

Green, C.H. *Catalogue of a Unique Collection of Cliff Dweller Ruins Taken from the Lately Descovered [sic] Ruins of Southwestern Colorado and Adjacent Parts of Utah, New Mexico and Arizona, Scientifically Estimated to Be the Oldest Relics in the World.* (ca. 1891): 1–35.

Green, Louis A. *Layman's Field Guide to Ancestral Puebloan Pottery Northern San Juan/Mesa Verde Region.* Montgomery, AL: Minuteman Press, 2010.

Gregory, Herbert E. "The Navajo Country: A Geographic and Hydrographic Reconnaissance of Parts of Arizona, New Mexico, and Utah." *United States*

Geological Survey, Water-Supply Paper 380. Washington, DC: Government Printing Office, 1916.

Gregory, Herbert E. "Scientific Explorations in Southern Utah." *American Journal of Science* 243 (October 1945): 527–49.

Gregory, Herbert E. "The San Juan Country: A Geographic and Geologic Reconnaissance of Southeastern Utah." *US Geological Survey, Professional Paper 188*. Washington, DC: Government Printing Office, 1938.

Groene, Scott, Executive Director. Southern Utah Wilderness Alliance membership letter. Fall 2016.

Gross, Mathew. "Bears Ears Campaign Surges Despite Official Utah's Rabid Opposition." *Redrock Wilderness* 33, no. 2 (Summer 2016).

Gulliford, Andrew. "Another Utah Asset: Dark Skies and the Stars Above." *Utah Adventure Journal* (Summer 2012): 12–3.

Gulliford, Andrew. "Bears Ears—Our New Backyard." *Utah Adventure Journal* (Mid-Winter 2017).

Gulliford, Andrew. *Boomtown Blues: Colorado Oil Shale*. Boulder: University Press of Colorado, 2003.

Gulliford, Andrew. "Canyon Country Controversy: A New National Monument or Conservation Area in Southern Utah?" *Utah Adventure Journal* (Spring 2015): 38–40.

Gulliford, Andrew. "Condors in the Canyons." *Archaeology Southwest* 33, nos. 1 and 2 (Winter and Spring 2019): 15.

Gulliford, Andrew. "Culture Clash: Tourism vs. Oil & Gas in Moab and Lessons from the Green River." *Utah Adventure Journal* (Fall 2014): 14–5.

Gulliford, Andrew. "Deadly Daughters, a Poisonous Past, and the Monticello Mill." *Utah Adventure Journal* (Early Spring 2018): 14–5.

Gulliford, Andrew, ed. *Outdoors in the Southwest: An Adventure Anthology*. Norman: University of Oklahoma Press, 2014.

Gulliford, Andrew, ed. *Preserving Western History*. Albuquerque: University of New Mexico Press, 2005.

Gulliford, Andrew. "Four Corners Odyssey: The Ill-Fated 1892 *Illustrated American* Exploring Expedition." *Inside/Outside Southwest* (April 2009): 14–6.

Gulliford, Andrew. "From the Silver Dollar Bar to the Bears Ears Education Center." *Utah Adventure Journal* (Summer 2018): 14–15.

Gulliford, Andrew. "Goddess of Glen Canyon." *Utah Adventure Journal* (Winter 2015): 14–5.

Gulliford, Andrew. "Handprints in the Canyon." *Utah Adventure Journal* (Fall 2012): 12.

Gulliford, Andrew. "Last of the Desert River Rats." *Utah Adventure Journal* (Winter 2013): 14.

Gulliford, Andrew. "Mapping Colorado: The Hayden Atlas Turns 130 Years Old." *Inside/Outside Southwest* (April/May 2007): 30–3.

Gulliford, Andrew. "Marie Ogden and the Home of Truth." *Utah Adventure Journal* (Spring 2017): 14–5.

Gulliford, Andrew. "New Rules for Moon House." *Utah Adventure Journal* (Summer 2011): 10.

Gulliford, Andrew. "Putting Ruess to Rest: Perhaps a Final Conclusion to a 1934 Southwest Mystery." *Utah Adventure Journal* (Summer 2017).

Gulliford, Andrew. "Race to the Rainbow: The Story of Finding Utah's Rainbow Bridge." *Utah Adventure Journal* (Early Spring 2015): 14–5.

Gulliford, Andrew. "Recapture Canyon, an Illegal ATV Trail, and a County Request." *Utah Adventure Journal* (Early Spring 2014): 14–5.

Gulliford, Andrew. "Remembering the Goddess of Glen Canyon—Katie Lee." *Utah Adventure Journal* (Mid-Winter 2018): 26–9.

Gulliford, Andrew. *Sacred Objects and Sacred Places: Preserving Tribal Traditions*. Boulder: University Press of Colorado, 2000.

Gulliford, Andrew. "Saving a Village One Stone House at a Time." *Utah Adventure Journal* (Winter 2018): 12–3.

Gulliford, Andrew. "Southeast Utah's Procession Panel: Ritual and Remembrance in Red Rock Country." *Utah Adventure Journal* (Fall 2016): 12–3.

Gulliford, Andrew. "Southeast Utah Sojourn: The 1892 Illustrated American Exploring Expedition," *Utah Adventure Journal* (Winter 2011): 10.

Gulliford, Andrew. "Stories on Stone: Protecting Prehistoric Rock Art." In *Rock Art: A Vision of a Vanishing Cultural Landscape,* edited by Jonathan Bailey. Denver: Johnson Books, 2019.

Gulliford, Andrew. "The Antiquities Act and the Conservation Legacy of Republicans." *Utah Adventure Journal* (Summer 2014): 14–5.

Gulliford, Andrew. "The Girl Ranger Who Broke the Sagebrush Ceiling." *Utah Adventure Journal* (Fall 2011): 10.

Gulliford, Andrew. "The Pothunting Problem: Thieves of Time in the American Southwest," *Utah Adventure Journal* (Spring 2012): 12–3.

Gulliford, Andrew. "The Struggle Over Bears Ears: Old West, New West, Next West." *Utah Adventure Journal* (Mid-Winter 2018).

Gulliford, Andrew. *The Woolly West: Colorado's Hidden History of Sheepscapes*. College Station: Texas A&M University Press, 2018.

Gulliford, Andrew. "Thoreau Visits Bears Ears." *The Gulch,* issue 12 (Spring 2020): 13–7

Gulliford, Andrew. "Utah Adventure in the Pleistocene: Hunting Mammoths in San Juan County." *Utah Adventure Journal* (Early Spring 2012): 10.

Gulliford, Andrew. "Utah Hikers and Recapture Wash—New Opportunities at a Mini-Mesa Verde." *Utah Adventure Journal* (Early Spring 2011): 10.

Gulliford, Andrew. "Vanishing Art: Pothunting and Skeleton Picnics in the American Southwest." *Inside/Outside Southwest* (October 2009): 20–3.

Hage, E. Wayne. *Storm Over Range Lands: Private Rights in Federal Lands*. Bellevue, WA: Free Enterprise Press, 1989.

Hanceford, Phil, et al. "Bears Ears National Monument Scoping Comments." Detailed report to Lance Porter. Monticello, UT: Bureau of Land Management, April 11, 2018.

Hargrave, Lyndon L. Letter to Mary Beckwith. April 28, 1959. Kent Frost Papers. Accession 1687; Macaw Sash. Box 23; Folder 6; Special Collections. Marriott Library. University of Utah.

Harmon, David, Francis P. McManamon, and Dwight T. Pitcaithley, eds. *The Antiquities Act: A Century of American Archaeology, Historic Preservation, and Nature Conservation.* Tucson: University of Arizona Press, 2006.

Harvey, Thomas J. *Rainbow Bridge to Monument Valley: Making the Modern Old West.* Norman: University of Oklahoma Press, 2011.

Hassell, Hank. *Rainbow Bridge: An Illustrated History.* Logan: Utah State University Press, 1999.

Heald, Weldon F. "Bold Plan to Save the Canyonlands." *Desert Magazine* (April 1962): 18–21.

Hedden, Bill. Executive Director. Grand Canyon Trust membership letter. October 2016.

Henderson, Al. "The Aneth Community: Oil Crisis in Navajoland." *The Indian Historian* 12, no. 1 (Winter 1979): 33–6.

Henderson, Randall. "19 Days on Utah Trails." Pts. 1 and 2. *Desert Magazine* (October 1949): 5–9; (November 1949): 19–25.

Henderson, Randall. "He Conquered the River and Died in an Airplane." *Desert Magazine* (1947): 2.

Henderson, Randall. "Just Between You and Me." *Desert Magazine* (1947): 46.

Henderson, Randall. "We Explored Dark Canyon." *Desert Magazine* (December 1946): 5–9.

Hewett, Edgar Lee. *Circular Relating to Historic and Prehistoric Ruins of the Southwest and Their Preservation.* Washington, DC: Government Printing Office, 1904.

Hewett, Edgar Lee. To the Secretary of the Interior, Archaeological Institute of America Application for Permit for Examination, Excavation, and Gathering of Objects of Antiquity in the state of Utah. Signed as Director of Work. Edgar L. Hewett, June 1, 1907. Reproduced from the National Archives, copy from the Utah Museum of Natural History.

Hillerman, Tony. *A Thief of Time*. New York: Harper & Row, 1988.

Hillerman, Tony. *The Great Taos Bank Robbery and Other Indian Country Affairs*. Albuquerque: University of New Mexico Press, 1973.

"Hole-in-the-Rock." *Desert Magazine* 26, no. 6 (June 1963): 3–4.

Holmes, William H. "Report on the Ancient Ruins of Southwestern Colorado, examined during the summers of 1875 and 1876." Extracted from the Tenth Annual Report of the Survey for the Year 1876. Washington, DC: Government Printing Office, 1879.

Holmes, William H. "Pottery of the Ancient Pueblos" in *Fourth Annual Report of the Bureau of Ethnology to the Secretary of the Smithsonian Institution, 1882–83*, 48th Cong. Mis. Doc. no. 42. Washington, DC: Government Printing Office, 1886.

HR871 (Representative Ruben Gallego). "Bears Ears Expansion and Respect for Sovereignty (BEARS) Act." February 2019.

HR3990 (Representative Rob Bishop). "National Monument Creation and Protection Act." October 2017.

HR4532 (Representative John Curtis). "'Shash Jaa' National Monument and Indian Creek National Monument Act." January 2018.

HR4518 (Representative Ruben Gallego). "Bears Ears National Monument Expansion Act." December 2017.

HR5780 (Representative Rob Bishop). "Utah Public Lands Initiative Act." July 2016.

Hull, Sharon, et al. "Turquoise Trade of the Ancestral Puebloan: Chaco and Beyond." *Journal of Archaeological Science* 45 (2014): 187–95.

Hunter, Lori M., and Michael B. Toney. "Religion and Attitudes Toward the Environment: A Comparison of Mormons and the General U.S. Population." *The Social Science Journal* 42 (2005): 25–38.

Hurst, Winston B., and Joe Pachak. *Spirit Windows: Native American Rock Art of Southeastern Utah.* Blanding: Spirit Windows Project and the Utah Endowment for the Humanities, 1989.

Hurst, Winston. "Colonizing the Dead: Early Archaeology in Western San Juan County." *Blue Mountain Shadows* 17 (1996): 2–13.

Hurst, Winston. "Deep History II: San Juan County's Archaeological Record," *Blue Mountain Shadows* 44 (Fall 2011): 3–74.

Hurst, Winston, ed. "Deep History: The Archaeological Record of San Juan County's Early Inhabitants." *Blue Mountain Shadows* 13 (Summer 1994): 3–81.

Hurst, Winston. "Ice Age Rock Art on the San Juan River?" *Blue Mountain Shadows* 44 (Fall 2011): 5–6.

Hyde, Philip. Letter to Senator Clair Engle. August 30, 1963. L58-RNPP, CANY Archives.

Indian Rights Association. "Protest of the Indian Rights Association Against the Proposed Removal of the Southern Ute Indians." Philadelphia. March 1890.

"In the News: Project Cerberus." *American Archaeology* 13, no. 3 (Fall 2009).

Irvine, Amy. "Open Wide: Can Indian Creek Swallow the Agendas of Climbers, Cowgirls and Conservationists?" *Climbing*, no. 216 (November 1, 2002): 65.

Irvine, Amy. *Trespass: Living at the Edge of the Promised Land.* New York: North Point Press, 2008.

Iverson, Peter. *Diné: A History of the Navajos.* Albuquerque: University of New Mexico Press, 2002.

Jacobs, Lynn. *Waste of the West: Public Lands Ranching.* Tucson: privately printed, 1991.

Jennings, Jesse D. "Early Man in Utah." *Utah Historical Quarterly* 28 (January 1960): 2–27.

Jensen, Frank. "A Long Weekend in Southeastern Utah." *Desert Magazine* (August 1960): 35–6.

Jensen, Frank. "He Founded: '. . . A Place Where the Best of Christianity and the Indian Way of Life Could Merge." *Desert Magazine* (May 1962): 12–3.

Jett, Stephen C., and John Thompson. "The Destruction of Navajo Orchards in 1864: Captain John Thompson's Report." *Arizona and the West* 16, no. 4 (Winter 1974): 365–78.

Jett, Stephen C., and Virginia E. Spencer. *Navajo Architecture: Forms, History, Distributions.* Tucson: University of Arizona Press, 1981.

Jewell, Sally. Secretary of the Interior. Letter to Gary Herbert, Governor of Utah. January 18, 2017. Utah State Institutional Trust Land Administration files.

Johannsen, Richard M. "Public Land Withdrawal Policy and the Antiquities Act." *Washington Law Review* 56 (1981): 439–65.

Jones, Allison, Jim Catlin, and Emanuel Vasquez. "The Ecological Importance and Biological Uniqueness of the Greater Canyonlands Ecoregion." Wild Utah Project. Submitted to the Southern Utah Wilderness Alliance. March 2011.

Jones, Kevin, T. *Standing on the Walls of Time: Ancient Art of Utah's Cliffs and Canyons.* Salt Lake City: University of Utah Press, 2019.

Jones, Marjorie C. "The Millennium as Envisioned by Marie Ogden." *Blue Mountain Shadows* 22 (Summer 2000): 72–7.

Judd, Neill M. "Beyond the Clay Hills." *National Geographic* (March 1924): 275–302.

Judd, Neil M. *Men Met Along the Trail: Adventures in Archaeology*. Salt Lake City: University of Utah Press, 2009.

Kamp, Kathryn A. *Children in the Prehistoric Puebloan Southwest*. Salt Lake City: University of Utah Press, 2002.

Kane, Francis Fisher, and Frank M. Ritter. "A Further Report to the Indian Rights Association on the Proposed Removal of the Southern Utes." January 20, 1892, 1–32.

Kantner, John. *Ancient Puebloan Southwest*. Cambridge, UK: Cambridge University Press, 2004.

Kearsley, Lisa. *San Juan River Guide: Montezuma Creek to Clay Hills Crossing.* Flagstaff, AZ: Shiva Press, 2014.

Kelley, Klara, and Harris Francis. *A Diné History of Navajoland*. Tucson: University of Arizona Press, 2019.

Kelly, Charles. "Chief Hoskaninni." *Utah Historical Quarterly* 21 (July 1953): 219–26.

Kelly, Charles. "Hoskaninni." *Desert Magazine* (July 1941): 6–9.

Kelly, Charles. "Proposed Escalante National Monument." *Desert Magazine* (February 1941): 21–2.

Kelly, Charles. "The Poke and Posey Wars." *Desert Magazine* (May 1965): 18–9.

Kelsey, Michael R. *Canyon Hiking Guide to the Colorado Plateau*. Provo, UT: Kelsey Publishing, 1995.

Kennedy, John F. President's State of the Union Address. January 11, 1962.

Kessell, John. *Whither the Waters: Mapping the Great Basin from Bernardo de Miera to John C. Fremont.* Albuquerque: University of New Mexico Press, 2017.

Kidder, Alfred Vincent, and Samuel J. Guernsey. *Archaeological Explorations in Northeastern Arizona.* Smithsonian Institution. Bureau of American Ethnology. Bulletin 65 Washington, DC: Government Printing Office, 1919.

King, Beth. "The Utah Navajos Relocation in the 1950s: Life Along the San Juan River." Originally published by the *Canyon Echo* and the San Juan County Historical Commission in July 1996. Posted online August 16, 2019 in *Canyon Echo.*

King, Thomas F. *Cultural Resource Laws & Practice.* Walnut Creek, CA: AltaMira, 1998.

Kirby, Don, and Joan Gentry. *The Anasazi Project.* Portland, OR: Nazraeli Press, 2012.

Kiser, Benjamin. "Bucking the White Elephant: Utah's Fight for Federal Management of the Public Domain, 1923–1934." *Utah Historical Quarterly* 88, no. 2 (Spring 2020): 165–80.

Knaut, Andrew. *The Pueblo Revolt of 1680: Conquest and Resistance in Seventeenth Century New Mexico.* Norman: University of Oklahoma Press, 1995.

Knipmeyer, James H. *Cass Hite: The Life of an Old Prospector.* Salt Lake City: University of Utah Press, 2016.

Knipmeyer, James H. *In Search of a Lost Race: The Illustrated American Expedition of 1892.* Bloomington, IN: Xlibris, 2006.

Kohler, Timothy A., Mark D. Varien, and Aaron M. Wright, eds. *Leaving Mesa Verde: Peril and Change in the Thirteenth Century Southwest.* Tucson: University of Arizona Press, 2010.

Kolbert, Elizabeth. "The Talk of the Town: Comment—Slash and Burn." *The New Yorker,* January 22, 2018, 17–8.

Kozak, David L. "Between a Rock and a Hard Place": Rock Climbing and Traditional Cultural Properties." *The Applied Anthropologist* 26, no. 2 (Fall 2006): 170–80.

Krech, Shephard. *The Ecological Indian: Myth and History.* New York: Patheon, 1999.

KUED, Public Television, Salt Lake City, Utah. "Battle Over Bears Ears," aired November 16, 2018, a Public Broadcasting System affiliate.

Lacey, Steve, and Pearl Baker. *Posey: The Last Indian War.* Salt Lake City, UT: Gibbs Smith, 2007.

Lambert, Neal. "Al Scorup: Cattleman of the Canyons." *Utah Historical Quarterly* 32 (Summer 1964): 301–20.

Lane, Remington W. "An Artist in the San Juan Country." *Harper's Weekly* 37 (December 9, 1893): 1174.

Lavender, David. "Mormon Cowboy." *Desert Magazine* (October 1940): 4–8.

Lavender, David. *One Man's West.* Lincoln: University of Nebraska Press, 1977.

Leake, Harvey. *Slim Woman: Louisa Wade Wetherill of Kayenta* (2nd printing). Blanding, UT: Edge of the Cedars State Park Museum, 2018.

LeBlanc, Steven A. *Constant Battles: The Myth of the Peaceful, Noble Savage*. New York: St. Martin's Press, 2003.

Lee, Katie. *All My Rivers Are Gone: A Journey of Discovery through Glen Canyon*. Boulder, CO: Johnson Books, 1998.

Lee, Katie. Letter to Kent and Fern Frost. October 9, 1957. Kent Frost Papers. Accession 1687; Katie Lee. Box 25; Folder 12; Special Collections. Marriott Library. University of Utah.

Lee, Katie. Letter to Kent Frost. July 30, 1958. Kent Frost Papers. Accession 1687; Katie Lee, Box 25; Folder 12; Special Collections. Marriott Library. University of Utah.

Lee, Katie. *Sandstone Seduction: Rivers and Lovers, Canyons and Friends*. Boulder, CO: Johnson Books, 2004.

Lee, Katie. *The Ghosts of Dandy Crossing*. Salt Lake City, UT: Dream Garden Press, 2014.

Lee, Mike, et al. "A Monumental Insult." *Deseret News*, October 8, 2021.

Lee, Ronald F. Supervisor of Historic Sites. Memorandum for the Director of the National Park Service. Re: Proposed Escalante National Park. February 25, 1940. Canyonlands NP Administrative Collection. Records. Southeast Utah Group Archives. National Park Service.

Lefler, Ellen. "Sheriff Newman and the Posey War." *Blue Mountain Shadows* IV (Spring 1989).

Lekson, Stephen. *A History of the Ancient Southwest*. Santa Fe, NM: School for Advanced Research Press, 2008.

Lekson, Stephen. *A Study of Southwestern Archaeology*. Salt Lake City: University of Utah Press, 2018.

Lekson, Stephen. *The Chaco Meridian: One Thousand Years of Political and Religious Power in the Ancient Southwest* (2nd ed.). New York: Rowman & Littlefield, 2015.

Lekson, Stephen. "War in the Southwest, War in the World," *American Antiquity* 67, no. 4 (October 2002): 607–24.

Leopold, Aldo. *A Sand County Almanac*. New York: Ballantine Books, 1970.

Leshy, John D. "Are U.S. Public Lands Unconstitutional?" *Hastings Law Journal* 69, issue, 2 (February 2018): 499–582.

Leshy, John D., *Debunking Creation Myths About America's Public Lands*. 2018 Wallace Stegner Lecture presented at the University of Utah. Salt Lake City: University of Utah Press, 2018.

Leupp, Francis E. "'Law or no Law' in Indian Administration." *Outlook* (January 30, 1909): 261–3.

Leupp, Francis E. *The Latest Phase of the Southern Ute Question: A Report*. Office of the Indian Rights Association, Philadelphia, September 30, 1895, 1–39.

Lewis, Richard Q., and Russell H. Campbell. "Geology and Uranium Deposits of Elk Ridge and Vicinity, San Juan County, Utah." Geological Survey

Professional Paper 474-B. Prepared on behalf of the US Atomic Energy Commission. Washington, DC: Government Printing Office, 1965.

Liebler, H. Baxter. *Boil My Heart for Me*. Salt Lake City: University of Utah Press, 1994.

Linford, Laurance D. *Navajo Places: History, Legend, Landscape*. Salt Lake City: University of Utah Press, 2000.

Lipe, William D., ed. "Tortuous and Fantastic: Cultural and Natural Wonders of Greater Cedar Mesa." *Archaeology Southwest* 28 (Summer and Fall 2014): 3–4.

Lipe, William D., et al. "Cultural and Genetic Contexts for Early Turkey Domestication in the Northern Southwest." *American Antiquity* 81, no. 1 (January 2016): 97–113.

Lipe, William D. "Grand Gulch: Three Days on the Road from Bluff." In *Camera, Spade and Pen: An Inside View of Southwestern Archaeology,* edited by Marnie Gaede. Tucson: University of Arizona Press, 1980.

Lipe, William D. "Recollections of Cedar Mesa Archaeology." *Blue Mountain Shadows* 50 (Fall 2014): 8–23.

Lipe, William D., et al. "Staying Warm in the Upland Southwest: A 'Supply Side' View of Turkey Feather Blanket Production." Pt. B. *Journal of Archaeological Science: Reports* 34 (December 2020).

Lister, Florence C. *Chaco's Vanished Past: Hogans, Tents, and Ruins*. Durango, CO: Durango Herald Small Press, 2008.

Lister, Florence C. *In the Shadow of the Rocks: Archaeology of the Chimney Rock District in Southwest Colorado* (2nd ed.). Durango, CO: Durango Herald Small Press, 2011.

Lister, Florence C. *Troweling Through Time: The First Century of Mesa Verdean Archaeology.* Albuquerque: University of New Mexico Press, 2004.

Lopez Whiteskunk, Regina. "Bears Ears Our Sacred Space." Speech at Durango, Colorado, Public Library. May 7, 2019.

Louderback, Lisbeth A. "Ancient Four Corners Potato." *Archaeology Southwest* 33, nos. 1 and 2 (Winter/Spring 2019): 53–4.

Lund, Christian. "Raiders of the Lost Art." *Utah Holiday* 14, no. 5 (February 1985): 40–52.

Lyman, Albert R. *Indians and Outlaws: Settling of the San Juan Frontier*. Salt Lake City, UT: Publishers Press, 1962.

Macfarlane, Robert. *Mountains of the Mind: Adventures in Reaching the Summit*. New York: Vintage Books, 2004.

Macfarlane, Robert. *The Old Ways*. New York: Penguin Books, 2012.

Macfarlane, Robert. *The Wild Places*. New York: Penguin Books, 2007.

Macomb, J.N., and J.S. Newberry. *Report of the Exploring Expedition from Santa Fe, New Mexico to the Junction of the Grand and Green Rivers of the Great Colorado of the West, in 1859; With Geological Report*. Washington, DC: Government Printing Office, 1876.

Madsen, Steven K. *Exploring Desert Stone: John N. Macomb's 1859 Expedition to the Canyonlands of the Colorado*. Logan: Utah State University Press, 2010.

Maffly, Brian. "Legislative Resolution: Drilling Is 'Best Use' for Cedar Mesa and San Rafael Swell." *Salt Lake Tribune*, March 9, 2015.

Maffly, Brian. "Unhappy with 'Lip Service' from Utah Delegation, Tribes to Take Request for Bears Ears Monument Straight to Obama." *Salt Lake Tribune*, December 31, 2015.

Maffly, Brian. "Utah AG Mounting Legal Challenge to Biden's Order Restoring Bears Ears and Grand Staircase Monuments." *Salt Lake Tribune*, October 21, 2021.

Maffly, Brian. "With a Biden Win, Bears Ears and Grand Staircase Monuments May Soon Be Restored." *Salt Lake Tribune*, December 10, 2020.

Malin, Stephanie A., and Peggy Petrzelka. "Left in the Dust: Uranium's Legacy and Victims of Mill Tailings Exposure in Monticello, Utah." *Society and Natural Resources* 23, no. 12 (November 2010): 1187–200.

Malin, Stephanie. *The Price of Nuclear Power: Uranium Communities and Environmental Justice*. New Brunswick, NJ: Rutgers University Press, 2015.

Malotki, Ekkehart, and Henry D. Wallace. "Columbian Mammoth Petroglyphs from the San Juan River near Bluff, Utah, United States." *Rock Art Research* 28, no. 2 (2011): 143–4.

Manley, Dave. *Ancient Galleries of Cedar Mesa*. Moab, UT: Canyonlands Natural History Association, 2016.

Manning, Steven. "The Lobed-Circle Image in Basketmaker Petroglyphs of Southeastern Utah." *Utah Archaeology* 5, no. 1 (1992): 1–37.

Marcario, Rose. "Patagonia CEO: This Is Why We're Suing President Trump." *Time,* December 6, 2017.

Martin, Debra L., "Ripped Flesh and Torn Souls," In *Invisible Citizens: Captives and Their Consequences,* edited by Catherine M. Cameron. Salt Lake City: University of Utah Press, Foundations of Archaeological Inquiry, 2008.

Matheson, Scott M. Governor of Utah. Letter to Mr. Charles R. Head, acting Director, Operations Division, Office of Civilian Radioactive Waste Management. US Department of Energy. July 9, 1984. CANY 299/03-77, Canyonlands NP Administrative Collection, Records. Southeast Utah Group Archives. National Park Service.

Matson, G.R., William D. Lipe, and William R. Haase. "Adaptational Continuities and Occupational Discontinuities: The Cedar Mesa Anasazi." *Journal of Field Archaeology* 15 (1988): 245–64.

McBrayer, Justin, and Sarah Roberts-Cady. "The Case for Preserving Bears Ears." *Ethics, Policy & Environment: A Journal of Philosophy and Geography* 21, no. 1: 48–51.

McCool, Daniel. Expert Witness Report, *Navajo Nation v. San Juan County, Utah.* Case. No. 2:12-cv-00039-RS, August 18, 2015, 117.

Mcintosh, Heidi. "Gutting America's National Treasures Is Unlawful and Unwise." *Time,* March 31, 2017.

McLoyd, C., and Graham, C. *Catalogue and Description of a Very Large Collection of Prehistoric Relics, Obtained in the Cliff Houses and Caves of*

Southeastern Utah. Special Collections, Harold B. Lee Library, Brigham Young University, 1984.

McManamon, Francis P. "The Antiquities Act and How Theodore Roosevelt Shaped It." *The George Wright Forum* 31, no. 3 (2014): 324–44.

McNitt, Frank. *Navajo Wars: Military Campaigns, Slave Raids, and Reprisals.* Albuquerque: University of New Mexico Press, 1972.

McNitt, Frank. *Richard Wetherill Anasazi: Pioneer Explorer of Southwestern Ruins.* Albuquerque: University of New Mexico Press, 1957.

McPherson, Robert S., and Susan Rhodes Neal. *Mapping the Four Corners: Narrating the Hayden Survey of 1875.* Norman: University of Oklahoma Press, 2016.

McPherson, Robert S. *A History of San Juan County.* Salt Lake City: Utah State Historical Society, San Juan County Commission, 1995.

McPherson, Robert S. *As if the Land Owned Us: An Ethnohistory of the White Mesa Utes.* Salt Lake City: University of Utah Press, 2011.

McPherson, Robert S. *Comb Ridge and its People: The Ethnohistory of a Rock.* Logan: Utah State University Press, 2009.

McPherson, Robert S. *Dinéjí Na 'Nitin: Navajo Traditional Teachings and History.* Boulder: University Press of Colorado, 2012.

McPherson, Robert S. *Fighting in Canyon Country: Native American Conflict, 500 AD to the 1920s.* Indianapolis, IN: Dog Ear Publishing, 2016.

McPherson, Robert S. "Howard R. Antes and the Navajo Faith Mission: Evangelist of Southeastern Utah." *Utah Historical Quarterly* 65, no. 1 (Winter 1997): 4–24.

McPherson, Robert S. *Life in a Corner: Cultural Episodes in Southeastern Utah, 1880–1950.* Norman: University of Oklahoma Press, 2015.

McPherson, Robert S. *Navajo Land, Navajo Culture: The Utah Experience in the Twentieth Century.* Norman: University of Oklahoma Press, 2001.

McPherson, Robert S. "Navajos, Mormons, and Henry L. Mitchell: Cauldron of Conflict on the San Juan." *Utah Historical Quarterly* 55, no. 1 (Winter 1987): 50–65.

McPherson, Robert S. "Paiute Posey and the Last White Uprising." *Utah Historical Quarterly* 53 (Summer 1985): 248–67.

McPherson, Robert S. "Power, Prayers, and Protection: Comb Ridge as a Case Study in Navajo Thought." *American Indian Culture & Research Journal* 34, issue 1 (2010): 1–23.

McPherson, Robert S. *Sacred Land, Sacred View.* Provo, UT: Charles Redd Center for Western Studies, Brigham Young University, 1992.

McPherson, Robert S. *The Northern Navajo Frontier, 1860–1900.* Logan: Utah State University Press, 1991.

McPherson, Robert S. *Viewing the Ancestors: Perceptions of the Anaasazi, Mokwic, and Hisatsinom.* Norman: University of Oklahoma Press, 2014.

Mehl, Chris. "National Monuments and Public Policy." *Public Land and Resources Committee Newsletter,* American Bar Association: Section of Environment, Energy and Resources 15, no. 1 (December 2017).

Meinig, D.W. "The Mormon Culture Region: Strategies and Patterns in the Geography of the American West, 1847–1964." *ANNALS of the Association of American Geographers* 55, no. 2 (June 1965): 191–220.

Meloy, Ellen. *The Last Cheater's Waltz: Beauty and Violence in the Desert Southwest.* Tucson: University of Arizona Press, 1999.

Meloy, Ellen. *The Anthropology of Turquoise: Meditations on Landscape, Art, and Spirit.* New York: Pantheon Books, 2002.

Meloy, Ellen. *Eating Stone: Imagination and the Loss of the Wild.* New York: Vintage Books, 2005.

Mesa Verde Foundation Press Release. October 8, 2020.

Miller, David E. *Hole-In-The-Rock: An Epic in the Colonization of the Great American West.* Salt Lake City: University of Utah Press, 1996.

Momaday, Scott N. *The Way to Rainy Mountain.* Albuquerque: University of New Mexico Press, 1969.

Montgomery, Clarence P. Acting Director. NPS to Senator Clair Engle. October 16, 1963. L58-RNPP CANY Archives, Canyonlands NP Administrative Collection. Records. Southeast Utah Group Archives. National Park Service.

Montgomery, Henry. "Pre-Historic Man in Utah." *The Archaeologist* II, no. 8 (August 1894): 227–34.

Monticello City Council. "Bears Ears National Monument Opposition." Resolution No. 2016-10. August 9, 2016.

Monticello Mill Interpretive Plaque. Monticello, Utah. 2017.

Moon, Samuel. *Tall Sheep: Harry Goulding Monument Valley Trader.* Norman: University of Oklahoma Press, 1992.

Moorehead, Warren K. "The Field Diary of an Archaeological Collector." 1902.

Moore, John F., III. "The Enigma of Marie Ogden," *Blue Mountain Shadows* 36 (Spring 2007): 75–8.

Morehouse, Barbara J. *A Place Called Grand Canyon: Contested Geographies.* Tucson: University of Arizona Press, 1996.

Morgan, T.J., Commissioner. "Protest of the Indian Rights Association Against the Proposed Removal of the Southern Ute Indians, Reasons Urged for this Removal." Philadelphia, Indian Rights Association. March 1890.

Morman, Todd Allin. *Many Nations Under Many Gods: Public Land Management and American Indian Sacred Sites.* Norman: University Press of Oklahoma, 2018.

Morris, Earl H., and Robert F. Burgh. *Anasazi Basketry—Basket Maker II through Pueblo III . . . A Study Based on Specimens from the San Juan River Country.* Washington, DC: Carnegie Institution of Washington, Publication 533, 1941.

Morris, Earl H. "An Unexplored Area of the Southwest." *Natural History* 22 (November-December 1922): 499–515.

Moseley, M. Edward. "The Discovery and Definition of Basketmaker, 1890–1914." *Masterkey* 40 (October-December 1966): 140–54.

Nash, Gerald D. *The Federal Landscape: An Economic History of the Twentieth Century West.* Tucson: University of Arizona Press, 1999.
National Congress of American Indians. Resolution #EC-15-002. "Supporting the Presidential Proclamation of the Bears Ears National Monument, Including Collaborative Management Between Tribal Nations and the Federal Agencies." September 20, 2015.
National Geographic. *Grand Gulch-Cedar Mesa Plateau*, BLM-Monticello Field Office, #706 Trails Illustrated Topographic Map, 2013.
National Geographic. *Manti-La Sal National Forest*, Trails Illustrated Topographic Map, 2008.
National Park Service. Acting Regional Director to the Director. Memo. June 7, 1963. L58 CANY, Canyonlands NP Administrative Collection. Records. Southeast Utah Group Archives. National Park Service.
National Park Service. Position Statement, Proposed Nuclear Waste Repository—Gibson Dome. July 1982. CANY 200/03-69, Canyonlands NP Administrative Collection. Records. Southeast Utah Group Archives. National Park Service.
National Trust for Historic Preservation. "11 Most Endangered Places 2016: Bears Ears and Ancestral Places of Southeast Utah."
Native American Graves Protection and Repatriation Act, 23 U.S.C ch. 32 §§ 3001-13 (1990).
"Navajos go into Uranium Business." *Life Magazine* (June 4, 1951): 61–5.
Needles District. Canyonlands National Park Visitor Register. CANY 299/02-51, Canyonlands NP Administrative Collection, Records. Southeast Utah Group Archives. National Park Service.
Nelson, Katherine Metcalf. "Bluff: Dead or Alive, the Best Old Town in Utah." *Utah Holiday* (June 1985): 69–74.
Nelson, Nancy. *Any Time, Any Place, Any River: The Nevills of Mexican Hat.* Flagstaff, AZ: Red Lake Books, 1991.
Nelson, Nels. "Grand Gulch Region, Utah, 1920." Report for the American Museum of Natural History, New York City.
Nelson, Paul T. *Wrecks of Human Ambition: A History of Utah's Canyon Country to 1936.* Salt Lake City: University of Utah Press, 2014.
Newell, Philip. "The Whispering Mountains." *Arizona Highways* (July 1956): 4–9.
Nicholas, Liza, Elaine M. Bapis, and Thomas J. Harvey, eds. *Imagining the Big Open: Nature, Identity, and Play in the New West.* Salt Lake City: University of Utah Press, 2003.
Nordby, Larry B. "Control Point/Defensive Architecture at Mesa Verde During the 13th Century." Presentation at the 67th Annual Meeting, Society for American Archaeology. Denver, Colorado. March 2002.
Nordenskiöld, Gustaf. Telegram to Erik Nordenskiöld. September 17, 1891. Copy at Center of Southwest Studies, Fort Lewis College, Durango, Colorado.

Nordhaus, Hannah. "Battle for the American West." *National Geographic* (November 2018): 42–67.

Norris, Frank. "The Antiquities Act and the Acreage Debate." *The George Wright Forum* 23, no. 3 (2006): 6–16.

Norris, Scott, ed. *Discovered Country: Tourism and Survival in the American West.* Albuquerque, NM: Stone Ladder Press, 1994.

"Not So Fast: Trump's Attack on National Monuments Will Fail." *Redrock Wilderness* Southern Utah Wilderness Alliance (Autumn/Winter 2017).

Nuclear Repository Elk Ridge Site. Information with map on Waste Terminal Storage Program Activities in Utah. CANY 299, 03-69, Canyonlands NP Administrative Collection. Records. Southeast Utah Group Archives. National Park Service.

Nusbaum, Jesse L. Memo. NABR 65/05-123 in Natural Bridges National Monument Records. Canyonlands NP Administrative Collection. Records. Southeast Utah Group Archives. National Park Service.

Nusbaum, Jesse L. "Certain Aspects of the Proposed Escalante National Monument in Southeastern Utah." In *Region III Quarterly* 1, no. 2 (October 1939). Canyonlands NP Administrative Collection. Records. Southeast Utah Group Archives. National Park Service.

Obama, Barack. Proclamation 9558. "Establishment of the Bears Ears National Monument." December 28, 2016. 82FR 1139. Federal Register. Document Number 2017-00038.

Oppelt, Norman T. "Pottery and Other Intrusive Materials in Mesa Verde National Park." *Southwestern Lore* 68, no. 4 (Winter 2002): 1–10.

Organic Administration Act, 16 U.S.C. §§ 473-478 (amended 1976).

Orr, Diane, film director. *Lost Forever: Everett Ruess.* 2000.

Pachak, Joe. "Early Rock Art on the San Juan River." *Blue Mountain Shadows* 13 (Summer 1994): 16–21.

Pacific Legal Foundation. "New AEI Study Says President Trump Can Revoke National Monuments," Press release, March 28, 2017.

Parker, Patricia L., ed. "Keepers of the Treasures: Protecting Historic Properties and Cultural Traditions on Indian Lands: A Report on Tribal Preservation Funding Needs Submitted to Congress." Washington, DC: US Department of the Interior, National Park Service, Interagency Resources Division, 1990.

Parker, Patricia L., ed. "Traditional Cultural Properties: What You Do and How We Think." *CRM* 16 (1993): 1–64.

Parman, Donald L. "The 'Big Stick' in Indian Affairs: The Bai-a-lil-le Incident in 1909." *Arizona and the West* 20, no. 4 (Winter 1978): 343–60.

Pasternak, Judy. *Yellow Dirt.* New York: Free Press, 2011.

Paul, Terri L., ed. *Edge of the Cedars State Park Museum Collections.* Virginia Beach, VA: Donning Company Publishers, 2009.

Pavlik, Bruce M., et al. "Plant Species Richness at Archaeological Sites Suggest Ecological Legacy of Indigenous Subsistence on the Colorado Plateau." *Proceedings of the National Academy of Sciences* 118, no. 21 (2021).

Payner, Robert L., "The Effect of the Uranium and Petroleum Industries Upon the Economy of San Juan County, Utah." Master's thesis, Brigham Young University, 1964.

Pepper, George H. "The Ancient Basketmakers of Southeastern Utah." Supplement to *American Museum Journal* 11, no. 4. Guide Leaflet no. 6 (April 1902): 1–26.

Perkins, Cornelia Adams, Marian Gardner Nielson, and Lenora Butt Jones. *Saga of San Juan.* San Juan County Chapter Daughters of Utah Pioneers, 1968.

Petersen, David. *Cedar Mesa: A Place Where Spirits Dwell.* Tucson: University of Arizona Press, 2002.

Petersen, David. *Natural Bridges: The Story of Wind, Water & Sand.* Moab, UT: Canyonlands Natural History Association, 2014.

Petersen, Tim. "People Often Ask Me About Bears Ears." *Colorado Plateau Advocate* (Spring-Summer 2020).

Peterson, Charles S. *Look to the Mountains: Southeastern Utah and the La Sal National Forest.* Provo, UT: Brigham Young University Press, 1975.

Pick, Richard D. *Images of Bears Ears: Bears Ears National Monument.* Privately printed, n.d.

Pierson Lloyd. "Archaeological Resources of the Beef Basin, Needles, Salt Creek Mesa Area." Field Investigation Report. Proposed Needles Recreation Area. September 1959. August 1960 revised. US Department of the Interior. Region III. National Park Service. CANY 36607, Folder 659—Needles Area Report. Records. Southeast Utah Group Archives. National Park Service.

Pinkley, Jean. MVNP archaeologist. Mesa Verde National Park, Administrative History. Appendix B "Early Museum Collections from Mesa Verde." ca. 1960s.

Planning and Research Associates. Salt Lake City. "Master Plan Goals and Policies, San Juan County, Utah." Bureau of Community Development. University of Utah. September 1967. Document in the Kent Frost Papers. Special Collections. Marriott Library. University of Utah.

Podmore, Zak. *Confluence.* Salt Lake City, UT: Torrey House Press, 2019.

Podmore, Zak. "Phil Lyman on the Costs of His County's Legal Battles." *Four Corners Free Press,* May 2, 2018.

Podmore, Zak. "San Juan County Asks President-Elect Joe Biden to Immediately Restore Bears Ears National Monument." *Salt Lake Tribune,* December 3, 2020.

Podmore, Zak. "San Juan County Frustrations Spill Out in the Open with Ballot Drive and Allegations of Racism." *Salt Lake Tribune,* August 25, 2019.

Podmore, Zak. "San Juan County Paid Nearly $500K to Louisiana Law Firm to Lobby for Bears Ears Reductions." *Salt Lake Tribune,* July 28, 2019.

Pomeroy, Earl. *In Search of the Golden West: The Tourist in Western America.* New York: Knopf, 1957.
"Pothunters in Cottonwood Wash." *Canyon Echo,* February 1996.
Powell, Allan Kent, ed. *San Juan County, Utah: People, Resources and History.* Salt Lake City: Utah State Historical Society, 1983.
Powell, John Wesley. *Report on the Lands of the Arid Region of the United States, with a More Detailed Account of the Lands of Utah: With Maps* (2nd ed.). Washington, DC, 1879.
Powell, Robert L. "Procession Panel Site Comb Ridge. San Juan County, Utah, 42SA21153." 1991.
Preliminary Hearing, *State of Utah v. Jeanne and James Redd,* March 20, 1997, in the Seventh Judicial District Court, Monticello Court, San Juan County State of Utah, 46–8.
"Preservation of Historic and Prehistoric Ruins, Etc., Hearing Before the Subcommittee of the Committee on Public Lands of the United States Senate on Bill S.1427 and S.5603." Washington, DC: Government Printing Office, 1904.
"President Donald J. Trump Stands with Local Communities Against Government Overreach on Land Management." Office of the Press Secretary, The White House. December 4, 2017.
Preston, Douglas. "A Reporter at Large: Cannibals of the Canyon." *The New Yorker* (November 30, 1998): 76–89.
Price, Patricia L. *Dry Place: Landscapes of Belonging and Exclusion.* Minneapolis: University of Minnesota Press, 2004.
Price, Raye. "Family Adventure." *Desert Magazine* (May 1966): 28–30.
"Project Cerberus." *American Archaeology* (Fall 2009).
"Proposed Comb Wash Integrated Watershed Plan and San Juan Resource Area Management Plan Amendment and Revised Environmental Assessment." February 1999.
Prudden, T. Mitchell. "An Elder Brother to the Cliff Dwellers." *Harper's New Monthly Magazine* 95 (1897): 55–62.
Prudden, T. Mitchell. *On the Great American Plateau.* New York: G.P. Putnam & Sons, 1906.
Prudden, T. Mitchell. "The Prehistoric Ruins of the San Juan Watershed in Utah, Arizona, Colorado and New Mexico." *American Anthropologist* N.S. 5 (1903): 224–88.
Pyle, Ernie. *Ernie Pyle's Southwest.* Desert-Southwest Publishers, 2003.
Pyle, Ernie. "Four Corners and Thereabouts." In *Home Country,* edited Pyle newspaper columns. New York: William Sloan Associates, 1947: 391–408.
Quintano, Jen Jackson. *Blow Sand in his Soul: Bates Wilson, the Heart of Canyonlands.* Moab, UT: Friends of Arches and Canyonlands Parks, 2014.
Rasband, James R. "The Future of the Antiquities Act." *Journal of Land Resources and Environmental Law* 21 (2001): 619–34.

Rasband, James R., "Stroke of the Pen, Law of the Land?" J. Reuben Clark Law School. Brigham Young University. Research Paper No. 17-31. Proceedings of the 63rd Annual Rocky Mountain Mineral Law Institute. 21-1 Rocky Mountain Mineral Law Foundation. 2017: 1–29.

Reagan, Douglas P. "The Ecological Context of Basketmaker Rock Art." *Southwestern Lore* (2014): 13–29.

Redd, J. Wiley. "History of the Natural Bridges." One-page typescript, no date. NABR 65/06-156, Natural Bridges National Monument Records. Southeast Utah Group Archives. National Park Service.

Redford, Robert. "Obama Must Protect Sacred Utah Land." *Time,* August 16, 2016.

Reese, April. "Scientists Sue to Protect Utah Monument—and Fossils That Could Rewrite Earth's History." *Science Magazine,* January 17, 2019.

Reilly, P.T. "The Lost World of Glen Canyon." *Utah Historical Quarterly* 63 (Spring 1995): 122–34.

"Relics of the Cliff-Dwellers: Mr. Moorehead's Purchase of the McLoyd Collection for the World's Fair." *The Illustrated American,* August 27, 1892.

Report. San Juan County Sheriff's Office. Case #9601-26. Ben Naranjo, Deputy, n.d. Redd Files, State Institutional Trust Land Administration.

Resolution 12-8-2020-1. "A Joint Resolution Opposing the San Juan County Commission's Resolution Regarding Bears Ears." *San Juan Record,* January 18, 2021.

Reynolds, Judith, and David Reynolds. *Nordenskiold of Mesa Verde.* Privately printed, Xlibris, 2006.

Richardson, Elmo. "Federal Park Policy in Utah: The Escalante National Monument Controversy of 1935–1940." *Utah Historical Quarterly* 33 (Spring 1965): 190–233.

Righter, Robert W. *Crucible for Conservation: The Struggle for Grand Teton National Park.* Moose, WY: Grand Teton Natural History Association, 1982.

Riis, Jacob August. *How the Other Half Lives, Studies Among the Tenements of New York.* New York: C. Scribner's Sons, 1890.

Riis, John. *Ranger Trails.* Bend, OR: Wilderness Associates, 2008. First published 1934.

Ringholz, Raye C. *Uranium Frenzy: Boom and Bust on the Colorado Plateau.* New York: Norton, 1989.

Roberts, David. *A Newer World: Kit Carson, John C. Fremont and the Claiming of the American West.* New York: Simon & Schuster, 2000.

Roberts, David. "Canyon Confidential." *National Geographic Adventure* (March/April 2001): 92–103.

Roberts, David. *In Search of the Old Ones.* New York: Simon & Schuster, 1996.

Roberts, David. *The Bears Ears: A Human History of America's Most Endangered Wilderness.* New York: Norton, 2021.

Roberts, Paul Henley, and L.F. Kneip. *Hoof Prints on Forest Ranges: The Early Years of National Forest Range Administration.* San Antonio, TX: Naylor, 1963.

Roberts, Phil. *Cody's Cave: National Monuments and the Politics of Public Lands in the 20th Century West*. Laramie, WY: Skyline West Press, 2012.

Roberts, Ryan, and Jenny Hurst. "Indian Education." *Blue Mountain Shadows* 9 (Winter 1991): 69–74.

Robinson, Rebecca. *Voices from Bears Ears: Seeking Common Ground on Sacred Land*. Tucson: University of Arizona Press, 2018.

Rogers, Jedediah S., and Matthew C. Godfrey, eds. *The Earth Will Appear as the Garden of Eden: Essays on Mormon Environmental History*. Salt Lake City: University of Utah, 2019.

Rogers, Jedediah S. *Roads in the Wilderness: Conflict in Canyon Country*. Salt Lake City: University of Utah Press, 2013.

Rogers, John D. "Piute Posey and the Last Indian Uprising." Typescript. Filed in Lloyd. L. Young Folder. Utah State Historical Society. Salt Lake City, Utah.

Rogers-Iversen, Kristen. *Interwoven: Junipers and the Web of Being*. Salt Lake City: University of Utah Press, 2018.

Rohn, Arthur H., and William M. Ferguson. *Puebloan Ruins of the Southwest*. Albuquerque: University of New Mexico Press, 2006.

Rollins, Royce. "It's Never Drab in Moab." *Desert Magazine* (January 1965): 21–2.

Rommes, Donald J., and William D. Lipe. *Cliff Dwellers of Cedar Mesa: The Culture, Sites, and Exodus of the Ancestral Puebloans*. Moab, UT: Canyonlands Natural History Association, 2013.

Rose, Mark. "Beyond Stone & Bone: Hearts and Minds in Utah." *Archaeology Magazine*, Archaeological Institute of America, October 9, 2009.

Rothman, Hal K. *America's National Monuments: The Politics of Preservation*. Lawrence: University Press of Kansas, 1989.

Rothman, Hal K. *Devil's Bargains: Tourism in the Twentieth-Century American West*. Lawrence: University Press of Kansas, 2000.

Rothman, Hal K. "Pokey's Paradox: Tourism and Transformation on the Western Navajo Reservation," In *Reopening the American West*, edited by Hal Rothman. Tucson: University of Arizona Press, 1998.

Rothman, Hal K. *The Culture of Tourism, the Tourism of Culture: Selling the Past to the Present in the American Southwest*. Albuquerque: University of New Mexico Press, 2003.

Rothman, Hal. "The Antiquities Act and National Monuments: A Progressive Conservation Legacy." *CRM*, no. 4 (1999).

Rowland-Shea, Jenny. "Bears Ears Cultural Area: The Most Vulnerable U.S. Site for Looting, Vandalism, and Grave Robbing." Center for American Progress. June 13, 2016.

Rowley, William. *U.S. Forest Service Grazing and Rangelands*. College Station: Texas A&M Press, 1985.

Ruiz, Larry, film director. *The Language of the Landscape*. 2019.

Runyan, Curtis. "Cowgirl Conservation: A Deal to Protect the Heart of Utah's Red Canyonlands May Change the Face of Ranching in the West." *Nature Conservancy* (Winter 2010): 2–7.

Ruple, John C. "Can Trump Redevelop America's Monumental Legacy?" *Public Land and Resources Committee Newsletter,* American Bar Association: Section of Environment, Energy and Resources 15, no. 1 (December 2017).

Ruple, John C. "The Transfer of Public Lands Movement: The Battle to Take 'Back' Lands That Were Never Theirs." *Colorado Natural Resources, Energy & Environmental Review* 29, no. 1 (January 2018): 3–78.

Ruple, John C. "The Trump Administration and Lessons Not Learned From Prior National Monument Modifications." *Harvard Environmental Law Review* Vol. 43. (2020): 1-76.

Rutzick, Mark C. "Environmental Law & Property Rights: Modern Remedies for Antiquated Laws: Challenging National Monument Designations Under the 1906 Antiquities Act." *Engage* 11, issue 2 (September 2010).

S.2354 (Senator Tom Udall). "America's Natural Treasures of Immeasurable Quality Unite, Inspire, and Together Improve the Economies of States Act of 2018—The Antiquities Act of 2018."

S.3193 (Senator Mike Lee) "Protecting Utah's Rural Economy (PURE) Act." July 11, 2018.

Sager, Merel S. Report submitted February 17, 1937. Folder 654A, CANY 36607, Canyonlands NP Administrative Collection. Records. Southeast Utah Group Archives. National Park Service.

Sagstetter, Beth, and Bill Sagstetter. *The Cliff Dwellings Speak: Exploring the Ancient Ruins of the Greater American Southwest.* Denver: Benchmark Publishing, 2010.

Salt Lake City Chamber of Commerce. *Life in Utah 2019.*

Sando, Joe. *Pueblo Nations: Eight Centuries of Pueblo Indian History.* Santa Fe, NM: Clear light Publishers, 1992.

San Juan County Commission. Letter to Honorable Wallace F. Bennett, US Senator. October 2, 1963 and associated letters from Senator Bennett and US Senator Frank E. Moss. CANY 339, Folder 671. Records. Southeast Utah Group Archives. National Park Service.

Sargent, Kay. "On a Dig in Southeastern Utah." *Beehive History* 3 (1978): 3–7.

Savonen, Carol. "Oh! The Fun We Had! The Bears Ears National Broadwalk." *Broadsides: Great Old Broads for Wilderness* 27, no. 1 (Winter-Spring 2017).

Schaafsma, Polly. "Head Trophies and Scalping," In *The Taking and Displaying of Human Body Parts as Trophies of Amerindians,* edited by R.J. Chacon and D.H. Dye, Interdisciplinary Contributions to Archaeology. Boston: Springer Publications, 2007.

Schaafsma, Polly. *The Rock Art of Utah.* Cambridge, MA: Peabody Museum of Archaeology and Ethnology, Harvard University, 1971.

Schaafsma, Polly. *The Rock Art of Utah.* Salt Lake City: University of Utah Press, 1994.

Schimel, Kate, and Brooke Warren. "Recreation Is Redefining the Value of the West's Public Lands." *High Country News* (May 14, 2018): 9.

Schmieding, Samuel J. "From Controversy to Compromise to Cooperation: The Administrative History of Canyonlands National Park." National Park Service, 2008.

Schroedl, Alan R. "The Grand Canyon Figurine Complex." *American Antiquity* 42, no. 2 (April 1977): 254–65.

Schultheis, Rob. *The Hidden West*. New York: Lyons & Burford, 1996.

Scott, Doug. *The Enduring Wilderness: Protecting our Natural Heritage Through the Wilderness Act*. Golden, CO: Fulcrum Publishing, 2004.

S.C.R. 4 (Michael E. Noel). Utah Concurrent Resolution Regarding the Creation of National Monuments. 2015.

Seamon, Richard, et al. Davillier Law Group. Comments prepared for the Utah Commission for the Stewardship of Public Lands in a report on Bears Ears National Monument and the Antiquities Act submitted to the Honorable Ryan Zinke. Secretary of the Department of the Interior. May 25, 2017.

Secakuku, Ferrell. Letter to William Benge, Grand County Attorney. May 16, 1996. State Institutional Trust Land Administration files.

"Secretary of the Interior Udall Envisions a 'Golden Circle' of National Parks and Monuments," news release, National Park Service, Region Three Office, Santa Fe, New Mexico. August 2, 1961. CANY 339, Folder 124. Records, Southeast Utah Group Archives, National Park Service.

Seymour, Deni J., ed. *From the Land of Ever Winter to the American Southwest: Athabaskan Migration, Mobility, and Ethnogenesis*. Salt Lake City: University of Utah Press, 2012.

Sharrock, Floyd W., and Edward G. Kean. *Carnegie Museum Collection from Southeast Utah*. University of Utah Department of Anthropology. Anthropological Papers. No. 57 Glen Canyon Series. No. 16, January 1962.

Sharrock, Floyd W. "The Hazzard Collection." *Archives of Archaeology* 23, Washington, DC and Madison, WI: Society for American Archaeology and the University of Wisconsin Press, 1963: 1–307.

Sharp, Kathleen. "The Rescue Mission: An Exclusive Look at the Greatest Haul of Native American Artifacts, Ever." *Smithsonian Magazine* (November 2015): 40–9.

Shelton, Charles E. "Mechanical 'Mules.'" *Desert Magazine* (February 1960): 16–9.

Shelton, W.T. San Juan School, Shiprock, New Mexico. Letter to the Commissioner of Indian Affairs. July 19, 1910.

Shepherd, John F. "Up the Grand Staircase: Executive Withdrawals and the Future of the Antiquities Act." Proceedings of the Forty-Third Annual Rocky Mountain Mineral Law Institute. Denver, Colorado. Rocky Mountain Mineral Law Foundation, Denver, Colorado. 1997.

Shogren, Elizabeth. "The Fate of National Monuments." *High Country News,* (August 21, 2017): 5–6.

Shogren, Elizabeth. "Lawsuits Challenge Trump's Trims." *High Country News,* (December 19, 2017): https://www.hcn.org/issues/50.1/monuments-lawsuits-challenge-trumps-shrinking-of-utah-national-monuments..

Shumway, Brett. "Pot Hunting in San Juan County." *Beehive History* 012 (1986): 28–30.

Shumway, Gary, ed. "Cottonwood Mining." *Blue Mountain Shadows* 25 (Winter 2001): 1–81.

Shumway, Gary Lee, "The Development of the Uranium Industry in San Juan County, Utah," Master's thesis, Brigham Young University, 1964.

Shumway, Gary L. *This Part of the Vineyard: Centennial Overview of the History of Blanding, Utah.* Yorba Linda, CA: Shumway Family History Publishing, 2005.

Shumway, Gary L., and Ken Hochfield. *They Call It Home: The Southeastern Utah Collection: The Communities of San Juan County, Utah, 1972–1973.* Cortez, CO: Southwest Printing, 2013.

Silbernagel, Robert. *Troubled Trails: The Meeker Affair and the Expulsion of Utes from Colorado.* Salt Lake City: University of Utah Press, 2011.

Simmons, Virginia McConnell. *Drifting West: The Calamities of James White and Charles Baker.* Boulder: University Press of Colorado, 2007.

Simms, Steven R. *Traces of Fremont: Society and Rock Art in Ancient Utah.* Salt Lake City: University of Utah Press, 2010.

Simon, Chris. *My Canyonlands: The Adventurous Life of Kent Frost.* Film by Sageland Media, 2008.

Silver, Ken. "The Yellowed Archives of Yellowcake." *Public Health Reports* 111, no. 2 (March-April 1996): 116–25.

Silvey, Frank. "When San Juan County was Given to the Southern Ute Indians—A Historical Experience of the Early Nineties." A-S-I3 (13). Manuscript at Utah State Historical Society. Salt Lake City, Utah.

Sjogren, Morgan. "Drive Thru-Protest." *The Gulch,* issue 9 (2019): 18–21.

Sjogren, Morgan. *The Best Bears Ears National Monument Hikes* Golden: Colorado Mountain Club Press, 2018.

Smith, H. Jay. "The Cliff Dwellers." Pamphlet. The H. Jay Smith Exploring Company. World's Columbian Exposition, 1893.

Snead, James E. *Ruins and Rivals: The Making of Southwest Archaeology.* Tucson: University of Arizona Press, 2001.

Solomon, Chris. "Overturning Bears Ears Is a Long Shot, but That Doesn't Mean Republicans Won't Try." *Outside* (December 2016).

Sorenson, Dan. "Wonder Mineral: Utah's Uranium." *Utah Historical Quarterly* 31 (Summer 1963): 280–90.

Southern Utah Wilderness Alliance. "Bears Ears National Monument: The First Truly Native American National Monument in History!" Flyer, 2017.

Sprague, Marshall. *Massacre: The Tragedy at White River.* Lincoln: University of Nebraska Press, 1980.

Sproul, David Kent. *A Bridge Between Cultures: An Administrative History of Rainbow Bridge National Monument.* Cultural Resources Selections, No. 18. Denver: Intermountain Region of the National Park Service, 2001.

Squillace, Mark, et al. "Presidents Lack the Authority to Abolish or Diminish National Monuments." *103 Virginia Law Review Online 55* (2017): 55–71.

Squillace, Mark, et al. "The Monumental Legacy of the Antiquities Act of 1906." *Georgia Law Review* 37, no. 2 (Winter 2003).

Stanton, Robert Brewster. *Colorado River Controversies.* Boulder, NV: Westwater Books, 1982. First published 1932.

State of Utah v. Jeanne Redd, Preliminary Hearing Case No. 9827-63, in the Seventh Judicial District Court in and for San Juan County, Utah, October 8, 1998.

Steen, Charlie R., ed. "The Natural Bridges of White Canyon: A Diary of H.L.A. Culmer, 1905." *Utah Historical Quarterly* 40 (1972): 55–87.

Stegner, Wallace. *The Gathering of Zion: The Story of the Mormon Trail.* Salt Lake City: Westwater Press, 1964.

Stegner, Wallace. *Mormon Country.* Lincoln: University of Nebraska Press, 2003. First published 1942.

Steinmetz, Katy. "Donald Trump's Move to Shrink Two National Monuments Sets Stage For Battle Over 111-Year-Old Law." *Time,* December 5, 2017.

Steinmetz, Katy. "Tribes Celebrated When This Region Became a National Monument. Now They're Suing to Get it Back." *Time,* June 1, 2018.

Steinmetz, Katy. "Trump's Other Big Fight Over Monuments." *Time,* August 24, 2017.

Stevens, Bill, and Katie Stevens. *Dark Canyon Trail Guide.* Moab, UT: Canyonlands Natural History Association, 1994.

Stevenson, Gene M. *Canyon Country Explorations & River Lore: The Remarkable Resilient Life of Kenny Frost.* Bluff, UT: Living Earth Studios, 2019.

Stiles, Jim. *Brave New West: Morphing Moab at the Speed of Greed.* Tucson: University of Arizona Press, 2007.

Stiles, Jim. "The Industrial Borg Comes to San Juan County: Is Resistance Futile?" *Blue Mountain Shadows* 57 (Spring 2018): 72–81.

Stiles, Jim. "The Blanding Raids: Shame and Hypocrisy All Around." *The Canyon Country Zephyr* Online (July 30, 2019).

Stokes, M.A., and T.L. Smiley. "Tree-Ring Dates from the Navajo Land Claim I. The Northern Sector." *Tree-Ring Bulletin* 25 (1963): 8–18.

Stoll, Mark. "Religion Irradiates the Wilderness." In *American Wilderness: A New History,* edited by Michael Lewis. New York: Oxford University Press, 2004.

Strom, Stephen E. *Bears Ears: Views from a Sacred Land.* George F. Thompson Publishing, American Land Publishing Project. Tucson: University of Arizona Press, 2018.

Strutin, Michael. *Chaco: A Cultural Legacy.* Tucson, Arizona: Southwest Parks & Monuments Association, 1994.

Stryker, Perrin. "The Great Uranium Rush." *Fortune* (August 1954): 89–93.

Stuart, David. *Anasazi America*. Albuquerque: University of New Mexico Press, 2000.

Sundeen, Mark. "Utah Wanted All the Tourists. Then It Got Them." *Outside Magazine* Online (January 29, 2020).

Taft, William L. Presidential Proclamation Establishing Rainbow Bridge National Monument. NABR 65/06-156, Canyonlands NP Administrative Collection. Records. Southeast Utah Group Archives. National Park Service.

Tassoni, Peter Francis. *A Hiking Guide to Cedar Mesa*. Salt Lake City: University of Utah Press, 2001.

Tate, LaVerne, and the San Juan County Historical Society. *Early San Juan County, Utah*. Charleston, SC: Arcadia Publishing, 2008.

Tate, LaVerne, ed. "Cedar Mesa—Also Includes Spirit Bird Cave and Sand Island Depictions." *Blue Mountain Shadows* 50 (Fall 2014): 1–61.

Taylor, P.A.M., and L.J. Arrington. "Religion and Planning in the Far West: The First Generation of Mormons in Utah." *The Economic History Review,* New Series 11, no. 1 (1958): 71–86.

Temple, Eric, film director. *A Voice in the Wilderness: Edward Abbey*. 2007

Tenakhongva, Clark. Hopi Vice Chairman. Speech at the Friends of Cedar Mesa Annual Conference. Bluff, Utah. March 7, 2020.

Thayne, Stanley J. "The Home of Truth: The Metaphysical World of Marie Ogden," Master's thesis, Brigham Young University, November 2009.

The Archaeologist by H. [Henry Montgomery?]. "Mummies in the San Juan Valley." Recent Discoveries 2 (1894): 190–1.

The Archaeologist by H. [Henry Montgomery?] "Recent Finds in Utah." Collectors' Department 2 (1894): 154–5.

The Archaeologist by H. [Henry Montgomery?]. Review of "Catalogue of Cliff House and Cavern Relics." McLoyd and Graham's Utah Collection 2 (1894): 184.

The Economist. "Bears Ears and Gold Butte Are the Latest Battlegrounds in a Long-Running Debate about Federal Lands in the West." January 14, 2017.

The Illustrated American. July 16, 1892.

Thompson, Jonathan. "A Monumental Divide: The Tribal Bid for Bears Ears Raises Tough Questions about Homelands." *High Country News* (October 31, 2016): 12–21.

Thompson, Jonathan. "Bears Ears National Monument Is a Go: Despite Compromises, Opposition Is Riled Up." *High Country News* (January 23, 2017): 5–6.

Thompson, Jonathan. "The Danger of Local Hands on Public Lands." *High Country News*. March 19, 2018. https://www.hcn.org/issues/50.5/public-lands-the-danger-of-local-hands-on-public-lands.

Throgmorton, Kellam. "Rock Art, Architecture, and Social Groups at the Basketmaker III-Pueblo I Transition: Evidence from the Procession Panel, Southeast Utah." *Kiva: Journal of Southwestern Anthropology and History* 83, no. 2 (2017): 137–61.

Thybony, Scott. *Canyon Country Parklands: Treasures of the Great Plateau.* Washington, DC: National Geographic Society, 1993.

Thybony, Scott. *The Disappearances: A Story of Exploration, Murder, and Mystery in the American West.* Salt Lake City: University of Utah Press, 2016.

Till, Jonathan, "Chacoan Roads and Road-Associated Sites in the Lower San Juan Region: Assessing the Role of Chacoan Influences in the Northwestern Periphery." Master's thesis, University of Colorado—Boulder, 2001.

Toll, Roger W. Letter to the director of the National Park Service. September 21, 1935. CANY 339/007-654, Canyonlands NP Administrative Collection. Records. Southeast Utah Group Archives. National Park Service.

Topping, Gary. *Glen Canyon and the San Juan Country.* Moscow: University of Idaho Press, 1997.

Treaty Between the United States of America and the Navajo Tribe of Indians, 1868, with a record of the discussions that led to its signing. Published in cooperation with the Navajo Tribe as the eighth in a continuing series commemorating the Navajo Centennial. Las Vegas: KC Publications, 1968.

Trump, Donald. Proclamation 9681. "Modifying the Bears Ears National Monument." December 4, 2017. 82FR 58081. Federal Register. Document Number 2017-26709.

Turner, Christy G. "A Reign of Terror: Butchered Human Bones Point to Cannibals in Chaco Canyon." *Discovering Archaeology* (May/June 1999).

Turner, Christy G., and Jacqueline A. Turner. *Man Corn: Cannibalism and Violence in the Prehistoric American Southwest.* Salt Lake City: University of Utah Press, 1999.

Turner, Jack. *Early Images of the Southwest: The Lantern Slides of Ansel F. Hall.* Denver: Roberts Rinehart, 1998.

Uglesich, Jessica, et al. "Paleontology of Bears Ears National Monument (Utah, USA): History of Exploration, Study, and Designation." *Geology of the Intermountain West* 7 (2020).

Unger, Don. "A Brief History of Mining Reclamation in Navajo Country." Report for the Navajo Abandoned Mining Lands Program © 2019. Navajo Tribal Authority. Report submitted January 2019.

University of Utah. Accession Records. 1925–1926 Collections in southeast Utah. Natural History Museum of Utah.

US Court of Appeals, Tenth Circuit. *UNITED STATES of America, Plaintiff-Appellee, V. Earl K. SHUMWAY, Defendant-Appellant,* Nos. 95-4201, 96-4000, decided May 6, 1997.

US Department of Agriculture. Fact Sheet on Criollo Cattle, n.d.

US Department of the Interior, Bureau of Land Management. "Bears Ears National Monument: Draft Monument Management Plans and Environmental Impact Statement *Shash Jaa* and Indian Creek Units, Executive Summary." August 2018.

US Department of the Interior, Bureau of Land Management. Environmental Assessment. DOI-BLM-UT-Y020-2012-0001. Hole-in-the-Rock

Foundation Trekking SRP. Finding of No Significant Impact. December 2015. Signed January 12, 2016.

US Department of the Interior, Bureau of Land Management. Incident Record. February 9, 1996. Redd Files. State Institutional Trust Land Administration.

US Department of the Interior. "Report on Restoring National Monuments: Prepared in Response to Executive Order 13990." June 2021.

Utah Bureau of Land Management. "Proposed Comb Wash Integrated Watershed Plan and San Juan Resource Management Plan (RMP) Amendment." 1997–1998.

Utah Code Annotated, 1953, Volume 1B, 2019 Replacement, Titles 1–9, Lexis Nexis, 644–5.

Utah Code Annotated, § 76-6-9.

Utah Code Annotated, 76-9-704.

Utah Code Annotated, Title 53C.

Utah Department of Transportation. *Resolution: State Route 211*. October 15, 1971.

Utah School & Institutional Trust Lands Administration v. Dr. James R. Redd and Jeanne Redd, Complaint Civil No. 9707-15, filed in the Seventh District Court for San Juan County, State of Utah, February 24, 1997. Redd Files, State Institutional Trust Land Administration.

Utah School and Institutional Trust Lands Administration v. Dr. James R. Redd and Jeanne Redd, Stipulation of Settlement, Case No. 9707-15CV, January 14, 2003.

Valentine, John F. *Lonesome Trails of San Juan: The Ranching Legacy of J.A. (Al) Scorup*. Provo, UT: Privately printed, 2002.

Voigt, William. *Public Grazing Lands: Use and Misuse by Industry and Government*. Rutgers, NJ: Rutgers University Press, 1976.

Walker, Don D. "The Carlisles: Cattle Barons of the Upper Basin." *Utah Historical Quarterly* 32 (Summer 1964): 268–84.

Washburn, Dorothy K., William N. Washburn, and Petia A. Shipkova. "Cacao Consumption During the 8th Century at Alkali Ridge, Southeastern Utah." *Journal of Archaeological Science* 40.4 (October 2014).

Watkins, T.H. *Righteous Pilgrim: The Life and Times of Harold L. Ickes, 1874–1952*. New York: Henry Holt, 1990.

Watkins, T.H. *The Redrock Chronicles*. Baltimore: Johns Hopkins University Press, 2000.

Weisiger, Marsha. *Dreaming of Sheep in Navajo Country*. Seattle: University of Washington Press, 2009.

Wetherill, B.K. Letter to Superintendent. Smithsonian Institute. Washington, DC, 1889. Copy courtesy of Harvey Leake.

Wetherill John, custodian. "Betatakin." Supplement of the June Report of the Southwestern Monuments. June 1934.

Wetherill, Louisa Wade, and Harvey Leake, compilers. *Wolfkiller: Lessons from a Nineteenth Century Navajo Shepherd*. Layton, UT: Gibbs-Smith, 2007.

Wetherill, Richard. "Expedition Notes 1896–1897." American Museum of Natural History. New York.

Wetherill, Richard. Letter to the Editor. *The Antiquarian* 1 (1897): 248.

Wetherill, Richard to G.F. Pollock, Acting Commissioner. Land Office. Washington, DC, from Putnam, NM. January 14, 1906. Copy courtesy of Harvey Leake.

White, Richard. *The Roots of Dependency*. Lincoln: University of Nebraska Press, 1983.

Wilde, Kathryn M. "The San Juan: The Four Corners River." *Plateau* 62, no. 4 (1991).

Wilkinson, Charles. *Fire on the Plateau: Conflict and Endurance in the American Southwest.* Washington, DC: Island Press, 1999.

Wilkinson, Charles. "The Greatness of the Bears Ears National Monument." Duane A. Smith Lecture Series. Center of Southwest Studies. Fort Lewis College. Durango, Colorado. March 22, 2018.

Williams, Terry Tempest. *Red: Passion and Patience in the Desert*. New York: Vintage Books, 2002.

Wilshusen, Richard, Gregson Schachner, and James R. Allison. *Crucible of Pueblos: The Early Pueblo Period in the Northern Southwest*. Monograph 71. Los Angeles: Cotsen Institute of Archaeology Press, UCLA, 2012.

Wilson, Lanny O. "Distribution and Ecology of the Desert Bighorn Sheep in Southeastern Utah." Master's thesis, Utah State University, 1968.

Wilson, Woodrow. Presidential Proclamation. NABR 65/06-156, Canyonlands NP Administrative Collection. Records. Southeast Utah Group Archives. National Park Service.

Wintch, Kenneth L. "The Miracle of CRM on Trust Lands." *Utah Archaeology* 21, no. 1 (2008): 121–8.

Witze, Alexandra. "When the Gambler Came to Chaco." *American Archaeology* 22, no. 2 (Summer 2018).

Worby, Rebecca. "Zinke Listened at Bears Ears, but Supporters Felt Unheard." *High Country News* (May 29, 2017): 5.

Wrobel, David M., and Patrick T. Long, eds. *Seeing and Being Seen: Tourism in the American West.* Lawrence: University Press of Kansas, 2001.

Wright, Rigby. Witness interview by Dawn J. Soper, SITLA attorney, February 23, 1998. Redd Files. State Institutional Trust Land Administration.

Wuerthner, George, and Mollie Matteson, eds. *Welfare Ranching: The Subsidized Destruction of the American West.* Washington, DC: Island Press and the Foundation for Deep Ecology, 2002.

Wyatt, Alexandra M. "Antiquities Act: Scope of Authority for Modification of National Monuments." Congressional Research Service. CRS Report No. R44687. Nov. 14, 2016.

Wyman, Leland C., and Stuart K. Harris. *The Ethnobotany of the Kayenta Navajo: An Analysis of the John and Louisa Wetherill Ethnobotanical Collection.* University of New Mexico Publications in Biology no. 5. Albuquerque: University of New Mexico Press, 1951.

Yoo, John and Todd Gaziano. "Presidential Authority to Revoke or Reduce National Monument Designations." American Enterprise Institute, March 2017.

Young et al. v. Felornia et al. (two cases) No. 7772, Supreme Court of Utah, May 21, 1952, 646.

Young, Karl. "Wild Cows of the San Juan." *Utah Historical Quarterly* 32 (Summer 1964): 252–67.

Young, William R. "The 1923 Indian Uprising in San Juan County, Utah." Typescript. Filed in Lloyd. L. Young Folder, Utah State Historical Society, Salt Lake City, Utah.

Zinke, Ryan. "Memorandum for the President, Subject: Final Report Summarizing Findings of the Review of Designations Under the Antiquities Act." Dec. 5, 2017.

Zwinger, Ann. *Wind in the Rock: The Canyonlands of Southeastern Utah*. Tucson: University of Arizona Press, 1978.

Index

Page numbers in italics refer to figures.